MANAGEMENT ACCOUNTING

SECOND EDITION

MANAGEMENT ACCOUNTING

ANTHONY A. ATKINSON
University of Waterloo

RAJIV D. BANKER
University of Minnesota

ROBERT S. KAPLAN
Harvard University

S. MARK YOUNG
University of Southern California

PRENTICE HALL, UPPER SADDLE RIVER, NJ 07458

Management accounting / Anthony A. Atkinson . . . [et al.]. — [2nd ed.]
    p. cm.—(The Robert S. Kaplan series in management
accounting)
    Includes bibliographical references and indexes.
    ISBN 0-13-255761-4
    1. Managerial accounting.   I. Atkinson, Anthony A.   II. Series.
HF5657.4.M328   1997
658.15′11—dc20   96-34705
             CIP

Editor in Chief: Richard Wohl
Executive Editor: P.J. Boardman
Assistant Editor: Natacha St. Hill
Editorial Assistant: Jane Avery
Director of Development: Steve Deitmer
Editorial Coordination: Monotype Editorial Services, Inc.
Managing Editor: Katherine Evancie
Production Coordinator: David Cotugno
Senior Manufacturing Supervisor: Paul Smolenski
Manufacturing Manager: Vincent Scelta
Electronic Artist: Warren Fischbach
Senior Designer: Suzanne Behnke
Design Director: Patricia Wosczyk
Interior Design: Suzanne Behnke
Cover Design: Suzanne Behnke
Illustrator (Interior): Warren Fischbach
Composition: Monotype Composition Co., Inc.

©1997, 1995 by Prentice-Hall, Inc.
A Simon & Schuster Company
Upper Saddle River, New Jersey 07458

Printed in the United States of America
10 9 8 7 6 5 4 3

ISBN 0-13-255761-4

Prentice-Hall International (UK) Limited, *London*
Prentice-Hall of Australia Pty. Limited, *Sydney*
Prentice-Hall Canada, Inc., *Toronto*
Prentice-Hall Hispanoamericana, S.A., *Mexico*
Prentice-Hall of India Private Limited, *New Delhi*
Prentice-Hall of Japan, Inc., *Tokyo*
Simon & Schuster Asia Pte. Ltd., *Singapore*
Editora Prentice-Hall do Brasil, Ltda., *Rio de Janeiro*

*This Book Is Dedicated
to Our Parents and Families*

BRIEF CONTENTS

CONTENTS

1

MANAGEMENT ACCOUNTING: INFORMATION THAT CREATES VALUE   1

THE ORGANIZATION AS A SYSTEM OF ACTIVITIES   42

3

COST CONCEPTS   86

4

COST BEHAVIOR   140

5

BASIC PRODUCT COSTING SYSTEMS   202

TWO-STAGE ALLOCATIONS AND ACTIVITY-BASED COSTING SYSTEMS   246

PRICING AND PRODUCT-MIX DECISIONS   304

PROCESS AND ACTIVITY DECISIONS   358

9

BUDGETING: RESOURCE ALLOCATION TO ACHIEVE ORGANIZATIONAL OBJECTIVES   404

10

Capital Budgeting   458

11

PLANNING AND CONTROL   500

12

FINANCIAL CONTROL   548

13

CONTEMPORARY MANAGEMENT ACCOUNTING: METHODS TO STAY COMPETITIVE   606

14

COMPENSATION ISSUES 644

15

MANAGEMENT ACCOUNTING AND CONTROL SYSTEM DESIGN: BEHAVIORAL FACTORS AND CHANGE MANAGEMENT   688

PREFACE

Management Accounting, second edition, has been written to introduce students to the vital role that management accounting information plays in organizations. Today, management accounting information is used for decision-making, learning, planning, and controlling activities. The information that management accounting systems produce supports the operational and strategic needs of the enterprise. Measures of the economic condition of the enterprise—such as the cost and profitability of the organization's products, services, and customers—are available only from management accounting systems.

Employees use management accounting information to receive rapid feedback on their performance so that they can learn from the recent past and improve for the future. Used in this way, management accounting information supports the organization's continuous learning and improvement activities. Management accounting information measures the economic performance of decentralized operating units such as business units, divisions, and departments. It provides feedback to senior management about the units' performance and also serves as the linkage between the strategy of the organization and the execution of that strategy in individual operating units.

INTENDED AUDIENCE

Several audiences will find the study of management accounting principles to be interesting and valuable. First, obviously, are individuals who expect to become management accountants. Historically, public practice with professional accounting and auditing firms was the glamour field for accounting students. Now the challenging new environment for manufacturing, service, not-for-profit, and governmental organizations has created exciting opportunities for management accountants. Until quite recently, financial people in organizations played staff roles. They were scorekeepers, sitting apart from the action, making sure that the organization's records complied with external regulatory procedures. They also issued periodic retrospective reports on internal operations.

In today's competitive environment, management accountants have become part of the management team, participating in formulating and implementing strategy. Management accountants can translate strategic intent into operational and managerial measures. Rather than just being caretakers of data and producers of historical reports, they can become the designers of an organization's critical management information systems.

Unfortunately, education of management accountants has not kept pace with these new opportunities. A research project sponsored by the Institute of Management Accountants and the Financial Executives Institute (IMA/FEI) surveyed U.S. corporate accounting and financial executives about the relative importance of various accounting knowledge and skill areas (AKSAs) and the extent to which entry level accountants bring these AKSAs to their first job. The four AKSAs rated as most important for management accountants were budgeting, product and service costing, control and performance evaluation, and strategic cost management, including activity-based costing. These four AKSAs, however, are the fields where the largest gap between corporate expectations and actual preparation of entry-level accountants exists. The areas in which management accountants were over-trained, relative to corporate needs, included taxation, external auditing, and FASB pronouncements.

This book's intense focus on demands for managerial accounting information provides comprehensive treatments of the IMA/FEI report's four most highly rated accounting knowledge and skill areas and should contribute to closing the gap between corporate expectations on the one hand and student preparation and performance in management accounting positions on the other hand. For individuals who aspire to a career in management accounting, this book provides a valuable perspective on how the measures and information they produce as management accountants create value in manufacturing, service, and government/not-for-profit organizations.

Many students who take an introductory management accounting course, however, do not expect to become management accountants. Nonetheless, their time in a management accounting class is well spent. For example, scientists and engineers benefit from studying modern management accounting practices. Organizations use management accounting information to measure the impact and success of engineers' and scientists' product and process designs. Proposed investments in new products, new projects, and new equipment will all be viewed through the lens of the organization's management accounting system. Knowing the rules of the measurement game and being able to understand and explain when organizational management accounting systems could be hindering the company's goal for technological excellence and innovation will be powerful assets for technologists.

Another important audience consists of the individuals who expect to become managers, either general managers who control organizations or the leaders of important departments such as market research, investment analysis, human resources, research and development, information systems, and strategic planning. A modern management accounting course will help general managers and staff members understand the active role they must play in demanding excellence from their organization's management accounting systems.

Managers must learn that the design of management accounting systems is too important to be left solely to management accountants. For many years, managers were intimidated by the professional training and certification of the accounting people within organizations. These managers were passive consumers of the information produced by the organization's accounting systems. While recognizing that the information from these systems was generally late, reported at too aggregate a level, plagued with arbitrary allocations, and frequently distorted, it was the only accounting system available. Managers expressed their feelings toward their accounting system by describing it as "a system designed by accountants for accountants."

Competitive challenges today require that management accounting systems have a customer focus that provides valuable information to company managers rather than simply serving the needs of the accounting staff. Managers should learn that management accounting systems can provide timely, accurate, and relevant information for them. Managers must insist that their management accounting staff redesign any systems that do not meet these criteria. This book addresses the demands for information for managers in line and staff positions, technical personnel, and front-line employees. It also illustrates how individuals aspiring to become management accounting professionals can design and operate information systems that are valuable for their organizations.

CONCEPTUAL FRAMEWORK

Management Accounting, second edition, uses activities—the collection of tasks and processes performed by organizational employees to create value for customers—to provide a unified framework for the textual material. Chapter 1, "Management Accounting: Information That Creates Value," introduces the nature of management accounting information and describes how it must be customized to the different needs of front-line operators, middle managers, and senior executives. The demand for management accounting information is derived from explicit managerial needs such as making decisions about products, services and customers; improving existing activities and processes; and aligning organizational activities toward long-term strategic objectives. This chapter introduces the reasons that leading manufacturing and service organizations are adopting activity-based costing; sharing financial and operating information on a timely basis with front-line employees; and guiding strategy implementation through a balanced system of financial and nonfinancial measures of activities, processes, and outcomes. Chapter 2, "The Organization as a System of Activities," builds on this activity framework and illustrates how managers can develop and use management accounting information to improve activity performance.

Chapter 3, "Cost Concepts," introduces basic cost concepts within an activity framework. It integrates recent advances in the foundations of activity costing into a general framework for describing cost behavior. Chapter 4, "Cost Behavior," builds on the activity-based framework established in Chapter 3 by highlighting the distinction between the cost of supplying organizational resources and the cost of using organizational resources to produce and deliver products and services to customers. This key distinction provides a rich foundation for describing cost behavior, embedding it in a general management framework that incorporates the demands for organizational resources, the nature of contracting for organizational resources, and management actions that, over time, adjust the supply of organizational resources to current and anticipated demands.

Chapter 5, "Basic Product Costing Systems," introduces the basics of product costing, such as job order and process cost systems. This material is presented using the activity costing foundation established in Chapter 3 and 4. Chapter 6, "Two-Stage Allocations and Activity-Based Costing Systems," extends this foundation by introducing activity-based cost (ABC) systems, including the two-stage process of assigning service department costs to production departments and activities, and then from cost centers and activities down to products and services. The chapter identifies the distortions arising from traditional costing systems that rely only on volume-related cost drivers. ABC systems use unit, batch, and product-sustaining cost drivers to avoid these distortions. Selling and distribution costs also are treated as components of product and customer costs.

With the foundations of using activity-based costing for measuring the costs of products, services, and customers established in Chapters 5 and 6, Chapter 7,

"Pricing and Product-Mix Decisions," illustrates how managers use this information for decisions such as short- and long-term pricing and selection of product mix. In Chapter 8, "Process and Activity Decisions," students learn how managers use cost information to make decisions that enhance profitability through activity and process improvements. This chapter integrates management accounting information with organizational improvement initiatives, such as total quality management and cycle time (just-in-time) management.

Chapters 1 through 8 represent a new approach to teaching management accounting. These chapters derive the demand for managerial accounting information from an integrated treatment of organizational objectives, an orientation to meeting customer expectations, and a focus on activities as the unit of analysis for measurement of cost, quality, and time.

Chapter 9, "Budgeting: Resource Allocation to Achieve Organizational Objectives," builds on the activity framework of Chapters 1 through 8 by forecasting the supply and spending on resources based on the demands by customers for products and services. Chapter 9 shows how short-term fixed expenses arise from authorizations made in the budgeting process. The chapter not only provides the analytic aspects of budgeting, but it also recognizes the behavioral effects of how people react to budgets. Chapter 10, "Capital Budgeting," extends the budgeting process to incorporate the acquisition of long-lived assets through capital budgeting and discounted cash flow procedures.

Chapter 11, "Planning and Control," revisits themes established in Chapters 1 and 2 of how the organization plans and develops goals for its various stakeholders: external shareholders, customers, suppliers, employees, and communities in which it operates. This chapter introduces formal planning and control procedures that enable the organization to achieve its desired goals. Chapter 12, "Financial Control," deals with the particular issues arising from the use of financial controls, including responsibility centers and associated performance measurement systems, such as flexible budgets and return-on-investment metrics. The strengths as well as the weaknesses of financial control systems are discussed.

Chapter 13, "Contemporary Management Accounting," is a new chapter for the second edition. It introduces the innovative management accounting procedures that leading organizations are using. Working with a total life cycle costing approach as an organizing framework, the chapter integrates target costing, kaizen costing, quality costing, and benchmarking, and it illustrates how each method improves decision making and performance.

The final two chapters address incentive, behavioral, and organizational issues that arise when using management accounting information. Chapter 14, "Compensation Issues," describes how compensation systems help to align employees' motivation, incentives, and rewards with achieving overall organizational goals. Chapter 15, "Management Accounting and Control System Design," brings together several important topics related to effective implementation and use of management accounting systems. It discusses the impact of the design of such systems on managers' motivation and behavior.

The entire text blends contemporary theory and the latest thinking in management accounting with practical applications and actual company experiences. A supplementary readings book, specifically designed to complement and support *Management Accounting*, second edition, and described later in the preface, enables students and instructors to study important issues in greater depth.

EMPHASIS ON REAL-WORLD EXAMPLES

Recognizing that today's students respond best to material drawn from actual events at actual companies, we have made a concerted effort to support our text with examples wherever possible.

The emphasis on actual business settings goes well beyond the use of examples within the textual narrative: The text is also well illustrated with full-color and black-and-white illustrations taken from the annual reports and newsletters of over a hundred companies. These photos add to the richness of the text's real-world flavor and emphasize that management accounting information has actual, tangible applications in a variety of workplace settings. From Microsoft's Windows '95 to EMI Records Group, these examples help make management accounting more relevant to students.

Consider This . . . features are boxed inserts that focus on a particular point of interest. Some of these features look at current or emerging practices in management accounting, such as ethics in budgeting. Other Consider This . . . boxes offer an insight into an actual company's operations. Management accounting comes alive in these features, which look at Pizza Hut, Walt Disney, Bristol-Myers Squibb, General Mills, Whirlpool, and scores of other businesses.

The text is supplemented with a set of **videotapes** containing actual footage of operations supplied by Fortune 500 service and manufacturing companies. Videos are also available containing excerpts from a variety of ABC News programs that deal with management accounting topics. A special series, *On Location!*, contains footage, custom-made, to accompany *Management Accounting.*

REVISIONS FOR THE SECOND EDITION

Changes in Content and Sequence

The sequence of chapters in *Management Accounting*, second edition, has been revised so that the basic cost concepts, from Chapter 3 ("Cost Concepts") to Chapter 8 ("Process and Activity Decisions") are covered in order, without interruption. Other important changes follow.

- Chapter 1 introduces the Balanced Scorecard, a measurement system that includes financial and nonfinancial measures of performance. The balanced scorecard is the framework for much of the text's presentation.

- Coverage of JIT, which appeared in the second chapter in the first edition, has been shortened and moved to Chapter 8, "Process and Activity Decisions."

- Budgeting for Operations, which had been the fifth chapter in the first edition, now appears as Chapter 9. In this way we move from basic cost ideas—Chapter 3, "Cost Concepts," and Chapter 4, "Cost Behavior"—directly into the sequence of chapters that focus on activity-based costing and activity-based management. Chapter 5 ("Basic Product Costing Systems"), Chapter 6 ("Two-Stage Allocations and Activity-Based Costing Systems"), Chapter 7 ("Pricing and Product-Mix Decisions"), and Chapter 8 ("Process and Activity Decisions") evolve most effectively in this improved sequence.

- Chapter 13, "Contemporary Management Accounting: Methods to Stay Competitive," is a new chapter that addresses innovative management accounting procedures, including benchmarking and life-cycle, target, quality, and kaizen costing.
- Much of the mathematical presentation has been taken out of the running text and is now displayed. This presentation will help students find appropriate mathematical references as they work through the assignment material.

Changes in Assignment Material

We have considerably improved the assignment material in this revision.

- Problem material has been revised for clarity and coverage. Each chapter has at least four new problems.
- Problems are now divided into two categories, Fundamental and Challenging. This division eases the instructor's task in making assignments. Also, students are able to evaluate their progress by understanding the degree of difficulty in the problems.
- Each exercise, problem, and case now has a label stating its topical coverage, which further helps the instructor in making assignments.
- Midchapter summary problems and end-of-chapter summary problems, with fully worked-out solutions, have been added as appropriate. These features give students a benchmark for their understanding of the chapter's content and a framework to which they can refer as they work on their assignments.

A Special Note on Numerical Exhibits

Data in some exhibits were produced using a computer spreadsheet. When the exhibits are printed they may show only four or five significant digits even though the computer is calculating the results with more significant digits. For example, when the computer multiplies $1 million by 0.348609425, it obtains the correct answer as 3,486,094.25 but may only report the answer to four significant digits, as 3,486,000. You should assume that the figures reported in the exhibits are correct although they may differ in the last digit from what you calculate based on the other numbers in the exhibit because of this rounding effect.

Special Features

Each chapter begins with a set of **Learning Objectives** to give students a preview of what material the chapter covers. These learning objectives appear again in the margins of the text adjacent to where the objectives are first addressed. They serve as a roadmap for the first read and for quick reference in review.

Key terms are displayed in bold-face type when first introduced in the text. Marginal definitions are provided for these key terms, which also serve as a vehicle for student review.

Chapters end with a **Summary,** which reinforces important topics. The **Key Term** list, with the terms referenced to the page where they are defined, follows. We then present the **Assignment Material,** which offers a range of Questions, Exercises, Problems, and Cases.

The end of the book offers a complete glossary and company and subject indexes.

SUPPLEMENTS AND SERVICE FOR THE INSTRUCTOR

THE PRENTICE HALL ACCOUNTING AND TAXATION HOTLINE 1-800-227-1816/or Hotline E-Mail: patti_dant@prenhall.com.   Prentice Hall's unique Accounting and Taxation Hotline is your direct link to satisfying all your adoption needs! By calling our toll-free telephone number, you can receive information on Prentice Hall's Accounting and Tax texts and supplements. The Hotline will also process your orders and keep you up-to-date on the upcoming Prentice Hall Accounting Seminars for Educators (PHASE) in your area.

INSTRUCTOR'S MANUAL/VIDEO GUIDE.   This supplement provides an overview, an outline, and a 10-minute quiz for each text chapter. In addition, the *Instructor's Manual* suggests readings that appear in the supplemental text *Readings in Management Accounting* by S. Mark Young. These are transition notes for faculty found after each chapter overview. The Video Guide, another component of the *Instructor's Manual*, provides a brief synopsis of the video content, suggested assignment material, and discussion questions for each video found in the ABC/PH Video Library for *Management Accounting*.

SOLUTIONS MANUAL/CHECK FIGURES.   Solutions for all questions, exercises, problems, and cases in the text are provided in the *Solutions Manual*. Each solution has been triple-checked for accuracy. A list of check figures provides key amounts for all numerical exercises, problems, and cases. Check figures are also available in quantity for the classroom by contacting the Prentice Hall Accounting and Taxation Hotline.

SOLUTIONS TRANSPARENCIES.   Every page of the *Solutions Manual* has been recreated as an acetate for use on the overhead projector.

TEST ITEM FILE.   The *Test Item File* contains approximately 1,500 components, including true/false questions, multiple-choice questions, exercises, problems, and critical-thinking questions.

PRENTICE HALL CUSTOM TEST.   Available in both DOS and WINDOWS, this easy-to-use computerized testing program is available on 3.5″ diskettes. This user-friendly program allows you to create an exam and evaluate and track student results. The *PH Custom Test* also provides on-line testing capabilities. Test material is drawn from the *Test Item File*.

PH PROFESSOR: A Classroom Presentation on PowerPoint for *Management Accounting*.   PowerPoint slides are available for each chapter of the text. This computerized supplement by Jamie Doran provides the instructor with an interactive presentation, which outlines the chapter material using colorful graphics and charts. It is not necessary to have PowerPoint in order to run the presentation. However, having PowerPoint will provide instructors with the flexibility to add slides or modify the existing ones to meet course needs.

TEACHING TRANSPARENCIES.   Derived from the *PH Professor: A Classroom Presentation on PowerPoint for Management Accounting* are four-color teaching transparencies that instructors can use on an overhead projector.

THE ABC NEWS/PRENTICE HALL VIDEO LIBRARY *ON LOCATION!* FOR *MANAGEMENT ACCOUNTING*.   Video is a dynamic way to enhance your classroom lectures, and the quality of the video material and how well it relates to your course can still make all the difference. For these reasons, Prentice Hall and ABC News have worked together to bring you the best and most comprehensive video ancillary available on the college market.

ABC NEWS.   Through its wide variety of award-winning programs, such as "Nightline," "Business World," "On Business," This Week with David Brinkley," "World News Tonight," and "The Wall Street Journal Report," ABC offers a resource for feature and documentary-style videos to enhance text concepts and applications. The programs have extremely high production quality, present substantial content, and feature well-versed, well-known anchors as hosts.

ON LOCATION!   These videos, commissioned exclusively for Prentice Hall, are included in the *ABC/Prentice Hall Video Library On Location for Management Accounting*. Broadcast journalism and accounting education meet to create a series of custom produced case videos. These videos contain all the fast-paced and engaging qualities of TV and focus on the successful management accounting activities of several companies. You can take your students *On Location* to companies such as the Ritz-Carlton, Grand Canyon Railway, Nally & Gibson Georgetown, Inc., and Deer Valley Ski Resort. Each video runs approximately eight to ten minutes.

　　The video library features plant-tour footage provided by Fortune 500 service and manufacturing companies such as Chrysler, Avnet, Con Edison, and Quaker State as well as footage on the Malcolm Baldrige Award Winners of 1990 and 1991. A Video Guide in the *Instructor's Manual* helps instructors carefully integrate the videos into classroom lectures.

INSTRUCTOR'S GUIDE TO USING READINGS IN MANAGEMENT ACCOUNTING.   This guide links *Readings in Management Accounting*, by S. Mark Young, to topics found in current management accounting texts. The discussion questions at the end of each reading invite students to test their analytical skills.

PRENTICE HALL'S WEBSITE FOR MANAGEMENT ACTIVITY.   The Prentice Hall Website for *Management Accounting* located at http://www.prenhall.com/phbusiness is a new resource that ties directly with the text. It provides up-to-date news articles relating to management accounting as well as numerous teaching resources and activities for the classroom. The Prentice Hall website also provides links to the websites of companies highlighted in the book to give students the opportunity to explore the businesses they are studying.

Supplements for the Student

STUDY GUIDE. For each chapter in the text, the *Study Guide* by S. Mark Young and Ella Mae Matsumura provides an overview, a review, and a self-test to help students prepare for examinations.

POWER NOTES. This convenient tool contains print-outs of each Power-Point slide and additional space for taking notes. Power Notes allow students to focus their attention on the class lecture and take down additional explanations and examples given by the instructor. This efficient note-taking supplement is also a great tool for studying!

READINGS IN MANAGEMENT ACCOUNTING. This supplement by S. Mark Young is a compilation of recent business press and academic articles that parallel the contents of the book. Sources include *The Journal of Cost Management, Management Accounting, The Wall Street Journal, Fortune Magazine, The Harvard Business Review,* and other sources. The introduction for each chapter summarizes key points in the provided readings. Each reading concludes with a thought-provoking question.

SPREADSHEET TEMPLATES. Students can use these templates by Albert Fisher to solve selected exercises and problems from the text. The documentation includes a short tutorial on how to use Excel as well as step-by-step instructions for completing each template. Students need not have an in-depth knowledge of spreadsheet programming techniques. Rather, the templates are designed to focus students on the appropriate accounting concepts. Spreadsheet solutions are available on disk to the instructor upon adoption of the text.

CAREER PATHS IN ACCOUNTING CD-ROM. Winner of the New Media INVISION Gold Award in Education, separately or with the text, this CD-ROM provides students with a dynamic, interactive job-searching tool. Included are workshops in career planning, resume writing, and interviewing skills. Students can learn the latest market trends and facts as well as the skills required to get the right job. In addition, the CD-ROM provides the student with salary information, video clips describing specific jobs, and profiles of practitioners in the field.

ACTIVITIES IN MANAGEMENT ACCOUNTING. Show your students the importance of teamwork and let them experience reading, analyzing, interpreting, and evaluating management accounting information for business decision making. This workbook by Martha Doran contains interactive learning assignments designed to help students see beyond the technical aspects of accounting through active learning. A variety of real-world situations will give students the opportunity to practice the concepts taught in the classroom. In addition, these group activities fulfill the AECC recommendations by providing students with the chance to practice and improve their writing, speaking, and reasoning skills. An *Instructor's Manual* provides a summary overview for each activity. The notes also highlight important content and process objectives, and provide step-by-step instructions for running each activity.

ACKNOWLEDGMENTS

We would very much like to take this opportunity to thank the many professors who reviewed this textbook at various stages of its development:

Onker N. Basu, University of Akron
Jacob G. Birnberg, University of Pittsburgh
Donald E. Bostrom, University of North Dakota
H. David Brecht, California State University, Sacramento
Wayne G. Bremser, Villanova University
Marvelyn R. Burnette, Wichita State University
Hsihui Chang, National Chengchi University
Susan R. Cockrell, East Texas State University
Maureen Crane, California State University, Fresno
Timothy A. Farmer, University of Missouri-St. Louis
David R. Fordham, James Madison University
George F. Gardner, Bemidji State University
Paul Gemmiti, State University of New York College at Cobleskill
Edward S. Goodhart, Shippensburg University
Mahendra Gupta, Washington University, St. Louis
M. Shamsul Haque, Howard University
Larry P. Hegstad, Pacific Lutheran College
Dolan R. Hinson, University of North Carolina at Charlotte
Susan B. Hughes, Butler University
Fred H. Jacobs, Michigan State University
Douglas A. Johnson, Arizona State University
Donald E. Keller, California State University, Long Beach
G. William Kennedy, Stonehill College
Zafar U. Khan, Eastern Michigan University
Leslie Kren, University of Wisconsin-Milwaukee
Alan Larris, University of Akron
Chi-Wen Jevons Lee, Tulane University
Seok-Young Lee, Sungshin Women's University
Robert Lin, California State University, Hayward
Thomas Lin, University of Southern California
Frank C. Lordi, Widener University
Kenneth A. Merchant, University of Southern California
Gerald M. Myers, Pacific Lutheran University
Brian A. O'Doherty, East Carolina University
Priscilla R. Reis, Idaho State University
Richard A. Rivers, Southern Illinois University at Carbondale
Michael D. Shields, University of Memphis
Donald R. Simons, University of Wisconsin-Oshkosh
Kimberly J. Smith, College of William and Mary
Donn W. Vickrey, University of San Diego
Joseph Weintrop, Baruch College of the City University of New York
Lourdes Ferreira White, University of Baltimore
James W. Woolley, University of Utah
William F. Yancey, Texas Christian University
Thomas L. Zeller, Loyola University-Chicago

The following people class-tested the textbook:

Felix E. Amenkhienan, Radford University
Hsihui Chang, National Chengchi University
Timothy A. Farmer, University of Missouri-St. Louis
Sanford C. Gunn, State University of New York at Buffalo
Scott K. Jones, University of Delaware
Debra Hua Lu, St. Cloud State University
Gerald M. Myers, Pacific Lutheran University
Linda S. Staniszewski, University of Southern Mississippi
Scott Stovall, Harding University
Audrey G. Taylor, Wayne State University

The following people contributed their insight in a focus group:

Thomas M. Carment, Northeastern State University, Oklahoma
Nancy T. Hill, DePaul University
Brian Leventhal, University of Illinois-Chicago
Karen Tabak, Maryville University
Thomas L. Zeller, Loyola University-Chicago

We would also like to thank people on the Prentice Hall team who contributed so much to this project: Jane Avery, Suzanne Behnke, P.J. Boardman, Patti Dant, Steve Deitmer, Deborah H. Emry, Katherine Evancie, Leslye Givarz, Joanne Jay, Natacha St. Hill, Vincent Scelta, Audra Silverie, Paul Smolenski, Richard Wohl, and Patricia Wosczyk.

The authors and publisher would also like to thank Ella Mae Matsumura for her valuable contributions and efforts in the completion of this manuscript.

A.A.A.
R.D.B.
R.S.K.
S.M.Y.

ANTHONY A. ATKINSON is currently the Society of Management Accountants of Ontario Professor in the School of Accountancy at the University of Waterloo. Atkinson received a Bachelor of Commerce and M.B.A. degrees from Queen's University in Kingston, Ontario, M.S. and Ph.D. in Industrial Administration degrees from Carnegie-Mellon University in Pittsburgh, and the designation of Certified Management Accountant in Nova Scotia. He has written or co-authored two texts, monographs, and over 35 articles on performance measurement and costing. In 1989, the Canadian Academic Accounting Association awarded Atkinson the Haim Falk Prize for Distinguished Contribution to Accounting Thought for his monograph that studied transfer pricing practice in six Canadian companies. He has served on the editorial boards of two professional and five academic journals and in 1996 was appointed Editor Elect of the Journal of Management Accounting Research. Atkinson also served as a member of the Canadian government's Cost Standards Advisory Committee, for which he developed the costing principles it now requires of government contractors.

RAJIV D. BANKER has taught at Carnegie-Mellon University, University of Minnesota and Dartmouth College. Banker graduated from the University of Bombay at the top of his class and received a doctorate in business administration from Harvard University. He received two awards for teaching excellence at Carnegie-Mellon University and the Outstanding Teacher Award at the University of Minnesota.

Banker has published more than 90 articles in leading research journals in accounting, information systems, computer science, operations management, management science, and economics, including articles in the *Accounting Review*, *Journal of Accounting and Economics*, and the *Journal of Accounting Research*. He has received five awards for his research articles. Banker's current research in management accounting includes issues pertaining to strategic cost management, activity-based costing, costs of quality, and value of performance-based incentive plans, among other issues. His research has been supported by the National Science Foundation, the Institute of Management Accountants, and several leading corporations.

ROBERT S. KAPLAN

since 1984 has been the Arthur Lowes Dickinson Professor of Accounting at the Harvard Business School. Formerly, he was on the faculty of the Graduate School of Industrial Administration at Carnegie-Mellon University and served as Dean of that school from 1977 to 1983. He received a B.S. and M.S. in Electrical Engineering from M.I.T. and a Ph.D. in Operations Research from Cornell University. In 1994, he was awarded an honorary doctorate from the University of Stuttgart.

Kaplan has authored or coauthored more than 100 papers and 8 books. Kaplan received the Outstanding Accounting Educator Award in 1988 from the American Accounting Association (AAA) and the 1994 CIMA Award from the Chartered Institute of Management Accountants (U.K.) for Outstanding Contributions to the Accountancy Profession.

Recent publications include *The Balanced Scorecard: Translating Strategy into Action* (Harvard Business School Press, 1996) and a four-part video tape series "Measuring Corporate Performance," which presents concepts and companies' experiences with activity-based cost management and the Balanced Scorecard.

Kaplan consults on the design of performance and cost management systems with many leading companies in North America and Europe.

S. MARK YOUNG

Professor of Accounting at the Leventhal School of Accounting at the University of Southern California, is Associate Editor of the *Journal of Management Accounting Research* and past Associate Editor of *The Accounting Review*. He also serves on several other major editorial boards including *Accounting, Organizations and Society*. Young received an A.B. from Oberlin College, an M.Acc. from The Ohio State University, and a Ph.D. from the University of Pittsburgh. He is the recipient of four outstanding teaching awards at the undergraduate and graduate levels, including the Golden Apple Teaching Award from the MBA Program at USC. He has published over 40 papers and made over 100 presentations of his research in Europe, Asia, Australia, and the United States. Young has been a KPMG Peat Marwick Faculty Fellow and has received research grants from the National Science Foundation, The Institute of Management Accountants, the Consortium for Advanced Manufacturing International, The Institute of Internal Auditors, and the Center for Innovation Management Studies. In 1994, together with coauthor Frank Selto, Young won the Management Accounting Section's (AAA) Notable Contribution to the Management Accounting Literature Award. Most recently, Dr. Young has conducted research or consulted with Nevada Power Company, Texas Instruments, the Economic Analysis Corporation, First Data Corporation, Chrysler, and General Motors.

MANAGEMENT ACCOUNTING

1

MANAGEMENT ACCOUNTING: INFORMATION THAT CREATES VALUE

CHAPTER OBJECTIVES

After reading this chapter,
you will be able to

1. appreciate the important role that management accounting information plays in both manufacturing and service organizations

2. discuss the significant differences between management accounting and financial accounting

3. understand how different people in the organization have different demands for management accounting information

4. appreciate how management accounting creates value for organizations and how it relates to operations, marketing, and strategy

5. explain why management accounting information must include both financial and nonfinancial information

6. understand why activities should be the primary focus for measuring and managing performance in organizations

7. discuss the role for multiple performance measures—financial and nonfinancial—to translate the organization's strategy into specific objectives and measures

GREEN'S GROCERY

Courtesy **Frank Siteman/Stock, Boston**

Art Shaw, a consultant in an international accounting firm, was interviewing for the corporate **controller**'s job at Green's Grocery, a regional supermarket chain in the Southwestern United States. Green's Grocery had a dominant market share in its region with sales in excess of $4 billion annually.

Bill Fuller, the president of Green's Grocery, had met Art at a recent conference where Art was giving a talk describing some new **cost management systems** being installed in electronics and automobile companies. Fuller spent several hours explaining why he wanted a new type of corporate controller for his food retailing company:

> Green's Grocery has a slim profit margin yet is one of the most profitable supermarket chains in the United States. We earn a 4% pretax return on sales, almost twice the industry average, but we're facing major challenges ahead. Some of the large retail chains, like Wal-Mart, have built discount-food stores in our area that offer prices significantly below ours. These discount stores don't offer the wide assortment of products, brands, flavors, and sizes that Green's does, but their rock-bottom prices are attracting many of our customers.

> I have a lot of options for changing the way Green's does business to become more profitable and more competitive, but I don't have a sound basis for making these decisions. I don't really know much about my cost structure, such as where my operations may be making or losing money. Our financial reporting systems seem to be fine—revenues and expenses are accurately recorded, and the auditors are more than pleased when they verify our records against actual physical assets. But I don't understand the relevant costs for making decisions about the number of different items and brands we should be offering to our customers, new supplier relationships, pricing, expansion of our private label offerings, and size of the stores.

> For example, although consumers value our large variety, I think the cost of this variety may be too high for us. Generating $20 million of annual sales from the 40,000 items we stock in one of our stores must be more expensive than getting the same $20 million in sales from the 5000 items that the discounters offer. The much higher variety we offer requires us to build and operate larger stores in order to display each item. It also forces us to purchase from many different suppliers. Undoubtedly, we have higher warehousing,

Controller
An organization's senior finance and accounting executive; prepares and interprets financial information for managers, investors, and creditors.

Cost management systems
Information systems that report on the costs of an organization's activities, processes, products, services, and customers; used for a variety of decision-making and improvement activities.

merchandising, and transportation costs from the larger variety. How can I balance the benefits to the consumer for a larger variety if I don't know the costs associated with the larger assortment we offer?

Also, some of our best suppliers are asking us to allow them to plan their production and distribution schedules based on information communicated electronically from our point-of-sale terminals—a practice known as electronic data interchange, or EDI. The synchronization of suppliers' production and supply based on actual consumer purchases, may produce enormous savings in operating expenses, inventory, and space requirements both for them and for us. If we can quantify these cost savings, the suppliers may sell us their products at lower prices. We can then offer the products at lower markups because of our lower operating expenses. This would substantially reduce and perhaps eliminate the price gap between our supermarkets and the discount stores.

In addition to such potential cost savings, we have another opportunity to consider. Some high-quality private label suppliers have developed products in very important categories for us, such as cola beverages, cookies, pet foods, and salad dressings. These suppliers claim that the quality of their products is indistinguishable from the best nationally advertised brands. The private label suppliers are willing to charge us much lower prices than the national brand manufacturers, which would allow us to earn a higher profit margin on their products while still offering them to consumers at lower prices than the national brands. Many of the national brand manufacturers, however, already operate very efficiently with us. Coca-Cola and Pepsi Cola, for example, deliver directly to our stores. Their salespersons drive to each of our stores and stock the shelves so that we don't have to do any work to get their products ready for sale. The private label suppliers, on the other hand, ship their products to our warehouses where we receive the goods, put them into inventory, store them, schedule them for delivery to our retail stores, deliver them, and place them onto our store shelves. I wonder if the apparently higher margins we may earn on private-label products may not be used up by the costs of performing all these extra activities.

As another issue, I must decide about which departments we should have in our stores. Every store must contain space for traditional packaged goods sold in cans, boxes, jars, and plastic containers; a dairy department that requires refrigerated shelves and will generate spoilage and frequent consumer returns; and a frozen goods department, again with expensive fixtures and high-energy consumption. Recently, we have added sections that sell health and beauty aids; a bakery; a fresh deli; and a prepared-foods section. Although our excellent financial-reporting systems enable us to know the total amount of store operating expense quite accurately, I have no idea how to relate this total operating expense to all the individual departments. Are we making money in the bakery and deli sections? We need to know where we can make operating improvements to enhance productivity and efficiency.

I also need a good cost-management system to help my store managers manage their daily operations more efficiently. What kinds of reports can the system produce to help my store managers monitor and control their labor staffing policies, merchandise availability, inventory efficiencies, and utility consumption?

If operational improvements are not enough to generate profitability, perhaps we can **outsource** some of our departments to more efficient contractors and allow them to operate these departments in the space we would rent to them. Maybe we can eliminate some of the noncritical categories entirely, which would enable us to build smaller stores in the future. Also, store managers keep thinking about new product categories that we can put into our stores—fresh flowers, wine, beer, liquor, stationery, books, magazines, and small toys. While all of these seem like good ideas from a gross margin basis (sales price less the purchase cost of the items), they may not be profitable when the costs of all the resources of the store, including space, merchandise inventory, and store personnel are accurately assigned to these categories.

Our current controller came from the same accounting firm where you now work, but his experience was all in the audit side and he seems to have little idea about managers' needs for information for decision-making and control. Can we apply the management accounting ideas now being used in electronics and automotive companies to the supermarket business?

Art Shaw wondered whether new management accounting concepts introduced successfully in many manufacturing companies could be applied to a service business like retailing. Should he leave a growing consulting business with his manufacturing clients to be an innovator on applying modern cost- and performance-measurement approaches to service businesses?

The challenges that Bill Fuller proposed to Art Shaw are examples of how managers in organizations need management accounting information for decision-making and control. Management accounting systems enable organizations to collect, process, store, and report information for a variety of vital operational and managerial decisions.

Outsource
The process of selecting an outside organization (a supplier) to provide a good or service previously produced internally. Outsourcing is typically done because the outside supplier can supply the good or service at lower cost or higher quality.

MANAGEMENT ACCOUNTING INFORMATION

What Is Management Accounting Information?

Management accounting is the process of identifying, measuring, reporting, and analyzing information about the economic events of organizations.[1] One example

Management accounting
The process of producing financial and operating information for organizational employees and managers. The process should be driven by the informational needs of individuals *internal* to the organization and should guide their operating and investment decisions.

---

[1] A more complete definition of management accounting appears in Appendix 1A.

Management accounting information
Financial and operating data about an organization's activities, processes, operating units, products, services, and customers; e.g., the calculated cost of a product, an activity, or a department in a recent time period.

of **management accounting information** is the reported expenses of an operating department, such as the bakery department in a grocery store. Other examples are the calculated costs of producing a product; delivering a service, performing an activity and business process; and serving a customer. Management accounting information is one of the primary informational sources for decision making and control in organizations. Management accounting systems produce information that helps workers, managers, and executives make better decisions and improve their organization's processes and performance.

Traditionally, management accounting information has been financial, that is, it has been denominated in a currency such as dollars or francs. Recently however, management accounting information has expanded to encompass operational or physical (nonfinancial) information, such as quality and process times, as well as more subjective information such as measurements of customer satisfaction, employee capabilities, and new product performance.

How Does Management Accounting Information Help Managers?

OBJECTIVE 1.1

Appreciate the important role that management accounting information plays in both manufacturing and service organizations.

Measures of the economic condition of the enterprise, such as the cost and profitability of the organization's products, services, customers, and activities, are available only from management accounting systems. In addition, management accounting information measures the economic performance of decentralized operating units, such as business units, divisions, and departments. These measures of economic performance link the strategy of the organization to the execution of the strategy by individual operating units. Management accounting information is also one of the primary means by which operators/workers, middle managers, and executives receive feedback on their performance, enabling them to learn from the past and improve for the future.

Ultimately, organizations succeed and prosper by designing products and services that customers value, producing these products and services and distributing them to customers with efficient operating processes and marketing and selling the organization's outputs effectively to customers. Although management accounting information cannot guarantee success in these critical organizational activities, inadequate and distorted signals from management accounting systems will cause companies to encounter severe difficulties. Effective management accounting systems can create considerable value by providing timely and accurate information about the activities required for the success of today's organizations.

Financial accounting
The process of producing financial statements for external constituencies—people outside the organization, such as shareholders, creditors, and governmental authorities. This process is heavily constrained by standard-setting, regulatory, and tax authorities and the auditing requirements of independent accountants (contrast with management accounting).

DIFFERENCES BETWEEN MANAGEMENT ACCOUNTING AND FINANCIAL ACCOUNTING

Financial accounting deals with reporting and communicating economic information about an organization to external constituencies: shareholders, creditors (bankers, bondholders, and suppliers), regulators, and governmental tax authorities. Financial accounting information communicates to outsiders the consequences of the decisions and process improvements made by managers and employees. The financial accounting process is constrained by mandated reporting requirements of external regulatory authorities, such as the Financial Accounting Standards Board (FASB) and the Securities and Exchange Commission (SEC) in the United States, as well as by governmental tax agencies. As a consequence, financial accounting tends to be rules driven, and students of financial accounting study the journal entries and procedures that generate the mandated financial statements.

In contrast, Bill Fuller's request to Art Shaw in the opening vignette illustrates that management accounting must provide economic information to internal constituencies: operators/workers, middle managers, and senior executives. Companies have great discretion in the design of their management accounting systems. Managers should use this discretion to design systems that provide information for helping employees make good decisions about their organization's financial, physical, and human resources, as well as their products, services, processes, suppliers, and customers. The information from management accounting systems should help employees learn how to do the following:

OBJECTIVE 1.2·

Discuss the significant differences between management accounting and financial accounting.

1. Improve the quality of operations.
2. Lower the cost of operations.
3. Increase the responsiveness of operations for customer needs.

Therefore, management accounting students focus on the decisions and informational needs of organizational participants. Exhibit 1-1 provides an overview of the basic features of financial and management accounting and illustrates the contrast between them.

EXHIBIT 1-1
Financial and Management Accounting Basic Features

	Financial Accounting	**Managerial Accounting**
Audience	*External:* Stockholders, creditors, tax authorities	*Internal:* Workers, managers, executives
Purpose	Report on past performance to external parties; contracts with owners and lenders	Inform internal decisions made by employees and managers; feedback and control on operating performance
Timeliness	Delayed; historical	Current, future oriented
Restrictions	Regulated; rules driven by generally accepted accounting principles and government authorities	No regulations; systems and information determined by management to meet strategic and operational needs
Type of Information	Financial measurements only	Financial plus operational and physical measurements on processes, technologies, suppliers, customers, and competitors
Nature of Information	Objective, auditable, reliable, consistent, precise	More subjective and judgmental; valid, relevant, accurate
Scope	Highly aggregate; report on entire organization	Disaggregate; inform local decisions and actions

CONSIDER THIS . . .

Management Accounting in 19th-Century Enterprises

TEXTILE INDUSTRY   The demand for management accounting information can be traced back to the early stages of the industrial revolution in textile mills, in armories that built weapons, and in other manufacturing operations. For example, records of early 19th-century textile mills show that textile mill managers received information about the hourly cost of converting raw material (cotton) into intermediate products (thread and yarn) and finished products (fabric) and the cost per pound of output by departments and for each worker.

The owners used such managerial accounting information for two different purposes:

1. To control and improve efficiency.
2. For pricing and product mix decisions.

For example, managers measured the efficiency of the process that converted raw cotton into finished yarn and fabric. Managers compared productivity among workers and tracked the productivity of individual workers over several periods of time. The managers used this information to provide additional compensation for the most productive workers and serve as production targets for less efficient workers. This information helped to maintain and improve the efficiency of critical internal processes.

For decision-making purposes, the cost information helped managers determine when additional purchases of new machinery might be justified by higher productivity. Managers also used information on products' costs and profitability to set piecework wages for workers and to establish target prices for selling fabric or yarn, particularly for items that were specialized and customized for individual orders.

RAILROAD INDUSTRY   The railroad organizations that developed in the mid-19th century were enormous and complex enterprises that could not have functioned effectively without extensive management accounting information to provide summary measures of performance for decentralized and dispersed managers. Financial managers in the railroads developed measures such as cost per ton mile for individual commodity types and for each geographic segment of operations. They developed and used a new measure called the operating ratio that measured the ratio of operating expenses to revenues. Managers used this measure both for operational control, to evaluate the efficiency of operations of local managers and for product costing to measure the profitability of various types of business: passenger versus freight, region by region. These measures enabled local managers to take actions based on the unique information they had about local conditions that were consistent with maximizing profits for the entire railroad.

OTHER COMPANIES   Steel mills, such as those owned and operated by Andrew Carnegie, measured daily the cost of materials, labor, and energy inputs used to produce steel and rails. Carnegie used the cost information for operational control—to evaluate the performance of department managers, foremen, and workers and to check the quality and mix of raw materials. He also used the cost information to evaluate investments that offered improvements for processes and products. For nonstandardized products, such as steel for bridges, the cost information was the basis for pricing decisions. The company would not accept a contract unless it had a careful analysis and estimate of the costs involved.

Companies that manufactured discrete customized products, such as machine tools, had to understand the costs of resources used to produce each item. This information determined the profitability of producing different product lines and helped determine the prices that would be offered, particularly for customized products, to prospective customers. Engineers in the scientific management movement, such as Frederick Taylor, developed procedures to measure in considerable detail the quantity of materials and the labor and machine time required to manufacture individual products. This information was collected primarily to improve and control the efficiency of production operations, but it also served as an input to product-costing calculations. The costing techniques developed at that time persisted for many decades and still can be found in many of today's organizations.

Source: This section draws on material in Chapters 2 and 3 of H. Thomas Johnson and Robert S. Kaplan, *Relevance Lost: The Rise and Fall of Management Accounting* (Boston: Harvard Business School Press, 1987).

From this brief description, it may seem logical that the accounting process should start by determining the information needed for internal purposes, and after designing excellent management accounting system address the needs of external constituencies for information about the aggregate economic impact of these internal decisions. Indeed, in the 19th century, companies' accounting systems were designed to meet the decision-making and control needs of managers.

During the past century, however, accounting for external constituencies became quite demanding because of the increased regulation and numbers of standards for external reporting (from the FASB and SEC, for example, in the U.S.). The demands of these external constituents led many organizations to place more emphasis on developing information for external financial reporting than for internal managerial decision making and control. As a result, management accounting systems in most organizations proved inadequate for changing and challenging competitive, technological, and market conditions.

The management accounting practices described in this book are derived from the information and decision needs of an organization's managers and employees, not from requirements to prepare statements for external constituencies.

DIVERSITY OF MANAGEMENT ACCOUNTING INFORMATION

We can illustrate the diverse uses for management accounting information with a relatively simple example. Consider the operation of an automobile dealership. What are the varied uses of operational and financial information in this type of organization? How does the demand for managerial accounting information vary among employees at different levels of the organization?

Repair Mechanic

Dennis Mitchell is an automobile mechanic who repairs and maintains cars. Dennis performs many standard activities for which much prior knowledge already exists. For example, he frequently replaces brakes; installs a new muffler or exhaust system; lubricates the car; changes the oil and oil filter; or performs a tune-up. These tasks have been done thousands of times before by mechanics at this dealership and at auto-repair facilities all over the world. Thus, *labor time standards* probably exist for the amount of time Dennis should take to perform each of these tasks as well as *materials quantity standards* for the amount of materials and supplies required for the maintenance or repair.

Since Dennis may wish to assess his efficiency in performing maintenance and repairs, the management accounting system should provide him with the information about the actual time required and the actual parts and materials used for each job. Dennis can use this information to determine whether he is performing at the normal efficiency assumed in establishing the labor time and materials quantity standards for this activity. In addition to the quantity of materials and labor time used, some repair jobs may require testing the automobile on specialized equipment or using that special equipment as part of the repair process itself. Dennis will find it helpful to know how much time each job required on specialized equipment. Management accountants can develop, relatively easily, information on the standards for labor time, machine time, and materials usage for the most repetitive tasks. Employees use this information to monitor, control, and improve the efficiency with which they use resources, such as their labor time, equipment use, and materials consumption, for repetitive tasks.

After Dennis finishes a maintenance- or repair-procedure, he performs a quality check by starting the car and testing whether it runs properly. If he finds a defect, he replaces the faulty part, either a bad part or a badly installed part, and continues to work on the car until it works properly. This information about the quality of the work performed is also valuable in assessing how well Dennis is performing his job.

In addition to routine tasks, Dennis is frequently asked to do some nonstandard work. For example, Dennis may have to fix an engine that is not working properly when neither the owner nor he currently knows the cause for the malfunction or to repair a car that has suffered considerable damage in an accident. In both these cases, the full extent of the required repairs are not known until Dennis starts working on the car. He will record the actual time spent on the job, which equipment was used, and for how long the equipment was used as well as the quantity and identity of parts and materials used to bring the car back into working condition. Then the manager of the repair shop will use this information to determine the price charged to the customer for the nonstandard repairs. This example shows how management accounting information can help in pricing decisions for nonstandard and customized services.

Paper moves through a modern paper machine at about 14 meters per second. Tiny holes in the web of paper can create costly problems. Mead Corporation, a paper maker, designed a computer-based artificial intelligence system that uses 1,200 sensing devices and computer systems to control some 750 process variables in paper making. *Courtesy* William Taufic

INFORMATIONAL SUMMARY.   The information used by Dennis, a frontline employee, includes data on the quantity of materials, supplies, labor and machine time used to produce a service. The information also includes data on the quantity of outputs Dennis produced: the number of repair jobs completed. Finally, it includes quality information, such as the proportion of repairs successfully completed without additional rework and the number of defects detected while producing the service.

At this simple level, we can see the role for a wide variety of quantitative information for employees such as Dennis, but so far not much of a role for financial information. This is typical of traditional organizations, in which employees and operators are directed to perform prescribed tasks. In such situations, they receive quantitative summaries of their performance but are told little about the economic or financial consequences of the work they perform. We will return to this issue later as we discuss how front-line employees can do their jobs even better if they receive financial information related to their work. For now assume that production and service workers primarily use quantitative operational data, rather than financial information, for their day-to-day tasks.

INFORMATIONAL FREQUENCY.   In addition to the amount and type of information provided to Dennis, with what frequency should it be provided? Dennis produces outputs, such as repaired cars, continually throughout the day. Therefore, he needs daily or even individual job summaries if he is to learn how well he is performing and where opportunities for improvement may exist. He is not likely to value a monthly report that contains only summary and aggregate information about factors like these:

1. The total parts and materials used in car repairs
2. The total time used during the month to repair cars including both actual time and the difference between actual and standard times allowed for the repairs
3. The total time spent reworking defects during the month

Dennis would *not* be able to relate such a highly aggregated and delayed report to each of the repair jobs he performed during the month.

To summarize at the operational level the relevant information provided to employees should include accurate quantitative information about inputs used—the labor and machine times, materials, parts and supplies; the outputs produced; and the quality of service or production process. The information should be timely, which means daily or after each job, so that the operator is aware at the time of any discrepancies between actual and standard or historical performance. As long as operators are performing standard, repetitive tasks, they apparently have little need for financial or cost data.

Manager of the Service Department

What are the information needs of Jennifer Pratt, the manager of the service department? Jennifer supervises the two dozen mechanics who work in the department as well as the service representatives who discuss proposed maintenance and repairs with customers and return repaired cars to them.

Jennifer wants information about the use of the service department's resources. Since mechanics are paid for an eight-hour shift whether they are working on jobs or not, she will want a report that compares the number of hours actually spent repairing and maintaining cars with the number of hours for which mechanics are paid. This will help her see whether the department currently has unused capacity or whether it is operating at full capacity. If productive work is consistently below capacity (so that mechanics are often not working on jobs), Jennifer can consider reducing the size of the service department; if the department is consistently working *at capacity*, she can contemplate adding additional resources, such as extra mechanics and another service bay to handle the greater demand.

To assess the *efficiency* of the mechanics as measured by the quantity of resources used for maintenance and repairs, she may want to compare the actual labor times, machine times, and quantity of materials and supplies used on individual jobs to the standards established for those jobs. Jennifer will want to determine which mechanics are working more efficiently than others and which are using more resources than expected. (The topic of determining cost standards, and comparing actual costs to standard costs will be discussed in Chapter 3.) Jennifer will also monitor the quality of the work performed—which jobs or mechanics are generating defects, rework, and customer complaints. The information about the efficiency and quality of work performed will direct her attention to mechanics who may need additional education and training so that they can accomplish their jobs more efficiently and with fewer defects. Also, by identifying the highest quality and most productive mechanics, she can encourage them to share their knowledge and techniques with the less productive, more defect-prone mechanics.

In addition to monitoring capacity use, efficiency, and quality of work performed, Jennifer may need information on the profitability of the service operation. She will receive a weekly or monthly report on the profit or loss generated by the service department. In addition to this aggregate report, she may want a more detailed report on the profitability according to the type of service performed, such as muffler repairs, tune-ups, oil changes, and brake replacements. To prepare this report, management accountants must be able to assign the total service department's expenses to the costs of performing each type of service (a topic that will be discussed in Chapters 5 and 6). Jennifer can then calculate the profitability of each type of service by linking its costs with the revenue generated by the service job. She can use the profitability information on this report to modify prices and to choose an appropriate product mix. For example, she may learn that certain jobs can be performed more efficiently by outsourcing: subcontracting the jobs to local mechanics in the area rather than handling them internally. She can also establish marketing and promotion policies to attract the most profitable maintenance and repair business to the service department. If certain types of jobs appear to be losing money, she can work with the mechanics to see how to perform these jobs at a lower cost.

Jennifer can use the cost estimates for each type of service when she estimates repair costs for used cars acquired as trade-ins when customers purchase new cars. Cost information also helps her make decisions about whether to acquire additional equipment to allow mechanics to perform certain jobs that are not currently possible with existing equipment. In summary, Jennifer will use information about the cost of individual types of maintenance and repair jobs to inform her decisions on pricing; product mix (which repair jobs are more profitable to promote); capacity expansion (adding service bays, mechanics, or new equipment); capacity contraction (reducing the number of mechanics); outsourcing (contracting with local repair shops for certain types of service work); process improvement (performing service jobs faster using fewer supplies and materials); and bidding for new business. These important decisions—made by middle- and upper-level managers in almost all organizations—require accurate management accounting information about current and future operations.

Manager of the Dealership

Barry Beck is the president of the dealership that employs Dennis Mitchell and Jennifer Pratt. Barry is obviously concerned with the overall profitability of the dealership but has less need than Dennis or Jennifer for information to monitor hourly and daily operations or the profit and loss on individual jobs and car sales. Barry receives a monthly, perhaps weekly, financial report on the dealership's profitability broken down by its major operating departments: new car sales, used car sales, car repairs and service, and parts sales. This report requires a reasonable assignment of dealer expenses to the individual operating departments. This means deciding how much of the dealership's people, building, and equipment resources are devoted to the various lines of business: new car sales, fleet sales, used car sales, repairs and service, and sales of parts. This information enables Barry to monitor whether any operating department is falling short of its profit plan. It highlights the likely causes for unexpected shifts in profitability, such as variations in volume, mix, quality, and pricing. Barry will also want to compare the performance of his dealership with that of similar dealerships in terms of volume, efficiency, and profitability. This creates a demand for acquiring external data about the best practices of competitors or other comparable organizations: a practice now referred to as **benchmarking.** (Benchmarking is discussed in Chapters 2 and 13.)

Barry will also want to see financial and operating statistics on **critical success factors,** that is, those factors that indicate whether the organization is creating long-term value and profitability. Critical success factors include the number of cars sold and the margins on car sales by type of vehicle, revenue per employee in the service department, customer-satisfaction indexes, and number of customer complaints.

Many automobile companies now send questionnaires to recent car buyers to assess the quality of the buying experience up through the delivery of the car to the customer. Barry will want to monitor his dealership's scores on this survey over time to ensure that the trend is positive. In addition, he will compare his score to that of other dealers to determine how well his operations are performing relative to competition. As another measure of how well his dealership is doing against competitors, he will measure market share—the percent of total automobile sales and service in his local area that his dealership captures. If customer satisfaction and market share are declining or below levels of targeted competitors, Barry may need to consider improvements in advertising, sales-force training, pricing, and customer service to regain and enhance his market position. Customer retention—the percent of customers who return to the dealership for their next car purchase—will also be a critical long-term success factor for his company.

The information used by a senior executive like Barry Beck—the profitability of products, services, and customers; market opportunities and competitive threats; customer loyalty and satisfaction; and technological innovations—are examples of the **strategic information** that is critical for informing and guiding the decisions of a company's senior executives.

Benchmarking
The process of studying and comparing how other organizations perform similar activities and processes. The other organizations can be either internal or external to the firm and are selected because they are known to have excellent performance for the benchmarked process.

Critical success factors
The elements, such as quality, time, cost reduction, innovativeness, customer service, or product performance, that create long-term profitability for the organization.

Strategic information
Information that guides the long-term decision making of the organization. Strategic information can include the profitability of products, services, and customers; competitor behavior and performance; customer preferences and trends; market opportunities and threats; and technological innovations.

FUNCTIONS OF MANAGEMENT ACCOUNTING

Management accounting information assists several different organizational functions—operational control, product and customer costing, management control, and strategic control—as shown in Exhibit 1-2.

The demand for management accounting information differs depending on the level of the organization. At the operator (front-line) level where raw materials or purchased parts are converted into finished products and where services are performed for customers, information is needed primarily to control and improve operations. The information is disaggregate and frequent; it is more physical and operational than financial and economic. As one moves higher up in the organization, middle managers supervise work and make decisions about financial and physical resources, products, services, and customers. These managers may receive management accounting information less frequently and the information is more aggregate. They use it to receive warning signals about aspects of operations that are different from expectations. Middle managers also use management accounting information to help them make better plans and decisions.

OBJECTIVE 1.3

Understand how different people in the organization have different demands for management accounting information.

Operational control
The process of providing feedback to employees and their managers about the efficiency of activities being performed.

Product costing
The process of measuring and assigning the costs of the activities performed to design and produce individual products (and services, for nonmanufacturing companies).

Customer costing
The process of assigning marketing, selling, distribution, and administrative costs to individual customers so that the cost of serving each customer can be calculated.

Management control
The process of providing information about the performance of managers and operating units.

Strategic control
The process of providing information about the competitive performance of the overall business unit, both financially and in meeting customers' expectations.

EXHIBIT 1-2
Functions of Management Accounting Information

Operational control	Provide feedback information about the efficiency and quality of tasks performed
Product and customer costing	Measure the costs of resources used to produce a product or service and market and deliver the product or service to customers
Management control	Provide information about the performance of managers and operating units
Strategic control	Provide information about the enterprise's financial and long-run competitive performance, market conditions, customer preferences, and technological innovations

Executives at the highest organizational levels receive management accounting information that summarizes transactions and events occurring at the individual operator, customer, and department levels; they use this information to support decisions that have long-term consequences for the organization. Executives typically receive management accounting information less frequently since it is used for strategic rather than operational decisions. Historically, senior-level executives have used financial information almost exclusively, using this aggregate information to assess the overall economics of the events occurring throughout the organization.

Recently however, senior executives like Barry Beck monitor a more balanced set of performance indicators that includes much more nonfinancial information, particularly information about these factors:

1. Customers and markets
2. Innovations in products and services
3. Overall quality, process time, and cost of critical internal processes
4. Capabilities of the organization's employees and systems

This balanced scorecard of business performance enables senior executives not only to monitor past performance but also to understand the drivers of future performance.

From the automobile dealership example, you can see that management accountants must customize both the content and the frequency of management accounting information to the different tasks performed by employees, managers, and executives at each level of the organization. Management accountants cannot expect a single standard set of reports to serve all employee and managerial needs. This need to customize management accounting information to the particular decision, learning, and control needs of employees and managers is an important theme throughout this book.

*20*TH-CENTURY DEVELOPMENTS IN MANAGEMENT CONTROL

The operations of an automobile dealership are relatively simple in comparison to the operations of many organizations. The dealership is an example of a company operating at a single location with a limited set of product lines—new cars, used cars, repair parts, and service—in a single industry—retail car sales and service. Today many companies, such as General Electric, Motorola, Mercedes-Benz, and Matsushita, operate hundreds of plants around the world that produce diverse products in several different industries. Managers of such large, diversified, and complex companies require management accounting information to help them allocate physical, financial, and human resources among their operating divisions and to monitor and control their diverse operations. The origins of using management accounting information in diversified companies can be traced to the experiences in the early 20th century of two companies: DuPont and General Motors.[2]

DuPont: One of the First Diversified Corporations

Many innovations in management accounting systems occurred in the early decades of the 20th century to support the growth of multiple-division diversified corporations. The DuPont Company was the prototype of a vertically integrated manufacturing organization. DuPont acquired raw materials from suppliers and processed these materials through several stages to produce a diversified mix of chemical products that companies in several different industries used. The senior executives of such a diversified company had to devise advanced techniques to coordinate operating activities in their different divisions. These techniques included an **operating budget,** the document that forecasts revenues and expenses during the next operating period including monthly forecasts of sales, production, and operating expenses (a topic that will be covered in depth in Chapter 9), as well as a **capital budget,** the document that authorizes spending for resources with multiyear useful lives, such as plant and equipment (a topic that will be covered in depth in Chapter 10).

DuPont's headquarters office collected for several managerial purposes daily and weekly data on sales, payroll, and manufacturing costs from all the company's mills and branch sales offices. The senior executives used this information to do the following activities:

1. Coordinate operations.
2. Monitor production and sales efficiencies.
3. Plan the growth among the company's diverse activities.
4. Evaluate and control the performance of the company's three main functional operating departments: manufacturing, distribution, and purchasing.

Operating budget
The document that forecasts revenues and expenses during the next operating period, typically a year. The operating budget also authorizes spending on discretionary activities, such as research and development, advertising, maintenance, and employee training.

Capital budget
The management document that authorizes spending for resources, such as plant and equipment, that will have multiyear useful lifetimes.

---

[2] See details on the DuPont and General Motors innovations in management accounting in Chapter 4 of Johnson and Kaplan, *Relevance Lost.*

Return on investment
The calculation that relates the profitability of an organizational unit to the investment required to generate that profitability. Often written as the return on sales multiplied by the ratio of sales to assets (or investment) employed.

Perhaps the most enduring of the innovations introduced at DuPont was the development of the **return-on-investment** (ROI) performance measure. The ROI measure combined both these measures:

Profitability Measure

$$Return\ on\ Sales\ =\ Operating\ Income\ \div\ Sales$$

Asset or Capital Utilization Measure

$$Sales\ \div\ Investment$$

This meant using a single number to evaluate performance:

$$\text{ROI} = \frac{\text{Operating Income}}{\text{Investment}} = \frac{\text{Operating Income}}{\text{Sales}} \times \frac{\text{Sales}}{\text{Investment}}$$

DuPont used the ROI figure as the single best performance measure to plan, evaluate, and control the profit earned for the company's owners. The senior managers at DuPont used new types of economic information, such as the ROI measure, to help them decide which of their divisions should receive additional capital to expand capacity. The use of return on investment as a financial performance measurement and control signal will be discussed in depth in Chapter 12 of this text.

General Motors: Innovative Management Accounting Systems

Decentralized responsibility
Senior corporate managers give local division managers the rights to make decisions on pricing, product mix, customer relationships, resource acquisition, materials sourcing, and operating processes without having to seek approval from higher-level managers. Decentralized responsibility allows local managers to make decisions rapidly based on their superior access to information about local opportunities and threats.

Centralized control
The management process by which senior executives receive periodic information about decentralized divisional operations to ensure that division managers are making decisions and taking actions that contribute to overall corporate goals.

Around 1920 Donaldson Brown, the chief financial officer of DuPont left the company to become CFO for General Motors under its new chief executive officer, Alfred Sloan. Under Sloan's and Brown's leadership, General Motors introduced many management accounting initiatives to accomplish the company's guiding operating philosophy, "centralized control with decentralized responsibility." **Decentralized responsibility** refers to the authority that local-division managers have to make their own decisions without having to seek higher approval on pricing, product mix, customer relationships, product design, acquisition of materials, and appropriate operating processes. Decentralization allows managers to use their superior access to information about local opportunities and operating conditions to make better and more timely decisions. **Centralized control** of decentralized operations is accomplished by having corporate managers receive periodic financial information about divisional operations and profitability. This summary financial information helps assure the senior managers that their division managers were making decisions and taking actions contributing to overall corporate goals. Chapter 11 describes these systems of financial control which senior executives use to monitor and control the outcomes and decisions made by managers of decentralized operating units.

Brown's and Sloan's management accounting systems at General Motors included:

1. **An Annual Operating Budgeting Process.** This process determined whether the plans of each division were consistent and coordinated with the plans of other divisions, that is, a sales division should not expect to sell more than a manufacturing division expects to produce. The annual budgeting

process also identified the capital requirements of the various divisions and made decisions about how the funds would be generated and subsequently allocated to the divisions. The annual budgeting process ensured consistency between top management's financial goals and each division manager's operating targets.

2. **Weekly Sales Reports and Monthly Flexible Budgets.**[3] The sales reports promptly indicated if actual sales were deviating from the estimates used to prepare the budget and operating plan. **Flexible budgets** provided forecasts of what expenses should have been given the actual volume and mix of production and sales in the most recent period. The system of providing weekly sales reports and flexible budgets gave feedback to division managers about current operations so they could take actions to adjust quickly to changes in the company's operating environment.

   Flexible budget
   A forecast of what expenses should have been given the actual volume and mix of production and sales.

3. **Annual Divisional Performance Reports Including Return on Investment.** The annual performance report gave top management information that enabled them to allocate both resources and management compensation among divisions using uniform and agreed-upon performance criteria, such as return on investment. Sloan greatly valued the ROI measure stating: "No other principle with which I am acquainted serves better than rate of return as an objective aid to business judgment."

The General Motors' management accounting system enabled a complex organization to plan, coordinate, control, and evaluate the operations of multiple, somewhat independent operating divisions, such as Chevrolet, Pontiac, and Fisher Body. It enabled the managers of these divisions to pursue aggressively their individual financial, operating, design, and marketing objectives while contributing in a coherent fashion to the overall wealth of the corporation. Sloan's and Brown's initiatives played a critical role in creating an enormously successful enterprise during the 1920 to 1970 time period. Unfortunately, between 1970 and 1990 General Motors experienced severe difficulties when its senior managers failed to use and adopt these procedures effectively for the new competitive challenges from European and Japanese carmakers.

Service Organizations

The major changes that manufacturing companies have experienced in recent years have also occurred in virtually all types of service organizations. Service companies have existed for hundreds of years; their importance in modern economies has increased substantially during the 20th century. See Exhibit 1-3 for examples of service industries and companies.

Demand for Management Accounting Information

Service companies differ from manufacturing companies in several ways. The most obvious difference is that service companies do not produce a tangible product.

---

[3] Flexible budgets forecast expected expenses at the volume and mix of production and sales that actually occurred in a period. We discuss flexible budgets in Chapter 11.

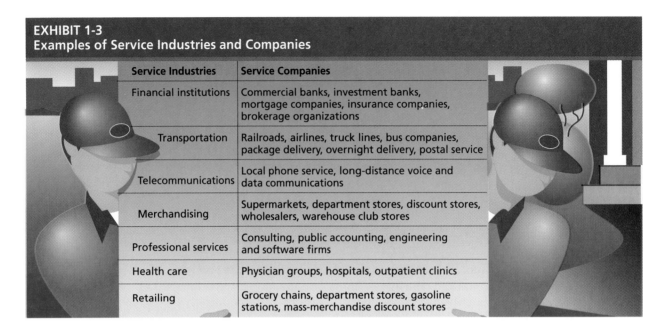

EXHIBIT 1-3
Examples of Service Industries and Companies

Service Industries	Service Companies
Financial institutions	Commercial banks, investment banks, mortgage companies, insurance companies, brokerage organizations
Transportation	Railroads, airlines, truck lines, bus companies, package delivery, overnight delivery, postal service
Telecommunications	Local phone service, long-distance voice and data communications
Merchandising	Supermarkets, department stores, discount stores, wholesalers, warehouse club stores
Professional services	Consulting, public accounting, engineering and software firms
Health care	Physician groups, hospitals, outpatient clinics
Retailing	Grocery chains, department stores, gasoline stations, mass-merchandise discount stores

Less obviously, employees in service companies like Green's Grocery have more direct contact with customers. Thus, service companies must be especially sensitive to the timeliness and the quality of the service their employees provide to their customers. Customers of service companies immediately notice defects and delays in service delivery. The consequences from such defects can be severe as dissatisfied customers choose alternative suppliers after an unhappy experience.

Managers in service companies, however, have historically used management accounting information far less intensively than managers in manufacturing companies. Service company managers did use financial information to budget and control spending in their functional departments. But even though service companies are frequently as complex and diversified as manufacturing companies, managers usually did not know the costs of the services they produced and delivered nor the cost of serving different types of customers. For example, Bill Fuller, the president of Green's Grocery, may know how much is spent at each store and warehouse. But he does not know the costs to receive a case of peas from a supplier, store it in a warehouse, deliver it to the store, and stock it on a delivery store shelf where the consumer can buy it. (Chapter 6 will describe how companies can measure the cost of these activities.)

Such a lack of accurate information about the cost of operations probably occurred because most service companies have long operated in benign, noncompetitive markets. Many service companies have been highly regulated until recently. In Europe many service organizations, such as railroads, airlines, and telecommunications, were not even private companies but government-owned-and-operated monopolies. Managers in regulated, government-owned service organizations have little demand to measure the cost of their individual products, services, and customers; there are no strong pressures for efficiency and productivity improvements. Regulators set prices to cover the operating costs of inefficient companies. Laws and regulations prevent more efficient competitors from entering the markets in which regulated or government-owned service companies operate. Taxpayer funds subsidize any losses in government-operated companies. And many independent service companies have only local rather than national or global competition.

In these noncompetitive environments, managers of service companies were not under great pressure to lower costs, improve the quality and efficiency of operations, introduce new products that made profits, or eliminate products and services that were incurring losses. Since managers were not making such decisions, their demand for information to help them make such decisions was virtually nonexistent. Consequently, the management accounting systems in most service organizations were simple. They allowed managers to budget expenses by operating department and to measure/monitor actual spending against these functional departmental budgets. Service companies were not the hothouses for management accounting innovations that occurred in 19th-century railroad, steel, and machine-tool companies as well as in the emerging 20th-century industrial giants such as DuPont and General Motors.

CHANGING COMPETITIVE ENVIRONMENT

During the last quarter of the 20th century, the competitive environment for both service and manufacturing companies has become far more challenging and demanding. As a consequence, today's companies demand different and better management accounting information.

Service Companies' Deregulation and Competition

The deregulation movement in North America and Europe since the 1970s has completely changed the ground rules under which many service companies operate. Pricing, product mix, and geographic and competitive restrictions have been virtually eliminated in the financial services industry. Transportation companies can now enter and leave markets and determine the prices at which they offer services to customers. Telecommunications companies now compete aggressively on price, quality, and service. Health-care reimbursement is shifting away from pure cost-recovery schemes. Even government monopolies, such as the postal service, are today experiencing competition from private companies. For example, Federal Express and UPS offer overnight delivery of letters and packages; telecommunication companies allow documents to be sent via facsimile transmission; and new technologies permit the transmission of messages and documents on international electronic mail networks. New entrants of efficient mass merchandisers, whether of food, office supplies, home furnishings, or pet supplies, have transformed retailing into a far more competitive industry. Managers of service companies now require information to improve the quality, timeliness, and efficiency of the activities they perform, as well as to make decisions about individual products, services, and customers.

Manufacturing Organizations in the Global Environment

Starting in the mid1970s, manufacturing companies in North America and Europe encountered severe competition from overseas companies that offered high-quality products at low prices. Global networks for raising and disbursing capital, for acquiring and transporting raw materials, and for distributing finished goods allowed the best manufacturers in whatever country they were located to access local domestic markets throughout the world. No longer was it sufficient for a company to have cost and quality parity against its domestic competitors. A company could survive and prosper only if its costs, quality, and product capabilities were as good as those of the best companies in the world.

The traditional systems that manufacturing companies had used for decades to measure product costs, however, were now supplying highly distorted information. These systems failed to assign accurately the costs of their large and growing indirect and support resources required to design, produce, market, sell, and deliver products and services. The errors introduced by costing systems that no longer reflected the economics of contemporary operations were causing managers, designers, and operators to make incorrect decisions. Product engineers were designing automobiles and electronic instruments with too many special and unique components as well as too many options. These designs greatly raised purchasing, materials handling, and manufacturing costs. Companies that attempted to reach new market segments and new geographic regions often learned that the additional revenue from these initiatives failed by substantial amounts to cover the extra costs required to design, produce, deliver, sell, and service products for the new segments and regions.

New Demands for Management Accounting Information

With a much more competitive environment, managers in both manufacturing and service companies need to have accurate, relevant information about their actual costs. For manufacturing companies, managers need this information to do the following:

OBJECTIVE 1.4

Appreciate how management accounting creates value for organizations and how it relates to operations, marketing, and strategy.

1. Help engineers design products that can be produced efficiently.
2. Signal where improvements in quality, efficiency, and speed are needed in manufacturing operations.
3. Guide product mix decisions.
4. Choose among alternative suppliers.
5. Negotiate about price, product features, quality, delivery, and service with customers.

Managers in service companies need to accurately measure the cost and profitability of their product lines, market segments, and individual products and customers. Both manufacturing and service company managers need operational-control systems that will enhance the cost-improvement, quality-improvement, and process-time reduction activities of their employees.

*C*ONSIDER THIS . . .

Looking for Labor Savings: Automobile Manufacturers Shift Work to Suppliers

Automobile-parts suppliers are playing a bigger role in the design and assembly of new vehicles for automobile manufacturers. Previously, the manufacturers' engineers designed the components of the vehicle—from the brakes to the upholstery—and asked suppliers to build the parts to specifications. Now parts suppliers say they are being asked to design components, forcing them to hire more engineers. "Basically, we're looking for more full-service suppliers. We want them to design, engineer and deliver components," said a Ford spokesperson. Lear Seating gets compo-

nents from other suppliers and then assembles the seats for Ford automobiles. Lear says it is set up to deliver automakers a completely assembled interior, including seats, armrests, doors, and instrument panels.

Automobile manufacturers say they have to find ways to bring costs down and make new cars affordable. Using suppliers for design and assembly work is just one of many ways. Ford says the practice and other savings identified by suppliers have helped it cut the cost of making each vehicle by more than $700.

An employee in a Lear Seating plant is assembling seats that will be installed by an automaker in a new car the following day. Just-in-time processes enable the supplier to sequence its production so that the seats can be stacked and delivered in the exact order they will be used when cars are assembled in the automaker's plant. *Courtesy* **Lear Seating Corporation**

Management accountants are now satisfying this demand for better information through the use of activity-based costing systems that measure more accurately the costs of activities, products, services, and customers; operational control systems that provide timely feedback for learning and improvement; and balanced scorecards that link current decisions and actions to long-term financial benefits. We will briefly introduce each of these innovations in the remainder of this chapter; they are covered in much more depth in the remainder of this book.

Role for Activity-Based Cost Systems

ASSIGNING INDIRECT AND SUPPORT EXPENSES. Manufacturing and service organizations are now introducing activity-based costing, or ABC, as it is frequently called, to overcome the inability of traditional cost systems to accurately assign their indirect and support costs. Many manufacturing companies now have indirect costs that are more than five or ten times their direct labor costs. Traditional management accounting systems allocate these indirect costs to products based on direct labor and thereby introduce enormous distortions in the costs assigned to products and customers.

Activity-based costing (ABC) systems avoid arbitrary allocations and subsequent cost distortions by first assigning the costs of resources to the activities using the resources. Then the activity costs are assigned to the products, services, and customers creating the demand for or benefiting from the activities performed. This means that the cost of purchasing is assigned to the items purchased, the cost of designing products is assigned to the new products designed, and the cost of assisting customers is assigned to the individual customers. Several chapters in the book are devoted to developing the theory (Chapters 3 and 4) and application (Chapters 5 to 7) of activity-based costing for management decision making.

ACTIVITY-BASED MANAGEMENT. Companies initially use activity-based costing to analyze historical financial data. They assign operating expenses of the most recent period to the products and services produced and customers served during that period. This process enables managers to learn the actual costs of activities and processes performed in the last period and the profitability of the previous period's products, services, and customers. This information becomes the basis for actions, often referred to as **activity-based management (ABM)** in the upcoming period. ABM includes making decisions to do the following:

1. Modify pricing, product mix, and customer mix.
2. Enhance supplier and customer relationships.
3. Improve the design of products and services.
4. Perform activities more efficiently.
5. Eliminate the need to perform certain activities that do not create any customer value.

For example, ABM includes current efforts to re-engineer and improve business processes and invest in new technologies that reduce the cost of performing critical activities.

Today leading companies also are using their activity-based cost systems in a proactive, predictive mode. Instead of just providing historical data inputs to their activity-based cost systems, these companies are using budgeted data to estimate activity and process costs for future periods. In addition, they are estimating the future

Activity-based costing
A procedure that measures the costs of objects, such as products, services, and customers. Activity-based costing (ABC) first assigns resource costs to the activities performed by the organization. Then activity costs are assigned to the products, customers, and services that benefit from or are creating the demand for the activities.

Activity-based management
The management processes that use the information provided by an activity-based cost analysis to improve organizational profitability. Activity-based management (ABM) includes performing activities more efficiently, eliminating the need to perform certain activities that do not add value for customers, improving the design of products, and developing better relationships with customers and suppliers. The goal of ABM is to enable customer needs to be satisfied while making fewer demands on organizational resources.

costs of producing products and servicing customers. Such forecasts enable managers to make better decisions in advance of actual events and to influence future cost behavior in a more powerful manner. For example, by using activity-based cost systems in the budgeting processes, managers can adjust the supply of resources (people, equipment, and facilities) in future periods to the estimated demands for activities and processes for the forecasted quantity and mix of products, services, and customers. *When managers use activity-based cost systems as the foundation of their budgeting systems, many organizational costs previously considered to be fixed become variable because managers can adjust the supply of resources to the potential demands for their use.* We discuss the use of ABC in a budgeting mode in more detail in Chapter 9.

CONSIDER THIS...

Procter & Gamble's Plan to Reward Efficiency

Procter & Gamble (P&G) plans a new price incentive intended to influence the trade to adopt more efficient practices in logistics and promotions. Wholesalers and retail distributors who partner with P&G in eliminating inefficiencies in the distribution stream will be awarded with lower prices on P&G products. That's the basis for P&G's latest grocery-supply-chain initiative, dubbed Streamlined Logistics II (SLII). The new pricing initiative is characterized by an additional tier of discount prices for participating retailers.

Dean Skadberg, the company's director of industry affairs said: "If customers will accept certain efficient operating principles, we will pass our internal savings on in the form of a lower list price." Primary features of the SLII initiatives include the following:

EFFICIENT ORDERING AND BILLING. Customers will be able to automate all orders and billing using **electronic data interchange (EDI)**—the exchange of data directly between suppliers' and customers' computers; this will improve speed and accuracy and reduce the need for manual intervention.

EFFICIENT DELIVERY. Retailers will be rewarded for picking up backhaul loads on schedule and for unloading P&G deliveries in two hours or less. P&G will also use its Chep pallet pool system (pallets already used for transport in the manufacturing process) for all its shipments except for a few paper items.

EFFICIENT PROMOTION. P&G will streamline its offerings of display-ready unit loads from its current level of more than 400 options down to 100 choices that reflect the company's biggest brands and best-selling items.

COMARKETING. The company will build on its existing account-customized direct-mail marketing programs by offering a custom-published family magazine that can be configured and distributed to meet retailers' marketing objectives.

ACTIVITY-BASED COSTING. The company is making intensive use of ABC techniques to identify the per-case cost of inefficient industry practices and the amounts that can be saved by improving those practices.

Skadberg commented as follows:

> One of the real objectives was to reduce complexities that we had built into our own systems. We were averaging 27,000 manual interventions monthly in our order and invoice process, or 31% of orders. We have now reduced that in one year to 5000 per month or less than 6% on orders.

Many of those interventions were a result of complexities in the company's order and pricing systems.

> "Last year we were implementing something like 55 pricing changes per day with 100 brands. Those changes were in large part promotion related. Multiply that by 17 different pricing brackets and the complexity was enormous."

Skadberg predicted that the total savings to P&G from the cost-cutting initiatives like value pricing and continuous replenishment could be as much as $50 million. According to an industry study, delivery and receiving efficiencies represented more than $2.5 billion annually in potential cost savings to the industry.

Source: Supermarket News, September 4, 1995, p. 1; U.S. Distribution Journal, October 15, 1995, p. 10.

Improvement of Operational Control Systems

The system for calculating activity, product, and customer costs was not the only management accounting system that proved inadequate in the changed competitive and technological environment. With their monthly summaries of financial performance, companies' operational control systems were sending reports too late for operators and managers to take corrective action. Also, the information on these reports was too aggregate to allow operators to learn about the causes of any unfavorable performance. One financial officer remarked:

> To understand the problem of delayed and aggregate financial information, you could think of the department manager as a bowler, throwing a ball at pins every minute. But we don't let the bowler see how many pins he has knocked down with each throw. At the end of the month we close the books, calculate the total number of pins knocked down during the month, compare this total with a standard, and report the total and the variance back to the bowler. If the total number is below standard, we ask the bowler for an explanation and encourage him to do better next period. We're beginning to understand that we won't turn out many world-class bowlers with this type of reporting system.[4]

The monthly performance reports of many operating departments had also become filled with cost allocations so that managers were being held accountable for performance that was neither under their control nor traceable to them. The costs of corporate- or factory-level resources, such as the heat and lighting in the building or the landscaping outside, were being allocated arbitrarily to individual departments even though the departments were not responsible for these costs. For example, referring again to the bowling alley scenario, think about the accountants, after a ball is thrown down each of an establishment's 35 bowling lanes, counting all the pins knocked down in the entire establishment, then dividing by 35, and reporting back the average to every bowler: 8.25714.[5] Such a number may be quite accurate (it does represent the mean number of pins knocked down per alley), but it is completely useless to each individual bowler. Bowlers want to see their own score, not the mean average. Bowlers do not want this number contaminated or influenced by the actions of others over which they have no control.

CHANGING THE NATURE OF WORK FROM CONTROLLING TO INFORMING.   The distorted and delayed signals from management accounting systems were symptomatic of even deeper changes occurring in organizations. The very nature of work was undergoing radical transformations. Work standards and standard costs were innovations established a century ago by engineers in the scientific management movement.[6] The system of work and cost standards repre-

---

[4] R. S. Kaplan, "Texas Eastman Company," Harvard Business School Case #9-130-039, pp. 6–7.

[5] Many accountants like to report all results using six significant digits. It makes them feel that they are very accurate. In truth, they are merely being precise but are usually quite inaccurate (the first digit may be wrong). In management accounting, we prefer to be vaguely accurate (that is, get the first digit correct) rather than precisely wrong.

[6] See discussion in last paragraph of "Management Accounting in 19th-Century Enterprises," p.6.

sented a philosophy by which engineers and managers determined operators' tasks. Operators were instructed to follow these procedures, and the system of measurement (comparing actual results to the predetermined standards) was used to check whether the workers had followed these procedures.

In the current vigorous global competition that companies are now confronting, however, performance against historical standards is no longer adequate. **Continuous improvement** of performance is necessary to match or stay ahead of leading competitors. Continuous improvement refers to the ongoing processes by which employees problem-solve and search for methods to reduce and eliminate waste, improve quality, and reduce defects.

Many managers now realize that perhaps the best source of new ideas for continually improving performance must come from their front-line operators— the people who are closest to the work being performed. These operators see the types of defects occurring and the principal causes of these defects. Allowing employees to take such actions without explicit authorization from middle managers and senior executives has come to be known as **employee empowerment.**[7]

Companies that truly delegate decisions to employees encourage their employees to solve problems and devise new approaches for performing work and satisfying customers. To implement such improvements, however, the employees cannot be held strictly to standards predetermined by engineers and managers. Rather, they need freedom to experiment with solutions designed to fix the root causes of defects. They also need information:

1. To identify the source and likely causes of defects.

2. To see immediately the consequences from attempts to fix the causes of the defects.

In this **total quality management (TQM)** philosophy, operators become problem-solvers. They are part of the process that helps find solutions for eliminating defective output, waste, and activities that do not add value to customers. Thus, the role of operators is changing. They no longer just follow standard operating procedures and monitor the machines producing output. They now must quickly identify problems as they arise, devise countermeasures for the problems, implement the countermeasures, and test and validate that the problems have been solved by these countermeasures. For these responsibilities, the operators need new information to assist their problem-solving activities, not to control them against preset and soon-to-become-obsolete standards. Today management accounting information is shifting away from its historical emphasis on controlling the actions of employees. Instead, managers are deploying new forms of management accounting information to assist and empower the employees for their continuous-improvement activities.

Continuous improvement
The ongoing processes by which employees continually problem solve and search for methods to reduce and eliminate waste, improve quality and reduce defects, shorten response and cycle times, and design products that are simpler to manufacture, deliver, and service.

Employee empowerment
Managers give employees who are closest to operating processes, customers, and suppliers the right to make decisions. Employees are encouraged to solve problems and devise creative new approaches for performing work and satisfying customers.

Total quality management
A management philosophy that attempts to eliminate all defects, waste, and activities that do not add value to customers; also refers to an organizational commitment to customer satisfaction.

---

[7] Unfortunately, some companies preach employee empowerment but don't practice it. They solicit suggestions and advice from front-line employees, but then don't act upon the information they receive. Or, they tell employees that it is now their responsibility to improve a process (work faster, produce more, and with fewer defects) but don't provide the employees with training, or with the information the employees need, including relevant financial information, or the authority to make changes to improve operations. Such rhetoric without real delegation of decision making leads to frustration and cynicism. See, C. Argyris, "Good Communication That Blocks Learning," *Harvard Business Review* (July-August 1994), pp. 77–85.

CONSIDER THIS . . .

How a Manufacturer Focused Its Activities to Win a National Quality Award

Armstrong World Industries' Building Products Division received one of two Malcolm Baldrige National Quality Awards in 1995. The stock price closed up 2⅛ to 56⅞ on the day the award was announced. Among the results reported were these:

1. Operating profit jumped to $87 million in 1994, a 500% increase over the previous year based on a revenue increase of 7.4% to $628 million.

2. Two of the division's seven production plants boasted over three million consecutive work hours without serious injury or accident—an industry record.

3. Annual sales per manufacturing employee jumped 40% since 1991. Output per manufacturing employee improved 39% since 1991 when Armstrong Building Products began using the quality criteria for the Baldrige award as a management tool.

4. Delivering the product within 30 minutes of the promised time occurred 97.3% of the time, up from a 93% on-time delivery rate in 1991 when the delivery window was four hours.

5. The cost of doing things poorly [often called the *cost of quality* or the *cost of nonconformance*] fell last year as a percentage of revenue to 6.8% from 10.8% in 1991. This measure covers improvements in seven key areas: scrap, machine downtime, customer claims, obsolescence, waste removal and disposal, occupational sickness and injury, and administrative and sales problems.

The effort involved the creation of 300 teams that involved all 2400 North American workers from the shop floor to the operations group.

Source: USA Today, October 17, 1995, p. 4B.

An Armstrong research technician prepares an acoustical chamber for testing whether the soundproofing properties of a new ceiling tile meet specifications. *Courtesy* **Armstrong World Industries**

ROLE FOR NONFINANCIAL INFORMATION.   Nonfinancial information about activities being performed is critical for improving internal processes and customer satisfaction. Employees must focus not just on reducing costs but also on how to improve quality, reduce **cycle times,** and satisfy customer needs. For these efforts, management accountants should supply employees with timely performance data on activities, such as defects, rework, scrap, yields, on-time delivery, **customer lead times,** and returns. LSI Logic, a designer and manufacturer of high-performance semiconductors, uses what it calls "the cycle of quality" to improve process performance. The cycle of quality at LSI Logic involves four steps:

1. Identify the problem.
2. Monitor the problem to assess its severity.
3. Analyze the problem to find its causes.
4. Correct the problem.

As Exhibit 1-4 shows, nonfinancial information about cycle time, quality, safety, and management culture plays an important role in focusing and evaluating the cycle-of-quality activities. The percentages shown in this pie chart represent the proportion of the cycle-of-quality activities devoted to each area of the business.

SHARING FINANCIAL INFORMATION WITH FRONT-LINE EMPLOY-EES.   Among the many interesting changes underway in providing relevant information to assist operators in their quality- and process-improvement activities is an expanded role for financial information. Previously operators received, at best, only operational or physical information: quantities of inputs used, time required

Cycle times
The time required to perform a process. For example, the cycle time to install a muffler could be 36 minutes, to transport a case of goods from a warehouse to a retail outlet could be 22 hours, and to produce a semiconductor chip from raw materials could be 18 days.

Customer lead time
The time from when a customer first requests a good or service until the customer receives the requested good or service. For example, the lead time for receiving a hamburger from a fast food outlet could be 6 minutes, for receiving a mortgage approval could be 21 days, and for receiving a complex medical instrument could be 8 months.

EXHIBIT 1-4
LSI Logic Activity Report

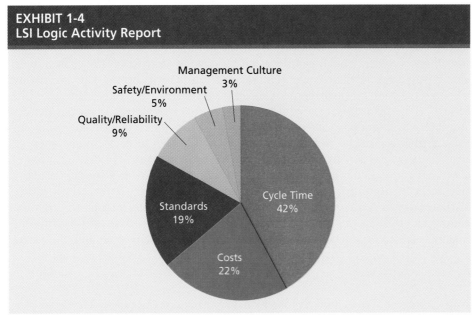

Source: LSI Logic Corporation, *1992 Annual Report,* p. 6.

to complete a task, quality of work accomplished. This type of nonfinancial information helped operators in their quality- and process-improvement activities.

Operators, however, can also benefit from seeing financial information about the resources they are using. For example, they can decide whether to replace the tooling in a machine so that the output has more consistent quality. As operators modify and redesign processes, they should be concerned not only with improving cycle times, quality, yields, and productivity but also with lowering the cost of performing work. For this purpose, several innovating organizations are now sharing for the first time financial information with operators to enable them to do the following:

1. Identify the opportunities for significant cost reduction.
2. Set priorities for improvement projects.
3. Make tradeoffs among alternative ways to improve operations.
4. Evaluate proposed investments to improve operations.
5. Assess the consequences of their improvement activities.

In summary, an important theme for this book is the role for management accounting information to provide information to employees for their problem-solving and continuous improvement activities.[8] This book stresses the use of financial and nonfinancial information to assist local decision making. It de-emphasizes the traditional role of cost accounting information for controlling operator performance. This shift in emphasis mirrors the shift occurring in practice from a command-and-control philosophy to an inform-and-improve philosophy for an organization's employees.

<table>
<tr><td>

OBJECTIVE 1.6

Understand why activities should be the primary focus for measuring and managing performance in organizations.

</td></tr>
</table>

Measuring and Managing Activities

The themes of activity-based cost systems, operational control systems, and expanded use of nonfinancial information for guiding employees' continuous-improvement activities can all be integrated by viewing activities as the central focus of any organization. The measurement of activities will be the key organizing principle for studying management accounting information. Activities should be viewed as the mechanism by which organizational resources and employees accomplish work. Operational control information provides financial and nonfinancial information on the cost, quality, and time required to perform activities. In turn, management accountants can use the operational control information to develop performance measures and targets that will signal how well individual activities are contributing to the complete set of processes performed to satisfy customer needs. Activities also are the unit of measurement for cost information leading naturally to the use of activity-based cost systems. Activities provide the linkage between organizational spending on resources (people, equipment, materials and supplies, and energy) and the products and services produced and delivered to customers.

---

[8] This new approach of giving decision authority and relevant, real-time information to front-line employees so that they can solve problems and increase quality and output, is described in R. S. Kaplan, "Texas Eastman Company," HBS Case #9-190-039; and R. S. Kaplan and A. Sweeney, "Romeo Engine Plant," HBS Case #9-194-932.

The focus on activities also directs managers' attention to crossfunctional business processes. Traditional costing systems emphasize budgets and spending control within departmental and functional boundaries. Business processes, however, such as procurement, order fulfillment, and customer administration draw resources from many departments. Performance measures on time, quality, and cost, should be applied to entire business processes—not just to efficiencies for individual workers, machines, or departments. Only when management accountants use a cross-functional, activity-based approach can managers see the current performance of their business processes and direct their efforts to improving these fundamental business processes.

Balanced Scorecard

A focus on business processes is also at the heart of the **Balanced Scorecard,** a measurement system for clarifying, communicating, and implementing business strategy.[9] The information-age environment for both manufacturing and service organizations requires new capabilities for competitive success. The ability to mobilize and exploit intangible or intellectual assets has become as important for companies as investing in and managing physical, tangible assets. Companies' intangible assets enable them to do the following:

Balanced Scorecard
A measurement and management system that views a business unit's performance from four perspectives: financial, customer, internal business process, and learning and growth.

1. Develop customer relationships that retain the loyalty of existing customers and enable the organization to reach new customer segments.
2. Introduce innovative products and services desired by targeted customer segments.
3. Produce customized products and services at low cost, high quality, and with short lead times.
4. Mobilize employee skills and motivation for continuous improvements in process capabilities, quality, and response times.
5. Deploy information technology, data bases, and systems.

Unfortunately, traditional short-term financial performance measures do not measure the increase in value when companies improve their capabilities and intangible assets. Even worse, measured short-term financial performance can improve even when companies reduce their spending on intangible assets.

The Balanced Scorecard remedies this defect in financial-measurement and financial-control systems. It retains the financial measures of past performance but also adds measures from three additional perspectives: customer, internal business processes, and learning and growth. These four perspectives together provide the framework for the Balanced Scorecard. (See Exhibit 1-5.)

FINANCIAL MEASURES OF POST PERFORMANCE. Financial measures such as return on investment have already been discussed. Innovations in the Balanced Scorecard occur in the three other perspectives that represent what the organization must succeed at to deliver outstanding future financial performance.

[9] R. S. Kaplan and D. P. Norton, "The Balanced Scorecard: Measures that Drive Performance," *Harvard Business Review* (January-February 1992), pp. 71–79.

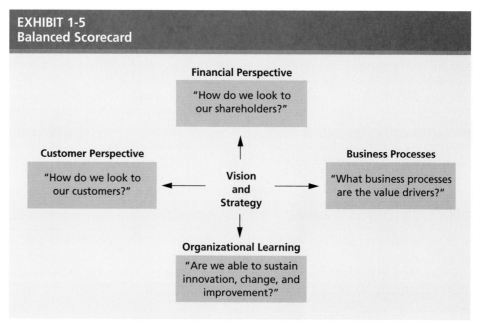

EXHIBIT 1-5
Balanced Scorecard

Source: Robert S. Kaplan and David P. Norton, "Using the Balanced Scorecard as a Strategic Management System," *Harvard Business Review* (January-February 1996).

CUSTOMER. In the customer perspective of the Balanced Scorecard, managers identify the customer and market segments in which the business unit will compete as well as the measures of the business unit's performance in these targeted segments. The customer perspective typically includes several core measures that represent the successful outcomes from a well-formulated and well-implemented strategy, such as customer satisfaction, customer retention, new customer acquisition, customer profitability, and market and account share in targeted segments. The customer perspective can also include specific measures, such as short lead times, on-time delivery, or the number of new products and services that lead to improvements in the core customer measures.

INTERNAL BUSINESS PROCESS. For the measures in the internal-business-process perspective, executives emphasize measures for the internal processes that will have the greatest impact on enhancing customer relationships and achieving the organization's financial objectives. See Exhibit 1-6 for these examples of internal-business processes:

1. **The Innovation Process.** Creating entirely new products and services to meet the emerging needs of current and future customers.

2. **The Operations Process.** Delivering existing products and services to existing customers, efficiently, reliably, and responsively.

3. **The Post-Sale Service Process.** Satisfying customers after the sale with prompt attention to their concerns and as needed with field service and technical support.

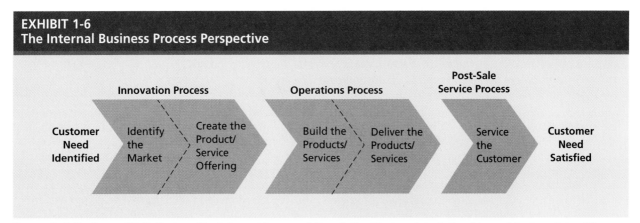

Source: R. S. Kaplan and D. P. Norton, *The Balanced Scorecard: Translating Strategy into Action* (Harvard Business School Press: Boston, Mass., 1996), Chapter 5.

LEARNING AND GROWTH.   The fourth balanced scorecard perspective, learning and growth, identifies what the organization must do to improve its capabilities for excellent internal processes that deliver value to customers and shareholders. Organizational learning and growth arises from sources such as people and systems. Typical measures for the learning and growth perspective include employee satisfaction, retention, training, and skills, and information system availability.

In summary, the Balanced Scorecard translates business strategy into objectives and measures across a balanced set of perspectives. While retaining an interest in short-term performance via the financial perspective, the Balanced Scorecard also measures the factors expected to lead to superior future financial and competitive performance. Corporate executives use the scorecard to measure how their business units create value for current and future customers, how they must build and enhance internal capabilities, and the investment in people and systems necessary to improve future performance. We describe the use of the Balanced Scorecard as the unifying framework for companies' planning and control processes in Chapter 10.

> **OBJECTIVE 1.7**
>
> Discuss the role for multiple performance measures—financial and nonfinancial—to translate the organization's strategy into specific objectives and measures.

BEHAVIORAL IMPLICATIONS OF MANAGEMENT ACCOUNTING INFORMATION

We have stressed the role for management accounting information to assist the decisions and problem-solving activities of operators and managers. Information is never neutral, however. Just the act of measuring and informing affects the individuals involved. This principle occurs even in physical phenomena in which the Heisenberg uncertainty principle notes that the act of measuring the position or velocity of a particle affects the particle's position or velocity. The intrusive effect of measurement is more pronounced when dealing with humans rather than particles. As measurements are made on operations and especially on individuals and groups, their behavior changes. People react to measurements. They focus on the variables or behavior being measured and spend less attention on variables and

*C*ONSIDER THIS . . .

Activity-Based Costing and the Balanced Scorecard Working Together to Communicate the Company's Cost and Revenue Functions

Activity-based costing can be viewed as estimating the organization's cost function by identifying the factors that generate the demand for spending on resources. Students in introductory economics see a simple cost function where the only driver of cost is the output quantity of a single product. Management accountants are now extending the economists' single-product cost curve by building ABC systems that reveal the economics of complex multiproduct, multiprocess, and multicustomer organizations. In these organizations, costs are driven not just by output quantities but by the mix, variety, and complexity of products, services, and customers, as well as the efficiency with which organizational activities and processes are performed.

While ABC can develop cost functions for the firm, an even more interesting question is what creates revenues. Students in introductory economics courses are familiar with the demand curve for a single product where the quantity demanded of a product is a function solely of the product's price. In actual situations, the quantity that is demanded of a product or service is a function of price plus many other factors as well. These other factors include but are not limited to the quality of the product, service, and supplier; the lead time and reliability for delivering the product; the reputation and image of the seller or supplier; and the innovativeness and functionality of the product. The customer and internal business process perspectives of the Balanced Scorecard help to specify those attributes of the product, service, and relationships that customers value and hence are expected to lead to future sales. The learning and growth perspective highlights how investments in employees and systems can improve future customer and internal business process performance. This specification enables the Balanced Scorecard to serve as the organization's revenue function, helping managers to understand what they have to produce and deliver to customers to generate current and future sales.

Thus, an organization with a well-specified activity-based cost model of its entire operations and a Balanced Scorecard measuring the factors that create current and future revenues will have the foundation for predicting both its cost and its revenue-generating functions.

behavior not measured. Some people have recognized this phenomenon by declaring: "What gets measured gets managed" or "If I can't measure it, I can't manage it."

In addition, if managers attempt to introduce or redesign cost and performance measurement systems, people familiar with the previous systems resist. These people have acquired expertise in the use and occasional misuse of the old system and are concerned with whether their experience and expertise are transferable to the new system. People may also feel committed to the decisions and actions taken based on the information the old system produced. These actions may no longer seem valid based on the information produced by a newly installed management accounting system. Thus, a new management system can lead to embarrassment and threat, a trigger for reactions against change.[10]

Even more importantly, when the measurements are used not just for information, planning, and decision making, but also for control, evaluation, and reward, employees and managers place great pressure on the measurements themselves. Managers may take unexpected and undesirable actions to influence their score on the performance measure.

---

[10] C. Argyris and R. S. Kaplan, "Implementing New Knowledge: The Case of Activity-Based Costing," *Accounting Horizons* (September 1994), pp. 83–105.

Management accountants must understand and anticipate the reactions of individuals to information and measurements. The design and introduction of new measurements and systems must be accompanied with an analysis of the behavioral and organizational reactions to the measurements. The later chapters in the book, especially Chapter 15, address behavioral and organizational issues that management accountants will confront when designing, installing, and operating management accounting systems.

GREEN'S GROCERY REVISITED

Art Shaw, the consultant being interviewed at Green's Grocery, now understands the considerable opportunities and challenges he would face as the new controller for Green's Grocery. He must design systems that will inform organizational employees about the efficiency, cost, and profitability of their activities. This information will serve the several business purposes shown in Exhibit 1-7. The

EXHIBIT 1-7 Business Purposes of Management Accounting Information	
Business Purpose	**Role for Management Accounting Information**
Operational control	Provide feedback information about the quality, timeliness, and efficiency of tasks performed and the performance of individuals and operating units. This information would be useful to a store manager to assess inventory levels, inventory turnover, and stockouts by item, as well as to manage checkout and stocking labor staffing levels and efficiency.
Product and customer costing	Measure the costs of resources used to produce a product or service and market and deliver the product or service to customers; assess the profitability of the organization's products and services by linking resources generated—that is, revenues from the sale of the products and services—to the costs of resources required for their design, production, sales, delivery, and service. Green Grocery store managers will want detailed information on the profitability of all categories in the store (for example, frozen goods, bakery, and dry grocery products, such as detergent, canned soups, and beverages), as well as profitability for individual brands and items (size, flavor) within brands. Cost and profitability by supplier will enable the managers to optimize their choice of vendors and the preferred methods for working with the selected vendors.
Organizational performance measurement	Develop performance measures for decentralized organizational units to promote organizational performance that is consistent with business unit strategy and facilitates coordination with other business units. Summary financial measures will enable Bill Fuller, president of Green's Grocery, to assess the relative profit performance of each store in the chain as well as the efficiency of each distribution center. Nonfinancial measures for each store, such as market share, customer satisfaction, stockouts, and returns, will provide additional measures of store performance.

information about the economics of supplier relationships will be the basis of discussions with national brand and private label manufacturers about the breadth of product line that Green's Grocery offers in its stores, the method of supplying the stores with merchandise, the price and method of ordering and paying for the merchandise, and the expected performance for on-time delivery and merchandise availability.

Art must also devise systems that will provide day-to-day feedback to store employees on key operating statistics, such as merchandise availability, stockouts, customer returns, defective merchandise, and sales and gross margins by categories and brands. Shaw must develop and manage a strategic information system for the owner, Bill Fuller, that reports on profits by store, by supplier, and by category. Shaw will also formulate operating and capital budgets that will help Fuller and his store and merchandise managers plan their business for the coming year and for several years into the future. These budgets articulate the financial consequences of the grocery chain's strategy for growth and future profitability. Beyond the financial forecasts embodied in the budget and business plans, Art may also wish to help the organization build a Balanced Scorecard that communicates the company's long-term strategy and its critical success factors—market share and satisfaction for customers; time, quality, and cost of internal processes; and employee skills and motivation and system capabilities—to all organizational participants.

SUMMARY

Management accounting has become an exciting discipline that is undergoing major changes to reflect the challenging new environment that organizations all over the world now face. Accurate, timely, and relevant information on the economics and performance of organizations are crucial to organizational success. This chapter has introduced the different informational needs for operators/workers, middle managers, and senior executives. It described the different tasks that are informed by management accounting information: operational control, product and customer costing, management control, and strategy implementation and control. Individuals will use both financial and nonfinancial information as they perform their tasks. The focus on the costs incurred and the value created by organizational activities and processes will provide a central focus for management accounting information. The design of management accounting systems and the use and interpretation of the management accounting information that is the output from these systems are now critical to the success of both manufacturing and service organizations in today's globally competitive and technologically challenging environment. This textbook introduces the opportunities for enhancing organizational performance through effective design and use of management accounting systems.

KEY TERMS

Activity-based costing, p. 20

Activity-based management, p. 20

Balanced Scorecard, p. 27

Benchmarking, p. 11

Capital budget, p. 13

Centralized control, p. 14

Continuous improvement, p. 23

Controller, p. 1

Cost management systems, p. 1

Critical success factors, p. 11

Customer costing, p. 12

Customer lead time, p. 25

Cycle times, p. 25

Decentralized responsibility, p. 14

Employee empowerment, p. 23

Financial accounting, p. 4

Flexible budget, p. 15

Management accounting, p. 3

Management accounting information, p. 4

Management control, p. 12

Operating budget, p. 13

Operational control, p. 12

Outsource, p. 3

Product costing, p. 12

Return on investment, p. 14

Strategic control, p. 12

Strategic information, p. 11

Total quality management, p. 23

APPENDIX 1-1

Definition of Management Accounting

Management accounting has been defined by the Institute of Management Accountants as the process of identification, measurement, accumulation, analysis, preparation, interpretation, and communication of financial information used by management to plan, evaluate, and control within an organization and to assure appropriate use of and accountability for its resources.[11]

Identification	Recognizing and evaluating business transactions and other economic events for appropriate accounting action.
Measurement	Quantifying, including estimating, business transactions or other economic events that have occurred or forecasts of those that may occur.
Accumulation	Devising disciplined and consistent approaches to recording and classifying appropriate business transactions and other economic events.
Analysis	Determining the reasons for the reported activity and their relationship with other economic events and circumstances.
Preparation and Interpretation	Coordinating accounting and/or planning data to provide information presented logically, which includes, if appropriate, the conclusions drawn from those data.
Communication	Reporting pertinent information to management and others for internal and external uses.
Planning	Quantifying and interpreting the effects of planned transactions and other economic events on the organization; planning, which includes strategic, tactical, and operating aspects, requires that the accountant provide quantitative historical and prospective information to facilitate planning; this includes participation in developing the planning system, setting obtainable goals, and choosing appropriate means of monitoring the progress toward the goals.
Evaluating	Judging implications of historical and expected events and helping to choose the optimum course of action; evaluating includes translating data into trends and relationships; communicating the conclusions derived from the analyses effectively and promptly.
Controlling	Assuring the integrity of financial information concerning an organization's activities and resources; monitoring and measuring performance and inducing

---

[11] *Statements on Management Accounting 1A*, "Definition of Management Accounting" (National Association of Accountants, March 19, 1981). The Institute of Management Accountants (formerly known as the National Association of Accountants) is the U.S. professional society of practitioners and academics who are interested in the design and operations of management accounting systems in organizations.

	any corrective actions required to return the activity to its intended course; providing information to executives operating in functional areas who can use it to achieve desirable performance.
Assuring Accountability Resources	Implementing a system of reporting that is aligned with organizational responsibilities and contributes to the effective use of resources and measurement of management performance; transmitting management's goals and objectives throughout the organization in the form of assigned responsibilities, which is a basis for identifying accountability; providing an accounting and reporting system that will accumulate and report appropriate revenues, expenses, assets, liabilities, and related quantitative information to managers who will then have better control over these elements.
External Reporting	Preparing financial reports based on generally accepted accounting principles or other appropriate bases for nonmanagement groups, such as shareholders, creditors, regulatory agencies, and tax authorities; participating in the process of developing the accounting principles that underlie external reporting.

■ QUESTIONS

1-1 Why do operators/workers, middle managers, and senior executives have different informational needs?

1-2 Why do a company's operators/workers, managers, and executives have different informational needs than do shareholders and external suppliers of capital?

1-3 Why may financial information alone be insufficient for the informational needs of operators/workers, managers, and executives?

1-4 What forces have caused management accounting systems designed decades ago to become less relevant and less valuable for organizational employees in today's globally competitive environment?

1-5 How does the role for management accounting systems change as the environment becomes more competitive?

1-6 What is the impact of shifting the role of management accounting information from controlling workers and operators to informing the continuous improvement activities of these workers and operators?

1-7 What information do employees need about activities performed in the organization?

1-8 How does measuring the cost of activities differ from the traditional cost accounting function of allocating costs to products for inventory valuation?

1-9 How can managers use information on the cost of activities and business processes?

1-10 Why are managers interested (or not interested) in assigning resource costs to products, services, and customers?

1-11 What, if any, are the differences between the management accounting information needed in manufacturing organizations and that needed in service organizations?

1-12 Why might senior executives need measures besides financial ones to assess how well their business performed in the most recent period?

■ EXERCISES

1-13 *Different information needs* Consider the operation of a fast-food company with hundreds of retail outlets scattered about the country. Identify the management accounting information needs for
   (a) The manager of a local fast-food outlet that prepares food and serves it to customers who walk in or pick it up in a drive-through window
   (b) The regional manager who supervises the operations of all the retail outlets in a three-state region
   (c) Senior management located at the company's corporate headquarters. Consider specifically the information needs of the president and the vice presidents of operations and marketing
Be sure to address the content, frequency, and timeliness of information needed by these different managers.

1-14 *Different information needs* Consider the operation of a hospital. Identify the management accounting information needs for

   (a) The managers of (1) a patient unit, where patients stay while being treated for illness or while recuperating from an operation, and (2) the radiology department, where patients obtain X rays and receive radiological treatment

   (b) The manager of the nursing service, who hires and assigns nurses to all patient units and to specialty services such as the operating room, emergency room, recovery room, and radiology room

   (c) The chief executive officer of the hospital

Be sure to address the content, frequency, and timeliness of information needed by these different managers.

1-15 ***Different information needs***   Consider the operation of Green's Grocery. Identify the management accounting information needs for

   (a) The category manager of frozen foods, responsible for all the frozen food product lines, brands, and individual product units (stock-keeping units, or SKUs)

   (b) The manager of a single grocery store

   (c) Bill Fuller, the president of Green's Grocery

Be sure to address the content, frequency, and timeliness of information needed by these different managers.

■ PROBLEMS

Fundamental Problems

1-16 ***Differences between financial and managerial accounting***   Many German companies have their management accounting department as part of the manufacturing operations group rather than as part of the corporate finance department. These German companies operate two separate accounting departments. One performs financial accounting functions for shareholders and tax authorities; the other maintains and operates the costing system for manufacturing operations.

REQUIRED

What are the advantages and disadvantages of having separate departments for financial accounting and management accounting?

1-17 ***Role for nonfinancial information for senior executives; Balanced Scorecard***   A recent article on the decline of a U.S. corporation described the information provided and the reward structure of senior managers: "Summarized data on sales and sales growth were displayed on senior executives' instrument panels and the managerial reward system gave generous weight to sales volume. In contrast, the senior executives' dashboard lacked summarized information on field failures, their effect on customer relations, the performance of competing machines, the growing cancer of failure-prone features, and the extent of customer defections."[12]

REQUIRED

   (a) Shouldn't senior executives be responsible for delivering excellent financial performance to shareholders, leaving the details of customer relations, engineering design, and manufacturing operations to the vice presidents and managers of these various departments?

   (b) Are financial measures alone sufficient to measure the performance of an organization during a period and to use as a basis for compensating the senior executives of an organization? Why or why not?

   (c) What problems, if any, arise from monitoring and rewarding senior executives by a combination of financial and nonfinancial measures?

---

[12] J. Juran, "Made in U.S.A.: A Renaissance in Quality," *Harvard Business Review* (July–August 1993).

1-18 *Differences between financial and managerial accounting*   The controller of a German machine tool company believed that historical cost depreciation was inadequate for assigning the cost of using expensive machinery to individual parts and products. Each year he estimated the replacement cost of each machine and calculated depreciation, based on the machine's replacement cost, to be included in the machine-hour rate used to assign machine expenses to the parts produced on that machine. Additionally, the controller included an interest charge, based on 50% of the machine's replacement value, into the machine-hour rate. The interest rate was an average of the 3- to 5-year interest rate on government and high-grade corporate securities.

As a consequence of these two decisions (charging replacement cost rather than historical cost and imputing a capital charge for the use of capital equipment), the product cost figures used internally by company managers were inconsistent with the numbers that were needed for inventory valuation for financial and tax reporting. The accounting staff had to perform a tedious reconciliation process at the end of each year to back out the interest and replacement value costs from the cost of goods sold and inventory values before they could prepare the financial statements.

REQUIRED

(a) Why would the controller introduce additional complications into the company's costing system by assigning replacement value depreciation costs and imputed interest costs to the company's parts and products?

(b) Why should management accountants create extra work for the organization by deliberately adopting policies for internal costing that violate the generally accepted accounting principles that must be used for external reporting?

1-19 *Role for financial information for continuous improvement*   Consider an organization that has empowered its employees, asking them to improve the quality, productivity, and responsiveness of their processes that involve repetitive work. This work could arise in a manufacturing setting, such as assembling cars or producing chemicals, or in a service setting, such as processing invoices or responding to customer orders and requests. Clearly the workers would benefit from feedback on the quality (defects, yields) and process times of the work they were doing to suggest where they could make improvements. Identify the role, if any, for sharing financial information as well with these employees to help them in their efforts to improve quality, productivity, and process times. Be specific about the types of financial information that would be helpful as well as the specific decisions or actions that could be made better by supplementing physical and operational information with financial information.

■ CASES

1-20 *Information for employee empowerment*   A U.S. automobile components plant had recently been reorganized so that quality and employee teamwork were to be the guiding principles for all managers and workers. One production worker described the difference:

> In the old production environment, we were not paid to think. The foreman told us what to do, and we did it even if we knew he was wrong. Now, the team decides what to do. Our voices are heard. All middle management has been cut out, including foremen and superintendents. Management relies on us, the team members, to make decisions. Salary people help us make these decisions; the production

and manufacturing engineers work for us. They are always saying, "We work for you. What do you need?" And they listen to us.

The plant controller commented as follows:

In traditional factories, the financial system viewed people as variable costs. If you had a production problem, you sent people home to reduce your variable costs. Here, we do not send people home. Our production people are viewed as problem solvers, not as variable costs.

REQUIRED

(a) What information needs did the production workers have in the old environment?

(b) What information do you recommend be supplied to the production workers in the new environment that emphasizes quality, defect reduction, problem solving, and teamwork?

1-21 ***Role for financial information for continuous improvement*** The manager of a large semiconductor production department expressed his disdain for the cost information he was presently supplied with:

Cost variances are useless to me.[13] I don't want to ever have to look at a cost variance, monthly or weekly. Daily, I look at sales dollars, bookings, and on-time delivery (OTD)-the percent of orders on time. Weekly, I look at a variety of quality reports including the outgoing quality control report on items passing the final test before shipment to the customer, in-process quality, and yields. Yield is a good surrogate for cost and quality. Monthly, I do look at the financial reports. I look closely at my fixed expenses and compare these to the budgets, especially on discretionary items like travel and maintenance. I also watch headcount.

But the financial systems still don't tell me where I am wasting money. I expect that if I make operating improvements, costs should go down, but I don't worry about the linkage too much. The organizational dynamics make it difficult to link cause and effect precisely.

REQUIRED

Comment on this production manager's assessment of his limited use for financial and cost summaries of performance. For what purposes, if any, are cost and financial information helpful to operating people? How should the management accountant determine the appropriate blend between financial and nonfinancial information for operating people?

1-22 ***Part proliferation: role for activity-based costing*** An article in the *Wall Street Journal* (June 23, 1993) reported on the major changes occurring in General Motors. Its new CEO, John Smith, had been installed after the board of directors requested the resignation of Robert Stempel, the previous CEO.

Last year [John Smith's] North American Strategy Board identified 30 components that could be simplified for 1994 models. Currently, GM has 64 different versions of the cruise control/turn signal mechanism. It plans to pare that to 24 versions next year, and the following year to just 8. The tooling for each one costs GM's A.C. Rochester division about $250,000. Smith said, "We've been talking about too many parts doing the same job for 25 years but we weren't focused on it." [Note that the tooling cost is

---

[13] We will study cost variances in later chapters. For purposes of working this problem, it is sufficient to recognize that a cost variance represents the difference between the cost actually assigned to a production department and the cost that was expected or budgeted for that department.

only one component of the cost of proliferating components. Other costs include the design and engineering costs for each different component, purchasing costs, setup and scheduling costs, plus the stocking and service costs for every individual component in each automobile dealership (including Beck's Motors) around the country.]

GM's proliferation of parts is mind-boggling. GM makes or buys 139 different hood hinges, compared with 1 for Ford. . . . Saginaw's Plant Six juggles parts for 167 different steering columns-down from 250 last year but still far from the goal of fewer than 40 by decade's end.

This approach increased GM's costs exponentially. Not only does the company pay far more engineers than competitors to design steering columns, but it needs extra tools and extra people to move parts around, and it has suffered from quality glitches when workers confused one steering column with another.

REQUIRED

(a) How could an inaccurate and distorted product costing system have contributed to the overproliferation of parts and components that General Motors executives have only recently recognized?

(b) What characteristics should a new cost system have that would enable it to signal accurately to product designers and market researchers about the cost of customization and variety?

1-23 ***Role for activity-based cost systems in implementing strategy*** Consider the case of the Cott Corporation, a Canadian private label producer of high-quality cola beverages. (Review the discussion about Green's Grocery, the opening vignette in this chapter.) Cott is attempting to get grocery retailers to stock its cola beverages, as a lower price alternative to the international brands, Coca Cola and Pepsi Cola. The international brands (Coke and Pepsi) deliver directly to the retailer's store and stock their product on the retailer's shelves. Cott, in contrast, delivers to the retailer's warehouse or distribution center, leaving the retailer to move the product to the shelves of its various retail outlets. Cott offers substantially lower prices to the retailers, and, in addition, is willing to work with the grocery retailer to customize the cola beverage to the retailer's specification, develop special packaging for the retailer, including labeling the beverage with the retailer's name (a practice known as "retailer branding,"; e.g., "Safeway Select Cola"), offer a full variety of carbonated beverages (diet, caffeine-free, multiple flavors, multiple sizes and packaging options), and develop a marketing and merchandising strategy for the retailer for the private label beverage.

REQUIRED

What activity-based cost systems should Cott be building to help it implement its strategy successfully? Be sure you think about the entire value chain of Cott's operations, including both suppliers and customers.

1-24 ***Financial versus management accounting: role for activity-based cost systems in privatization of government services*** The mayor of Gotham City is dissatisfied with rising costs and deteriorating quality of the services provided by the municipal workers, particularly in the Transportation Department: paving roads, repairing potholes, and cleaning the streets. He is contemplating privatizing these services by out-sourcing the business to independent, private contractors. The mayor has demanded that his staff develop an activity-based cost system for municipal services, however, before proceeding with his privatization initiative, declaring, "Introducing competition and privatization to government services requires real cost information. You can't compete out if you are using fake money." Currently, the accounting and financial systems of Gotham City report only how much is being spent in each department, by type of expenditure: payroll, benefits, materials, vehicles, equipment (including computers and telephones) and supplies.

REQUIRED

(a) Before outsourcing to the private sector, why does the mayor want to develop activity-based cost estimates of the current cost of performing these municipal services?

(b) After building activity-based cost models, should this information be shared with the municipal workers? Why or why not? How might the workers use the ABC information?

1-25 ***Role for Balanced Scorecard in monitoring and reporting on performance***   Organizations in the public and nonprofit sector, such as government agencies and charitable social service entities, have financial systems that budget expenses and monitor and control actual spending. Identify why these organizations should consider developing a balanced scorecard of measurements to monitor and report on their performance. What should be the various perspectives in such a balanced scorecard of measurements?

2

THE ORGANIZATION AS A SYSTEM OF ACTIVITIES

EMI RECORDS GROUP

Current hits account for 60% of sales in the music business. This means that music manufacturing and distribution systems must be able to respond quickly to changing tastes. In the early 1990s, most music industry observers recognized EMI Records Group, a music distributor, as an outstanding model of how *not* to do things. Other than signing and representing popular recording artists like the Rolling Stones and Garth Brooks, EMI seemed incapable of doing anything well. EMI often took 20 days to fill customer orders—more than twice the industry average of 8 days. EMI was able to correctly or completely fill customer orders only 81% of the time. Despite operating three massive warehouses, all filled with inventory, stock shortages were chronic. This abysmal performance caused retailers to order early and overstock new releases because they could return unsold inventory that EMI usually scrapped for refunds. Sale items that had been promoted in cooperative advertising were often unavailable. Beyond wasting advertising funds, EMI's lack of reliability created customer ill will toward the various EMI labels and caused problems for retailers. EMI also incurred excessive costs relating to correcting errors made in filling initial orders. Retailers complained that delivery delays on everyday items caused lost sales and increased inventory-related costs. The retailers were demanding better service. EMI knew that its distribution system was creating excessive distribution-related and return-related costs and massive amounts of customer dissatisfaction. These factors were seriously eroding its profit performance.

The EMI Records Group example illustrates the impact of poor information and improper procedures that can exist in today's organizations. The focus of this chapter is on the organization itself—its nature and purpose; its customer focus; and, especially, its activities. Understanding these important elements about organizations is critical for interested parties, both inside and outside the organization.

One of management's most important roles is to ensure that the organization achieves its objectives. This requires developing and using information so that the organization consumes the fewest possible resources in completing its activities. Looking at the fundamental features of organizations can help us better understand how an organization like EMI Records Group may identify and correct its problems in order to survive.

ORGANIZATIONS AND THEIR CUSTOMERS

Organizations are collections of people, equipment, and capital. Organizations come in all sizes and forms: government agencies, fast-food chains, religious groups, multinational automobile manufacturers, student societies, special interest groups, and performing arts groups. While there are many things that organizations do *not* have in common, they all have one thing in common—their customers.

Organizations perform activities that provide goods or services, called *products*, to their customers. It does not matter whether the organization is profit seeking or not or whether it is a manufacturing or service organization. Every organization has customers, and no organization can exist indefinitely if it fails to meet its customers' needs.[1] Therefore, understanding the organization's activities and customers is critical for the people who design and operate the organization's processes.

THE ORGANIZATION AS A SEQUENCE OF ACTIVITIES OR VALUE CHAIN

OBJECTIVE 2.1

Understand the idea of the organization as a sequence of activities in a value chain.

Value chain
A sequence of activities whose objective is to provide a product to a customer or to provide an intermediate good or service in a larger value chain.

Think of the organization as a sequence of activities whose output is a good or service delivered to the organization's customer. For example, a library gives a customer a needed book or information; a government employment agency helps a client find a job; a theater group provides its audience with entertainment; and a computer manufacturer provides a customer with a computer. An organization can be defined by how it organizes and manages its sequence of activities. A sequence of activities that creates a good or service can be viewed as a **value chain** since each step in the chain *should add something that the customer values* to the product.

Consider the activities at Mike's Custom Doors, a company that manufactures doors to order. Concerned about declining sales and profits, Michael Roy, the owner, wonders what can be done to reverse these trends. The major activities at Mike's Custom Doors include taking customer orders, buying raw materials and equipment, hiring and training employees, making doors, shipping doors to customers, billing customers, paying suppliers and employees, and handling customer complaints.

Activities

Activity
A unit of work, or task, with a specific goal. Examples of activities are grading a student's examination, issuing a Medicare check, and painting an automobile.

An **activity** is a unit of work, or task, with a specific goal, such as purchasing raw materials, like steel, at Mike's Custom Doors; making a hamburger in a restaurant; interviewing a client in a welfare office; or setting up a machine in a factory. There are four broad classes of activities in the value chain. Exhibit 2-1 summarizes these activities.

[1] Most people can think of organizations that exist without apparent consideration of customers' needs. Governments are often, and sometimes unfairly, mentioned as examples. The claim here is that this cannot continue indefinitely, not that at every instant in time the organization must meet its customers' needs.

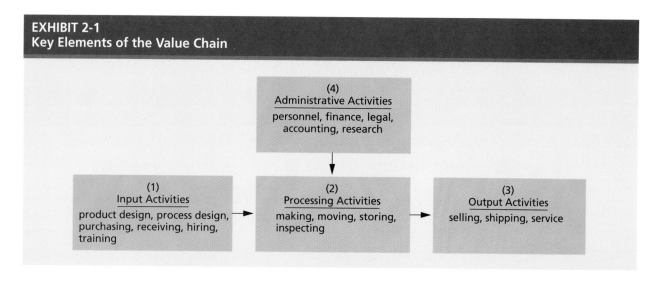

EXHIBIT 2-1
Key Elements of the Value Chain

1. **Input activities, or activities related to getting ready to make a product.** These include product and market research and development; hiring and training employees; and buying raw materials, components, and equipment.

2. **Processing activities, or activities related to making a product.** These include operating machines or using tools to make a product; moving work in process around the facility; storing work in process; and inspecting partially completed work.

3. **Output activities, or activities related to dealing with a customer.** These include selling activities; billing activities; service activities; and delivering activities.

4. **Administrative activities, or other activities that support the first three activities.** These include administrative functions, such as personnel, payroll, data processing, legal services, accounting, and general administration.

The Customer's Perspective as a Means of Focusing the Value Chain

Because the value chain focuses on providing a product to a customer, it makes sense to evaluate the management and operations of the value chain's activities from the customer's perspective. If the final customer is the end point of the value chain, then each link in the value chain is the customer of the previous link. If each link in the value chain focuses on meeting its customer's needs, the organization can deliver the product that the final customer wants.

Suppose that the primary activities in Mike's Custom Doors include cutting the steel, shaping the steel, assembling the door, doing finishing operations on the door, and painting the door as shown in Exhibit 2-2. The value chain idea implies that, when evaluating operations and undertaking improvement activities, employees in each department should think of the employees in the next department as their customers. Therefore, each department in the value chain has a supplier

OBJECTIVE 2.2

Appreciate the role of the customer in defining the focus of the activities in the value chain.

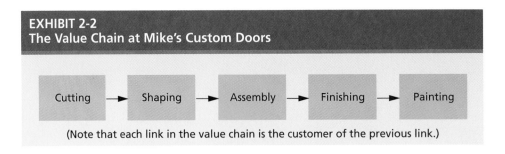

EXHIBIT 2-2
The Value Chain at Mike's Custom Doors

Cutting → Shaping → Assembly → Finishing → Painting

(Note that each link in the value chain is the customer of the previous link.)

department and a customer department. This is a simple but powerful way of providing focus and coordination in an organization that literally may have thousands of activities in the value chain.

Tempering the Customer Focus of the Value Chain

A focus on customers is just part of an organization's story. An organization cannot focus exclusively on customers, because doing so could result in the following:

1. Meeting customers' requirements at any cost, delivering products at too low a price, or offering features and services whose cost customers are unwilling to pay.
2. Making products that customers want but that may expose employees to dangerous working conditions.

This employee at Alberto-Culver Company, a manufacturer of consumer health care products, is part of a value chain designed to decrease response time, improve service to customers, reduce logistical costs, and improve order-filling accuracy. The picture shows automated palletizing systems that are an important part of this logistical system. Note the scanner in the employee's hand and the computer display device beside his right knee. Scanners provide employees with information about order-filling requirements, which is often obtained directly from the customer's computer. Employees provide the computers that control the logistical process with information about each order's status. This real-time information exchange between employees and computers is a common characteristic of modern logistical systems. *Source* Alberto-Culver Company, Annual Report, 1994, p. 10

3. Making illegal products that some customers may want but that may prompt legal or other sanctions from the community.

Therefore, the focus of the value chain on customers must be tempered by the organization's objectives, which are defined by the organization's owners and tempered by the organization's other stakeholders.[2]

THE ORGANIZATION'S PURPOSE

Having a well-defined and well-understood purpose is one of the most important ingredients for an organization's success. A clear statement of purpose focuses attention in the organization on what matters and allows the organization to delegate decision-making responsibility to people at all levels. There is evidence that such a focus improves the organization's ability to achieve its stated objectives. **Objectives** are the organization's broad purposes that, in turn, reflect what the organization's owners, or principals, expect the organization to accomplish.[3]

Objectives
The broad purposes of an organization that reflect the objectives of the stakeholders whose interests the organization deems primary.

Choosing the Organization's Objectives

The responsibility for choosing the organization's objectives belongs to the organization's board of directors and its senior management. The organization's objectives define the organization's core purpose which, in turn, provides the basis for evaluating everything the organization does.

The scope and nature of organization objectives differ widely. Governments presumably want to improve the quality of life for their citizens. Social service organizations want to provide services to their target beneficiaries. Profit-seeking organizations want to earn profits for their owners. Or do they?

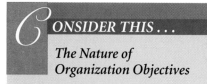

CONSIDER THIS . . .

The Nature of Organization Objectives

Peter Drucker describes the importance of having a clear statement of organization objectives as follows: "Because the modern organization is comprised of specialists, each with his or her own narrow area of expertise, its mission must be crystal clear. The organization must be single-minded or its members will become confused. They will follow their own specialty rather than apply it to the common task. They will each define 'results' in terms of their own specialty and impose its values on the organization. Only a focused and common mission will hold the organization together and enable it to produce."

Source: Peter F. Drucker, "The New Society of Organizations," *Harvard Business Review*, Volume 70, Number 5, 1992, pp. 95–104.

---

[2] **Stakeholders** are the people, groups of people, or institutions that define the organization's success or affect the organization's ability to achieve its objectives. An organization's stakeholders usually include customers, employees, suppliers, owners, and the general community. Since customers define the focus and purpose of most of the organization's activities, they are the focus of this chapter. Chapter 11 discusses the role of the organization's owners in defining the organization's objectives and the role of its other stakeholders in shaping organization strategies and the nature of its activities. In summary, the contributions and requirements of employees, suppliers, owners, and the community serve to *define the environment and the general constraints that the organization must recognize* in its customer-related operations. Specifically, stakeholder requirements define the constraints on the value chain that the organization designs and manages to deliver products to its customers.

[3] A *Wall Street Journal* article ("Visioning Missions Becomes its Own Mission", January 7, 1994, p. B1) cited a study that suggested that "visionary" companies outperform a control group by more than 6:1. These visionary companies were distinguished by setting ambitious goals, communicating them to employees, and following a core ideology.

Stakeholders
Groups of people who, or institutions that, have a legitimate claim on having an organization's objectives reflect their requirements. Stakeholders include customers, employees, partners, owners, and the community.

It is not hard to find profit-seeking organizations that pursue social policies that conflict with the objective of maximizing profits. For example, Ben and Jerry's, a dairy products manufacturer, has stated that one of its policies is to buy milk exclusively from Vermont farmers, whether such locally produced milk costs more or not. The Body Shop, a manufacturer of bath and beauty products, has indicated that it intends to pursue social goals, even if doing so offends prospective customers or creates additional costs. Many organizations have indicated that they are willing, to some extent, to sacrifice profits to pursue goals relating to other stakeholders.

Exhibit 2-3 summarizes this idea. In this chapter we are concerned with the right column in Exhibit 2-3, which is labeled the domain of management accounting. Chapter 11 discusses the issues in the left column in Exhibit 2-3, which define the scope and purpose of the management accounting system.

There is no single criterion based on economic, ethical, or social standards that those who evaluate organization objectives can use to evaluate an organization's objectives. There is no basis on which to say that an organization like the Body Shop, which pursues social causes, is better or worse than another organization that pursues only profit objectives. Casual observation suggests that organizations that pursue purely economic objectives for their shareholders tend to be larger, with more widely held shares. Organizations that pursue other than purely shareholder-based objectives tend to be smaller and more closely held, with the objectives often reflecting the owners' values. The only valid criterion to use in judging an organization's statement of objectives is whether the statement is clear and whether all organization members understand it.

Organization Objectives and Management Accounting

Organization control
The activity of assessing the value chain's performance from the perspective of the organization's objectives.

Management accountants need to understand the source and scope of an organization's objectives because they evaluate the organization's performance relative to its objectives. The activity of assessing the value chain's performance from the perspective of the organization's objectives is called **organization control.**

Chapter 11 explains how the organization's objectives are the foundation for its planning and control system. Therefore, management accountants must have a clear understanding of the nature and scope of organization objectives and, in a particular setting, the specific objectives that the organization selects. This means that the design of an effective management accounting system should be contingent on the unique nature of the organization, its objectives, and the strategies that it pursues to achieve those objectives. A management accounting system cannot be designed in isolation from the organizational context in which it must

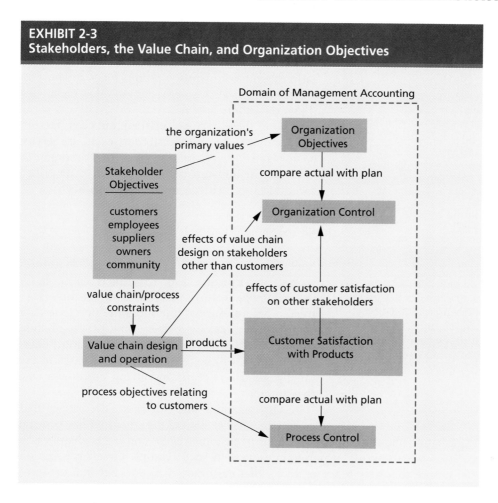

EXHIBIT 2-3
Stakeholders, the Value Chain, and Organization Objectives

operate and be used. Thus, it is impossible to *develop a standard management accounting system for all organizations.*

Using Information to Manage the Value Chain

Process control is the activity of assessing the value chain's ability to meet customer requirements. Organizations establish processes and systems to achieve certain outcomes that contribute to meeting their long term objectives. For example, a process may focus on the goal of customer service to achieve the longer run objective of increased profitability. Process control is short-cycle, sometimes continuous control and measures and compares short-term performance to short-run targets or standards.

Process control
The activity of assessing the operating performance of a single process or the entire value chain in meeting customer requirements.

Performance Measures in Process Control

Process control focuses on directing, evaluating, and improving the processes the organization uses to deliver products to its customers. Therefore, customer expectations define the performance measures in process control.

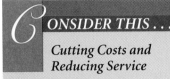

CONSIDER THIS . . .

Cutting Costs and Reducing Service

In their zeal to cut costs, some organizations cut service. Proctor & Gamble and General Foods, large competitors in the coffee market, were slow to react to the customer move to gourmet coffee brands. In fact, a preoccupation with cutting costs led to a decrease in product service as large competitors substituted cheaper robusta beans with higher-quality arabica beans. In another effort to reduce costs, large competitors developed the facilities to process larger batches of coffee, which reduced the processing cost but also reduced the freshness of the resulting product. These manufacturers failed to realize that a significant group of customers were willing to pay more for a better product (that is, higher service) and that their cost-cutting activities were alienating those customers. Cost cutting should focus on eliminating elements of service that customers do not want or unnecessary production steps—not on eliminating services that customers value.

Critical success factors
Elements of performance required for an organization's success, for example, for *customers*, service, quality, and cost; for *employees*, job satisfaction and safety; for *partners and owners*, an adequate return on investment; and for *the community*, conformance to laws.

Critical performance indicators
Performance measures used to assess an organization's performance on its critical success factors.

Service
The product's tangible and intangible features promised to the customer; service is also known as value in use.

Customer Expectations

Customers, as the ultimate consumers of an organization's products, provide a unique focus and purpose for the organization's activities or value chain. But what do customers want?

The three process **critical success factors,** which reflect what most customers want, are service, quality, and cost. We call the measures that organizations use to measure performance on their critical success factors, **critical performance indicators.**

Service

Service refers both to the product's tangible features, such as performance, taste, and functionality, and to its intangible features, such as how customers are treated before, during, and after the purchase decision. In short, service is everything promised about the product that the customer receives and values.[4] Some people call service the product's value in use. Giving good service means giving customers what they want.

Organizations find out about the service their customers expect by asking them. This provides information about changes and trends in customer tastes and helps identify what most customers want,[5] which is important for two reasons. First, organizations can ensure that they make products that customers will buy. Second, organizations can ensure that they do not build features or attributes into products for which customers will not pay. Many organizations have made the mistake of assuming that they know what their customers want without confirming this information directly with the customers themselves.

Therefore, service is what customers pay for. In turn, the amount that customers are willing to pay for the product reflects the service they *expect* from the product. For Mike's Custom Doors, service means how it treats its customers when they order a door, what it offers in the style and functionality of its product line, and how it treats its customers after the sale, particularly regarding delivery promises and after-sales problems or complaints.

Some service elements can be measured easily. For example, when customers want a prompt response to an order, organizations can measure the total time re-

---

[4] This is a very broad definition of service that you may find unfamiliar. However, understanding the breadth of this definition is important in what follows. See, for example, Ronald Henkoff, "Service is Everybody's Business", *Fortune*, June 27, 1994, pp. 48–60. The author describes service as the ultimate strategic imperative which is driven by the reality that, increasingly, all physical goods are becoming commodities and that service is how organizations now differentiate each other. "What counts most is the way that service is built into something—the way the product is designed and delivered, billed and bundled, explained and installed, repaired and renewed. Product quality, once a competitive advantage, is now just the ante into the game."

[5] Since most organizations cannot ask all customers what they want, organizations have to rely on sample information to make inferences about what the customer population wants.

quired to take an order, manufacture the product, and deliver the product to the customer. Organizations also measure how well their products have performed in practice, either by monitoring product returns and warranty claims or by soliciting comments directly from customers.

Some service elements are difficult to measure directly since they reflect the customer's subjective valuation of the product's various attributes. Therefore, organizations often measure performance on intangible features indirectly. For example, a performance measure like sales volume is a measure of revealed customer valuation.

Quality

Quality is defined as conformance to specifications. Quality is the difference between what the customer is promised and what the customer receives. Quality is *not* the difference between what the customer wants and what the customer gets because organizations cannot control or be responsible for meeting unknown or unreasonable customer expectations. Instead, organizations can be responsible only for keeping their promises to customers. In this way, the definition of quality is made relative to this definition of service. Exhibit 2-4 summarizes the elements of service and quality for a restaurant meal and a new television.

When quality is bad, production has to be either reworked or destroyed. This causes the cost per unit of good production to increase. As quality improves, scrap and rework decrease, as do costs.

Many people associate the quality of a product with its performance, attributes, or features. For example, many people believe that a Rolls Royce has higher quality than a Buick because it has more features. For our purposes, the differences between the performance, attributes, and features of a Buick and a Rolls Royce result in them being classified as different products with different services rather than being classified as the same product, a car, with different qualities. When we define quality as conformance to specifications, Buicks have higher quality than Rolls Royces because, on average, customer surveys report that Buicks have fewer defects per vehicle than Rolls Royces.

Quality is important to customers because they expect to get what they have paid for. Expectations determine what the customer is willing to pay. Thus, quality is judged relative to expectations. For example, customers expect more from a meal in a five-star restaurant than from one in a fast-food restaurant. Quality is also related to how each product lives up to the customer's expectations. In the case of Mike's Custom Doors, quality relates to the relationship between expectations relating to the door (its looks, functionality, and treatment of the customer before and after buying the door). An organization that has established a reputation for high quality, such as Toyota, has customers who feel that they have a low risk of being disappointed. As organizations get better at keeping promises to customers, quality goes up, and

Quality
The difference between the promised and the realized level of service; conformance to specifications.

Red Lobster requires its suppliers to inspect every piece of fish they supply to meet their high quality standards. Candling involves using a lighted background to inspect fish fillets. *Courtesy* **Greg Edwards**

EXHIBIT 2-4
The Relationship Between Service and Quality

Service/Quality	Restaurant Meal	Television Set
Element of Service What the customer experienced relating to each facet of the product that is relevant to the customer	Reservation process, restaurant ambiance, wait to be seated, treatment by host or hostess, wait for service, treatment by server, wait for meal, meal taste and presentation, wait for bill, treatment during departure	Ordering process, treatment by sales staff, delivery process and treatment by delivery personnel, television performance, treatment by service personnel, adequacy of response to service requests
Elements of Quality Comparison of what actually happened, that is, service, with expectations of service	Did the reservation process work as expected in terms of both the process itself and the timing of the meal? Was the restaurant's ambiance as expected? Was there an excessive wait to be seated? Was the host's or hostess's manner appropriate? Was the wait for service excessive? Was the server's behavior appropriate? Was the wait for the meal excessive? Was the meal as expected? Was the wait for the bill excessive? Was the treatment during departure reasonable?	Was the process of finding the product as expected? Was the treatment by sales staff as expected? Were delivery promises kept, and was the behavior of the delivery staff reasonable? Did the television perform as expected? Was the time taken by service personnel to respond to problems reasonable? Were service requests handled satisfactorily?

the customer's assessment increases that expected services will be realized. Exhibit 2-5 summarizes the relationship between service and quality.

Costs

Costs
Resources used to provide a product or service.

Costs reflect the resources that the organization uses to provide products or services. Accomplishing the same things with fewer resources and, therefore, lower costs means that the organization is becoming more efficient. Cost is important because of the relationship between a product's cost and its price. In the long run, the price received for a product must cover its costs, or the organization will stop making that product. Since customers will buy the product with the lowest price if all other things are equal, keeping costs at a minimum provides an organization with a strong competitive advantage.

Monitoring Overall Customer-Related Performance

If customers value service, quality, and cost performance, then the organization must measure these attributes using critical performance indicators. This is part of the process of managing the value chains that organizations have designed and

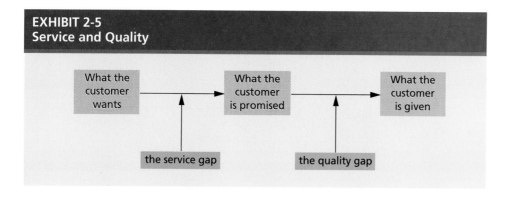

EXHIBIT 2-5
Service and Quality

operate to deliver products to their customers. Exhibit 2-6 summarizes these important performance measures.[6]

Many customer performance measures, or performance indicators, are made and evaluated continuously because they relate to the daily operation and management of the value chain's activities. Although measures that do not relate to customers—such as employee and supplier satisfaction, employee and supplier turnover, return on owners' investment, and the organization's image in the community—are important performance measures for the organization to monitor, organizations usually monitor these non-customer performance measures less frequently because they are influenced primarily by longer-term, more periodic decisions reflecting the production process and organization design or discretionary expenditures, such as a donation to a charity.

EXHIBIT 2-6
Customer Performance

Critical Success Factor	Examples of Critical Performance Indicators
Service	Number of customers, number of new customers, number of customers lost, market share, purchases per customer, time to serve customers during peak periods, time to respond to customer orders, time taken to resolve customer complaints
Quality	Number of customer complaints per 1000 orders filled, customer satisfaction surveys, percent on-time delivery, returns, warranty claims
Cost	Ratio of costs to revenues, ratio of amount of material in final product to amount of material purchased, cost of a particular activity, customer profitability, ratio of labor allowed for work done to total labor, sales per hour during peak operations

[6] The measures in Exhibit 2-6 relate to the external or final customers. Organizations can also develop customer performance measures for internal customers. Internally, performance measures usually relate to conformance, particularly relating to quality and meeting delivery schedules.

CONSIDER THIS . . .

The Nature of Effective and Efficient

Effective and *efficient* are two terms that management accountants use frequently. Each of these terms has a very special meaning.

Effective is a process characteristic that refers to the ability of a process to achieve its objectives. For example, suppose that a post office is using a mail sorter whose error rate is 3%. The post office buys a new machine with the objective of reducing the error rate. The new machine's error rate is 1.5%. Because the machine has achieved its objective, it is effective.

Efficient is a process characteristic that refers to the ability to use the fewest possible resources to do something. For example, suppose that one steel mill uses 100 tons of raw steel to make 80 tons of finished product and a second steel mill uses 90 tons of raw

steel to make 80 tons of the same finished product. The second steel mill is more efficient than the first because it uses less raw steel to produce the same amount of final product.

Effectiveness and efficiency are very different issues that managers attack differently. Effectiveness is determined by the process design, which is evaluated and changed periodically. Efficiency is determined jointly by the process design and how the process operates each day.

Professor Charles T. Horngren, a renowned management accounting educator, made this point when he said "killing a fly with a hammer is effective but it is not efficient."

Sometimes it is necessary to continuously monitor noncustomer-related measures of organization performance, especially for high-risk systems that can cause serious problems. For example, because their working environment provides a high potential for personal injury, most steel mills continuously monitor and report accidents involving personal injury. Because their facilities provide a high potential for environmental damage, most paper mills continuously monitor and report environmental incidents, such as accidental spills. Finally, because their environment provides a high potential for political damage, most political parties continuously monitor and report political incidents such as reported misdeeds by party members.

Suppose Mike Roy can purchase a new steel cutting machine for Mike's Custom Doors that will reduce costs by creating less scrap steel and rework. This would reduce costs, thereby allowing Mike to lower his prices while improving profit performance. This option is attractive to both customers and the owner. However, suppose that Mike decides not to buy this machine because he feels that its design and operating characteristics create unacceptable safety risks for employees. This example illustrates how issues relating to meeting employee, supplier, owner, and community needs are usually affected by long-term decisions relating to the value chain's design. These decisions are reconsidered periodically when planners re-evaluate the process design.

Performance Measurement

Performance measurement
The measuring of the performance of an activity or a value chain.

Performance measurement is the activity of measuring the performance of an activity or the entire value chain. Performance measurement is perhaps the most important, most misunderstood, and most difficult task in management accounting. An effective system of operations performance measurement contains critical performance indicators (performance measures) that do the following:

1. Consider each activity and the organization itself from *the customer's perspective.*
2. Evaluate each activity using *customer-validated* measures of performance.
3. Consider all facets of activity performance that affect customers and are therefore *comprehensive.*
4. Provide *feedback* to help organization members identify problems and opportunities for improvement.

REFLECTING THE CUSTOMER PERSPECTIVE.   Performance measures should communicate and summarize the things that are critical to the organization's success in meeting customer requirements. Although this seems very basic, many organizations fail to measure systematically what their customers want and value. Customer-focused performance measures help organization members manage the value chain's processes and activities by concentrating their attention on improving what matters to the customer. For example, if all employees at Mike's Custom Doors know that customers require fast service and reliable products that are delivered on time at a low price, these employees can manage their activities accordingly even if they do not deal directly with customers. Maintenance personnel can interpret these objectives to mean that equipment should be maintained so that it will not fail and cause unnecessary production delays and excess costs.

USING THE CUSTOMER'S VALIDATION—OUTPUTS AND OUTCOMES.
Performance measures should be external, or customer validated, rather than internal to the organization. They should reflect an understanding of the difference between the output and outcome of activities. This requires the ability to define precisely what customers value.

An **output** is a physical measure of activity, such as the number of units produced or the amount of time spent doing something. An **outcome** is how the customer values the result of the activity, such as the number of good units of production or the amount of client satisfaction generated by a service.

Exhibit 2-7 provides some examples of inputs, outputs, and outcomes. Inputs are the resources that the organization uses to make something. Outputs are the things that organizations often measure because they are physical and therefore easily measured objectively. Many organizations assess productivity as the ratio of outputs over inputs. For example, fish, meat, and chicken processing plants routinely measure material productivity (also called yield) by dividing the weight of salable product produced by the weight of raw material.

However, since outcomes are what customers value, they provide a better measure of what the

Output
A physical measure of production or activity, such as the number of units produced or the amount of time spent doing something.

Outcome
The value attributed to the result of an activity by the customer, for example, the number of good units of production and the amount of client satisfaction generated by a service.

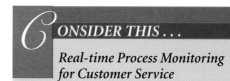

CONSIDER THIS . . .

Real-time Process Monitoring for Customer Service

Caribbean Satellite Services, Inc., installs transceivers in cargo containers. The transceivers monitor the container's position and its internal temperature and humidity. This information is transmitted first to a satellite and then to the company's computer. This information allows Caribbean Satellite Services' customers to monitor the position and condition of their containers. It also allows shippers to advise their customers of the position and estimated time of arrival of their shipment and provides the ability to adjust the temperature and humidity in the containers.

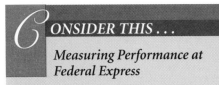

Measuring Performance at Federal Express

Federal Express measures 12 attributes of service. It weights the performance score on each attribute—the higher the customer aggravation caused by the performance failure, the higher the weight assigned to that attribute—to determine an overall service performance score, which it calls the service quality indicator. The score is computed and reported weekly.

Employees use the score to find the root causes of performance failures. For example, if mislabeled packages are causing service failures, procedures are designed to eliminate the causes of packages being mislabeled.

process is contributing to the organization. Outcomes are the things that the organization is in business to accomplish. Consider how misleading the material productivity measure of output weight divided by input weight might be in a meat-packing plant. The processing operation would get the same performance evaluation from turning raw material that might have been processed into prime rib roast into hamburger.[7]

Exhibit 2-8 summarizes the relationships between inputs, outputs, and outcomes in a university.

Most organizations choose to measure outputs (such as the number of pieces made, the number of words typed, and the number of shipments delivered) rather than outcomes (such as the number of pieces made that met customer requirements, the number of good words typed, and the number of shipments delivered without damage and on time). *The critical difference between outcome and output measurement is that outcome focuses on effectiveness in meeting customer requirements and output does not.* Therefore, an organization that focuses on improving outputs fails to distinguish between what is done and what is done that customers value.

REFLECTING COMPREHENSIVE INFORMATION. An effective program of performance measurement assesses all facets of relevant performance so that the decision maker is not motivated or influenced to trade off relevant but

EXHIBIT 2-7
Inputs, Outputs, and Outcomes

Organization	Input	Output	Outcome
Government Employment Office	Hours of counseling time paid for by the government	Number of hours counseled	Number of jobs found that meet clients' legitimate expectations
Police Street Patrols	Cost of patrolling	Hours spent patrolling	Effect of patrolling on crime rate
Research Laboratory	Number of laboratory worker hours paid for	Number of laboratory hours worked	Number of patents produced or the profitability of the products produced
Sawmill	Volume of logs processed	Volume of lumber created	Net realizable value of lumber created

[7] In fact, the processing operation might get more credit from doing this since the process would use more fat that otherwise might have been scrapped.

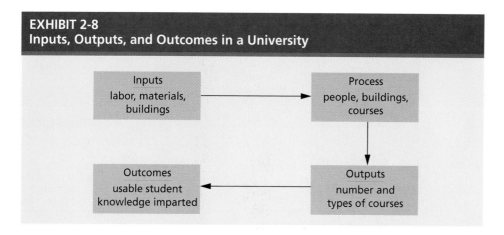

EXHIBIT 2-8
Inputs, Outputs, and Outcomes in a University

unmeasured facets of performance for performance on measured facets. Organizations must avoid falling into the trap of thinking "if we cannot measure what we want, then we will want what we can measure."[8] Focusing on a single performance measure can have severe consequences, as the subsequent examples show.

When Domino's Pizza promised its customers it would deliver pizzas to their homes within 30 minutes or provide a $3 refund, it was both defining and guaranteeing its service. What Domino's did not envision or intend was that young, often inexperienced drivers would race through the streets to meet the 30-minute service commitment. Consumers began to complain about the guarantee and told Domino's Pizza franchisees that they would rather wait longer for their pizzas so that these delivery people would drive more slowly and safely. Many Domino's franchisees felt the same way, told their drivers to slow down, and paid the $3 refund routinely and willingly. By focusing only on one facet of performance—speed—Domino's Pizza sent the message to its employees that speed alone, and not any other performance facet, like safety, counted. This matter became a crisis in December 1993 when a jury awarded $99 million to a woman who suffered head and spine injuries after she was broadsided by a Domino's Pizza driver who ran a red light. Shortly after this accident, Domino's discontinued its 30-minute delivery guarantee.

In the late 1970s and early 1980s, Harley Davidson, the motorcycle manufacturer, was struggling. In order to improve its cash flow company executives ordered factory personnel to speed up manufacturing and delivery. The result was that the factory literally followed these instructions and shipped motorcycles they knew were defective resulting in new motorcycles leaking oil in the dealers' showrooms.

Suppose that the counter staff at Mike's Custom Doors is told to take and fill orders quickly to improve the customer service rate. Customers who are unable to communicate their orders quickly (for example, they may be new to the business and unfamiliar with the product line or they may have language, vision, reading, or hearing problems) will frustrate the employees who may be evaluated on their sales rate. In turn, the employees might be rude to, or even ignore, customers

---

[8] The difficulty of finding performance measures that are aligned with intended performance, and the problems created when organizations use inappropriate performance measures, is well known in the organization behavior literature. For example, see Steven Kerr, "On the Folly of Rewarding A, While Hoping for B," *Academy of Management Journal*, Volume 18, Number 4, 1975, pp. 769–783.

Two critical success factors in the trucking industry are getting shipments to customers on time (customer service) and keeping trucks occupied in revenue-generating activities (efficiency). Improving service and efficiency requires information exchanges between the deployed truck drivers and their dispatchers. Rockwell International Corporation, a company specializing in electronics, has developed a device that helps truck drivers communicate with their dispatchers. The dispatcher sends the driver routing information (which helps to keep the trucks busy) while allowing the driver to send information about the status of a shipment (which helps to improve customer service). Many of these devices can be tracked by satellite so that the dispatcher is continuously and automatically advised about truck locations. *Source* **1994 Annual Report, Rockwell International Corporation, p. 8**

whom they believe may reduce their productivity. Therefore, the counter staff at Mike's Custom Doors should be told to focus on providing good service first and then working to improve speed.

PROVIDING FEEDBACK. Performance measures should be both understandable and tailored to the needs of the people who manage the organization's activities. An effective performance measurement program will help the people who manage the value chain identify problems and suggest solutions. This attribute reflects the purposeful nature of performance measurement in assessing operations and providing a meaningful guide for improvement.

Signal
Information provided to a decision maker. There are two types of signals: (1) a warning that there is a problem and (2) a diagnostic that identifies the problem.

Signals

A **signal** is information provided to a decision maker. Performance measures provide two types of useful signals: (1) warning signals and (2) diagnostic signals.

Warning Signals

The first signal is a *warning* that something is wrong in the same way that an increase in a person's body temperature above normal is a signal that something is wrong. The warning signal triggers an investigation to identify and correct the problem that triggered the signal. In business, deteriorating financial performance, such as falling sales, profits, or return on investment, are warning signals that the effectiveness or efficiency of the organization's value chain, or of its underlying processes, are decreasing. Supervisory personnel often use financial measures as warning signals to monitor ongoing processes for which they are responsible but do not manage directly. For example, at Mike's Custom Doors, declining sales and a declining profit as a percent of sales would be a signal to Mike that there are underlying problems relating to attracting customers (the revenue effect on profits) and controlling costs (the cost effect on profits) that need to be identified and corrected.

Diagnostic Signals

Diagnostic signals provide direct or indirect evidence of the nature of an underlying process problem and may even suggest a way to deal with the problem. For example, many automobiles have monitoring systems that can sense a loss of pressure in the braking system. If the monitoring system detects a problem, it stores a code in its memory to indicate the problem identified and signals the driver with a warning light that service is required. The driver, who may have little or no mechanical ability, is warned that there is something wrong that requires an expert's attention. Then the service mechanic can use a computer to access the stored code, which is a diagnostic signal that identifies why the monitoring system turned on the warning light.

In response to declining sales, which is a warning signal that some elements of the organization's processes are not meeting customer requirements, the marketing manager at Mike's Custom Doors may undertake a customer survey that identifies among other things that improperly finished doors are causing customer dissatisfaction and lost sales. This specific or diagnostic information focuses attention on finishing activities in the door manufacturing process that may require employee retraining, revised processes, or new machinery.

People who directly manage activities need both warning and diagnostic information to identify and solve the problems that require attention. Unfortunately, although some organizations gather diagnostic information on a systematic basis,[9] most diagnostic information is expensive. Therefore, most organizations use warning information, particularly financial information, to trigger episodic gathering of diagnostic information.

[9] There are two types of organizations that commonly use diagnostic information—those in the natural resource industries, such as oil and gas and pulp and paper, and those that use continuous processes, such as nylon manufacturers. In the case of natural resource industries, the primary concern is to monitor and control the use of raw materials, a major component of product costs. In the case of continuous processes, the primary concern is to detect and correct problems quickly because of the fast production rate. The process control equipment itself gathers the information that it uses to quickly identify and correct process problems.

The Costs and Benefits of Information

One of the primary differences between financial and management accounting is that financial accounting information is prescribed or required by the authorities who set external reporting standards. In contrast, management accounting information must always be justified by the benefits it provides the organization. Specifically, assessing these benefits involves estimating the increased profit resulting from developing and using information.

Therefore, companies should evaluate all management accounting information and control systems, at least intuitively, by comparing the costs and benefits of the proposed information and system. Many people believe that as costing systems become more complex, costs rise more quickly and benefits increase less rapidly.[10] Exhibit 2-9 shows the point where the marginal costs and benefits of information suggest is the optimal level of information to provide. The marginal value and marginal cost of information[11] are equal when the information quantity is about 10. Developing less or more than this amount of information is suboptimal. Clearly, neither management nor the management accountant is likely to be able to develop a detailed picture to compare the costs and benefits of information. However, the principle of comparing expected benefits with expected costs is important.

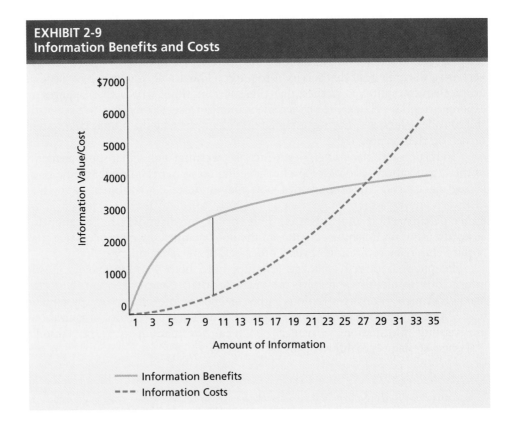

EXHIBIT 2-9
Information Benefits and Costs

---

[10] That is, the marginal value of information is falling and the marginal cost of developing information is increasing.

[11] In the picture, these marginal amounts respectively equal the slopes of the benefit and cost functions.

The principle illustrated here is that information system improvements, where expected costs outweigh expected benefits, are not justified. Therefore, management accountants must always be careful to compare the estimated costs and benefits of the information that they provide. Consequently, complex costing systems, such as the activity costing systems described in Chapter 7, may be economically desirable in some organizations and not in others.

Performance Measures as Aids in Operations Control

Performance measures are a critical part of operations control. **Control** is the set of methods and tools that organization members use to keep the organization on track toward achieving its objectives.

Control
The set of methods and tools that organization members use to keep the organization on track toward achieving its objectives.

The organization's customers determine operations' objectives within the context of the constraints defined by the organization's other stakeholders. Control may be exercised by (1) developing standard procedures that employees are told to follow or (2) hiring qualified people who understand the organization's objectives, telling them to do whatever they think best to help the organization achieve its objectives, using the control system to evaluate the resulting performance, thereby assessing how well they have done. For example, to illustrate the first type of control, Mike's Custom Doors may develop a standard way to set up a machine to cut steel and require that all machine setups follow this method. To illustrate the second type of control, Mike's Custom Doors may hire a manager who is told to do whatever she feels is necessary to achieve the owner's objectives.

Information is critical to both of these approaches to control. When control is used to *ensure compliance with standard operating procedures*, information is used to motivate people to follow rules and to verify that they follow them. When control is used to *motivate people to be creative in meeting customer objectives*, information is used to inform people and help them choose a course of action that helps the organization achieve its objectives.

PERFORMANCE STANDARDS

Once the organization has decided what critical performance indicators to measure and has developed a system to capture these measures, it must evaluate performance. Part of the performance evaluation process is to compare realized, or actual, performance with some standard or target performance level. A discrepancy between the actual and planned performance levels, such as failing to meet sales targets at Mike's Custom Doors, signals a potential problem. This, in turn, invokes a problem-solving exercise to determine first if there is a problem and, if so, to solve it.

Organizations develop performance standards in many different ways. Many organizations set performance standards based on *estimated potential*. For example, an engineer may study a bottling machine and conclude, based on its design and operating characteristics, that the machine should be able to fill 2500 bottles per hour. Or, based on *experience*, the manager at Mike's Custom Doors may feel that a worker should be able to finish a standard door in 35 minutes. Mike can evaluate actual performance relative to this standard of performance.

Other organizations set performance targets based on improving past performance. For example, a study of past performance may reveal that sewers in a shirt factory should complete 20 shirts per hour. Based on this information, the target for current performance may be set at 21 shirts per hour—a process of continuous improvement.

The problem with basing performance standards either on potential or on past performance is that these standards provide no sense of urgency. They do not reflect what is going on in the world outside the organization, particularly regarding what competitors are achieving. These internal standards usually are intended to encourage people to work harder or faster rather than smarter. Working smarter requires an emphasis on improving processes and eliminating things that do not improve the product's attributes. Pressures to work harder create organization friction if the people subjected to these standards challenge them either quietly or openly.

Cost as a Process Performance Measure

Our focus now shifts to cost, which management accounting practice uses as a major performance measure. Although cost seems to be a straightforward topic, some cost aspects require careful consideration.

Managing by the numbers
An approach to cost-cutting that focuses on reducing the budget, or cost allowance, allowed for a particular activity.

COSTS AND MANAGING BY THE NUMBERS.   In the past, cost information supported a process called **managing by the numbers.** When an organization is managed by the numbers, planners first decide the amount of cost reduction required and then reduce each facility's or department's budget by those amounts.

Managing by the numbers has three inherent problems:

1. It is ineffective.
2. It assumes that cost is the only relevant measure of an activity's performance.
3. It does not recognize the reasons for costs in an organization.

In the short run, a budget cut, such as a layoff, will cause employees to work harder to do the same things in the same way with fewer resources. This regime quickly tires employees. As employees tire of the faster pace, they will slow down and, as a result, there will be pressures to rehire the people who were laid off. Costs will then revert to their previous level. For example, Mike's Custom Doors may react to its low profits by reducing the number of employees. In the short run, the staff may respond by working harder and, perhaps, even by staying after their shift to catch up on maintenance and other activities that can be postponed and not affect production levels in the short run. However, they will soon tire of the faster pace and Mike will face strong pressures to rehire the people laid off.

Managing by the numbers makes no attempt to understand why costs exist in the organization. Rather, it assumes that costs are bad and, therefore, should be eliminated.

UNDERSTANDING THE CAUSES OF COSTS.   Effective cost control requires understanding how customer requirements create the need for activities and how activities, in turn, create costs. Improving cost performance, called *activity-management* or *activity-based management*, requires an examination of the need, efficiency, and effectiveness of existing activities and any new activities.

In an activity-management approach to cost improvement, a manufacturer, for example, may try to reduce costs by studying its current activities and developing plans to eliminate unnecessary activities and improve the performance of necessary activities. For example, a study of activities may indicate that 50% of labor costs in the factory relate to handling work in process, which adds nothing to the product attributes that customers value. Instead, handling activities reflect organization constraints, poor product design, and a poor factory layout. The organization may reduce the need for handling by redesigning the product, simplifying the process used to make the product, and rearranging the factory layout to reduce the need for handling. Then it would be possible to eliminate many material handling costs permanently without affecting the value of the product to the customer. This approach would not require that employees work harder to reduce costs. Instead the organization would reduce costs by eliminating unnecessary activities. Relative to competitors who continue to undertake extra handling activities, the organization with improved activity processes would acquire a permanent cost advantage. In the short run, other organizations that had not eliminated handling activities might sprint as the employees may do at Mike's Custom Doors in response to a cut in personnel. However, employees cannot maintain sprints over the long run because employees eventually tire of working harder to make up for inefficient product or process designs.

Eliminating activities that do not improve the product attributes that customers value is an effective way to cut costs. Philip Crosby, a noted quality guru of the 1980s, argued that "Quality is free." Crosby believes that $1 spent in preventing defective production will result in saving at least $1, and usually more, in the costs of detecting and fixing quality problems. At Mike's Custom Doors, for example, spending $500 to train an employee to avoid common mistakes is likely to repay itself many times over by reducing costs and customer ill will caused by those mistakes.

Information About Activities

Because of the performance improvement potential that results from improved activity management, many experts argue that organizations should develop activity data. Examples of activity data include the amount of time needed to make and deliver a product or service, materials handled, storage space used on the factory floor, and rework done. The organization manages by using the activity data rather than cost data. The activity data not only helps identify problems, but in many cases also suggests how to solve problems. Therefore, organizations can use activity information as diagnostic information to improve performance. At the same time, activity costs can serve as a warning signal of the cost of nonvalue-added activities and can be used to set priorities for efforts to improve the performance of value-added activities.

HOW ACTIVITIES CREATE COSTS.   Exhibit 2-10 shows, from left to right, how activities create costs. The activities required to make and deliver a product to the organization's customers create a demand for resources—materials, labor, and equipment. The acquisition and consumption of these resources create costs, which the accounting system measures.

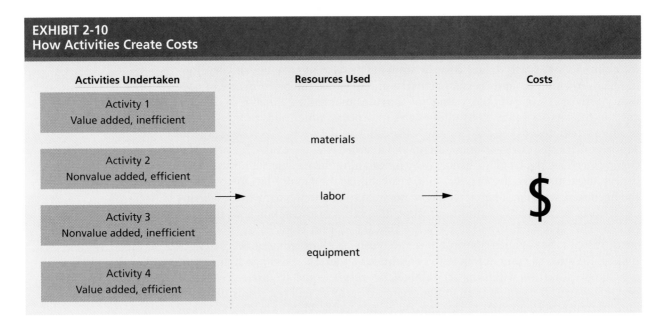

EXHIBIT 2-10
How Activities Create Costs

The most primitive approach to control is managing by the numbers. One example of this type of strategy, which is common in government, is to institute a hiring freeze. This reduces costs in the short run since the hiring freeze reduces the amount of labor that the organization unit is allowed to employ and pay. However, a hiring freeze does not reduce costs in the long run because it does not reduce the underlying demand for labor by eliminating the need for the activity that causes the demand for it.

VALUE-ADDED AND NONVALUE-ADDED ACTIVITIES AND COST PERFORMANCE. Exhibit 2-10 shows four types of activities, each of which has two indices. The first index identifies whether the activity is value-added or nonvalue-added. A **value-added activity** is an activity that, if eliminated, would in the long run reduce the product's service to the customer. For example, acquiring raw materials to make a product is a value-added activity because without them the organization would be unable to make the product. Painting an automobile is a value-added activity because customers want painted cars. We evaluate each value-added activity by how it contributes to the final product's service, quality, and cost.

Value-added activity
An activity that, if eliminated in the long run, would reduce the product's service to the customer.

Any activity that cannot be classified as value-added is a nonvalue-added activity.[12] A **nonvalue-added activity** presents an opportunity for cost reduction without reducing the product's service potential to the customer. It has the potential to reduce the organization's results on every facet of performance that the customer values.[13]

Nonvalue-added activity
An activity that presents the opportunity for cost reduction without reducing the product's service potential to the customer.

An organization undertakes nonvalue-added activities because the current

[12] Some people call the costs created by nonvalue-added activities and the costs created by the poor design of value-added activities *chronic waste* because these costs can be reduced only by eliminating the need to perform nonvalue-added activities or by redesigning activities to eliminate inefficiencies. *Sporadic waste* refers to inefficiencies created by the improper management and operation, rather than the design, of activities.

[13] Because they invariably involve handling work in process, and because handling often leads to damage, nonvalue-added activities often degrade, and never improve, quality. Because they are not done instantaneously, nonvalue-added activities decrease service by increasing processing time and by increasing the amount of time taken to discover mistakes, thereby increasing the number of mistakes that are made. Because they are never costless, nonvalue-added activities increase costs.

product design or process design requires them. For example, poor facility layout requires that work in process be moved during production; this is of no concern to the customer. Therefore, moving work in process around an office, a store, or a factory adds nothing to the value that the customer assigns to the product. Similarly, the customer does not know or care about rework, which is caused by failing to make the product right the first time. Rework creates additional costs for the organization that offers no additional customer value. The customer cares only that the product performs as expected and is unwilling to subsidize the excess costs of a manufacturer who has to rework production so that it meets the product specification.

Organizations cannot just eliminate their nonvalue-added activities. Instead, they must study and then change the underlying activity processes to eliminate nonvalue-added activities. Classifying an activity as nonvalue added indicates whether it will ever be possible to reduce and eventually eliminate the activity and, therefore, its related cost by improving the product design or process layout. For example, machine setup costs are nonvalue added since they do not modify the

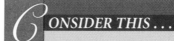

CONSIDER THIS...

The Effects of Eliminating Moving Activities

Henredon Furniture Industries makes frames that it supplies to furniture manufacturers. By reorganizing the plant so that the machines were grouped by what is needed to make a specific product (rather than locating all the same machines together), the following process improvements resulted: the time taken to complete an order was reduced from eight weeks to three; delivery performance improved from completing 42% of the orders in eight weeks to completing 99% of the orders in three weeks; and productivity improved 25%. These changes reduced factory processing costs by $500,000 beyond the expected sales increase resulting from the improved service potential.

Source: Michael J. Lemon, "Modern management and technology . . .", *National Productivity Review,* June 22, 1995, p. 61.

basic raw materials in the product. However, setup costs are necessary when companies use multipurpose machinery to make multiple customized products. Many companies now use dedicated factories or specialized lines either to eliminate setup costs or to reduce setup costs to almost zero by designing methods and equipment that can be set up quickly. Consider the example of transportation costs. Many suppliers have located their factories to minimize the total cost of transporting goods into and out of their facilities.

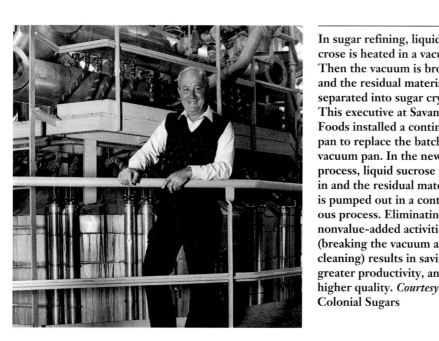

In sugar refining, liquid sucrose is heated in a vacuum. Then the vacuum is broken and the residual material is separated into sugar crystals. This executive at Savannah Foods installed a continuous pan to replace the batch vacuum pan. In the new process, liquid sucrose goes in and the residual material is pumped out in a continuous process. Eliminating two nonvalue-added activities (breaking the vacuum and cleaning) results in savings, greater productivity, and higher quality. *Courtesy* **Colonial Sugars**

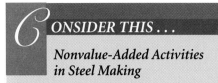

Nonvalue-Added Activities in Steel Making

A common way of making coil steel is to manufacture the raw steel, cast the raw steel into a large slab, allow the slab to cool, transport the slab to a rolling mill, reheat the slab, and then roll out the slab into the gauge (thickness) required.

Many people recognized that all intermediate steps in this process relating to cooling and reheating the slab were nonvalue-added and created considerable additional costs and time delays. This insight and knowledge drove people in the steel industry to develop a casting machine that could cast thin gauge steel directly from molten steel.

In the last few years this technology has been perfected, and raw steel can be cast into a thickness much closer to the finished gauge. This new technology eliminates all the intermediate steps and therefore the costs associated with making and handling slabs.

The drive to reduce or eliminate nonvalue-added activities is important because it allows organizations to permanently reduce the costs of making their goods or services without affecting the value the customer assigns to the product. Process re-engineering, or simply **re-engineering,** is a popular term that describes this process of finding and eliminating nonvalue-added activities.

Some activities are tricky to classify. For example, laws may require that a factory not pollute its environment. Therefore, pollution abatement equipment and its related activities may be thought of as value added. However, this is not entirely accurate because it may be possible to design a process or use raw materials or equipment that created no pollution, thus avoiding the cost of pollution abatement equipment.

We should always be careful in determining whether an activity is value added. For example, when considering wine-making activities, classifying storing as a value-added activity assumes that the only way to make fine wine is to store it and allow it to age. However, think of the advantage that a winery would have if it could make good wine that did not need long storage periods.

Re-engineering
The process of finding and eliminating nonvalue-added activities. Re-engineering involves evaluating the process objectives and redesigning the entire process to make it less costly.

Efficient
A process characteristic that refers to its ability to use the fewest possible resources to produce something.

Continuous improvement
The relentless search to document, understand, and improve the activities that the organization undertakes to meet its customers' requirements.

EFFICIENT AND INEFFICIENT ACTIVITIES AND COST PERFORMANCE. Exhibit 2-10 uses an index to classify activities as either efficient or inefficient. **Efficient** means that the performance of the activity consumes no excess resources. We can determine whether an activity's performance is efficient by comparing one company's performance with that of competitors. This process is called competitive benchmarking. For example, General Mills, a maker of breakfast cereals, studied how race car pit crews organized themselves to accomplish their activities (such as changing tires or adding fuel) in the least possible time. General Mills adapted the ideas that they got from studying these pit crews to develop a system for machinery changeovers in its factories. This system reduced average machine changeover time from 8 hours to 10 minutes. This improvement reduced costs and increased machine productivity. An inefficient activity requires more resources than necessary to produce the desired outcome. Many organizations have adopted a philosophy of continuously studying existing processes to discover better ways of doing them. This is called **continuous improvement,** which is the relentless search to document, understand, and improve the activities that the organization undertakes to meet its customers' requirements.

Activities 2 and 3 in Exhibit 2-10 should be eliminated because they add nothing to the product that the customer values. If the company eliminates these activities, it also eliminates a related demand for resources that in turn creates costs. Therefore, deleting nonvalue-added activities reduces the organization's long-term cost structure.

However, in the short run it may be impossible to change the process or product design that creates the need for nonvalue-added activities. Therefore, it may be beneficial to improve the efficiency of type 3 activities to reduce costs while working to eliminate the need to carry out these activities. Mike's Custom Doors, for example, may have a supervisor who inspects each door before it is shipped to the customer to ensure that it is complete and looks acceptable. This inspection cost is required because the employees have not been trained or are not trusted to inspect their own work. If the production process is redesigned, or re-engineered, to eliminate the possibility of defects or if the employees are taught how to inspect their own work and motivated to do the inspection properly, Mike can eliminate the need for the supervisor. However, until the employees have been trained to undertake self-inspection, Mike must use the supervisor and look for ways to improve (continuous improvement) the efficiency of the supervisor's inspection activities.

The inefficiency of a type 1 activity, a value-added activity that is being poorly done, may be caused by outdated machinery or poor operating procedures. Here, the solution to improve efficiency may be to provide employees with better work procedures, better designed workstation layouts, and better equipment.

General Motors set out to improve the process that assemblers used to make the complicated front seats for its Cadillacs. The assemblers were given worktables on wheels. In addition, the assemblers could adjust the height of the worktables so that they could see their work well and work comfortably. The company also redesigned the process of supplying the parts that went into the seats. The parts were put into bins along a U-shaped path about 10 meters long. The shape and length of the path minimized the distance the assembler had to travel. The bins highlighted inventory levels which, in turn, allowed the reduction of the parts inventory. At the same time, the bins provided a signal about when to restock parts. The assembler pushed the worktable along the path, taking the needed parts from the bins and assembling them into the seat. These simple changes improved both the efficiency of the assembly process and the quality of the seats.

Based on a study of competitor's practices, the manager at Mike's Custom Doors may reorganize the plant layout to minimize the movement of material and work in process. The redesigned layout may ensure that the equipment and people needed to complete a particular product or group of products are located close together; this minimizes materials handling.

Making such process improvements implies that we understand how activities create the demand for resources and in turn how resources consume costs. Benchmarking costs can result in warning signals that something is wrong. For example, the manager at Mike's Custom Doors may find out that on average the cost to make a door at Mike's Custom Doors is 5% higher than a competitor's costs. This benchmarking information should motivate the manager to explore the reasons for the difference.

Costs are warning signals rather than diagnostic signals because they signal the presence of excessive costs rather than the cause of the costs. To improve processes, organizations must understand how costs behave in order to attack the root causes of excess costs. Cost information also helps organization members set priorities for their efforts to eliminate nonva-

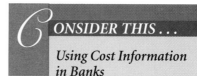

CONSIDER THIS . . .

Using Cost Information in Banks

Banks have traditionally used their interest spreads (the difference between what banks earn and pay on deposits) to cover the costs of the services they provide customers. However, as the financial services industry becomes more competitive, interest spreads have narrowed. At the same time, banks have been using new costing methods, discussed later in this book, to identify the costs of providing services to customers. As a result, many banks have begun to charge for high-cost specialized services that were formerly provided without charge. The banks argue that customers who demand specialized services should pay for those services themselves and not expect other customers to subsidize their consumption of these services. You may find it interesting to consider what may have forced the banks to adopt this strategy. Assume that their overall profit rate has remained unchanged.

lue-added activities or to improve value-added activities and nonvalue-added activities that cannot be eliminated in the short run. Organizations should direct their energies toward those opportunities where the benefits from eliminating or improving activities are the highest.

After studying costs, the manager at Mike's Custom Doors may estimate that the cost of wasted steel resulting from inefficient practices in processing orders and cutting the sheet steel is $8,000 per week and that the cost of labor wasted from an inefficient layout factory layout is $5,000 per week. Obviously both these activities should be improved, but Mike should attack the issues surrounding processing orders and cutting steel first because they promise higher cost savings if resolved.

OTHER STAKEHOLDERS' CRITERIA ON CLASSIFYING ACTIVITIES. Other stakeholders also define constraints that organizations must meet; some activities the organization undertakes, and the form of other activities, often reflect these constraints. For example, customers may want products at the lowest possible price. To keep costs low, an organization may spend as little as possible on employee safety and consequently create a dangerous working environment. Even if a dangerous work environment does *not* affect employee attitudes and performance, many governments consider dangerous work environments socially undesirable and have passed laws to regulate work environments. Therefore, dangerous work environments would fail to meet community expectations about the type of work environment that organizations should provide.

Similarly, although inspection is usually viewed as a nonvalue-added activity, sometimes the law requires it. For example, government contracting usually requires 100% inspection of parts critical to aircraft safety. Consumer product safety laws often require 100% inspection of the formulation of batches of chemicals used to prepare prescription drugs that are critical to a patient's life. Therefore, it is important to assess an activity to determine if it is value added and efficient within the constraints that all the organization's stakeholders define for its operations.

Chapter 11 will discuss how stakeholders other than customers affect the design and evaluation of activities in more detail.

Activity analysis
An approach to operations control that involves applying the steps of continuous improvement to an activity (also known as value analysis).

ACTIVITY, OR VALUE, ANALYSIS. **Activity analysis,** also known as value analysis, is an approach to operations control that became popular during the 1980s. An activity is any discrete task that an organization undertakes to make or deliver a product or service. Specifically, activity analysis includes four steps:

1. **Identify the process objectives** defined by what the customer wants or expects from the process.

2. **Chart** by recording from start to finish the activities used to complete the product or service.

3. **Classify** all activities as value-added or nonvalue-added.

4. **Continuously improve** the efficiency of all activities and plan to eliminate nonvalue-added activities.

Exhibit 2-11 summarizes these steps. Activity analysis is very useful in helping organizations identify opportunities to reduce costs and improve quality and processing time in a systematic way.

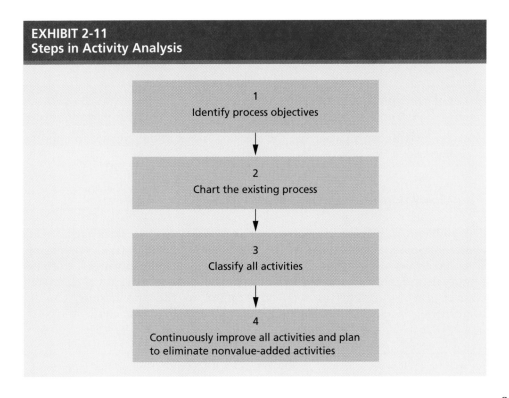

EXHIBIT 2-11
Steps in Activity Analysis

1
Identify process objectives

2
Chart the existing process

3
Classify all activities

4
Continuously improve all activities and plan to eliminate nonvalue-added activities

Storyboards

Storyboarding is the process of using a chart to depict all activities involved in a process. The idea behind storyboarding is to describe each individual activity in a process on a card that is then tacked onto a large board in the order in which it occurs in the process. The storyboard becomes a process flowchart. Writers and animators at the Walt Disney studios in the 1930s and 1940s used storyboards to design the sequence of events in its full-length animated feature films. Storyboards provide a visual, practical, and low-cost tool to use in activity analysis. They allow all the people who work on activities in the process to help identify and describe those activities.

After depicting the process on the storyboard, the next step is to identify how each activity on the storyboard contributes to the organization's success. For example, activities deemed to be value added could be shown on green cards. Activities deemed to be nonvalue added could be shown on red cards, which makes them highly visible targets for potential elimination. It is also a good idea to

Storyboarding
Using a chart to depict all activities involved in a process.

*C*ONSIDER THIS . . .

*Activity Analysis
in a Hospital*

A cross-functional team at the Victory Memorial Hospital tackled the problem of customer complaints about excessive waiting times in the emergency room department. The team began by developing a process flow diagram that described every step of a patient's visit to the emergency room department. Then it monitored the waiting times of three types of patients and identified the patient group that experienced the longest delays. The team then identified the five groups of factors that caused delays: people, machines, materials, methods, and environment. Waiting for test results was a major contributor to waiting time. The team then identified what factors were working against the reduction of waiting time for laboratory results and developed policies and procedures to reduce the delays.

record performance measurements for each activity's service, quality, and cost on its card. This provides a very visible and practical approach to identifying opportunities and setting priorities for improvement.

*E*MI RECORDS GROUP REVISITED

How did EMI Records Group use the ideas discussed in this chapter to improve its operations?

The Main Problem at EMI Records Group

The problems at EMI Records Group evolved from decision makers having inadequate information about the company's manufacturing and distribution systems. This caused the organization to carry far more inventory than needed, store inventory in multiple warehouses so that it could be found more easily, and have excessive costs for returns as suppliers adapted to the unreliable system by overordering stock that was later returned. EMI realized that minor improve-

---

Like all storyboards, this exhibit lays out each process activity clearly so that each activity can be studied in terms of its contribution to the overall process objectives.

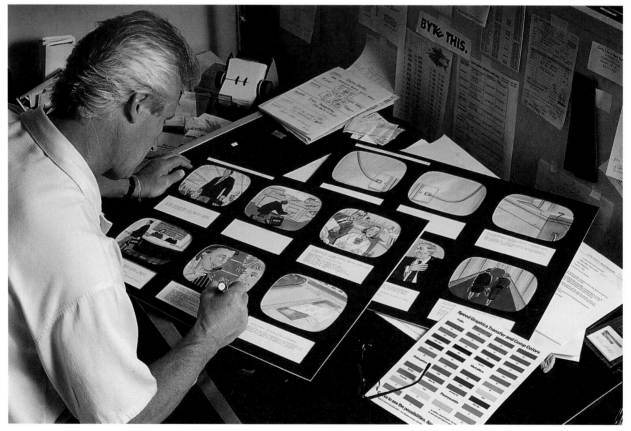

ments or just continuously improving the existing systems would not solve its woes. Instead, what it needed and what was undertaken was a massive re-engineering of its entire value chain.

Resolving the Operating Problems at EMI

The underlying objective in EMI's re-engineering process was to develop a reliable and flexible manufacturing and distribution system. With reliability and improved manufacturing, distribution, and information systems came shorter and less variable response times. This, in turn, reduced the need for customers to order too many products. These new systems also improved the distribution system's ability to resupply retailers when a recording's success exceeded expectations. This performance improvement reduced costs and increased sales.

Simultaneously EMI reorganized both the physical and recordkeeping processes associated with inventory. By reducing manufacturing cycle time and keeping track of inventory, EMI eliminated the need to store similar products in multiple warehouses.

The results were both dramatic and impressive: order filling time dropped from 20 days to 3 days for high-volume items and to 5 days for older stock. The order fill rate improved from 81% to 95%. This improved service performance improved sales. At the same time, process improvements lowered distribution and obsolescence costs by approximately 25% and reduced labor costs by about 30%. Inventory turns increased from 3 to 6 times per year, freeing up a considerable amount of warehouse space. Improved factory productivity reduced the need for the expensive practice of contracting out production. In addition to these measured improvements, the process improvements enhanced EMI Record Group's relations with its artists, customers, and consumers.

SUMMARY

The organization in its pursuit of objectives or purpose undertakes a sequence of activities designed to deliver a product (a physical good or a service) to its customers. It is important to evaluate this sequence of activities from the customers' perspective since they ultimately judge the product's acceptability. Service, quality, and cost are universal attributes that customers use to judge products. The organization's other stakeholders define constraints on the value chain that the organization designs and uses to meet customers' requirements.

Organization members need information about process details including cost to manage their sequence of activities by using the fewest possible resources to meet objectives. Helping organization members to develop the systems to capture and interpret this information defines a natural and useful role for management accountants in organizations.

Charting an organization's process activities and labeling them as value added or nonvalue added helps organization members continuously strive to improve the service, quality, and cost performance of all activities. In addition, in the longer run it allows them to eliminate activities that provide the opportunity for cost reduction without reducing the product's service potential to customers.

The activity perspective developed in this chapter provides the foundation for the balance of this book, which explores and develops the ideas and methods that people use to measure, assess, and improve the organization's activities.

A SUMMARY EXAMPLE

An article in *Management Accounting* magazine[14] describes how Xerox Corporation dealt with a problem that it identified in customer billing. The process began by identifying the billing error rate as 3.54% and estimating the cost of the errors to the organization. This included an estimate of the cost of mistake fixing and lost opportunities created by disaffected customers; this amounted to about $200,000 every six months. The company then formed a cross-functional team to consider the problem. The team first developed a fish bone (Ishikawa) diagram,[15] which had the effect of tying the cross-functional group together into an integrated team that recognized that the problem was multifaceted and multifunctional. The team then followed the following process to develop a solution:

1. Identify the problem.
2. Analyze the problem.
3. Generate potential solutions.
4. Select and plan a solution.
5. Implement and evaluate a solution.

The estimated cost of the project was $7000, and the effect of the solution was to reduce the cost of the billing errors by 54%.

KEY TERMS

Activity, p. 44	Organization control, p. 48
Activity analysis, p. 68	Outcome, p. 55
Continuous Improvement, p. 66	Output, p. 55
Control, p. 61	Performance measurement, p. 54
Costs, p. 52	Process control, p. 49
Critical performance indicators, p. 50	Quality, p. 51
	Re-engineering, p. 66
Critical success factors, p. 50	Service, p. 50
Effective, p. 54	Signal, p. 58
Efficient, p. 66	Stakeholders, p. 47
Managing by the numbers, p. 62	Storyboarding, p. 69
Nonvalue-added activity, p. 64	Value chain, p. 44
Objectives, p. 47	Value-added activity, p. 64

---

[14] David M. Buehlmann and Donald Stover, "How Xerox Solves Quality Problems," *Management Accounting,* September 1993, p. 33.

[15] This article illustrates the use of a fishbone diagram, an interesting and valuable tool that organizations use for process improvement.

ASSIGNMENT MATERIAL

■ QUESTIONS

2-1 What is an activity? Give an example.

2-2 What does control mean?

2-3 What is managing by the numbers?

2-4 What does continuous improvement mean?

2-5 What does effective mean?

2-6 What does efficient mean?

2-7 What is a critical performance indicator? Give an example of one for a university.

2-8 What are organization objectives?

2-9 Define outcome and output. Are they related? Explain.

2-10 Define service and quality. Are they related? Explain.

2-11 What is a signal?

2-12 What is cost and why is it important?

2-13 Define a value chain and give an example.

2-14 Define a value-added activity and give an example.

2-15 What is a critical success factor?

2-16 What is benchmarking?

2-17 What is process control?

■ EXERCISES

2-18 *What customers value*   Can you think of something other than service, quality, and cost that is important to a customer? Explain.

2-19 *What customers do not value*   Can you think of a product where one, or several, of the elements of service, quality, and cost are unimportant to the customer? Explain.

2-20 *Product service features*   For each of the following products, what are the three most important elements of service:
  (a) television set
  (b) university course
  (c) meal in an exclusive restaurant
  (d) meal that is taken away from a restaurant
  (e) container of milk
  (f) visit to the doctor
  (g) trip on an airplane
  (h) pair of jeans
  (i) novel
  (j) university text

2-21 *The elements of quality*   For each of the following products, suggest three measures of quality:
  (a) television set
  (b) university course
  (c) meal in an exclusive restaurant

    (d) meal that is taken away from a restaurant
    (e) container of milk
    (f) visit to the doctor
    (g) trip on an airplane
    (h) pair of jeans
    (i) novel
    (j) university text

2-22 *Customer focus*   Explain why the customer is the appropriate focus on the value chain. How do the organization's other stakeholders temper this focus?

2-23 *Cost as a customer consideration*   Can you think of any product where cost is not an issue? When we say that cost is not an issue, we mean that the customer will invest little or no effort to investigate opportunities to buy the required product at the lowest possible price.

2-24 *Using benchmarking*   Describe how you might use benchmarking to improve your study habits.

2-25 *Effectiveness and efficiency*   Give an example of an activity that is effective but not efficient. Why do you think that organizations sometimes design processes that accomplish activities effectively but not efficiently?

2-26 *Process charting*   Briefly describe, using a process flow chart, any process with which you are familiar. Identify two activities in the process that you think are nonvalue added and why you think that they are nonvalue added. You need not make this complicated. Describing something simple, like borrowing a book from the library, is good enough (but do not use this example).

2-27 *Role of auditing*   If inspection activities are nonvalue added, then auditing should be classified as an nonvalue-added activity. Explain why you agree or disagree.

2-28 *Inventory costs*   Many people have pointed to inventory-related costs as a good example of nonvalue-added costs. What are the costs of holding inventory?

2-29 *Input, output, and outcome*   Pick any job with which you are familiar. Do not use an example from the text. Give one example each of an input, output, and outcome measure for that job. Do you see any danger in using either input or output measures to assess performance on that job? Why?

■ PROBLEMS

Fundamental Problems

2-30 *The value chain in a university*   Describe the value chain in a university. Make sure that you identify each of the activities that a university undertakes and how each relates to the university's customers.

2-31 *Activities and critical success factors in a hospital*   What are the key activities in a hospital? What are the critical success factors in a hospital, and how might they be used to evaluate the key activities?

2-32 *Activities and critical success factors in a convenience store*   Describe the value chain in a neighborhood convenience store. What are the critical success factors, and how might they be used to evaluate the key activities?

2-33 *Critical success factors in the personal computer industry*   Identify the critical success factors for a manufacturer of personal computers and construct a performance measurement system that reflects those critical success factors.

2-34 *Outputs and outcomes*   Choose an activity or process that you know about. Define an output and an outcome. (Do not use an example from the text.) Explain how using the outcome measure would be more effective in promoting activity improvement efforts than using the output measure.

2-35 *Monitoring materials use*   Organizations in the natural resource sector of the economy, such as pulp and paper, meat packers, and organizations that process ores and metals, have developed and use perhaps the most sophisticated tools for monitoring and managing materials costs. Why do you think this is so?

2-36 *Nature of nonvalue-added costs*   Pick any business with which you have some familiarity. Identify three nonvalue-added costs, why they exist, and how the organization might eliminate those costs.

2-37 *Storyboards*   Draw a storyboard that documents the process of signing out a book in the library at your university or college.

Challenging Problems

2-38 *The nature of signals*   Use the context of grading a student's examination or assignment paper to illustrate the difference between a warning signal and a diagnostic signal.

2-39 *Critical success factors in a university*   Many organizations publish rankings of universities, and many of the universities complain about the way that these rankings are developed.

REQUIRED

 (a) Identify a university's critical success factors.
 (b) Based on the university's critical success factors, construct a performance measurement system for students enrolled in a university's business school.

2-40 *Performance measurement in the fast food industry*   Because of the competitiveness of the industry, monitoring performance in a fast food restaurant is critical for success.

REQUIRED

 (a) Identify a fast-food restaurant's critical success factors.
 (b) Identify the major activities in a fast-food restaurant.
 (c) Construct a performance measurement system for each activity that reflects the restaurant's critical success factors.

2-41 *Performance measurement in the airline industry*   Because of the competitiveness of the industry, monitoring performance in an airline is critical for success.

REQUIRED

 (a) Identify an airline's critical success factors.
 (b) Identify an airline's major activities.
 (c) Construct a performance measurement system for each activity that reflects the airline's critical success factors.

2-42 *Incomplete performance measurement*   Choose an activity or process that you know about. Define a performance measurement system that looks at only a part of what the process contributes to the organization. Explain how assessing performance on only a part of what the process contributes to the organization might promote inappropriate behavior.

2-43 *University examinations*   Consider the process of examinations in a university setting.

REQUIRED

 (a) What are the main activities in the examination process?
 (b) What resources does each main activity in the examination process consume?
 (c) Suppose that the university is faced with a cutback and reduces the available levels of the resources that you believe examinations consume. Explain what you think will happen.

2-44 ***Managing by the numbers*** Give an example of managing by the numbers. In view of its limitations, why do you think that managing by the numbers has attracted such a wide following?

2-45 ***Cost behavior*** Pick any business with which you have a reasonable amount of familiarity. Identify three primary causes of costs in this business. Given this, identify some effective ways to reduce costs.

■ CASES

2-46 ***Performance measurement and customer complaints*** Bob Eaton, Chrysler Corporation's Vice-Chairman, made the following observation about Chrysler employees whose jobs are to answer calls from customers with problems or complaints:

> The people who answer these phones have one of the most important jobs in the company. They are our front lines. They can have a more direct effect on sales than anyone else.

After noting that it can cost as much as five times more to get a new customer than it costs to keep one, and that, on average, a satisfied customer will recount his experience to 5 people and an unsatisfied customer to 35, Mr. Eaton went on to say this:

> Even the best salespeople sell only two or three cars a day. Our people on the phones deal with dozens of customers every day. How well they take care of our customers is critical.

REQUIRED

Design a performance measurement system for the Chrysler staff that takes these customer calls.

2-47 ***Competitive strategy*** Nalco Chemical Company makes industrial chemicals. The following material appeared in the December 1991 edition of the *Nalco News*, the company's employee newsletter.

> Our customers are concerned with just-in-time delivery, safe chemical delivery, and shorter lead times—in addition, many customers are setting higher requirements for us.
>
> Since 1985, our order volume has increased significantly. We hired an outside consultant to help us put all of our delivery functions under one umbrella called Operation Excellence. They helped us design a strategy to deliver products 100 percent of the time within the time frame that we agree upon with the customer. We want to improve overall delivery time by delivering 80 percent of our U.S. pounds to customers in 7 days or less. Right now we ship about 800 million pounds a year domestically, so that's a pretty tall order.
>
> This past July we shipped 16 percent of our orders within 7 days . . . In October it was 40 percent . . . In January we should reach 60 percent, and by April we are determined to reach our goal of 80 percent.
>
> 98.6 percent of our 7-day deliveries are on time; 94 percent of our 14-day deliveries are on time; and 97.5 percent of our 21-day deliveries are on time. Of course, our goal is to be 100 percent on time in all three categories within 6 months.
>
> To achieve these goals we are manufacturing certain products closer to the customers and are streamlining manufacturing processes so they are more cost effective. We are building a centralized finished goods warehouse at Clearing to help us more efficiently handle the large numbers of domestic orders—40 percent—that are shipped from that facility.

We also are installing a warehouse management software program to track all orders on a real-time basis, as well as installing a product-package forecasting system to predict what customers will be ordering. This means we can adjust our manufacturing to meet their needs. This will allow us to order raw materials more cost effectively, and we will have the time to get the right type of container to the plant to meet our manufacturing schedule.

Finally, all products will be bar coded and forklift trucks will have a video display screen to help select products at each location and minimize shipping errors. We have heard from our customers and we are responding. Quality is defined by excellent customer service, and this is our driving force toward excellence. We must never forget that the reason we are here is to serve our customers in a quality manner.

REQUIRED

(a) What competitive strategy does Nalco Chemical Company seem to have adopted?
(b) What do you think of the manner and level of the goals that Nalco Chemical Company has set for itself?
(c) What do you think about the way that the company has gone about improving service to its customers?

2-48 *Strategy and performance measurement*   In 1990, McDonnell Douglas Space Systems Company (MDSSC) used three primary strategic business objectives (SBOs). These SBOs are:

1. *Customer-focused:*   to become the preferred supplier in our key market segments.
2. *Cultural:*   to become a company that is the embodiment of total quality management.
3. *Financial:*   to achieve sales growth greater than 6% per year; to increase after-tax return on investment from 16.4% to 20% over the next 10 years.

MDSSC made the following statement about performance measurement:

We can measure our performance as a company against our SBOs. To achieve the goals that we have set, we need everyone to be involved. We need a road map created from objectives, flowing down throughout the organization, to identify all the tasks we need to reach our stated goals. Measuring our performance against those goals will help us to see how well we are doing.

The process at MDSSC was for senior management to create broad business unit objectives and then for each business unit to set its objectives to support the objectives of the larger group. In this way, objectives would flow down through the organization. Unit leaders were told the following:

Your team's objectives should be set high enough to challenge the group, but not so high that they cannot be reached.

For example, the Business and General Support group had the following Strategic Objectives:

1. Improve the quality of information & services by a factor of 5 in 3 years leading toward 100% quality.
2. Reduce all cycle times by 50%.
3. Reduce costs by 30% in 3 years.

The measurement process for each of these SBOs was defined as follows:

1. Customer feedback
2. Cycle time measurement systems, which measure the time the organization takes to do specific activities, such as ordering a part or making something
3. Cost measurement systems

REQUIRED

(a) What do you think of this system?
(b) Specifically, how would you measure customer feedback, cycle time, and costs?
(c) Identify how this system might be used in your university or college to improve operations. Your discussion should identify strategic business objectives and include specific measurements.

2-49 *Course registration as a process*   Consider the process of registering for courses at your university or college.

REQUIRED

(a) Draw a process flowchart that describes the process of registering for courses at your university or college.
(b) As a customer, what criteria do you use to evaluate the registration process?
(c) Label each activity that you have identified in the registration process as value added or nonvalue added.
(d) How might the registration process be reorganized to eliminate the nonvalue-added activities?
(e) How might the activities be reorganized to improve performance on the evaluative criteria that you think are important?
(f) Which activity would you improve first? Why?

2-50 *Critical success factors and performance measurement*   The fishing products industry has 5 critical success factors in the fishing products industry.

1. Keep costs down so that prices can be kept down.
2. Ensure that products meet stated, or expected, quality standards.
3. Ensure that the assigned quota of each species is harvested.
4. Ensure that the fish that are harvested are handled and processed in a way that maximizes their retail value.
5. Support growth by developing new products that are appealing to customers.

There are unique conditions affecting the fishing industry. Harvesting is constrained by two factors. A government regulatory agency sets quotas for each species of fish. The quotas specify the maximum amount of each species of fish that can be caught and the permissible fishing period. Because of equipment failure, weather conditions, and stock depletion, most firms are unable to catch their assigned quota of any given species.

Care has to be taken at each step in the process of harvesting and transporting the fish. During harvesting too many fish in the nets causes the fish to be crushed and bruised, resulting in a loss of quality. Fish begins to deteriorate the moment it is caught. Therefore, care has to be taken to pack the fish in ice in the ship's hold. Similarly, when the fish is discharged from the ship's hold into the processing plant, care has to be taken to ensure that the fish is not damaged or bruised.

Within the processing plant, care has to be taken to ensure that the fish is processed rapidly to prevent deterioration, carefully (to ensure that quality standards relating to color, form, and lack of parasites are met), effectively (to ensure that bones, skin, and blood are not left in the fish and, conversely, that excessive amounts of flesh are not removed with the bone), and efficiently (since many of the operations are manual, labor costs are significant).

The Down East Fishing Products Company (DEFPC) is organized into three responsibility units: (1) harvesting (the fleet of company owned ships and their crews used to harvest various species of fish); (2) processing (the processing plants used to process raw fish into the fresh, frozen, and cooked products wanted by the company's customers); and (3) marketing (responsible for creating the demand for the company's products).

Currently the performance of each of the three responsibility units is evaluated as follows:

Unit	Performance Evaluation
Harvesting	Tons of fish caught
Processing	Costs relative to flexible budget standards
Marketing	Sales increases over the previous year.

REQUIRED

Assess the current system that is used to evaluate the performance of each responsibility center at DEFPC. Make suggestions for any improvements.

2-51 ***Performance measurement and incentive contracting***   Speedy Copy operates a chain of copy centers located throughout North America. Usually located close to college and university campuses, Speedy Copy provides a variety of services that are organized into six business areas: (1) normal copying; (2) color copying; (3) binding; (4) graphics services (such as posters and business cards); (5) preparing readings packages for university courses (including obtaining copyright permissions); and (6) basic word-processing services.

Speedy Copy's approach to business is captured in its motto: *provide value to the customer while doing it right and fast.* The company's operations manual explains that market intelligence suggests that success in the copy business depends on (1) providing services that customers value; (2) providing a fast response to a customer request; (3) providing clear copies; (4) providing accurate duplication services (for example, ensure that a readings package is not missing any pages and that its pages are properly aligned); and (5) doing all of the above at a competitive cost.

You have recently been appointed the manager of a Speedy Copy center located near the campus of a small university (about 1800 students) located in a small town (population about 6000) in a predominately rural area. You and 27 other center managers report to a regional manager. You are paid a salary and a bonus that depends on the measured performance of the center that you manage.

Each quarter, each center manager negotiates performance targets that reflect local conditions and opportunities with the center manager's regional manager in each of the following areas:

1. Sales for each of the six business areas mentioned above
2. Costs as a percentage of sales in each of the six business areas
3. Product quality as determined by a random audit of output conducted during a surprise visit by a team from the regional office
4. Service as determined by the time required to complete a sample of jobs chosen by the audit teams (all jobs are logged in and logged out on the computer terminal at the customer service counter)
5. Customer satisfaction as determined by a quarterly survey of faculty and students at the nearby university (approved jointly by the center manager and the center manager's regional manager and is conducted by the regional manager's staff)

A performance score is computed as follows:

1. A score is determined for each of the five items of performance.
2. The scores on these five items are added to compute a total score.

The center manager's bonus is the percentage of the center manager's salary represented by the total score. The performance score on each of the five items of performance is determined as follows:

1. three points for meeting the target, plus or minus 3%
2. two points for missing target by between 3% and 5%
3. one point for missing target by between 5% and 8%
4. four points for exceeding the target by between 3% and 5%
5. five points for exceeding the target by between 5% and 8%

Performance that varies by more than 8% of target is excluded from the evaluation and is subjected to an immediate investigation by a committee comprised of (1) the center manager, (2) the regional manager, and (3) the regional controller.

REQUIRED

(a) Evaluate this performance measurement system by indicating why you like, or dislike, each of its relevant features.

(b) As part of your efforts to improve the quality of your products and the services provided to your customers, you have decided to develop a product and service quality monitoring system for your copy center. Suggest what type of system might be useful and why.

2-52 *Identifying value-added and nonvalue-added activities*   Woodpoint Furniture Manufacturing manufactures various lines of pine furniture. The plant is organized so that all similar functions are performed in one area, as shown in Exhibit 2-12. Most pieces of furniture are made in batches of 10 units.

Raw materials are ordered and stored in the raw materials storage area. When an order is issued for a batch of production, the wood needed to complete that batch is withdrawn from the raw materials area and taken to the saw area. There the wood is sawed into the pieces that are required for the production lot.

The pieces are then transferred to the sanding and planing area where they are stored awaiting processing in that area. When the machines are free, any sanding or planing is done on all the pieces in the batch. Any pieces that are damaged by the planing or sanding are reordered from the saw area. The other pieces in the lot are set aside in a storage area when pieces have to be reordered from the saw area.

When all the pieces have been sanded or planed, the pieces are then transferred to the assembly area where they are placed in a large bin to await assembly. Pieces are with-

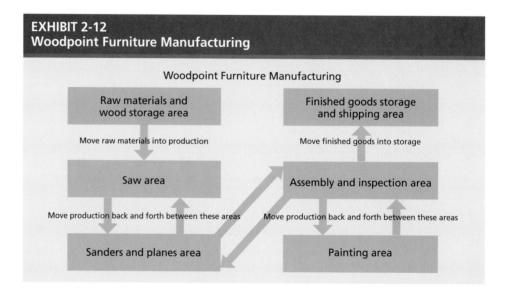

EXHIBIT 2-12
Woodpoint Furniture Manufacturing

Woodpoint Furniture Manufacturing

| Raw materials and wood storage area | Finished goods storage and shipping area |

Move raw materials into production   Move finished goods into storage

| Saw area | Assembly and inspection area |

Move production back and forth between these areas   Move production back and forth between these areas

| Sanders and planes area | Painting area |

EXHIBIT 2-13
From Modest Beginnings to Quality Steel Products

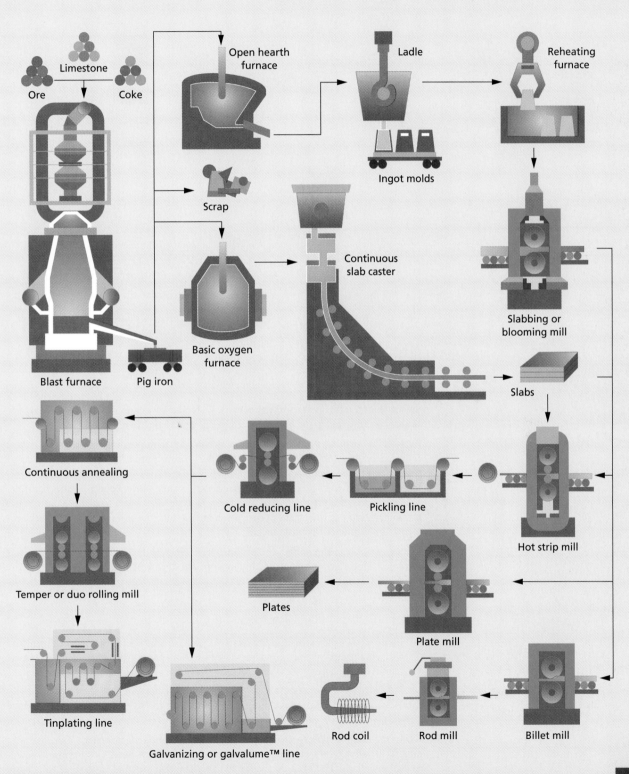

Limestone
Ore
Coke
Open hearth furnace
Ladle
Reheating furnace
Ingot molds
Scrap
Continuous slab caster
Basic oxygen furnace
Slabbing or blooming mill
Blast furnace
Pig iron
Slabs
Continuous annealing
Cold reducing line
Pickling line
Hot strip mill
Temper or duo rolling mill
Plates
Plate mill
Tinplating line
Rod coil
Rod mill
Billet mill
Galvanizing or galvalume™ line

Courtesy Bethlehem Steel Corporation

EXHIBIT 2-14
New Coilcast™ Production Process

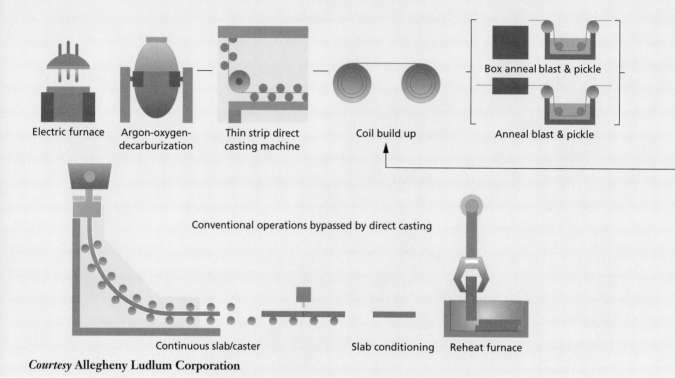

Box anneal blast & pickle

Electric furnace   Argon-oxygen-decarburization   Thin strip direct casting machine   Coil build up   Anneal blast & pickle

Conventional operations bypassed by direct casting

Continuous slab/caster   Slab conditioning   Reheat furnace

Courtesy **Allegheny Ludlum Corporation**

drawn from the bin as assembly proceeds. Defective or missing pieces are returned to the saw or sand and plane area where they are remanufactured.

As assembly proceeds or when assembly is completed, depending on the product, any required painting or staining is done in the painting area. Pieces to be stained or painted are transferred back and forth between the assembly and paint area on a trolley. There is a storage area in the paint department for pieces awaiting painting. Whenever assembly is halted to await pieces that have been sent for painting and staining, the rest of the pieces in that batch are put into the storage bin to await the return of the stained or painted pieces.

When assembly is completed, the product is checked by the quality inspector. Any defective products are returned to the appropriate department for rework. When the product is approved, it is packaged and put into final storage to await an order by the customer.

REQUIRED

(a) Identify the activities undertaken to make furniture in Woodpoint Furniture Manufacturing by drawing a process flowchart for a typical piece of furniture. Classify each activity on your process flow chart as a value-added or nonvalue-added activity.

(b) What critical performance indicators would you use to evaluate the performance of this manufacturing operation?

2-53 *Using the customer perspective to identify nonvalue-added activities* Consider Exhibit 2-13, which summarizes the activities at Bethlehem Steel Corporation's Sparrows Point Plant. The blast furnaces make the iron that is refined into steel. The basic

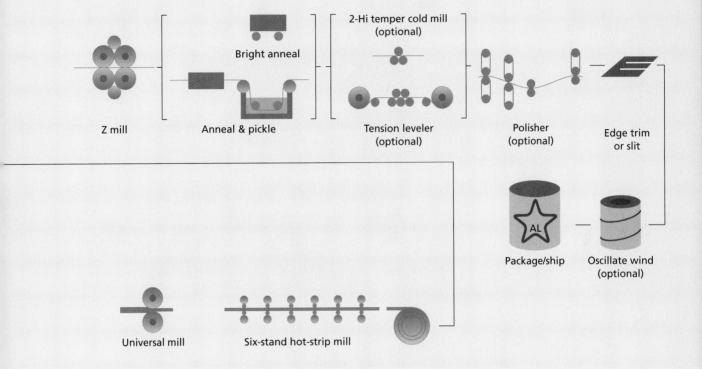

Z mill   Anneal & pickle   Bright anneal   2-Hi temper cold mill (optional)   Tension leveler (optional)   Polisher (optional)   Edge trim or slit   Package/ship   Oscillate wind (optional)   Universal mill   Six-stand hot-strip mill

oxygen furnaces and open hearth furnaces refine the iron into steel. The mix of iron, scrap, and alloys used to make the steel and the characteristics of the furnace determine the steel's properties, which include formability, strength, toughness, hardenability, and corrosion resistance. The continuous slab caster uses the steel from the basic oxygen furnace to make slabs of steel. The steel from the open-hearth furnace is poured into ingot molds for cooling.

When it has cooled and hardened, the steel ingot, weighing between 11,000 and 80,000 pounds, is removed from the mold and stored. When required, the ingots are reheated and moved to the blooming or slabbing mills, which transform the ingots into blooms (square or rectangular shape) or slabs (wide and flat shape), depending on the final product that the ingot will be used to make. This operation also improves the properties of the steel. The billet mill reduces blooms into 4-inch square billets that are shipped to the rod mill, which produces coils of rod that are then transformed into finished items such as wire. Plates are rolled from reheated slabs in the plate mill. The plates must be cut on all sides to the desired dimensions after rolling. Slabs are also used to make strip steel, which is either made into some final products directly or is subjected to finishing operations to make steel sheet or tinplate.

REQUIRED

(a) What do you think is critical to the customer in making a steel purchasing decision?
(b) Do you see any steps in this process that involve nonvalue-added activities?
(c) What might be the critical performance indicators in this process?

2-54 ***Charting process now*** Go to a restaurant. Chart the sequence of activities that occur from the time that you enter the restaurant until the time you leave. Are some of these activities unnecessary, or poorly designed? Does your evaluation of these activities depend on the type of restaurant, i.e., a fast-food restaurant or a formal dining establishment?

2-55 *Eliminating nonvalue-added activities* Exhibit 2-14 shows how Allegheny Ludlum, a steel company, eliminated nonvalue-added steps in the process of making steel coil. The top line in the exhibit shows how the company makes steel coil. Step 3 in this process (the thin strip direct casting machine) has replaced all the steps shown in the second line of the exhibit (labeled conventional operations bypassed by direct casting). In the past, steel was cast into huge slabs (an intermediate product) that was cooled, conditioned, reheated, rolled, and then coiled. Now the coil is cast directly eliminating all these steps.

Allegheny Ludlum expects that the thin strip direct casting machine will have costs of about 25% of steps it replaces, reduce manufacturing time (thereby reducing inventories and improving service to customers), reduce investment levels, and give the company the opportunity to make new products.

REQUIRED

(a) Creating the intermediate product (slabs) seems like such a waste of time and money compared to direct casting thin strips. In the past, when people used the operations that thin casting now allows steel makers to avoid as examples of nonvalue-added activities, steel makers argued that these conventional steps were a necessary part of making steel coil. Using library reference material, explain why steel companies used the slab approach and why so many people were convinced that using slabs to make steel was necessary and therefore value added.

(b) More generally, why do you think nonvalue-added activities exist in most organizations?

(c) Identify two existing processes in other industries that you think are analogous to the slab approach to making steel coil. Briefly describe each process and how it might be replaced the way thin strip direct casting replaced the need to make slabs.

2-56 *The clash between reducing costs to improve investor return and providing a work environment that employees expect* Read the article cited in the footnote below, by Robert Frank in the *Wall Street Journal*.[16] This article describes the clash between an organization that has developed standard operating rules to promote efficiency and quality and the workers who have to follow the rules.

> With a battalion of more than 3,000 industrial engineers, the company dictates every task for the employees. Drivers must step from their trucks with their right foot, fold their money face up, and carry packages under their left arm... It tells drivers how fast to walk (three feet per second), how many packages to pick up and deliver a day (400, on average), even how to hold their keys (teeth up, third finger)... Those (drivers) considered slow are accompanied by supervisors, who cajole and prod them with stopwatches and clipboards.

The article goes on to identify the pressures that demands for increased productivity and the ability to handle a widening product line has put on the employees. The article mentions that the Teamsters' Union, which represents the drivers at UPS, commissioned a study that claimed that the drivers at UPS scored in the 91st percentile of U.S. workers for job stress. One employee observed "But you just wonder how much more they can squeeze out of us before something breaks." What do you think of this? How can an organization decide when it has gone too far in its cost cutting efforts?

2-57 *Developing process performance measures* Exhibit 2-15 shows the canning cycle for Coca-Cola Bottling Operation. Study this diagram, and then identify the production performance measures that you think would be useful to evaluate this process and explain why you would use these performance measures.

---

[16] Robert Frank, "Driving Harder: As UPS Tries to Deliver More to Its Customers, Labor Problems Grow," *Wall Street Journal*, May 23, 1994, p. A1.

EXHIBIT 2-15
Canning Cycle at Coca-Cola Bottling Operation

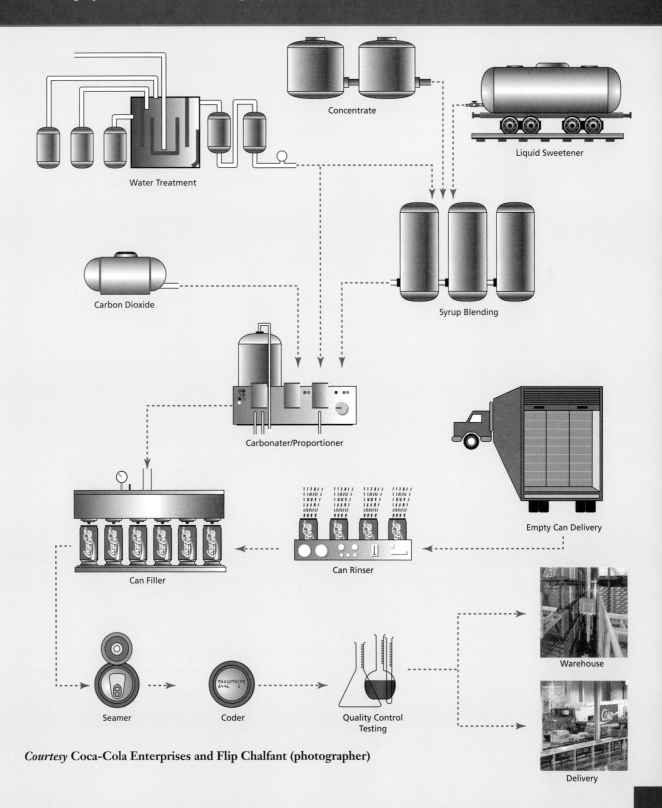

Concentrate

Liquid Sweetener

Water Treatment

Carbon Dioxide

Syrup Blending

Carbonater/Proportioner

Empty Can Delivery

Can Filler

Can Rinser

Warehouse

Seamer

Coder

Quality Control Testing

Delivery

Courtesy Coca-Cola Enterprises and Flip Chalfant (photographer)

3

COST CONCEPTS

LA MUSICA COMPANY

Courtesy **Comstock**

Maria Rosario had just joined the management team at the La Musica Company manufacturing plant in San Antonio, Texas. La Musica makes the plastic jewel cases that CDs come in. Maria had stepped up into this position after ten years in production engineering. Now she would report directly to Mike Mantly, manager in charge of the plant. Anxious to start in her new position, she stepped into Mike's office.

"Maria," Mike requested, "please prepare an analysis of how our decision to replace the old case-forming machines with the new automated machines will affect costs. The new machines should reduce *direct labor costs* considerably because they will require only one worker from now on. I also expect to see efficiency gains in *direct materials* because of the new machine's greater accuracy. I want you to pay special attention to *manufacturing support costs*. Although *facility-sustaining costs*, such as depreciation and insurance, will no doubt increase, we should obtain savings in other *support costs*, such as supervision, maintenance, materials handling, work-in-process inventory storage, and quality inspection."

Maria headed straight to the accounting department to check the plant's accounting records and find out how much the different types of costs had changed when the new automated pressing machines were installed.

Maria's situation is not unusual. Today's organizations require well-informed decision makers who must be knowledgeable about the cost on which they are basing their judgments.

Need for cost information

Managers often require cost information to help them make decisions, as indicated in the following examples:

- Product managers at Procter & Gamble evaluated market demand and product cost data for their own and their competitors' cereal brands before deciding to cut their prices in mid-1996.
- Comparison of manufacturing costs of various facilities was an important step in General Motors selection of plants that needed to be closed in 1994.
- Periodic decisions about routes and fares require managers at American Airlines to weigh the costs of deploying aircraft and personnel on a route against competitive market demand conditions that determine revenues.
- The *gain-sharing incentive plan*[1] at Whirlpool Corporation's washer and dryer component plants calls for paying bonuses to workers for attaining reductions in the ratio of manufacturing costs to **production volume.**
- Successful control of hospital operations at Humana Corporation, Inc., requires its managers to maintain a close check on both the amount of costs budgeted versus the amount spent by each department and the reimbursement of costs from insurance companies.

Production volume
Overall measure, such as number of units, of various products manufactured in a given time period.

In each case, managers used different types of costs to make the appropriate trade-offs for their specific decisions.

Product cost calculations influence most *product-pricing and product-mix decisions.* Managers monitor the cost of operating processes to ensure that the processes are kept under control and that the company uses resources efficiently. In addition, managers analyze costs carefully for nonroutine decisions, such as plant closures or additions of new airline routes. Therefore, they must understand a number of different cost concepts to be able to use the information generated by a cost accounting system appropriately for a wide variety of decisions and control purposes.

This chapter presents three basic frameworks useful for understanding the design of cost accounting systems in organizations.

1. First, we describe how cost accounting systems were designed traditionally to analyze costs by *function*, such as manufacturing, selling, or administration in order to value inventory for external financial reporting.
2. Second, we describe how to classify costs by *activities* as reflected in many systems designed recently and how to express and estimate the costs of activities in terms of cost equations. (Remember that Chapter 2 defined organizations as a sequence of activities.)
3. Third, inventory valuation for financial reports requires a historical or retrospective perspective on cost data, but for most managerial decisions, we need to predict what impact the decisions will have on future costs and revenues. Thus, we require a forward-looking, or prospective, perspective on cost data

---

[1] Gain-sharing incentive plans are designed to share productivity gains between workers and owners. They are based on an agreed-upon formula to quantify and share the gains.

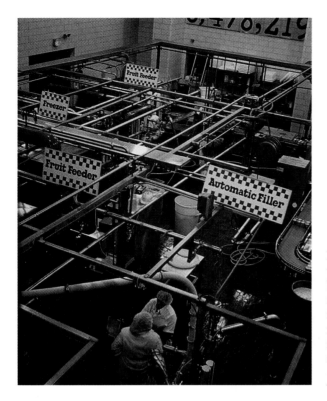

Helping decision makers understand the nature and behavior of costs in organizations, including this ice cream manufacturing facility, is one of the most important roles played by management accountants. *Courtesy* **Ben & Jerry's**

in management accounting systems. Therefore, in the final segment of this chapter, we describe the basic structure of standard cost accounting systems, which firms use both to estimate and predict cost behavior and to control costs by comparing actual costs with standard cost estimates.

Functional Cost Classifications

Accounting systems collect and analyze cost data to support managerial decision making. *Cost* is defined as the monetary value of goods and services expended to obtain current or future benefits. Costs are not necessarily the same as expenses. *Expenses* are reported in the income statement. They can represent costs for which benefits have already been received in the current fiscal period, such as cost of goods sold. Expenses can also represent **period costs,** such as advertising or research and development, whose benefits cannot be matched easily with the products or services sold in a specific fiscal period. **Product costs** are all the costs incurred for the volume and mix of products produced during the period. The portion of product costs assigned to the products actually sold in a period appears as expenses (cost of goods sold) in the income statement; the remaining portion of product costs is assigned to the products in inventory and appears as an asset in the balance sheet. Thus, expenses in a fiscal period may not include all the costs (monetary value of goods and services) expended during the year.

Traditionally, the basic structure of cost accounting systems has reflected the need to determine *product costs* for external financial statements. This calculation

OBJECTIVE 3.1

Classify costs based on their functions.

Period costs
Costs treated as expenses in the period in which they are incurred because they cannot be associated with the manufacture of products.

Product costs
Costs associated with the manufacture of products.

must satisfy external financial reporting requirements imposed by corporate, securities, and income tax laws. These external requirements specify which costs to assign to products to appear either as cost of goods sold or inventory as well as which costs to exclude from product cost calculations. In principle, cost accounting systems to support managerial decision making can be designed independently of such external reporting requirements. Systems designed in the past, however, economized on information-processing costs by adopting the structure imposed by external reporting requirements. Therefore, most cost accounting systems we observe in business firms today tend to be driven by the rules that determine product costs for inventory valuation and cost of goods sold.

Traditional cost accounting systems classify costs into manufacturing costs and nonmanufacturing costs based on their respective functions. (See Exhibit 3-1 and the information below.)

Manufacturing costs
All costs of transforming raw materials into finished products; classified as direct and indirect costs.

Nonmanufacturing costs
All costs other than manufacturing costs.

1. **Manufacturing Costs.** All costs of transforming raw materials into a finished product, for example, *direct costs* (direct materials, direct labor) and *indirect costs* (manufacturing support).

2. **Nonmanufacturing Costs.** All costs other than manufacturing costs.
   - *Distribution costs* are the costs of delivering finished products to customers.
   - *Selling costs* include sales personnel salaries and commissions and other sales office expenses.
   - *Marketing costs* include advertising and publicity expenses.
   - *Research and development costs* include expenditures for designing and bringing new products to the market.
   - *General and administrative costs* include expenses, such as the chief executive officer's salary and legal and accounting office costs that do not fall into any of the above categories.

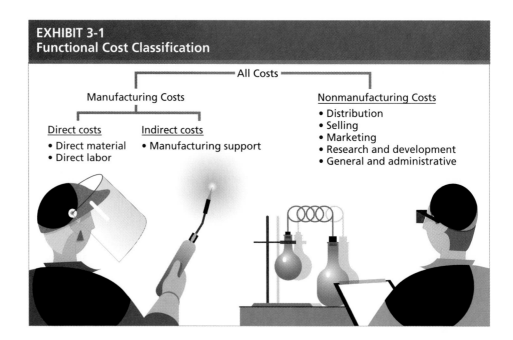

EXHIBIT 3-1
Functional Cost Classification

For external reporting purposes, only manufacturing costs are included in the valuation of finished goods inventories. Traditional cost accounting systems, therefore, provide for the analysis of these costs in great detail in order to assign them to products. All nonmanufacturing costs are treated as period costs and are reported as expenses without any additional analysis.

Direct manufacturing costs can be traced directly to a product. Examples of direct manufacturing costs include these:

- *Direct material costs* are the costs of all materials and parts that can be traced to the final product. For instance, if the manufacture of an automobile chassis requires 120 pounds of steel and the steel price is $11 per pound, the direct material cost per chassis is computed as follows: *Price Per Pound × Number of Pounds of Steel Per Chassis*, or $1320 ($11 × 120).

> **OBJECTIVE 3.2**
>
> Differentiate between direct and indirect costs.

Direct manufacturing costs
Costs that can be traced easily to the product manufactured or service rendered.

ONSIDER THIS . . .

Cost of Fringe Benefits for Employees

Bachman's, Inc. is a Minneapolis-based specialty retailer of garden products with 30 retail outlets ranging in size from large centers to small stores. It also operates commercial services, wholesale nurseries, and retail landscape businesses. Bachman's employs between 850 and 1400 workers depending on the time of year as several of its businesses—such as retail sales, landscaping, and nursery operations—are seasonal. It has many different job types: union and nonunion; full time, part time, and seasonal; regular and casual; and salaried, hourly, and commissioned. Each job type is entitled to a different set of benefits.

Until recently, Bachman's accounted for fringe benefits as support costs, assigning them to all its departments using the same flat rate of 26.5% of employee wages and salaries. However, Bachman's managers believed that the real benefit costs were different for different businesses depending on their employment patterns. Expecting fringe benefits costs to increase on average to 30% of employee wages and salaries within the next few years, Bachman's wanted to gain better control over them. Managers felt it was important to have a clear understanding of the impact of fringe benefits when faced with tough decisions such as whether to close a store or drop a business segment.

Bachman's now records and analyzes fringe benefits costs in more detail to trace them more accurately to the actual spending for individual departments. The pie chart below indicates that health insurance, social security (FICA), retirement and pension plans, unemployment, and workers'

compensation insurance are most of the fringe benefits costs. Social Security costs are 7.65% of labor wages for employees who do not exceed the FICA limit. The costs of most other benefits vary by employee job type, wage rate, and other drivers of the company's payment obligation. Bachman's found that, in general, retail stores had lower fringe benefit costs, averaging 17.8% of employee wages and salaries. In contrast, fringe benefit costs for businesses such as landscape and nursery with high workers' compensation and unemployment rates averaged 37%, well above the overall average of 26.5%.

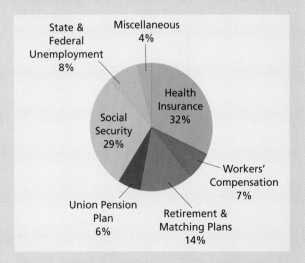

Source: D. Lockwood, "Allocating the Cost of Fringe Benefits," *Management Accounting,* November 1994, pp. 50–53.

■ *Direct labor costs* include the wages and fringe benefits paid to workers involved directly in manufacturing a product. If six workers spend 45 minutes each and the wage rate including benefits is $32 per hour, the direct labor cost is computed as follows: *Wage Rate Per Hour* × *Number of Direct Labor Hours*, or $144 ($32 × 6 × 45/60).

Direct manufacturing costs are assigned to products directly based on the measured quantity of the resources consumed for their manufacture. In general, direct costs can be expressed symbolically in terms of cost equations of the following form where:

C = cost of input resource
P = price per unit of resource
Q = quantity (number of units) of resource

$$C = P \times Q \qquad (3\text{-}1)$$

OBJECTIVE 3.3

Understand how support activity costs arise.

Indirect manufacturing costs
All manufacturing costs other than direct manufacturing costs.

Manufacturing support costs
Indirect cost of transforming raw materials into finished product; indirect manufacturing costs.

All other manufacturing costs are classified as **indirect manufacturing costs.** These costs are incurred to supply the resources required to perform various activities to support the production of different products. Therefore, we shall label these costs **manufacturing support costs.** Such costs are also referred to as *manufacturing overhead*, or *burden*. We prefer not to use these terms because they suggest incorrectly that support activity costs are not important, that they do not add value to the products manufactured, or that they cannot be analyzed mean-

The salaries and benefits paid to pilots, copilots, navigators, and flight engineers comprise about 9% of the total operating costs for an airline. These costs can be traced directly to the individual flights for which a flying crew is responsible. *Courtesy* **Rameshwar Das/ Monkmeyer Press Photo**

CONSIDER THIS . . .

Health Care Adds to the Cost of a Pizza

A Pepsico official testified before the U.S. Congress that requiring all employers to help pay for workers' health care under proposals considered by the U.S. Congress could add about 40 cents to the cost of an $11 pizza at the company's Pizza Hut chain.

The pie chart (right) displays different components of costs as a percent of revenues for typical chain-owned fast-food stores. Food costs include the costs of dough, tomato puree, and other materials needed for a pizza or meat, buns, lettuce, and tomato for a hamburger. Labor costs include workers' wages and fringe benefits. Store overhead costs include rent, utilities, depreciation, advertising, insurance, pilferage, and breakage. Corporate overhead costs include accounting, legal, and general administrative costs.

The Pepsico official testified that labor costs at Pizza Hut were 30% of sales—somewhat above the industry average. If employers are required to pay 12% of their payroll for health care, it would raise the cost of an $11 pizza by $11 × 30% × 12%, or 40 cents. This 3.6% increase (40 cents ÷ $11) in costs will force the company to raise the price of pizzas and cut back on the employment of entry-level workers.

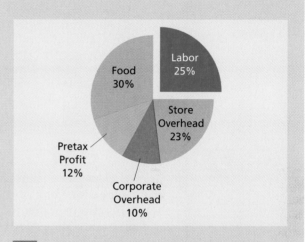

Source: Milt Freudenheim, "Pizza Hut Defends Its Insurance Plans," *New York Times,* July 23, 1994, p. 8.

ingfully. Manufacturing support costs include wages and benefits paid to production supervisors and workers engaged in activities that cannot be traced readily to individual products. Such support activities include purchasing and receiving materials; scheduling and expediting production; setting up machines; moving and storing raw materials and work in process; performing quality inspections; and providing packaging and shipping, machine maintenance, process and product engineering, plant upkeep, and janitorial services. Each of these activities is essential to the functioning of the plant, and most workers performing support activities help to produce several product lines. Because these activities are not performed for manufacturing a specific unit of a product, it is generally difficult to find a direct quantity measure to assign their costs to individual product units. Assigning indirect costs to products is often done using simple methods that are adequate for satisfying external reporting requirements.

LA MUSICA COMPANY REVISITED

Recall the introductory conversation at La Musica, in which the manager, Mike Mantley, asked Maria Rosario to estimate the impact on manufacturing costs from introducing new automated machines.

Maria examined the cost accounting records at the La Musica plant. She determined the direct material cost to be the cost of the plastic used to form the

EXHIBIT 3-2
La Musica Monthly Case-Forming Department Costs

Type of Cost	Before	After	Change
Direct materials	$22,400	19,900	$(2,500)
Direct labor	18,700	14,100	**(4,600)**
Support costs:			
Supervision	3,100	2,800	(300)
Materials handling	4,000	2,900	**(1,100)**
Storage	3,600	2,100	**(1,500)**
Inspection	3,000	2,000	(1,000)
Machine maintenance	2,600	3,800	1,200
Depreciation	5,700	9,100	3,400
Insurance	1,100	1,500	400
Total costs	$64,200	$58,200	$(6,000)

jewel cases. She identified the workers responsible for the case-forming activity and measured direct labor costs as the wages and benefits earned. Cost accounting records also indicated the amount of support costs assigned to the case-forming department. Thus, Maria was able to compile the information in Exhibit 3-2 for the monthly costs of the case-forming department, analyzed by function, both before and after the new automated machines were installed.

Maria determined that production volume had remained the same in the three months after the installation of the new machines as in the three months before. She was now in a position to estimate the impact of the machine changeover on various costs categorized by function.

Maria attributed the $6000 reduction in total costs to the efficiencies gained by the installation of the automated machines. In particular, the new machines resulted in less material waste and required fewer machine operators. In addition, the case-forming process was faster and more reliable, and it was possible to reduce nonvalue-added activities, such as materials handling and storage, after installing the new equipment. The net savings from these activities more than offset the increases in machine maintenance, depreciation, and insurance costs. The analysis of costs by function enabled Maria to understand the individual sources of the costs and benefits of installing the new automated machines.

COST STRUCTURE TODAY

The composition of manufacturing costs has changed substantially in recent years. In the early 1900s when many businesses first installed formal cost systems, direct labor represented a large proportion, sometimes 50% or more, of the total manufacturing costs. Direct materials cost was also substantial. As a result, cost accounting systems were designed to focus on measuring and controlling direct labor and materials, and they served this purpose admirably.

In today's industrial environment, however, direct labor is only a small portion of manufacturing costs. In the electronics industry, for instance, direct labor

The assembly line equipment at this factory needs to be set up for each new batch of pumps manufactured. The set-up of more complex pumps requires greater care and effort and demands more time from the set-up workers. *Courtesy* **David Joel/Tony Stone Images**

cost is often less than 5% of the total manufacturing cost. The cost of direct materials, however, remains important as it represents about 40% to 60% of the costs in many plants.

The big change in cost structure has been the much higher share that support costs represent. This change has occurred because of the shift toward greater automation, which requires more production engineering, scheduling, and machine setup activities; the emphasis on better customer service; and the increase in support activities required by a proliferation of multiple products. In addition to indirect manufacturing costs becoming more important, indirect costs associated with distribution, selling, marketing, and administrative activities have increased even as direct labor costs have continued to decline in recent years.

This change in cost structure has caused cost systems that were designed for manufacturing activities with high direct labor content to become obsolete. In the past, when direct material and direct labor costs were substantial, the cost systems were designed to monitor them in detail to ensure that they could be traced correctly to the individual products. When support activity costs were small, it was not crucial to understand how they arose or how to assign them carefully to products because assignments of these costs would be unlikely to lead to large product cost distortions. Now, however, when support activity costs contribute a significant part of the total costs, managers must understand and analyze them carefully. Therefore, today's designers of cost accounting systems pay special attention to support activity costs.

The Cost of Manufacturing Transactions

A recent study of 32 plants in the electronics, machinery, and automobile components industries reveals that manufacturing overhead costs on the average are approximately three times the direct labor costs. Direct material costs contribute the largest part of total manufacturing costs.

Components of Manufacturing Costs in
Three Industries

Cost	Electronics	Machinery	Automobile Components
Direct labor	8.4%	10.8%	7.8%
Direct material	65.2%	63.6%	67.5%
Manufacturing support	26.4%	25.6%	24.7%
Total	100.0%	100.0%	100.0%

For this sample of 32 plants, manufacturing support costs are strongly correlated to direct labor costs. But manufacturing support costs are more strongly correlated to measures of manufacturing transactions, as described by Miller and Vollman. (See "Consider This . . . What Drives Manufacturing Support Costs," on page 97.) In this study, the number of logistical transactions was measured by the average area for the movement and storage of work-in-process materials and the number of balancing transactions by the number of personnel assigned to purchasing and production planning activities. Quality transactions were measured by the number of personnel assigned to quality control and improvement activities and change transactions were measured by the number of engineering change orders.

Source: R. D. Banker, G. Potter, and R. G. Schroeder, "An Empirical Study of Manufacturing Overhead Cost Drivers," *Journal of Accounting and Economics,* January 1995, pp. 115–138.

ACTIVITY-BASED ANALYSIS OF INDIRECT AND SUPPORT COSTS

Direct material and direct labor costs are easy to explain because they can be traced directly to the products manufactured or services rendered by the organization. But to understand why support activity costs are incurred, we first need to analyze why a variety of activities are performed in an organization to support the production of goods and services.

Consider two plants located in Massachusetts that are operated by Jim and Barry's Ice Cream Company. The first plant, located in Springfield, manufactures only vanilla ice cream. The second plant, located in Worcester, produces a variety of ice cream flavors. Last year, the Springfield plant manufactured 600,000 gallons of vanilla ice cream. The Worcester plant also manufactured a total of 600,000 gallons, but it produced seven different flavors: 200,000 gallons each of chocolate and strawberry ice cream, and 40,000 gallons each of raspberry, raisins and nuts, orange, butterscotch, and pecan ice cream. Although both plants produce the same volume of ice cream using the same manufacturing process, significant differences exist between the two plants. Both plants use about the same amount of direct materials, such as cream and flavorings, and about the same number of direct labor hours and machine hours since both plants are making 600,000 gallons of ice cream per year. Yet the manufacturing costs for the Worcester plant are much higher than those for the Springfield plant.

Manufacturing support costs, which include the indirect costs of transforming raw materials into finished products, are higher at the Worcester plant be-

---

CONSIDER THIS . . .

What Drives Manufacturing Support Costs

Manufacturing executives indicate that controlling and reducing support costs only ranks behind quality and getting new products out on schedule as their primary concern. Support costs as a percent of value added in manufacturing have been increasing steadily over the past 100 years, while the proportion of direct labor costs has been decreasing. (Value added in manufacturing equals direct labor plus manufacturing support costs.) Production managers have been paying increased attention to support costs in today's environment because they have more leverage on improving productivity through cutting support costs than they do through pruning direct labor.

The critical step for managers in controlling support costs lies in developing a model that identifies the forces driving these costs. In a classic paper Miller and Vollman suggest that support costs in a plant are driven not by production volume but by the following four types of manufacturing transactions:

1. *Logistical transactions,* which involve ordering, executing, and confirming the movement of materials from one location to another. These transactions are processed, transcribed, and analyzed by workers on the shop floor as well as by workers in the receiving, expediting, shipping, data entry, and accounting departments.

2. *Balancing transactions,* which ensure that the supplies of materials, labor, and capacity are equal to the demand for these resources. Workers in purchasing; production and materials planning; production scheduling and control; and labor requirements planning take part in these transactions.

3. *Quality transactions,* which comprise quality control, including inspection and rework; quality improvement, including worker training, engineering, and supplier certification; and field support including warranty repairs.

4. *Change transactions,* which update manufacturing information systems to accommodate changes in engineering designs, schedules, routings, standards, materials specifications, and bills of material.

Source: J. G. Miller and T. E. Vollman, "The Hidden Factory," *Harvard Business Review,* September-October 1985, pp. 142–150.

---

cause it requires more indirect labor to perform support activities such as setting up the machines and quality testing ice cream color and flavor when changing from one batch of an ice cream flavor to another flavor; supervising the production and machine setup labor during and after changeover; storing and handling different materials; purchasing materials required for the manufacture and packing of different products; scheduling and expediting production; servicing different customer orders; and providing engineering support for different products. Manufacturing support costs increase with the volume of activities required to support production, and because the Worcester plant requires a greater volume of support activities, it incurs higher manufacturing support costs.

TYPES OF PRODUCTION ACTIVITIES

We classify production activities into four categories:

1. Unit related
2. Batch related
3. Product sustaining
4. Facility sustaining

OBJECTIVE 3.4

Discuss unit-related, batch-related, product-sustaining, and facility-sustaining activity cost drivers.

Unit-Related Activities

Unit-related activities
Activities whose levels are related to the number of units produced.

Unit-related activities are those whose volume or level is proportional to the number of units produced or to other measures, such as direct labor hours and machine hours, that are themselves proportional to the number of units produced. The indirect labor required for quality inspection that checks every item or 10% or 20% of items is evidently associated with the number of units produced. Uniform supervision of all activities performed by direct workers requires supervisory effort that is associated with the number of direct labor hours. The consumption of lubricating oil for machines and the energy required to operate the machines as well as the scheduled maintenance of machines after every 20,000 hours of use or after any specified amount of use are examples of manufacturing support costs that are proportional to machine hours. Since direct labor hours and machine hours themselves increase with the number of units produced, the use of many activities supporting production increases with the level of production.

Batch-Related Activities

Batch-related activities
Activities whose levels are related to the number of batches produced.

Batch-related activities are triggered by the number of batches produced rather than by the number of units manufactured. Machine setups, for instance, are required when beginning the production of a new batch of products. Once the machine has been set up, no additional setup effort is required whether we produce a batch of 100 units or 1000 units of the product. Since the *in-process materials* for a batch are moved together from one work center to the next, the cost of materials handling also tends to be associated with the number of batches rather than with the number of units in the batches. Similarly, indirect labor for *first-item quality inspections* (inspections of only the first unit in each batch) involves testing a fixed number of units for each batch produced rather than a percent of the entire batch. Therefore, the indirect labor required for such inspections is also associated with the number of batches.

Clerical effort expended to issue purchase orders or to receive materials from suppliers is a support activity associated with the number of purchase orders or with the number of deliveries rather than with the quantity of materials ordered. The cost of the purchased materials, such as cream and flavors at Jim and Barry's, depends on the quantity of materials ordered. However, the support costs of processing the paperwork for purchases depends only on the number of orders rather than the quantity ordered. Production scheduling is also considered a batch-related activity because it is performed for each production run that needs to be scheduled in a plant rather than for each unit produced in a production run.

Product-Sustaining Activities

Product-sustaining activities
Activities performed to support the production of individual products.

Product-sustaining activities support the production and sale of individual products. The larger the number of products and product lines, the higher the cost of product-sustaining activities. Examples include administrative efforts required to maintain drawings and labor and machine routings for each part; product engineering efforts to maintain coherent specifications such as the bill of materials for individual products and their component parts and their routing through different work centers in the plant; and the process engineering required to implement engineering change orders (ECOs). Engineering efforts to design and test process routines for products and perform product enhancements are also other examples of product-sustaining activities. Also, the need to expedite production orders increases as the number of products and customers serviced by a plant increases. Costs of obtaining patents or regulatory approval, such as Food and Drug Administration approval for new pharmaceutical drugs or food products, also increase with the number of products introduced.

At Jim and Barry's, product-sustaining activities include designing new ice cream flavors; developing, maintaining, and improving recipes; and designing packaging and marketing materials for individual ice cream flavors. The demand for these activities is higher in the Worcester plant with its seven products than in the Springfield plant, which produces only one product, even though both plants have identical total production volumes (600,000 gallons).

Facility-Sustaining Activities

Facility-sustaining activities are required to support the upkeep of the plant and the associated managerial infrastructure that makes production possible. These activities are not related to the number of individual products, the number of production runs, or the number of units manufactured. Examples include plant rental and depreciation, plant maintenance, insurance and taxes, housekeeping, landscaping, lighting, and security. In addition, facility-sustaining activities include those functions performed by the plant manager, plant accountants, and personnel managers.

Exhibit 3-3 displays the four categories of production-related activities in a hierarchical diagram as well as related activity cost driver information. Facility-

Facility-sustaining activities
Activities performed to provide the managerial infrastructure and to support the upkeep of the plant.

EXHIBIT 3-3
Categories of Activities and Their Activity Cost Drivers

Categories	Representative Activities	Activity Cost Drivers
Facility-sustaining activities	• Plant management • Accounting and personnel • Housekeeping, lighting • Rent, depreciation	• Square feet of space • Number of workers
Product-sustaining activities	• Product design • Parts administration • Engineering • Expediting production orders	• Number of products • Number of parts • Number of ECOs
Batch-related activities	• Machine setup • First item inspection • Purchase ordering • Materials handling • Production scheduling	• Setup hours • Inspection hours • Number of orders • Number of material moves • Number of production runs
Unit-related activities	• Every item inspection • Supervision of direct labor • Consumption of power and oils to run machines	• Number of units • Direct labor hours • Machine hours

sustaining activities are at the top of this hierarchy, followed by product-sustaining activities, batch-related activities, and, finally, unit-related activities, which are at the bottom. This hierarchy reflects the fact that the costs of batch-related activities are independent of unit-related activities, the costs of product-sustaining activities are fixed relative to both batch-related and unit-related measures, and finally the costs of facility-sustaining activities are independent of the number of products, batches, or units produced. This hierarchical classification of activities requires us to think about how to select measures, known as activity cost drivers, to assign the costs of these different types of activities to individual products.

Activity cost drivers

OBJECTIVE 3.5

Express the cost relations of activities and their drivers as equations.

Earlier in this chapter, we expressed the costs of direct materials and direct labor in terms of the following equations:

$$Cost\ of\ Steel\ =\ Price\ of\ Steel\ per\ Pound\ \times\ Number\ of\ Pounds\ of\ Steel$$
$$Cost\ of\ Direct\ Labor\ =\ Wage\ Rate\ per\ Hour\ \times\ Direct\ Labor\ Hours$$

Recall that, symbolically, equation 3-1 depicts these equations as follows where:

$$C\ =\ \text{cost of input resource}$$
$$P\ =\ \text{price per unit of resource}$$
$$Q\ =\ \text{quantity (number of units) of resource}$$

$$C\ =\ P\ \times\ Q \tag{3-1}$$

Although equation 3-1 works well for calculating direct costs, such precise and specific quantity measures are often not available conveniently or at a reasonable cost for most support activities. For instance, supervisors' salaries are usually regarded as indirect costs. In theory, we could require the supervisors to maintain detailed logs recording the actual time that they spend supervising the production of specific batches of products, which would allow these costs to be assigned *directly* to product units or batches. However, because they spend time on numerous batches in any given day, recording such detailed information would be cumbersome and time-consuming.[2]

Most designers of cost accounting systems prefer to attribute such support costs indirectly by developing surrogate quantity measures that are more readily available. For example, if supervisors spend their time supervising activities of direct workers more or less uniformly across all batches being produced, the amount of their time spent on different batches is likely to be proportional to the number of direct labor hours worked on those batches. Cost accounting systems, therefore, often use direct labor hours (*DLH*) as a surrogate quantity measure for supervisory effort. Such a quantity measure for an activity is referred to as an

---

[2] In contrast, partners in accounting firms and legal firms record the time they spend consulting with clients in meticulous detail because such records are required to bill the clients and no alternatives or surrogate measures of the partners' effort expended on different clients will suffice for this purpose.

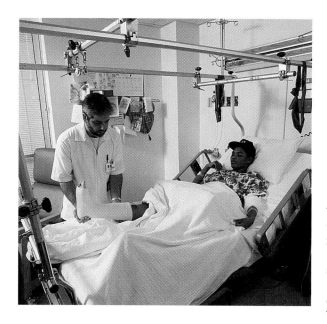

The total amount of nursing time required depends on the number of patients and the number of days the patients stay at the hospital. The activity cost driver for the missing services is the number of patient-days (number of patients × average number of days of stay). *Courtesy* **Billy E. Barnes/ Stock, Boston**

activity cost driver. The first supervision activity cost equation below can then be replaced by the second supervision activity cost equation:

Supervision Activity Cost = Supervision Wage Rate × Supervision Hours
Supervision Activity Cost = Supervision Activity Cost Driver Rate per DLH × DLH

Symbolically this looks like equation 3-2 below where:

C = the cost for the activity
R = the cost driver rate for the activity
X = the surrogate cost driver measure for the activity

$$C = R \times X \qquad (3\text{-}2)$$

Thus, activity cost drivers for the cost of support activities can be either direct measures, such as the number of supervision hours, or indirect surrogate measures, such as direct labor hours, that well approximate the quantity of activity performed.

Turn back now to Exhibit 3-3. It lists activity cost drivers for unit-related activities that are unit-level measures, cost drivers for batch-related activities that are batch-level measures, and so on. In choosing the appropriate cost driver, system designers consider how well the measure relates to the quantity of the activity performed and the convenience of collecting the information. For instance, the number of setup hours is commonly used as the cost driver for the machine setup activity. If, however, all batches of products require about the same number of hours to setup the machines, we could use the more easily measured quantity— the number of setups—as the activity cost driver because it is proportional to setup hours for every batch produced.

An additional point requires further attention. We expressed $C = R \times X$ in equation 3-2 to represent the activity cost equation. The **activity cost driver rate,**

Activity cost driver
Unit of measurement for the level (or quantity) of the activity performed.

Activity cost driver rate
Ratio of the cost of resources to provide an activity to the level of the capacity made available by those resources.

R, or the ratio of the cost of resources to provide an activity to the level of the capacity made available by those resources, however, is usually not readily available. By examining accounting records, we can determine the value of C, the total cost of performing the activity, and X, the total number of units of the cost driver for that activity. Thus, we can calculate the activity cost driver rate, R, from this information using the following equation:

$$R = C \div X \tag{3-3}$$

For instance, if the cost of setup operations, including setup workers' wages and benefits, is \$24,000 per month and if it makes 750 labor hours available for setup operations, then we calculate the setup activity cost driver rate to be \$32 (\$24,000 $\div$ 750) per setup hour. Next we can use the estimated activity cost driver rate, R, to assign activity costs to products. For instance, if the cost driver rate for the setup activity is \$32 per setup hour and if 200 setup hours are used for the production of Product A in January, then \$6,400 (\$32 $\times$ 200) of setup activity costs can be assigned to Product A in January. In such an assignment of support costs to products, activity cost driver rate and quantity are comparable to the price and quantity of a direct material or a direct labor cost.

Consideration of Multiple Activities

The multiproduct Worcester ice cream plant requires numerous activities to be performed. The same principles described for a single activity in the previous section apply directly to situations involving multiple activities. For example, suppose that a production process requires five activities: setup, scheduling, ordering, moving materials, and packaging. Using equation 3-3, we can determine a separate cost driver rate for each of these five activities so that we have this:

$$R_1 = \frac{C_1}{X_1}, R_2 = \frac{C_2}{X_2}, R_3 = \frac{C_3}{X_3}, R_4 = \frac{C_4}{X_4}, R_5 = \frac{C_5}{X_5} \tag{3-4}$$

The total of the support costs for the plant comprises the costs of each of the five activities. Therefore, we can write the total support costs, C, as follows:

$$\begin{aligned} C &= C_1 + C_2 + C_3 + C_4 + C_5 \\ &= R_1X_1 + R_2X_2 + R_3X_3 + R_4X_4 + R_5X_5 \end{aligned} \tag{3-5}$$

Notice that the total support cost is a *function of all five activity cost drivers* X_1, X_2, X_3, X_4, and X_5. Suppose that we use only one cost driver, for example, X_1, instead to describe the cost equation and determine an alternative cost driver rate, R', so that we arrive at this:

$$R' = \frac{C}{X_1} = \frac{C_1 + C_2 + C_3 + C_4 + C_5}{X_1} \tag{3-6}$$

If we write $C = R'X_1$ and use it for the estimation of costs, the estimates will be distorted when the quantities of the remaining cost drivers, X_2, X_3, X_4, and X_5, are not proportional to the selected driver X_1.

Cost Distortion with One Driver

To illustrate the formulas in equations 3-4 and 3-5, and how the use of only one cost driver distorts the estimation of costs, consider the following example. The true cost equation has two activity cost drivers:

$$X_1 = \text{direct labor hours}$$
$$X_2 = \text{setup hours}$$

and is given by $C = \$70X_1 + \$500X_2$.

The activity cost driver values in total for February 1997, are these:

$$X_1 = 1000 \text{ direct labor hours}$$
$$X_2 = 60 \text{ setup hours}$$

Therefore, the total costs are $100,000.

$$\$70 \times 1000 = \$ 70,000$$
$$\$500 \times 60 = \underline{\$ 30,000}$$
$$\$100,000$$

If the second cost driver, X_2 (setup hours) is not recognized and the cost accounting system is based on only one cost driver, X_1, direct labor hours, then the cost equation is estimated as this where $R_1' = \$100$ ($\$100,000 \div 1,000$):

$$C = R_1' \times X_1$$

This cost per direct labor hour is the apparent activity cost driver rate because all costs are allocated (for simplicity) by just this one cost driver.

Assume that the cost equation estimated using February 1997 data is applicable to March 1997 production. The values of the activity cost drivers associated with the production of a product A planned in March 1997 are these:

$$X_1 = 90 \text{ direct labor hours}$$
$$X_2 = 7 \text{ setup hours}$$

The cost equation based on only the first cost driver estimates the costs of product A as follows:

$$\textit{Estimated Cost of Product A} = R_1' \times X_1$$
$$= \$100 \times 90$$
$$= \$9,000$$

This estimate distorts the value of costs that should be attributed to product A because, in fact, the costs are these:

$$\text{True Cost of product A} = \$70X_1 + \$500X_2$$
$$= (\$70 \times 90) + (\$500 \times 7)$$
$$= \$6300 + \$3500$$
$$= \$9800$$

Such distortions always occur unless the values of the omitted cost driver (setup hours, in this case) vary exactly in proportion to the values of the included cost driver (direct labor hours).

The challenging task before us, therefore, is to identify all the principal activities performed in an organization and the appropriate cost drivers to use for each of these activities.

A MIDCHAPTER REVIEW PROBLEM

The following worked-out problem highlights the determination of support activity cost driver rates discussed so far. Now is a good point to take a moment to apply these concepts to a concrete example before moving on.

Goodhue Steel Tubes, Inc. is developing an activity-based cost system for its plant in Rochester, Minnesota. A task force comprising representatives from the controller's department, production departments, and plant engineering has compiled the following information about manufacturing support activities and costs:

Support Activity	Activity Cost	Activity Cost Driver	Planned Activity Level
Supervision of direct labor	$ 320,000	Direct labor hours	8,000
Machine setup labor	570,000	Number of setups	1,900
Machine maintenance	160,000	Machine hours	10,000
Product engineering	150,000	Engineering hours	1,500
Facility rent and maintenance	210,000	Square feet of area	7,000
Total	$ 1,410,000		

(a) Classify the manufacturing support activities as unit-related, batch-related, product-sustaining, or facility-sustaining activities.

(b) Determine the activity cost driver rate for each activity.

(c) Express total manufacturing support costs in the form of a linear equation.

(d) Determine the cost driver rate if direct labor hours is assumed to be the only cost driver for all manufacturing support costs.

(e) What is the equation for manufacturing support costs under the assumption in part (d) above?

This is the solution to this problem.

(a) Supervision of direct labor: Unit-related activity
   Machine setup labor: Batch-related activity
   Machine maintenance: Facility-sustaining activity
   Product engineering: Product-sustaining activity
   Facility rent and maintenance: Facility-sustaining activity

(b) Activity cost driver rates:

Activity	Activity Cost Planned Level	Rate
Supervision of direct labor	$\dfrac{\$320{,}000}{8000\ DLH}$	$40 per DLH
Machine setup labor	$\dfrac{\$570{,}000}{1900\ setups}$	$300 per setup
Machine maintenance	$\dfrac{\$160{,}000}{10{,}000\ mach.\ hrs.}$	$16 per mach. hr.
Product engineering	$\dfrac{\$150{,}000}{1500\ eng.\ hrs.}$	$100 per eng. hr.
Facility rent and maintenance	$\dfrac{\$210{,}000}{7000\ sq.\ ft.}$	$30 per sq. ft.

(c) Total manufacturing support costs =
    ($40 × *Direct Labor Hours*)
  + ($300 × *Number of Setups*)
  + ($16 × *Machine Hours*)
  + ($100 × *Engineering Hours*)
  + ($30 × *Square Feet*)

(d) If all manufacturing support costs are assumed to be driven by direct labor hours, then the cost driver rate is ($1,410,000 ÷ 8000) × *DLH* = $176.25 per direct labor hour.

(e) Under the assumption that all manufacturing support costs are driven by only direct labor hours, the cost equation is this:

Total Manufacturing Support Costs = $176.25 × *Direct Labor Hours*

IDENTIFYING ACTIVITY COSTS

OBJECTIVE 3.6

Discuss how to collect information to estimate activity costs.

Cost system designers must identify activities that consume the support resources, assign costs of these resources to the activities, select a cost driver measure for each activity, and determine the activity cost driver rate. These designers conduct detailed observations, examine cost accounting records, and interview knowledgeable and experienced managers to understand the activities performed by different organizational units.

Consider the study conducted by Linda Collins, manager in charge of cost analysis and planning at Montex Company. Montex makes steel and brass pumps at its four plants located in Minnesota, Indiana, Illinois, and Michigan. Linda first examined the accounting and payroll records at the Minnesota plant. She organized payroll costs including benefits by department and analyzed expenditure records to identify tools, supplies, and other costs with individual departments. Exhibit 3-4 shows the cost associated with two departments, machine setups and quality inspections, and the names of the managers of each department.

After collecting the departmental cost information, Linda interviewed the departmental managers to identify what activities the personnel in their departments

EXHIBIT 3-4
Montex Company
Departmental Costs for Two Representative Departments

Department	Machine Setups	Quality Inspections
Manager	Roger Smith	David Carlson
Wages and benefits	$406,000	$476,000
Tools, supplies, and other costs	110,000	26,000
Initial total costs	$516,000	$502,000
Add: Engineer's wages	0	38,000
Revised total costs	$516,000	$540,000

performed. Edited versions of these interviews with salient information appear below.

Linda first interviewed Roger Smith, manager of the machine setup department, who has been with Montex Company for 26 years.

Linda Collins: How many people do you have in your department?

Roger Smith: I supervise eight people. We had seven until last June, but because of the high workload we had to add Steve Swanson in the second half of last year. Steve is now a permanent worker in our department.

Linda Collins: What work do they do?

Roger Smith: All my people are responsible for setting up the machines.

Linda Collins: What drives the amount of work that they do?

Roger Smith: Well, setups are required each time they begin a production run. When the machine is available for the production run, our people go and set up the machine and inspect the first item produced to make sure that the machine is set up right.

Linda Collins: So the number of production runs or batches seems to drive your work not how large a run is?

Roger Smith: Yes, that is really the case. Setting up the machine takes the same time, whether we produce 60 pumps or 5 pumps.

Linda Collins: Do the setups for all batches take about the same amount of time?

Roger Smith: No. There are big differences, depending on the product for which we have to set up the machines. Some products have very complex specifications that require about three hours of setup time. Other products, such as P101, are much simpler, and we can set those up in only one-half hour.

Linda Collins: So the number of setup hours is perhaps the best measure of how much work the setup people perform for the manufacture of a product.

Roger Smith: Yes.

Linda Collins: How many hours of setup work can your crew perform in a year?

Roger Smith: Well, I expect about 1800 hours of productive time per year from each of my people. Last year we had 7.5 workers on average, so there were a total of 13,500 hours available for setup. This year we have 8 workers who will provide a total of 14,400 possible hours for setup.

Linda next interviewed David Carlson, an 18-year veteran at Montex, now in charge of the quality inspection department.

Linda Collins: How many people do you have in the quality inspection department?

David Carlson: I have 12 people in addition to myself. Three of them are responsible for inspecting materials received from our suppliers. The remaining nine are responsible for the final inspection of all our production. I supervise all of their work, so I spend about 25% of my time on receipt inspection and 75% on final inspection.

Linda Collins: Hmm. Let me see. Our payroll records indicate that there are only 11 people reporting to you in your department.

David Carlson: Yes, but Jon Wang from the production engineering department is now permanently assigned to me to help us with our final product inspections.

Linda Collins: (Checking her payroll records) That means I need to add another $38,000 in wages and benefits to your department and subtract it from the production engineering department. Your departmental costs, therefore, are $540,000. (See Exhibit 3-4.)

David Carlson: Yes.

Linda Collins: Let me move on. What determines the amount of work for your people who inspect material receipts?

David Carlson: We inspect every lot of materials we receive, so I suppose it is the number of material receipts.

Linda Collins: Does the amount of inspection time depend on the size of the lot?

David Carlson: Not unless it is an exceptionally large lot that we receive only once or twice a year. You see, we randomly inspect a fixed quantity from each batch of incoming materials. It normally takes only about one hour to record, inspect, and store each lot we receive.

Linda Collins: How many lots can you receive and inspect in a year with your present staff?

David Carlson: We can do up to 100 per week. Since the plant works 50 weeks in a year, I suppose that means that we can inspect 5000 materials receipts in a year.

Linda Collins: What triggers the work done by your people who are responsible for the final inspection of your production?

David Carlson: Company policy requires us to inspect every unit we produce, so it is the total number of units produced at the plant.

Linda Collins: Do all products require the same number of inspection hours?

David Carlson: Yes. We follow the same procedures for every pump we produce.

Linda Collins: How many pumps can your crew inspect in a year?

David Carlson: We can inspect 5000 pumps in a week, so it means that we can inspect 250,000 pumps in a year. You should realize, of course, that during some weeks when the production level is low in the plant, we do not inspect 5000 pumps and sometimes during peak production periods we work overtime to get the job completed.

DETERMINING ACTIVITY COST DRIVER RATES FOR MONTEX

How can we assimilate all this information to determine the cost driver rates for the activities performed by these two departments? The analysis requires five steps for each department:

STEP 1 Identify the activities performed by the organization.

STEP 2 Determine the cost of performing each activity.

STEP 3 Identify a cost driver for each activity.

STEP 4 Determine the number of units of the cost driver made available by the resources committed to each activity.

STEP 5 Divide the activity cost by the number of cost driver units made available to determine the activity cost driver rate.

Linda followed these steps to determine activity cost driver rates as follows:

Machine Setup Activity Cost Driver Rate

STEP 1 Roger Smith's department performs machine setups.

STEP 2 Last year, the cost of the resources to perform this activity was $516,000. (See Exhibit 3-4.)

STEP 3 The appropriate cost driver in this case is the number of setup hours rather than the number of setups because the setup time differs for different products.

STEP 4 The resources supplied, at the cost of $516,000, made 13,500 hours available for machine setups. (See discussion with Roger.)

STEP 5 The activity cost driver rate for the activity, performing setups, equals $38.22 per setup hour ($516,000 ÷ 13,500 hours).

Based on Roger's estimates for this year, 14,400 setup hours will be available. If we expect the costs of both wages and benefits and tools and supplies to increase proportionally with the number of setup hours made available, we would expect the total activity cost this year to be $550,368 ($38.22 × 14,400).

Material Receipts Activity and Final Inspection Activity Cost Driver Rates

STEP 1 David Carlson's department performs two different activities: inspecting materials received from suppliers and inspecting materials produced by Montex.

STEP 2 Linda Collins identified the people working on each of these two activities and apportioned David's salary and other costs between the two activities. She determined that last year's total department costs were $540,000. (See Exhibit 3-4.) The material receipts inspection activity cost $135,000 and the final inspection activity cost $405,000.

STEP 3 Linda selected the number of material receipts as the cost driver for the first activity, *inspection of materials from suppliers,* and the number of units produced as the cost driver for the second activity, *inspection of pumps produced.*

STEP 4 The resources made available for inspecting material receipts allow 5000 inspections to take place. Similarly, it is possible to inspect 250,000 finished pumps with the resources currently supplied for this activity.

STEP 5 The activity cost driver rate is $27 ($135,000 ÷ 5,000) per pump for materials receipt inspection. The cost driver rate is $1.62 ($405,000 ÷ 250,000) per pump for finished product inspection.

See Exhibit 3-5 for a summary of activity cost driver rates at Montex. Recall that these are only three *representative* activities performed at Montex Company, but if these three were the *only* activities, we would reflect support costs at Montex as follows:

$$\text{Support Cost} = (\$38.22 \times \text{Setup Hours}) + (\$27.00 \times \text{Material Receipts}) + (\$1.62 \times \text{Finished Pumps})$$

This represents the more general version of cost equation 3-5.

Notice that the expenditure for each activity in the machine setup department depends on the *amount of driver capacity made available not the actual use of the capacity* as long as this capacity for 13,500 setup hours is adequate for actual demand. The wages and benefits for the 7.5 setup workers and their supervisor and the associated costs of the tools, supplies, and other resources they require total $516,000. The total expenditure for this activity would have been the same amount even if the setup crew had been used for only 13,120 hours and had remained idle for the remaining 380 (13,500 − 13,120) hours. The cost for this activity, therefore, depends on the capacity that is made available, rather than on how much is actually used.

EXHIBIT 3-5
Montex Company
Cost Driver Rates for Three Representative Activities

Cost/Rate	Machine Setup Activity	Material Receipts Inspection Activity	Finished Product Inspection Activity
Total cost	$516,000	$135,000	$405,000
Cost driver	Setup hrs.	No. of receipts	No. of pumps
Capacity made available	13,500 hrs.	5,000 receipts	250,000 pumps
Cost driver rate	$38.22 per setup-hr.	$27.00 per receipt	$1.62 per pump

COST CONCEPTS FOR SERVICE ORGANIZATIONS

So far we have discussed cost concepts in the context of manufacturing organizations. How can we apply these concepts to service organizations, including both for-profit and not-for-profit organizations that do not perform manufacturing activities?

Distinguishing Characteristics of Service Organizations

Services produced cannot be inventoried for future sale. Therefore, cost accounting systems in most service organizations are not burdened with the financial reporting requirement to value inventory. Requirements for financial reporting, especially from the regulatory agencies of many for-profit and the funding agencies of not-for-profit service organizations, have often specified the structure of cost reports. These requirements have limited the use of external financial reports for internal managerial purposes. Many service organizations, however, have developed and maintained alternative cost accounting systems to facilitate managerial decision making. These alternative systems operate in parallel (at the same time) with their traditional financial reporting systems. This innovation has occurred because of decreased information processing costs and increased economic and fiscal pressure resulting from deregulation.

Another characteristic that often distinguishes service organizations from manufacturing plants reflects measuring outputs versus outcomes. The true output of a service organization is often difficult to measure because it represents a less tangible and measurable product than that from manufacturing operations. For example, at Montex, one can identify the number of satisfactorily produced pumps (output) and at Jim and Barry's, one can measure the gallons of ice cream produced. But how do we measure the output of a hospital, a school, a savings and loan bank, or a radio station? The answer is not straightforward or easy.

The difficulty in measuring output for service organizations raises special concerns about designing product costing and management control systems. Service organizations have few if any direct costs, such as direct labor or materials, associated with their outputs. As a result, many of the costs of service organizations are classified as indirect, and the concepts relating activity analysis and support costs become particularly salient as shown in the following example.

An Illustration for a Service Organization

Consider Riverside General Hospital, located on the banks of the Mississippi River in Minneapolis, Minnesota. Exhibit 3-6 displays 18 account names and related account expenses for the fiscal year 1997 collected from the hospital's financial ledger.

Holly Ward, Riverside's controller, identifies three principal uses for the cost accounting system at Riverside:

EXHIBIT 3-6 Riverside General Hospital Operating Costs for Fiscal Year 1997		
Account Number	**Account Name**	**Cost**
101	Nursing services	$ 2,973,154
102	Nursing administration	1,269,762
103	Pharmacy	496,629
104	Laboratory	312,347
105	Medical supplies	482,165
106	**Linen and laundry**	**358,736**
107	Dietary	813,148
108	Employee cafeteria	167,239
109	Housekeeping	706,308
110	Medical records and library	250,345
111	Social services	199,026
112	Patient scheduling and administration	60,238
113	Billing and collection	112,280
114	Plant operations	301,238
115	Plant maintenance	386,622
116	Medical equipment operations	496,275
117	Property insurance	38,350
118	Depreciation	960,573
	Total operating costs	$10,384,435

1. Determine the costs of resources used during a patient's stay. Some of these costs, such as pharmacy, are billed to the patient. More recently, hospital management has been comparing patient care costs with predetermined reimbursement rates to assess the hospital's profitability in treating patients in different diagnosis-related groups (DRGs).

2. Provide the planning basis for operating expenditures. If cost rates are known accurately, the hospital may be able to plan better for its staffing and other resource requirements based on forecasts of patient volume and mix.

3. Provide the basis for comparing the hospital's costs to those of other hospitals and for determining the best opportunities for reducing expenses.

These expectations for the role of the hospital's cost accounting system are similar to those for many manufacturing establishments. In each case, the organizations require a good understanding of cost behavior.

Holly does not find the distinction between direct and indirect costs very useful for her organization. Direct materials include pharmaceutical prescriptions and supplies, such as saline transfusions. Direct labor could include the actual hours of nursing service provided to the patient, but recording nursing hours daily for the individual patient treated would be cumbersome and not likely to be informative. Therefore, virtually all the costs in the hospital are classified as indirect costs. In contrast to our use earlier in this chapter of the term *indirect costs* to mean costs of supporting manufacturing operations, *indirect costs* for Riverside and for service organizations are often referred to as **operating costs.**

Operating costs
Indirect costs of producing services in a service organization.

	EXHIBIT 3-7 Riverside General Hospital Activity Cost Driver Rates for Fiscal Year 1997			
Number	**Activity**	**Cost Driver**	**Activity Level**	**Cost Driver**
101	Nursing services	Nursing hours	280,621	$10.5949
102	Nursing administration	Nursing hours	280,621	4.5248
103	Pharmacy	Direct		
104	Laboratory	Number of tests	80,224	3.8934
105	Medical supplies	Number of patient days	45,606	10.5724
106	**Linen and laundry**	**Pounds of laundry**	**840,749**	**0.4267**
107	Dietary	Number of meals	88,673	9.1702
108	Employee cafeteria	Number of nurse days	35,078	4.7676
109	Housekeeping	Square feet of space	23,798	29.6793
110	Medical records	Number of patients	8,367	29.9205
111	Social services	Number of patients	8,367	23.7870
112	Patient scheduling	Number of patients	8,367	7.1995
113	Billing and collection	Number of patients	8,367	13.4194
114	Plant operations	Square feet of space	23,798	12.6581
115	Plant maintenance	Square feet of space	23,798	16.2460
116	Equipment operation	Number of procedures	62,179	7.9814
117	Property insurance	Value of property	$21,567,322	0.1778%
118	Depreciation	Value of property	$21,567,322	4.4538%

Exhibit 3-7 presents the cost drivers identified by Holly Ward that correspond to the activities related to the cost accounts appearing in Exhibit 3-6. Activity cost driver rates are determined as ratios of the cost of the activity to the level of the activity capacity made available. For instance, the cost driver for linen and laundry is the number of pounds of laundry. The activity cost is $358,736. (See Exhibit 3-6, account number 106.) These resources make it possible to process 840,749 pounds of laundry resulting in an activity cost driver rate of $0.43 ($358,736 ÷ 840,749) per pound of laundry. (See Exhibit 3-7.) We summarize these rates in Exhibit 3-7.

Organizations often use such activity cost driver rates to estimate the activity costs when the level of activity changes. For instance, if the number of pounds of laundry is expected to decrease to 803,250, the linen and laundry costs are estimated to be $342,700 ($0.4267 × 803,250). One must be cautious, however, in using such rates as activity levels change. The amount of expenditure for an activity depends on the *capacity made available* rather than on the *actual consumption of the activity resources.* Therefore, it may not be possible to reduce costs as activity levels change if the capacity of resources made available cannot be reduced proportionally with the reduction in the demand placed on them.

Holly decided to develop a simple cost equation to estimate costs as a part of the hospital's annual budgeting process. She began by classifying the activities listed in Exhibit 3-7 into three distinct categories:

1. The first category comprises activities related to the number of patient days. Holly decided that the number of patient days is the best measure of the

"production volume" at the hospital, and activities related to it could be thought of as *unit-related* activities.

2. The second category comprises activities related to the number of patients admitted to the hospital, such as medical recordkeeping and patient billing. These activities are analogous to batch-related activities in a manufacturing establishment in the sense that the demand for them is related to the number of patients treated regardless of how many days they are actually hospitalized.

3. The third category includes facility-sustaining activities, such as plant operations and maintenance.

See these classifications in parts A, B, and C, respectively, of Exhibit 3-8.

EXHIBIT 3-8
Riverside General Hospital
Activity Classification

Number	Activity	Cost
A. Unit-Related Activities		
101	Nursing services	$2,973,154
102	Nursing administration	1,269,762
103	Pharmacy	496,629
104	Laboratory	312,347
105	Medical supplies	482,165
106	Linen and laundry	358,736
107	Dietary	813,148
108	Cafeteria	167,239
116	Equipment operation	496,275
	Total unit-related costs	**$7,369,455**
	Number of patient days	45,606
	Cost per patient day	$ 161.59
B. Batch-Related Activities		
110	Medical records	$ 250,345
111	Social services	199,026
112	Patient scheduling	60,238
113	Billing and collection	112,280
	Total batch-related costs	**$ 621,889**
	Number of patients	8,367
	Cost per patient	$ 74.33
C. Facility-Sustaining Activities		
109	Housekeeping	$ 706,308
114	Plant operations	301,238
115	Plant maintenance	386,622
117	Property insurance	38,350
118	Depreciation	960,573
	Total facility-sustaining costs	**$2,393,091**

Holly developed the following equation to represent the 1997 costs:

$$\text{Costs} = \underset{\text{Unit Related}}{} + \underset{\text{Batch Related}}{} + \underset{\text{Facility Sustaining}}{}$$
$$= (\$161.59 \times \text{Patient Days}) + (\$74.33 \times \text{Patients}) + \$2,393,091$$

The first two terms in the equation reflect the expectation that these costs will change as the number of patient days or patients change. (See parts A and B, Exhibit 3-8.) The last term represents the total facility-sustaining costs. (See part C, Exhibit 3-8.) Because Holly did not expect any significant changes in the amount of plant and equipment required, she believed that these costs would remain at the same level for the next year. In any case, these costs are independent of the number of patient days and the number of patients treated.

Holly used the activity cost driver rates obtained from the 1997 data to estimate costs for 1998 because the wage rates were frozen for 1998 at the 1997 level. She expected 43,000 patient days and 8200 patients for 1998. Inserting these values into the cost equation, she now estimates the total costs for 1998 as follows:

$$\begin{aligned}
\text{Costs} &= (\$161.59 \times 43,000) + (\$74.33 \times 8,200) + \$2,393,091 \\
&= \$6,948,370 + \$609,506 + \$2,393,091 \\
&= \$9,950,967
\end{aligned}$$

STANDARD COST ACCOUNTING SYSTEMS

Standard costs
Efficient and attainable benchmarks established in advance for the costs of activity resources that should be consumed by each product.

Cost accounting systems are often required not only to measure the actual costs incurred by the organization in the past period but also to project, or estimate, what the costs will be in the future. **Standard costs** are benchmarks based on standards established in advance for (1) the quantity of activity resources that should be consumed by each product or other unit of output and (2) the price of these resources. It is possible to estimate costs for different production and activity levels based on standards established for quantities and prices.

Most manufacturing organizations use some form of a standard cost system. Of the firms participating in a 1990 survey, 87% indicated that they used a standard cost system.[3] Most of these systems measure standard costs and actual costs and compare them to determine the variances between the standard and actual costs. Many new activity-based costing systems also rely on standard costs to estimate the consumption of different activity resources.

Why do the vast majority of firms use a standard cost system? There are three principal uses of such systems:

1. **Estimate Product Costs.** Standards are developed for the consumption of direct materials, direct labor, and support activity resources required by each product. Multiplying these quantity standards by the *standard prices* for the resources and adding all the resources consumed by a product yields standard costs for individual products. Then companies use these standard prod-

---

[3] Bruce R. Gaumnitz and Felix P. Kollaritsch, "Manufacturing Variances: Current Practice and Trends," *Journal of Cost Management*, Spring 1991, pp. 58–64.

CONSIDER THIS . . .

The Costs of Staying Airborne

Cost analysis is important in the airline industry, a major worldwide service industry. Airline managers need to decide whether to add new routes, discontinue existing routes, or adjust the number of daily flights on a route. The identification of costs with specific flights, however, is difficult for all airline firms since they have a high proportion of indirect costs. Only costs such as fuel, meals, and the salaries of pilots and flight attendants can be assigned directly to individual flights. Other costs, such as airplane depreciation; general administration; and the salaries of promotion and salespeople, ground service personnel, and maintenance staff are difficult to trace to individual flights. A study of 28 major U.S. airlines by Banker and Johnston indicates that only about 37.5% of the operating costs were direct costs. (Compare the classification of costs for this service industry with those for manufacturing firms, described on page 96.) Following the deregulation of the U.S. airline industry, many airlines have pursued new operating strategies. Airlines such as Northwest, USAir, and Delta schedule many of their flights through their hubs in Minneapolis, Pittsburgh, and Atlanta, respectively, because of the cost advantage that this strategy offers. Banker and Johnston find that the operating cost per passenger seat mile is lower for airline firms routing their flights through hubs. This cost advantage is even greater when the airline dominates the hub (controls more than 60% of the flights from the airport), as Northwest, U.S. Air, and Delta do at each of their hubs. Careful analysis of costs also helps managers make decisions about scheduling more flights per week on existing routes. Banker and Johnston find that adding a flight on an existing route results in lower flying operations costs and passenger service costs per passenger seat mile, but this cost advantage is offset partially by higher promotion and selling costs and traffic, and servicing costs per passenger seat mile.

Source: R. D. Banker and H. H. Johnson, "An Empirical Study of Cost Drivers in the U.S. Airline Industry," *The Accounting Review,* July 1993, pp. 586–601.

uct costs to help set bid prices for customer orders and evaluate product profitability.

2. **Budget for Costs and Expenditures.** Total costs representing the consumption of each activity can be estimated based on the *standard quantity of consumption* of an activity required to manufacture different products and the *planned production levels* for those products. Some organizations use these estimated costs to plan expenditures for a forthcoming period. Use of estimated costs for such purposes can be misleading in some cases because of the time lag that can occur between recognizing costs (representing consumption of activity resources) and incurring related expenditures for the acquisition of activity resources.

3. **Control Costs Relative to Standards.** Decision makers can compare actual costs with standard costs, with the expectation that the actual costs should approximately equal standard costs. Differences between actual and standard costs, or **cost variances,** can be analyzed further by distinguishing between the variance caused by *quantity variations* and that caused by *price variations.* Associating quantity and price variations with managers who are responsible for the related activities that create the variations allows organizations to motivate managers to attain the quantity and price targets embodied in the standards.

Cost variances
Differences between actual and standard costs.

CONSIDER THIS . . .

Trane Company's New Cost Accounting System

Trane Company is a subsidiary of American Standard, a leading worldwide producer of air-conditioning systems and bathroom and kitchen fixtures and fittings, and it is also a major European manufacturer of commercial vehicle braking systems. The Trane Company plant in Pueblo, Colorado, produces water chillers for commercial and industrial building air-conditioning applications.

A new cost accounting system has been designed and implemented at the Pueblo plant. The guiding principle in the design of the cost accounting system is that it should be *simple, low cost,* and *eliminate* unnecessary reporting procedures.

The new system is designed as a standard cost system to monitor cost changes. It has no detailed labor reporting because direct labor is less than 5% of product cost, and past experience indicated that the cost (people and computers) required to track actual labor would not pay for itself in the form of savings resulting from better monitoring management of the labor resource. The new system also *excludes* from materials costs all low-cost items (nuts, bolts, screws, labels, and the like), which represent 76% of the part numbers but only 3% of the total production costs. The costs of direct labor and low-cost parts are included instead in a new category, called *conversion costs,* which also includes costs previously classified as manufacturing support. As a result, the direct mate-

rials records focus only on 24% of the parts that comprise about 67% of the total production costs but present a greater opportunity for cost savings with better monitoring and management of materials.

Source: Ronald B. Clements and Charlene W. Spoede, "Trane's Soup Accounting: It's a System of Utter Practicality," *Management Accounting,* June 1992, pp. 46–52.

Trane's production and cost management uses no computerized shop-floor control or labor reporting system. *Courtesy* **Trane Co.**

Choosing the Level of Standards

How should companies determine the appropriate levels of standards to set? Should they set standards for the consumption of materials and labor based on the technical specifications for the process under *ideal conditions?* Or should they set the standards at the level that is most likely to occur given the known inefficiencies in the consumption of labor and materials so that plans based on such standards will be most accurate? Or should companies set standards that are somewhat more demanding than current levels to encourage continuous improvement?

Most experts recommend setting standards that represent *efficient and attainable* operating procedures. The choice depends on how standards influence the behavior of workers and managers whose performance is evaluated relative to the standards. A standard set at an average easy-to-achieve level will not motivate workers to exert effort to eliminate existing inefficiencies and to achieve a higher level of performance. On the other hand, if the standard is set too high and is difficult to attain even with considerable effort, workers may soon become frustrated and as a result may not work at all to achieve a level of performance that they perceive to be an impossible target. An efficient and attainable standard motivates higher levels of effort to eliminate inefficiencies. It also rewards performance sufficiently frequently to reinforce the worker's or manager's decisions to exert that extra effort.

A second principle to remember when choosing the level of standards is to ensure that all employees likely to be affected by the standards participate in their establishment. Employees who participate in this process are more likely to accept the level of standards as being fair and will be more motivated to attain the targets they represent.

Determination of Standards

To illustrate the idea of standard setting, consider the manufacture of Jim and Barry's ice cream. Each gallon of ice cream requires, on average, 0.19 pound of pulverized sugar. This estimate has been developed based on product engineering specifications and a careful analysis of past experience in making ice cream. Consultations with the purchasing department reveal that the price of sugar including freight to Jim and Barry's plant is $0.13 per pound. These two numbers represent quantity and price standards for consumption of sugar in the manufacture of ice cream at Jim and Barry's plant. Based on the quantity and price standards, the standard cost of sugar in a gallon of ice cream is $0.0247 (0.19 × $0.13). (See Exhibit 3-9.) Thus, we have this:

$$\text{Standard Cost} = \text{Standard Quantity} \times \text{Standard Price}$$

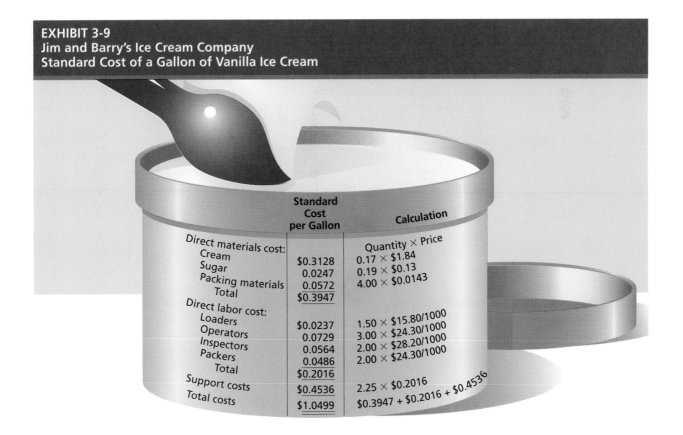

EXHIBIT 3-9
Jim and Barry's Ice Cream Company
Standard Cost of a Gallon of Vanilla Ice Cream

	Standard Cost per Gallon	Calculation
Direct materials cost:		Quantity × Price
Cream	$0.3128	0.17 × $1.84
Sugar	0.0247	0.19 × $0.13
Packing materials	0.0572	4.00 × $0.0143
Total	$0.3947	
Direct labor cost:		
Loaders	$0.0237	1.50 × $15.80/1000
Operators	0.0729	3.00 × $24.30/1000
Inspectors	0.0564	2.00 × $28.20/1000
Packers	0.0486	2.00 × $24.30/1000
Total	$0.2016	
Support costs	$0.4536	2.25 × $0.2016
Total costs	$1.0499	$0.3947 + $0.2016 + $0.4536

Direct labor standards for making ice cream are established in a similar manner. Companies often use industrial engineering studies of work, time, and motion to determine the amount of direct labor effort required for each operation. Ice cream is manufactured at Jim and Barry's Springfield plant in batches.

- For each batch produced, two loaders are required to work for 45 minutes, or 0.75 hours, each.
- For direct production, three hours of operator and machine time are required for each 1000 gallons produced. These represent quantity standards for the direct labor input.

Price standards are based on payroll information.

- The average wage of loaders is $10.40 per hour plus $5.40 per hour in benefits paid by the employer. Therefore, the price standard for loaders is set at $15.80 per hour. Thus, the standard cost of loader labor is $23.70 (2 $\times$ 0.75 $\times$ $15.80) per batch produced.
- The price standard for operators is set at $24.30 per hour, which consists of $15.90 in wages and $8.40 in benefits. Thus, the standard cost of operator labor is $0.0729 (3 $\times$ $24.30 $\div$ 1000) per gallon of ice cream (batches include 1000 gallons).
- Other direct labor per batch requires one inspector for two hours at $28.20 per hour, including benefits, and one packer for two hours at $24.30 per hour. (See Exhibit 3-9.)

Establishing, updating, and maintaining the information on direct materials and labor standards in a standard cost accounting system requires an enormous amount of time and effort. Setting up standards for support costs has usually received far less attention in many organizations.

Jim and Barry's, for instance, follows its traditional financial reporting system and uses a standard cost driver rate of 225% of direct labor cost.

- The rate is based on the estimate of $936,000 of annual support costs, which is 2.25 times the estimate of $416,000 for the direct labor costs for the year.
- The total standard direct labor cost (inclusive of loader, operator, inspector, and packer labor) is $0.2016 per gallon. Therefore, the standard support cost is set at $0.4536 ($0.2016 $\times$ 2.25) per gallon.

Such cost driver rates based on direct labor alone can often distort the estimates of support costs. The standard cost per gallon of ice cream at Jim and Barry's plant is determined as the sum of the standards for direct material, direct labor, and support costs as shown in Exhibit 3-9. Direct material costs are based on standards for cream (given), sugar (shown in detail in the text), and packing materials (given); direct labor includes standard costs for loaders and operators (shown in detail in the text) as well as inspectors and packers (given). In contrast, support cost standards are based only on direct labor cost.

Support activities are not directly traceable to the products; therefore, it is not possible to determine industrial engineering standards for support costs in the same way as for direct material or direct labor costs. Setting support cost stan-

Part of setting up a piece of equipment, and therefore an element in the standard setup cost, is to check the initial units of production from the equipment to ensure that they meet specification. These employees at the Colgate-Palmolive plant in Guayama, Puerto Rico, are ensuring that the initial production from this packaging line meets specifications. *Courtesy* **Colgate-Palmolive**

dards on the basis of direct labor, however, ignores why support activities are required or what drivers actually cause support costs. Therefore, it is better to establish standards that reflect the consumption of support activity resources by each product.

Consider the activity of setting up the machines for each new batch of ice cream at Jim and Barry's Worcester plant. Chocolate ice cream is made in a batch size of 10,000 gallons; each setup requires 30 minutes (0.5 hour) from two setup workers. The standard rate for the demand placed by chocolate ice cream on setup activity resources is 0.0001 (2 × 0.5 ÷ 10,000) setup hour per gallon of ice cream based on the given assumptions about the standard batch size and effort required. Because wages plus benefits cost $22.60 per hour on average for setup workers at the Worcester plant, the standard cost for setup is $0.00226 (0.0001 × $22.60) per gallon of chocolate ice cream.

In contrast, raisins and nuts ice cream is produced in a batch size of 500 gallons and requires 45 minutes (0.75 hour) each from two setup workers. The standard rate for the consumption of the setup activity is 0.003 (2 × 0.75 ÷ 500) setup hour per gallon of raisins and nuts ice cream; the setup cost is $0.0678 (0.003 × $22.60) per gallon.

Note that these *standard activity rates* represent only the rate of consumption of activity resources and that the corresponding standard costs represent the costs of the activity resources *consumed*. This should be distinguished from the amount expended on setup activity resources at the Worcester plant because the actual expenditure depends on the amount of activity resources *made available* (such as the number of setup workers employed) rather than *consumed*.

The Worcester plant employs two setup workers. Each setup worker works 36 hours a week. Therefore, 72 hours' worth of resources *are made available for the setup activity each week*, which costs a total of $1,627.20 (72 × $22.60). In the first week of August, the plant produced 35 batches of chocolate ice cream and 20 batches of raisins and nuts ice cream. To set up these 55 batches required 65 hours of setup activity resources:

$$35 \text{ chocolate batches } \times 0.5 \times 2 = 35 \text{ hr.}$$
$$20 \text{ raisins and nuts batches } \times 0.75 \times 2 = \underline{30 \text{ hr.}}$$
$$65 \text{ hr.}$$

The standard cost of these consumed resources is \$1,469.00 (65 × \$22.60), which differs from the amount of \$1,627.20 *actually spent* for the setup personnel.

OBJECTIVE 3.9

Understand the uses and limitations of standard cost systems.

These standard activity costs reflect the demand placed on different activity resources and are useful for long-term planning and deployment of resources for various activities. It would not be correct to use the standard costs for short-term (daily, weekly, or monthly) planning of expenditures on various activities.

Limitations of Standard Cost Systems

Many organizations use standard cost systems, but an important caveat is in order. The usefulness of these systems is restricted largely to settings in which the production technology is stable and the number of business changes taking place is small. If there is much volatility in the products or the manufacturing processes, the standards need to be changed frequently, which requires much organizational effort. Standards for product costs do not remain reliable for long in such settings, which implies that standards for the consumption of direct labor, materials, and other activity resources are not very useful as benchmarks to evaluate current production.

More importantly, however, overreliance on managing with a standard cost accounting system creates a mind-set of simply meeting the standards. It diverts attention from the organization's strategic needs to remain a step ahead of its present and potential competitors by being able to respond to a changing environment. In a stable environment, when the product and process innovations are not frequent or critical, maintaining costs at current levels is a strategic necessity for many organizations. The use of standards to control costs is often effective in such settings. But when the organization's strategic need is to focus its attention on constant innovation that anticipates customer requirements, preoccupation with meeting current or past standards can in fact be detrimental to organizational performance.

A SUMMARY EXAMPLE

Grazioli Company in Milan, Italy, manufactures brakes for motor vehicles. Presently, its support costs (*SUPPCOST*) are estimated as 75,000 lira per direct labor hour (*DLH*) as described in the following equation (KL means 1000 lira):

$$SUPPCOST = 75 \text{ KL} \times DLH$$

(One U.S. dollar equaled approximately 1400 lira in early 1996.)

The company's new controller, Paula Penzoli, noticed differences between the actual and estimated support costs when reviewing the monthly support cost reports. She believed that the present cost equation did not reflect several activities performed in the plant that were not driven by direct labor. They included activities such as materials handling, machine setup, quality inspection, production supervision, and production scheduling, as well as the costs of lubricating oils and power.

After conducting a detailed investigation, Paula decided to employ two additional cost drivers in specifying the support cost equation: (1) the number of quality inspections (*INSP*) and (2) the number of batches manufactured (*BATCH*). Although different products require different numbers of inspections, each inspection takes the same amount of time. Direct labor required per unit manufactured also differs for different products. Further, products manufactured in small batch sizes required as much material handling and machine setup activities as products made in large batch sizes. Therefore, to better estimate the support cost Paula developed the following equation:

$$SUPPCOST = (37.5 \text{ KL} \times DLH) + (150 \text{ KL} \times INSP) + (750 \text{ KL} \times BATCH)$$

Planned activity levels for the next two months and the average levels for the next year are as follows:

Month	DLH	INSP	BATCH
1	4000	180	150
2	4200	200	160
Average 1996	4000	200	160

(a) List unit-related and batch-related activities performed at Grazioli's plant.

(b) Estimate support costs using the current estimation procedure for each of the two months.

(c) Estimate support costs using the alternative equation developed by Paula for each of the two months.

(d) Explain why there is a difference between the two sets of estimates.

(e) Repeat steps (2) and (3) using the averages for the year. Explain why the difference between the two estimation procedures is small in this case.

Here is the solution to this problem. All amounts are expressed in thousand lira (KL).

(a) Unit-related activities: Quality inspection, production supervision, the cost of lubricating oils and power
Batch-related activities: Materials handling, machine setup, and production scheduling

(b) Estimated support costs based on direct labor hours only:
Month 1: 300,000 KL = 75 × 4000
Month 2: 315,000 KL = 75 × 4200

(c) Estimated support costs based on the new cost equation:
Month 1: 289,500 KL = (37.5 × 4000) + (150 × 180) + (750 × 150)
Month 2: 307,500 KL = (37.5 × 4200) + (150 × 200) + (750 × 160)

(d) The two sets of estimates differ because the cost equation $SUPPCOST = 75 \times DLH$ omits two important cost drivers that do not vary proportionally to direct labor hours.

(e) Estimated support costs based on the present equation:
$$\text{Average} = 300{,}000 \text{ KL} = 75 \times 4000$$
Estimated support costs based on the new equation:
$$\text{Average} = 300{,}000 \text{ KL} = (37.5 \times 4000) + (150 \times 200) + (750 \times 160)$$

The two cost equations provide the same estimates because they have been designed to fit the same cost data on average. But there can be large discrepancies in individual months as the relative proportions of the three cost drivers can differ each month from those on average.

SUMMARY

It is common to classify costs according to their *function*. Direct material and labor costs are costs that can be traced easily to the products manufactured or services rendered. Indirect or support costs are not easily traced to products and services. The proportion of support costs in the overall cost structure has increased considerably in recent years.

To understand why organizations find it necessary to incur support costs, we must analyze the activities performed in the organization. Cost drivers are direct or surrogate measures for the level of activity. Activity costs depend on the *level of capacity made available* for the activity rather than the actual use of that capacity. The cost driver rate for an activity is determined as the ratio of the cost of the activity to the level of capacity made available for the activity.

These basic cost concepts extend directly to service organizations. It is often more difficult to define outputs for a service organization, but the analysis of activity costs for a service organization resembles that for a manufacturing organization and can be even more important since few, if any, costs can be assigned directly to the outputs of service organizations.

Many organizations use standard cost systems that estimate costs of products, jobs, and production processes by developing standards for the consumption of materials, labor, and other activities. These standards are usually set at efficient and attainable levels. Updating standards is a costly operation, and, therefore, the use of a standard cost system may be difficult and expensive in fast-changing environments.

KEY TERMS

activity cost driver, p. 101
activity cost driver rate, p. 101
batch-related activities, p. 98
cost variances, p. 115
direct manufacturing costs, p. 91
facility-sustaining activities, p. 99
indirect manufacturing costs, p. 92
manufacturing costs, p. 90
manufacturing support costs, p. 92

nonmanufacturing costs, p. 90
operating costs, p. 111
period costs, p. 89
product costs, p. 89
production volume, p. 88
product-sustaining activities, p. 98
standard costs, p. 114
unit-related activities, p. 98

ASSIGNMENT MATERIAL

■ QUESTIONS

3-1 Why do different types of cost information need to be reported to support different managerial decisions?

3-2 What are some different uses of cost information?

3-3 Describe the difference between *costs* and *expenses*.

3-4 What categories of costs are classified by function?

3-5 Why do traditional cost accounting systems tend to analyze manufacturing costs in greater detail than they do other functional categories of costs?

3-6 What are the three principal categories into which manufacturing costs are classified?

3-7 How is it possible to distinguish direct costs from indirect costs?

3-8 How has the composition of manufacturing costs changed in recent years? How has this change affected the design of cost accounting systems?

3-9 What are the four categories of production activities? Explain the differences among them.

3-10 What do the terms *activity cost driver* and *activity cost driver rates* mean? What is the activity cost equation?

3-11 What happens when a cost accounting system omits a significant cost driver?

3-12 What five steps must be performed to determine the activity cost driver rates?

3-13 What are some special considerations in the design of cost accounting systems for service organizations?

3-14 What is the difference between *actual costs* and *standard costs*?

3-15 What are three benefits from using a standard cost accounting system?

3-16 Why should standards be *efficient* and *attainable*?

3-17 Why do estimates of cost driver costs based on activity standards often differ from the actual costs?

3-18 What are some caveats for organizations using standard cost accounting systems?

3-19 When would you prefer to use the number of setups instead of the number of setup hours as the cost driver measure for the setup activity?

■ EXERCISES

3-20 *Cost classification by function* Classify each of the following costs based on function.
(a) Direct labor
(b) Sales commissions
(c) Depreciation on delivery trucks
(d) Salary and bonus for the chief executive officer
(e) Direct materials
(f) Product design staff salaries
(g) Advertising
(h) Property taxes
(i) Accounting office staff salaries
(j) Customer credit evaluation staff salaries

3-21 *Components of manufacturing costs*   Classify each of the following manufacturing costs as direct materials, direct labor, or support activity costs.
(a) Insurance on manufacturing equipment
(b) Steel plates used in making an automobile body
(c) Wages of assembly workers
(d) Salaries of plant security personnel
(e) Rubber used in making tires
(f) Overtime premiums paid to assembly workers
(g) Depreciation on the factory building
(h) Cost of electric power to operate machines
(i) Production workers' holiday and vacation pay benefits
(j) Wages of materials-handling workers
(k) Grapes used to manufacture wine
(l) Quality inspection costs

3-22 *Cost classification by activity type*   Classify the following costs as unit-related, batch-related, product-sustaining, or facility-sustaining activity costs.
(a) Direct materials
(b) Setup labor wages
(c) Salaries of plant engineers responsible for executing engineering change orders
(d) Building depreciation
(e) Direct labor wages
(f) Purchase order clerk wages
(g) Product design engineer salaries
(h) Rent for plant building

3-23 *Cost classification by activity type*   Classify the following costs as unit-related, batch-related, product-sustaining, or facility-sustaining activity costs.
(a) Packing labor wages
(b) Materials-handling labor wages
(c) Part administrators' salaries
(d) Plant management salaries
(e) Production scheduling staff salaries
(f) Equipment maintenance
(g) Property taxes
(h) Production expediters' salaries
(i) Insurance for plant facility

3-24 *Cost classification by activity type*   Classify the following activities as unit-related, batch-related, product-sustaining, or facility-sustaining activities.
(a) Supervision of direct labor
(b) Supervision of setup labor
(c) Setup of machines for a new batch
(d) Making product engineering changes
(e) Quality inspection
(f) Moving materials from one machine to the next
(g) Production scheduling
(h) Accounting
(i) Sales support for individual product lines

3-25 *Cost classification by activity type*   Classify each of the following activities as unit-related, batch-related, product-sustaining, or facility-sustaining activities.
(a) Plant security
(b) Purchase ordering
(c) Direct materials consumption
(d) Workers' training

(e) Product development
(f) Electricity usage
(g) Factory depreciation
(h) Engineering change
(i) Quality inspection
(j) Direct labor

3-26 *Activity cost equation*   The support activity costs of the machining department at Wilmark Company's plant in Weston, Virginia, are represented by the equation given below where:

$$ACTCOST = \text{support activity costs}$$
$$SETUP = \text{the number of setups}$$
$$DLH = \text{direct labor hours}$$
$$MHCAP = \text{the machine-hour capacity available}$$

$$ACTCOST = (\$238 \times SETUP) + (\$11.50 \times DLH) + (\$9.75 \times MHCAP)$$

The planned levels of the cost drivers for June and July are as follows:

Month	Setup	DLH	MHCAP
June	100	700	1500
July	150	800	2500

What is the expected level of support activity costs for June and July?

3-27 *Activity cost driver rates*   Creathon Company's plant in Columbus, Ohio, manufactures two products: BR12 and BR15. Product BR15 has a more complex design and requires more setup time than BR12.

Setups for BR12 require two hours on average; setups for BR15 require three hours. Creathon's setup department employs 10 workers whose average wage is $10 per hour; fringe benefits cost 38% of the wages. Other costs for setup activities amount to $25 per setup. Creathon plans to use all 10 workers for 40 hours each for the first three weeks of the winter quarter. The amount of work for these three weeks is as follows:

Week	Number of Setups for Product BR12	Number of Setups for Product BR15
1	85	75
2	90	70
3	80	80

(a) Determine the actual setup activity cost driver rate based on (1) the number of setups and (2) the number of setup hours.
(b) Is either of the two activity cost driver rates or some other rate appropriate in this case? Why?

3-28 *Support activity cost equation*   Cuomo Company uses the following equation to estimate monthly support activity costs where:

$$DLH = \text{direct labor hours}$$
$$SETUP = \text{the number of setups}$$
$$INSP = \text{the number of inspections}$$

$$COST = (\$12 \times DLH) + (\$300 \times SETUP) + (\$180 \times INSP)$$

The estimated levels of these three activities for January, February, and March are these:

Month	DLH	SETUP	INSP
January	1400	250	100
February	1100	200	80
March	1200	210	85

Calculate the expected *total support activity costs* for the months of January, February, and March.

■ PROBLEMS

Fundamental Problems

3-29 ***Activity cost equations*** Eagan Electrical Instruments Company estimates manufacturing support activity costs (*SUPPCOST*) as 950% of direct labor costs (*DLCOST*):

$$SUPPCOST = 9.50 \times DLCOST$$

Eagan's controller, Jim Becker, is concerned that the actual manufacturing support activity costs have differed substantially from the estimates in recent months. He suspects that the problem is related to the use of only one cost driver. Jim identified the following three additional cost drivers that reflect support activities: number of material moves (*MOVE*), number of setups (*SETUP*), and number of machine hours (*MACH*). He developed the following alternative equation to estimate manufacturing support activity costs:

$$SUPPCOST = (\$1 \times DLCOST) + (\$200 \times MOVE) + (\$300 \times SETUP) \\ + (\$20 \times MACH)$$

Information for two recent months includes the following:

Cost and Quantity	May	June
Direct labor cost	$3000	$4200
Number of material moves	50	70
Number of setups	30	40
Number of machine hours	1000	1200

REQUIRED

(a) Estimate manufacturing support activity costs using both equations.
(b) Why do the two sets of estimates differ?
(c) Why will both methods fail to predict accurately the manufacturing support activity costs? Is one of the two methods likely to be more useful than the other? Explain.

3-30 ***Activity cost drivers and cost equation*** Mankato Company is developing an activity-based cost system. The company compiled the following information on support costs and activities:

Activity	Estimated Costs	Activity Cost Drivers	Planned Activity Level
Purchase ordering	$ 20,000	Number of orders	400
Maintenance	44,000	Machine hours	2,000
Power	36,000	Kilowatt hours	30,000
Setups	62,500	Number of setups	500
Supervision	48,000	Direct labor hours	4,000
Total	$210,500		

REQUIRED

Express the support activity cost as a linear equation in terms of the five activity cost drivers.

3-31 *Activity cost equation* PQR Company manufactures and sells Products P, Q, and R. The company uses the following equation to estimate support activity costs where LABHR is direct labor hours and MACHR is machine hours:

$$Total\ Support\ Activity\ Costs = \$100,000 + (\$13\ LABHR) + (\$6\ MACHR)$$

Estimated production levels and requirements for Products P, Q, and R for next month are as follows:

Quantity	Product P	Product Q	Product R
Number of units	4000	5000	8000
Direct labor hours per unit	2	3	4
Machine hours per unit	3	5	2

REQUIRED

Estimate the total support activity costs for the next month.

3-32 *Activity cost drivers and cost equations* Dallas Devices Company has accumulated this information about its operations:

Support Activity	Activity Cost	Activity Cost Driver	Committed Cost Driver Capacity
Power	$100,000	Kilowatt hours	200,000
Setups	400,000	Number of setups	10,000
Engineering	250,000	Engineering hours	2,500
Rent	200,000	Number of square feet	5,000

REQUIRED

(a) Classify the support activities as unit-related, batch-related, product-sustaining, or facility-sustaining activities.
(b) Determine the cost driver rate for each activity.
(c) Express total support activity costs in the form of a linear equation.

3-33 *Cost classification* The L.A. Dress Shop manufactures dresses and decorates them with custom designs for retail sales on the premises. The shop sold 5000 dresses last month. Costs incurred during the last month include the following:

Cost of fabric used in dresses	$60,000
Wages of dressmakers	5,000
Wages of dress designers	4,000
Wages of sales personnel	1,000
Wages of designers who experiment with new fabrics and dress designs	3,000

Wages of the employee who repairs the shop's pattern and sewing machines	2,000
Salary of the owner's secretary	1,200
Cost of the new sign displayed in front of the retail shop	400
Cost of electricity used in the pattern department	200
Depreciation on pattern machines and sewing machines	10,000
Cost of advertisements in local media	800
Cost of hiring a plane and a pilot to fly along the beach pulling a banner advertising the shop	1,400
Cost of insurance for the production employees	2,000
Rent for the building	6,000

Apportion the rent into different categories based on the following facts. Half of the building's first floor is used for administrative offices. The other half of it is used for a retail sales shop. The second floor is used for making dresses and storing of raw material.

REQUIRED

(a) Classify the above costs into one of the following categories: direct materials costs, direct labor costs, manufacturing support costs, distribution costs, selling costs, marketing costs, research and development costs, general and administrative costs. What is the total cost for each category?

(b) Classify the costs as unit-related, batch-related, product-sustaining, or facility-sustaining costs. What is the total cost for each category?

3-34 *Activity cost drivers*   The Simply French Restaurant has identified the following activities performed by its staff:

Set tables
Seat customers
Take orders
Cook food
Serve orders
Take dessert orders
Serve dessert
Present bills and collect
Clean tables

REQUIRED

(a) For each of the above activities, identify the cost driver.

(b) Explain why the cost driver for many of the above activities is the number of tables served and not the number of customers at the tables.

3-35 *Activity workload estimation*   The Abby Corporation, a chain of department stores, estimates the standard workload at its retail outlets in terms of the time required for the activities of (1) hanging new inventory; (2) selling merchandise; (3) handling complaints, inquiries, and returns; (4) taking markdowns; and (5) counting inventory. The following are the estimated average times for each of these five activities:

Activity	Average time required
Hanging new inventory	1 minute per piece hanged (*HANG*)
Selling merchandise	10 minutes per customer (*CUST*)
Handling complaints and returns	15 minutes per complaint (*CMPL*)
Taking markdowns	2 minutes per piece marked down (*MARK*)
Counting inventory	0.5 minute per piece counted (*COUN*)

Therefore, the standard workload (*WORKLOAD*) in minutes is represented by the following equation:

$$WORKLOAD = (1 \times HANG) + (10 \times CUST) + (15 \times CMPL)$$
$$+ (2 \times MARK) + (0.5 \times COUN)$$

The Abby Corporation uses these workload estimates to plan its staffing levels. Past experience indicates that it needs to provide for about 30% more time than the standard workload estimate to ensure that customer service is satisfactory. The Abby Corporation has a policy of hiring only full-time sales consultants working 40 hours a week. The following information pertains to the estimated levels for various activities cost drivers for the four weeks in June:

Week	HANG	CUST	CMPL	MARK	COUN
1	5000	4500	500	400	1000
2	6000	5000	400	300	1400
3	5500	4800	600	500	1500
4	6200	5500	550	600	2000

REQUIRED

Determine the number of full-time equivalent sales consultants that need to be hired in each of these four weeks.

3-36 *Activity productivity*   (See problem 3-35) The Abby Corporation wants to evaluate the performance of the managers of its three stores in Chicago, Illinois. The Abby Corporation evaluates a productivity measure for each store as a ratio of the standard workload hours to actual sales consultant hours. The standard workload (in minutes) is determined based on the following equation:

$$WORKLOAD = (1 \times HANG) + (10 \times CUST) + (15 \times CMPL)$$
$$+ (2 \times MARK) + (0.5 \times COUN)$$

The number of sales consultants hired and the actual quantity of work for the first week of July follow:

Store Location	Number of Sales Consultants	HANG	CUST	CMPL	MARK	COUN
Midtown	40	5000	4000	500	300	800
Downtown	50	7000	5700	600	500	1000
Uptown	29	4000	2500	400	800	900

REQUIRED

(a) Determine the standard workload hours for each of the three stores.
(b) Determine the productivity ratios for the three stores, and rank the store managers' performance based on the productivity ratio.

3-37 *Activity cost estimation*   Brashear Brass Company manufactures and sells three products: valves, pumps, and flow controllers. Estimated annual sales in units, labor hours per unit, and total manufacturing labor hours per year are presented below for these three products:

Product	Annual Sales in Units	Labor Hours per Unit	Manufacturing Labor Hours per Year
Valves	10,000	4	40,000
Pumps	20,000	5	100,000
Flow controllers	30,000	2	60,000
Total			200,000

Manufacturing support costs (*SUPPCOST*) for 1997 are estimated to be $1,600,000 based on a cost driver rate of $8 per direct labor hour (*DLHR*). Brashear Brass Company is considering changing the company's current support cost estimation method. Preliminary investigation revealed that the number of direct labor hours (*DLHR*), the number of machine hours (*MACHR*), the number of setups (*SETUP*), the number of production orders (*ORDER*), and the number of inspections (*INSP*) are important drivers of *SUPPCOST*. Sherry Kelton, the management accountant, estimated the same manufacturing support costs of $1,600,000 based on a detailed analysis of six support activities as follows:

Support Activity	Estimated Costs	Activity Cost Driver	Estimated Activity Level
Machine-related activity	$ 120,000	*MACHR*	60,000
Labor-related activity	400,000	*DLHR*	200,000
Machine setups	200,000	*SETUP*	4,000
Production orders	180,000	*ORDER*	800
Quality control	100,000	*INSP*	200
General factory	600,000	*MACHR*	60,000
Total	$1,600,000		

The planned levels of the five cost drivers for January and February 1997 are as follows:

Month	*MACHR*	*DLHR*	*SETUP*	*ORDER*	*INSP*
January	5000	16,500	300	70	15
February	6000	17,000	400	60	20

REQUIRED

(a) Develop the equation to estimate manufacturing support costs (*SUPPCOST*) based only on direct labor hours (*DLHR*).

(b) Develop the new equation to estimate manufacturing support costs (*SUPPCOST*) as a linear equation in terms of the five activity cost drivers.

(c) Using both equations, compute the expected level of manufacturing support costs for January and February 1997.

3-38 *Cost distortions*   Chang Computer Company currently estimates manufacturing support costs based on direct labor hours. Nia Chang, the marketing manager, recently read about distortions resulting from the use of these traditional methods. She convinced the controller to collect the following information for 1997 so she could compare the cost estimates based on the current method with those obtained using an activity-based system.

**ACTIVITY-BASED SYSTEM
COST ESTIMATE FOR 1997**

Activity	Estimated Cost	Activity Cost Driver
Maintenance	$1,000,000	Machine hours
Power	600,000	Kilowatt hours
Setups	300,000	Setup hours
Supervision	800,000	Direct labor hours
	$2,700,000	

The estimated and planned activity levels of the cost drivers for the year are given below:

Activity Cost Driver	Estimated Activity Level for 1997	Planned Level in January 1997
Machine hours	250,000	20,000
Kilowatt hours	200,000	16,000
Setup hours	150,000	12,500
Direct labor hours	400,000	40,000

REQUIRED

(a) Estimate support activity costs for January 1997 using the existing method based on direct labor hours.

(b) Classify the support activities as unit-related, batch-related, product-sustaining, or facility-sustaining activities.

(c) Determine the activity cost driver rate for each activity.

(d) Express the support cost as a linear equation in terms of the four activity cost drivers.

(e) Estimate support costs for January 1997 using this equation.

Challenging Problems

3-39 *Activity cost driver rates* The customer billing department at U.S. West Telecommunication, Inc., currently employs 25 billing clerks on annual contract. Each clerk works 160 hours per month. The average monthly wages of billing clerks, including benefits, amount to $2800. Other billing-related costs, including stationery and supplies, are $0.50 per billing.

The two types of customers are residential and business. For residential customers, billing takes on average 10 minutes to prepare; each business customer billing requires 15 minutes.

The following information pertains to the estimated number of customer billings for the months of June and July:

NUMBER OF BILLINGS

Month	Business Customers	Residential Customers
June	8,000	12,000
July	6,000	15,000

REQUIRED

(a) Determine the billing activity cost driver rate based on the expected number of billings.

(b) Determine the billing activity cost driver rate based on the expected number of billing labor hours.

(c) Compare the cost driver rates in (a) and (b) above. Which rate do you recommend? Why?

(d) Is there a better way to estimate the costs of this activity than using a single cost driver rate?

3-40 *Activity cost equations* Nestec Company estimated its manufacturing support activity costs (*SUPPCOST*) as 178% of its direct labor cost (*DLCOST*):

$$SUPPCOST = 1.78 \times DLCOST$$

Alan DeLeon recently joined the company as an assistant plant controller. He analyzed in detail the activities performed at the plant and recognized that support costs were incurred to perform activities related to setting up the machines (*SETUPS*, number of setups); handling customer orders (*ORDERS*, number of customer orders); and inspecting and shipping finished products and supervising direct labor (*SHPMNTS*, number of shipments). Therefore, he developed the following equation to estimate manufacturing support activity costs:

$$SUPPCOST = (\$0.90 \times DLCOST) + (\$180 \times SETUPS) + (\$60 \times ORDERS)$$
$$+ (\$80 \times SHPMNTS)$$

Planned activities for May and June are as follows:

Month	DLCOST	SETUPS	ORDERS	SHPMNTS
May	$85,000	212	132	386
June	91,000	208	104	312
Average for 12 months	80,000	200	120	340

REQUIRED

(a) Estimate the expected amount of manufacturing support activity costs for May and June using the old equation based only on direct labor cost.
(b) Estimate the expected manufacturing support activity costs for May and June using the equation developed by Alan DeLeon.
(c) Why is there a difference between the two sets of estimates? Which set of estimates is likely to be more accurate? Why?
(d) Repeat parts (a) and (b) using the averages for the year. Why are your comparisons different in this case?

3-41 *Activity cost equations*   Belinda Jackson, the controller of Jackson Company, is considering changing the company's current support activity cost estimation procedures (*SUPPCOST*), which are based on direct labor hours (*DLH*) as described by the following equation:

$$SUPPCOST = \$20 \times DLH$$

Her preliminary investigations revealed that the number of setups (*SETUP*) and the number of quality inspections (*INSP*) are important cost drivers in addition to the number of direct labor hours. She developed the following alternative equation to estimate support activity costs:

$$SUPPCOST = (\$10 \times DLH) + (\$250 \times SETUP) + (\$34 \times INSP)$$

Activity levels for May and June are as follows:

Month	DLH	SETUP	INSP
May	20,000	480	2400
June	18,000	430	2150

REQUIRED

(a) Estimate support activity costs for May and June using the current support activity cost estimation method based on *DLH*.
(b) Estimate support activity costs for May and June using Belinda's new equation.
(c) Explain why there is only a small difference between the two numbers.
(d) Do you agree with Belinda that the new method provides the more accurate estimates? Why?

3-42 *Cost classification*   Poker's is a small hamburger shop catering mainly to students at a nearby university. It is open for business from 11 A.M. until 11 P.M., Monday through Friday. The owner, Chip Poker, employs two cooks, one server, and a part-time janitor. Because there is no space for dining inside the shop, all orders are take-out orders.

Poker's sold 10,000 hamburgers last month. The average hamburger requires 1 hamburger bun, 8 ounces of meat, 4 ounces of cheese, one-half a leaf of lettuce, and $0.07 worth of other ingredients. Costs incurred during the last month include the following:

Meat	$5000
Cheese	1000
Bread	800
Lettuce	600
Other ingredients	700
Cook's wages	5000
Server's wages	1500
Janitor's wages	600
Utilities	500
Depreciation on equipment	300
Paper supplies (napkins and bags)	200
Rent	600
Advertisement in local newspaper	300

REQUIRED

(a) Classify these costs into one of the following categories: direct materials, direct labor, manufacturing support, selling support, and administrative support. What is the total cost for each category?

(b) Classify the costs as unit-related, batch-related, product-sustaining, or facility-sustaining costs. What is the total cost for each category?

3-43 *Activity cost equation*   The Skylock Savings and Loans Bank is developing an activity-based cost system for its teller department. A task force has identified five different activities: (1) process deposits, (2) process withdrawals, (3) answer customer inquiries, (4) sell negotiable instruments, and (5) balance drawer. By tracing the costs of operating the teller department to these five activities, the task force has compiled the following information regarding support costs and activities for one of its suburban branches.

Support Activity	Estimated Cost	Activity Cost Driver	Monthly Level
Process deposits	$29,630	Number of deposits processed	33,250
Process withdrawals	26,080	Number of withdrawals processed	22,750
Answer inquiries	24,860	Number of customer inquiries	45,000
Sell negotiable instruments	4,860	Number of negotiable instruments sold	1,100
Balance drawers	4,290	Number of drawers balanced	1,300
	$89,720		

REQUIRED

(a) Express the total support activity cost as a linear equation in terms of the five activity cost drivers.

(b) The task force has developed the following bill of activities for a typical checking account marketed to retired persons.

Support Activity	Average Monthly Volume
Process deposits	2.3
Process withdrawals	6.0
Answer customer inquiries	2.1
Sell negotiable instruments	0.5

Estimate the total monthly support costs for this checking account product.

3-44 *Activity cost driver rates* The Amos-Baker Company manufactures replacement parts for automobile engines and drive trains. Its purchasing department currently employs 10 purchasing clerks on quarterly contracts. Each clerk works 160 hours per month. The average monthly salary of a purchasing clerk, including benefits, amounts to $3200. Other purchase order related costs, including stationery and supplies, are $3 per purchase order.

There are two types of purchase orders: simple and complex. Complex purchase orders are for multiple parts with delivery spread out over several periods, and they often involve obtaining bids from multiple suppliers. A complex purchase order takes on average 60 minutes to fill; in contrast, each simple purchase order requires only 20 minutes on the average.

The following information pertains to the estimated number of purchase orders for the months of October, November, and December.

Month	Simple	Complex	Total
October	2100	900	3000
November	2400	800	3200
December	1800	1000	2800

REQUIRED

(a) Determine separate purchase order activity cost driver rates for the three months based on the expected number of purchase orders.
(b) Determine monthly purchase order activity cost driver rates based on the expected number of purchasing labor hours.
(c) Which of the two methods in (a) and (b) above do you recommend? Why?
(d) Are there any further refinements that should be made in determining the activity cost driver rates? Please explain.

3-45 *Activity cost equation* Rochester Hospital wants to develop a simple cost equation to estimate costs as a part of the hospital's annual budgeting process. Carole Grimaldi, Rochester's controller, collected information on 17 expense categories for the fiscal year 1996 from the hospital's financial ledgers. Carole identified the cost drivers for the activities corresponding to the expense accounts as follows:

Activity	Costs	Activity Cost Driver	Activity Level
Nursing services	$3,000,000	Nursing hours	280,000
Nursing administration	1,300,000	Nursing hours	280,000
Laboratory	300,000	Number of tests	80,000
Medical supplies	500,000	Number of patient days	50,000
Linen and laundry	400,000	Pounds of laundry	840,000
Dietary	800,000	Number of meals	90,000
Employee cafeteria	200,000	Number of nurse days	40,000

Housekeeping	700,000	Square feet of space	20,000
Medical records	250,000	Number of patients	8,000
Social services	200,000	Number of patients	8,000
Patient scheduling	60,000	Number of patients	8,000
Billing and collection	110,000	Number of patients	8,000
Plant operations	300,000	Square feet of space	20,000
Plant maintenance	400,000	Square feet of space	20,000
Equipment operation	500,000	Number of procedures	60,000
Property insurance	40,000	Value of property	$21,000,000
Depreciation	1,000,000	Value of property	$21,000,000

Carole classified the activities listed above into three distinct categories: The first category pertains to the activities related to the number of patient days. The second category pertains to the activities related to the number of patients admitted to the hospital. The third category includes facility-sustaining activities.

REQUIRED

(a) Classify the above activities and costs as unit-related activities, batch-related activities, or facility-sustaining activities.
(b) Express total support activity costs in the form of a linear equation using (1) patient days, (2) patients, and (3) fixed cost component.
(c) Carole expects 55,000 patient days and 9000 patients for 1997. Estimate the total support activity costs for 1997.

3-46 (Adapted from CMA December 1991) *Standard cost system*   Productivity and cost control can be improved by introducing cost standards in business operations. However, standards must be properly installed and administered to be effective. Consequently, careful attention must be paid to developing the standards. This development includes the selection of the operational activities for which performance is to be measured, the levels of performance required, the degree of participation by various departments, and the support of top management for this effort.

REQUIRED

(a) Discuss the criteria that should be considered when selecting the operational activities for which cost standards are to be established.
(b) Discuss the behavioral issues to be considered when selecting the level of performance to be incorporated into the cost standards.
(c) Discuss the role that each of the following departments should play in establishing the cost standards.
    1. Accounting department
    2. The department whose performance is being measured
    3. Industrial engineering department

3-47 (Adapted from CMA December 1990) *Variance analysis*   Mark-Wright, Inc. (MWI) is a specialty frozen-food processor located in the midwestern states. Since its founding in 1982, MWI has enjoyed a loyal local clientele willing to pay premium prices for the high-quality frozen foods it prepares from specialized recipes. In the last two years, the company has experienced rapid sales growth in its operating region and has had many inquiries about supplying its products on a national basis. To meet this growth, MWI expanded its processing capabilities, which resulted in increased production costs and distribution costs. Furthermore, MWI has been encountering pricing pressure from competitors outside its familiar Midwestern marketing region.

As MWI desires to continue its expansion, Jim Condon, CEO, engaged a consulting firm to assist MWI in determining its best course of action. The consulting firm concluded that although premium pricing is sustainable in some areas, MWI must make some price concessions if sales growth is to be achieved. Also, in order to maintain profit margins, costs must be reduced and controlled. The consulting firm recommended the institution of a standard cost system that would also facilitate budgeting of costs for different levels of demand that can be expected when serving an expanding market area.

Jim met with his management team and explained the recommendations of the consulting firm. He then assigned his managers the task of establishing standard costs. After discussing the situation with their respective staffs, the managers met to review the matter.

Sally Renkavitz, purchasing manager, advised that meeting expanded production would force MWI to obtain basic food supplies from vendors other than its usual sources. This change would entail increased costs for raw material and for shipping and could result in lower-quality supplies. Consequently, these increased costs would need to be made up by the processing department if current cost levels are to be maintained or reduced.

Stan Kuchepa, processing manager, countered that accelerating processing cycles to increase production coupled with the possibility of receiving lower-grade supplies, could result in a slip in quality and a greater product-rejection rate. Under these circumstances, per-unit labor use could not be maintained or reduced, and forecasting future unit-labor content would become very difficult.

Tom Lopez, production engineer, advised that if the equipment is not properly maintained and thoroughly cleaned at prescribed daily intervals, the quality and unique taste of the frozen food products will fail. Jack Reid, vice president of sales, stated that if quality cannot be maintained, MWI cannot expect to increase sales to the levels projected.

Jim listened to the problems his management team outlined. He advised them that if they could not agree on appropriate standards, he would have the consulting firm set them, and everyone would have to live with the results.

REQUIRED

(a) List the major advantages of using a standard cost system. List disadvantages that can result from using a standard cost system.
(b) Identify those people who should participate in setting standards, and describe the benefits of their participation in the standard-setting process. Explain the general features and characteristics associated with the introduction and operation of a standard cost system that make it an effective tool for cost control.
(c) What might happen if Jim has the outside consulting firm set the standards?

■ CASES

3-48 *Activity workload estimation* First Cherokee Bank uses standards to estimate the workload of its teller clerks. The standard amount of time for processing each of these transactions is withdrawal (*WTHDR*), 4.0 minutes; deposit (*DEPST*) 2.2 minutes; and transfer (*TRNSF*) of funds between accounts, 1.9 minutes. Total workload (in minutes) is estimated based on the following equation:

$$WORKLOAD = (4.0 \times WTHDR) + (2.2 \times DEPST) + (1.9 \times TRNSF)$$

First Cherokee uses these workload estimates to plan its staffing levels. Past experience indicates that it needs to provide for about 40% more time than the workload estimate to ensure that customers do not have to wait in line to be served for an unacceptably long time. The bank can hire either full-time tellers working 40 hours a week or part-time tellers working 20 hours a week. Estimates for the number of various teller transactions for the first five weeks of the fall quarter follow:

Week	*WITHDR*	*DEPST*	*TRNSF*
1	1450	1900	650
2	1600	2000	700
3	1550	1800	650
4	1650	1900	650
5	1500	2100	700

Determine the number of teller clerks that will be hired in each of these five weeks.

3-49 *Activity cost efficiency analysis* (See Case 3-48.) First Cherokee Bank compares the productivity of the teller labor across its 10 branches and determines a productivity measure for each branch as a ratio of the standard workload hours to actual teller hours. An overall productivity measure for the bank is also determined as a benchmark on the basis of averages across all branches. The following data are compiled for Week 11 operations for the 10 branches:

Branch	Produc- tivity Ratio	Full- Time Equiv- alent Tellers	Standard Workload (in minutes)	Number of With- drawals	Number of Deposits	Number of Transfers	Number of Customer Trans- actions
1	0.628	6	9,040	1,000	1,600	800	2,840
2	0.581	12	16,720	2,400	2,200	1,200	3,400
3	0.632	8	12,130	1,600	2,000	700	3,440
4	?	9	?	1,700	1,800	900	3,350
5	?	6	?	900	1,200	600	2,250
6	?	5	?	800	1,000	500	1,900
7	?	10	?	2,100	2,000	1,100	3,710
8	?	12	?	2,300	3,000	1,400	3,820
9	?	11	?	2,100	2,900	1,100	3,700
10	?	11	?	2,300	3,100	1,200	3,880
Average	?	9	13,261	1,720	2,080	950	3,229

Standard workload (in number of minutes) is determined based on the following equation:

$$WORKLOAD = (4.0 \times WTHDR) + (2.2 \times DEPST) + (1.9 \times TRNSF)$$

(a) Determine the productivity ratios for all 10 branches.

On reviewing these productivity measures, Nick Chow, First Cherokee Bank's new controller, realized that the productivity ratios were highest for the three city branches (branches 8, 9, and 10). All seven suburban branches were rated lower. On further inquiry, Nick determined that much of the teller's time was required for the initial interaction with each customer requiring service. This time was the same, whether the customer had multiple transactions (several different deposits or both a withdrawal and a deposit) or just one transaction to conduct. Recognizing this to be a batch-related cost, Nick altered the equation for workload as follows to explicitly include the number of customer transactions (*CSTRN*) as a cost driver to reflect the time spent interacting initially with the customer:

$$WORKLOAD = (1.6 \times CSTRN) + (4.0 \times WTHDR) + (2.2 \times DEPST)$$
$$+ (1.9 \times TRNSF)$$

(b) Determine the standard workload and the productivity ratio for each of the 10 branches with the new workload equation. Rank the branches and compare the new rankings with the previous rankings. Why do the rankings change? Which productivity measure is likely to be more useful?

3-50 *Activity workload estimation*   McGourmet, Inc., a chain of fast-food stores, estimates the standard workload at its restaurants in terms of the time required for the operations of order receiving (*ORDER*), cooking (*COOK*), and packing (*PACK*). On average, each order receipt takes 1.9 minutes, each cooking operation requires 3.6 minutes, and each packing operation (for take-out orders) needs 0.5 minute. Therefore, the estimation of standard workload (*WORKLOAD*) in number of minutes is represented by the following equation:

$$WORKLOAD = (1.9 \times ORDER) + (3.6 \times COOK) + (0.5 \times PACK)$$

McGourmet adds 30% to the standard workload estimate to determine its staffing requirements. Past experience has shown that customers do not need to wait very long because of this higher level of staffing. McGourmet hires only part-time workers for 20 hours per week and pays them $4.60 per hour including benefits. The following information pertains to the estimated levels for various activities for the four weeks in February:

Week	*ORDER*	*COOK*	*PACK*
1	5600	7200	1150
2	5800	7900	1200
3	6000	8600	1400
4	5800	7600	1100

Determine the number of workers hired for each of the 4 weeks and the total labor cost for February.

3-51 *Activity cost efficiency analysis*   (See Case 3-50.) McGourmet, Inc. uses a productivity measure, defined as the ratio of standard workload hours to actual worker hours, to evaluate the performance of the managers in its five stores in Pittsburgh, Pennsylvania. The standard workload (in minutes) is estimated based on the following equation:

$$WORKLOAD = (1.9 \times ORDER) + (3.6 \times COOK) + (0.5 \times PACK)$$

The number of workers hired and the actual quantity of work for the first week of March are as follows:

Store Location	Number of Workers	Order Receipts	Cooking Operations	Packing Operations	Products Offered
			Quantity of		
Oakland	134	20,000	25,000	2,600	9
Northside	45	6,000	8,400	720	11
Shadyside	88	11,000	13,000	800	16
Downtown	160	23,000	28,000	2,000	9
Southside	65	8,000	12,000	1,400	14

(a) Determine the standard workload hours. Rank the store managers' performance based on the productivity ratio.

Upon receiving the performance report, two managers who were ranked at the bottom argued that the number of products offered in the store also should be considered in estimating workload because more products add more complexity to the operations.

(b) How should McGourmet's controller address this concern?

4

COST BEHAVIOR

RIVERSIDE GENERAL HOSPITAL

"Look at how much our costs in 1997 increased compared to last year. In 1996 our costs were $206.50 per patient day, but this year it is costing us $227.70 to care for one patient for one day. Are our operations becoming more inefficient?" asked Eric Nelson, executive director of Riverside General Hospital. "What can we do to bring our costs back in line with those for 1996?"

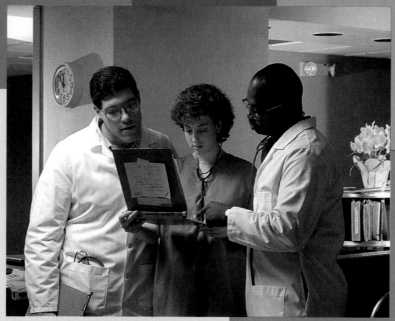

Courtesy **Chip Henderson/ Tony Stone Images**

"Our problem is that changes in demographics in our region have caused a more than 5% reduction in the number of patients treated. About 23% of our costs are *fixed costs*—costs that do not vary with the changes in the number of patients or patient days. Therefore, our costs have not decreased proportionally with the decrease in output," replied Holly Ward, the hospital's controller. "If we can't stimulate an increase in the demand for our services, then we must make some hard decisions to reduce our capacity and cut our fixed costs."

"With the present demographics and trends in medical-care treatment, I don't believe we'll be able to increase the number of our patient days," Eric said. "We must bring our costs down so that they will be in line with the decline in the number of patient days. How much do we need to reduce our fixed costs in order to break even?"

Riverside General Hospital would break even if its total revenues were exactly equal to its total costs.

"Well, if we continue to have 8,367 patients and 45,606 patient days of service, as we had in 1997 and if our present average reimbursement rate does not change, we must reduce our fixed costs by almost 15% to break even," Holly answered, after performing some quick calculations on the back of an envelope.

This scenario is repeated many times in all kinds of organizations. Managers like Eric Nelson and Holly Ward must understand how costs behave relative to variations in the level of activities performed.

Cost behavior and production volume

Concerns about how *costs behave* in response to changes in production volume are the focus of decision makers in almost all industries. For example, erosion in customer demand at Sears Roebuck and Company led to an increase of almost 0.5% in compensation costs for its sales force to more than 6% of sales. This increase prompted managerial action to control these costs. Similarly, the drastic reduction in capacity announced in early 1995 by IBM translated into a reduction of nearly 20% in its **breakeven point** (the production level at which sales volume results in zero profit), reassuring investors about its financial viability even with a lower market share.

Analysis of cost behavior is also important for the airline industry. Airline executives closely monitor an operating statistic called *load factor,* the proportion of the airline's flying capacity (number of seats) that is filled with paying passengers. Airlines work hard at cost control to bring their *breakeven load factor* down below 60% because most airlines have difficulty sustaining load factors above that level. This means that they attempt to ensure that a load factor of only 60% of capacity is sufficient for revenues to cover expenses.

Understanding the behavior of costs in response to changes in production and sales activity levels is clearly critical for the management of many organizations.

Breakeven point
Production level at which sales volume results in zero profit.

Fixed Versus Variable Costs

OBJECTIVE 4.1

Identify the difference between fixed and variable costs.

Costs are related to the levels of multiple activity cost drivers as described in Chapter 3. But managers are often interested in how costs change with a change in the level of one important cost driver, the volume of production, because many marketing, production, and investment decisions affect production volume. To supply this information to managers, organizations traditionally classify costs into fixed costs and variable costs based on their behavior in response to changes in production volume.

Fixed costs do not change with changes in the level of production (or sales) over short periods of time. Rent and insurance for a plant facility, for instance, will not change even if production drops by 5-10%.

Variable costs change in proportion to changes in the level of production (or sales). Direct material costs, for instance, may be expected to increase by 20% when production increases by 20%.

If sales personnel are paid a flat salary, selling costs are fixed; if instead they receive a commission for every unit sold, selling costs are variable.

Recall the discussion about Jim and Barry's Ice Cream Company in Chapter 3. Consider some of the distribution costs for Jim and Barry's. They lease five refrigerated trucks for a quarterly lease payment of $2000 per truck to distribute ice cream to vendors all over New England. The company also incurs costs for gas and maintenance to operate the trucks. These gas and maintenance costs increase with the number of trips varying at the rate of $0.48 cents per mile traveled. As the production of ice cream increases in the summer months, the number of trips increases for the five trucks. Let us consider how costs change with production.

Truck rental cost is a fixed cost because it remains the same for different production volumes. (See Exhibit 4-1.) At either 400,000 or 800,000 gallons of pro-

Fixed costs
Costs that are independent of the level of production (or sales).

Variable costs
Costs that change proportionally with production (or sales) volume. They represent resources whose consumption can be adjusted to match the demand placed for them.

The cost of mechanics' salaries and benefits at an automobile repair shop depends on the number of mechanics hired for the work. The amount of time the mechanics actually work depends on the number of customers and the complexity of the repair order. *Courtesy* J. Jacobsen/The Image Works

duction, total rental costs remain at $10,000 for the five trucks. Exhibit 4-2 shows the graph of these fixed costs (FC) plotted for different levels of production (Q). It reveals a horizontal straight line, which signifies the same level of cost for different levels of production.

    Now consider the behavior of fixed cost per unit volume by referring to the data in Exhibit 4-1 and the related graph presented in Exhibit 4-3. Notice that the fixed *cost per unit volume* (per gallon) *declines* when production increases because the same amount of fixed costs is spread over more units. Although fixed costs *per*

EXHIBIT 4-1
Jim and Barry's Ice Cream Company
Quarterly Truck Rental Cost

Quarterly Production in Gallons	Miles Traveled	Total Rental Cost	Cost per Gallon*	Cost per Mile**
400,000	32,000	$10,000	$0.0250	$0.3125
500,000	40,000	10,000	0.0200	0.2500
600,000	48,000	10,000	0.0167	0.2083
700,000	56,000	10,000	0.0143	0.1786
800,000	64,000	10,000	0.0125	0.1563

*Cost per Gallon = Rental Cost ÷ Number of Gallons
**Cost per Mile = Rental Cost ÷ Miles Traveled

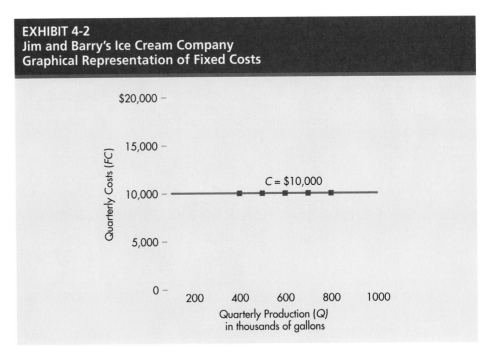

EXHIBIT 4-2
Jim and Barry's Ice Cream Company
Graphical Representation of Fixed Costs

unit volume (*FC* ÷ *Q*) decrease as the amount of production (*Q*) increases, do *not* jump to the conclusion that fixed costs depend on the volume of production.

In contrast, total variable costs (*VC*) change proportionally with production changes while variable costs *per unit volume* (*VC* ÷ *Q*) remain the same at all lev-

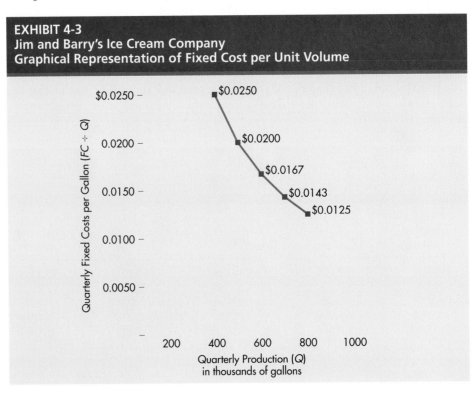

EXHIBIT 4-3
Jim and Barry's Ice Cream Company
Graphical Representation of Fixed Cost per Unit Volume

els of production (Q). See Exhibit 4-4, which shows the cost per gallon at $.0384 regardless of production volume. The graph in Exhibit 4-5 displays a horizontal straight line, signifying that the variable costs per unit volume do not change with production volume.

Gas and maintenance costs are variable costs with respect to the number of miles traveled for Jim and Barry's because the costs increase with increases in the production and sale of ice cream. The activity cost driver for these costs is the number of miles traveled. Notice that this is a *unit-related measure*, a measure that

---

EXHIBIT 4-4
Jim and Barry's Ice Cream Company
Quarterly Gas and Maintenance Costs

Quarterly Production in Gallons	Miles Traveled	Total Gas and Maintenance Costs	Cost Per Gallon*	Cost Per Mile**
400,000	32,000	$15,360	$0.0384	$0.4800
500,000	40,000	19,200	0.0384	0.4800
600,000	48,000	23,040	0.0384	0.4800
700,000	56,000	26,880	0.0384	0.4800
800,000	64,000	30,720	0.0384	0.4800

Cost per gallon = Total Gas and Maintenance Costs ÷ Number of Gallons
**Cost per Mile = Total Gas and Maintenance Costs ÷ Miles Traveled*

EXHIBIT 4-5
Jim and Barry's Ice Cream Company
Graphical Representation of Variable Cost per Unit Volume

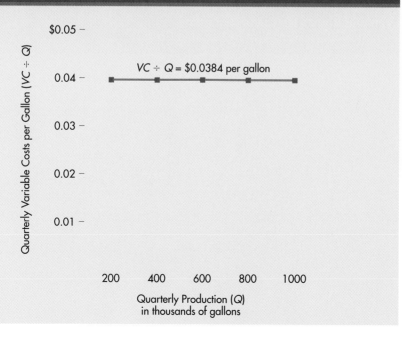

is proportional to the number of units produced or sold. In fact, for this example, the number of miles traveled is *perfectly correlated* with the number of gallons produced. The sale of *every* additional 100,000 gallons of ice cream requires the trucks to travel an additional 8000 miles for their distribution trips. Although we may not find such a perfect relationship in practice, all unit-related cost drivers will be closely proportional to the number of units produced. Therefore, activity costs that vary proportionally with a unit-related cost driver are usually *variable costs.*

Exhibit 4-6 presents the plot of these variable costs. It reveals a straight line passing through the origin, whose slope equals the variable cost rate of $0.0384 ($0.48 × 8,000 ÷ 100,000) per gallon of ice cream. That is, the variable cost rate of $0.0384 is obtained by multiplying $0.48, the cost per mile, by 0.08, which represents the rate of 8000 miles required for every additional 100,000 gallons of ice cream produced.

Mixed Costs

In contrast, the activity cost driver for the truck rental costs is the number of trucks, which is a facility-sustaining activity measure. This measure is independent of the number of gallons produced; therefore, we classify the cost of truck rental costs as a fixed cost.

The total truck operating cost is the sum of two components: (1) truck rental cost and (2) gas and maintenance costs. The first component is a fixed cost; the second is a variable cost. Exhibit 4-7 shows the tabulations of these costs, which appear as a straight line when graphed. (See Exhibit 4-8.) The intercept on the vertical axis is $10,000, which corresponds to the amount of fixed truck rental

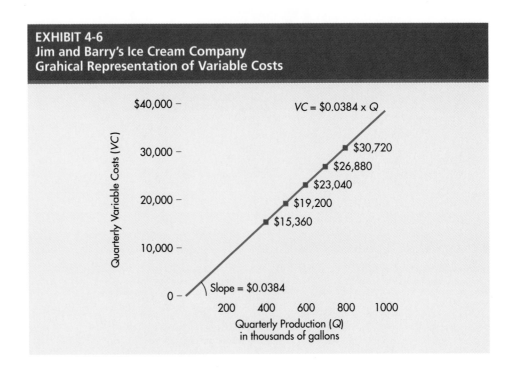

EXHIBIT 4-6
Jim and Barry's Ice Cream Company
Grahical Representation of Variable Costs

EXHIBIT 4-7
Jim and Barry's Ice Cream Company
Total Truck Operating Costs

Quarterly Production in Gallons	Fixed Cost Component	Variable Cost Component	Total Costs	Cost per Gallon*
400,000	$10,000	$15,360	$25,360	$0.0634
500,000	10,000	19,200	29,200	0.0584
600,000	10,000	23,040	33,040	0.0551
700,000	10,000	26,880	36,880	0.0527
800,000	10,000	30,720	40,720	0.0509

Cost per Gallon = Total Costs ÷ Number of Gallons

costs depicted in Exhibit 4-2. Its slope is equal to the variable cost rate of $0.0384 per gallon of ice cream as depicted in Exhibit 4-6.

The total truck operating cost is one example of **mixed costs,** which include both fixed and variable cost components. We can write the cost equation for the total truck operating cost as follows:

Truck Operating Costs = $10,000 + (0.0384 × *Production in Gallons*)

Although this example focuses on a specific type of distribution cost, we can apply a similar fixed and variable cost analysis to *all* manufacturing, selling, and

Mixed costs
Costs comprising both fixed and variable cost components.

EXHIBIT 4-8
Jim and Barry's Ice Cream Company
Graphical Representation of Mixed Costs

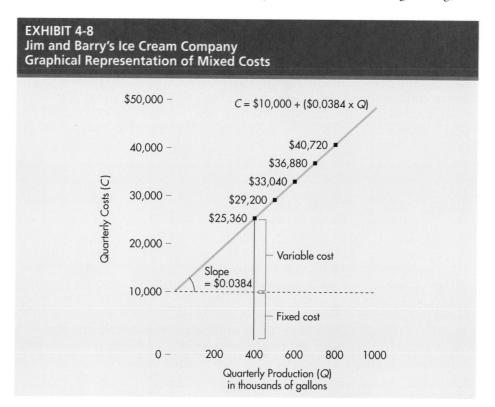

other costs incurred by an organization. Then we can represent total costs in terms of the following linear equation:

$$\textit{Total Costs} = \textit{Fixed Costs} + (\textit{Variable Cost Rate} \times \textit{Quantity of Production}) \quad (4\text{-}1)$$

or

$$C = F + (V \times Q)$$

Representing Activity Costs as Fixed or Variable Costs

Now compare equation (4-1) with our earlier representation of total costs as the sum of all activity costs, which appeared in equation (3-5) in Chapter 3.

$$C = R_1 X_1 + R_2 X_2 + R_3 X_3 + R_4 X_4 + R_5 X_5$$

where R_1, R_2, R_3, R_4 and R_5 are the cost driver rates for five activities. As we have observed, many of the activity cost drivers, $(X_1, X_2, X_3, X_4, X_5)$, especially those that are unit-related measures, are closely related to the production volume, Q. When examined over a sufficiently long period of time in which managers have the flexibility to adjust *the level* of resources performing batch-related activities, some of the batch-related measures also vary with the production volume.

For example, let X_1, X_2, and X_3 be the three activity cost drivers that are highly correlated with production volume, Q, and let X_4 and X_5 be the remaining two activity cost drivers that are independent of Q. Thus, the first three activity cost drivers vary with production volume, but the last two activity cost drivers remain fixed when the production level changes. In the Jim and Barry's example, recall that the activity cost driver, *miles traveled*, was perfectly correlated with production volume (*number of gallons*), but that the activity cost driver, number of trucks, was independent of the production volume. Then, we can express *total* variable costs as $R_1 X_1 + R_2 X_2 + R_3 X_3$. The variable cost rate, V, would be

$$V = \frac{R_1 X_1 + R_2 X_2 + R_3 X_3}{Q} \quad (4\text{-}2)$$

The total fixed costs, F, in this case, are

$$F = R_4 X_4 + R_5 X_5 \quad (4\text{-}3)$$

The representation of costs in terms of variable and fixed costs has the advantage of providing a quick perspective of the *behavior of costs* with respect to changes in production volume. However, it is evident that this representation suppresses considerable detail about how costs are generated as activities are performed. A detailed representation of an organization's costs in terms of activity costs is necessary to obtain a good understanding of its cost structure and manage its activities efficiently. The simple representation of costs as fixed and variable is appropriate when the activity cost drivers are either *almost* perfectly correlated with production volume or *almost* fixed with respect to production volume.

Costs in an Economic Framework

If you have already had a course in economics, you will wonder how this accounting representation of costs can be interpreted in an economics framework. In many introductory economics textbooks, costs are represented by *an inverted S-shaped curve,* as displayed in Exhibit 4-9. According to this **cost curve,** at low production levels *costs increase at a decreasing rate* with volume (the curve is *concave* in this re-

Cost curve
Graph of costs plotted against activity cost driver or production volume.

EXHIBIT 4-9
Relevant Range and the Economist's Representation of the Cost Curve

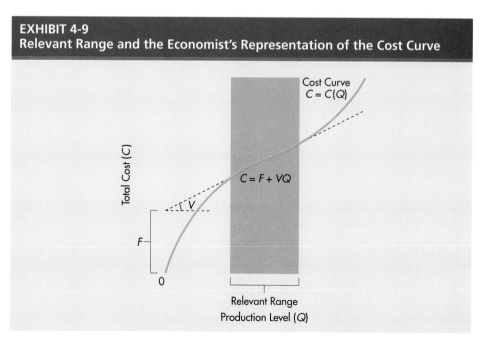

Economies of scale
Decreasing average costs with increases in production volume.

Capacity constraints
Limitations on the quantity that can be produced because the capacity committed for some activity resources (such as plant space or number of machines) cannot be changed in the short run.

Diseconomies of scale
Increasing average costs with increases in production volume.

Relevant range
The range of production levels over which the classification of a cost as fixed or variable is appropriate.

gion) because organizations are assumed to enjoy **economies of scale** that reduce average product costs. These economies of scale, or decreasing average costs with increases in production volume, typically arise from being able to produce more output without having to increase fixed costs. This effect is similar to the mixed cost curve shown in Exhibit 4-8. Once the production level reaches **capacity constraints** imposed by fixed resources, costs are assumed to increase at an increasing rate as **diseconomies of scale,** or increasing average costs with increases in production volume, prevail. For example, small increases in volume beyond existing capacity may require the firm to acquire additional capacity, at considerable cost.[1]

This is a useful theoretical representation of cost opportunities available to any firm in a particular industry over its entire range of possible production levels. For most managerial decisions, however, accountants need to generate cost estimates that are applicable over the much smaller range of production levels where a specific firm normally contemplates its regular operations to be. This smaller range of relevant production levels is called the **relevant range,** or the range of production levels over which the classification of costs as fixed or variable is appropriate. The linear equations described earlier often provide good approximations of the behavior of costs for that firm within the relevant range. For instance, consider the shaded region in Exhibit 4-9 that defines the relevant range.

$$C = F + VQ$$

The linear equation above fits the part of the cost curve that falls within this relevant range. Thus, when we extend in a straight line the segment of the cost curve falling within the relevant range (see dotted line), it begins to resemble the diagram in Exhibit 4-8 with the extended line displaying an intercept equal to F on the vertical axis and a slope equal to V.

This representation of the cost curve as a straight line over the relevant range is only an approximation used to simplify our analysis. In individual cases encountered in practice, it is important to be careful to examine whether the assumption about the cost equation is valid.

The Step Function Cost Curve

A common departure from the assumption that the cost equation applies over the relevant range is a *step function* cost curve. In our example of Jim and Barry's Ice Cream Company, when the production level is very high the five trucks will not be adequate to distribute the product and the company may need to rent an additional truck to meet the workload. The addition of a new truck would step up the truck rental cost from $10,000 to $12,000 per quarter. Exhibit 4-10 depicts such a step function cost curve. The relevant range in this case is restricted to within one step. If, however, decision makers contemplate production levels beyond a single step, they must consider different levels of fixed costs explicitly. In the Jim and Barry's example, the different levels are expressed as the following where Q^{MAX} is the maximum volume that can be handled with only five trucks:

---

[1] The representation of *total costs* as an inverted S-shaped curve corresponds to *marginal costs* decreasing with production volume at first as economies of scale are realized and marginal costs increasing with production volume as capacity constraints begin to impose diseconomies of scale. (Marginal costs are the costs of producing an additional unit of the output).

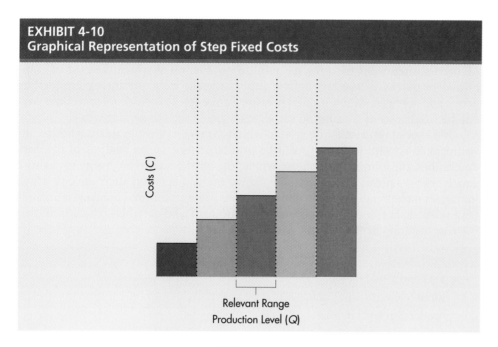

EXHIBIT 4-10
Graphical Representation of Step Fixed Costs

Costs (C)

Relevant Range
Production Level (Q)

If $Q < Q^{\text{MAX}}$
$C = \$10,000 + (0.0384 \times Q)$.
If $Q > Q^{\text{MAX}}$
$C = \$12,000 + (0.0384 \times Q)$.

If the steps in the cost function are relatively wide, that is, the costs remain the same over a wide range of production volumes, the costs are referred to as **step fixed costs.** If instead, the steps are relatively narrow, for example, when materials can be purchased only in whole units not in fractions, such costs are referred to as **step variable costs** because the cost curve is approximated closely by a single straight line. Exhibit 4-11 displays an example of step variable costs graphically.

Step fixed costs
Costs that increase in relatively wide discrete steps.

Step variable costs
Costs that increase in relatively narrow discrete steps.

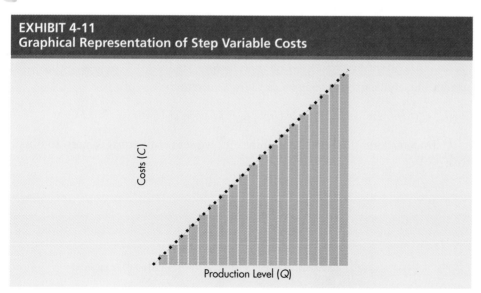

EXHIBIT 4-11
Graphical Representation of Step Variable Costs

Costs (C)

Production Level (Q)

BREAKEVEN ANALYSIS

Managers often want to know the level of production at which the cost of committed resources is covered by the profits earned from producing and selling goods and services. As mentioned previously, the level at which sales volume covers the fixed costs of committed resources is called the *breakeven point*.

Of special interest is the case in which managers must evaluate whether investment in a business venture will be profitable. Breakeven analysis in this case determines the output volume at which the profit from the business venture equals zero—a profit that can also be earned under a decision alternative in which managers make no investment in the business. The traditional breakeven analysis here relies on the decomposition of costs into fixed and variable costs. Recall that the cost equation can be written as follows where:

C = total cost
F = fixed cost
V = variable cost rate per unit
Q = production level in units

$$C = F + (V \times Q)$$

If the production of Q units is sold at a price of P per unit, sales revenue totals $P \times Q$.[2] The profit for the firm from this operation is given by the following equation:

$$
\begin{aligned}
Profit &= Revenues - Costs \\
&= (P \times Q) - [F + (V \times Q)] \qquad \text{(4-4)} \\
&= [(P - V) \times Q] - F
\end{aligned}
$$

Contribution margin per unit
Difference between the price and variable cost per unit.

The difference $(P - V)$ between the price and the variable cost per unit is defined to be the **contribution margin per unit.** If we increase production and sales by one unit, the sales revenue would increase by the amount of the sales price (P), and the total costs would increase by the amount of variable cost per unit (V). Therefore, the contribution margin per unit is the net increase $(P - V)$ in the profit when we increase production and sales by one unit. It is the amount that each unit produced and sold contributes to covering the fixed costs and earning profit. The above profit equation can now be written:

$$Profit = (Contribution\ Margin\ per\ Unit \times Production\ in\ Units) - Fixed\ Costs \qquad \text{(4-5)}$$

To determine the breakeven point, Q^0, we set profit equal to zero to obtain this:

$$0 = [(P - V) \times Q^0] - F$$

$$Q^0 = \frac{F}{P - V}$$

---

[2] For most breakeven analysis problems, sales and production levels are assumed to be equal.

Thus the breakeven point is obtained in this case by dividing the fixed cost by the contribution margin per unit of output:

$$Breakeven\ Point\ in\ Units\ =\ \frac{Fixed\ Costs}{Contribution\ Margin\ Per\ Unit} \qquad (4\text{-}6)$$

We can illustrate this breakeven analysis by means of the graphs shown in Exhibit 4-12. Such a set of graphs is often referred to as a breakeven chart, which depicts sales revenues, and fixed, variable, and total costs with a breakeven point at the intersection of the sales revenue and total cost curves. To construct a breakeven chart, we first draw a horizontal line to represent the fixed costs and then add on the variable costs to the fixed costs for different levels of production (and sales), as in Exhibit 4-8, to obtain the total cost curve. Next we draw a line through the origin to represent the total sales revenues, which increase proportionally with the production (and sales) volume. The breakeven point is indicated by the point at which the total cost curve intersects the total sales revenue curve because profit equals zero when total costs equal total sales revenues. Breakeven analysis in this case helps managers learn about how large sales volume must be for the contribution margin (price per unit less variable cost per unit) from sales to just equal the fixed cost of supplying committed resources to perform activities required by the volume of sales.

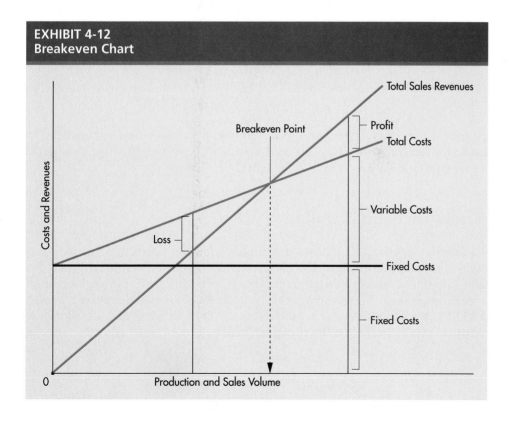

EXHIBIT 4-12
Breakeven Chart

Target Profit

Breakeven analysis can be extended easily to address the case in which we need to determine the production volume necessary to obtain a target profit level, T. We write the profit equation as

$$T = [(P - V) \times Q^T] - F$$
$$(P - V) \times Q^T = F + T$$
$$Q^T = \frac{F + T}{P - V} \tag{4-7}$$
$$= \frac{Fixed\ Cost\ +\ Target\ Profit}{Contribution\ Margin\ Per\ Unit}$$

The profitability target can also be expressed in terms of the profit-to-sales ratio (profit ÷ sales) instead of dollars of profit. The volume at which the target profit to sales ratio is attained can be determined by adjusting the approach we used above.

We begin as before with the expression for profit: $[(P - V) \times Q] - F$. The profit-to-sales ratio is obtained by dividing the above expression for profit by the expression $P \times Q$ for sales. The resulting fraction is then equated to the target profit-to-sales ratio, Z, to determine the production volume Q^Z at which the target profit-to-sales ratio is attained:

$$\frac{[(P - V) \times Q^Z] - F}{PQ^Z} = Z \tag{4-8}$$

$$[(P - V) \times Q^Z] - F = ZPQ^Z$$
$$(P - V - ZP) \times Q^Z = F$$
$$Q^Z = \frac{F}{P - V - ZP}$$

Some students choose to commit these formulas to memory. You will likely find it more convenient, however, to proceed from basic principles by writing down the profit equation and equating it to the target as required.

Breakeven Point in Dollars

Breakeven analysis also applies when production level is expressed in monetary units. Consider Martha Jacobs' decision to rent a booth at the local fair to sell Jim and Barry's ice cream in eight different flavors. She plans to set the price of the ice cream by adding 25% to its variable cost. Martha must also incur fixed costs of $800 to rent the stall and a portable freezer. How many dollars of sales must Martha make to break even on this enterprise?

$$Sales = 1.25 \times Variable\ Cost$$
$$Variable\ Cost = \frac{Sales}{1.25} = 0.80 \times Sales$$

Martha's pricing policy (25% markup over variable costs) leads to variable costs of $0.80 for each $1.00 of sales. The contribution margin is 20% [($1.00 − $0.80) ÷ $1.00] of sales.

The contribution margin *expressed as a percent of sales* is also referred to as the **contribution margin ratio.** To determine the breakeven point, we employ our earlier formula, treating $1.00 as the unit of measurement for the production level Q. Therefore, contribution margin per dollar (one unit of measurement) of sales is $1.00 − $0.80, and the breakeven point, Q^0, is given by this formula:

Contribution margin ratio
Contribution margin expressed as a percent of sales.

$$Q^0 = \textit{Fixed Costs} \div \textit{Contribution Margin}$$
$$= \$800 \div (\$1.00 - \$0.80)$$
$$= \$800 \div \$0.20$$
$$= \$4,000$$

The breakeven quantity is expressed in dollars because our unit of measurement is $1. Martha must earn $4000 of sales revenues to break even on her $800 commitment of fixed resources for booth and freezer rental.

*C*ONSIDER THIS . . .

Pittsburgh's Pirates May Sail Away

In 1988, Pittsburgh's city government and corporate leaders together bought the Pirates, the city's baseball team, to keep major league baseball in Pittsburgh. Operating in a small metropolitan area with a population of about two million, the Pirates faced financial problems in the 1980s and 1990s. The 1988 buyout contract provides for the ownership to revert to the city if the team amasses operating losses of $10 million or more in any consecutive three-year period. The city is expected to sell the team in this case.

In 1988, the Pirates had a breakeven point of 1.4 million tickets. With a steep increase in the team's payroll, the Pirates had to sell more than two million tickets in 1990 to break even. How were the breakeven points estimated?

The team's payroll in 1988 was $6.2 million. Administrative and other fixed operating costs amounted to $4.1 million. Revenues from television and radio broadcast rights and from concessions were $1.9 million. The contribution margin was $6 per ticket. The Pirates break even if the total revenues from ticket sales and broadcast rights equal the total payroll and administrative costs:

$$\textit{Breakeven Point} =$$

$$\frac{\textit{Payroll Costs} + \textit{Administrative Costs} - \textit{Broadcast Revenues}}{\textit{Contribution Margin Per Ticket}}$$

$$= \frac{\$6.2 \text{ million} + \$4.1 \text{ million} - \$1.9 \text{ million}}{\$6 \text{ per ticket}}$$

$$= 1.4 \text{ million tickets}$$

Can you determine how the breakeven point will change if the Pirates add high-priced talented players to strengthen their roster and increase their payroll by 58% to $9.8 million? (Answer: The breakeven point increases to two million tickets.) Can you determine how many tickets the Pirates (with the $9.8 million payroll) must sell to keep their annual operating losses under $3.333 million? (Answer: 1.445 million tickets.)

Source: "How Business Went to Bat for the Pirates," *Business Week,* July 18, 1988, p. 98; "Pittsburgh's Pirates May Have to Sail Away," *Business Week,* April 16, 1990, p. 78; W. Wucinich, "Profit Is the Name of the Game," *Management Accounting,* February 1991, pp. 58–59.

RIVERSIDE GENERAL HOSPITAL REVISITED

Let us return to Riverside General Hospital. Holly Ward, the controller at Riverside, developed the following cost equation:

$$Costs = \$2,393,091 + (\$161.59 \times Patient\ Days) + (\$74.33 \times Patients)$$

The average reimbursement rate is expected to remain at $220 per patient day. The number of patients and patient days for 1998 are expected to remain at the 1997 levels of 8,367 patients and 45,606 patient days. How much must the fixed costs be reduced if Riverside General is to break even?

Holly's back-of-the-envelope calculations indicated that fixed costs must be reduced by almost 15% to break even. How did she reach this conclusion?

Because the number of patients and of patient days are expected to be 8,367 and 45,606 respectively, the costs varying with these two measures of output are estimated to be $621,889 ($74.33 × 8,367) and $7,369,455 ($161.59 × 45,606). (See Exhibit 3-8.) Our objective is to determine the reduction required in fixed costs; therefore, we shall denote fixed costs by the symbol F, and write the costs as follows:

$$Costs = F + \$7,369,455 + \$621,889$$
$$= F + \$7,991,344$$

Revenues are $220 per day for 45,606 patient days.

$$Revenues = \$220 \times 45,606$$
$$= \$10,033,320$$

To break even, we must have this equation:

$$0 = Revenues - Costs$$
$$0 = \$10,033,320 - F - \$7,991,344$$
$$F = \$2,041,976$$

Because the fixed costs are $2,393,091 at present, they must be reduced by 14.67% [($2,393,091 − $2,041,976) ÷ $2,393,091], or nearly 15%, for Riverside to break even.

BREAKEVEN ANALYSIS AND CAPACITY UTILIZATION

You may wonder whether breakeven analysis is restricted only to the types of situations we have described so far. For a managerial application of this analytical method in a more complex setting, consider Regal Airlines, which is evaluating a proposal to introduce a daily Boeing 757 round-trip flight on the New York to Los Angeles route. The costs involved in adding this flight include the following:

1. Airplane equipment rental and airport gate rental fees of $136,000 per week
2. Maintenance and other ground staff costs of $32,000 per week
3. Flight crew's salaries and benefits of $48,000 per week

4. Fuel costs of $6500 per one-way flight, that is, $91,000 for the 14 one-way flights per week.

Discretionary advertising expenditure of $40,000 per week is planned to support the new operation. Commissions paid to travel agents average 10% of sales. The aircraft can hold 80 passengers in its specially designed comfortable seating configuration, and the average one-way fare is $600 per passenger.

How many passengers must fly on this daily flight for Regal Airlines to break even on this new operation? All costs except sales commissions become fixed once the decisions to operate and advertise the route are made. Direct labor (flying crew) and direct materials (fuel) do not vary with the output (number of passengers) in this case. The fixed costs amount to $347,000 per week. Each one-way passenger ticket contributes $540. Regal Airlines must have at least 642.6 ($347,000 ÷ $540) passengers per week or 45.9 (642.6 ÷ 14) passengers per flight on average to break even.

Weekly fixed costs:	
Airport gate rental fees	$136,000
Maintenance and ground staff costs	32,000
Flight crew salaries and benefits	48,000
Fuel costs	91,000
Advertising	40,000
Total	$347,000

One-way passenger ticket revenue:	
Revenue per passenger	$600
Commission paid to travel agents (10%)	−60
Total	$540

Airline executives monitor the load factor, or capacity utilization, for each route on a daily basis. *Load factor* is measured as the ratio of the number of passengers per flight to the number of seats available per flight. Regal can expect to break even on this route when its load factor is 57.4% (45.9 ÷ 80).

Step Fixed Costs and Multiple Breakeven Points

The breakeven point is determined by dividing the fixed costs by the contribution margin per unit. When the cost curve is characterized by step fixed costs, however, we need to consider a different amount of fixed costs corresponding to each step. Therefore, in principle, we could compute a breakeven point for each level of fixed costs. Some of these computed breakeven points may not be feasible because they may violate the limits imposed by the relevant range corresponding to the level of fixed costs considered in their computation.

Consider Regal Airlines once again. Regal has determined that the number of additional passengers wanting to fly on its Los-Angeles-to-New-York route is less than the 643 it requires to breakeven with a daily flight schedule. It is now considering a truncated flight schedule of only 10 or 12 one-way flights (instead of 14) per week by not scheduling flights on Saturday and/or Sunday. Fixed costs will be only $306,000 if it schedules 10 flights and $327,000 if it schedules 12 flights, instead of the $347,000 of fixed costs when it schedules 14 flights. Fixed costs will be lower because Regal can plan to reduce airport gate rental commitments, hire fewer ground staff and flying crew, and incur lower fuel costs. Thus, these costs behave as step fixed costs. How many passengers must Regal Airlines fly each week to break even?

If Regal decides to schedule only 10 flights per week, its breakeven point will be 566.7 passengers per week, or 56.7 passengers per flight on average, a 70.8% load factor. If it decides to schedule 12 flights per week, instead, its breakeven point will be 605.6 passengers per week, or 50.5 passengers per flight on average, a 63.1% load factor.

Breakeven point at 10 flights per week:

$$\frac{\text{Fixed costs, \$306,000}}{\text{Per passenger revenue, \$540}} = 566.7 \text{ passengers per week}$$

$$\frac{566.7 \text{ passengers per week}}{10 \text{ flights}} = 56.7 \text{ average passengers per flight}$$

$$\frac{56.7 \text{ average passengers per flight}}{80 \text{ total capacity}} = 70.8\% \text{ load factor}$$

Breakeven point at 12 flights per week:

$$\frac{\text{Fixed costs, \$327,000}}{\text{Per passenger revenue, \$540}} = 605.6 \text{ passengers per week}$$

$$\frac{605.6 \text{ passengers per week}}{12 \text{ flights}} = 50.5 \text{ average passengers per flight}$$

$$\frac{50.5 \text{ average passengers per flight}}{80 \text{ total capacity}} = 63.1\% \text{ load factor}$$

Notice that there are different breakeven points, depending on Regal management's decision concerning the level of capacity to make available. With the lower capacity level (10 flights), fewer passengers are required each week for the airline to break even. This decision also implies that the airline must achieve a higher load factor on its weekday flights to break even.

Cost Variability and Level of Analysis

Next consider the decision by National Airlines, Inc. regarding the number of flights to operate on the air shuttle route between New York and Boston. Its advertising, personnel, and other expenditures to support the operation in New York and Boston amount to $150,000 per week. Flying crew, fuel, and other flight-related expenditures amount to $7500 per flight. Aircraft rental and airport gate fees are $6500 per week per flight. In addition, ground support personnel cost $4000 per flight as company policy seeks to maintain quality service even as volume increases. National pays a commission of 8% to travel agents on a one-way fare of $160 per passenger. A full flight carries 100 passengers.

How many flights must National Airlines operate to break even if it expects the load factor to be 70% per flight? The analysis in Exhibit 4-13 indicates that National must operate 58 round-trip flights each week to break even.

We see in the examples of Regal Airlines and National Airlines that the behavior of costs depends on the level of analysis. When the number of flights has already been decided, as in the Regal example, only a small portion of the costs vary with the number of passengers. When a decision about the number of flights is considered, as in the National example, we can treat all flight-related costs as varying with volume (number of flights) in an analysis to determine the breakeven point.

A Planning Model

Understanding cost behavior also helps management to determine the level of operation likely to maximize profits. Suppose the load factor for National Airlines is not expected to equal 70% for each flight. Instead, the load factor is expected to

OBJECTIVE 4.3

Capture the relationship among revenues, costs incurred, and production volumes by sketching a planning model.

EXHIBIT 4-13
National Airlines
Breakeven Point Analysis

Description	Amount	Calculations
Revenue per passenger	$160.00	
Sales commission	$12.80	8% × $160
Contribution per passenger	$147.20	$160 − $12.80 sales commission
Passengers per flight	70	0.70 load factor × 100 capacity available
Net revenue per round-trip flight	$20,608.00	2 trips × 70 passengers × $147.20 contribution per passenger
Cost per round-trip flight	$18,000.00	$7,500 crew salaries + $6,500 aircraft and gate rental + $4,000 support personnel
Contribution per flight	$2,608.00	$20,608 − $18,000
Costs not varying with flights	$150,000.00	advertising, personnel, and the like
Breakeven point	57.5 round-trip flights per week	$150,000 ÷ 2,608

EXHIBIT 4-14
National Airlines
Cost and Revenue Behavior

Factor	Calculation
Net profit	*Total revenues − Total expenses*
Total revenue	*Average fare × Number of passengers*
Number of passengers	*2 × Number of round-trip flights per day × 7 days × Average load factor*
Average load factor	*0.92 − 0.04 × (Number of round-trip flights per day − 1)*
Total expenses	*Commission costs + Flying crew and fuel costs + Aircraft rental and gate fees + Ground support costs + Advertising and other costs*
Commission costs	*0.08 × Total revenues*
Flying crew and fuel costs	*$7500 × Number of round-trip flights per day × 7*
Aircraft rental and gate fees	*$6500 × Number of round-trip flights per day × 7*
Ground support costs	*$4000 × Number of round-trip flights per day × 7*
Advertising and other costs	$150,000

EXHIBIT 4-15
National Airlines
Weekly Profits for Different Number of Flights

Equation in Exhibit 4-14	Number of Round-Trip Flights per Day						
	1	**2**	**3**	**4**	**5**	**6**	**7**
Average load Factor	92%	88%	84%	80%	76%	72%	68%
No. of passengers	1,288	2,464	3,528	4,480	5,320	6,048	6,664
Total revenue	206,080	394,240	564,480	716,800	851,200	967,680	1,066,240
Commission costs	16,486	31,539	45,158	57,344	68,096	77,414	85,299
Flying crew and fuel costs	7,500	15,000	22,500	30,000	37,500	45,000	52,500
Aircraft rental and gate fees	6,500	13,000	19,500	26,000	32,500	39,000	45,500
Ground support costs	4,000	8,000	12,000	16,000	20,000	24,000	28,000
Advertising and other costs	150,000	150,000	150,000	150,000	150,000	150,000	150,000
Total expenses	184,486	217,539	249,158	279,344	308,096	335,414	361,299
Net profit	21,594	176,701	315,322	437,456	543,104	632,266	704,941

be 92% for the first flight scheduled in each direction. Each additional round-trip flight is expected to result in a decline in average load factor by 4% on all flights. How many round-trip flights should National Airlines operate?

It is possible to derive an algebraic expression to determine the number of flights that maximize profits, but the expression depends on the specific relationship between the expected demand (load factor) and the proposed supply (number of flights). The more general skill to be learned here is the ability to understand the basic equations that project profits as described in Exhibit 4-14.

The equations in Exhibit 4-14 specify the *behavior of costs* and revenues and enable us to determine the *best choice* using a spreadsheet model. Such articulation forms the basis for developing a *planning model* for the firm. Critical for this purpose is a thorough understanding of what drives costs and revenues and the way that each of them is related to factors that managers can control.

Exhibit 4-15 summarizes the cost and revenue implications of operating different numbers of flights. The numbers in this table are derived from the equations specified in the planning model in Exhibit 4-14. Exhibit 4-16 displays the graph of profits plotted against the number of flights. Looking at the graph, we can see that the profits are the highest when National operates 11 round-trip flights.

A MIDCHAPTER REVIEW PROBLEM

Tony's Pizza delivers 12-inch pepperoni pizzas for phoned-in orders. Each pizza sells for $10. The manager, Tony Pena, has projected the following costs corresponding to sales of 10,000 and 12,000 pizzas for the next month's operation:

Number of Round-Trip Flights per Day							
8	**9**	**10**	**11**	**12**	**13**	**14**	**15**
64%	60%	56%	52%	48%	44%	40%	36%
7,168	7,560	7,840	8,008	8,064	8,008	7,840	7,560
1,146,880	1,209,600	1,254,400	1,281,280	1,290,240	1,281,280	1,254,400	1,209,600
91,750	96,768	100,352	102,502	103,219	102,502	100,352	96,768
60,000	67,500	75,000	82,500	90,000	97,500	105,000	112,500
52,000	58,500	65,000	71,500	78,000	84,500	91,000	97,500
32,000	36,000	40,000	44,000	48,000	52,000	56,000	60,000
150,000	150,000	150,000	150,000	150,000	150,000	150,000	150,000
385,750	408,768	430,352	450,502	469,219	486,502	502,352	516,768
761,130	800,832	824,048	830,778	821,021	794,778	752,048	692,832

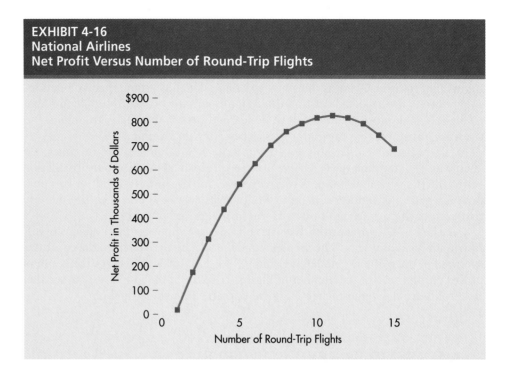

EXHIBIT 4-16
National Airlines
Net Profit Versus Number of Round-Trip Flights

TONY'S PIZZA
PROJECTED COSTS FOR NEXT MONTH

	Number of Pizzas Sold	
Cost Items	**10,000**	**12,000**
Dough	$ 4,000	$ 4,800
Toppings	2,500	3,000
Cheese	4,500	5,400
Tomatoes	3,000	3,600
Energy	4,000	4,500
Kitchen personnel	3,000	3,000
Delivery personnel	2,200	2,640
Car expenses	3,500	3,800
Facilities	10,000	10,000
Advertisement	4,500	4,500
Total costs	$41,200	$45,240

(a) Classify these costs as variable, fixed, or mixed. Express each item in terms of a cost equation in the form $C = F + (V \times Q)$.

(b) Determine the contribution margin per pizza.

(c) Determine the breakeven sales level in number of pizzas.

(d) Determine the sales level in number of pizzas that will generate a profit of $9000 for the next month.

The following is the solution to this problem:

Item	Cost Type	Fixed Cost	Variable Cost
Dough	variable	$ 0	$0.40
Toppings	variable	0	0.25
Cheese	variable	0	0.45
Tomatoes	variable	0	0.30
Energy	mixed	1,500*	0.25**
Kitchen personnel	fixed	3,000	0
Delivery personnel	variable	0	2.20
Car expenses	mixed	2,000***	0.15****
Facilities	fixed	10,000	0
Advertisement	fixed	4,500	0
Total		$21,000	$4.00

* $4,500 − ($0.25 × 12,000) = $1,500
** ($4,500 − 4,000) ÷ (12,000 − 10,000) = $0.25
*** $3,800 − ($0.15 × 12,000) = $2,000
**** ($3,800 − 3,500) ÷ (12,000 − 10,000) = $0.15

(b) Contribution Margin per Pizza $= \$10 - \$4$
$= \$6$

(c) Let X be the number of pizzas to break even.

$$\$6 \times X - \$21,000 = \$0$$

$$X = \frac{21,000}{6} = 3500 \text{ pizzas}$$

(d) Let X be the number of pizzas that will generate a profit of $9000.

$$\$6 \times X - \$21,000 = \$9000$$
$$\$6 \times X = \$30,000$$
$$X = 5000 \text{ pizzas}$$

SUPPLY VERSUS USAGE OF ACTIVITY RESOURCES

Understanding the *behavior of costs* is sometimes challenging because cost behavior is contingent on time frame, range of activity levels, and a variety of other factors. For instance, the cost driver for direct materials is the number of units produced. Direct labor hours, the cost driver for direct labor cost, is also a unit-related measure. Therefore, it is commonly assumed that both direct material and direct labor costs are variable. This assumption is not always correct.

A more precise way to think of *variable costs* is that they represent resources whose supply can be adjusted to match the demand placed for them. If only 100 automobile chassis are manufactured instead of a planned 110, steel for 100 chassis will be used up and the steel for the remaining 10 chassis can be inventoried to be used later. Therefore, direct material costs are usually variable even in the short term. In contrast, the supply of direct labor resources often cannot be changed readily in response to short-term fluctuations in production levels. Workers are

OBJECTIVE 4.4

Discuss the importance of knowing how commitment and usage of activity resources influence cost variability.

usually paid a fixed amount of wages for a day or a week, whether they are occupied productively for the entire period or not. Thus labor costs may be relatively inflexible, that is, fixed in the short run so that direct labor costs may not vary exactly in proportion with production volume.[3]

Consider the Carex Muffler Company, which specializes in same-day service. Cars brought in by 8:00 A.M. are guaranteed to be serviced before 6:15 P.M. The shop has eight service bays. As many as 8 mechanics can be hired on a 8:00 A.M. to 4:00 P.M. daily shift to service the automobiles. Each muffler replacement takes a mechanic 45 minutes (0.75 hours). In a day's work, therefore, allowing for a 30-minute break for lunch, a mechanic is expected to service 10 cars (7.5 hours ÷ 0.75 hours per car).

The number of customers seeking muffler repairs fluctuates daily. If the number of jobs is less than 10 times the number of mechanics on any day, some mechanics will be idle for a period of time. If the number of jobs exceeds the available capacity, some mechanics may be asked to work overtime to ensure that all cars are serviced before 6:15 P.M. the same day. Regular wages, including benefits, average $30 per hour. Overtime wages include a 50% premium in addition to the regular wages. Exhibit 4-17 summarizes the daily direct labor costs for different numbers of customer orders (jobs).

The *cost driver* for the muffler replacement activity is the number of mechanic hours. By hiring 8 mechanics, Carex has committed to paying regular wages for at least 64 mechanic hours (8 mechanics × 8 hours per day). The committed cost, therefore, is $1920 ($30 per hour × 64 hours). These committed resources supply a capacity of 60 hours (7.5 hours/day/mechanic × 8 mechanics), which is sufficient to service 80 jobs (10 jobs per mechanic × 8 mechanics). Additional resources are required *if and only if* the actual demand exceeds 80 jobs. When the demand is for 80 or fewer jobs (see columns for 50, 60, and 70 orders in Exhibit 4-17), some of the available 60 hours of mechanic labor are not used for muffler repairs. Since the mechanics have been hired for the entire day, they will be paid for some idle time. When the demand is for more than 80 jobs (see the 90- and 100-order columns), overtime is required.

If the actual demand is Q jobs, with $Q > 80$, then these hours of overtime are required:[4]

$$0.75 \times (Q - 80) = 0.75Q - 60$$

Regular wages for overtime are as follows:

$$\$30 \times (0.75Q - 60)$$

The 50% overtime premium amounts to this:

$$.50 \times \$30 \times (0.75Q - 60)$$

The total overtime wages amount to

$$1.50 \times \$30 \times (0.75Q - 60)$$

---

[3] Many Asian and European companies consider direct labor costs to be fixed because they find it difficult to adjust the number of workers employed in response to changes in the production level.

[4] Overtime equals the number of jobs exceeding the capacity for 80 jobs with regular time (that is, $Q - 80$ jobs) multiplied by the 0.75 hour required to service each job. Alternatively, you can view overtime as the difference between the time required to service Q jobs, that is, 0.75 Q hours, less the 60 hours of capacity made available by hiring eight mechanics.

EXHIBIT 4-17
Carex Muffler Company
Daily Direct Labor Costs

Labor Item	Number of Daily Customer Orders					
	50	60	70	80	90	100
Number of mechanics	8	8	8	8	8	8
Total demand for labor hours: *Number of orders* × 0.75 *Hour per Order*	37.5	45	52.5	60	67.5	75
Available regular time labor hours: 7.5 *Hours per day* × *Number of Mechanics*	60	60	60	60	60	60
Idle time in hours	22.5	15	7.5	0	0	0
Overtime in hours	0	0	0	0	7.5	15
Total regular wages: *(8 mechanics* × *$30 per Hour* × *8 Hours)*	$1920	$1920	$1920	$1920	$1920	$1920
Total overtime wages	0	0	0	0	$337.50	$675.00
Total direct labor costs	$1920	$1920	$1920	$1920	$2257.50	$2595
Direct labor costs per job: *Total Direct Labor Costs* ÷ *Number of Orders*	$38.40	$32.00	$27.43	$24.00	$25.08	$25.95

The cost equation, therefore, has two forms. When the number of muffler repairs is less than 80, the *committed resources* (the mechanics) represent a fixed cost. When the required demand for the resource available for muffler repairs exceeds the available capacity (80 jobs), then it is necessary to add on the cost for the overtime hours. We can write the cost equations for Carex Muffler Company as follows:

When $Q \leq 80$:

$C = \$1920$

When $Q > 80$:

$C = \$1920 + 1.50 \times \$30 \times (0.75Q - 60)$

The graph in Exhibit 4-18 plots the total direct labor costs for different numbers of daily customer orders (jobs). We see that total costs remain fixed at $1920 until the supply of available resource capacity (80 jobs) is fully used. Then total costs increase with the number of jobs ($2257.50 for 90 orders and $2595.00 for 100 orders) because overtime is required to meet the additional demand for mechanic time.

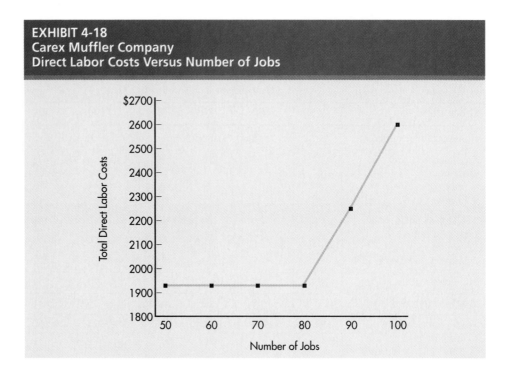

EXHIBIT 4-18
Carex Muffler Company
Direct Labor Costs Versus Number of Jobs

Normal Costs

OBJECTIVE 4.5

Understand the significance of the normal costs of an activity.

Exhibit 4-19 displays the graph of the average labor cost per job plotted against the number of daily jobs. We see that the average or unit costs depend on the number of daily customer orders. Average unit costs are lowest when the demand for direct labor exactly matches the available capacity at 80 jobs. We define the normal unit cost of an activity to be the cost per unit capacity at the point where the demand for the activity exactly equals the available capacity:

$$\textit{Normal Unit Cost} = \frac{\textit{Regular Cost of Providing Capacity}}{\textit{Capacity Made Available}}$$

$$= \$1920 \div 80 \text{ jobs} \qquad\qquad (4\text{-}9)$$

$$= \$24 \text{ per job}$$

Suppose Carex management could wait to hire mechanics until it knew the actual customer demand for muffler repairs each day or had complete flexibility in adjusting the number of mechanic hours to meet actual demand. At the regular wage rate of $32 per hour ($30 × 8 ÷ 7.5), the cost per job would be $24 ($32 per hour × 0.75 hour per job). Thus, **normal unit costs** of an activity measure the average or unit costs *as if* the activity were perfectly variable. This cost information is useful for determining a benchmark for long-run product prices.[5]

Normal unit cost
The average cost of the activity when the demand for the activity exactly equals the capacity made available by the resources committed to the activity.

When demand is less than the available capacity supplied and managers cannot adjust the supply of labor to actual demand, then actual unit costs will be

[5] The use of normal costs in product prices will be discussed in detail in Chapter 7. See also R. D. Banker and J. S. Hughes, "Product Costing and Pricing," *The Accounting Review*, July 1994, pp. 479–494.

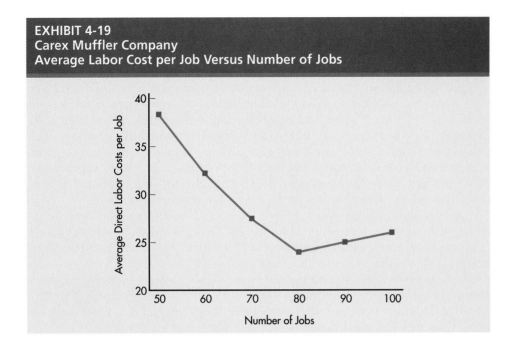

EXHIBIT 4-19
Carex Muffler Company
Average Labor Cost per Job Versus Number of Jobs

higher than normal unit costs because of idle time. The actual unit costs are also higher than the normal unit costs when demand exceeds available capacity because an overtime premium must be paid. Notice that the definition of the normal unit cost of an activity *extends and formalizes* the definition of activity cost driver rates from Chapter 3 in the present context of supply and usage of activity resources.

We previously defined the activity cost driver rate as activity costs divided by the number of units of the activity cost driver. The precise definition presented here requires the following:

1. The *activity costs* in the numerator must be the regular cost only (excluding additional costs, such as overtime) to provide the normal capacity of activity resources.

2. The *number of units of the activity cost driver* in the denominator represents the *capacity made available* by the resources committed to the activity.

RESOURCE FLEXIBILITY AND COST VARIABILITY

Managers try to operate at a low unit-cost level by maintaining flexibility in the use of resources. For example, U.S. automobile and steel manufacturing firms, such as the Saturn division of General Motors, obtained a concession from their labor unions in recent years to eliminate or greatly reduce worker job categories so that potentially idle workers could be deployed to perform different tasks.

Many plants provide incentives for workers to acquire multiple skills so that they can perform many different tasks. These incentives include changes in compensation, such as paying for knowledge available (in workers) rather than for the particular job they happen to be performing at any given time. Managers also try to plan production well in advance to smooth out demand for direct labor and

OBJECTIVE 4.6

Explain why activity costs tend to be variable in the long run.

other manufacturing resources and thereby eliminate the incidence of idle time. Smoothing is often attained, however, at the cost of increasing the levels of inventory or increasing the lead time for meeting customer orders.

If direct workers are paid on a piece-rate basis for units produced and shipped, direct labor costs vary in proportion to volume. More commonly, however, plants hire workers on a daily, weekly, monthly, or some other time basis. In such cases, we have seen that because of idle time and overtime, direct labor costs measured on a daily basis will not usually vary directly with the corresponding production volume. When considering direct labor costs over a longer duration, however, these costs are more likely to vary with production. This occurs because managers have more flexibility over the longer term to adjust staffing levels to meet anticipated seasonal or long-term changes in production volume.

For example, managers at the Carex Muffler Company have the flexibility to temporarily add extra mechanics on some days. Demand on Friday is high because people repair their cars in anticipation of weekend driving needs. Demand on Monday is also high because repair shops are closed over the weekend. Generally, the demand on Fridays and Mondays varies from 76 to 92 jobs and averages 84 jobs. Demand on Tuesdays and Thursdays averages 75 jobs, and on Wednesdays it averages only 66. Carex managers attempt to adjust the number of mechanics daily depending on the expected demand on each day. Therefore, eight mechanics work on Mondays and Fridays, seven on Tuesdays and Thursdays, and six on Wednesdays.

Exhibit 4-20 lists the actual demand for 20 days in September 1997. The direct labor cost each day comprises both the fixed cost of the committed resources and the additional cost for the overtime hours. The cost equation that applies here is as described before except that we now have different equations, depending on whether there are eight, seven, or six mechanics.

If there are N mechanics, the number of hours available is $(7.5 \times N)$ hours. A demand of Q jobs requires $(0.75 \times Q)$ hours because each job requires 0.75 hours to complete. No overtime is required as long as the demand for the activity resource $(0.75 \times Q)$ is no more than the amount of committed resources $(7.5 \times N)$; that is, when $Q \leq 10 \times N$.[6] This cost equation can be written as this:

When $Q \leq 10 \times N$:
$C = \$30 \times 8 \times N$

When $Q > 10 \times N$:
$C = \$30 \times 8 \times N + 1.5 \times \$30 \times (0.75 \times Q - 7.5 \times N)$

For instance, on Tuesday, September 2, seven mechanics were employed and 73 jobs were ordered. Thus, 2.25 hours of overtime were required to meet the demand, and total direct labor costs were $1781.25.

$$\frac{\text{Total hrs. required}}{\text{hrs.}} = 0.75 \text{ hrs. per job} \times 73 \text{ jobs} = 54.75 \text{ hrs.}$$

$$\frac{\text{Regular hrs.}}{\text{hrs.}} = 7.5 \text{ hrs. per mechanic} \times 7 \text{ mechanics} = \underline{52.5 \text{ hrs.}}$$

$$\text{Overtime hrs. required} = \underline{2.25 \text{ hrs.}}$$

[6] If $0.75 \times Q \leq (7.5 \times N)$, then $Q \leq (7.5 \div 0.75 \times N) = 10 \times N$.

EXHIBIT 4-20
Carex Muffler Company
September 1997 Demand and Direct Labor Costs

Day	Date	Number of Mechanics	Number of Jobs	Idle Time (Hours)	Overtime (Hours)	Direct Labor Cost	Average Cost per Job
Mon.	9/1	8	89	0.00	6.75	$2,223.75	$24.99
Tue.	9/2	7	73	0.00	2.25	1,781.25	24.40
Wed.	9/3	6	70	0.00	7.50	1,777.50	25.39
Thu.	9/4	7	81	0.00	8.25	2,051.25	25.32
Fri.	9/5	8	86	0.00	4.50	2,122.50	24.68
Mon.	9/8	8	87	0.00	5.25	2,156.25	24.78
Tue.	9/9	7	82	0.00	9.00	2,085.00	25.43
Wed.	9/10	6	71	0.00	8.25	1,811.25	25.51
Thu.	9/11	7	78	0.00	6.00	1,950.00	25.00
Fri.	9/12	8	79	0.75	0.00	1,920.00	24.30
Mon.	9/15	8	84	0.00	3.00	2,055.00	24.46
Tue.	9/16	7	77	0.00	5.25	1,916.25	24.89
Wed.	9/17	6	60	0.00	0.00	1,440.00	24.00
Thu.	9/18	7	75	0.00	3.75	1,848.75	24.65
Fri.	9/19	8	85	0.00	3.75	2,088.75	24.57
Mon.	9/22	8	80	0.00	0.00	1,920.00	24.00
Tue.	9/23	7	76	0.00	4.50	1,882.50	24.77
Wed.	9/24	6	63	0.00	2.25	1,541.25	24.46
Thu.	9/25	7	67	2.25	0.00	1,680.00	25.07
Fri.	9/26	8	83	0.00	2.25	2,021.25	24.35
						Average	$24.75

Direct labor costs:

$30 per hr. $\times$ 8 hrs. $\times$ 7 mechanics = $1680.00
1.5 (time and a half for overtime) $\times$ $30 per hr. $\times$ 2.25 hrs = $ 101.25
Total $1781.25

Since $Q = 73$ jobs is greater than the available capacity of $10 \times 7 = 70$ jobs with the 7 mechanics,

$$C = (\$30 \times 8 \times 7) + (1.5 \times \$30 \times (0.75 \times 73 - 7.5 \times 7))$$
$$= \$1,680.00 + \$101.25$$
$$= \$1,781.25$$

Unit costs were $24.40 ($1781.25 ÷ 73).

Exhibit 4-21 shows actual labor costs plotted against the production volume (number of jobs) for the 20 days in September. You can now see that the costs vary more or less in proportion to the number of jobs. This picture contrasts with the cost curve shown in Exhibit 4-18, which describes the relationship between costs and production if the number of mechanics is fixed at eight. This variability of costs over a longer period arises because managers are using their hiring flexibility to adjust the quantity of resources (number of mechanics) supplied each day to match the expected demand for them.

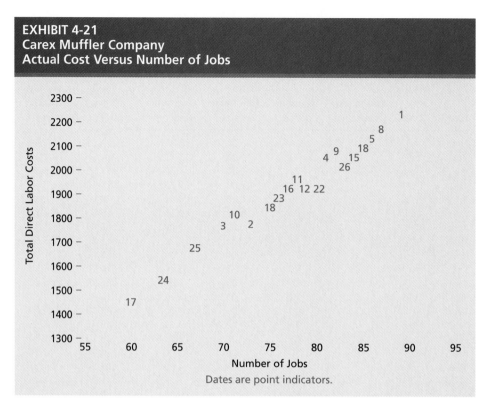

Exhibit 4-22 displays the unit costs plotted against the production volume (number of jobs). Notice that, unlike the corresponding graph in Exhibit 4-19, the unit costs are aligned around a horizontal straight line. This is consistent with the

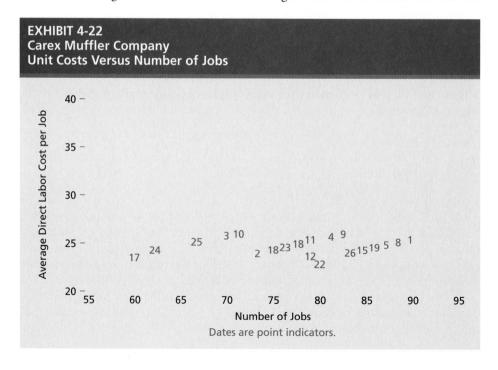

notion that the *variable cost rate* is independent of the production level. You will also notice that the *average cost of $24.75* per job is higher than the normal cost of $24.00 per job because in actual operations both overtime and idle time costs are incurred because managers cannot forecast demand exactly or supply resources (mechanics) in exactly the demanded quantities. (See the last line in Exhibit 4-20.)

Cost Behavior

Cost behavior describes the way costs change with changes in activity cost drivers or with production volume. The key concept for understanding cost behavior is to recognize that managers must commit to supplying many production resources before knowing the actual demand for them. In this case, the cost of supplying these resources is incurred whether or not the resources are fully used to perform productive work. The cost of these resources will appear to be fixed with respect to actual production volume as long as the capacity of the resources supplied is not exceeded.

The supply of other resources, however, such as materials or power to operate machines, can be adjusted easily to match precisely the demand placed for them. The cost of such resources is said to be variable with production activity.

The supply of resources such as direct labor cannot usually be adjusted to demand in the very short run. Such costs are fixed over the short-term horizon, but in the longer run managers can make adjustments by adding, retrenching, or redeploying workers to match the anticipated demand for direct labor. Therefore, the cost of direct labor appears to vary with production volume over longer-term horizons.

The behavior of many other manufacturing costs can be explained in a similar way depending on the different degrees of commitment required for different types of resources. For the personnel who perform support activities, such as materials handling and scheduling, management can adjust the number of workers and hence the total costs of these resources with relative ease. In contrast, management has much less flexibility in changing the plant capacity and therefore in adjusting the support costs associated with rent and insurance. Costs related to materials handling and scheduling are therefore relatively more variable, but rent and insurance costs are relatively more fixed with respect to production levels.[7]

Variability of costs also depends on the time frame considered. In the Carex Muffler Company example, managers have no flexibility in adjusting the number of mechanics within any given day. Therefore, for a period as short as a day the direct labor costs are fixed unless the capacity is exceeded. However, for longer time periods Carex management can increase or decrease the number of mechanics so that the direct labor costs appear to vary with production volume (number of jobs). Over a sufficiently long period of time, the supply of almost all activity resources is flexible so that their costs will vary with production volume when considered over the long-term. Typically, the costs of activity resources that are flexible in the short- to medium-term are classified as *variable*, while the costs of activity resources that can be adjusted only in the long run are classified as *fixed*.

Cost behavior
The way costs change with changes in activity cost drivers or with production volume.

---

[7] R. D. Banker and H. Chang, "Flexibility of Activity Resources and Behavior of Activity Costs," *Chinese Accounting Review*, September 1994, pp. 22–51.

This recently completed cracking unit at a Shell Oil Refinery cost many millions of dollars to build but reduced the company's need to purchase gasoline from other refiners. By building this unit, Shell has substituted a cost committed when the resource capacity was acquired (the depreciation on this unit) for a cost incurred only when resources are used (the cost paid to suppliers for refined oil products). *Courtesy* **Don Teiwes/Shell Oil**

Variability of Support Activity Costs

Support activity resources may be any of the following:

1. Flexible
2. Discretionary
3. Committed

Flexible resources
Resources that are acquired as needed; their costs vary with production activity; examples include indirect materials and electric power to operate machines.

Discretionary costs
Costs resulting from strategic and tactical decisions of managers; examples include advertising, publicity, and research and development.

Flexible resources are acquired as needed; their costs vary with the production activity. Examples include indirect materials and the electric power to operate machines.

The use of discretionary resources is not directly related to the production volume. Such **discretionary costs** result from strategic and tactical decisions of managers and include, for example, expenditures made for advertising, publicity, and research and development. In these cases, the expenditure for the activity resource influences the production level in the long run instead of the production level influencing the consumption of the activity resource. Costs of discretionary activities are therefore usually considered to be fixed with respect to production volume.

Committed resources are made available before their demand is known precisely. These resources cannot be reduced in case the demand is actually less than the capacity made available. Commitment for some resources may be for the short run, such as for materials handling and supervision. For some other resources, like plant equipment and facilities, the commitment may extend over a longer term. The usage of committed resources varies with the actual volume and mix of products. As the volume and complexity of production increase, the capacity of committed resources made available may be inadequate to support actual production.

Our examination of the variation in direct material and direct labor costs relative to production volume is meaningful because these costs can be traced directly to each product manufactured and sold. By definition, support costs cannot be traced to products in this fashion. Therefore, an important first step in the analysis of support costs is to identify each activity's cost driver.

Recall that support costs arise because of the performance of a number of different activities to support production or sales. Each activity may be associated with a direct or surrogate measure, referred to as its *activity cost driver*. For instance, the number of purchase orders is an activity cost driver for purchase department costs, and the numbers of setups and batches produced are activity cost drivers for setup and materials handling personnel costs. The number of active parts maintained and the number of engineering change orders (ECOs) are activity cost drivers for the engineering support activity costs.

In the case of direct labor, managers first determine the level of resources to make available for production and then the actual production volume determines the demand for available resources. This structure for the supply and usage of resources applies to many activities that comprise manufacturing support costs. Managers commit to incurring the expense for support activities when they hire personnel and provide them with the tools and facilities to perform their activities. The expense levels are influenced by the managers' expectations about the requirement for each activity. The actual demand for each activity and the consumption of its resources are related in turn to the actual production volume and mix.

Consider this example. If it takes two hours to set up a machine for each new batch and 36 hours are available per week from each setup worker supplied, the employment of 10 setup workers provides the capacity for 180 setups per week (10 workers $\times$ 36 hours $\div$ 2 hours per setup). If weekly wages (including benefits) average $720 per worker, the total expense for setup labor is $7200. We also can measure the cost per unit of the activity capacity made available for production. In this case, for each setup that can be done with the available capacity, the labor cost averages $40 ($7,200 $\div$ 180 setups). The normal unit cost of the setup labor activity is thus $40 per setup.

The actual demand for setups in a period depends on the number of batches of products manufactured. If two million units are manufactured in the first week of April in batches of average size of 12,500, then 160 setups (2,000,000 $\div$ 12,500) are required. There is, however, capacity for 180 setups. Therefore, the *unused capacity* for the first week of April is 20 setups (180 $-$ 160), or equivalently the idle time for setup labor is 40 hours ($2 \times 20 = (10 \times 36) - (2 \times 160)$). The expenditure for setup labor remains, therefore, at $7200 for the 10 workers employed at the plant since the setup workers come to work each day prepared to do as many setups as they can. The *actual* average cost per setup for the first week of April is $45 ($7200 $\div$ 160), which exceeds the normal cost of $40 per setup because of the unused capacity during that week.

This flexible manufacturing cell, manufactured by Cincinnati Milicron, allows manufacturers to produce a wide variety of products on a single machine. The machine's flexibility allows fast, low-cost setups, as the machine is converted from making one part to making another part. *Courtesy* Cincinnati Milicron

Costs of Multiple Products and Activities

OBJECTIVE 4.7

Link the costs of indirect and support resources to the production of multiple products.

The thinking behind commitment and consumption of activity resources becomes more complicated when more than one product is produced and sold. In this case, managers must also consider the relative mix of products when estimating activity costs. Different customers may require products to be manufactured in different-size batches. A product manufactured in batches of 10,000 units requires twice as many setups for the same volume of production as a product manufactured in batches of 20,000 units. Also, some products may require much longer setup times than others. As a result, the demand for support activities can vary considerably as the product mix changes.

Consider Global Glass Company's plant that manufactures glass bottles of three different sizes: two ounces, four ounces, and six ounces. Indirect labor costs include setup of the glass-extrusion machines and quality inspection of every finished bottle.

Proper setup is important because improper settings lead to higher defect and rejection rates. Setup workers, therefore, have specialized skills and many years of experience in working with the glass-extrusion machine. The plant employs 10 setup workers. Each worker can work up to 36 hours a week setting up the machines. The average weekly wages including benefits are $720 per worker. Because the smaller bottles are more difficult to manufacture, a job order for the two-ounce bottles requires more time per setup than for the larger bottles. Even if bottles with the same dimensions are to be manufactured in successive jobs, a new setup is required for each job because each customer wants a different and distinctive design for its bottles. Thus the demand for setup labor varies with both the number and type of job.

Quality inspection is not as specialized as setup work at Global Glass. The plant maintains some flexibility in adjusting the supply of inspection workers with changes in the expected number of customer orders. In the past two years, however, the plant has maintained 52 inspectors on its payroll. They are paid $630 (including benefits) per week on average and work 36 hours each week. Plant operations are scheduled for three shifts each day around the clock so that no overtime is possible. If resource capacity committed at the outset is not adequate, the company delays the execution and delivery of customer orders, which results in the loss of goodwill and potential sales. The demand for quality inspection varies approximately with the number of bottles manufactured. Exhibit 4-23 presents detailed data for support activity requirements.

Exhibit 4-24 shows actual production data for three weeks. In week 1, for instance, the two-ounce bottles required 80 setups (800,000 bottles produced ÷ 10,000 batch size). These setups took 176 hours (2.2 hours per setup × 80 setups). In addition, four-ounce bottles required 100 setup hours (2 × 1,000,000 ÷ 20,000), and six-ounce bottles required 64 setup hours (2 × 400,000 ÷ 12,500). In comparison with the total of 340 setup hours (176 + 100 + 64) required for production in week 1 (see Exhibit 4-25), the company supplied resources capable of performing 360 hours of setup work (10 workers × 36 hours per worker). Therefore, 20 hours of setup work resources supplied were not used.

Exhibit 4-26 shows calculations for quality inspection hours required each week. In week 3, for instance, 800 hours (1,000,000 ÷ 1,250) of quality inspection were required for two-ounce bottles, 720 hours (900,000 ÷ 1,250) for four-ounce bottles, and 400 hours (400,000 ÷ 1,000) for six-ounce bottles. In comparison with the total requirement of 1920 hours (800 + 720 + 400) of quality inspection, only 1872 hours (52 inspectors × 36 hours) of inspection worker time were supplied. Because the quantity of resources supplied was less than the quantity demanded, some jobs were delayed and the plant shop floor became congested with work in progress.

EXHIBIT 4-23
Global Glass Company
Support Activity Requirements

Bottle Size	Hours per Setup	Batch Size	Bottles Inspected per Hour
2 ounces	2.2	10,000	1,250
4 ounces	2.0	20,000	1,250
6 ounces	2.0	12,500	1,000

EXHIBIT 4-24
Global Glass Company
Actual Production Quantities in Number of Bottles

Bottle Size	Week 1	Week 2	Week 3
2 ounces	800,000	900,000	1,000,000
4 ounces	1,000,000	900,000	900,000
6 ounces	400,000	500,000	400,000

EXHIBIT 4-25
Global Glass Company
Setup Hours Required

Bottle Size	Number of Setups =	Bottles Produced ÷	Batch Size	Setup Hours =	Hours per Setup ×	Number of Setups
	Week 1	Week 2	Week 3	Week 1	Week 2	Week 3
2 ounces	80 = 800,000 ÷ 10,000	90 = 900,000 ÷ 10,000	100 = 1,000,000 ÷ 10,000	176 = 2.2 × 80	198 = 2.2 × 90	220 = 2.2 × 100
4 ounces	50 = 1,000,000 ÷ 20,000	45 = 900,000 ÷ 20,000	45 = 900,000 ÷ 20,000	100 = 2.0 × 50	90 = 2.0 × 45	90 = 2.0 × 45
6 ounces	32 = 400,000 ÷ 12,500	40 = 500,000 ÷ 12,500	32 = 400,000 ÷ 12,500	64 = 2.0 × 32	80 = 2.0 × 40	64 = 2.0 × 32
Total Setup Hours Required				340	368	374

The costs of lost sales or goodwill because of delays or the costs of expediting delayed jobs in a congested plant do not show up as setup or inspection expenses in a conventional income statement. Nonetheless, these are important costs for managers to track and control to make the right decisions about the number of support activity workers to employ and of customer jobs to accept.[8]

EXHIBIT 4-26
Global Glass Company
Inspection Hours Required

Bottle Size	Inspection Hours Required =	Bottles Produced ÷	Bottles Inspected Per Hour
	Week 1	Week 2	Week 3
2 ounces	640 = 800,000 ÷ 1,250	720 = 900,000 ÷ 1,250	800 = 1,000,000 ÷ 1,250
4 ounces	800 = 1,000,000 ÷ 1,250	720 = 900,000 ÷ 1,250	720 = 900,000 ÷ 1,250
6 ounces	400 = 400,000 ÷ 1,000	500 = 500,000 ÷ 1,000	400 = 400,000 ÷ 1,000
Total Inspection Hours Required	1,840	1,940	1,920

[8] R. D. Banker, S. M. Datar, and S. Kekre, "Relevant Costs, Congestion, and Stochasticity in Production," *Journal of Accounting and Economics*, Fall 1988, pp. 171–198.

Many vineyards operate their own bottle manufacturing plants. At this San Joaquin Valley vineyard
plant, workers must carefully set up the bottle-
forming machines to ensure that bottles are manufactured as designed and are free of defects.
Courtesy Ted Streshinsky/Photo 20-20

Expenditure Versus Consumption of Activity Resources

Exhibit 4-27 summarizes the resource supply and resource usage levels for both setup and quality inspection activities at Global Glass. The expenditure for setup and inspection labor ($7200 + $32,760) that shows up on the financial accounting statements does not change each week because it depends only on the managerial decision about the number of workers supplied in the time period. The actual usage of the resources supplied, however, depends on the production volume. Therefore, we find that the amount of idle time each week changes because of unused resource capacity or due to production delays attributable to resource shortages.

> **OBJECTIVE 4.8**
>
> Understand the difference between the costs of resources supplied and the costs of resources used for an activity.

Even when a permanent change in the production levels produces repeated unused or excess capacity for an activity, managers often delay adjusting the quantity of resources supplied for an activity to match the new demands for the resources. When the production level goes down, committed activity resources often remain in place for several months before the managers find an alternative use for the excess resources or make the politically difficult decision to permanently eliminate the surplus resources. When production increases place a demand on an activity that exceeds the present available capacity, workers often work longer or faster in the short run or else production is delayed. Eventually of course excess demand adversely affects performance, and managers must make more resource capacity available for the activity to relieve the overload. Therefore, there is often a lag between the production demands on activity resources and expenditures for the resource capacity supplied to perform the activities.

Although total expenditure levels are monitored in conventional financial accounting statements, the measurement of the specific demands placed on activity resources is sometimes ignored by cost accounting systems. A well-designed cost system seeks to measure the activity resources required to manufacture a product. It enables managers to recognize that changes in the demand for activity resources must be followed by corresponding changes in the expenditures to supply resources to perform the activities.

EXHIBIT 4-27
Global Glass Company
Setup and Quality Inspection Expenditures

Expense	Setup Activity			Quality Inspection		
	Week 1	Week 2	Week 3	Week 1	Week 2	Week 3
Number of workers employed	10	10	10	52	52	52
Total number of hours available per week (*Number of Workers* × 36)	360	360	360	1,872	1,872	1,872
Total number of hours required (see Exhibits 4-25, 4-26)	340	368	374	1,840	1,940	1,920
Idle time hours (*Hours Available − Hours Required*, if positive; otherwise zero)	20	0	0	32	0	0
Resource shortage hours (*Hours Required − Hours Available*, if positive; otherwise zero)	0	8	14	0	68	48
(10 setup workers × 720 weekly wages, and 52 inspections × 630 weekly wages)	$7,200	$7,200	$7,200	$32,760	$32,760	$32,760

Recall our previous definition of normal unit cost as the average cost at the point where activity demand equals available capacity. In other words, the *normal activity cost* of a product measures the demand placed by the product for the resources required to perform an activity charged at the normal unit cost rate for that activity. Exhibit 4-28 presents the normal unit costs for the activity resources (setup and quality inspection) required by the sizes of bottles that Global Glass produces. Because wages of $720 are paid weekly for a capacity of 36 hours for setups, the normal cost per setup hour is $20 ($720 ÷ 36). To manufacture 100,000 two-ounce bottles in batch sizes of 10,000, we need 10 (100,000 ÷ 10,000) batches. Each batch setup requires 2.2 hours. (See Exhibit 4-23). Therefore, the normal cost of setup activity for 100,000 two-ounce bottles is $440 (2.2 hours per setup × 10 batches × $20 setup cost per hour). We determine the normal costs for the quality-inspection activity in a similar manner. Each hour of quality inspection costs $17.50 ($630 ÷ 36 hours available). Because two-ounce bottles are inspected at the rate of 1250 each hour it requires 80 hours ($100,000 ÷ 1,250) to inspect 100,000 two-ounce bottles. (See Exhibit 4-23.) Therefore, the normal cost of the quality-inspection activity required to manufacture 100,000, two-ounce bottles is $1400 (80 hours × $17.50 per hour).

C ONSIDER THIS . . .

Nursing Activity Resource Consumption Model at Braintree Hospital

Braintree Hospital is a private rehabilitation hospital providing in-patient and out-patient treatment. It is one of the largest rehabilitation network care providers in the United States with 168 beds on site.

Patients entering with physical disabilities due to neurological and orthopedic disease or injury are normally diagnosed as having one of the following: stroke, spinal cord injury, congenital deformity, amputation, major multiple trauma, femur fracture, brain injury, polyarthritis and joint replacement, neurological disorders, burns, and neoplasms. The patient's average stay is approximately 21 days, during which time the individual progresses through a comprehensive program aimed at restoring and maintaining functional abilities.

Traditionally, the cost of nursing is factored into the daily room charge for a hospital. For example, a rate of $500 to $800 per day covers the 24-hour nursing availability for the patient. Nursing expenses, primarily labor costs, are part of the cost driver rate included in the patient's daily bill. The same fixed charges are applied to all patients.

The problem with this typical convention is that not all patients use nursing services in equal amounts. As a result, fixed charges are not always related to the nursing services that individual patients utilize. Further, nursing services are available on call to handle possible patient emergencies, and their value is not readily identifiable with individual patients.

Typically, nursing services in the hospital comprise a varied skill mix: professional registered nurses (RNs), licensed practical nurses (LPNs), and ancillary nursing assistants (NAs). These professionals have different levels of education, training, and hospital experience. Teams of nurses administer medication, maintain daily patient records, assist the physicians with medical care, monitor medical devices, conduct routine tests, and so on. They are responsible for the routine jobs of feeding and bathing the patients, ensuring their safety, and most importantly providing them personal care and comfort.

The professional RN is licensed to perform all of the many nursing functions in the hospital but usually concentrates on the more seriously ill or demanding patients. The other nursing team members normally work with the RNs to deliver care to their group of patients. Thus, a team with varying skill levels delivers the array of nursing services. There is a hierarchy of nursing from the RN to the NA with pay scales ranging from $26 per hour to $8 per hour depending on specific position, skills, and education.

The amount of nursing services required by different patients varies widely, which the health care industry has now recognized. Third-party payers (including insurance companies and Medicare) are demanding that they pay only for the services actually used by the patient and at the lowest price.

Mary-Jean Crockett, vice president of nursing, recognized that nursing service delivery needed to be understood better. She was determined to find an easy, reliable, and fair method to ascertain the amount, mix, and resulting cost of nursing services consumed by individual patients. She also wanted a more accurate approach to forecasting the skills mix required in the care of patients within particular diagnostic groups.

After conducting a detailed process analysis, Mary-Jean and her staff team determined that routine events such as performing vital sign tests, administering medication, and changing beds were easy to predict. The percent of baseline routine nursing time could vary from 5% to 70% depending on the medical problem and length of hospital stay. For example, a new brain-injury patient requires constant care, and routine nursing may account for just 5% of the total daily nursing services consumed. A burn patient about to be discharged may be quite self-sufficient, but routine care may represent 70% of the total daily nursing services consumed. The staff team believed that nonroutine events were the drivers behind the varying levels of the nursing services consumed each day.

The team amassed detailed daily data over a period of several months on the amount and type of service provided by each nurse to individual patients classified by their diagnostic groups. A further analysis of these data demonstrated that the consumption of nursing services is a function of both patient diagnosis and the length of hospital stay. Most patients have a large consumption of nursing services during the initial period of their stay and over time the consumption declines.

A matrix was built and all the activities performed by various skill levels were determined for each category of patient illness and tracked over the length of hospital stay by patient category. The team had developed the *nursing activity resource consumption model* for the hospital, which was a model of the activities consumed by each patient by category, detailing the amount of nursing services from each nursing skill level. Patient load and mix projections could be translated into nursing resource consumption patterns. This information changed the economic focus of the managers from simply filling beds to seeking those patients who have a consumption pattern compatible with the available mix of nursing services. Managers now adjusted the nursing mix for the forecasted consumption level. Armed with these new cost data, the hospital could also unbundle the previously fixed single nursing services charge and negotiate rate and fees with the third-party payers depending on actual circumstances.

Source: Lawrence P. Carr, "Unbundling the Cost of Hospitalization," *Management Accounting*, November 1993, pp. 43–48.

EXHIBIT 4-28
Global Glass Company
Normal Activity Costs

Bottle Size	Normal Costs Per 100,000 Bottles	
	Setup Activity	Quality Inspection
2 ounces	$440 (2.2 × 10 × $720 ÷ 36)	$1,400 (80 × $630 ÷ 36)
4 ounces	$200 (2 × 5 × $720 ÷ 36)	$1,400 (80 × $630 ÷ 36)
6 ounces	$320 (2 × 8 × $720 ÷ 36)	$1,750 (100 × $630 ÷ 36)

Chapter 6 extends this discussion by showing that activity-based costing systems determine product costs by aggregating normal costs over *all* the activities required to support the production of each product.

Breakeven Analysis of Committed Resources

We can apply breakeven analysis to decisions about the quantity of committed resources to supply. Consider Carex Muffler Company, which is trying to decide whether to employ seven or eight mechanics. What is the number of daily jobs at

As demand for products increased, Ball Corporation added a fourth beverage can manufacturing line in this plant. The line can make 2,000 cans per minute. The cost of resources committed to this fourth line was traded off against the contribution earned from the additional cans manufactured on this line. *Courtesy* Ball Corporation

which managers are indifferent about whether seven or eight mechanics are sup-plied?[9] This is the breakeven number of jobs for this decision.

To answer this question, let Q denote the number of daily jobs. Recall that each mechanic can service 10 jobs in a day. If there are fewer than 70 jobs in a day, evidently no more than seven mechanics need be employed. If there are more than 80 jobs in a day, eight mechanics must be employed to minimize overtime work. We shall consider, therefore, Q between 70 and 80 ($70 < Q < 80$) to find the value Q^0 at which the costs for the two alternatives (employing seven or eight mechanics) are equal. Note that revenues from Q jobs are the same whether seven or eight mechanics are employed.

If eight mechanics are employed and Q is less than 80, there will be idle time and the direct labor cost will only be the committed regular wages for the eight mechanics. Costs, or C, would be this:

$$
\begin{aligned}
C &= \$30 \text{ per hour} \times 8 \text{ hours} \times 8 \text{ workers} \qquad (4\text{-}10) \\
&= \$1920 \text{ when } N = 8
\end{aligned}
$$

If seven mechanics are employed and Q is greater than 70, $[(0.75 \text{ hours per job} \times Q) - (7.5 \text{ hours per day} \times 7 \text{ mechanics})]$ hours of overtime will be required. Following our earlier analysis, we can write the direct labor cost as this:

$$
\begin{aligned}
C &= (\$30 \times 8 \times 7) + (1.5 \times \$30)[(0.75 \times Q) - (7.5 \times 7)] \\
&= \$1680 + [(\$33.75 \times Q) - \$2362.50] \qquad (4\text{-}11) \\
&= (\$33.75 \times Q) - \$682.50) \text{ when } N = 7
\end{aligned}
$$

At the breakeven point, Q^0, the two cost expressions are equal. Therefore, the following applies:

$$
\begin{aligned}
(\$33.75 \times Q^0) - \$682.50 &= \$1920 \\
\$33.75 \times Q^0 &= \$1920 + \$682.50 \\
\$33.75 \times Q^0 &= \$2602.50 \\
Q^0 &= \$2602.50 \div \$33.75 \\
&= 77.11
\end{aligned}
$$

The two cost expressions are graphed in Exhibit 4-29, which also depicts the breakeven point (77.11) as the point of intersection of the two graphs.

The breakeven analysis indicates that if 77 or fewer orders are expected on any particular day, only seven or fewer mechanics should be employed; if 78 or more orders are expected, eight or more mechanics should be employed. Break-even analysis in this case helps managers choose between supplying additional quantities of resources (increasing the amount of fixed costs) or paying higher variable costs (due to overtime pay) should a high level of demand be realized.

A SUMMARY EXAMPLE

Let's consider some of this chapter's key points by working through the following problem.

---

[9] The output (number of jobs) and therefore the revenues under both options are the same. Consequently, the comparison of profits to determine the breakeven point reduces to a comparison of only the costs in this case.

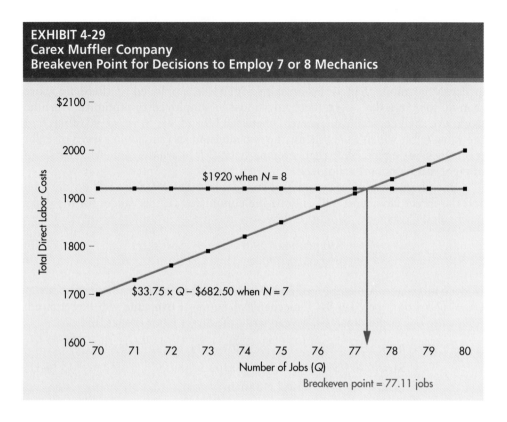

EXHIBIT 4-29
Carex Muffler Company
Breakeven Point for Decisions to Employ 7 or 8 Mechanics

$1920 when N = 8

$33.75 x Q − $682.50 when N = 7

Total Direct Labor Costs

Number of Jobs (Q)

Breakeven point = 77.11 jobs

Bob's Barber Shop offers two types of haircuts: regular and special. Bob employs 10 full-time hairdressers who work eight hours on Saturdays and Sundays and six hours on Tuesdays, Wednesdays, Thursdays, and Fridays. The shop is closed on Mondays. Average weekly wages including fringe benefits are $400 per week. If the workload on any day exceeds the available staff time, however, some hairdressers are asked to work overtime. The overtime wage rate is $15 per hour. Each regular haircut takes 30 minutes, and each special haircut takes 60 minutes.

The following information pertains to the expected demand for the two types of haircuts:

BOB'S BARBER SHOP
EXPECTED DEMAND FOR HAIRCUTS

Day	Regular	Special
Weekdays (except Monday)	44	25
Saturday	56	45
Sunday	66	59

(a) Determine the idle time (in terms of hairdresser labor hours) or overtime that is expected each day.
(b) Determine the total weekly hairdresser labor costs to service the expected demand with the present staffing levels.
(c) Determine the staffing levels that will minimize the labor cost for servicing the expected demand. Assume that the shop remains closed on Mon-

days but that the number of full-time hairdressers (working 40 hours per week) can be changed, as can the number of hours assigned to each day, although the weekly total must be 40 hours per week per hairdresser.

The following is the solution to this problem.

(a)

Day	Hours Available	Hours Required	Idle Hours	Overtime Hours
Weekdays (except Monday)	60 (10 × 6)	47 (44 × 0.5 + 25)	13	0
Saturday	80 (10 × 8)	73 (56 × 0.5 + 45)	7	0
Sunday	80 (10 × 8)	92 (66 × 0.5 + 59)	0	12

(b) Regular wages $4000   ($400 × 10)

     Overtime costs   180   ($15 × 12)

     Total weekly labor costs $4,180

(c) Expected total demand: 353 hours   [(47 × 4) + 73 + 92]

     Full-time equivalents: 8.825 hairdressers   (353 ÷ 40)

(Full-time equivalents are determined based on the regular work time of 40 hours per worker).

Overtime wages at $15 per hour will exceed the weekly wages ($400) of an additional hairdresser if the number of overtime hours exceeds 26.667 ($400 ÷ $15) or equivalently overtime exceeds 0.667 ($26.67 ÷ $40) full-time equivalent hairdressers. Because 0.825 is larger than 0.667, Bob is better off hiring the additional hairdresser. Therefore, he should hire nine full-time hairdressers to minimize the labor cost to service the expected demand.

SUMMARY

Managers need to understand the behavior of costs so that they can estimate the impact of their decisions. A number of factors, including the range of activity levels and time frames, influences the way costs behave. The flexibility available to managers in adjusting the quantity of activity resources supplied to match the demand placed on them determines the variability of different types of costs.

In hiring personnel to work machines or support production, managers commit to capacities for performing various production activities. These capacity decisions determine the expenditure levels for the activities. These expenditures will not change based on actual activity volumes; that is, they represent fixed costs. In contrast, the quantity of resources that are used as opposed to committed during the period depends on the actual volume of production. However, since the quantity of resources committed is not always the same as the quantity of resources used, expenditures on activity resources do not necessarily vary with actual volume of production. An exception is resources, such as direct materials, that are supplied only as used and therefore represent variable costs.

Understanding the relationships between production, activity use, and expenditure enables managers to develop planning models and perform breakeven analysis. The breakeven point is the production level at which sales revenue exactly equals the fixed and variable costs. Breakeven analysis is useful for evaluating company alternatives and the changes in profitability with changes in production and sales activity levels.

KEY TERMS

breakeven point, p. 142

capacity constraints, p. 150

committed resources, p. 173

contribution margin per unit, p. 152

contribution margin ratio, p. 155

cost behavior, p. 171

cost curve, p. 149

discretionary costs, p. 172

diseconomies of scale, p. 150

economies of scale, p. 150

fixed costs, p. 142

flexible resources, p. 172

mixed costs, p. 147

normal unit costs, p. 166

relevant range, p. 150

step fixed costs, p. 151

step variable costs, p. 151

variable costs, p. 142

ASSIGNMENT MATERIAL

■ QUESTIONS

4-1 Why are a firm's profits more sensitive to demand fluctuations when a high proportion of its costs are fixed?

4-2 "Variable cost per unit remains the same for different levels of production, but fixed cost per unit decreases with increases in production." Do you agree with this statement? Explain.

4-3 How can you reconcile the economist's representation of costs as an inverted S-shaped curve with the accountant's representation of costs as a straight line?

4-4 What is the linear equation representing cost in terms of volume of production? What are each of the components of the equation?

4-5 What is the difference between discretionary and committed costs?

4-6 How does each of the following costs change with increases in the volume of production?
(a) Total variable cost
(b) Total fixed cost
(c) Variable cost per unit produced
(d) Fixed cost per unit produced

4-7 What does the term *relevant range* mean? Why is it important to consider what the relevant range is in individual applications?

4-8 What is the difference between each of these five cost terms?
(a) Fixed costs
(b) Variable costs
(c) Mixed costs
(d) Step fixed costs
(e) Step variable costs.
Illustrate your answer.

4-9 What does the term *contribution margin* per unit mean? How is contribution margin used in cost analysis to support managerial decisions?

4-10 What does the term *breakeven point* mean?

4-11 "Sales force compensation can be a fixed cost or a variable cost." Do you agree with this statement? Explain.

4-12 "Direct costs are always variable costs." Do you agree with this statement? Explain.

4-13 Why are unit-related support costs likely to be considered variable costs?

4-14 Why are facility-sustaining support costs likely to be considered fixed costs?

4-15 What is the difference between step fixed and step variable costs? Give an example of each type of cost.

4-16 "Presence of idle time and overtime indicates that direct labor is not a variable cost in the short run." Do you agree with this statement?

4-17 Activity resources are committed in advance, leading to idle time or overtime when the demand placed on activity resources is *realized*. When is the average cost of the activity the lowest in these circumstances?

4-18 Why are activity costs more likely to be variable when managers have greater flexibility in adjusting the level of resources committed for the activity?

4-19 Why is there often a delay before activity resources are adjusted downward in response to a permanent decline in the demand placed on them?

4-20 "Activity-based costs measuring the demand placed on activity resources are not good measures to help when budgeting for related activity expenses." Do you agree with this statement? Explain.

■ EXERCISES

4-21 *Classification of cost behavior*   Classify each of the following as a variable, fixed, or mixed cost.
(a) Salaries of production supervisors
(b) Wages of production workers
(c) Salary of the chief executive officer
(d) Charges for janitorial services
(e) Commissions paid to sales personnel
(f) Advertising expenses
(g) Salaries of billing clerks
(h) Electricity used to operate machines
(i) Lubricants for machines
(j) Maintenance for machines

4-22 *Classification of cost behavior*   Classify each of the following as a variable, fixed, or mixed cost.
(a) Paper used in newspaper production
(b) Steel used in automobile production
(c) Wood used in furniture production
(d) Glue used in furniture production
(e) Depreciation of factory equipment
(f) Depreciation of shipping truck
(g) Gasoline used to deliver products
(h) Boxes used for packing products
(i) Rent for factory building
(j) Factory insurance

4-23 *Breakeven price*   The Metropolitan Museum of Art in New York is organizing a special five-week exhibition of a collection of Henri Matisse's work. Insurance, security, utilities, and other facility-related costs total $20,000 per day. Costs of setting up the exhibit and transporting the works of art are $350,000. The museum expects an average of 6000 visitors a day to view this exhibit. Determine the amount the museum must charge each patron to break even.

4-24 *Contribution margin analysis*   Packer Parkas Company budgets sales revenues at $900,000, variable costs at $585,000, and fixed costs at $140,000 for the year 1997.

REQUIRED

(a) What is Packer's contribution margin ratio?
(b) Determine the sales revenue it must generate to break even.
(c) Determine the sales revenue required to earn (pretax) income equal to 20% of revenue.
(d) Packer is considering increasing its advertising expenses by $38,500. How much of an increase in sales is necessary from expanded advertising to justify this expenditure?

4-25 *Support cost evaluation* Omega Corporation uses the following equation to estimate support costs based only on direct labor hours (*DLH*):

$$Support\ Costs\ =\ \$800,\!000\ +\ (\$40 \times DLH)$$

A consultant has developed the following alternative equation that recognizes machine-hours (MH) also as a cost driver:

$$Support\ Costs\ =\ \$500,\!000\ +\ (\$35 \times DLH)\ +\ (\$60 \times MH)$$

Data for two recent months include the following:

Hours	February	April
Direct labor hours	7500	6000
Machine hours	5000	5500

REQUIRED

(a) Estimate the total support costs for the two months using the equation based on *DLH*.
(b) Estimate the total support costs for the two months using the new equation.
(c) How did the fixed support costs change in the new equation? Why?
(d) Compare the two equations to explain the *direction* of the difference in the estimated support costs with these equations.

4-26 *Support cost equation* The activity costs for Parker's Pizza Shop in March 1997 include the following:

Cost Item	Cost Driver Quantity	Cost Driver Rate	Total
Dough	1200 lb	$ 0.25	$ 300
Other ingredients	600 lb	0.60	360
Energy	120 kwh	0.20	24
Kitchen personnel	240 hrs	8.00	1920
Delivery personnel	360 hrs	6.00	2160
Car expenses	2 cars	2000.00	4000
Facility expenses	300 sq ft	12.00	3600
Total costs			$12,364

Parker's Pizza sold 1200 pizzas in March 1997 at the average price of $11 per pizza.

REQUIRED

(a) Classify the preceding costs as fixed or variable costs.
(b) Based on your classification of the costs, determine the values for *F* and *V* in the following cost equation:

$$Total\ Costs\ =\ F\ +\ (V \times Number\ of\ Pizzas)$$

4-27 *Actual versus normal costs* Hiawatha Company manufactures three products: HW1, HW2, and HW3. Support activities include setting up the machines and packing the finished product. The plant employs five setup workers and 10 packing workers. Each worker can work up to 40 hours a week. However, overtime work is performed, if necessary, to meet actual work load demand.

The average hourly wages are $20 including fringe benefits. The overtime premium is 50% of regular wages. Demand for setup and packing labor varies by the type of product produced. Detailed data for each product include the following:

Product	Hours per Setup	Batch Size	Units Packed per Hour
HW1	2	5,000	2,000
HW2	3	20,000	5,000
HW3	4	25,000	2,000

The actual production data for the first two weeks of January 1998 follow:

	Units Manufactured	
Product	Week 1	Week 2
HW1	100,000	120,000
HW2	600,000	400,000
HW3	500,000	500,000

REQUIRED

(a) Prepare a schedule of actual costs of the two support activities for the first two weeks of January 1998.

(b) Compare the actual average costs of the support activities with their normal costs.

4-28 *Comparison of alternative cost behavior*   Jeren Company is considering replacing its existing cutting machine with a new machine that will help reduce its defect rate. Relevant information for the two machines includes the following:

Cost Item	Existing Machine	New Machine
Monthly fixed costs	$32,000	$40,000
Variable cost per unit	44	40
Sales price per unit	55	55

REQUIRED

(a) Determine the sales level, in number of units, at which the costs are the same for both machines.

(b) Determine the sales level in dollars at which the use of the new machine results in a 10% profit on sales (Profit/Sales) ratio.

4-29 *Cost variability and decision context*   Second City Airlines operates 35 scheduled round-trip flights between New York and Chicago each week. It charges a fixed one-way fare of $140 per passenger. Second City Airlines can carry 150 passengers per flight. Fuel and other flight-related costs are $5000 per flight. On-flight meal costs are $5 per passenger. Sales commissions averaging 5% of sales is paid to travel agents. Flying crew, ground crew, advertising, and other administrative expenditures for the New York-Chicago route amount to $400,000 each week.

REQUIRED

(a) How many passengers must each of the 70 one-way flights have on average to make a total profit of $180,000?

(b) If the load factor is 60% on all flights, how many flights must Second City Airlines operate on this route to earn a total profit of $80,000?

(c) Are fuel costs variable or fixed?

4-30 *Capacity level and contribution analysis*   Extel Corporation's Wedmark, California, plant manufactures chips used in PC486 computers. Its installed capacity is 2000 chips per week. The selling price is $100 per chip. Production this quarter is 1600 chips per week. Total costs of production this week at 80% of capacity level comprise $75,000 of fixed costs and $80,000 of variable costs.

REQUIRED

(a) At what level of activity will the plant break even?
(b) What will the plant's profit be if it operates at capacity?
(c) If the plant's accounting system reports fixed cost per unit using its installed capacity level as the base, what is the reported cost per unit?
(d) Suppose that a new customer offers $80 per chip for an order of 200 chips per week for delivery beginning this quarter. If this order is accepted, production will increase from 1600 chips at present to 1800 chips per week. Should the company accept the order?

4-31 *Comparison of alternative choices*   Seattle Sonic Company has recently developed a new product, SUPER79. It is debating whether to (1) establish its own distribution network or (2) engage independent sales agents to market the new product.

The information pertaining to the two options includes the following:

Cost Item	Establish Own Network	Engage Sales Agents
Sales commission	5%	20%
Annual fixed selling expenses	$300,000	$0

The selling price of SUPER79 is targeted to be $20 per unit. Unit variable manufacturing cost is $9 and fixed manufacturing cost is $900,000.

REQUIRED

(a) Determine Seattle Sonic Company's estimated breakeven point for its SUPER79 operations under each of the two options for marketing the product.
(b) Which of the two options should Seattle Sonic Company adopt to market SUPER79? Why?

■ PROBLEMS

Fundamental Problems

4-32 *Comparison of alternative cost behavior*   Premier Products, Inc., is considering replacing its existing machine with a new faster machine that will produce a more reliable product and will turn around customer orders in a shorter period. This change is expected to increase the sales price and fixed costs but not the variable costs.

Cost Item	Old Machine	New Machine
Monthly fixed costs	$120,000	$250,000
Variable cost per unit	14	14
Sales price per unit	18	20

REQUIRED

(a) Determine the breakeven point *in units* for the two machines.

(b) Determine the sales level *in units* at which the use of the *new* machine will achieve a 10% target profit-to-sales ratio.

(c) Determine the sales level *in units* at which profits will be the same for either the old or the new machine.

(d) Which machine represents a lower risk of incurring a loss? Explain why.

(e) Determine the sales level *in units* at which the profit-to-sales ratio will be equal with either machine.

4-33 *Contribution margin analysis*   Tenneco, Inc., produces three models of tennis rackets: standard, deluxe, and pro. Sales and cost information for 1997 follows:

Item	Standard	Deluxe	Pro
Sales (in units)	100,000	50,000	50,000
Sales price per unit	$30	$40	$50
Variable manufacturing cost per unit	$17	$20	$25

Fixed manufacturing support costs are $800,000, and fixed selling and administrative costs are $400,000. In addition, the company pays its sales representatives a commission equal to 10% of the price of each racket sold.

REQUIRED

(a) If the sales price of deluxe rackets decreases by 10%, its sales are expected to increase 30%, but sales of standard rackets are expected to decrease by 5% as some potential buyers of standard rackets will upgrade to deluxe rackets. What will be the impact of this decision on Tenneco's profits?

(b) Ignore Part (a). Suppose that Tenneco decides to increase its advertising by $50,000 instead of cutting the price of standard rackets. This is expected to increase sales of all three models by 2% each. Is this decision advisable?

(c) The incentive created by sales commissions has led Tenneco's sales force to push the higher-priced rackets more than the lower-priced ones. Is this in the best interest of the company?

4-34 *Contribution margin and breakeven analysis*   The following information pertains to Torasic Company's budgeted income statement for the month of June 1998:

Sales (1200 units @ $250)	$300,000
Variable cost	−150,000
Contribution margin	$150,000
Fixed cost	−200,000
Net loss	($50,000)

REQUIRED

(a) Determine the company's breakeven point in both units and dollars.

(b) The sales manager believes that a $22,500 increase in the monthly advertising expenses will result in a considerable increase in sales. How much of an increase in sales must result from increased advertising to justify this expenditure?

(c) The sales manager believes that an advertising expenditure increase of $22,500 coupled with a 10% reduction in the selling price will double the sales quantity. Determine the net income (or loss) if these proposed changes are adopted.

4-35 *Commitment and consumption of activity resources*   Classic Containers Company specializes in making high-quality customized containers to order. Its agreement with the labor union ensures employment for all its employees and a fixed payroll of

$80,000 per month including fringe benefits. This payroll makes available 4000 labor hours each month to work on orders the firm receives. The monthly wages must be paid even if the workers remain idle due to lack of work. If additional labor hours are required to complete jobs, overtime costs $30 per labor hour.

Each job requires four labor hours for machine setup and 0.05 labor hours per container. Variable costs comprise $1.60 per container for materials and $8.00 per labor hour for support expenses (energy, maintenance, and so forth). In addition, the firm must pay $20,000 per month for selling, general, and administrative expenses and $36,000 per month lease payments for machinery and physical facilities.

In April 1997, the firm won 90 orders, of which 60 were for 800 containers each and 30 were for 1600 containers each. Determine the total costs for April.

4-36 *Contribution and breakeven analysis*   Air Peanut Company manufactures and sells roasted peanut packets to commercial airlines. Price and cost data per 100 packets of peanuts follow:

Estimated annual sales volume = 11,535,700 packets

Selling price	$35.00
Variable costs:	
Raw materials	$16.00
Direct labor	7.00
Manufacturing support	4.00
Selling expenses	1.60
Total variable costs per batch	$28.60
Annual fixed costs:	
Manufacturing support	$192,000
Selling and administrative	276,000
Total fixed costs	$468,000

REQUIRED

(a) Determine Air Peanut's breakeven point.
(b) How many packets does Air Peanut have to sell to earn $156,000?
(c) Air Peanut expects its direct labor costs to increase by 5% next year. How many units will it have to sell next year to break even if the selling price remains unchanged?
(d) If Air Peanut's direct labor costs increase by 5%, what selling price must it charge to maintain the same contribution margin to sales ratio?

Challenging Problems

4-37 *Cost behavior in a hospital*   Magnolia Medical Institute operates a 100-bed hospital and offers a number of specialized medical services. Because of the reputation Magnolia has developed over the years, demand for these services is strong. Magnolia's hospital facility and equipment are leased on a long-term basis.

The hospital charges $100 per patient day. During November 1997, the total service volume at the hospital was measured as 2000 patient days. During December 1997, the service volume was 2300 patient days. Costs for November and December follow:

Month	November	December
Number of Patient Days	2,000	2,300
Costs:		
Wages, nurses	$ 28,600	$ 32,890
Wages, aides	11,400	12,660
Laboratory	18,400	20,260
Pharmacy	25,000	28,750
Laundry	17,000	19,550
Administration	22,000	22,000
Facility and equipment	60,000	60,000
Total costs	$182,400	$194,010

Magnolia Medical Clinic estimates the cost of each of these activities by using a linear equation of this form:

$$Cost = F + V \times Number\ of\ Patient\ Days$$

REQUIRED

(a) Classify each cost as fixed, variable, or mixed.
(b) Determine the values of the parameters F and V for each of the seven activities.
(c) The hospital's administrator has estimated that the hospital will average 2300 patient days per month. How much will the hospital need to charge per patient day to break even at this level of activity?

4-38 *Cost structure and competitive strategy* Alpha Corporation and Beta Corporation compete directly against each other, selling the same product of identical quality but employing different manufacturing processes and selling methods. The estimated costs and prices for the two firms follow:

Prices/Costs	Alpha Corporation	Beta Corporation
Sales price per unit	$9.00	$8.00
Direct materials costs per unit	$1.90	$2.25
Direct labor costs per unit	$1.25	$2.40
Variable manufacturing support per unit	$1.10	$1.15
Fixed manufacturing support costs	$675,000	$450,000
Advertising and fixed selling costs	$350,000	$400,000
Sales commission	4% of price	0
Sales units (number of)	350,000	400,000
Capacity units (number of)	500,000	400,000

REQUIRED

(a) Determine the estimated breakeven points in annual sales units for the two firms.
(b) Determine the annual sales volume at which the two firms have the same manufacturing costs. Explain the circumstances under which one of the two firms enjoys a competitive cost advantage.
(c) How low can Alpha Corporation price its product and still break even, assuming that its sales volume stays at its existing level?
(d) Recommend a coherent competitive strategy for Alpha Corporation. Explain your answer by critically evaluating Alpha's current strategy.

4-39 *Multiple breakeven points* In September 1997, Capetini Capacitor Company sold capacitors to its distributors for $250 per capacitor. The sales level of 3000 capacitors per month was less than the single-shift capacity of 4400 capacitors at its plant located in San Diego, California. Variable production costs were $100 per capacitor, and fixed production costs were $200,000 per month. In addition, variable selling and distribution support costs are $20 per capacitor and fixed selling and distribution support costs are $62,500 per month.

At the suggestion of the marketing department, Capetini reduced the sales price to $200 in October 1997 and increased the monthly advertising budget by $17,500. Sales are expected to increase to 6800 capacitors per month. If the demand exceeds the single-shift capacity of 4400 capacitors, the plant needs to be operated in two shifts. Two-shift operation will increase monthly fixed production costs to $310,000.

REQUIRED

(a) Determine the contribution margin per capacitor in September 1997.
(b) Determine the sales level *in number of capacitors* at which the profit-to-sales ratio would be 10%.
(c) Determine the two breakeven points for October 1997.
(d) Determine the sales level *in number of capacitors* at which the profit-to-sales ratio in October is the same as the actual profit-to-sales ratio in September. Is there more than one possible sales level at which this equality would occur?

4-40 *Actual versus normal costs*   The billing department of Union Credit Card Company in Wilmington, Delaware, employs 20 workers on a weekly basis. They are each paid $600 for 40 hours per week. Each worker can handle 12 billings per hour on average. If the number of billings requires more than the available number of labor hours, overtime work is scheduled. A 50% overtime premium is paid in addition to regular wage. Workload information for the first eight weeks of 1998 follows:

Week	Number of Billings
1	10,080
2	9,060
3	11,240
4	8,320
5	12,720
6	10,220
7	9,880
8	8,790

REQUIRED

(a) Determine the normal unit cost per billing.
(b) Graph the total billing costs as a function of the number of billings for the first eight weeks of operation in 1997.
(c) Graph the average cost per billing as a function of the number of billings for the first eight weeks of operation in 1997.

4-41 *Commitment of activity resources*   Crown Cable Company provides cable television service in the Richfield metropolitan area. The company hires only full-time service persons working 40 hours a week at $18 per hour including fringe benefits. Service persons handle additional service demand by working overtime at the rate of $24 per hour. The service manager uses standards for estimating the workload and staffing requirements. Each service person can handle an average of six calls in an eight-hour work day. The estimated number of service calls for the first three weeks of October 1997 follow:

Week	Service Calls
1	1280
2	1340
3	1200

REQUIRED

(a) Determine the number of service persons that will be hired in each of these three weeks to minimize costs.

(b) Estimate the service labor cost for each of the three weeks.

(c) Suppose that the company cannot change the staffing level from week to week. Estimate the service labor costs assuming that the same number (38, 39, 40, 41, 42, 43, 44, or 45) of workers is hired for all three weeks. How much do costs increase under this restriction?

4-42 *Actual versus normal costs*   Allegheny Medical Clinic is a county-owned facility that provides outpatient services to the residents of Allegheny County five days a week. It formerly employed eight full-time nurses and 15 full-time aides in annual contracts. Average wages have remained at $500 and $300 per week in the past two years for nurses and aides, respectively. Because of recent budget cuts, clinic management has cut back two nurse and three aide positions. It employs temporary workers in months when higher workloads are anticipated.

Each patient must be serviced by both a nurse and an aide. On average, a regular nurse can service 20 outpatients in a day. Each outpatient visit also requires aides' service time. Each regular aide can service on average 10 outpatients in a day. Temporary workers are paid the same average daily wages as regular nurses and aides but they are not as efficient. They can service on average 20% fewer outpatients than regular workers.

The following information pertains to the first three months of 1997:

ALLEGHENY MEDICAL CLINIC PERSONNEL NEEDS
FOR FIRST QUARTER 1997

| | Regular | | Temporary | | Average Patient |
Month	Nurses	Aides	Nurses	Aides	Visits Per Day
January	6	12	1	2	130
February	6	12	0	0	120
March	6	12	2	4	145

Determine the normal and actual cost per patient visit for each month.

4-43 *Multiple breakeven points*   In October 1996, Saldanha Sports Company sold soccer balls to its distributors for $18 each. The sales level of 40,000 soccer balls was less than the single shift capacity of 50,000 soccer balls at their plant in Granville, South Carolina.

These are the costs for October 1996:

Direct labor costs	$	2 per ball
Direct materials costs		4 per ball
Variable manufacturing support costs		3 per ball
Fixed manufacturing support costs		122,000 per month
Variable selling and administrative costs		2 per ball
Fixed selling and administrative costs		52,200 per month

REQUIRED

(a) Compute the contribution margin per soccer ball in October 1996.

(b) Compute the gross margin per soccer ball in October 1996.

(c) Compute the sales level in number of soccer balls at which the profit on sales is 10%.

The marketing manager has decided to reduce the price to $16.75 per soccer ball for November 1996 and increase the monthly advertising budget by $17,275. The expectation is that these actions will increase sales to 63,000 soccer balls. If sales exceed

50,000 soccer balls, the plant will need to operate two shifts and the fixed manufacturing costs will increase to $232,400.

REQUIRED

  (d) Compute the two breakeven points for November 1996.
  (e) Compute the sales level in number of soccer balls at which the profit under the new marketing plan, is $32,775. Is there more than one possible sales level at which the profit is $32,775?

4-44 *Multiple breakeven points* The aluminum can industry experiences large fluctuations in production and sales because of the seasonal nature of the food products that are canned. Tom Jenkins, the manager of the Fresno, California plant of Canalum Company has projected the following costs corresponding to production volumes of 20,000 and 50,000 cans:

CANALUM COMPANY
COSTS VERSUS PRODUCTION LEVELS

	Production Levels	
Cost Category	20,000 cans	50,000 cans
Direct material	$ 60,000	$150,000
Direct labor	100,000	250,000
Depreciation	85,000	85,000
Indirect labor	70,000	160,000
Power costs	40,000	100,000
Supervision*	50,000	50,000

*The capacity of a single eight-hour shift is 60,000 cans per month. If a second shift is added, supervisory costs will increase by $35,000.

The Canalum Company estimates the cost of each of these activities by using linear equations of the following form:

$$Cost = F + (V \times Number\ of\ Cans)$$

REQUIRED

  (a) Classify each cost as fixed, variable, mixed, or step fixed.
  (b) Determine the values of the parameters F and V for each of the six cost categories.
  (c) Estimate the total manufacturing costs for production volumes of 60,000, 90,000 and 110,000 cans.

4-45 (Adapted from CPA November 1993) *Multiple breakeven points* Green Company is a medical laboratory that performs tests for patients referred by physicians. Green anticipates performing up to 12,000 tests during the month of October 1996. Relevant information is as follows:

At the low range of activity (0 to 5999 tests performed):

Sales price per test	$	120
Variable costs per test		40
Fixed costs		320,000

At the high range of activity (6000 to 12,000 tests performed):

Sales price per test	$	120
Variable costs per test		40
Fixed costs		560,000

Compared to industry averages for laboratories operating at the low range of activity, Green has a lower sales price per test, higher fixed costs, and the same breakeven point in the number of tests performed. At the high range of activity, Green's sales price per test and fixed costs are the same as industry averages, and Green's variable costs are lower.

REQUIRED

(a) Classify each of the following costs as fixed or variable and categorize it as one of the following: (1) direct materials costs, (2) direct labor costs, (3) support costs for laboratory testing, or (4) general and administrative costs.

Office manager's salary
Cost of electricity to run laboratory equipment
Hourly wages of part-time technicians who perform tests
Cost of lubricant used on laboratory equipment
Cost of distilled water used in tests
Depreciation on laboratory equipment
Depreciation on laboratory building
Cost of expensive binders in which test results are given to physicians

(b) Determine the contribution margin per test.
(c) Determine the two breakeven points in number of tests for October 1996.
(d) Determine the sales level in number of tests performed to achieve a target profit of $200,000.
(e) Determine if each of the following items for Green Company is greater than, less than, or the same as the industry average.

Variable costs at low activity range
Contribution margin at high activity range
Breakeven point at high activity range

4-46 *Contribution margin analysis*   The Monteiro Manufacturing Corporation manufactures and sells folding umbrellas. The corporation's condensed income statement for 1996 follows:

Sales (200,000 units)		$1,000,000
Cost of goods sold		600,000
Gross margin		400,000
Selling expenses	$150,000	
Administrative expenses	100,000	250,000
Net profit (before income taxes)		$ 150,000

Monteiro's budget committee has estimated the following changes for 1997:

30% increase in number of units sold
20% increase in material cost per unit
15% increase in direct labor cost per unit
10% increase in variable indirect cost per unit
5% increase in indirect fixed costs
8% increase in selling expenses, arising solely from increased volume
6% increase in administrative expenses, reflecting anticipated higher wage and supply price levels; any changes in administrative expenses caused solely by increased sales volume are considered immaterial

As inventory quantities remain fairly constant, the budget committee considered that for budget purposes any change in inventory valuation can be ignored. The composition of the cost of a unit of finished product during 1996 for materials, direct labor, and manufacturing support, respectively, was in the ratio of 3 to 2 to 1. In 1996,

$40,000 of manufacturing support was for fixed costs. No changes in production methods or credit policies were contemplated for 1997.

REQUIRED

(a) Compute the unit sales price at which the Monteiro Manufacturing Corporation must sell its umbrellas in 1997 in order to earn a budgeted profit of $200,000.

(b) Unhappy about the prospect of an increase in selling price, Monteiro's sales manager wants to know how many units must be sold at the old price to earn the $200,000 budgeted profit. Compute the number of units which must be sold at the old price to earn $200,000.

(c) Believing that the estimated increase in sales is overly optimistic, one of the company's directors wants to know what annual profit is likely if the selling price determined in (a) is adopted but the increase in sales volume is only 10%. Compute the budgeted profit in this case.

4-47 *Competitive contribution margin analysis* Johnson Company and Smith Company are the two competing firms offering limousine service from the Charlesburg airport. While Johnson pays most of its employees on a per-ride basis, Smith prefers to pay its employees fixed salaries. Information about the cost structures of the two firms is given below:

COMPETING LIMOUSINE SERVICE BIDS
FROM CHARLESBURG AIRPORT

	Per Ride Data	
Cost Category	**Johnson Company**	**Smith Company**
Selling price	$30	$30
Variable cost	24	15
Contribution margin	$6	$15
Fixed costs per year	$300,000	$1,500,000

REQUIRED

(a) Calculate the breakeven point in the number of rides for both firms.

(b) Draw two graphs plotting profit as a function of the number of rides for the two firms. Such graphs are sometimes called profit-volume charts.

(c) Explain which firm's cost structure is more profitable.

(d) Explain which firm's cost structure is riskier.

4-48 (Adapted from CPA May 1993) *Contribution margins for multiple products* The following budget information for the year ending December 31, 1996, pertains to Rust Manufacturing Company's operations:

	Product		
Budget Item	**Ace**	**Bell**	**Total Costs**
Budgeted sales in units	200,000	100,000	
Selling price per unit	$40	$20	
Direct materials cost per unit	$8	$3	
Direct labor hours per unit	2	1	
Depreciation			$200,000
Rent			$130,000
Other manufacturing costs			$500,000
Selling costs			$180,000
General and administrative costs			$40,000

The following information is also provided:

1. Rust has no beginning inventory. Production is planned so that it will equal the number of units sold.
2. The cost of direct labor is $5 per hour.
3. Depreciation and rent are fixed costs within the relevant range of production. Additional costs would be incurred for extra machinery and factory space if production is increased beyond current available capacity.
4. Rust allocates depreciation proportional to machinery use and rent proportional to factory space. Budgeted usage is as follows:

Depreciation Item	Ace	Bell
Machinery	70%	30%
Factory space	60%	40%

5. Other manufacturing support costs include variable costs equal to 10% of direct labor and also include various fixed costs. None of the miscellaneous fixed manufacturing support costs depend on the level of activity, although support costs attributable to a specific product are avoidable if that product's production ceases. Other manufacturing support costs are allocated between Ace and Bell based on a percent of budgeted direct labor.
6. Rust's selling and general administrative costs are fixed.
7. Rust allocates selling costs on the basis of a number of units sold at Ace and Bell.
8. Rust allocates general and administrative costs on the basis of sales revenue.

REQUIRED

(a) Prepare a schedule, using separate columns for Ace and Bell, showing budgeted sales, variable costs, contribution margin, fixed costs, and pretax operating profit for the year ending December 31, 1996.
(b) Calculate the contribution margin per unit and the pretax operating profit per unit for Ace and for Bell.
(c) Calculate the effect on pretax operating profit resulting from a 10% decrease in sales and production of each product.
(d) What may be a problem with the above analysis?

4-49 *Breakeven analysis*   The Herschel Candy Company produces a single product—a chocolate almond bar which sells for $0.40 per bar. The variable costs for each bar (sugar, chocolate, almonds, wrapper, and labor) total $0.25. The total monthly fixed costs are $60,000. During March 1997, one million bars were sold. The president of Herschel Candy Company was not satisfied with its performance and is considering the following options to increase the company's profitability:

1. Increase advertising
2. Increase the quality of the bar's ingredients and simultaneously increase the selling price
3. Increase the selling price with no change in ingredients.

REQUIRED

(a) The sales manager is confident that an intensive advertising campaign will double sales volume. If the company president's goal is to increase this month's profits by 50% over last month's, what is the maximum amount that can be spent on advertising that doubles sales volume?
(b) Assume that the company increases the quality of its ingredients, thus increasing variable costs to $0.30 per bar. How much must the selling price be increased to maintain the same breakeven point?
(c) Assume next that the company has decided to increase its selling price to $0.50 per bar with no change in advertising or ingredients. Compute the sales volume in

units that would be needed at the new price for the company to earn the same profit as in March 1997.

■ CASES

4-50 *Flexibility in committing activity resources*   Dr. Barbara Barker is the head of the pathology laboratory at Barrington Medical Center in Mobile, Alabama. Dr. Barker estimates the amount of work for her laboratory staff by classifying the pathology tests into three categories: simple routine, simple nonroutine, and complex. She expects a simple-routine test to require two hours, a simple-nonroutine test to require 2.5 hours, and a complex test to require four hours of staff time. She estimates the demand for each of the three types of tests for June through August to be the following:

Month	Simple Routine	Simple Nonroutine	Complex
June	800	250	450
July	600	200	400
August	750	225	450

Laboratory staff salaries including fringe benefits average $3600 per month. Each worker works 150 hours per month. If the hospital work load exceeds the available staff time, Dr. Barker has the tests performed at a neighboring private pathology laboratory that charges $80 for a simple-routine test, $100 for a simple-nonroutine test, and $160 for a complex test.

Dr. Barker is thinking of employing 20 to 27 workers. Because of the difficulty in hiring reliable workers, Barrington's chief administrator has instructed her to employ laboratory staff for at least one quarter.

REQUIRED

(a) Determine how many workers Dr. Barker should employ to minimize the costs of performing the tests. What is the minimum cost?
(b) Suppose the easy availability of experienced laboratory staff allows Barrington Medical Center to change staffing loads each month. Determine the number of workers Dr. Barker should hire each month in these circumstances. What is the minimum cost?

4-51 *Commitment and consumption of activity resources*   Steelmax, Inc. sells office furniture in the Chicago metropolitan area. To better serve its business customers, Steelmax recently introduced a new same-day service. Any order placed before 2 P.M. is delivered the same day.

Steelmax hires five workers on an eight-hour daily shift to deliver the office furniture. Each delivery takes 30 minutes on average. If the number of customer orders exceeds the available capacity on some days, workers are asked to work overtime to ensure that all customer orders are delivered the same day. Regular wages are $12 per hour. Overtime wages include a 50% premium in addition to the regular wages.

The Steelmax management has noticed considerable fluctuation in the number of customer orders from day to day over the last three months as shown here:

Day of the Week	Average Number of Orders
Monday	65
Tuesday	70
Wednesday	80
Thursday	85
Friday	95

Steelmax has now decided to pursue a more flexible hiring policy. It will reduce the number of delivery workers to four on Mondays and Tuesdays and increase the number to six on Fridays.

REQUIRED

(a) Determine the total and unit delivery cost when the number of daily customer orders is 70, 80, or 90.

(b) Determine the expected total delivery cost per day and the expected delivery cost per customer order based on both the old and the new hiring policy. What is the expected value per week of the new flexible hiring policy?

4-52 *Complex behavior of activity costs* Over the past 15 years, Anthony's Autoshop has developed a reputation for reliable repairs and has grown from a one-person operation to a nine-person operation including one manager and eight skilled auto mechanics. In recent years, however, competition from mass merchandisers has eroded business volume and profits, leading the owner, Anthony Axle, to ask his manager to take a closer look at the cost structure of the autoshop.

The manager determined that direct materials (parts and components) are identified with individual jobs and charged directly to the customer. Direct labor (mechanics) is also identified with individual jobs and charged at a prespecified rate to the customers. The salary and benefits for a senior mechanic are $65,000 per year; for a junior mechanic, they are $45,000 per year. Each mechanic can work up to 1750 hours in a year on customer jobs, but if there are not enough jobs to keep each of them busy, the cost of their compensation still will have to be incurred. The manager's salary and benefits amount to $75,000 per year. In addition, the following fixed costs are also incurred each year:

Rent	$36,000
Insurance	6,000
Utilities	6,000
Supplies	9,000
Machine maintenance	8,000
Machine depreciation	21,800
Total costs	$86,800

Because material costs are recovered directly from the customers, the profitability of the operation depends on the volume of business and the hourly rate charged for labor. At present, Anthony's Autoshop charges $51.06 per hour for all its jobs. Anthony said he would not consider firing any of the four senior mechanics because he believes it is difficult to get workers with their skills and loyalty to the firm, but he is willing to consider releasing one or two of the junior mechanics.

REQUIRED

(a) Determine the total fixed costs including personnel costs for each of the following three staffing levels:

Option	Senior Mechanics	Junior Mechanics
X	4	4
Y	4	3
Z	4	2

(b) What is the contribution margin per hour worked on customer jobs?

(c) Determine the *minimum* number of hours that must be charged to customer jobs for the autoshop to earn an annual profit of $50,000.

(d) Determine the *minimum* number of hours that must be charged to customer jobs for the autoshop to earn an annual profit equal to 10% of labor billing revenues (excluding charges for parts).

(e) Business is expected to increase if one more senior mechanic is hired. How much new business (in terms of hours charged to customer jobs) must be generated to justify adding a fifth senior mechanic?

5

Basic Product
Costing Systems

ARCHIE'S AUTO SERVICE COMPANY

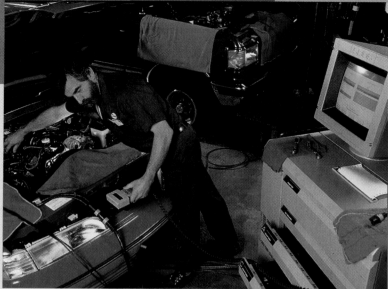

Courtesy **Blair Seitz/Photo Researchers Inc.**

Archibald Austin started Archie's Auto Service Company in 1974. Over a period of two decades, he built it into a business with more than $1 million in billings each year and a strong reputation for high-quality auto repair work. In the past three years, however, Archie lost a considerable amount of business to quick service operations such as Carex Muffler Company for simple jobs including exhaust system replacements. Increased competition from companies such as Carex cut into his sales volume and profit margins, and his take-home income from the business declined precipitously.

Archie has expanded his auto shop considerably since its opening more than 20 years ago. The shop now has five service bays and employs five mechanics, two of whom are highly skilled and trained in doing complex repair jobs. The salary and benefits of $60,000 for each expert mechanic exceeds the average compensation of the other three mechanics by almost $25,000. The three junior mechanics primarily work on routine repairs, such as brake relinings and muffler replacements.

Archie's accountant, Ace Acton, asked Archie to explain the problem that led to poor financial performance over the last two years: "Archie, your net income looks terrible. What has happened to your business?"

Archie responded: "Specialized operators like Carex Muffler Company have taken away most of my simple repair business with their low prices. How can they price their jobs so low and still make a profit?"

Ace encouraged Archie with this response: "Let me take a look at your job order costing system. I may be able to find the answer to that question."

As the consultation with Ace Acton shows, management accountants today must be able to understand how to calculate the cost of products and services. What costs should be included as part of product costs and why? How should such costs be calculated, accumulated, and reported to decision makers to help them in their planning and operating decisions?

JOB ORDER COSTING SYSTEMS

Job order costing system
System for estimating costs of manufacturing products for a job.

A **job order costing system** is a common method for estimating product costs in firms that have several distinct products. A job order costing system estimates costs of manufacturing products for different jobs required for specific customer orders.

Products may differ in their materials content and the hours of labor and machine time required to manufacture them. Products also may differ in the demand they place on support activity resources or in response to special customer needs that may lead to customized production, such as when different product characteristics are targeted for different markets. With such product and customer variety, managers want to understand the costs of individual products so that they can assess product and customer profitability.

Many firms are also required to bid on jobs before customers decide to place an order with them. Costs need to be estimated for each job in order to prepare a bid. Job order costing systems provide the means to estimate these costs.

Components of a Job Bid Sheet

Job bid sheet
Format for estimating job costs.

Exhibit 5-1 displays a **job bid sheet,** a format for estimating job costs. Vernon Valve Company, a manufacturer of a variety of special valves for several large customers, uses this sheet to bid its jobs. The bid sheet has five distinct panels. Panel 1 identifies the customer, the product, and the quantity of valves (number of units) required. Panel 2 lists all the materials required to complete the job. For each item of material, the quantity required is estimated based on *standard engineering specifications.* For instance, each unit of valve L181 requires 2.4 pounds of bar steel stock. Therefore, the order for 1500 units of L181 requires 3600 pounds of bar steel stock. The current price of $11.30 per pound is obtained from records maintained and updated by the purchasing department. With these inputs the cost of bar steel stock required for this job can be calculated as $40,680 ($11.30 price per pound $\times$ 3600 pounds).

The third panel lists the amount of direct labor required for the job. These estimates are obtained from *industrial engineering specifications* developed on the basis of *work and motion* studies or by *analogy with comparable standard products.* For instance, at a major steel company, engineering staff studies how workers perform each task necessary to make steel to customer specifications so that they can estimate how much time each task requires. Project managers at a software system development firm compare new project specifications with projects they have managed before to estimate the amount of programmer time required to develop the new software system.

At Vernon Valve, industrial engineers have estimated that 0.6 assembly hours are required per valve. Therefore, 900 assembly hours (1500 units $\times$ 0.6 hours per unit) are required for 1500 valves. After estimating the direct labor hours required for a job, Vernon Valve must determine a separate wage rate for each grade of labor required for the operations performed to manufacture the valves. The wage rate for assembly workers is $18 per hour, so that the 900 assembly hours are estimated to cost $16,200 (900 hours $\times$ $18 wage rate per hour).

The fourth panel of the bid sheet contains estimates for cost driver costs. Vernon assigns support costs to jobs based on the number of machine hours and

EXHIBIT 5-1
Vernon Valve Company
Job Bid Sheet

Panel 1	Bid Number: J4369		Date: July 6, 1997	
	Customer: Michigan Motors			
	Product: Automobile engine valves (valve L181)			
	Engineering Design Number: JDR-103		Number of Units: 1,500	

Panel 2	**Direct Materials**	**Quantity**	**Price**	**Amount**
	Bar steel stock	**3600 lb**	**$11.30**	**$ 40,680**
	Subassembly	1500 units	39.00	58,500
	Total direct materials			$ 99,180

Panel 3	**Direct Labor**	**Hours**	**Rate**	**Amount**
	Lathe operators	480	$26.00	$ 12,480
	Assembly workers	**900**	**18.00**	**16,200**
	Total direct labor	1380		$ 28,680

Panel 4	**Support Costs**			**Amount**
	600 machine hours @ $40 support costs			$ 24,000
	1380 direct labor hours @ $36.00 per hour			49,680
	Total support costs			$ 73,680

Panel 5	**Total Costs**			**Amount**
	Direct Materials + Direct Labor + Support Costs			$201,540
	Add 25% margin			50,385
	Bid price			$251,925
	Unit cost			$ 134.36
	Unit price			$ 167.95

direct labor hours expected for the job. For this purpose, Vernon uses two cost driver rates, based on the assumption that all manufacturing support costs are related either to machines or direct labor. The company classifies manufacturing support costs into two cost pools, based on whether the cost drivers are machine hours or direct labor hours, and computes a separate cost driver rate for each of the two cost pools. (Subsequent sections will describe the procedure for calculating cost driver rates in detail.) To obtain the total amount of support costs allocated to the job, an analyst multiplies the number of machine hours (600) and the number of direct labor hours required for the job (1380) by their respective cost driver rates ($40 per machine hour and $36 per direct labor hour). Then the Vernon Valve analyst adds the two estimates to obtain a total of $73,680.

600 machine hours × $40 cost driver rate per machine hour = $24,000
1380 labor hours × $36 cost driver rate per labor hour = $49,680
Total $73,680

Panel 5 of the job bid sheet shows the total costs estimated for the job, $201,540, obtained by adding together the total direct materials, total direct labor, and total support costs ($99,180 + $28,680 + $73,680).

Job Costs and Markup

Job costs
Total of direct material, direct labor, and support costs estimated for or identified with a job.

Markup or margin
Amount of profit added to estimated job costs to arrive at bid price.

Markup rate
Ratio of the markup amount to the estimated costs for a job.

Rate of return
Ratio of net income to investment (also called *return on investment*).

The total of direct material, direct labor, and support costs for the job is referred to as the **job costs.** Most firms **mark up** the job costs by adding an additional amount, or **margin,** to create a profit on the job. The total job costs plus the margin equals the bid price. At Vernon Valve, the **markup rate,** or the percent by which job costs are marked up, is 25%. The markup rate depends on a variety of factors, including the amount of support costs excluded from the *cost driver rate* (for example, corporate-level costs); the target **rate of return** (ratio of net income to investment) desired by the corporation; competitive intensity; past bidding strategies adopted by key competitors; demand conditions; and overall product-market strategies.

The markup rate may differ for different product groups and for different market segments, depending on local conditions. It also may change over time as conditions change. For instance, managers may decide to decrease profit margins when demand is weak and unused production capacity is likely to be available, but may use higher markups to create higher profits when demand is expected to be

---

*C*ONSIDER THIS . . .

Costing Bicycles

Paramount Cycles, based in Dayton, Ohio, is a manufacturer of high-quality bicycles for children and adults. Paramount cycles are sold primarily through specialty bicycle shops.

Paramount uses a standard cost accounting system to estimate the cost per bicycle for each model it manufactures. Engineering standards are developed for material quantity and labor hours for each part and for each operation. The industrial engineering department also provides lists for parts and component materials for each bicycle. By multiplying material quantity by estimated cost obtained from the purchasing manager, the finance department is able to calculate direct material cost. Manufacturing records of direct labor hours required for each job are used with labor costs per hour, estimated by the personnel department, to calculate direct labor cost for each bicycle. A cost driver rate is determined by dividing the annual budgeted support cost by the budgeted direct labor dollars to obtain a support cost rate per direct labor dollar. The total of direct material, direct labor, and support costs is used as the cost of a bicycle for both inventory valuation and for product pricing.

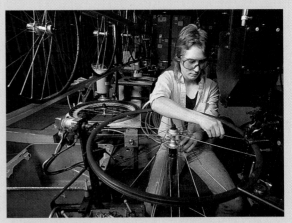

***Courtesy* Henry Horenstein/Stock, Boston**

Source: "Paramount Cycle Company," Harvard Business School, Case 180-069.

high and little unused production capacity exists. (Chapter 7 presents the issue of how costs are related to prices in greater detail.)

Determination of Cost Driver Rates

As discussed previously, determining realistic cost driver rates has become increasingly important in recent years because support costs now comprise a large portion of the total costs in many industries. Notice that allocated support costs in the Vernon Valve example ($73,680) are more than twice the direct labor costs ($28,680) and almost as much as direct materials costs ($99,180). In addition, many firms now recognize that support costs are not related to just one or even two factors, such as direct labor hours or machine hours, but that several different factors may be driving costs. Firms are now taking greater care when analyzing support costs by identifying which costs should relate to what cost driver. For instance, costs identified with the activity of setting up machines are related to the cost driver as set-up hours. All costs associated with a cost driver, such as set-up hours, are accumulated separately. Each subset of total support costs that can be associated with a distinct cost driver is referred to as a **cost pool.**

Each cost pool has a separate **cost driver rate.** The cost driver rate is the ratio of the normal cost (as defined in Chapter 4) of a support activity accumulated in the cost pool to the normal level of the cost driver for the activity:

$$Activity\ Cost\ Driver\ Rate\ =\ \frac{Normal\ Cost\ of\ Support\ Activity}{Normal\ Level\ of\ Cost\ Driver} \qquad (5\text{-}1)$$

Recall that the normal cost of the support activity is the cost of the resources committed to the particular activity. The normal level of the activity cost driver is the long-term capacity made available by the amount of resources committed to a support activity. For example, if 10 setup workers are hired at weekly wages including benefits of $810 each and if each worker has the time to complete 15 setups in a week, then the normal cost for the setup activity is $8100 per week ($810 $\times$ 10 workers). This makes available a capacity for performing 150 setups in a week (15 setups $\times$ 10 workers). Then the cost driver rate for the setup activity is $54 per setup ($8100 normal cost $\div$ 150 setup capacity). The normal cost of a support activity, therefore, excludes fluctuations in costs caused by short-term adjustments such as overtime payments. The normal level of the support activity cost driver also excludes short-term variations in demand as reflected in overtime or idle time. Because the ratio shown in equation 5-1 is based on normal costs and normal cost driver levels, the rate remains stable over time and does not fluctuate as activity levels change in the short run. As a result, this activity cost driver rate does not change simply because of short-run changes in external factors that do not affect the efficiency or price of the activity resources.

Problems Using Fluctuating Cost Driver Rates

Consider the support activity cost driver rate based on machine hours at Vernon Valve Company. The cost pool includes machine depreciation, maintenance, power, and other machine-related costs. The normal machine-related costs amount to $900,000 per year; the normal capacity made available is 20,000 machine hours per year, or 5000 machine hours (20,000 ÷ 4) per quarter. Therefore, the machine-related cost driver rate is $45 per machine hour ($900,000 ÷ 20,000 hours).

The *actual* machine usage varies each quarter because of fluctuations in demand. Machine hours used are 5400 in the spring quarter, 4500 in the summer, 5000 in the fall, and 3600 in the winter. The normal level of the cost driver is the capacity of 5000 machine hours made available each quarter by the installed machines in the plant. This capacity is exceeded in the spring quarter by operating the machines overtime beyond regular shift hours.

Machine-related costs each quarter are $225,000. If the rate for machine-related costs is based on quarterly *cost driver levels* instead of the normal levels, the rate increases as the demand for the machine activity falls, and the rate decreases as the demand increases. For example, as the number of machine hours decreases from 5400 in the spring to 4500 in the summer, the cost driver rate increases from $41.67 per machine hour for spring to $50.00 per machine hour for summer. (See Exhibit 5-2.) In contrast, the cost driver rate based on normal costs and normal activity levels remains fixed at $45.00 per machine hour ($225,000 ÷ 5000 hours) throughout the year because costs depend on the machine capacity made available and not on the season.

Determination of cost driver rates based on planned or actual short-term usage results in higher rates in periods of lower demand. In such job costing systems, job costs appear to be higher in time periods when demand is lower. If bid prices are based on estimated job costs, the firm is likely to end up bidding higher prices during periods of low demand when, in fact, it should have been considering lowering prices. The higher bid price can further decrease demand, which, in turn, leads to higher cost driver rates and even higher prices. Thus, the firm can enter an unnecessary death spiral as cost driver rates increase, leading to higher bid prices and ultimately even lower demand for its products. Conversely, cost driver rates can appear low in such a cost system when demand is high and capacity is short. This leads to attracting additional business just when the company should be raising prices to ration demand.

EXHIBIT 5-2
Cost Driver Rate and Quarterly Cost Driver Levels

Quarter	Details*	Overhead Rate per Machine Hour
Spring	$\dfrac{\$225,000}{5,400}$	$41.67
Summer	$\dfrac{\$225,000}{4,500}$	50.00
Fall	$\dfrac{\$225,000}{5,000}$	45.00
Winter	$\dfrac{\$225,000}{3,600}$	62.50

$$*\text{Cost Driver Rate} = \frac{\textit{Quarterly actual costs}}{\textit{Quarterly actual machine hours}}$$

Support activity costs are caused by the *level of capacity of each activity that is made available rather than the level of actual usage of these committed resources.* Therefore, the activity cost driver rate should be calculated based on *the normal cost per unit of the activity level committed.* Determining the cost driver rate by dividing the budgeted or actual cost per unit by the budgeted or actual use of that activity will produce misleading product costs.

ARCHIE'S AUTO SERVICE REVISITED

Let us return to the case of Archie's Auto Service Company. Ace prepared the following description of the cost accounting system used to prepare bids for Archie's customers' jobs. (See Exhibit 5-3.)

System Description

A cost estimate is prepared for each customer job, as shown in Exhibit 5-3. After initially checking the customer's car, Archie prepares a list of replacement parts (Archie's direct materials) required. He consults his authorized dealer price book to obtain list prices for the parts. He also consults his blue book to obtain the number of standard labor hours for the work required to service the car. Then he multiplies standard hours by the combined labor, support activities cost, and

EXHIBIT 5-3
Archie's Auto Service
Cost Estimate for Customer Job

	Estimate Number: 1732			Date: August 9, 1997	

	Customer Name: Brandon Briggs

	Address: 43 Bridget Blvd. Bournemouth

PARTS

	Part	Quantity	List Price	Amount	Total
Direct materials	Muffler	1	$38.00	$38.00	$ 38.00
	Tailpipe	1	15.00	15.00	15.00
	Total parts				$ 53.00

LABOR

Direct labor, support costs, and markup	Replacement of exhaust systems 2 hours @ $61.20 per hour	**$122.40**
	Total labor	**$122.40**
	Total costs	**$175.40**

Prepared by: Archie Austin

markup rate of $61.20 per hour. The combined conversion cost rate includes the following:

Mechanic's wages and benefits

Shop support activity costs including tools and machine depreciation

Markup of 20% to provide a reasonable profit for Archie

The total cost estimate, or bid price, is the sum of the replacement parts cost and the labor cost charged at the combined labor, support conversion, and markup rate.

Ace investigated further how the combined labor, support activities cost, and markup rate of $61.20 per hour was determined. He examined the accounting and operating records in detail to prepare the following summary of costs budgeted for 1995:

Salaries of two expert mechanics	
($60,000 each; total of 3600 billable hours)	$120,000
Salaries of three regular mechanics	
($35,000 each; total of 5400 billable hours)	105,000
Fringe benefits	90,000
General and administrative costs	26,000
Depreciation and maintenance on physical facilities,	
bays, equipment, etc.	64,000
Depreciation and maintenance on special tools and	
machines (3600 machine hours)	54,000
Total costs	$459,000

The combined processing cost (labor and support activity) driver rate in dollars is determined by dividing the total costs ($459,000) by the total billable hours (3600 + 5400 hours) and then multiplying by 1.20 to represent a markup of 20%.

$$Present\ Cost\ Driver\ Rate\ =\ \frac{\$459,000}{3600\ +\ 5400}\ \times\ 1.20$$

$$=\ \$61.20\ per\ labor\ hour$$

OBJECTIVE 5.4

Evaluate a cost system to understand whether it is likely to distort product costs.

Ace determined that Archie's company had lost considerable business for simple jobs, such as exhaust system replacement and brake relining, that did not require expert mechanics or specialized tools and machines. The present job costing system was deficient in not distinguishing between the expert and regular types of labor and in not recognizing that *some of the support activity costs—$54,000 for depreciation and maintenance—resulted from the availability of special tools and machines.* The costs of expert and regular labor and special tools and machines were all bundled together into a single cost driver rate of $61.20 per labor hour. This average rate did not reflect the differences between jobs that required expert or regular labor and/or whether jobs required the use of special tools and machines.

This type of simple cost system is often referred to as a peanut butter spreading approach since the cost of all types of resources—different labor skills, different machine types, and different support resources—are allocated across all jobs regardless of whether a job uses particular resources or not.

Recommended System Changes

Ace recommended that instead of using a single conversion cost driver rate, Archie's should use the following four different cost driver rates:

1. Expert labor wage rate
2. Other labor wage rate
3. Depreciation and maintenance on physical plant
4. Depreciation and maintenance on special tools

The labor and support activity costs should be separated, therefore, into the four cost pools depicted in Exhibit 5-4. To do this, it is necessary first to apportion fringe benefits between the two types of labor costs (expert and regular mechanics) in the ratio of their respective costs. Then the company should determine its labor rates by dividing the total costs for wages and apportioned fringe benefits by the respective billable hours in each labor category and then adding a 20% markup. (See Exhibit 5-5.) Notice that both support activity costs and markup are included in the *labor rate* here. In contrast, Vernon Valve added markup after determining *all* product costs—materials, labor, and support activity. (See Exhibit 5-1, Panel 5.) Both methods are common in practice. Archie's method of calculating a combined conversion cost driver rate is used more in service organizations; Vernon's method of separating labor from support costs is common in manufacturing and trading establishments.

The machine-related activity rate for special tools and machines is $18 per machine hour (1.20 markup × $54,000 costs ÷ 3600 hours). The remaining support activity costs comprising general/administrative costs and depreciation/maintenance on physical facilities, bays, and equipment are expected to be related

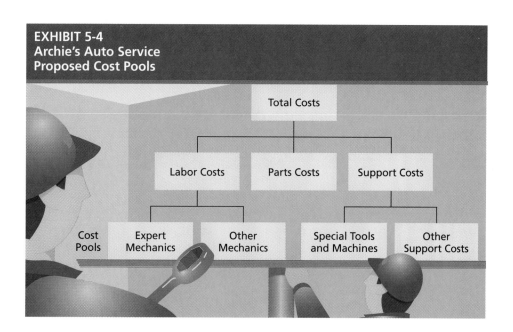

EXHIBIT 5-4
Archie's Auto Service
Proposed Cost Pools

EXHIBIT 5-5
Archie's Auto Service
Labor Rates

Elements	Expert Mechanics	Other Mechanics
Wages	$120,000	$105,000
Fringe benefits	48,000	42,000
Total costs	$168,000	$147,000
Markup	20%	20%
Total cost plus markup	$201,600	$176,400
Total billable hours	3,600	5,400
Labor rate per hour	$56.00	$32.67

$$\frac{\$90,000 \text{ benefits} \times \$120,000}{\$120,000 \text{ salaries of expert mechanics} + \$105,000 \text{ salaries of other mechanics}}$$

$$\frac{\$90,000 \text{ benefits} \times \$105,000}{\$120,000 \text{ salaries of expert mechanics} + \$105,000 \text{ salaries of other mechanics}}$$

to total labor hours of both types of mechanics. Therefore, the formula to determine the remaining support activity cost driver rate is this:

$$\begin{array}{l} \textit{Support} \\ \textit{Activity} \\ \textit{Cost} \\ \textit{Driver} \\ \textit{Rate} \end{array} = \frac{1.20 \text{ markup} \times (\$26,000 \text{ G\&A} + \$64,000 \text{ depreciation})}{3600 \text{ expert mechanics' billable hours} + 5400 \text{ other mechanics' billable hours}}$$

$$= \$12 \text{ per labor hour}$$

New Cost Accounting System Illustrated

To illustrate how the new cost accounting system provides better information about job costs, Ace picks two representative jobs. Details of the work requirement for these two jobs appear in Exhibit 5-6. The first job involves the replace-

EXHIBIT 5-6
Archie's Auto Service
Costs Under the Old Job Costing System

Work Description		Job 1732 Replacement of Exhaust System		Job 2326 Rebuilding Engine Valves
Parts cost		$53		$412
Labor Hours:				
Expert mechanic hours	0		4	
Other mechanic hours	2		2	
Total labor hours		2		6
Special tools and machine hours		0		4

ment of an exhaust system, a simple job that requires neither expert mechanics nor special tools and machines. The second job is relatively complex and involves rebuilding engine valves.

Under the previous system, job 1732 (replacement of the exhaust system) is costed out at $175.40 [$53.00 parts + (2 hours × $61.20) (old support activity cost driver rate)], including the 20% markup for profit. Under the new system, the cost of the same job is estimated to be $142.34, including the same 20% markup for profit. (See Exhibit 5-7.) The new system reveals that job 1732 actually costs less than what appeared to be the case under the previous system. The previous system overcosted the job because the single support activity cost driver rate of $61.20 per labor hour wrongly applied a portion of the expert mechanic wages and special tools and machines costs to the job although this simple job did not use any of these specialized and expensive resources. Thus, with the new cost system Archie's may be able to win back some of its lost business for simple jobs by lowering the price but not the profit margin.

In contrast, the costs of the more complex job 2326 (rebuilding engine valves) increase from $779.20 [$412 parts + (6 hours × $61.20) (old support activity cost driver rate)] to $845.34 when the new system is used and the higher costs of expert labor and special tools are recognized. (See Exhibit 5-7.) Thus, the correct assignment of costs reveals that Archie currently may be underpricing the services of his expert mechanics using special tools. Although this underpricing means that he is getting these more complex jobs, he is making much less profit and perhaps even taking a loss on these jobs than the present costing system leads him to believe. In addition, he is running out of capacity on the relatively more expensive resources for the complex activities by attracting business that does not cover the costs of these resources.

The difference between the old and the new product costing systems results from the difference in the structure of the cost pools. The new system recognizes two types of labor and support activity costs that include costs of special tools and machines not required for all jobs.

EXHIBIT 5-7
Archie's Auto Service
Costs Under the New Job Costing System

	Job 1732	Job 2326
Parts cost	$53.00	$412.00
Expert mechanics	0	$224.00 (4 hours × $56 wage rate)
Other mechanics	$65.34 (2 hours × $32.67 wage rate)	$65.34 (2 hours × $32.67)
Special tools support	0	$72.00 (4 hours × $18 cost driver rate)
Other support	$24.00 (2 hours × $12 overhead rate)	$72.00 (6 hours × $12 cost driver rate)
Total costs	**$142.34**	**$845.34**

CONSIDER THIS . . .

Sentry Group

Sentry Group, based in Rochester, New York, manufactures fireproof and insulated metal products, including safes, containers, and files for home and office use. Production of steel parts for metal safes starts in the press department where cold-rolled steel is cut to the proper length and width on shear presses. Door jambs and frames are spot-welded to add strength and create a smoother appearance; door hinges are welded to add durability. When all welding is finished, the safe frame and door are filled with vermiculite insulation (a mixture of water, chemicals, and cement) and set aside to cure for 24 hours. When the insulation is dry, safe pieces are cleaned and painted. When the pieces are dry, the safe frame, door, and lock are assembled to form a completed safe, which is then packed for shipment.

Sentry Group uses a standard cost accounting system. Material and labor standards are reviewed annually and updated as necessary. There are six production departments for metal products: press; spot welding; mig welding; insulation; clean and paint; and final assembly. Labor costs for each production department are divided into direct labor and indirect labor (such as materials handling). The direct labor cost of each product is calculated by summing the standard hours per unit for each production department and multiplying the result by the company's average labor rate. Standard materials costs are calculated by the standard price per unit of each item of materials used in its production.

Support costs include five major elements: indirect labor in production departments, other production department costs, general plant costs, shipping and receiving costs, and maintenance costs. The cost driver rate is determined annually by dividing the total support costs of the previous year by the total direct labor costs. The resulting cost driver rate is multiplied by the direct labor content of each product to obtain the support cost per unit of that product. All other manufacturing costs, including engineering, quality control, and materials management—along with selling and general and administrative expenses—are considered period costs and not included in product costs.

Sentry Group is considering changing to an activity-based costing system to obtain more accurate estimates of its product costs.

Source: "Sentry Group," Harvard Business School, Case 190-124.

Number of Cost Pools

You may ask the question: How many cost pools should there be? Cost accounting systems in many German firms use more than 1000 cost pools. The general principle to use in determining the number of pools is to use separate cost pools if the cost or productivity of resources is different and if the pattern of demand varies across resources. Exhibit 5-8 displays the trade-offs involved in choosing the level of accuracy of a product costing system. The increase in measurement costs required by a more detailed cost system must be traded off against the benefit of increased accuracy in estimating product costs. If cost and productivity differences between resources are small, more cost pools will not make much of a difference in the accuracy of product cost estimates. In such a case, the benefits of decreasing errors, such as those that resulted in Archie losing simple jobs, will be relatively small and not sufficient to justify the increased cost of more cost pools.

A MIDCHAPTER REVIEW PROBLEM

Marymount Electronics Corporation manufactures two types of electronic devices that measure, display, and transmit information about process temperature

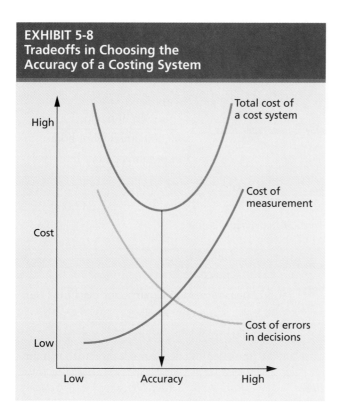

EXHIBIT 5-8
Tradeoffs in Choosing the
Accuracy of a Costing System

and pressure as well as automatically control them within specified ranges. Its plant has two production departments: fabrication and assembly. Manufacturing support costs and activity levels for the two departments for 1997 are estimated to be the following:

Costs and Hours	Fabrication	Assembly	Total
Manufacturing support costs	$800,000	$600,000	$1,400,000
Direct labor hours	25,000	75,000	100,000
Machine hours	25,000	25,000	50,000

Direct labor hours and machine hours required for job MM737 are estimated to be the following:

Hours	Fabrication	Assembly	Total
Direct labor hours (DLH)	320	900	1220
Machine hours (MH)	100	150	250

(a) Assume that a single, plantwide predetermined cost driver rate based on direct labor hours is used to estimate manufacturing support costs for bidding on individual jobs. Determine the cost driver rate and estimate manufacturing support costs for job MM737.

(b) Determine the departmental cost driver rates and estimate manufacturing support costs for job MM737 assuming instead that machine hours are used as the cost driver for the fabrication department and that direct labor hours are used as the cost driver for the assembly department.

The following is a solution to (a) and (b) above:

(a) *Plantwide Cost Driver Rate* $= \dfrac{\$1,400,000}{100,000 \text{ direct labor hours}}$

$= \$14$ per direct labor hour

Estimated Manufacturing Support Costs for Job MM737 $= \$14 \times (320 + 900)$
$= \$17,080$

(b) *Departmental Cost Driver Rates*

Fabrication $= \dfrac{\$800,000}{25,000 \text{ machine hours}}$

$= \$32$ per fabrication department machine hour

Assembly $= \dfrac{\$600,000}{75,000 \text{ direct labor hours}}$

$= \$8$ per assembly department direct labor hour

Department	Rate	Cost Driver	Support Costs
Fabrication	$32	100 MH	$ 3200
Assembly	8	900 DLH	7200
Total			$10,400

OBJECTIVE 5.5

Explain the importance of recording actual costs and comparing them with estimated costs.

RECORDING ACTUAL JOB COSTS

In addition to *preparing* bids, job order cost accounting systems also record costs *actually* incurred on individual jobs as they are produced. This process allows comparison of actual costs with the estimated costs to determine whether unexpected variations occurred in the quantity (efficiency) or prices of the various resources used.

Consider job J4369 of the Vernon Valve Company on page 204. Once Vernon has received the customer order and scheduled production, the company prepares a **materials requisition note** listing materials required to begin production. The materials requisition note M47624 lists the bar steel stock required for initial machining work. (See Exhibit 5-9.) Vernon obtains steel requirements from engineering specifications for part design JDR-103 identified in the customer order. On receipt of the materials requisition note, the stores department issues the bar steel stock and moves the materials to the machining department.

Materials requisition note
A note instructing the stores department to issue materials to the shop floor in order to commence production.

The 720 pounds of materials issued are for 20% of the total order. The customer requires delivery spread over several months, and Vernon Valve schedules production for meeting delivery schedules, a production system called a *pull system*. This production order is for 300 L181 valves (20% of the total customer order for 1500 L181 valves.) (See Exhibit 5-1.) Each valve requires 2.4 pounds of

EXHIBIT 5-9
Vernon Valve Company
Materials Requisition Note

Materials Requisition Note Number: M47624   Date: August 2, 1997
From: Machining Department

Approved by: Mike Machina   Machining Supervisor
                      Steve Stuart   Stores Supervisor
Job Number: J4369

Engineering Design: JDR-103

Identification Number	Description	Quantity	Rate	Amount
24203	Bar steel stock	720 lb	$11.50	$8280.00

materials; therefore, 720 pounds (300 valves $\times$ 2.4 pounds per valve) of bar steel stock has been requisitioned. Since the actual price of bar steel is $11.50 per pound, the actual cost of the requisitioned material is $8280 (720 $\times$ $11.50).

Once the machining department receives the materials, the supervisor assigns specific lathe operators to the job. A record of the time the operators spend working on a job is recorded on a **time cards,** such as the one shown in Exhibit 5-10 for machinist William Wiley (employee number M16).

After the completion of machining work, workers either store the machined bars as work in process or move them to the assembly department if they are scheduled for assembly. The just-in-time pull system that Vernon Valve uses moves the materials almost immediately to the next department. The assembly department then prepares an additional materials requisition note to have the stores department issue the appropriate subassemblies. The assembly workers also prepare time cards to record the time they spend on job J4369.

Time card
Record of hours spent by each worker each day or week on different jobs.

EXHIBIT 5-10
Vernon Valve Company
Worker Time Card

TIME CARD

Employee Number: M16   Name: William Wiley

Date: August 2, 1997   Department: Machining

Checked by: Mike Machina   Machining Supervisor

Job Number	Start Time	Stop Time	Total Hours	Wage Rate	Amount
J4369	6:00	10:00	4	$28.00	$112.00
J4362	10:00	1:00	3	28.00	84.00
J4371	2:00	3:00	1	28.00	28.00
Total			8		$224.00

Job cost sheet
Format for recording actual job costs.

Copies of all materials requisition notes and worker time cards are forwarded to the accounting department, which then posts them on a **job cost sheet,** shown in Exhibit 5-11. Even if time cards are recorded in an integrated computerized information system instead of a manual accounting system, job cost sheets are prepared using data obtained from actual materials requisition and actual time card records. The time records may come from workers entering data into a computer terminal or by passing an electronic wand over a bar code on the job.

Finally, the system calculates total costs for the portion of the job completed. The structure of the job cost sheet is similar to that of the job bid sheet, except that the direct material and direct labor costs on the job cost sheet represent ac-

---

EXHIBIT 5-11
Vernon Valve Company
Job Cost Sheet

Panel 1
Job number: J4369   Date: August 12, 1997
Customer: Michigan Motors
Product: Automobile engine valves
Engineering design number: JDR-103
Total number of units ordered: 1500

Panel 2

Materials Requisition Number	Description	Quantity	Price	Amount
M47624	Bar steel stock	720 lb	$11.50	$ 8,280.00
A35161	Subassemblies	290 units	38.00	11,020.00
Total direct materials cost				$19,300.00

Panel 3

Dates	Employee Number	Hours	Rate	Amount
8/2, 8/3, 8/4, 8/5	M16	24	$28.00	$ 672.00
8/2, 8/3, 8/4, 8/5	M18, M19	64	26.00	1,664.00
8/6, 8/7, 8/8, 8/9, 8/10	A25, A26, A27	120	18.00	2,160.00
8/6, 8/7, 8/8, 8/9, 8/10	A32, A34, A35	60	17.00	1,020.00
Total direct labor cost		268		$5,516.00

Panel 4

Support Costs	Amount
117 Machine hours @ $40 per hour	$ 4,680.00
268 Direct labor hours @ $36 per hour	9,648.00
Total support costs	$14,328.00

Panel 5

Total cost	$39,144.00
Number of units produced	290
Cost per unit	$134.98
Projected unit cost	$134.36

tual costs incurred on the job. Direct material costs include $11,020 for subassemblies, in addition to $8,280 for 720 pounds of bar steel stock recorded in materials requisition note M47624. (See Exhibit 5-9.) Referring to Exhibit 5-11, we see that direct labor costs comprise the hours charged by three machinists (M16, M18, M19 lathe operators) and six assembly workers (A25, A26, A27, A32, A34, A35) for this job. (This includes the four hours charged for employee number M16 on August 2 as recorded in the time card described in Exhibit 5-10.) Support costs are applied to the job based on actual machine hours (117 hours) and direct labor hours (268 hours). The same predetermined support cost driver rates ($40 per machine hour and $36 per direct labor hour) as in the job bid sheet are used because actual total support costs for the plant will not be known until the end of the fiscal period. (See Exhibit 5-1, panel 4.)

Total costs are determined as before by adding together the direct material, direct labor, and support activity costs applied to the job to date. It is now possible to compare these to the costs on the bid sheet. Notice that the actual unit costs of $134.98 ($39,144 total cost ÷ 290 units produced) for the portion of the job completed through August 12, 1997 are higher than the unit costs of $134.36 ($201,540 total cost ÷ 1500 units) estimated on the job bid sheet. (See Exhibits 5-11, panel 5, and 5-1, panel 5.) The next section presents methods useful for analyzing the reasons for the differences between actual and bid costs.

BASIC VARIANCE ANALYSIS

Variance analysis is the set of procedures used by managers to help them understand the source of differences (variances) between actual and estimated costs. Variance analysis can help managers in several ways. If managers learn that specific actions they took on some jobs helped lower the actual costs of these jobs, then they can obtain further cost savings by repeating those actions on similar jobs in the future. If managers can identify the factors causing actual costs to be higher than expected, then they may be able to take the necessary actions to prevent those factors from recurring in the future. And if they learn that cost changes are likely to be permanent, they can update their cost information when bidding for future jobs.

Because Vernon Valve has completed only a part of job J4369, it is necessary to prorate the estimated costs in the job bid sheet. Exhibit 5-12 shows these prorated calculations. For instance, each valve requires 2.4 pounds of bar steel stock (3600 [pounds of bar steel stock] ÷ 1500 [valves]); therefore, 696 pounds (2.4 pounds per valve × 290 valves) should be required for the 290 valves manufactured. At the price of $11.30 per pound of steel, the estimated cost of bar steel required is $7864.80.

First-Level Variances

Column 3 of Exhibit 5-13 displays the **first-level variances** for different cost items. The first-level variance for a cost item is the *difference between the actual and estimated costs for that cost item.* Variances are "favorable," or "F," if *the actual costs are less than estimated costs.* "Unfavorable," or "U," variances arise when actual costs exceed estimated costs. A variance is favorable when the variance indicates

Variance analysis
Decomposition of differences between actual and estimated costs into amounts related to specific factors causing the variance between actual and estimated costs.

First-level variance
Difference between actual and estimated costs for a cost item.

EXHIBIT 5-12
Vernon Valve Company
Prorated Cost Estimates for 290 Valves

Cost	Estimated Quantity Required for 290 Valves	Estimated Rate	Estimated Cost
Direct materials:			
Bar steel stock	2.4 lb × 290 = 696 lb	$11.30	$ 7,864.80
Subassemblies	1 × 290 = 290 units	39.00	11,310.00
			$19,174.80
Direct labor:			
Lathe operators	0.32 × 290 = 92.8 hrs.	$26.00	$ 2,412.80
Assembly workers	0.60 × 290 = 174 hrs.	18.00	3,132.00
			$ 5,544.80
Support Costs:			
Based on machine hours	0.40 × 290 = 116 hrs.	$40.00	$ 4,640.00
Based on direct labor hours	0.92 × 290 = 266.8 hrs.	36.00	9,604.80
			$14,244.80

EXHIBIT 5-13
Vernon Valve Company
First-Level Analysis of Variances

Cost	(1) Estimated Cost From Exhibit 5-12	(2) Actual Cost From Exhibit 5-11	(3) First-Level Variance [(1) − (2)]	(4) Variance per Valve [(3) ÷ 290]
Direct materials:				
Bar steel stock	$ 7,864.80	$ 8,280.00	$415.20 U	$1.43 U
Subassemblies	11,310.00	11,020.00	290.00 F	1.00 F
	$19,174.80	$19,300.00	$125.20 U	$0.43 U
Direct labor:				
Lathe operators	$ 2,412.80	$ 2,336.00*	$ 76.80 F	$0.26 F
Assembly workers	3,132.00	3,180.00*	48.00 U	0.16 U
	$5,544.80	$5,516.00	$ 28.80 F	$0.10 F
Support Costs:				
Based on machine hours	$ 4,640.00	$ 4,680.00	$ 40.00 U	$0.14 U
Based on direct labor hours	9,604.80	9,648.00	$ 43.20 U	0.15 U
	$14,244.80	$14,328.00	$ 83.20 U	$0.29 U
Total costs	$38,964.40	$39,144.00	$179.60 U	**$0.62 U**

*From panel 3 in Exhibit 5-11: $2,336 = $672 + $1,664 and $3,180 = $2,160 + $1,020

that actual profits are higher than those estimated and, therefore, that actual costs are lower than those estimated, or unfavorable when the variance indicates that the actual profits are less than those estimated and, therefore, that actual costs are higher than those estimated. In this example, the first-level cost variance for bar steel is $415.20 unfavorable ($8280.00 actual bar steel cost − $7864.80 estimated cost of bar steel required).

Second-Level Variances

First-level direct material and direct labor variances can be analyzed or decomposed further into efficiency (use) and price variances, which are referred to as **second-level variances**, as shown in Exhibit 5-14. To illustrate this analysis, consider the decomposition of the bar steel cost variance.

Second-level variance analysis
Analysis of a first-level variance into efficiency and price variances.

MATERIAL USAGE AND PRICE VARIANCES.   The material usage variance is determined by using the following formula where:

AQ = actual quantity of materials used
SQ = estimated or standard quantity of materials required
SP = estimated or standard price of materials

$$Usage\ Variance = (AQ - SQ) \times SP \qquad (5\text{-}2)$$
$$= (720 - 696) \times \$11.30$$
$$= \$271.20\ U$$

OBJECTIVE 5.6

Understand the relevance of performing an analysis of variances between actual and estimated costs including first- and second-level variances.

EXHIBIT 5-14
Vernon Valve Company
Second-Level Analysis of Variances

Item		Amount	Total
Direct material:			
Bar steel stock			
Usage variance	(720 − 696) × $11.30	**$271.20 U**	
Price variance	($11.50 − $11.30) × 720	**144.00 U**	**$415.20 U**
Subassemblies			
Usage variance	(290 − 290) × $39	$ 0.00	
Price variance	($38 − $39) × 290	290.00 F	290.00 F
Total direct material variance			$125.20 U
Direct labor:			
Lathe operators			
Efficiency variance	(88 − 92.8) × $26	$124.80 F	
Rate variance	($28 − $26) × 24 + ($26 − $26) × 64	48.00 U	$ 76.80 F
Assembly workers			
Efficiency variance	(180 − 174) × $18	$108.00 U	
Rate variance	($18 − $18) × 120 + ($17 − $18) × 60	60.00 F	48.00 U
Total direct labor variance			$ 28.80 F

Positive cost variances are unfavorable because they indicate that actual costs exceeded estimated costs. Negative cost variances are favorable since actual costs were less than estimated costs. In this case, the positive variance ($271.20) indicates that more bar steel was used than estimated at the time of bidding for the job. This inefficient use contributed to increasing the actual costs by an additional $271.20 from the amount estimated.

Material price variance for bar steel stock is calculated using the following formula where:

$$AP = \text{actual price of materials}$$
$$SP = \text{estimated or standard price of materials}$$
$$AQ = \text{actual quantity of materials used}$$

$$Price\ Variance = (AP - SP) \times AQ \tag{5-3}$$
$$= (\$11.50 - \$11.30) \times 720$$
$$= \$144.00\ U$$

Thus, we have decomposed the total variance for the cost of bar steel stock into a material usage and a material price variance. When we add these two second-level variances together ($271.20 U + $144.00 U), we obtain the total first-level variance for bar steel stock ($415.20 U). (See Exhibit 5-13.)

The general result relating first- and second-level variances is verified easily by adding together the algebraic formulas for material usage and price variances. The sum of the second-level variances is this:

$$\begin{aligned}
\text{Sum of Second-}&\\
\text{Level Variances} &= Usage\ Variance + Price\ Variance \tag{5-4}\\
&= [(AQ - SQ) \times SP] + [(AP - SP) \times AQ]\\
&= (AQ \times SP) - (SQ \times SP) + (AP \times AQ) - (SP \times AQ)\\
&= (AP \times AQ) - (SQ \times SP)\\
&= Actual\ Cost - Estimated\ Cost\\
&= Total\ (First\text{-}Level)\ Variance
\end{aligned}$$

MATERIAL PRICE VARIANCE IDENTIFIED WITH PURCHASING FUNCTION. Vernon Valve purchases materials as required for individual jobs. With this procedure, material purchases can be identified directly with specific jobs so that it makes sense to determine a material price variance separately for each job. More commonly, however, materials used in several jobs are purchased in larger quantities and stored until requisitioned for individual jobs. In these situations, it is common to separate out the material price variance *at the time of the purchase* and to charge jobs for materials only at their standard prices. This procedure identifies an aggregate material price variance for the purchasing function instead of at the level of individual jobs described previously. In other words, the actual material cost recorded in a job cost sheet equals *standard* price times *actual* quantity ($SP \times AQ$) instead of the *actual* price times *actual* quantity ($AP \times AQ$) used in Exhibit 5-11, panel 2, for Vernon Valve. The first-level variance is the difference between actual and estimated costs, which in this case is this:

$$\begin{aligned}
First\text{-}Level\ Variance &= Actual\ Costs - Estimated\ Costs \tag{5-5}\\
&= (SP \times AQ) - (SP \times SQ)\\
&= SP \times (AQ - SQ)
\end{aligned}$$

This is the same as the material usage variance calculated in the second-level variance analysis in (5-2). Thus, only the material usage variance is identified with individual jobs, and the material price variance is associated in the aggregate directly with the purchasing function.

EFFICIENCY AND WAGE RATE VARIANCES FOR DIRECT LABOR COSTS. The labor cost variances are determined in a manner very similar to that described for material usage and price variances. The formulas follow where:

AH = actual number of direct labor hours
AR = actual wage rate
SH = estimated or standard number of direct labor hours
SR = estimated or standard wage rate

$$\textit{Efficiency Variance} = (AH - SH) \times SR \qquad (5\text{-}6)$$

$$\textit{Rate Variance} = (AR - SR) \times AH \qquad (5\text{-}7)$$

As before total cost variance is computed as follows:

$\textit{Efficiency Variance} + \textit{Rate Variance}$
$\quad = (AH - SH) \times SR + (AR - SR) \times AH$
$\quad = (AH \times SR) - (SH \times SR) + (AR \times AH) - (SR \times AH)$
$\quad = (AR \times AH) - (SR \times SH)$
$\quad = \textit{Actual Cost} - \textit{Estimated Cost}$
$\quad = \textit{Total Cost Variance}$

Some organizations use technology to correct chronic unfavorable material usage variances. Pentair, Inc. uses this electronic measuring system to ensure that sheet metal parts are cut to exact specifications. By reducing waste and rework, this machine reduces material and labor use. *Courtesy* Pentair, Inc.

SECOND-LEVEL ANALYSIS OF SUPPORT ACTIVITY COST VARIANCES. Second-level support activity cost variance analysis is not necessary because the same predetermined cost driver rates are actually used for charging support activity costs to specific jobs. Even companies that calculate actual material and labor costs for each individual job almost always use a standard rate for assigning support activity costs to jobs. All variation between actual and estimated support activity costs for a job, therefore, arises from differences in the number of units of the basis on which support activity costs are applied to jobs (direct labor hours and machine hours in the case of Vernon Valve).

Managerial Use of Job Cost Variance Information

How can the managers at Vernon Valve use the information provided by the first- and second-level variance analysis reports in Exhibits 5-13 and 5-14? They would find it reassuring to know that the actual costs exceed the estimated costs by only $0.62 per valve—an amount that is less than 0.05% of the bid price. However, many interesting details appear when analyzing this small overall variance for the completed part of the job into its components.

As noted earlier, inefficiency in the use of bar steel stock is indicated by the unfavorable second-level material usage variance. The reasons for the excess usage need to be investigated. Further inquiry revealed that higher than estimated waste in the use of bar steel stock occurred because of a breakdown of the lathe machine after it produced several defective pieces that had to be rejected. This problem has since been corrected; therefore, bar steel consumption was not expected to exhibit unfavorable usage variance for the rest of the job. Furthermore, although bar steel prices were higher than estimated, the material price variance indicated that the purchasing manager had been successful in saving $1 per valve in the price of subassemblies.

This packing area is the end of a multistage system used in a Colgate-Palmolive plant in Puerto Rico to make fabric softener. The costs associated with this batch of production would be accumulated at each stage (blending, filling, and packaging) and allocated to the batch of production to determine the cost per unit for blending, filling, and packaging. *Courtesy* Richard Alcorn/Colgate-Palmolive

At this chemical plant, products are manufactured continuously. The process has multiple stages, with different chemical reactions occurring in different cells. *Courtesy* **Tom Carroll/Phototake**

Inquiries pursuant to labor cost variance analysis revealed that more experienced lathe operators worked on this job. The unfavorable rate variance due to their higher wages was more than offset by the favorable labor usage because of their higher efficiency. In contrast, less experienced assembly workers with lower wages had been assigned to this job. The resulting favorable wage rate variance, however, was not adequate to compensate for the unfavorable efficiency variance. In both cases, therefore, the variance information suggests that the use of the higher paid but more experienced workers should result in lower costs for the rest of this job.

Vernon analyzes and reports the direct cost variances for each job. In companies that work on a large number of small jobs, these variances are aggregated for all jobs completed in a month and only the total variances for the month are reported to managers. This procedure avoids presenting a lot of potentially confusing detail in the variance analysis reports. The principles for analyzing these variances, however, remain the same as those employed at Vernon.

Multistage Process Costing Systems

For many plants engaged in continuous processing, such as those in the chemicals, basic metals, pharmaceuticals, grain milling and processing, and electric utilities industries, production flows continuously, semicontinuously (that is, continuously, but with a few interruptions), or in large batches from one process stage to the next. At each successive process stage, there is further progress toward converting

CONSIDER THIS...

Computerized Job Costing System Keeps a Ship Builder on an Even Keel

Atlantic Dry Dock Corporation does ship repairs and conversions on the banks of St. John's River east of Jacksonville, Florida. It obtains business by bidding on jobs. Preparation of a bid requires an analysis of job specifications, which are often supplied by the customer. The job estimator must understand and interpret the specifications in terms of the materials and labor required. Occasionally a customer simply comes in and says, "Fix my boat, she broke." In such a case, the estimator must develop the work scope that forms a part of the contract with the customer.

Job specifications are often converted into specific material items and labor tasks by referring to similarities and differences with past jobs that can be looked up in a computerized database. Material requirements, availability, and prices are also determined by accessing a computerized database. Experienced estimators must often rely on their judgment to determine labor hours required for a job and categorize them by trade and skill levels. Labor is usually the largest cost item, and the setting and review of labor rates is the most critical to the success of the bid. Costs of consumable supplies, hand tools, and small equipment purchased or rented for use on a particular job are charged directly to that job as direct material costs. Support costs are relatively small compared to the direct material and labor costs and are *ignored* for the preparation of bids and job costing purposes at Atlantic Dry Dock.

During the progress of the work on a job, the variance between the actual job costs and the bid estimates is analyzed at the end of each week. In this business, large variances occur frequently. For example, after sandblasters clean the ship's hull down to bare metal, a thunderstorm may come along, get the metal wet before it can be primed, cause it to rust, and additional sandblasting may be required. Not all variances are explained so easily. Sometimes shipfitters and welders encounter a structural beam, a pipe or a bulkhead not where it was thought to be from a study

of the drawings or an inspection of the vessel; this may require a different repair procedure and cause a significant labor variance. Understanding and explaining variances is considered to be an important part of the learning process for estimators, workers, and managers at Atlantic Dry Dock Corporation.

***Courtesy* Brian Seed/Tony Stone Images**

Source: T. L. Barton and F. M. Cole, "Atlantic Dry Dock's Unique Cost Estimation System," *Management Accounting,* October 1994, pp. 32–40.

---

the raw materials into the finished product. In contrast to a job shop manufacturing establishment, in continuous processing it is necessary first to determine costs for each stage of the process and then to assign their costs to individual products.

The design of product costing systems in such process-oriented plants enables measurement of the costs of converting the raw materials during a time period to be made separately for each process stage. These conversion costs are applied to products as they pass through successive process stages. This system for determining product costs, known as a **multistage process costing system,** is common in process-oriented industries. We find multistage process costing systems also in some discrete parts manufacturing plants such as those producing automobile components, small appliances, and electronic instruments and computers.

     The common feature in all these settings is that the products manufactured are all relatively homogeneous. Few and relatively small differences occur in the production requirements for batches of different products. As a result, it is not necessary to maintain separate cost records for individual jobs. Instead costs are measured only for process stages and cost variances are determined only at the level of the process stages instead of at the level of individual jobs.

Multistage process costing system
System for determining product costs in multi-stage processing industries.

Comparison with Job Order Costing

Multistage process costing systems have the same objective as job order costing systems. Both types of systems assign material, labor, and manufacturing support activity costs to products. Some important differences, however, do exist between the two systems. (See Exhibit 5-15.) Note that the factors in column 1 highlight the major points for consideration.

OBJECTIVE 5.8

Understand the significance of differences between job order costing and multistage-process costing systems.

Process Costing Illustrated

Consider the product costing system at Calcut Chemical Company's plant that processes organic chemical products through three stages: (1) mixing and blending, (2) reaction chamber, and (3) pulverizing and packing. (See Exhibit 5-16). First, Calcut Chemical estimates costs for these three stages as shown in Exhibit 5-17. These costs include production labor assigned to each stage, support labor performing tasks, such as materials handling and setup, and laboratory testing.

EXHIBIT 5-15
Differences Between Job Order and Multistage Process Costing Systems

Factors	Job Order Costing System	Multistage Process Costing System
Production	(a) Carried out in many different jobs	(a) Carried out continuously, semi-continuously, or in large batches
Production requirements	(b) Different for different jobs	(b) Homogeneous across products or jobs
Costs	(c) Measured for individual jobs	(c) Measured for individual process stages
Variances	(d) Between actual and estimated direct materials and direct labor costs are determined for individual jobs	(d) Between actual and estimated costs are determined for individual process stages

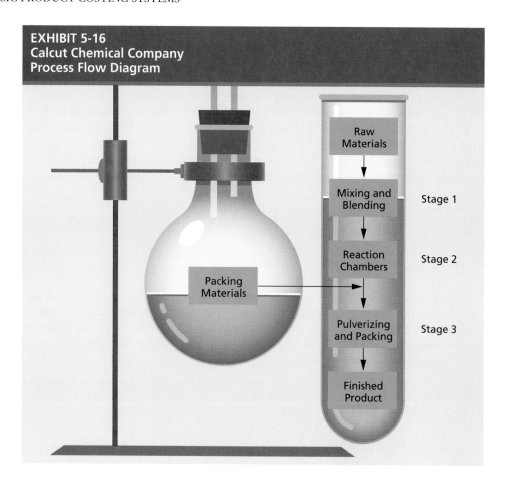

EXHIBIT 5-16
Calcut Chemical Company
Process Flow Diagram

EXHIBIT 5-17
Calcut Chemical Company
Estimated Process Costs for 1997

	Mixing and Blending	Reaction Chambers	Pulverizing and Packing
Production labor	$230,000	$1,040,000	$360,000
Engineering support	20,000	46,000	22,000
Materials handling	18,000	18,000	27,000
Equipment maintenance	10,000	32,000	8,000
Laboratory expenses	20,000	20,000	4,000
Depreciation	40,000	160,000	48,000
Power	32,000	78,000	24,000
General and administrative	16,000	16,000	16,000
Total conversion costs	$386,000	$1,410,000	$509,000
Total number of process hours	8,760	35,040	8,760
Conversion cost per process hour	$44.06	$40.24	$58.11

We refer to the total cost of all the activities performed at each stage of the process as the **conversion costs** for that stage. That is, conversion costs are the costs to convert the materials or product at each stage. The total estimated conversion costs for each stage are divided by the corresponding total number of process hours to obtain the estimated conversion cost driver rate per process hour for that stage.

Conversion costs
Costs of production labor and support activities to convert the materials or product at each process stage.

Consider two representative products, G307 and G309, manufactured and sold by Calcut Chemical. (See Exhibit 5-18.) Both products are derivatives of ethyl oleate and require the same basic raw materials, which cost $1240 per ton of finished product. The product G309 requires $234 of packing materials per ton, almost 60% more than the $146 of packing materials per ton required for G307. The first product, G307, requires the following:

6 hours per ton for mixing and blending

24 hours of reaction time

4 hours for pulverizing and packing

The second product, G309, requires the same processing time for the mixing and blending and for the reaction chamber stages. But because of the special requirements of the customers, it needs twice as much processing time for pulverizing and packing (eight versus four hours). Exhibit 5-18 presents the costs per ton of the two products.

To determine individual product costs, it is necessary to (1) identify the costs of the material input required at various stages and (2) add the estimated conversion costs for all the process stages to the material costs. For example, as Exhibit 5-18 shows, material costs per ton of product G307 include $1240 of raw materials required initially for the mixing and blending stage and $146 of packing materials used at the final pulverizing and packing stage.

The product conversion costs for each process stage are estimated by multiplying the number of process hours for that stage by the corresponding conver-

EXHIBIT 5-18
Calcut Chemical Company
Product Costs per Ton

Costs	G307		G309	
Materials:				
Raw materials	$1240.00		$1240.00	
Packing materials	146.00		234.00	
	$1386.00		$1474.00	
Conversion costs:				
Mixing and blending	$ 264.36	(6 hrs.)	$ 264.36	(6 hrs.)
Reaction chamber	965.76	(24 hrs.)	965.76	(24 hrs.)
Pulverizing and packing	232.44	(4 hrs.)	464.88	(8 hrs.)
Total conversion costs	$1462.56		$1695.00	
Total cost	$2848.56		$3169.00	

CONSIDER THIS . . .

Product Costing at Kenco Engineering

Kenco Engineering, Inc. is a family-owned firm with about $5 million in sales per year. It enjoys a reputation as a producer of high-quality cutting-edge tools made of steel impregnated with tungsten. These tools are used in construction, road building, and mining power equipment. The firm's key proprietary process is merging tungsten carbide chips with a steel plate. When the company's profit margins were good, management felt little need to collect much cost data and control costs. However, when the company experienced its first losses, it was time to implement detailed and accurate cost standards.

The new costing system divides the production process into three stages: tungsten crushing, steel cutting, and conversion processing (merging tungsten and steel). Because crushed tungsten may be purchased on the open market, it is a candidate for outsourcing. Costs assigned to the tungsten-crushing process are based on the long-term costs of operation that can be avoided if crushed tungsten is purchased from outside. This costing method yields the relevant cost of the process, which management needs in deciding whether or not to outsource.

In the past, the steel-cutting operation required an overhead crane, a cutting machine, and storage areas because steel was ordered in huge sheets and cut in house. Kenco now has precut steel delivered on a just-in-time basis by a preferred supplier; most internal costs for this operation have been eliminated.

Conversion processing has five distinct steps: bevelling, bolt-hole cutting, tungsten impregnating, straightening, and drilling. The critical, capacity-limiting step is the proprietary tungsten impregnating. Purposely, the other four steps have greater capacity and do not limit this expensive activity. The tungsten process is expected to run 80%

of the available time under normal efficient operating circumstances.

There exists only one common cost pool for all five steps of conversion processing. This pool includes costs for all overhead and all labor; they are assigned to the products in the proportion of the time spent on the tungsten-impregnating process based on its normal capacity. Only the time spent on this one step is considered for assigning costs. The other four steps are ignored because tungsten impregnating is the critical process that cannot be outsourced and therefore limits capacity. For example, reducing setup time in the bevelling step would not reduce production cycle time or generate any cost savings.

The bid sheet at Kenco Engineering breaks the cost of each product into setup, tungsten crushing, steel cutting, conversion processing, and so on. Bid prices also reflect prevailing market forces. Therefore, profit margins vary widely from one product to the next. Products with low gross-profit percents receive priority attention from Kenco managers.

Most Kenco products are customized orders, but all products have several attributes in common. Therefore, knowledge from past jobs helps improve efficiency and future bidding. For example, one job required that numerous tungsten strips make several passes through a tungsten-impregnating machine. Analysis of actual job costs revealed a negative gross profit. After engineering consultation, the product was redesigned to use a smaller number of critically placed tungsten strips and the product became profitable.

Source: James T. Mackey and Vernon H. Hughes, "Decision Focused Costing at Kenco," *Management Accounting*, May 1993, pp. 22–26.

sion cost driver rate per process hour. For instance, the conversion costs per ton of product G307 are $264.36 (6 hours × $44.06 conversion cost driver rate for the mixing and blending stage), $965.76 (24 hours × $40.24 conversion cost driver rate for the reaction chamber stage), and $232.44 (4 hours × $58.11 conversion cost driver rate for the pulverizing and packing stage). (See Exhibit 5-18.) The conversion costs per ton of product G309 are the same for the first two stages but are higher at $464.88 (8 hours × $58.11) for the pulverizing and packing stage, as noted before.

EXHIBIT 5-19
Calcut Chemical Company
First-Level Variance Analysis for Mixing and Blending Process Stage

Cost Item	Actual Costs	Estimated Costs	First-Level Variance
Production labor	$236,000	$230,000	$6,000 U
Engineering support	20,400	20,000	400 U
Materials handling	19,000	18,000	1,000 U
Equipment maintenance	9,800	10,000	200 F
Laboratory expenses	20,800	20,000	800 U
Depreciation	40,000	40,000	0
Power	31,600	32,000	400 F
General and administrative	16,000	16,000	8,760
Total conversion costs	$393,600	$386,000	$7,600
Total number of process hours	8,760	8,760	0
Conversion costs per process hour	$44.93	$44.06	$0.87 U

Variance Analysis in Process Costing Systems

Multistage process costing systems accumulate *actual* costs incurred during a period for each process stage. Knowing actual conversion costs allows calculation of a variance analysis between actual and estimated costs for individual process stages, just as in a job order cost system.

Actual conversion costs for the mixing and blending process stage are presented in Exhibit 5-19. As in the case of the previous job order costing example, first-level variances represent the difference between actual and estimated costs for a cost category. In this case, the variances for production labor, engineering support, materials handling, and laboratory costs are unfavorable because their actual costs exceed the estimated costs. Variances for equipment maintenance and power are favorable because their actual costs are less than estimated costs.

A SUMMARY EXAMPLE

We turn now to a problem that reviews some of this chapter's most important points. Mars Electronic Company manufactures a variety of electronic components. In April 1997, the company received an invitation from Precision Appliances, Inc., to bid on an order of 1000 units of component ICB371 that must be delivered by August 16, 1997. The following are the standard requirements and prices for 1000 units of ICB371:

	Quantity	Price
Direct material	2000 units	$10 per unit
Direct labor	1000 hours	10 per hour

The cost of support resources is assigned to jobs based on direct labor hours (a single cost driver rate system). The estimated support costs and direct labor hours for 1997 are $300,000 and 50,000 hours, respectively.

Mars has a policy to add a 20% markup to estimated job costs to arrive at the bid price.

(a) Prepare a job bid sheet to determine the bid price for this job.

Assume next that Precision Appliances, Inc., accepted Mars' bid. After producing and delivering the 1000 units of ICB371 to Precision on August 4, Mars' management accountants compiled the following information about this job:

	Actual Quantity	*Actual Price*
Direct material	2100 units	$ 9.75 per unit
Direct labor	1000 hours	$11.00 per hour

(b) Prepare a job cost sheet to record the actual costs incurred on this job.
(c) What were the total direct material and direct labor cost variances? What does their sum equal?
(d) What was the direct material purchase price variance? What was the direct material quantity variance? What does their sum equal?
(e) What was the direct labor rate variance? What was the direct labor efficiency variance? What does their sum equal?

The following are solutions to (a) through (e).

(a) Mars Electronic Company: Job bid sheet ICB-PR1-B
Date: April 15, 1997
Customer: Precision Appliances, Inc.
Product: ICB371
Number of units: 1,000 units

	Quantity	*Price*	*Amount*
Direct material	2000 units	$10 per unit	$20,000
Direct labor	1000 hours	10 per hour	10,000
Manufacturing support		6 per direct labor hour	6,000
Total estimated costs			$36,000
Markup (20%)			7,200
Bid price			$43,200

(b) Mars Electronic Company: Job cost sheet ICB-PR1-C
Date: August 4, 1996
Customer: Precision Appliances, Inc.
Product: ICB371
Number of units: 1,000 units

	Quantity	*Price*	*Amount*
Direct materials	2100 units	$ 9.75 per unit	$20,475
Direct labor	1000 hours	11.00 per hour	11,000
Manufacturing support		6.00 per direct labor hour	6,000
Total actual costs			$37,475

(c) *Total Direct Materials Cost Variance* $=$ *Actual Direct Material Cost* $-$ *Standard Direct Material Cost*

$$= \$20,475 \ - \ \$20,000$$
$$= \$475 \text{ U}$$

Total Direct Labor Cost Variance $=$ *Actual Direct Labor Cost* $-$ *Standard Direct Labor Cost*

$$= \$11,000 \ - \ \$10,000$$
$$= \$1,000 \text{ U}$$

Sum of Total Direct Material and Direct Labor Cost Variances $=$ $\$475$ U $+$ $\$1000$ U

$$= \$1475 \text{ U}$$
$$= \$37,475 \ - \ \$36,000$$
$$= \text{\textit{Total actual cost}} \ - \ \text{\textit{Total estimated cost}}$$

(d) *Direct Material Purchase Price Variance* $= (AP - SP) \times AQ = (\$9.75 - \$10) \times 2100$

$$= \$525 \text{ F}$$

Direct Material Quantity Variance $= (AQ - SQ) \times SP = (2100 - 2000) \times \$10$

$$= \$1,000 \text{ U}$$

Sum of Direct Material Price and Quantity Variances $=$ *Total Direct Material Cost Variance (see part c)*

$$= \$525 \text{ F} \ + \ \$1000 \text{ U}$$
$$= \$475 \text{ U}$$

(e)   *Direct
Labor Rate* $=$ $(AR - SR) \times AH$
Variance

$$= (\$11 - \$10) \times 1000$$
$$= \$1000 \text{ U}$$

*Direct
Labor
Efficiency* $=$ $(AH - SH) \times SR$
Variance

$$= (1000 - 1000) \times \$10$$
$$= \$0$$

*Sum of
Direct Labor
Rate and* $=$ *Total Direct Labor Cost Variance (see part c)*
*Efficiency
Variances*

$$= \$1000 \text{ U} + \$0$$
$$= \$1000 \text{ U}$$

SUMMARY

This chapter describes the basic principles underlying product costing systems. These systems are used to estimate and then measure actual costs of discrete job orders and products produced in continuous process industries. Although these systems are described here as two different costing systems, many costing systems observed in practice exhibit elements of both systems. Both types of cost systems identify materials and labor costs directly with jobs or products. Both systems also assign the remainder of costs to jobs or products on the basis of predetermined cost driver rates.

The support cost driver rate should be determined as the normal cost per unit of capacity of support activity that is made available. If the cost driver rate is based instead on actual or budgeted activity levels that fluctuate over time, then support activity costs will be understated in periods of high demand and will be overstated in periods of low demand. If product costing systems do not adequately reflect the systematic differences in prices and productivity of materials and labor resources and of factors driving support activity costs, the resultant job or product costs are likely to be distorted. In particular, if there are several grades of labor with widely differing productivity levels and wage rates but only a single common rate is used for all labor, then product costs are likely to be distorted for products that require different grades of labor in different proportions. Similarly, if support costs are caused by multiple cost drivers but only a single cost driver rate (a peanut butter spreading approach) is employed to assign all support costs, then product costs are likely to be distorted for products that require different proportions of the multiple cost drivers.

Most companies need to estimate product costs before actually manufacturing the products so that they can bid on jobs or price the products. Job bid sheets are prepared to calculate the estimated costs for a job. If the bid based on these estimated costs is accepted, then a job cost sheet is prepared to record the actual costs of production for the job. Recording actual costs enables companies to perform a variance analysis, comparing actual costs to the estimated costs. Variances between actual and estimated costs are analyzed into components such as materials price, materials usage, labor rate, and labor efficiency variances so companies can understand the factors contributing to the difference between actual and estimated costs. Based on this variance analysis, companies can revise their product costs or take actions that improve operations by retaining practices that led to favorable variances and eliminating the causes of unfavorable variances.

KEY TERMS

conversion costs, p. 229

cost driver rate, p. 207

cost pool, p. 207

first-level variances, p. 219

job bid sheet, p. 204

job cost sheet, p. 218

job costs, p. 206

job order costing system, p. 204

markup or margin, p. 206

markup rate, p. 206

materials requisition note, p. 216

multistage process costing system, p. 227

rate of return, p. 206

second-level variance analysis, p. 221

time card, p. 217

variance analysis, p. 219

ASSIGNMENT MATERIAL

■ QUESTIONS

5-1 Why do costs need to be estimated for individual jobs?

5-2 What information is presented in a typical job bid sheet?

5-3 What is the source of the information to estimate the cost of materials?

5-4 What is the source of the information to estimate the direct labor cost?

5-5 How are support activity cost driver rates determined?

5-6 How is support activity cost estimated for individual jobs?

5-7 What is the *markup* rate? On what factors does it depend?

5-8 What is a *cost pool*? Why are multiple cost pools required?

5-9 What problem arises when cost driver rates are based on planned or actual short-term usage instead of normal usage? Why?

5-10 What is the *normal cost* of a support activity? What is the *normal usage level* of a cost driver?

5-11 "Use of a peanut butter spreading approach of a single cost driver rate when there are multiple cost drivers leads to distortions in job costs." Do you agree with this statement? Explain.

5-12 What is the managerial use of tracking actual costs of individual jobs?

5-13 What documents initiate the recording of actual direct materials and direct labor costs for individual jobs?

5-14 Why are *predetermined* cost driver rates used when recording actual job costs?

5-15 How does analysis of reasons for variances between actual and estimated job costs help managers?

5-16 What is the difference between the first and the second levels of variance analysis?

5-17 "If more experienced workers work on the job than planned in developing the labor standards, the labor efficiency variance is likely to be favorable but the labor wage variance is likely to be unfavorable." Do you agree with this statement? Explain.

5-18 Why is it useful to decompose a first-level variance into a price variance and a quantity variance?

5-19 What effect will the purchase and use of cheaper, lower-quality materials likely have on price and quantity components of both materials and labor variances?

5-20 What does the term *conversion costs* mean?

5-21 What considerations are important in estimating product costs in continuous processing plants?

5-22 Why do variations in yield rates across products introduce additional complexity in estimating product costs?

■ EXERCISES

5-23 *Plantwide versus departmental rates* Wright Wood Products has two production departments: cutting and assembly. The company has been using a single predetermined cost driver rate based on plantwide direct labor hours. The estimates for 1997 follow:

	Cutting	Assembly	Total
Manufacturing support	$25,000	$35,000	$60,000
Direct labor hours	1000	3000	4000
Machine hours	4000	2000	6000

(a) What was the single plant-wide cost driver rate for 1997?
(b) Determine departmental cost driver rates based on direct labor hours for assembly and machine-hours for cutting.

5-24 *Variance analysis*   The following information is available for job KL37 for Burjor Company:

Actual:
Materials used: 10,500 pounds purchased at $2.50 per pound
Direct labor: 1800 hours at $12 per hour
Units produced: 500

Standard:
Materials: 20 pounds per unit at a price of $2.20 per pound
Direct labor: 4 hours per unit at a wage rate of $10 per hour

(a) Determine the material price variance and quantity variance.
(b) Determine the direct labor rate variance and efficiency variance.

5-25 *Variance analysis*   Phiroze Company employs a standard cost system. Job 8822 is for the manufacture of 500 units of the product P521. The company's standards for one unit of the product P521 are as follows:

	Quantity	Price
Direct material	5 oz	$2 per oz
Direct labor	2 hrs.	$10 per hr.

The job requires 2800 ounces of raw material costing $5880. An unfavorable labor rate variance of $250 and a favorable labor efficiency variance of $100 also were determined for this job.

(a) What was the direct material purchase price variance?
(b) What was the direct material quantity variance?
(c) Determine the actual quantity of direct labor hours used on job 8822.
(d) Determine the actual direct labor costs incurred for job 8822.

5-26 *Variance analysis*   Each unit of job Y7023 has standard requirements of 5 pounds of raw material at a price of $100 per pound and 0.5 hours of direct labor at $12 per hour. To produce 9,000 units of this product, job Y7023 actually required 40,000 pounds of the raw material costing $97 per pound. The job used a total of 5,000 direct labor hours costing a total of $60,000.

(a) Determine the material price and quantity variances.
(b) Assume that the materials used on this job were purchased from a new supplier. Would you recommend continuing with this new supplier? Why or why not?
(c) Determine the direct labor rate and efficiency variances.

5-27 ***Standard costs versus actual costs***   Assembly of the product P13 requires one unit of component X, two units of component Y, and three units of component Z. Job J1372 produced 220 units of P13. The following information pertains to material variances for this job, analyzed by component:

	X	**Y**	**Z**
Price variance	160U	120F	192U
Usage variance	168U	100U	84F

The actual prices were $0.30 more, $0.20 less, and $0.50 more per unit for components X, Y, and Z, respectively, than their standard prices.

(a) Determine the number of units consumed of each component.
(b) Determine the standard price per unit of each component.

5-28 *Process costs*   Health Foods Company produces and sells canned vegetable juice. The ingredients are first combined in the blending department and then packed in gallon cans in the canning department. The following information pertains to the blending department for January 1997.

Item	**Price per Gal**	**Gal**
Ingredient A	$0.40	10,000
Ingredient B	0.60	20,000
Vegetable juice		27,000
Materials loss		3,000

Conversion costs for the blending department are $0.55 per gallon for January 1997.

(a) Determine the yield rate.
(b) Determine the cost per gallon of blended vegetable juice before canning.

5-29 *Process costs*   Washington Chemical Company manufactures and sells Goody, a product that sells for $10 per pound. The manufacturing process also yields one pound of a waste product called Baddy in the production of every 10 pounds of Goody. Disposal of the waste product costs $1 per pound. During March 1995, the company manufactured 200,000 pounds of Goody. Total manufacturing costs were as follows:

Direct materials	$232,000
Direct labor	120,000
Manufacturing support costs	60,000
Total costs	$412,000

Determine the cost per pound of Goody.

■ PROBLEMS

Fundamental Problems

5-30 *Job cost sheet*   Portland Electronics, Inc. delivered 1,000 custom-designed computer monitors on February 10 to its customer Video Shack; they had been ordered on January 1. The following cost information was compiled in connection with this order:

Direct materials used:
Part A327: 1 unit costing $60 per monitor
Part B149: 1 unit costing $120 per monitor

Direct labor used:
Assembly: 6 hours per monitor at the rate of $10 per hour
Inspection: 1 hour per monitor at the rate of $12 per hour

In addition, manufacturing support costs are applied to the job at the rate of $5 per direct labor hour. The selling price for each monitor is $350.

(a) Prepare a job cost sheet for this job.
(b) Determine the cost per monitor.

5-31 *Job cost sheet*   The following costs pertain to job 379 at Baker Auto Shop.

	Quantity	Price
Direct materials:		
Engine oil	11 ounces	$ 2 per ounce
Lubricant	2 ounces	3 per ounce
Direct labor	3 hours	15 per hour
Support costs (based on direct labor hours):		10 per hour

Prepare a job cost sheet for Baker Auto Shop.

5-32 *Job cost sheet*   Duluth Metalworks Company has two departments, milling and assembly. The company uses a job costing system that employs a single, plantwide support cost driver rate to apply support costs to jobs on the basis of direct labor hours. The following estimates are for May 1997:

	Milling	**Assembly**
Support costs	$120,000	$160,000
Direct labor hours	8,000	12,000
Machine hours	12,000	6,000

The following information pertains to job 691, which was started and completed during May 1997:

	Milling	**Assembly**
Direct labor hours	10	40
Machine hours	18	8
Direct materials costs	$800	$50
Direct labor costs	$100	$600

(a) Prepare a job cost sheet for job 691.
(b) Assume next that instead of using a single, plantwide support cost driver rate, the company uses machine hours and direct labor hours as cost drivers for the application of support costs in the milling and assembly departments, respectively. Prepare a job cost sheet for job 691.

5-33 *Variance Analysis*   The Sudbury, South Carolina, plant of Saldanha Sports Company has the following standards for its soccer ball production.

Standards:
Material (leather) per soccer ball	0.25 yard
Material price per yard	$16
Direct labor hours per soccer ball	0.20 hours
Wage rate per direct labor hour	$10 per hour

Actual Results for October 1996:
Purchased and used 13,000 yards of raw material for $205,150.
Beginning raw material inventory was zero yards.
Paid for 8240 direct labor hours at $9.50 per hour.
Manufactured 40,000 soccer balls.

REQUIRED

Determine the following variances for October 1996:
(a) Total direct material cost variance
(b) Total direct labor cost variance
(c) Direct material purchase price variance
(d) Direct material quantity variance
(e) Direct labor rate variance
(f) Direct labor-efficiency variance

5-34 *Job costing*   The Gonzalez Company uses a job order costing system at its Green Bay, Wisconsin, plant. The plant has a machining department and a finishing department. The company uses two cost driver rates for allocating manufacturing support costs to job orders: one on the basis of machine hours for allocating machining department support costs and the other on the basis of direct labor cost for allocating the finishing department support costs. Estimates for 1997 follow:

	Machining Department	**Finishing Department**
Manufacturing support cost	$500,000	$400,000
Machine hours	20,000	2,000
Direct labor hours	5,000	22,000
Direct labor cost	$150,000	$500,000

REQUIRED

(a) Determine the two departmental cost driver rates.
(b) During the month of January 1997, cost records for Job 134 show the following:

	Machining Department	**Finishing Department**
Direct materials cost	$12,000	$2,000
Direct labor cost	$300	$1,200
Direct labor hours	10	50
Machine hours	80	8

Determine the total costs charged to Job 134 in January 1997.

(c) Explain why Gonzalez Company uses two different cost driver rates in its job costing system.

5-35 *Standard versus actual costs*   For each of the following two jobs manufacturing two different products, determine the missing amounts for items (a) through (h).

Item	Job 321	Job 322
Units produced	200	(e)
Standards per unit:		
Material quantity	5 lb	(f)
Material price	$2 per lb	$3 per lb
Labor hours	2 hrs.	3 hrs.
Labor rate	$15 per hr.	$12 per hr.
Actual consumption:		
Material quantity	(a)	1000 lb
Material cost	$2000	(g)
Labor hours	(b)	(h)
Labor cost	(c)	$5800
Variances:		
Material quantity	(d)	$100 F
Material price	$50 U	$500 F
Labor hour	$100 F	$50 U
Labor rate	$60 U	$200 F

5-36 *Job costing* The Goldstein Company employs a job order cost system to account for its costs. There are three production departments. Separate departmental cost driver rates are employed because the demand for support activities for the three departments is very different. All jobs generally pass through all three production departments. Data regarding the hourly direct labor rates, cost driver rates, and three jobs on which work was done during the month of April 1997 appears below. Job 101 and job 102 were completed during April, while job 103 was not completed as of April 30, 1997. The costs charged to jobs not completed at the end of a month are shown as work in process at the end of that month and at the beginning of the next month.

Production Departments	Direct Labor Rate	Cost Driver Rates
Department 1	$12	150% of direct material cost
Department 2	18	$8 per machine hour
Department 3	15	200% of direct labor cost

	Job 101	**Job 102**	**Job 103**
Beginning work in process	$25,500	$32,400	$0
Direct materials:			
Department 1	$40,000	$26,000	$58,000
Department 2	3,000	5,000	14,000
Department 3	0	0	0
Direct labor hours:			
Department 1	500	400	300
Department 2	200	250	350
Department 3	1500	1800	2500
Machine hours:			
Department 1	0	0	0
Department 2	1200	1500	2700
Department 3	150	300	200

REQUIRED

(a) Determine the total cost of completed job 101.
(b) Determine the total cost of completed job 102.
(c) Determine the ending balance of work in process for job 103 as of April 30, 1997.

Challenging Problems

5-37 *Plantwide versus departmental rates* Bravo Steel Company supplies structural steel products to the construction industry. Its plant has three production departments: cutting, grinding, and drilling. The estimated support activity cost and direct labor and machine hour levels for each department for June 1997 follow:

	Cutting	Grinding	Drilling
Support activity cost	$42,000	$192,000	$228,000
Direct labor hours	5,000	8,000	12,000
Machine hours	80,000	40,000	30,000

The direct labor and machine hours consumed by job ST101 are as follows:

	Cutting	Grinding	Drilling
Direct labor hours	2,000	2,500	3,000
Machine hours	20,000	3,000	2,000

(a) Assume that a single, plantwide predetermined cost driver rate is used on the basis of direct labor hours. Determine the support cost applied to job ST101.

(b) Determine the departmental support cost driver rate and support costs applied to job ST101, assuming that machine hours are used as the cost driver application base in the cutting department and that direct labor hours are used as the cost driver for the grinding and drilling departments.

5-38 *Variance analysis, process costing* Trieste Toy Company manufactures only one product, called Robot Ranger. The company uses a standard cost system and has established the following standards per unit of Robot Ranger.

	Standard Quantity	Standard Price	Standard Cost
Direct materials	3.0 pounds	$12 per pound	$ 36.00
Direct labor	1.2 hours	15 per hour	18.00
			$54.00

During November 1996, the following activity was recorded by the company for the production of Robot Ranger.

(1) The company produced 6000 units during the month.

(2) A total of 21,000 pounds of material were purchased at a cost of $241,500.

(3) There was no beginning inventory of materials on hand to start the month; 1800 pounds of materials remained in the warehouse unused.

(4) The company employs 40 persons to work on the production of Robot Ranger. During November, each worked an average of 160 hours at an average rate of $16 per hour.

The company's management wishes to determine the efficiency of the activities related to the production of Robot Ranger.

REQUIRED

(a) For direct materials used in the production of Robot Ranger:

■ Compute direct material purchase price variance and direct material quantity variance.

■ The direct materials were purchased from a new supplier who is anxious to enter into a long-term purchase contract. Would you recommend that the company sign the contract? Explain.

(b) For direct labor employed in the production of Robot Ranger:

■ Compute direct labor rate variance and direct labor efficiency variance.

■ In the past, the 40 persons employed in the production of Robot Ranger consisted of 16 experienced workers and 24 inexperienced assistants. During November, the company experimented with 20 experienced workers and 20 inexperienced assistants. Would you recommend that the new labor mix be continued? Explain.

5-39 *Charging for service activity costs* Airporter Service Company operates scheduled coach service from Boston's Logan Airport to downtown Boston and to Cambridge. A common scheduling service center at the airport is responsible for ticketing and customer service for both routes. The service center is regularly staffed to service traffic of 2400 passengers per week: two-thirds for downtown Boston passengers and the balance for Cambridge passengers. The costs of this service center are $7200 per week normally, but they are higher in weeks when additional help is required to service higher traffic levels. The service center costs and number of passengers serviced during the five weeks of August follow:

Week	Cost	Boston Passengers	Cambridge Passengers
1	$7200	1600	800
2	7200	1500	900
3	7600	1650	800
4	7800	1700	850
5	7200	1700	700

How much of the service center costs should be charged to the Boston service, and how much to the Cambridge service? Explain why your method should be preferred over the other alternatives.

5-40 *Variance analysis, process costs in service industry*   (Adapted from CMA, June 1989) Mountain View Hospital has adopted a standard cost accounting system for evaluation and control of nursing labor. Diagnosis Related Groups (DRGs), instituted by the U.S. government for health insurance reimbursement, are used as the output measure in the standard cost system. A *DRG* is a patient classification scheme that perceives hospitals to be multiproduct firms where inpatient treatment procedures are related to the numbers and types of patient ailments treated. Mountain View Hospital has developed standard nursing times for the treatment of each DRG classification, and nursing labor hours are assumed to vary with the number of DRGs treated within a time period.

The nursing unit on the fourth floor treats patients with four DRG classifications. The unit is staffed with registered nurses (RNs), licensed practical nurses (LPNs), and aides. The standard nursing hours and salary rates are as follows.

	Fourth Floor Nursing Unit Standard Hours		
DRG Classification	RN	LPN	Aide
1	6	4	5
2	26	16	10
3	10	5	4
4	12	7	10

Standard Hourly Rates	
RN	$12
LPN	8
Aide	6

For the month of May 1997, the results of operations for the fourth floor nursing unit are presented below.

Actual Number of Patients	
DRG 1	250
DRG 2	90
DRG 3	240
DRG 4	140
	720

	RN	LPN	Aide
Actual hours	8,150	4,300	4,400
Actual salary	$100,245	$35,260	$25,300
Actual hourly rate	$12.30	$8.20	$5.75

The accountant for Mountain View Hospital calculated the following standard times for the fourth floor nursing unit for May 1997.

DRG Classification	No. of Patients	Standard Hours/DRG			Total Standard Hours		
		RN	LPN	Aide	RN	LPN	Aide
1	250	6	4	5	1500	1000	1250
2	90	26	16	10	2340	1440	900
3	240	10	5	4	2400	1200	960
4	140	12	7	10	1680	980	1400
					7920	4620	4510

The hospital calculates labor variances for each reporting period by labor classification (RN, LPN, Aide). The variances are used by nursing supervisors and hospital administration to evaluate the performance of nursing labor.

REQUIRED

Calculate the total nursing labor variance for the fourth floor nursing unit of Mountain View Hospital for May 1997, indicating how much of this variance is attributed to the following for each class of nurses:

(a) labor efficiency
(b) rate differences

5-41 *Variance analysis, Job costing* Asahi USA, Inc. is a Denver, Colorado based subsidiary of a Japanese company manufacturing specialty tools. Asahi USA employs a standard cost system. Presented below are standards per unit of one of its products, tool KJ79. This tool requires as direct materials a special chrome steel.

	Standard Quantity	Standard Price	Standard Cost
Direct materials	8 pounds	$18 per pound	$144
Direct labor	2.5 hours	$ 8 per hour	20
			$164

During November 1996, Asahi USA started and completed job KJX86 to manufacture 1900 units of tool KJ79. It purchased 16,000 pounds of the special chrome steel for tool KJ79 at a total cost of $304,000. The total direct labor charged to Job KJX86 was $37,800. Job KJX86 actually consumed 14,250 pounds of the special chrome steel and 5000 direct labor hours.

REQUIRED

(a) For job KJX86, do the following:
   (i)   Compute the direct material purchase price variance.
   (ii) Compute the direct material quantity variance.
   (iii) Compute the direct labor rate variance.
   (iv) Compute the direct labor efficiency variance.

Use "U" or "F" to indicate whether the variances are unfavorable or favorable.

(b) Prepare a plausible explanation for the variances.

■ CASE

5-42 *Alternative job costing systems*   Refer to the facts presented in Case 4-52 about the operations of Anthony's Autoshop. The following additional information is available:

The present job costing system uses a single conversion rate for all jobs. The cost driver rate is currently determined by dividing estimated total labor and support costs by expected hours charged to customers. The eight mechanics are expected to be busy on customer jobs for 95% of the total available time. The price of $51.06 per hour is determined by adding a markup of x% to the cost driver rate, that is $51.06 = [1 + (x/100)] \times$ cost driver rate. Note that all personnel costs are included in conversion costs at present.

The manager is considering switching to the use of two rates, one for class A repairs and another for class B repairs. Electronic ignition system repairs or internal carburetor repairs are examples of Class A repairs. Class A repairs require careful measurements and adjustments with equipment such as an oscilloscope or infrared gas analyzer. Class B repairs are simple repairs such as shock absorber replacements or exhaust part replacements. Class A repairs can be done only by senior mechanics; class B repairs are done mainly by junior mechanics. Half of the hours charged to customers are expected to be for class A repairs, and the other half are for class B repairs. Because class A repairs are expected to account for all of the senior mechanic time and most of the machine usage, 60% of the total costs (including personnel costs) are attributable to class A repairs and the remaining 40% to class B repairs.

(a) Determine the markup of x% currently used.

(b) Determine the two new rates, one for class A repairs and another for class B repairs, using the same markup of x% that you determined in (a) above.

(c) The following are expected labor hours anticipated for 2 customer jobs:

Job No.	Description	Class A Repairs	Class B Repairs
101	Carburetor repairs	4.5 hr.	1.5 hr.
102	Exhaust replacement	none	2.0 hr.

Determine the price to be charged for each of the two jobs under the present accounting system and under the proposed accounting system.

(d) What change in service mix is likely to result from the proposed price change?

6

TWO-STAGE ALLOCATIONS AND ACTIVITY-BASED COSTING SYSTEMS

MEDEQUIP

"We have been very successful with our new product line over the last two years. Sales reports from every market indicate sales growth of 25% or better for the new line. You report a gross margin of 80% for all of our new products, yet our operating profits have gone down almost 20%," said Charles Eager to his controller, Kendra Rivers. "Please explain to me why our financial performance does not reflect the excellent sales performance."

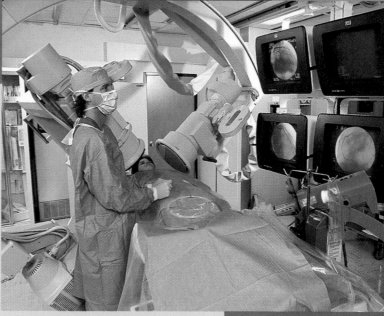

Courtesy **Bob Daemmrich/The Image Works**

Charles Eager had assumed the post of the chief executive officer of Medequip, Inc. in 1996. Medequip is a Minneapolis-based manufacturer of equipment for bacteriological analysis with about $32 million in annual sales. Soon after taking over the helm at Medequip, Eager introduced a new line of equipment for special hematological (blood) analysis to beef up the old product line, whose growth rate had begun to slow down. The Medequip sales force was able to sell the old products several units at a time to medium and large hospitals, but the new products need to be sold one unit at a time to special pathology laboratories. The sales force adapted well to the need to service this new group of customers, and sales of the new product line indicated a good response to its efforts.

The present product costing system reports only a 25% gross margin on average for the old products, in contrast to the 80% gross margin on average for the new products. Medequip found that the sales of its old product line were declining in a market that was growing slowly. In contrast, its new product line had captured more than 30% of the market share despite its apparently high gross margins. The new line now accounted for approximately 33% of Medequip's sales revenues. Although overall sales had grown, *selling and administrative expenses had increased more than expected*, and Kendra found that Medequip profits had declined in each of the last two years.

As Kendra thought more about the possible factors that might explain declining profitability, she decided to take a closer look at the cost accounting system. She wanted to understand why actual costs were higher than those projected based on the product costs determined using Medequip's existing product costing system.

TWO-STAGE COST ALLOCATION METHOD

Cost accounting systems assign operating expenses to products with a two-stage procedure. First, expenses are assigned to production departments and then, in the second stage, production department expenses are assigned to the products. Let's begin by discussing how departmental structure influences the first-stage allocation process and then move to examples of the use of specific allocation methods.

The Effect of Departmental Structure on Allocation

Production departments
Departments directly responsible for some of the work of converting raw materials into finished products.

Many plants are organized into departments that are responsible for performing designated activities. Departments that have direct responsibility for converting raw materials into finished products are called **production departments.** In a manufacturing plant such as Medequip, casting, machining, assembly, and packing are production departments. Departments performing activities that support

Ball Corporation, which manufactures metal and glass containers, uses Computer-Aided-Design to develop containers that meet customer requirements while providing for ease in manufacturability. The cost of this product designer and the equipment he is using must be assigned to the product lines that benefit from the design work. The challenge facing the management accountant in this operation would be to choose the appropriate cost driver(s) to use to allocate the product design costs. *Courtesy* Ball Corporation

production, such as machine maintenance, machine setup, production engineering, and production scheduling, are **service departments.** All service department costs are indirect support activity costs because they do not arise from direct production activities.

Conventional product costing systems assign indirect costs to jobs or products in two stages. In the first stage, the system identifies indirect costs with various production and service departments, and then all of the service department costs are allocated to production departments. In the second stage, the system assigns the accumulated indirect costs for the production departments to individual jobs or products based on predetermined departmental cost driver rates. (See Exhibit 6-1.)

At the Medequip plant there are four production departments: casting, machining, assembly, and packing. In addition, there are five service departments: machine maintenance, machine setup, production scheduling, production engineering, and general and administrative. The cost accounting system accumulates costs separately for each of these nine departments.

Costs accumulated for the four production departments include supervision, supplies, and machine depreciation costs. Costs for the five service departments include the salaries, wages, and benefits of the engineers and workers who are responsible for these activities as well as the costs of the tools and materials they use. Costs for the general and administrative service department include the salaries and benefits for plant managerial staff, rent, heating and lighting, and janitorial services.

Service departments
Departments that perform activities that support production but are not responsible for any of the conversion stages.

OBJECTIVE 6.1

Understand why the difference between production and service departments is important.

OBJECTIVE 6.2

Discuss the importance and method of allocation of service department costs to production departments.

EXHIBIT 6-1
Two-Stage Cost Allocation System

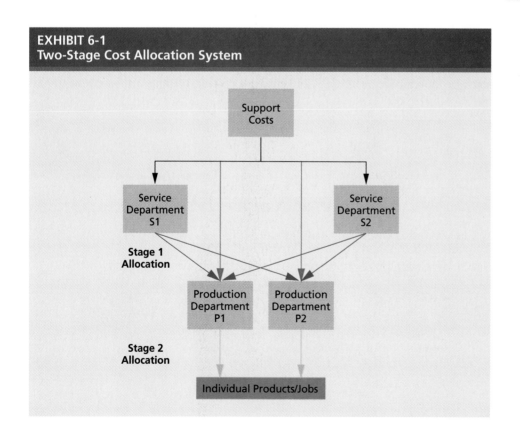

Stage 1 Cost Allocations

The first step in Stage 1 of the cost allocation procedure involves estimation of the normal manufacturing support costs incurred in each department. The following summary reflects the total support costs for the nine departments, which are depicted in Exhibit 6-2:

MEDEQUIP

ESTIMATE OF MANUFACTURING SUPPORT COSTS

Departments	Support Costs
Production:	
Casting	$ 65,600
Machining	131,600
Assembly	51,000
Packing	29,600
Service:	
Machine maintenance	160,000
Machine setup	300,000
Production scheduling	120,000
Production engineering	180,000
General and administrative	90,000
Total manufacturing support costs	$1,127,800

Because jobs are worked on in production departments, it is relatively easy to identify the number of direct labor and machine hours for individual jobs in each production department. Conventional costing systems are based on the as-

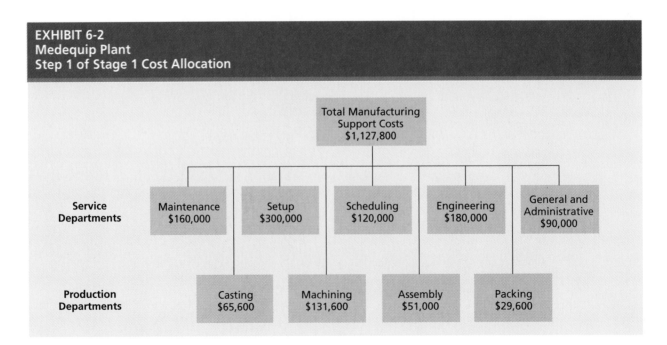

EXHIBIT 6-2
Medequip Plant
Step 1 of Stage 1 Cost Allocation

sumption that we cannot obtain *direct* measures of use of service departments' resources on individual jobs as conveniently as we can of production departments' resources because jobs are worked on only in production departments. Therefore, conventional costing systems allocate the service department costs first to the production departments before assigning them to individual jobs. This assignment of costs from the service departments to production departments is the second step in Stage 1 of the cost allocation procedure. There are several different methods of allocating service department costs. We shall describe only the basic principles of **Stage 1 allocations** with reference to a specific method.

Direct Allocation Method

The **direct allocation method** is a simple method that allocates the service department costs directly to the production departments, ignoring the possibility that some of the activities of a service department may benefit other service departments in addition to the production departments. Other allocation methods are designed to reflect situations in which considerable interaction occurs between service departments. The **sequential allocation method** allocates service department costs one service department at a time in sequential order. The **reciprocal allocation method** determines service department cost allocations simultaneously. Appendix 6-1 presents a discussion of these two methods in more detail. Here we describe only the direct allocation method.

Allocation Bases at Medequip

Allocation of costs requires the identification for each service department of a basis, or cost driver, that best reflects and measures the activity performed by that department. The Medequip plant uses the following bases to allocate service department costs by the direct allocation method.

Stage 1 allocations
Identification of costs with individual production and service departments (step 1), followed by allocation of service department costs to production departments (step 2).

Direct allocation method
A simple method to allocate service department costs to production departments that ignores interdependencies between service departments.

Sequential allocation method
A method that recognizes interdependencies between service departments and allocates service department costs one service department at a time in a sequential order.

Reciprocal allocation method
A method to determine service department cost allocations simultaneously that recognizes the reciprocity between pairs of service departments.

Data processing costs are significant in most large organizations. This employee in Upjohn's Administrative Computer Center, a service department, has developed a system that administrators can use to mail reports to customers and that customers can use to retrieve reports electronically. This system improves the report delivery cycle time and reduces the amount of paper used by Upjohn by about 2.5 million pages each month. This new system means that the costs in this department can no longer be allocated based on report pages printed, a common method of allocating computer center costs. *Courtesy* The Upjohn Company

Service Department	*Allocation Basis*
Machine maintenance	Book value of machines in each production department
Machine setup	Number of setups in each production department
Production scheduling	Number of machine hours in each production department
Production engineering	Number of direct labor hours in each production department
General and administrative	Number of square feet occupied by each production department

The allocation bases do not always perfectly reflect the activities that generate service department costs. For example, the number of hours of setup work in each production department is a better basis than the number of setups for allocating setup department costs if the time required per setup differs across production departments. Similarly, expected maintenance hours for each department is a better measure for allocating machine maintenance costs than the book value of machines. However, there must be a trade-off between the additional cost of collecting such information against the potential benefits of the greater accuracy that its use may provide. For instance, Medequip did not believe that the costs of obtaining information about maintenance hours in each department justified the benefit from the greater accuracy it might provide. Therefore, the company uses the book value of machines to allocate maintenance costs because this measure is easily available.

It is often difficult to obtain any reasonable measures to allocate the costs of product-sustaining or facility-sustaining activities to production departments. Production scheduling, engineering, and plant administration activities do not benefit specific production departments although their use may differ across dif-

EXHIBIT 6-3
Medequip
Allocation Bases Values for Production Departments

Allocation Bases	Production Departments				Totals
	Casting	Machining	Assembly	Packing	
Book value of machines	$300,000	$600,000	$180,000	$120,000	$1,200,000
Number of setups	200	400	200	200	1,000
Machine hours	6,000	22,000	9,000	3,000	40,000
Direct labor hours	2,000	11,000	6,000	6,000	25,000
Square feet	6,000	9,000	9,000	6,000	30,000

ferent products. Medequip uses machine hours and direct labor hours as the bases to allocate these costs to the production departments. Keep in mind the previous discussion about external financial reporting requirements, such as the valuation of inventory, which have influenced the design of product costing systems in the past. As a result, the objective of most conventional product costing systems, such as the one at the Medequip plant, is to assign all manufacturing costs to jobs and products.

Exhibit 6-3 presents the allocation bases and their values for the production departments at Medequip. The allocation of normal costs of the service departments to the production departments is made in proportion to their *respective allocation basis value.*

To complete the allocation procedure for Stage 1, do the following:

1. Obtain the ratio of allocation of machine maintenance service costs to the casting department. To illustrate, consider the ratio 0.250 in the top left hand corner of Exhibit 6-4. This is the ratio of $300,000, the book value of the machines in the casting department, to $1,200,000, the total book value of machines in the four production departments.

$$\underbrace{\$300,000 \div \$1,200,000}_{\substack{\uparrow \\ \text{see Exhibit 6-3}}} = \underbrace{0.250}_{\substack{\uparrow \\ \text{see Exhibit 6-4}}}$$

2. Determine the amount of service department costs allocated to the production department costs by multiplying the allocation ratio by the corresponding service department costs. (See Exhibit 6-5.) For example, the casting department receives $40,000 of machine maintenance service department costs.

$$\underbrace{0.250 \times \$160,000}_{\substack{\uparrow \\ \text{see Exhibit 6-2}}} = \underbrace{\$40,000}_{\substack{\uparrow \\ \text{see Exhibit 6-5}}}$$

3. Add the allocated costs from the service departments to the costs originally identified with the production departments.

$$\overset{\substack{\text{see Exhibit 6-2} \\ \downarrow}}{\$65,600} + \overset{\substack{\text{see Exhibit 6-5} \\ \downarrow}}{\underbrace{\$150,400}} = \overset{\downarrow}{\$216,000}$$

$$\underbrace{}_{\downarrow}$$

$$\$40,000 + \$60,000 + \$18,000 + \$14,400 + \$18,000$$

This completes Stage 1 of the cost allocation procedure. The $1,127,800 of both service and production departmental costs for the Medequip plant were allocated to the production departments as follows: $216,000 to casting; $503,800 to machining; $232,200 to assembly; and $175,800 to packing. (See Exhibit 6-6.) During Stage 2 of the allocation procedure, these amounts are used to determine the departmental cost driver rates for assignment of these costs to the jobs worked on in each production department.

EXHIBIT 6-4
Medequip
Allocation Ratios

Service Department	Allocation Basis	PRODUCTION DEPARTMENTS				
		Casting	Machining	Assembly	Packing	Totals
Machine maintenance	Book value of machines	0.250	0.500	0.150	0.100	1.000
Machine setup	Number of setups	0.200	0.400	0.200	0.200	1.000
Production scheduling	Machine hours	0.150	0.550	0.225	0.075	1.000
Production engineering	Direct labor hours	0.080	0.440	0.240	0.240	1.000
General & administrative	Square feet	0.200	0.300	0.300	0.200	1.000

Stage 2 Cost Allocations

Stage 2 allocations
Assignment of costs accumulated in production departments to individual products.

Stage 2 allocations require the identification of appropriate cost drivers for each production department and assign production department costs to jobs and products while they are worked on in the departments. Conventional cost accounting systems use unit-related cost drivers, such as the number of units made, the number of direct labor hours (or direct labor cost), and the number of machine hours. Medequip uses machine hours as the cost driver for the casting and machining de-

EXHIBIT 6-5
Medequip
Allocation of Service Department Costs to Production Departments

Service Department Costs	PRODUCTION DEPARTMENTS			
	Casting	Machining	Assembly	Packing
Support costs identified directly in step 1 of stage 1 allocations	$ 65,600	$131,600	$ 51,000	$ 29,600
Allocated from service department in step 2 of stage 1:				
Machine maintenance	40,000	80,000	24,000	16,000
Machine setup	60,000	120,000	60,000	60,000
Production scheduling	18,000	66,000	27,000	9,000
Production engineering	14,400	79,200	43,200	43,200
General and administrative	18,000	27,000	27,000	18,000
Total support costs for the production departments	$216,000	$503,800	$232,200	$175,800

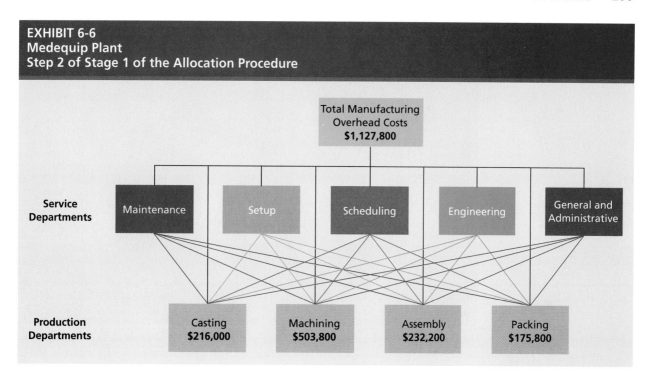

EXHIBIT 6-6
Medequip Plant
Step 2 of Stage 1 of the Allocation Procedure

partments because of their high reliance on machines for the operations performed in these departments. The assembly and packing operations are more labor intensive; therefore, Medequip uses direct labor hours as the cost driver in these two departments. (See Exhibit 6-7.)

Dividing the indirect costs accumulated in each production department by the total number of units of the corresponding cost driver results in obtaining cost driver rates for each department. To illustrate, the total indirect support costs from Stage 1 are $216,000 for the casting department, with total machine hours estimated to be 6,000. Therefore, the cost driver rate for the casting department is $36 per machine hour ($216,000 ÷ 6,000).

OBJECTIVE 6.3

Identify and use the two stages of cost allocations and understand the differences between them.

EXHIBIT 6-7
Medequip
Stage 2: Cost Driver Rates for Production Departments

	PRODUCTION DEPARTMENTS			
	Casting	**Machining**	**Assembly**	**Packing**
Total support costs (from step 2 of stage 1)	$216,000	$503,800	$232,200	$175,800
Allocation basis	Machine hours	Machine hours	Direct labor hours	Direct labor hours
Total machine hours	6,000	22,000	9,000	3,000
Total direct labor hours	2,000	11,000	6,000	6,000
Allocation rate	$36.00	$22.90	$38.70	$29.30

This maintenance department employee at a Wheeling-Pittsburgh steel mill designed an effective way to balance the cost associated with premature parts replacement and the cost of equipment failure to determine the best time to undertake preventative maintenance on equipment. The number of hours worked might be a way of allocating the cost of this employee's activities to the production department so that product costs will reflect the cost of his contribution. *Courtesy* Wheeling-Pittsburgh Steel

Support costs are applied to each job as it is worked on in the production departments. Exhibit 6-8 presents data on the number of machine and direct labor hours incurred on two representative jobs, J189-4 and J273-2, in each production department. Job J189-4 involves the production of a batch of 12 units of E189, bacterial analysis equipment in the old product line. Job J273-2 is for the produc-

EXHIBIT 6-8 Medequip Machine and Labor Hours for Two Representative Jobs		
	Job J189-4 (Old Product Line)	**Job J273-2 (New Product Line)**
Machine hours:		
Casting	30	16
Machining	140	56
Assembly	60	24
Packing	20	18
Direct labor hours:		
Casting	18	7
Machining	70	28
Assembly	40	16
Packing	40	16

tion of a batch of five units of E273, one of the new products whose sales have been increasing rapidly.

Exhibits 6-9 and 6-10 present the costs for direct materials, direct labor, and support costs applied to these two jobs. Recall from Chapter 5 that direct material costs are identified with the jobs based on requisition notes issued for materials required in the casting department, subassemblies required in the assembly department, and packing materials required in the packing department. Direct labor costs are determined by multiplying the number of direct labor hours by the labor wage rate applicable to each department. (See Exhibit 6-8.) The wage rate is higher in the machining department than in the packing department because more skilled workers are required for machining operations.

To obtain support costs for the jobs J189-4 (Exhibit 6-9) and J273-2 (Exhibit 6-10), multiply the number of machine hours by the departmental cost driver rate for the casting and machining departments, and the number of direct labor hours by the cost driver rate for the assembly and packing departments (See Exhibits 6-9, 6-10, and 6-7.) Notice that the number of machine-hours and direct labor hours used for these calculations correspond to the amount of time spent on the job in a particular department rather than on the *totals* for the job in the entire plant. The total manufacturing costs for each job are the sum of the direct material, direct labor, and support costs. To obtain the manufacturing cost per unit, divide total manufacturing costs for the job by the number of units produced in the job.

EXHIBIT 6-9
Medequip
Application of Support Costs to Job J189-4

Item	Costs	Calculation Details
Direct materials costs:		
Casting	$ 2,658.40	
Assembly	1,446.60	*given*
Packing	632.80	
Total materials costs	$ 4,737.80	
Direct labor costs:		
Casting	$ 331.20	18 × $18.40
Machining	1,666.00	70 × $23.80
Assembly	632.00	40 × $15.80 *given*
Packing	528.00	40 × $13.20
Total direct labor costs	$ 3,157.20	
Support costs:		
Casting	$ 1,080.00	30 × $36.00
Machining	3,206.00	140 × $22.90 *see*
Assembly	1,548.00	40 × $38.70 *Exhibit 6-7*
Packing	1,172.00	40 × $29.30
Total support costs	$ 7,006.00	
Total manufacturing costs	$14,901.00	
Number of units	12	
Cost per unit	$1,241.75	

EXHIBIT 6-10
Medequip
Application of Support Costs to Job J273-2

Item	Costs	Calculation Details
Direct materials costs:		
Casting	$1,186.60	
Assembly	788.80	*given*
Packing	491.40	
Total materials costs	**$2,466.80**	
Direct labor costs:		
Casting	$ 128.80	7 × $18.40
Machining	666.40	28 × $23.80
Assembly	252.80	16 × $15.80 *given*
Packing	211.20	16 × $13.20
Total direct labor costs	**$1,259.20**	
Support costs:		
Casting	$ 576.00	16 × $36.00
Machining	1,282.40	56 × $22.90 *see*
Assembly	619.20	16 × $38.70 *Exhibit 6-7*
Packing	468.80	16 × $29.30
Total support costs	**$2,946.40**	
Total manufacturing costs	**$6,672.40**	
Number of units	5	
Cost per unit	$1,334.48	

DISTORTIONS CAUSED BY TWO-STAGE ALLOCATIONS. Product costing systems installed in many plants employ the two-stage allocation method just described. The structure of these systems, however, can actually distort product costs. Consider the following example.

Assume that Minnetka, a company that makes steel valves, has a plant that is organized into three departments: machine setups, which is a service department, and machining and assembly, which are both production departments. Total setup costs of $200,000 are assigned $120,000 to the machining and $80,000 to the assembly departments in proportion to the respective setup hours of 480 and 320 in the two production departments.

The plant manufactures two products, labeled A and B, shown in Exhibit 6-11. From the information regarding setup costs above, the setup activity costs driver is this:

$$\$200,000 \div (480 + 320 \text{ setup hours}) = \$250 \text{ per hour}$$

Intuitively, it would seem logical to charge products A and B the following for setup costs:

Product A

$$\$250 \times (5 \text{ setup hours} \div 800 \text{ units}) = \$1.5625$$

EXHIBIT 6-11
Minnetka Production Factors
Products A and B

	PRODUCTS	
Relevant Factors	**A**	**B**
Batch size in number of units	800	200
Setup hours required:		
Machining	3	3
Assembly	2	2
Normal production in number of units	64,000	16,000
Normal production in number of batches	80	80

Product B

$$\$250 \times (5 \text{ setup hours} \div 200 \text{ units}) = \$6.2500$$

Let us see now how the two-stage allocation method actually charges setup costs to the products A and B. Stage 2 assigns support costs to products based on machine hours for both production departments at Minnetka. Both products require 0.1 machine hours per unit in each department, machining and assembly. Each department has a total of 8000 machine hours.

$$0.1 \times (64,000 + 16,000 \text{ units of normal production}) = 8000$$

Newsprint machines at this plant spin the pulp at 45 miles per hour and convert it into finished newsprint in 10 seconds. The setting-up operation is costly because it involves the use of skilled workers and expensive equipment. Because costs associated with this setup would include the cost of the workers and the equipment, the management accountant would have to use several cost drivers to allocate setup costs to production runs. *Courtesy* **Media General**

Therefore, these are the cost driver rates:

Machining department

$$\$15 \text{ per machine hour } = \$120,000 \text{ setup costs } \div 8000 \text{ machine hours}$$

Assembly department

$$\$10 \text{ per machine hour } = \$80,000 \text{ setup costs } \div 8000 \text{ machine hours}$$

Both products A and B are charged $2.50 per unit for setup costs:

$$\$2.50 = (0.1 \times \$15) + (0.1 \times \$10)$$

Product A is overcosted because it is charged more than its share of setup costs ($2.50 instead of $1.5625). In contrast, product B is undercosted because it is charged less ($2.50 instead of $6.25) than the costs of resources actually used for setups of product B. Why does the two-stage allocation method distort product costs in this manner?

REASON FOR TWO-STAGE ALLOCATION DISTORTION.   The reason for the distortion is the break in the link between the cause for the support activity costs (setup hours) and the basis for assignment of the costs to the individual products (machine hours). Two related factors contribute to these cost distortions:

1. Allocations based on unit-related measures
2. Differences in relative consumption ratios

Both products A and B have the same number of machine hours per unit; therefore, both are assigned the same amount of setup costs ($2.50 per unit). In

CONSIDER THIS . . .

Strategic Cost Allocation at Hitachi

Hitachi Corporation operates the world's largest factory devoted exclusively to the manufacture of video cassette recorders (VCRs). The Hitachi VCR plant is highly automated, but it continues to use direct labor as the basis for allocating manufacturing support costs. The accountants at Hitachi have purposely designed the cost accounting system such that support costs allocation distorts the actual production process in the plant's automated environment. Hitachi's top management is convinced that reducing direct labor is strategically essential for continuous cost improvement, and it is committed to aggressive automation to promote long-term competitiveness. Allocating support costs based on direct labor makes direct labor appear much more costly than it is in the short term, and as a result it creates the desired strong incentives for managers to replace direct labor with automated machinery.

At another Hitachi plant, which manufactures refrigeration and air-conditioning equipment, support costs are allocated based on the number of parts in product models in an effort to influence engineers' design decisions. Hitachi believes that the complexity associated with a large number of parts, especially custom parts, leads to a significant increase in manufacturing support costs. In plants assembling diverse products, reducing the number of parts and promoting the use of standard parts across product lines can lower support costs dramatically and also lower materials costs by creating possibilities for more aggressive volume buying. Allocating support costs based on the number of parts creates the desired incentives to reduce the number of parts at this plant.

Source: T. Hiromoto, "Another Hidden Edge—Japanese Management Accounting," *Harvard Business Review,* July-August 1988, pp. 22–26.

reality, however, the demand for setup activity is less for product A because it is produced in larger batches. It is charged the same rate as for product B because of the use of machine hours as the cost driver in the second stage of allocations. Conventional two-stage allocation methods use unit-related cost drivers to allocate support activity costs in the second stage, even when the demand for these activities is driven, in fact, by batch-related and product-sustaining cost drivers such as setups and engineering changes.

Cost distortions are greater when the difference between the relative proportion of the cost driver for the activity (setup hours) and the relative proportion of the basis for second-stage assignment of support costs (machine hours) is greater. Product A needs 0.00625 setup hours per unit (5 ÷ 800) on average, but product B needs more—0.02500 setup hours per unit (5 ÷ 200). Both products need the same number of machine hours per unit. The *actual* consumption ratio of product A to product B for setup activity is 1:4 (that is, 0.00625 ÷ 0.02500) based on the ratio of the actual cost driver, setup hours. But the *apparent* consumption ratio used to allocate setup costs is 1:1 based on machine hours (0.1 ÷ 0.1). This difference in the actual cost driver consumption ratio and the unit-level cost drivers used by conventional systems results in overcosting product A and undercosting product B.

Such distortions could be eliminated if we designed a costing system that used the actual cost driver for *each* support activity to assign costs directly to the products. This is the logic underlying the development of activity-based costing systems.

A MIDCHAPTER REVIEW PROBLEM

The following numerical problem illustrates the calculations involved in a two-stage allocation method for assigning costs to individual jobs and products. This concrete example will help apply concepts discussed so far before moving on to a discussion of activity-based costing systems.

Seven Springs Company is engaged in the manufacture of a variety of leaf springs, hot wound springs, and coiled flat springs at its plant in Concord, New Hampshire. The plant has two service departments: supervision and administration (department S1); and machine maintenance and engineering (department S2). There are also two production departments: fabrication (department P1) and assembly (department P2). Total manufacturing support costs for *all* production jobs in 1996 and the cost drivers for the four departments are listed below:

SEVEN SPRINGS COMPANY
MANUFACTURING SUPPORT COSTS FOR 1996

Department	Support Costs	Cost Driver
S1	$ 750,000	Direct labor hours (*DLH*)
S2	600,000	Machine hours (*MH*)
P1	250,000	Machine hours (*MH*)
P2	340,000	Direct labor hours (*DLH*)
Total	$1,940,000	

In the first stage, service department costs are allocated to the production departments based on the quantity of service cost drivers consumed by the production departments. These consumption levels are as follows:

SEVEN SPRINGS COMPANY QUANTITY OF SERVICE COST DRIVERS

Department	DLH	MH
P1	20,000	20,000
P2	30,000	10,000
Total	50,000	30,000

In the second stage, support costs accumulated in the production departments are allocated to jobs based on the quantity of production department activity cost driver consumed by each job. The cost driver resources consumed in the two production departments by job J96-73 are as follows:

SEVEN SPRINGS COMPANY QUANTITY OF PRODUCTION DEPARTMENT ACTIVITY COST DRIVERS

Department	DLH	MH
P1	100	80
P2	100	50

REQUIRED

Determine the manufacturing support costs allocated to job J96-73.

SOLUTION

SEVEN SPRINGS COMPANY
MANUFACTURING SUPPORT COSTS OF JOB J96-73

Step	Stage 1 Allocation	Dept. P1	Dept. P2
1	Directly traced	$250,000	$340,000
2	Allocated from Dept. S1	300,000[a]	450,000[b]
	Allocated from Dept. S2	400,000[c]	200,000[d]
	Total support costs	$950,000	$990,000
	Cost driver level	20,000	30,000
	Cost driver rate	$47.50 per *MH*	$33.00 per *DLH*

Stage 2 Allocation

From Dept. P1	$3800[e]
From Dept. P2	3300[f]
Total support costs for Job J96-73	$7100

[a] $750,000 $\times \dfrac{20,000}{50,000}$ = $300,000   [b] $750,000 $\times \dfrac{30,000}{50,000}$ = $450,000

[c] $600,000 $\times \dfrac{20,000}{30,000}$ = $400,000   [d] $600,000 $\times \dfrac{10,000}{30,000}$ = $200,000

[e] $47.50 $\times$ 80 (Dept. P1-*MH*) = $3800   [f] $33.00 $\times$ 100 (Dept. P2-*DLH*) = $3300

ACTIVITY-BASED COSTING SYSTEMS

The fundamental assumption of the two-stage allocation method is the absence of a strong direct link between the support activities and the products manufactured. For this reason, service department costs are first allocated to production departments in the conventional two-stage allocation method.

The Basis of Activity-Based Costing

Activity-based costing rejects this assumption and instead develops the idea of cost drivers that *directly link the activities performed to the products manufactured.* These cost drivers measure the average demand placed on each activity by the various products. Then activity costs are assigned to products in proportion to the demand that the products place on average on the activities. This usually eliminates the need for the second step in Stage 1 allocations that allocates service department costs to production departments before assigning them to individual jobs and products.[1] Exhibit 6-12 summarizes and compares the various stages and steps in the conventional and activity-based costing systems.

Activity-based costing systems
Product costing systems that assign support costs to products in the proportion of the demand each product places on various activities.

OBJECTIVE 6.5

Use activity-based costing systems to estimate product costs.

CONSIDER THIS . . .

Activity-Based Costing Helps AT&T

Throughout its history, the telephone business has been regulated in North America. Regulators have determined pricing formulas under a mandate established by political processes. The Federal Communications Commission developed its methods for establishing prices on the basis of cost plus an allowable profit. Regulatory requirements detailed cost allocation procedures that were followed by AT&T.

AT&T's breakup into smaller, more focused business units, combined with gradual relaxation of price regulation, has made understanding and managing, rather than simply allocating, costs critical. As a result, AT&T managers decided to implement an activity-based costing (ABC) system to understand the activities driving their business.

The business billing center was selected for an ABC pilot project. Billing activities included monitoring billing records; editing checks; validating data; correcting errors; and printing, sorting, and dispatching invoices to business customers. A cross-functional team prepared a schematic flowchart of the business and operational relationships

to identify how resources and activities related to each other and to trace outputs from the activities to services provided to each customer.

The cost of service provided to different types of customers was determined by identifying activity and cost driver consumption characteristics. Deciding on activity cost drivers was relatively straightforward because team members from the various business functions were familiar with the operations. Some of the drivers selected were number of customer accounts tested, change requests, service orders, customer locations, printer hours, and pages printed.

AT&T managers find the pilot ABC model to be an innovative tool for managing costs and an education in enhancing the operation of their business. It has led to improvements in internal operating processes, supplier relationships, and customer satisfaction.

Source: T. Hobdy, J. Thomson, and P. Sharman, "Activity-Based Management at AT&T," *Management Accounting,* April 1994, pp. 35–39.

---

[1] Even with ABC, those service department costs that do, in fact, provide service to other service departments or to production departments are assigned using the sequential or reciprocal methods as in traditional systems. (See Appendix 6-1.)

CONSIDER THIS . . .

Is ABC Worth the Investment?

In 1994, the Institute of Management Accountants conducted a fax survey to determine if readers of its monthly magazine, Management Accounting, believed ABC was worth the investment. Most respondents agreed that it was worthwhile. The main reasons cited for implementing an ABC system included more accurate product costs, improved performance measurements, and more relevant cost data for decision-making purposes.

The most common problems reported in the survey were difficulty in determining cost drivers, the additional work that implementation required, lack of

commitment from people from whom input was required, and need for a dedicated team to implement ABC. The principal reason for dissatisfaction with ABC was the lack of action by some managers to improve profitability using the results of the ABC analysis.

Difficulties in implementing new cost management systems, such as an ABC system, are discussed in more detail in Chapter 15.

Source: S. Jayson, "ABC *Is* Worth the Investment," *Management Accounting,* April 1994, p. 27.

Activity-Based Costing at the Medequip Plant

Consider once again the allocation of manufacturing support costs at the Medequip plant. Stage 1 of the activity-based cost allocation procedure involves identifying activities, their cost drivers, and the corresponding costs incurred to perform the activities. Exhibit 6-13 lists the activities and their costs at Medequip. The total manufacturing support costs of $1,127,800 are distributed over 13 activities. In some cases, such as with machine maintenance at the Medequip plant, an activity may correspond exactly to a service department, but such a one-to-one correspondence is not necessary. For example, activities such as materials handling and materials movement may be performed by workers in several different departments.

EXHIBIT 6-12
Comparison of the Structure of Two Product Costing Systems

Conventional Two-Stage Allocation System	Activity-Based Costing System
Stage 1	**Stage 1**
Step 1: Trace all support costs to production and service departments cost pools	Trace all support costs to activity cost pools associated with distinct activity cost drivers
Step 2: Allocate service departments costs to production departments	
Stage 2	**Stage 2**
Assign costs to jobs or products based on production departments' cost driver rates (computed as ratios of support costs accumulated in each production department to the corresponding level of a unit-related measure of production volume in the department)	Assign costs to jobs/products based on activity cost driver rates (computed as ratios of support costs accumulated in each activity cost pool to the corresponding level of the activity cost driver)

EXHIBIT 6-13
Medequip
Activities, Cost Drivers, and Cost Driver Rates

No.	Activity	Total Costs	Cost Drivers	Total Cost Driver Levels	Cost Driver Rates
1	Supervision: casting	$ 26,000	Casting setup hours	500	$52.00
2	Supervision: machining	39,600	Machining setup hours	600	66.00
3	Supervision: assembly	42,000	Assembly direct labor hours	6,000	7.00
4	Supervision: packing	23,600	Packing direct labor hours	6,000	3.93
5	Depreciation: casting	39,600	Casting machine hours	6,000	6.60
6	Depreciation: machining	92,000	Machining machine hours	22,000	4.18
7	Depreciation: assembly	9,000	Assembly machine hours	9,000	1.00
8	Depreciation: packing	6,000	Packing machine hours	3,000	2.00
9	Machine maintenance	160,000	Total machine hours	40,000	4.00
10	Machine setup	300,000	Total other machine setup hours	300	1,000.00
11	Production scheduling	120,000	Number of batches	500	240.00
12	Production engineering	180,000	Engineering change orders.	200	900.00
13	General and administrative	90,000	Total machine hours	40,000	2.25
	Total	$1,127,800			

Referring to Exhibit 6-13, we can see that support costs for each of the four production departments at the Medequip plant are traced to one of two activities: supervision or machine depreciation. Supervision in casting and machining departments (numbers 1 and 2) at the Medequip plant is required at the beginning of each batch to ensure that it is set up right. Therefore, setup hours in the casting and machining departments are used as the cost drivers for the supervision activity in the two departments. In contrast, supervision in the assembly and the packing departments (numbers 3 and 4) extends over the entire time of a job. Therefore, departmental direct labor hours are used as the cost drivers in these departments. Depreciation costs (numbers 5-8) are associated with the use of machines in all four departments, and, accordingly, departmental machine hours are used as the cost drivers. Total machine hours, total setup hours, number of batches, and engineering change orders are the cost drivers for machine maintenance, machine setup, production scheduling, and production engineering activities (numbers 9-12, respectively). The general and administrative costs (number 13) arise from a facility-sustaining activity represented by the capacity made available at the plant. Therefore, these costs are allocated to jobs on the basis of their total machine hours.

Stage 2 allocations to assign support activity costs to jobs and products are based on separate cost driver rates for the activities. The estimated total cost for an activity shown in Exhibit 6-13, column 3, is divided by the corresponding estimated total amount for its cost driver, column 5, to obtain the activity cost driver rate, column 6. For instance, the rate of $900 per engineering change order for activity 12, production engineering, is obtained as the ratio of the total cost, $180,000, to the total cost driver level, 200.

Support activity costs are assigned to individual jobs on the basis of their respective cost driver levels. Exhibit 6-14 presents this information for jobs J189-4 and J273-2. Exhibit 6-15 displays the costs assigned to the two jobs.

EXHIBIT 6-14
Medequip, Inc.: Activity Cost Driver Values for Two Representative Jobs

Activity	Cost Driver	Job J189-4	Job J273-2
1	Casting setup hours	1.0	1.0
2	Machining setup hours	1.2	1.2
3	Assembly direct labor hours	40.0	16.0
4	Packing direct labor hours	40.0	16.0
5	Casting machine hours	40.0	16.0
6	Machining machine hours	140.0	56.0
7	Assembly machine hours	60.0	24.0
8	Packing machine hours	20.0	18.0
9	Total machine hours	260.0	114.0
10	Total setup hours	2.2	2.2
11	Number of batches	1.0	1.0
12	Engineering change orders	0.4	0.3
13	Total machine-hours	260.0	114.0

EXHIBIT 6-15
Medequip
Activity-Based Costs for Two Representative Jobs

Item	JOB J189-4 Costs	JOB J189-4 Calculation Details	JOB J273-2 Costs	JOB J273-2 Calculation Details
Direct material costs	$4,737.80	see Exhibit 6-9	$2,466.80	See Exhibit 6-10
Direct labor costs	3,157.20	see Exhibit 6-9	1,259.20	See Exhibit 6-10
Support costs:				
Supervision				
1. Casting	52.00	1.0 × $52.00	52.00	1.0 × $52.00
2. Machining	79.20	1.2 × $66.00	79.20	1.2 × $66.00
3. Assembly	280.00	40.0 × $7.00	112.00	16.0 × $7.00
4. Packing	157.20	40.0 × $3.93	62.88	16.0 × $3.93
Depreciation				
5. Casting	264.00	40.0 × $6.60	105.60	16.0 × $6.60
6. Machining	585.20	140.0 × $4.18	234.08	56.0 × $4.18
7. Assembly	60.00	60.0 × $1.00	24.00	24.0 × $1.00
8. Packing	40.00	20.0 × $2.00	36.00	18.0 × $2.00
9. Machine maintenance	1,040.00	260.0 × $4.00	456.00	114.0 × $4.00
10. Machine setup	2,200.00	2.2 × $1,000.00	2,200.00	2.2 × $1,000.00
11. Production scheduling	240.00	1.0 × $240.00	240.00	1.0 × $240.00
12. Production engineering	360.00	0.4 × $900.00	270.00	0.3 × $900.00
13. General and administrative	585.00	260 × $2.25	256.50	114.0 × $2.25
Total support costs	$5,942.60		$4,128.26	
Total manufacturing costs	$13,837.60		$7,854.26	
Number of units	12	See Exhibit 6-9	5	See Exhibit 6-10
Cost per unit	$1,153.13	$13,837.60 ÷ 12	$1,570.85	$7,854.26 ÷ 5

CONSIDER THIS . . .

Activity-Based Costing at a Hewlett-Packard Plant

In 1989, Hewlett-Packard (HP) implemented an ABC system at its Boise Surface Mount Center (BSMC) plant in Idaho. The plant manufactures about 50 different electronic circuit boards for internal customers within HP. With surface-mount technology, patches of a semiliquid solder are placed on the surface of a circuit board and electronic components are placed on the solder patches. Then the board goes through an oven to melt the solder to form a strong mechanical board and a reliable electronic circuit. The process is highly automated with computer-controlled machines that can select more than 100 different components each minute from the correct reel and place each one on the surface of the board within a tolerance of four-thousandths of an inch. Production volumes for each board fluctuate from a few hundred to several thousand per month.

Prior to adopting ABC, the BSMC plant applied all manufacturing support as a percent of direct materials cost. The ABC system uses 10 different cost pools and drivers, as shown below:

Cost Pools	Activity Cost Drivers
1. Panel operations	Percent of a whole panel; if one panel contains four individual boards, then each board is charged 25% of the panel rate
2. Small component placement	Number of "small" components placed on the board's surface
3. Medium component placement	Number of medium-sized components placed on the board's surface
4. Large component placement	Number of large components placed on the board's surface
5. Through-hole component insertion	Number of components with wires that are inserted through holes on the board
6. Hand load component placement	Minutes required to place all components that must be hand-loaded rather than automatically placed on the board.
7. Material procurement & handling	Number of unique parts in the board
8. Scheduling	Number of scheduling hours
9. Assembly setup	Number of minutes of setup time
10. Test & rework	Number of minutes of test and rework time for each board

The BSMC plant compared the costs of its 57 products under the old and the new costing systems to evaluate the extent of cost distortion caused by the old system. Their findings follow:

Distortion Caused by the Old System, Expressed as a Percent Difference from ABC Cost	Number of Products
Undercosted:	
More than 100%	1
Between 50% and 100%	5
Between 20% and 50%	6
Between 5% and 20%	23
Little Change:	
Less than 5% under- or overcosted	13
Overcosted:	
Between 5% and 20%	9
Total	57

Under the old costing system, products with low material costs had low amounts of manufacturing support costs assigned to them. The ABC system indicated that several of these products were undercosted by the old system. It also indicated that nine large-volume products that had high material costs were overcosted by the old system.

Courtesy **Hewlett-Packard**

Source: C. M. Merz and A. Hardy, "ABC Puts Accountants on Design Team at HP," *Management Accounting,* September 1993, pp. 22–27.

Notice that the costs assigned to job J273-2 under activity-based costing ($1570.85) are much higher than those assigned under the conventional method ($1334.48). (See Exhibit 6-10.) Job J273-2 is smaller than job J189-4; therefore, the conventional method assigns fewer costs to job J273-2. This occurs because Stage 2 allocations are in proportion to the unit-related machine-hour and direct labor hour cost drivers instead of the true activity cost drivers for the job.

This distortion is corrected in activity-based costing because setup and other batch-related activity costs are assigned to the jobs on the basis of batch-related cost drivers, and product engineering and other product-sustaining activity costs are assigned to the jobs on the basis of product-sustaining cost drivers.

SELLING AND DISTRIBUTION ACTIVITIES

OBJECTIVE 6.6

Assign selling and distribution costs to products.

You will have noticed so far that all the product costing systems described in this and the previous chapter considered only manufacturing costs but not selling and distribution costs. This focus on manufacturing costs is typical of conventional cost accounting systems because only manufacturing costs can be considered in valuing inventories for external financial reporting purposes. External financial reporting requires accountants to design cost accounting systems that track manufacturing costs and allocate them between costs of goods sold and inventories on hand.

In the first three quarters of the 20th century without the help of inexpensive electronic data-processing facilities, accountants did not want to be burdened with the responsibility for maintaining multiple accounting systems. Therefore, external reporting requirements also dictated the structure of the product cost systems for internal managerial decision-making.

Conventional product costing systems either completely excluded selling and distribution and other nonmanufacturing costs or assigned them to products on a rather arbitrary basis, such as relative sales value, manufacturing cost, conversion cost, or gross margin. Neither of these methods reflected the demand for the selling and distribution activities placed by different products sold to different types of customers through different distribution channels.

When costs for selling and distribution, corporate, administrative, research and development, and other nonmanufacturing activities were small relative to manufacturing costs, excluding these costs from the product costing system did not have a significant impact on the validity of managerial decisions. Recently, however, with the increasing emphasis on customer orientation and technological innovation to obtain a competitive edge, selling, distribution, and technology expenses have been growing. Many managers want to understand which products demand more of selling, distribution, technology, and other nonmanufacturing activities and determine how to incorporate products' different consumption patterns into the determination of product costs.

Selling and Distribution Costs at Medequip

Let us return to our discussion of product costs at the Medequip plant. Kendra Rivers, Medequip's controller, assigned two of her brightest young accountants and one experienced sales manager to a task force responsible for analyzing selling and distribution costs.

*C*ONSIDER THIS . . .

Activity-Based Costing Helps Food Companies Reach Full Potential

From little more than a footnote three years ago, activity-based costing (ABC) has emerged as a key component of the Efficient Consumer Response (ECR) process. Jack Haedicke, vice president of activity-based management at Kraft Foods, says, "You cannot do ECR unless you understand your internal costs, your costs to serve your customers, and your customers' profitability on your product. If you don't understand ABC, you're not going to be able to partner, to redesign your supply chain, or to understand category profitability when your product gets to the retailer's shelf." One of the first joint-industry reports on ECR was "Performance Measurement: Applying Value Chain Analysis to the Grocery Industry." The study employs ABC techniques to define the specific activities performed by trading partners within each of the several value chains that exist in the grocery industry—self-distributing retailers, wholesaler supplied systems, and direct store delivery. A study conducted by Ernst & Young in October 1994 found that 41% of food manufacturers were using or piloting an ABC system. The same was true for 26% of distributors, 36% of retailers, and 21% of brokers surveyed. Another 50% of manufacturers said they were planning to pilot an ABC system in the near future, as did 43% of distributors, 29% of retailers, and 48% of brokers.

Activity-based costing has also served as a powerful tool for the management of stock-keeping units (SKUs), that is, the different products carried in inventory. Ralph Drayer, vice president of product supply and customer business development at P&G comments, "When you take an item-by-item

elimination approach, you never really achieve the full value of rationalizing your SKU line-up. It's important to really zero-base it, to start from the beginning. We've employed ABC techniques to do that in our ongoing SKU rationalization efforts, enabling us to make effective reductions in our SKUs."

An industry consultant noted that the other major context for applying ABC in grocery companies is to enhance their re-engineering efforts. "They are using ABC to ask how big are the activities in each work flow, and how much are they costing. From this data, they can develop a cost baseline for today's process and then show the potential return on investment of the redesigned process, thus adding a dimension of financial support to the business case for process improvement." Drayer of P&G added, "For us, it has certainly heightened the focus on those indirect activities that were not previously analyzed as a contribution to costs of individual items and processes."

At Kraft, ABC is being used to assign corporate support costs to a variety of processes and cost objects based on actual resource consumption with the objective of better understanding the company's distribution value chain. These include analyses at the customer and SKU level. Haedicke comments, "We've identified that our cost to serve customers can vary from 1% to 8% of sales through distribution. We consider that a key finding."

Source: U.S. Distribution Journal, November 15, 1995, pp. 15–18.

The task force determined that there were seven selling and distribution activities performed at Medequip. (See Exhibit 6-16.) These activities include *order-getting* activities—such as marketing management, marketing travel, distributing sales catalogs, and providing customer service—and *order-filling* activities such as order execution, warehousing, and shipping.

The task force also correlated costs directly with the seven activities based on the personnel, facilities, equipment, and services required for each activity. (See Exhibit 6-17.) The costs for each activity are further separated into each of the two major product lines: bacterial analysis and hematology equipment. There are more customer service and order execution costs assigned to the new hematology equipment line because it has more demanding but fewer customers than the bacterial analysis line. Customers of the new line also purchase fewer units than do the customers for the bacterial-analysis line.

EXHIBIT 6-16
Medequip
Selling and Distribution Activities

Type of Activity	Description of Activity
Order getting	1. *Marketing Management:* Salaries and benefits of marketing managers, depreciation and maintenance on facilities and equipment used by them, power, telephone charges, and supplies. Allocated to product groups based on estimated proportion of time spent on each group.
	2. *Marketing Travel:* Travel and entertainment expenditures. The new hematological equipment products business required much more travel to build up a network of new customers because each customer ordered only one unit. Allocated to product groups based on business purpose.
	3. *Sales Catalog:* Costs of developing, printing, and mailing sales catalog to current and potential customers. Allocated to product groups based on number of mailings.
	4. *Customer Service:* Salaries and benefits of customer service representatives and costs of equipment and supplies used by them. Hematological equipment product group required more customer service hours because the product designs were new and product installations were dispersed. Allocated to product groups based on estimated proportion of time spent on each group.
Order filling	5. *Order Execution:* Salaries and benefits of staff responsible for contacting customers before receiving and after filling orders, coordinating production to schedule deliveries, invoicing, and collection. Allocated to product groups based on estimated proportion of time spent on each group.
	6. *Warehousing:* Costs of storing finished goods inventory in the warehouse awaiting shipment to customers. Allocated to product groups based on their inventory levels.
	7. *Shipping:* Costs of shipping finished goods to customers. Directly identified with product groups based on shipping records.

Exhibit 6-18 displays the cost drivers and cost driver rates for the seven selling and distribution activities. The amount of time and effort spent on customer service (number 4), for instance, depends largely on the number of units installed. As in the case of manufacturing support activities, the cost driver rate is determined by dividing the activity costs by the cost driver levels. Thus, there are two separate cost driver rates for the two product lines because they differ so much in the quantity of the sales-support activities required for them. For instance, the customer-service-activity cost driver rate for the older bacterial analysis equipment product line is $110 per unit, which is obtained by dividing the cost of $26,400 by the number of units, 240. (See Exhibit 6-17.) The cost driver rate for the hematological equipment product line is $420 per unit ($50,400 ÷ 120), which reflects the higher intensity of demand for the customer-service activity for the new product line.

EXHIBIT 6-17
Medequip
Selling and Distribution Activity Costs

Activities	Totals	ACTIVITY COSTS AND ALLOCATION TO PRODUCT GROUPS	
		Bacterial Analysis Equipment	Hematology Equipment
1. Marketing management	$ 97,800	$ 52,800	$ 45,000
2. Marketing travel	49,800	12,000	37,800
3. Sales catalog	48,000	18,000	30,000
4. Customer service	76,800	26,400	50,400
5. Order execution	146,000	56,000	90,000
6. Warehousing	46,800	28,800	18,000
7. Shipping	99,000	54,000	45,000
Totals	$564,200	$248,000	$316,200

Differences in the consumption of sales-support activities by jobs J189-4 and J273-2 are also reflected in the cost driver data collected by the task force. (See Exhibit 6-19.) The impact of these differences in activity consumption rates on the product costs is apparent from the data shown in Exhibit 6-20. Activity costs are assigned to jobs as before based on cost driver rates and quantities. For instance, customer-service-activity cost of $1320 is assigned to job J189-4, which had 12 units (see Exhibit 6-19) at the rate of $110 per unit (see Exhibit 6-18). Job

EXHIBIT 6-18
Medequip
Cost Driver Rates for Selling and Distribution Activities

Activity	Cost Driver	BACTERIAL ANALYSIS EQUIPMENT			HEMATOLOGICAL EQUIPMENT		
		Allocated Activity Cost	Cost Driver Level	Cost Driver Rate	Allocated Activity Cost	Cost Driver Level	Cost Driver Rate
1. Marketing management	Sales $	$52,800	$528,000	10.00%	$45,000	$300,000	15.00%
2. Marketing travel	Order Qty.	12,000	80	$150.00	37,800	120	$315.00
3. Sales catalog	Order Qty.	18,000	80	$225.00	30,000	120	$250.00
4. Customer service	Order Qty.	26,400	240	$110.00	50,400	120	$420.00
5. Order execution	Order Qty.	56,000	80	$700.00	90,000	120	$750.00
6. Warehousing	Avg. Inv. Vol.	28,800	5,760	$5.00	18,000	3,600	$5.00
7. Shipping	Units × Mi	54,000	72,000	$0.75	45,000	60,000	$0.75

EXHIBIT 6-19
Medequip
Selling and Distribution Cost Drivers for Two Representative Jobs

Activity	Cost Driver	Job J189-4	Job J273-2
1	Sales dollars	$26,400	$12,500
2	Number of orders	4	5
3	Number of orders	4	5
4	Number of units	12	5
5	Number of orders	4	5
6	Average inventory volume	864 c.ft.	540 c.ft.
7	Units × miles	3600	2500

J273-2 is charged $2100 for customer service activity for its five units (see Exhibit 6-20) because of the higher cost driver rate of $420 per unit (see Exhibit 6-18) for the new product line.

The mechanics of assigning the selling and distribution costs are very similar to those described earlier for manufacturing-service activities. However, the additional analysis of sales-support activities can provide useful insight about differences in the cost of the sales and marketing-activity resources consumed by different product lines, types of customers, or market segments.

EXHIBIT 6-20
Medequip
Selling and Distribution Costs for Two Representative Jobs

Activity	JOB J189-4		JOB J273-2	
	Costs	Details*	Costs	Details*
1. Marketing management	$ 2,640.00	0.10 × $26,400	$ 1,875.00	0.15 × $12,500
2. Marketing travel	600.00	4 × $150	1,575.00	5 × $315
3. Sales catalog	900.00	4 × $225	1,250.00	5 × $250
4. Customer service	1,320.00	12 × $110	2,100.00	5 × $420
5. Order execution	2,800.00	4 × $700	3,750.00	5 × 750
6. Warehousing	4,320.00	864 × $5	2,700.00	540 × $5
7. Shipping	2,700.00	3,600 × $0.75	1,875.00	2,500 × $0.75
Total selling and distribution costs	$15,280.00		$15,125.00	
Number of units	12		5	
Selling and distribution costs per unit	$1,273.33	$15,280 ÷ 12	$3,025.00	$15,125 ÷ 5
Manufacturing costs per unit	1,153.13	see Exhibit 6-15	1,570.85	see Exhibit 6-15
Total costs per unit	$2,426.46		$4,595.85	

* Refer to Exhibits 6-18 and 6-19 for the source of these numbers.

A SUMMARY EXAMPLE

The Winona plant of Minnehaha Electronic Company manufactures two products: CD107 and CD635. The company has established the following three cost pools for its manufacturing support costs:

MINNEHAHA ELECTRONIC COMPANY
WINONA PLANT'S COST POOLS FOR CD107 AND CD635

Cost Pool	Manufacturing Support Costs
S	$640,000
P1	400,000
P2	200,000
Total	$1,240,000

Pool S includes all support activity costs at the plant. Pools P1 and P2 include support costs traced directly to the two production departments, fabrication (P1) and assembly (P2), respectively. The current cost accounting system at the plant employs a two-stage cost allocation method that first allocates manufacturing support costs in pool S to the pools P1 and P2 on the basis of machine hours and then assigns the accumulated manufacturing costs in the pools P1 and P2 to the two products on the basis of direct labor hours. A separate cost driver rate is computed for each of the two production departments. The direct labor wage rate including benefits is $15 per hour.

The following information was collected from plant records for June 1997:

MINNEHAHA ELECTRONIC COMPANY
WINONA PLANT'S DIRECT LABOR HOURS FOR JUNE 1997

	Direct Labor Hours (DLH)		
Department	CD107	CD635	Total
Fabrication (P1)	20,000	20,000	40,000
Assembly (P2)	25,000	15,000	40,000
Total	45,000	35,000	80,000

MINNEHAHA ELECTRONIC COMPANY
WINONA PLANT'S MACHINE HOURS FOR JUNE 1997

	Machine-Hours (MH)		
Department	CD107	CD635	Total
Fabrication (P1)	27,000	18,000	45,000
Assembly (P2)	20,000	15,000	35,000
Total	47,000	33,000	80,000
Sales price per unit	$260	$220	
Direct material cost per unit	$80	$40	
Units produced and sold	8,000	6,000	

The plant is considering implementing an activity-based costing system. The controller has compiled the following information to reassign the manufacturing support costs for June 1997 from the existing cost pools (S, P1, P2) to five new activity cost pools:

MINNEHAHA ELECTRONIC COMPANY
WINONA PLANT'S NEW ACTIVITY COST POOLS FOR JUNE 1997

Activity Cost Drivers	Existing Cost Pool			Total
	S	P1	P2	
P1-DLH	$ 40,000	$ 40,000	$ 0	$ 80,000
P2-DLH	150,000	0	80,000	230,000
P1-MH	50,000	110,000	0	160,000
P2-MH	60,000	0	40,000	100,000
Setup hours	340,000	250,000	80,000	670,000
Totals	$640,000	$400,000	$200,000	$1,240,000

The number of setups in June 1997 was 1000 for each of the two products, but each setup for CD 107 takes twice as long as a setup for CD635.

(a) Determine the product cost per unit for both CD107 and CD635 using the existing cost accounting system.
(b) Determine the product cost per unit for the two products using the proposed activity-based costing system.
(c) Explain why the product costs differ in the two cost accounting systems.

The solutions follow.

(a) Existing Cost Accounting Systems

Stage 1 Allocation

Item	Department P1	Department P2
Directly identified support costs	$400,000	$200,000
Allocated from S	360,000[a]	280,000[b]
Total support costs	$760,000	$480,000
DLH	40,000	40,000
Cost driver rate	$19 per DLH	$12 per DLH

[a] $640,000 × (45,000 ÷ 80,000) = $360,000
[b] $640,000 × (35,000 ÷ 80,000) = $280,000

Stage 2 Allocation

Allocated from Department	CD107		CD635	
P1 ($19.00 × 20,000)	$380,000	($19.00 × 20,000)	$380,000
P2 ($12.00 × 25,000)	300,000	($12.00 × 15,000)	180,000
Total support costs	$680,000		$560,000

	CD107			CD635
Direct materials				
($80 × 8,000)	$ 640,000	($40 × 6,000)		$ 240,000
Direct labor				
($15 × 45,000)	675,000	($15 × 35,000)		525,000
Support costs				
(From Stage 2)	680,000	(From Stage 2)		560,000
Total costs	$1,995,000			$1,325,000
Number of units	8,000			6,000
Unit cost				
($1,995,000 ÷ 8,000)	$249.38	($1,325,000 ÷ 6,000)		$220.83
Sales price	$260.00			$220.00
Gross margin				
($260.00 − $249.38)	$10.62	($220.00 − $220.83)		($0.83)

(b) Activity-Based Costing System

Cost Driver		CD107
P1-DLH	$80,000 × (20,000 ÷ 40,000)	$ 40,000
P2-DLH	$230,000 × (25,000 ÷ 40,000)	143,750
P1-MH	$160,000 × (27,000 ÷ 45,000)	96,000
P2-MH	$100,000 × (20,000 ÷ 35,000)	57,143
Setup hours	$670,000 × [2,000 ÷ (2,000 + 1,000)] =	$446,667
Total		$783,560

Cost Driver		CD35
P1-DLH	$80,000 × (20,000 ÷ 40,000)	$ 40,000
P2-DLH	$230,000 × (15,000 ÷ 40,000)	86,250
P1-MH	$160,000 × (18,000 ÷ 45,000)	64,000
P2-MH	$100,000 × (15,000 ÷ 35,000)	42,857
Setup hours	$670,000 × [1,000 ÷ (2,000 + 1,000)] =	223,333
Total		$456,440

Product Costing	CD107			CD635
Direct material ($80 × 8,000)	$ 640,000	($40 × 6,000)		$ 240,000
Direct labor ($15 × 45,000)	675,000	($15 × 35,000)		525,000
Support costs (from activity		(from activity		
cost analysis)	783,560	cost analysis)		456,440
Total costs	$2,098,560			$1,221,440
Number of units	8,000			6,000
Unit cost ($2,098,560 ÷ 8,000)	$262.32	($1,221,440 ÷ 6,000)		$203.57
Sales price	$260.00			$220.00
Gross margin ($260.00 − $262.32)	($2.32)	($220.00 − $203.57)		$16.43

(c) Product CD107 was undercosted and CD635 was overcosted under the existing system because the existing system ignored two important facts:

1. More than half of support costs are caused by the setup activity
2. A unit of CD107 requires twice as much setup-activity resources as a unit of CD635.

SUMMARY

This chapter describes the two stages of allocations typically used in conventional product-costing procedures. The first stage traces all support costs including those pertaining to support services to the production departments in two steps. The second stage assigns the support costs accumulated in the production departments to individual products based on unit-related measures, such as direct labor hours or machine hours. With conventional costing systems, products manufactured in small batches or in small annual volumes are undercosted because batch-related and product-sustaining costs are assigned only in proportion to the number of units.

Activity-based costing corrects these distortions by using separate cost drivers for different activities and assigning costs to products based on unit-related, batch-related, product-sustaining, or facility-sustaining cost drivers as appropriate. Activity-based costing principles also apply to nonmanufacturing costs, such as selling and distribution, as well as to service industries.

KEY TERMS

activity-based costing systems, p. 263
direct allocation method, p. 251
production departments, p. 248
reciprocal allocation method, p. 251

sequential allocation method, p. 251
service departments, p. 249
stage 1 allocations, p. 251
stage 2 allocations, p. 254

APPENDIX 6-1

Sequential and Reciprocal Allocation Methods

Companies use several different methods to allocate service department costs to production departments. Sequential and reciprocal allocation methods are used when service departments consume services provided by other service departments.

Sequential Allocation Method

Companies use the sequential method under the following condition: There is no pair of service departments where each department in that pair consumes a significant proportion of the services produced by the other department in that pair. To illustrate this method, consider a plant with two production departments, machining and assembly, and two service departments, power and engineering. Service department costs are allocated on the basis of kilowatt hours and engineering hours, respectively. Exhibit 6-21 displays the directly attributable costs of the four-departments and their consumption of the two services.

The sequential allocation method requires that the service departments are first arranged in order so that a service department can receive costs allocated from another service department only *before* its own costs are allocated to other departments. Once a service department's costs are allocated, no costs of other departments can be allocated back to it.

In this example, the power department does not receive engineering services, but the engineering department uses power. Therefore, in the sequential method, the power department costs are allocated first, followed by allocation of the engineering department costs. The total cost of a service department allocated to other departments equals the amount directly identified with the service department *plus* the amount allocated earlier to the service department from other service departments.

EXHIBIT 6-21
Directly Identified Costs and Service Consumption Levels

Item	SERVICE DEPARTMENTS		PRODUCTION DEPARTMENTS		
	Power	Engineering	Machining	Assembly	Totals
Directly identified costs	$320,000	$180,000	$120,000	$ 80,000	$700,000
Consumption of service:					
Kilowatt hours	0	100,000	480,000	220,000	800,000
Engineering hours	0	0	2,000	2,000	4,000
Allocation ratios:					
Power	0	0.125	0.600	0.275	1.000
Engineering	0	0	0.500	0.500	1.000

$$
\begin{array}{ccc}
\textit{Total} & \textit{Directly} & \textit{Costs} \\
\textit{Costs} & = \textit{Identified} & + \textit{Allocated} \\
\textit{Allocated} & \textit{Costs} & \textit{to It}
\end{array}
$$

These costs are allocated to the other service and production departments in proportion to their consumption of the service as detailed in Exhibit 6-21. Therefore, for the allocation of the costs of the power department, the allocation ratios in Exhibit 6-21 are based on the consumption of power by the engineering, machining, and assembly departments. The allocation ratios for the engineering service are based on the consumption by the machining and the assembly departments. Exhibit 6-22 shows the resulting allocations.

Power department costs are allocated first because it does not consume any other service. Engineering department costs are allocated next. Allocated costs of $220,000 for engineering are the directly identified costs of $180,000 plus the costs allocated to the engineering department from the power department of $40,000. Notice that no costs are allocated back to the power department.

If both the service departments in this example consumed each other's services, the reciprocal allocation method is appropriate. The sequential method ignores or suppresses such reciprocal relations.

Reciprocal Allocation Method

This method recognizes reciprocal interactions between different service departments. We shall alter the consumption data in Exhibit 6-21 to illustrate this method. Notice that the information in Exhibit 6-23 is the same as that in Exhibit 6-21, except that the power department also consumes 1000 hours of engineering service.

The sequential method does not work in this situation because when the engineering department's costs are allocated, 20% must be allocated back to the power department whose costs were already allocated. This would leave unallocated costs in the power department. If we were to allocate this new balance in the power department on the basis of the same allocation ratios as before, we would

EXHIBIT 6-22
Sequentially Allocated Costs

	SERVICE DEPARTMENTS		PRODUCTION DEPARTMENTS	
Item	Power	Engineering	Machining	Assembly
Directly identified costs	$ 320,000	$ 180,000	$120,000	$ 80,000
Allocation of power department costs	(320,000)	40,000	192,000	88,000
Allocation of engineering department costs	0	(220,000)	110,000	110,000
Totals	$ 0	$ 0	$422,000	$278,000

EXHIBIT 6-23
Directly Identified Costs and Service Consumption Levels

Item	SERVICE DEPARTMENTS Power	SERVICE DEPARTMENTS Engineering	PRODUCTION DEPARTMENTS Machining	PRODUCTION DEPARTMENTS Assembly	Totals
Directly identified costs	$320,000	$180,000	$120,000	$ 80,000	$700,000
Consumption of service:					
Kilowatt hours	0	100,000	480,000	220,000	800,000
Engineering hours	1,000	0	2,000	2,000	5,000
Allocation ratios:					
Power	0	0.125	0.600	0.275	1.000
Engineering	0.200	0	0.400	0.400	1.000

be left with unallocated costs in the engineering department. In principle, of course, we could repeat these sequential allocations until the unallocated balance of costs became negligible. The same result, however, can be obtained by using the algebraic approach of the reciprocal allocation method.

We shall denote the total costs to be allocated for the power department as P and those for the engineering department as E. Using the equation previously developed, we can find the total costs to be allocated to the power department:

$$\begin{array}{ccc} \textit{Total} & \textit{Directly} & \textit{Costs} \\ \textit{Costs} & = \textit{Identified} + \textit{Allocated} \\ \textit{Allocated} & \textit{Costs} & \textit{to It} \end{array}$$

Because the power department consumes 20% of the engineering services, we have

$$P = \$320,000 + 0.20E \qquad (6\text{-}1)$$

Also, because the engineering department uses 12.5% of the power consumed in the plant, we have

$$E = \$180,000 + 0.125P \qquad (6\text{-}2)$$

Equations (6-1) and (6-2) thus recognize that the power department's total costs include a 20% share of the engineering department's total costs, and the engineering department's total costs include a 12.5% share of the power department's costs. We can now solve these two equations simultaneously. For this purpose, we shall substitute the expression for E into the first equation for P.

$$\begin{aligned} P &= \$320,000 + 0.20\,(\$180,000 + 0.125P) \\ P &= \$320,000 + \$36,000 + 0.025P \\ 0.975P &= \$356,000 \\ P &= \$365,128 \end{aligned}$$

We also can solve for E by substituting this value of P in the second equation.

$$E = \$180,000 + 0.125\ (\$365,128)$$
$$E = \$180,000 + \$45,641$$
$$E = \$225,641$$

Now that we have determined the total costs for the two service departments, we can calculate the amounts to be allocated to the two production departments using the allocation ratios in Exhibit 6-23. These cost allocations appear in Exhibit 6-24. Notice that the allocations are different from those obtained in the earlier illustration for the sequential method because we began with different data. The power department's total costs were higher because it also consumed some engineering services. Because the machining department consumed a relatively larger amount of power, we find that in this case the costs allocated to it are also higher.

EXHIBIT 6-24
Reciprocally Allocated Costs

Item	SERVICE DEPARTMENTS		PRODUCTION DEPARTMENTS	
	Power	Engineering	Machining	Assembly
Directly identified costs	$ 320,000	$ 180,000	$120,000	$ 80,000
Allocation of power department costs	(365,128)	45,641	219,077	100,410
Allocation of engineering department costs	45,128	(225,641)	90,256	90,256
Totals	$ 0	$ 0	$429,333	$270,666

ASSIGNMENT MATERIAL

QUESTIONS

6-1 What is the difference between *production departments* and *service departments?*

6-2 What are the two stages of cost allocations in conventional product-costing systems?

6-3 Why do conventional product-costing systems allocate service department costs first to the production departments before assigning them to individual jobs?

6-4 What are the different situations for which direct, sequential, and reciprocal allocation methods are designed?

6-5 What is the difference between the cost drivers typically used in the first stage and those used in the second stage of conventional product costing systems?

6-6 Why are conventional two-stage cost allocation systems likely to systematically distort product costs?

6-7 What are two factors that contribute to cost distortions resulting from the use of conventional, two-stage cost allocation systems?

6-8 What fundamental assumption implicit in conventional two-stage cost-allocation systems is rejected in activity-based costing systems?

6-9 How do activity-based costing systems avoid distortions in allocations of batch-related costs?

6-10 Why do conventional product costing systems often exclude selling and distribution costs?

6-11 What recent changes have made it more important to have nonmanufacturing costs assigned to products, product lines, or market segments?

6-12 Why are conventional product-costing systems more likely to distort product costs in highly automated plants? How do activity-based costing systems deal with such a situation?

6-13 "Conventional product costing systems are likely to overcost high-volume products." Do you agree with this statement? Explain.

6-14 How are allocation bases selected in the two stages of conventional product costing systems?

6-15 How are cost drivers selected in activity-based costing systems?

6-16 "Activity-based costing systems yield more accurate product costs than conventional systems because they use more cost drivers to assign support costs to products." Do you agree with this statement? Explain.

6-17 What are *cost pools?* How is the appropriate number of cost pools selected?

EXERCISES

6-18 *Activity cost drivers* Identify a cost driver for each of the following activities:
  (a) Machine maintenance
  (b) Machine setup
  (c) Utilities
  (d) Quality control
  (e) Material ordering

(f) Production scheduling
(g) Factory depreciation
(h) Warehouse expense
(i) Production supervision
(j) Payroll accounting
(k) Custodial service
(l) General and administration

6-19 *Product costing systems and product profitability*   Potter Corporation has gained considerable market share in recent years for its specialty, low-volume, complex line of products, but the gain has been offset by a loss in market share for its high-volume simple line of products. This has resulted in a net decline in its overall profitability. Advise management about specific changes that may be required in its cost accounting system, and explain why the existing system may be inadequate.

6-20 *Service department cost allocation, direct method*   San Miguel Company has two production departments, assembly and finishing, and two service departments, machine setup and inspection. Machine setup costs are allocated on the basis of number of setups while inspection costs are allocated on the basis of number of direct labor hours. Selected information on the four departments follows:

Item	Direct Costs	Number of Setups	Direct Labor Hours
Machine setup	$40,000	0	0
Inspection	15,000	0	0
Assembly	25,000	300	200
Finishing	20,000	100	500

REQUIRED

(a) Using the direct method, determine the amount of machine setup costs allocated to the two production departments.
(b) Using the direct method, determine the amount of inspection costs allocated to the two production departments.

6-21 *Product profitability analysis*   Dance Division of Nitterhouse Video Company markets two dance videos: jazz and rap. To motivate the sales of the two videos, the company offers its marketing personnel a sales commission of 10% of the sales price for each copy they sell. Selected data for the two videos for February 1997 follow:

Item	Jazz	Rap
Unit price	$20	$30
Manufacturing costs:		
Material	6	12
Labor	4	6
Support	2	3
Number of copies sold	5000	8000

The monthly fixed selling expenses of $80,000 are allocated equally to the two videos. Although the demand for the jazz videos is still very strong, the company has been experiencing losses on its sales over the last six months. The owner of Nitterhouse Video Company has asked your opinion on whether the jazz video should be discontinued. What course of action do you recommend? Explain.

6-22 *Activity-based costs*   VG Company has identified the following cost pools and cost drivers:

Cost Pools	Activity Costs	Cost Drivers
Machine setup	$360,000	6,000 setup hours
Materials handling	100,000	50,000 pounds of material
Electric power	40,000	80,000 kilowatt hours

The following cost information pertains to the production of V203 and G179:

Item	V203	G179
Number of units produced	5,000	15,000
Direct materials cost	$25,000	$33,000
Direct labor cost	$14,000	$16,000
Number of setup hours	120	150
Pounds of material used	5,000	10,000
Kilowatt hours	2,000	3,000

Determine the unit cost for each of the two products using activity-based costing.

6-23 **Sequential allocation**   *(Appendix)* Cooper Company has two service departments and two production departments. Information on annual manufacturing support costs and cost drivers follows:

Item	SERVICE DEPARTMENT		PRODUCTION DEPARTMENT	
	S1	S2	P1	P2
Support costs	$65,000	$55,000	$160,000	$240,000
Direct labor hours	2,000	1,500	2,000	3,000
Number of square feet	800	1,200	2,400	2,600

The company allocates service department costs using the sequential method. First, S1 costs are allocated on direct labor hours. Next, S2 costs are allocated based on square footage. The square footage for S1 is assumed to be zero for this purpose. Determine the total support costs allocated to each of the two production departments.

■ PROBLEMS

Fundamental Problems

6-24 **Cost distortions**   Normal manufacturing support costs of McInnes Company for September 1997 are as follows:

Cost Pools	Normal Costs
Power	$40,000
Materials handling	90,000
Setups	80,000
Quality inspections	40,000
Total	$250,000

The present cost accounting system allocates support costs to final products based on machine hours. Estimated machine hours for September 1997 are 50,000. After losing several bids recently, Roy McInnes, the president, asked the controller to implement an activity-based costing system because he was told that activity-based costing provides more accurate product cost estimates. The controller collected the following data:

Activities	Cost Drivers	Available Capacity	Costs
Electric power	Kilowatt hours	20,000 kwh	$40,000
Materials handling	Material moves	5,000 moves	90,000
Setup	Machine setups	1,000 setups	80,000
Quality inspection	Number of inspections	2,000 inspections	40,000

The company recently received a request for a bid to supply 1,000 units of its product M5. The following estimates were prepared for the production of 1,000 units of M5:

Item	Amount
Direct materials costs	$20,000
Direct labor cost	$18,000
Machine hours	1,800
Direct labor hours	2,000
Kilowatt hours of electricity	2,000
Number of material moves	40
Number of machine setups	5
Number of quality inspections	20

REQUIRED

(a) What is the estimated cost per unit of M5 under the present cost accounting system?

(b) What is the estimated cost per unit of M5 if activity-based costing is used?

6-25 *Comparison of two costing systems*   Ferreira Company has established the following cost pools for 1997:

Cost Pools	Committed Costs	Cost Drivers	Level
Maintenance	$20,000	Machine hours	10,000
Materials handling	25,000	Number of moves	250
Machine setup	30,000	Setup hours	1,000
Inspection	25,000	Number of inspections	500
Total	$100,000		

The following information pertains to two representative jobs completed during January 1997:

Item	J101	J102
Direct materials cost	$10,000	$7,500
Direct labor cost	$8,000	$5,500
Number of units	2,000	1,500
Direct labor hours	640	400
Machine hours	700	650
Number of material moves	40	15
Number of setup hours	80	40
Number of inspections	35	15

REQUIRED

(a) Determine the unit cost of each job using machine hours to allocate all support costs.

(b) Determine the unit cost of each job using activity-based costing.
(c) Which of the two methods produces more accurate estimates of job costs? Explain.

6-26 *Sequential and reciprocal allocation*   *(Appendix)* Stephens Company has two service departments (S1 and S2) and two production departments (P1 and P2). In July 1997, directly identified support costs were $300,000 for S1 and $300,000 for S2. Information on the consumption of their services follows:

Supplying Department	User Department			
	S1	**S2**	**P1**	**P2**
S1	0%	40%	30%	30%
S2	25%	0%	25%	50%

REQUIRED

(a) Determine the service department costs allocated to the two production departments using the direct method.
(b) Determine the service department costs allocated to the two production departments using the sequential method beginning with the allocation of S1 department costs.
(c) Determine the service department costs allocated to the two production departments using the reciprocal method.

6-27 *Cost distortions*   Ehsan Electronics Company manufactures two products, X21 and Y37, at its manufacturing plant in Duluth, Minnesota. For many years the company has used a simple plantwide manufacturing support cost rate based on direct labor hours. A new plant accountant suggested that the company may be able to assign support costs to products more accurately by using an activity-based costing system that relies on a separate rate for each manufacturing activity that causes support costs.

After studying the plant's manufacturing activities and costs, the plant accountant has collected the following data for 1996:

Item	X21	Y37
Units produced and sold	50,000	100,000
Direct labor hours used	100,000	300,000
Direct labor cost	1,000,000	4,500,000
Number of times handled	40,000	20,000
Number of parts	12,000	8,000
Number of design changes	2,000	1,000
Number of product setups	8,000	6,000

The accountant has also determined that actual manufacturing support costs incurred during 1996 were as follows:

Cost Pool	Activity Costs
Handling	$ 3,000,000
Number of parts	2,400,000
Design changes	3,300,000
Setups	2,800,000
Total	$11,500,000

The direct materials cost for product X21 is $120 per unit, while for product Y37 it is $140 per unit.

(a) Determine the unit cost of each product using direct labor hours to allocate all manufacturing support costs.

(b) Determine the unit cost of each product using activity-based costing.

6-28 **Product profitability analysis**   Kidspack, Inc. has recently expanded its line of backpacks to include high quality, lightweight hiker backpacks. This new model uses more expensive material and takes longer to produce. While a basic school backpack can be cut and sewn together in 30 minutes, a hiker backpack takes 45 minutes to cut and sew together. The school model is produced in batches of 1000 packs while the hiker model is produced in batches of 100 packs. Each batch requires inspection time of one hour. Using direct labor hours to allocate manufacturing support costs, product profitability is analyzed as follows:

Item	School Backpacks	Hiker Backpacks
Sales	$10.00	$30.00
Less:		
Direct Materials	2.00	10.00
Direct Labor	2.00	3.00
Manufacturing Support	3.00	4.50
Gross Margin	$3.00	$12.50
Selling/Administrative	0.50	1.00
Profit	$2.50	$11.50
Sales Volume	90,000	6,000

Angel Johnson, the controller at Kidspack, believes that activity-based costing may be a more accurate way of measuring the costs of the two models. She has allocated manufacturing support costs to the following activity pools.

			COST DRIVER DEMANDED	
Activity	Activity Costs	Activity Driver	School Model	Hiker Model
Cutting and Sewing	$ 19,800	Direct labor hours	45,000	4,500
Orders	97,500	Number of orders	450	200
Inspections	179,700	Number of inspections	?	?
Total	$297,000			

REQUIRED

(a) The method of allocation does not affect the total manufacturing support costs. Only the amounts allocated to individual products change. Explain why Angel should care about how these costs are allocated.

(b) Using activity-based costing, calculate the manufacturing support cost per unit for each of the two models.

(c) Analyze product profitability using activity-based costs.

6-29 **Direct, sequential, and reciprocal allocation**   *(Appendix)* The managers of Bruell Brush Company are discussing ways to allocate the cost of service departments such as quality control and maintenance to the production departments. To aid them in this discussion, the controller has provided the following information:

Item	Quality Control	Maintenance	Machining	Assembly	Total
Support costs					
before allocation	$350,000	$200,000	$400,000	$300,000	$1,250,000
Machine hours	0	0	50,000	0	50,000
Direct labor hours	0	0	0	25,000	25,000
Hours of service:					
Quality Control	0	7,000	21,000	7,000	35,000
Maintenance	10,000	0	18,000	12,000	40,000

REQUIRED

(a) Using the direct method of allocating service department costs, compute the total service costs allocated to the assembly department.

(b) Using the direct method of allocating service department costs, compute the total amount of support costs per machine hour for the machining department.

(c) Using the sequential method of allocating service department costs beginning with quality control, compute the maintenance costs allocated to the assembly department.

(d) Using the reciprocal method of allocating service department costs, compute the total amount of quality control costs allocated to the other departments.

6-30 *Job bid sheet*   The Jackson Manufacturing Company produces machine parts on a job order basis. The company operates two service departments (maintenance and power) and two production departments (machining and finishing). The support costs of the maintenance department are allocated on the basis of *maintenance hours* and those of the power department on the basis of *kilowatt hours*. The company allocates support costs to job orders on a *machine-hour* basis for the machining department and on a *direct-labor-hour* basis for the finishing department. The following estimates are provided for 1997.

	SERVICE DEPARTMENT		PRODUCTION DEPARTMENT	
Item	Maintenance	Power	Machining	Finishing
Manufacturing support costs	$200,000	$100,000	$500,000	$400,000
Maintenance hours	0	3,000	6,000	2,000
Kilowatt hours	50,000	0	100,000	150,000
Direct labor hours	0	0	10,000	50,000
Machine hours	0	0	20,000	5,000

REQUIRED

(a) Allocate service department costs to production departments using the *direct* method.

(b) Compute the manufacturing support cost driver rate for each production department.

(c) During the month of November 1996, the accounting records of the company show the following data for job 431:

Item	Machining	Finishing
Direct labor hours	50	200
Machine hours	100	10
Direct materials cost	$2,700	$1,600
Direct labor cost	$600	$2,000

Compute the total manufacturing cost of job 431. If there are 100 units in job 431, what is the unit cost?

6-31 *Job bid sheet, Appendix*   Sanders Manufacturing Company produces electronic components on a job order basis. Most business is gained through bidding on jobs. Most firms competing with Sanders bid full cost plus a 30% markup. Recently, with the expectation of gaining more sales, Sanders dropped its markup from 40% to 30%. The company operates two service departments and two production departments. Manufacturing support costs and normal activity levels for each department are given below.

Item	SERVICE DEPARTMENT		PRODUCTION DEPARTMENT	
	Personnel	Maintenance	Machining	Assembly
Support costs	$100,000	$200,000	$400,000	$300,000
Number of employees	5	5	5	40
Maintenance hours	1,500	200	7,500	1,000
Machine hours	0	0	10,000	1,000
Direct labor hours	0	0	1,000	10,000

Support costs of the personnel department are allocated on the basis of employees and those of the maintenance department on the basis of maintenance hours. Departmental rates are used to assign costs to products. The machining department uses machine hours, and the assembly department uses direct labor hours for this purpose.

The firm is preparing to bid on a job 781 that requires three machine hours per unit produced in the machining department and five direct labor hours per unit produced in the assembly department. The expected direct materials and direct labor costs per unit are $450.

REQUIRED

(a) Allocate the service department costs to the production departments using the direct method.
(b) Determine the bid price per unit produced for job 781 using the direct method.
(c) Assume that the support costs of the service department incurring the greatest costs are allocated first, and allocate the service department costs to the production departments using the sequential method.
(d) Determine the bid price per unit produced for job 781 using the sequential method in (c).

6-32 *Direct, sequential, and reciprocal allocation*   (*Appendix*) Boston Box Company has two service departments, maintenance and grounds, and two production departments, fabricating and assembly. Management has decided to allocate maintenance costs on the basis of machine hours used by the departments and grounds costs on the basis of square feet occupied by the departments. The following data appear in the company's records for 1997:

Item	Maintenance	Grounds	Fabricating	Assembly
Machine hours	0	1,500	12,000	6,000
Square feet	3,000	0	15,000	20,000
Support costs	$18,000	$14,000	$45,000	$25,000

REQUIRED

(a) Allocate service department costs to the production departments using the direct method.

(b) Allocate service department costs to the production departments using the sequential method, assuming that the costs of the service department incurring the greatest cost are allocated first.

(c) Allocate service department costs to the production departments using the reciprocal method.

Challenging Problems

6-33 ***Product profitability analysis***   Ittner Company manufactures two models of electronic valves for automobile engines. The design of valve IO23 is simpler than that for valve IO29. Ittner Company's plant has two service departments, S1 and S2, and two production departments, P1 and P2. Total support costs for 1996 were $600,000. Of this total, $100,000 was traced to S1, $160,000 traced to S2, $200,000 traced to P1, and $140,000 traced to P2. The existing cost accounting system allocates support costs in the following two stages. In Stage 1, costs of service department S1 are allocated to the production departments based on the proportion of their respective machine hours, and S2 costs are allocated in the proportion of their total direct labor hours. In Stage 2, separate cost driver rates are determined for the two production departments on the basis of direct labor hours (*DLH*) to assign support costs to two products. The direct labor wage rate is $10 per hour in both production departments.

| Product | Total Direct Labor Hours | | |
	P1	P2	Total
IO23	1,500	2,000	3,500
IO29	1,500	3,000	4,500
Total	3,000	5,000	8,000
Machine hours	400	600	

An activity-based costing system has been proposed; it traces production support costs to four cost pools, each identified with a unique cost driver as presented in the following table:

| Activity | Activity Costs | COST DRIVER LEVELS | | |
		Total	IO23	IO29
P1 *DLH*	$ 90,000	3,000	1,500	1,500
P2 *DLH*	100,000	5,000	2,000	3,000
Setup hours	200,000	200	50	150
Number of inspections	210,000	500	150	350
Total support costs	$600,000			

Other relevant information follows:

Item	IO23	IO29
Sales price per unit	$120	$150
Materials cost per unit	60	80
Number of units sold	5,000	6,000

REQUIRED

(a) Determine unit product costs using the existing accounting system.

(b) Determine unit product costs using the proposed ABC method.

(c) Explain the principal reason that the existing two-stage cost allocation system may be distorting product costs.

(d) Analyze the profitability of the two products. What should Ittner do to improve its profitability?

6-34 *Cost distortions* Anderson Company uses a conventional two-stage cost allocation system. In the first stage, all manufacturing support costs are assigned to two production departments, P1 and P2, based on machine hours. In the second stage, direct labor hours are used to allocate support costs to individual products.

Anderson Company manufactures two products, X and Y, for which the following information is available:

Item	Product X	Product Y
Units sold	1,000	3,000
Direct materials cost per unit	$60	$50
Direct labor wage rate per hour	$25	$15
Direct labor hours in P1 per unit	2	1
Direct labor hours in P2 per unit	1	3

During 1997 manufacturing support costs totaled $200,000. Machine hours in production departments P1 and P2 were 5000 and 15,000 hours, respectively. Direct labor hours in production departments P1 and P2 were 5000 and 10,000, respectively.

Anderson Company is considering implementing an activity-based costing system. Its controller has compiled the following information for activity cost analysis:

Activity	Activity Costs	Activity Cost Driver	Activity Support Driver Rate	COST DRIVER DEMANDED X	COST DRIVER DEMANDED Y
Material movement	$ 30,000	Number of production runs	$30 per run	200	800
Machine setups	100,000	Number of setups	$500 per setup	50	150
Quality inspections	50,000	Number of units	$12.50 per unit	1,000	3,000
Shipment	20,000	Number of shipments	$100 per shipment	50	150
Total support costs	$200,000				

REQUIRED

(a) Determine the unit costs for each of the two products under the existing cost accounting system.

(b) Determine the unit costs for each of the two products if the proposed ABC system is adopted.

6-35 *Comparison of cost systems* Kallapur Company manufactures two products: SK33 and SK77. Manufacturing support costs are estimated to be $2 million for the current year. Estimated unit cost and production data follow:

Item	SK33	SK77
Direct materials cost	$30	$45
Direct labor cost ($12 per hour)	$24	$60
Estimated production in units	25,000	15,000

REQUIRED

    (a) Estimate the manufacturing cost per unit of each product if support costs are assigned to products on the basis of number of units produced.

    (b) How does your answer change if support costs are assigned to products on the basis of direct labor hours?

Assume next that the company's manufacturing support costs can be traced to four activities as follows:

Activity Cost Driver	Activity Costs	Cost Driver	COST DRIVER UNITS DEMANDED BY	
			SK33	SK77
Machine setups	$ 400,000	Number of setups	100	400
Purchase ordering	600,000	Number of orders	200	100
Machine hours	500,000	Number of machine hours	2,000	6,000
Inspection and shipments	500,000	Number of shipments	200	300
Total	$2,000,000			

    (c) Estimate the manufacturing cost per unit of each product if an activity-based costing approach is used.

6-36 *Job bid price* *(Appendix)* Sherman Company manufactures and sells small pumps made to customer specifications. It has two service departments and two production departments. Information on March 1997 operations follows:

Item	SERVICE DEPARTMENT		PRODUCTION DEPARTMENT	
	Maintenance	Power	Casting	Assembly
Support costs	$750,000	$450,000	$150,000	$110,000
Machine hours	0	80,000	80,000	40,000
Kilowatt hours	40,000	0	200,000	160,000
Direct labor hours	0	0	100,000	60,000

Separate cost driver rates are determined on the basis of machine hours for the casting department and on the basis of direct labor hours for the assembly department. It takes one machine hour to manufacture a pump in the casting department and 0.5 labor hour to assemble a pump in the assembly department. Direct labor and material costs amount to $32 per pump.

A prospective customer has requested a bid on a two-year contract to purchase 1000 pumps every month. Sherman Company has a policy of adding a 25% markup to the full manufacturing cost to determine the bid.

REQUIRED

    (a) What is the bid price when the direct method is used?

    (b) What is the bid price when the sequential method that begins by allocating maintenance department costs is used?

    (c) What is the bid price when the reciprocal method is used?

6-37 *Product cost distortions* The Manhattan Company manufactures two models of compact disc players: a deluxe model and a regular model. The company has manufactured the regular model for years; the deluxe model was introduced recently to tap a new segment of the market. Since the introduction of the deluxe model, the company's profits have steadily declined and management has become increasingly concerned about the accuracy of its costing system. Sales of the deluxe model have been increasing rapidly.

The current cost accounting system allocates manufacturing support costs to the two products on the basis of direct labor hours. For 1997, the company has estimated that it will incur $1 million in manufacturing support cost and produce 5000 units of the deluxe model and 40,000 units of the regular model. The deluxe model requires two hours of direct labor and the regular model requires one hour. Material and labor costs per unit and selling price per unit are as follows:

Item	Deluxe	Regular
Direct materials cost	$45	$30
Direct labor cost	$20	$10
Selling price	$140	$80

REQUIRED

(a) Compute the manufacturing support cost driver rate for 1997.

(b) Determine the cost to manufacture one unit of each model.

The company has decided to allocate manufacturing support costs based on four activities. The amount of manufacturing support cost traceable to the four activities for 1997 are given below:

Activity	Cost Driver	Cost	COST DRIVER DEMANDED		
			Total	Deluxe	Regular
Purchase orders	number of orders	$ 180,000	600	200	400
Quality control	number of inspections	250,000	2,000	1,000	1,000
Production setups	number of setups	220,000	200	100	100
Machine maintenance	machine hours	350,000	35,000	20,000	15,000
		$1,000,000			

(c) Using the activity-based costing data presented above, compute the total cost to manufacture one unit of each model.

(d) Compare the manufacturing activity resources demanded per unit of the regular model and per unit of the deluxe model. Why did the old costing system undercost the deluxe model?

(e) Is the deluxe model as profitable as the company thinks it is under the old costing system? Explain.

(f) What should Manhattan Company do to improve its profitability?

6-38 *Activity-based costing* (Adapted from CMA, June 1992) Alaire Corporation manufactures several different types of printed circuit boards; however, two of the boards account for the majority of the company's sales. The first of these boards, a TV circuit board, has been a standard in the industry for several years. The market for this type of board is competitive and therefore price sensitive. Alaire plans to sell 65,000 of the TV boards in 1998 at a price of $150 per unit. The second high-volume product, a PC circuit board, is a recent addition to Alaire's product line. Because the PC board incorporates the latest technology, it can be sold at a premium price; the 1998 plans include the sale of 45,000 PC boards at $300 per unit.

Alaire's management group is meeting to discuss strategies for 1998, and the current topic of conversation is how to spend the sales and promotion dollars for next year. The sales manager believes that the market share for the TV board could be expanded by concentrating Alaire's promotional efforts in this area. In response to this suggestion, the production manager said, "Why don't you go after a bigger market for the PC board? The cost sheets that I get show that the contribution from the PC board is more than double the contribution from the TV board. I know we get a premium price for the PC board; selling it should help overall profitability."

Alaire uses a standard cost system, and the following data apply to the TV and PC boards.

Item	TV Board	PC Board
Direct materials	$80	$140
Direct labor	1.5 hours	4 hours
Machine time	0.5 hour	1.5 hours

Variable manufacturing support costs are applied on the basis of direct labor hours. For 1998, variable manufacturing support costs are budgeted at $1,110,000, and direct labor hours are estimated at 277,500. The hourly rates for machine time and direct labor are $10 and $14, respectively. Alaire applies a materials handling charge of 10% of materials cost; this materials handling charge is not included in variable manufacturing support costs. Total 1998 expenditures for material are budgeted at $11,500,000.

Ed Welch, Alaire's controller, believes that before the management group proceeds with the discussion about allocating sales and promotional dollars to individual products, it may be worthwhile to look at these products on the basis of the activities involved in their production. Welch has prepared the schedule shown below for the management group.

Costs	Budgeted Cost	Cost Driver	Annual Activity for Cost Driver
Material support costs:			
Procurement	$ 400,000	Number of parts	4,000,000
Production scheduling	220,000	Number of boards	110,000
Packaging and shipping	440,000	Number of boards	110,000
Total costs	$1,060,000		
Variable support costs:			
Machine setup	$ 446,000	Number of setups	278,750
Hazardous waste disposal	38,000	Pounds of waste	16,000
Quality control	560,000	Number of inspections	160,000
General supplies	66,000	Number of boards	110,000
Total costs	$ 1,110,000		
Manufacturing support costs:			
Machine insertion	$1,200,000	Number of parts	3,000,000
Manual insertion	4,000,000	Number of parts	1,000,000
Wave soldering	132,000	Number of boards	110,000
Total costs	$5,332,000		

Required per Unit	TV Board	PC Board
Parts	25	55
Machine insertions	24	35
Manual insertions	1	20
Machine setups	2	3
Hazardous waste	0.02 lb	0.35 lb
Inspections	1	2

"Using this information," Welch explained, "we can calculate an activity-based cost for each TV board and each PC board and then compare it to the standard cost we have been using. The only cost that remains the same for both cost methods is the cost of direct materials. The cost drivers will replace the direct labor, machine time, and support costs in the standard cost."

REQUIRED

(a) Identify at least four general advantages that are associated with activity-based costing.

(b) On the basis of standard costs, calculate the total contribution expected in 1998 for Alaire Corporation's products: (1) the TV board and (2) the PC board.

(c) On the basis of activity-based costs, calculate the total contribution expected in 1998 for Alaire Corporation's two products.

(d) Explain how the comparison of the results of the two costing methods may impact the decisions made by Alaire Corporation's management group.

6-39 *Manufacturing support cost driver rates* (Adapted from CMA, December 1990) Moss Manufacturing has just completed a major change in its quality control (QC) process. Previously, products had been reviewed by QC inspectors at the end of each major process, and the company's 10 QC inspectors were charged as direct labor to the operation or job. In an effort to improve efficiency and quality, a computer video QC system was purchased for $250,000. The system consists of a minicomputer, 15 video cameras, other peripheral hardware, and software.

The new system uses cameras stationed by QC engineers at key points in the production process. Each time an operation changes or there is a new operation, the cameras are moved and a new master picture is loaded into the computer by a QC engineer. The camera takes pictures of the units in process, and the computer compares them to the picture of a good unit. Any differences are sent to a QC engineer who removes the bad units and discusses the flaws with the production supervisors. The new system has replaced the 10 QC inspectors with two QC engineers.

The operating costs of the new QC system, including the salaries of the QC engineers, have been included as manufacturing support in calculating the company's plant-wide manufacturing support cost rate, which is based on direct labor dollars.

Josephine Gugliemo, the company's president, is confused. Her vice-president of production has told her how efficient the new system is; yet there is a large increase in the manufacturing support cost driver rate. The computation of the rate before and after automation is shown below.

Item	Before	After
Budgeted support costs	$1,900,000	$2,100,000
Budgeted direct labor costs	1,000,000	700,000
Budgeted cost driver rate	190%	300%

"Three hundred percent," lamented the president. "How can we compete with such a high manufacturing support cost driver rate?"

REQUIRED

(a) Define manufacturing support costs, and cite three examples of typical costs that would be included in this category. Explain why companies develop manufacturing support cost driver rates.

(b) Explain why the increase in the cost driver rate should not have a negative financial impact on Moss Manufacturing.

(c) Explain, in the greatest detail possible, how Moss Manufacturing could change its accounting system to eliminate confusion over product costs.

(d) Discuss how an activity-based costing system may benefit Moss Manufacturing.

■ CASES

6-40 *Comparison of two costing systems*   The Redwood City plant of Crimson Components Company makes two types of rotators, R361 and R572, for automobile engines. The old cost accounting system at the plant traced support costs to four cost pools:

Cost Pool	Support Costs	Cost Driver
S1	$1,176,000	Direct labor cost
S2	1,120,000	Machine hours
P1	480,000	—
P2	780,000	—
	$3,556,000	

Pool S1 included service activity costs related to setups, production scheduling, plant administration, janitorial services, materials handling, and shipping. Pool S2 included activity costs related to machine maintenance and repair, rent, insurance, power, and utilities. Pools P1 and P2 included supervisors' wages, idle time, and indirect materials for the two production departments, casting and machining, respectively.

The old accounting system allocated support costs in Pools S1 and S2 to the two production departments using *direct labor cost* and *machine hours*, respectively, as the cost drivers. Then the accumulated support costs in pools P1 and P2 were applied to the products on the basis of direct labor hours. A separate rate was determined for each of the two production departments. The direct labor wage rate is $15 per hour in casting and $18 per hour in machining.

Department	DIRECT LABOR HOURS (DLH)			Direct Labor Costs
	R361	R572	Total	
Casting (P1)	60,000	20,000	80,000	$1,200,000
Machining (P2)	72,000	48,000	120,000	2,160,000
Totals	132,000	68,000	200,000	$3,360,000

Department	MACHINE HOURS (MH)		
	R361	R572	Totals
Casting (P1)	30,000	10,000	40,000
Machining (P2)	72,000	48,000	120,000
Totals	102,000	58,000	160,000

Item	R361	R572
Sales price per unit	$19	$20
Sales units	500,000	400,000
Number of orders	1,000	1,000
Number of setups	2,000	4,000
Materials cost per unit	$8	$10

Now the plant has implemented an activity-based costing system. The following table presents the amounts from the old cost pools that are traced to each of the new activity cost pools.

Activity	OLD COST POOLS				
Cost Drivers	S1	S2	P1	P2	Total
P1 *DLH*	$ 120,000	$ 0	$120,000	$ 0	$ 240,000
P2 *DLH*	240,000	0	0	120,000	360,000
Setup hours	816,000	80,000	240,000	540,000	1,676,000
P1 *MH*	0	260,000	120,000	0	380,000
P2 *MH*	0	780,000	0	120,000	900,000
	$1,176,000	$1,120,000	$480,000	$780,000	$3,556,000

Setups for R572 are 50% more complex than those for R361, that is, each R572 setup takes 1.5 times as long as one R361 setup.

REQUIRED

(a) Determine the product costs per unit using the old system. Show all intermediate steps for both Stage 1 and Stage 2 allocations, including departmental cost driver rates and a breakdown of product costs into each of their components.
(b) Determine the product costs per unit using the new system.
(c) Explain the intuitive reason that the product costs differ under the two accounting systems.
(d) What should Crimson Components do to improve the profitability of its Redwood City plant?
(e) Describe how experienced production and sales managers are likely to react to the new product costs.

6-41 *Activity-based costing*   The Fishburn plant of Hibeem Electronics Corporation makes two types of wafers, W101 and W202, for electronic instruments. The old cost accounting system at the plant traced support costs to *three cost pools.*

Cost Pools	Support Costs	Cost Drivers
S	$1,740,000	Machine hours
P1	680,000	—
P2	240,000	—
	$2,660,000	

Pool S included all service activity costs at the plant. Pools P1 and P2 included support costs traced directly to the two production departments, photolithography and assembly, respectively.

The old cost accounting system allocated costs in pool S to the two production departments on the basis of *machine hours.* Then the accumulated costs in P1 and P2 were applied to the products on the basis of direct labor hours. A separate rate was computed for each of the two production departments. The direct labor wage rate is $20 per hour. The following data were compiled from plant records for January:

	DIRECT LABOR HOURS (*DLH*)		
Department	**W101**	**W202**	**Totals**
Photolithography (P1)	80,000	20,000	100,000
Assembly (P2)	40,000	20,000	60,000
	120,000	40,000	160,000

	MACHINE HOURS (*MH*)		
Department	**W101**	**W202**	**Total**
Photolithography (P1)	80,000	30,000	110,000
Assembly (P2)	20,000	15,000	35,000
	100,000	45,000	145,000

Item	**W101**	**W202**
Sales price per unit	$11.50	$12.25
Sales units	600,000	300,000
Number of orders	1,000	1,000
Number of setups	2,000	4,000
Materials cost per unit	$ 4.00	$ 5.00

Now the plant has implemented an activity-based costing system. The following table presents the amounts from the old cost pools that are traced to each of the new activity cost pools.

Activity Cost Drivers	OLD COST POOLS			
	S	**P1**	**P2**	**Total**
P1-*DLH*	$ 180,000	$140,000	$ 0	$ 320,000
P2-*DLH*	120,000	0	60,000	180,000
Setup hours	900,000	390,000	145,000	1,435,000
P1-*MH*	400,000	150,000	0	550,000
P2-*MH*	140,000	0	35,000	175,000
	$1,740,000	$680,000	$240,000	$2,660,000

Each W202 setup takes 1.25 times as long as a W101 setup.

REQUIRED

(a) Determine the product costs per unit using the old system. Show all intermediate steps for both Stage 1 and Stage 2 allocations, including departmental cost driver rates and a breakdown of product costs into each of their components.
(b) Determine the product costs per unit using the new system.
(c) Explain the intuitive reason that the product costs are different under the two accounting systems.
(d) What should Hibeem Electronics Corporation do to improve the profitability of its Fishburn plant?

6-42 *Activity-based costing*   Sandra Slaughter, senior vice president for sales for Showman Shoes, Inc., noticed that the company had substantially increased its market share for the high-quality boomer boots (BB) and lost market share for the lower-quality lazy loafers (LL). Sandra found that Showman's prices were lower than the competitors' for BB but higher for LL. She did not understand the reasons for these price differences because all companies used the same production technology and were equally efficient.

The manufacturing process is relatively simple. Showman's manufacturing facility has a cutting department and an assembly department. The high-quality BB is produced in small batches (1000 pairs of shoes each), and the lower-quality LL is produced in large batches (3000 pairs each). Sandra has asked you, the company's new controller, to analyze the product costing method to see if the product prices should be changed.

The company currently uses a plantwide cost driver rate based on direct labor hours. The rate is computed at the beginning of the year using the following budgeted data:

Total manufacturing support costs	$1,200,000
Total direct labor hours	49,000
Total machine-hours	49,400
Total setup hours	520

Your assistant has provided you with the following additional information about the production of batches of BB and LL:

EACH BATCH OF (BB): 1000 PAIRS

Item	Cutting	Assembly	Totals
Direct labor hours	80	120	200
Machine hours	160	120	280
Setup hours	3	1	4
Direct costs	$7,500	$6,000	$13,500

EACH BATCH OF (LL): 3000 PAIRS

Item	Cutting	Assembly	Totals
Direct labor hours	150	180	330
Machine hours	150	120	270
Setup hours	1	1	2
Direct costs	$9,000	$7,200	$16,200

On further inquiry, your assistant has been able to trace the support costs to the two service departments and the two production departments and to identify the following details for potential cost drivers for the service departments.

Item	Maintenance	Setup	Cutting	Assembly	Totals
Support costs	$160,000	$400,000	$440,000	$200,000	$1,200,000
Direct labor hours	0	0	21,400	27,600	49,000
Machine hours	0	0	27,800	21,600	49,400
Setup hours	0	0	340	180	520

Your assistant has also collected the following information on activities and their cost drivers:

Support Activities	Cost	Activity Category	Cost Driver
Maintenance	$160,000	Product sustaining	Machine hours
Setups	400,000	Batch related	Setup hours
Cutting supervision	280,000	Batch related	Setup hours
Cutting depreciation	160,000	Facility sustaining	Machine hours
Assembly supervision	160,000	Unit related	Direct labor hours
Assembly depreciation	40,000	Facility sustaining	Machine hours

REQUIRED

(a) Using a single, plantwide cost driver rate based on direct labor hours, determine the costs per pair of BB and LL.

(b) Determine the costs per pair of BB and LL using departmental cost driver rates based on machine hours for the cutting department and direct labor hours for the assembly department. Allocate service department costs using the direct method.

(c) Determine the costs per pair of BB and LL using activity-based costing.

(d) Explain why unit costs for product BB are higher when departmental cost driver rates are used than when a single plantwide rate is used.

(e) Explain why activity-based costs for product LL are lower than the corresponding costs based on a single plantwide rate.

6-43 **Product profitability analysis**   Petersen Pneumatic Company makes three products. Its manufacturing plant in Petersburg has three production departments and three service departments.

Department	Support Costs
Machining (MC)	$ 40,000
Plating (PL)	50,000
Assembly (AS)	15,000
Purchasing and inventory (PI)	50,000
Setup and scheduling (SS)	120,000
Quality control (QC)	70,000

Support costs are first traced to the six departments. The old cost accounting system allocated the service department costs to the production departments using the following cost drivers:

Department	Cost Driver
PI	Materials cost (*MAT*)
SS	Direct labor hours (*DLH*)
QC	Machine hours (*MCH*)

The old cost accounting system applied support costs to the three products on the basis of direct labor hours. A different cost driver rate was determined for each department. The direct labor wage rate at the plant is $10 per hour.

Department	DIRECT LABOR HOURS (*DLH*)			Machine Hours (*MCH*)
	GT101	GT102	GT103	
MC	7,000	2,800	2,200	5,200
PL	3,500	1,700	1,800	1,900
AS	2,500	1,000	1,000	2,900

	PRODUCT SALES		BATCH-RELATED DRIVERS		MATERIALS COST PER UNIT	
Product	Price	Sales Units	Orders	Setups	MC	PL
GT101	$1.25	500,000	25	110	$0.30	$0.10
GT102	1.20	200,000	10	43	0.25	0.10
GT103	1.30	200,000	40	166	0.28	0.10

The profitability of the Petersburg plant has been declining for the past three years despite the successful introduction of the new product GT103, which has now captured more than 60% share of its segment of the industry. In an attempt to understand the reasons for its declining profitability, the company has appointed a special task force.

The task force is considering a new cost accounting system based on activity analysis. This system employs five cost drivers: three departmental *DLH*, setups (*SET*), and orders (*ORD*). Each departmental cost pool is divided into homogeneous cost pools identified with a unique driver. The following table presents the percent of the departmental support costs that are put in each of the homogeneous cost pools. The total amounts in the five cost pools are allocated to the three products based on their respective cost drivers.

Department	*DLH*	*SET*	*ORD*
MC	30%	70%	0%
PL	70%	30%	0%
AS	60%	40%	0%
PI	0%	40%	60%
SS	?	?	?
QC	0%	70%	30%

Peter Gamble is the leader of the task force responsible for activity-based cost analysis. He interviewed Nola Morris, who was responsible for the setup and scheduling department, to determine the cost drivers for the departmental support costs.

Gamble:
  How many people work in the setup and scheduling department?
Morris:
  I have 12 people who work on setups. Three more are responsible for production scheduling. I spend most of my time supervising them.
Gamble:
  How do you assign setup workers to production jobs?
Morris:
  Almost all the time they set up machines in the machining department. The effort depends only on the number of setups.
Gamble:
  On what does the time spent on scheduling depend?
Morris:
  It depends on the number of orders.
Gamble:
  So a large batch or order will require the same amount of setup and scheduling time as a small batch or order.
Morris:
  Yes, that's right.

REQUIRED

(a) List the reasons that the old cost accounting system at Petersen Pneumatic may be distorting its product costs.

(b) Determine the product costs per unit using both the old and new cost accounting systems. Show all the intermediate steps including the cost driver rates, amounts in the three new cost pools, and a breakdown of product costs into each of their components.

(c) Analyze the profitability of the three products. What insight is provided by the new profitability analysis? What should Petersen Pneumatic do to improve the profitability of its Petersburg plant?

(d) Mike Meservy is a veteran production manager and Shannon Corinth is a marketing manager with considerable experience as a salesperson. Discuss how each of them is likely to react to your analysis and recommendations. Explain how their expected reactions may affect the way you will present your recommendations.

6-44 *Product profitability analysis*   Pharaoh Phawcetts, Inc., manufactures two models of faucets: a regular and a deluxe model. The deluxe model, introduced just two years ago, has been very successful. It now accounts for more than half of the firm's profits as evidenced by the following income statement for 1996:

Item	Total	Regular	Deluxe
Sales	$2,400,000	$1,200,000	$1,200,000
Cost of goods sold	1,540,000	771,000	769,000
Gross margin	$ 860,000	$ 429,000	$ 431,000
Selling/administrative expenses	500,000	250,000	250,000
Net income	$ 360,000	$ 179,000	$ 181,000
Number of units	500,000	300,000	200,000

Its manufacturing plant in Phoenix, Arizona, has two production departments: a machining department and an assembly department. The cost of goods sold included $720,000 in production support costs. The plant accountant traced $192,000 of the production support costs to the machining department and $168,000 to the assembly department. The balance of $360,000 was attributed to the various service departments, and in Stage 1 of the existing cost allocation system, it was allocated to the machining and the assembly departments in the proportion of their respective machine hours. In Stage 2, separate cost driver rates were determined for the two production departments based on their respective direct labor hours to assign the support costs to the two products.

	TOTAL DIRECT LABOR AND MACHINE HOURS		
Product	Machining Department	Assembly Department	Totals
Regular	15,000 *DLH*	3,000 *DLH*	18,000 *DLH*
Deluxe	13,000 *DLH*	5,000 *DLH*	18,000 *DLH*
Total *DLH*	28,000 *DLH*	8,000 *DLH*	36,000 *DLH*
Total machine hours	52,000 *MH*	8,000 *MH*	60,000 *MH*

The direct labor wage rate is $10.00 per hour. Direct materials cost is $0.80 per unit of the regular model and for the deluxe model is $1.10 per unit. An average customer order for the regular model is for 5000 faucets, but for the deluxe model, each order is for 2000 units. The machines required a setup for each order. Three hours are required per machine setup for the regular model; the more complex deluxe model requires five hours per setup.

Pharaoh Phawcetts' profitability has been declining for the past two years despite the successful introduction of the deluxe model, which has now captured over 65% share of its segment of the industry. Market share for the regular model has decreased to 12%. In an attempt to understand the reasons for its declining profitability, the company has appointed a special task force.

The task force is considering a new cost accounting system based on activity analysis. This system employs four cost drivers: two departmental direct labor hours, setup hours, and number of orders. Production support costs are traced to four homogeneous cost pools, each identified with a unique driver as presented in the following table.

| | | TRACEABLE NUMBER OF UNITS OF COST DRIVER | | |
Activity Cost Driver	Costs	Total	Regular	Deluxe
Machining *DLH*	$112,000	?	?	?
Assembly *DLH*	96,000	?	?	?
Setup hours	272,000	?	?	?
Number of orders	240,000	?	?	?
Total manufacturing support costs	$720,000			

The task force also analyzed selling and administrative expenses. These costs included 5% sales commission on regular models and 10% on deluxe models. Advertising and promotion expenses were $50,000 for the regular model and $90,000 for the deluxe model. The remaining $180,000 of selling and administrative expenses are attributed equally to the two products.

REQUIRED

(a) Determine the product costs per unit using the existing cost accounting system. Show all the intermediate steps including the cost driver rates and a breakdown of product costs into each of their components.

(b) Determine the product costs and profits per unit using the new activity-based costing system. Show all the intermediate steps including the cost driver rates and components of product costs.

(c) Explain the principal reasons that the old cost accounting system at Pharaoh Phawcetts may be distorting its product costs and profitability. Support your answer with numbers when necessary.

(d) Analyze the profitability of the two products. What insight does the new profitability analysis provide? What should Pharaoh Phawcetts do to improve its profitability? What options may be available?

(e) Ryan O'Reilley is a marketing manager with considerable experience as a salesperson. Discuss how he is likely to react to your analysis and recommendations.

6-45 *Cost distortions* Sweditrak Corporation manufactures two models of its exercise equipment: regular (REG) and deluxe (DLX). Its plant has two production departments, fabrication (FAB) and assembly (ASM), and two service departments, maintenance (MNT) and quality control (QLC). The parts for each model are manufactured in the fabrication department and put together in the assembly department. The maintenance department supports both production departments, and QLC performs all inspections for both production departments. Each unit of both products needs one inspection in each production department. Each inspection takes 30 and 60 minutes for REG and DLX models, respectively. The two production departments have set the following standards for direct material cost, direct labor cost, and machine hours for each unit of product.

| | FABRICATION | | ASSEMBLY | |
Item	REG	DLX	REG	DLX
Direct materials cost	$40.00	$80.00	$10.00	$20.00
Direct labor cost	20.00	40.00	20.00	30.00
Machine hours	2.0	3.0	1.0	2.0

The average wage rate for direct labor is $10 per hour. The following table gives the production volume and support costs for the past two weeks:

| | PRODUCTION VOLUME | | SUPPORT COSTS | |
Week	REG	DLX	MNT	QLC
45	450	430	$35,000	$63,100
46	450	450	$35,400	$63,500

The present cost accounting system assigns support costs in MNT to the production departments on the basis of machine hours and assigns QLC costs to the two production departments on the basis of the number of inspections. The accumulated costs in FAB and ASM are applied to products based on direct labor hours.

The company is considering implementing an activity-based costing system using machine hours as the cost driver for MNT cost and inspection hours as the cost driver for QLC cost.

REQUIRED

(a) Using the present cost accounting system, determine the product costs per unit for each product for the two weeks.

(b) Using the proposed ABC system, determine the unit product costs for each product for the two weeks.

7

PRICING AND PRODUCT-MIX DECISIONS

PRECISION SPRINGS

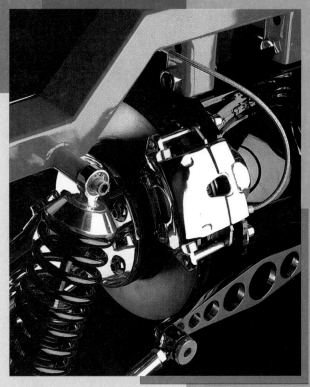

"We cannot possibly make a profit if we sell at a price below costs. The quarterly product cost reports from the accounting department indicate a cost of $2.79 per pound for our 0.25-inch steel springs. I do not see any benefit in your proposal to accept Genair's offer to buy 120,000 pounds of our 0.25-inch springs at only $2.48 per pound. How can we survive in this business if we keep slashing our prices?"

Bob Smith is the owner and president of Precision Springs, a manufacturer of high-precision steel springs for industrial customers. He was meeting with Mike Gaston, his marketing manager, and Alex Reed, his controller, to evaluate an offer from Genair Corporation to purchase a large quantity of 0.25-inch springs at sharply reduced prices. His outburst followed Alex

Courtesy **Paul Avis/Liaison International**

Reed's comments about the costs and price of this product.

> "Our accounting records show that the full cost of the 0.25-inch springs is $2.79 per pound, comprising $1.38 of direct materials, $0.76 of direct labor, and $0.65 of manufacturing support costs. We usually mark up our products 30% over costs, which implies a markup of $0.84 and a price of $3.63 per pound for the 0.25-inch springs. This means that Genair is demanding a discount of $1.15 per pound, which is almost 32% off our normal price," Alex had observed earlier.

Mike realized that Alex's comments about the product costs and Bob's reaction to it meant that he could not justify his proposal simply by appealing to the value of developing a reputable firm such as Genair Corporation as a large customer. He had to make a case for accepting a lower price by comparing the price with the **incremental costs (or revenues)** of producing the springs. (The **incremental cost per unit** of a product is the amount by which the total costs of production and sales increase when one additional unit of that product is produced and sold.)

> "It is true that the full cost of the 0.25-inch springs is $2.79, but that includes $0.65 of manufacturing support costs. We know that manufacturing support costs comprise rent, depreciation, insurance, heating and lighting, janitorial services, and so on. These are fixed costs and will not increase if we accept Genair's order. So the only costs we need to consider are materials and labor, which add up to only $2.14. Even at a price of $2.48, we can earn a margin of $0.34 per pound," Mike explained.

> "Mike is right about rent, depreciation, and insurance being fixed costs," replied Alex. "But such fixed costs are only 60% of our total manufacturing

Incremental costs/ revenues
The amount by which costs/revenues change if one particular decision is made instead of another.

Incremental cost per unit
The amount by which the total costs of production and sales increase when one additional unit of that product is produced and sold.

support at present. Support activities also include supervision, setups, and inspection, whose costs will increase if we accept the Genair order. Variable manufacturing costs for the 0.25-inch springs are $1.38 direct materials, $0.76 direct labor, plus $0.26 variable support activity costs. This adds up to $2.40 of variable costs, so it seems we would have a contribution margin of $0.08 per pound. But that is before we consider selling and distribution costs, which will, I believe, add another $0.23 to the variable costs of the 0.25-inch springs. I figure the total variable costs to be $2.63 per pound, which is more than the offer of only $2.48 per pound."

"Well, should we counter Genair's offer by suggesting that we would accept it for a $2.70 price? That would earn us a contribution margin of $0.07 per pound by your calculations."

Before Alex could respond, Bob interrupted this discussion:

"I am very confused by all this talk about only variable costs. Costs are costs. I pay for rent and insurance just as I pay our workers and our suppliers. If our customers do not pay me a price that covers all our costs—both fixed and variable—I cannot possibly make money in this business."

ROLE OF PRODUCT COSTS IN PRICING AND PRODUCT-MIX DECISIONS

The situation described at Precision Springs applies to most firms that need to make decisions about establishing or accepting a price for their products. Firms also need to determine whether they should offer discounts for large orders or to valued customers. Understanding how to analyze product costs is important for making such pricing decisions. Even when prices are set by overall market supply and demand forces and the firm has little or no influence on product prices, the firm still has to decide the best mix of products to manufacture and sell, given their market prices and margins (price less relevant costs) and their use of capacity resources. Once again, a proper analysis of product costs is important when determining the most profitable mix of products. In a related vein, product cost analysis also is significant when a firm is deciding how best to deploy marketing and promotion resources, including how much commission (or how many other incentives) to provide the sales force for different products and how large a discount to offer off list prices.

An important function of the management accountant, therefore, is to supply the cost information that helps to support these types of decisions. Management accountants in many organizations supply product cost reports periodically to help marketing departments make pricing and product mix decisions. In addition, management accountants also prepare special analyses and reports to facilitate the evaluation of specific offers or bids. To design such cost reports and perform such analyses properly, management accountants must understand how to use cost information in making these decisions.

Short- and Long-Term Pricing Considerations

Firms must consider both the *short-term* and *long-term* consequences of their decisions. Recall from Chapter 4 that the costs of many resources committed to activities are likely to be fixed costs in the short term because firms cannot easily alter the capacities made available for many production and support activities. Consequently, for short-term decisions, it is important to pay special attention to whether surplus capacity is available for additional production or whether shortages of available capacity limit additional production alternatives. Of special concern here is the time period involved in the contract in which the firm must commit production capacity to the particular order it is evaluating. The time period is relevant because a long-term capacity commitment to a marginally profitable order may prevent the firm from deploying its capacity for more profitable products or orders should demand for such products arise in the future.

If production is constrained by inadequate capacity, a firm needs to consider whether overtime production or the use of subcontractors can help augment capacity in the short term. In the long term, managers have considerably more flexibility in adjusting the capacities of activity resources to match the demand for these resources to produce various products. Decisions about whether to introduce new products or to eliminate existing products have long-term consequences. Therefore, our emphasis here is to analyze how such decisions will affect the demand placed on activity resources by each product.

We also shall classify decisions based on whether the firm can influence the price of its products. If the firm is one of a large number of firms in an industry and if there is little to distinguish the products of different firms from each other, economic theory tells us that the prices will be set by aggregate market forces of supply and demand so that no one firm can influence the prices significantly by its own decisions. For instance, in commodity businesses, such as grains, meat, and sugar, traders in the commodity markets set prices based on industry supply and demand. Similarly, if prices are set by one or more large firms leading an industry, a small firm on the fringe must match the prices set by the industry leaders. In such a situation, a small firm is a **price taker** because it chooses its product mix given the prices set in the marketplace for its products.

In contrast, firms in an industry with relatively few competing firms and firms enjoying large market shares and exercising leadership in an industry must decide what prices to set for their products. Firms in industries in which products are highly customized or otherwise differentiated from each other because of special features, characteristics, or customer service also need to set the prices for their differentiated products. Such firms are **price setters.** In such cases, production follows the pricing decision as they receive customer orders in response to the announced prices.

We shall consider four different situations in this chapter as shown in Exhibit 7-1. We begin the next section by considering the short-term product-mix decision of a price-taker firm (quadrant 1). Then we analyze short-term pricing decisions for a price-setter firm (quadrant 2) and follow with an examination of long-term benchmark prices for a price-setter firm (quadrant 3). Finally, we return

Price taker
A firm that has little or no influence on the industry supply and demand forces and consequently on the prices of its products.

Price setter
A firm that sets or bids the prices of its products because it enjoys a significant market share in its industry segment.

EXHIBIT 7-1
Classification of Pricing and Product-Mix Decisions

Decision Type	Price-Taker Firm	Price-Setter Firm
Short-term decisions	1	2
Long-term decisions	4	3

to the price-taker firm and consider the long-term evaluation of product and customer profitability for that type of firm (quadrant 4).

SHORT-TERM PRODUCT-MIX DECISIONS

Production decisions by a firm with a very small market share in its industry have little impact on the overall industry supply and demand and, therefore, on the prices of the firm's products. Such is the case in high-volume manufacturing in-

CONSIDER THIS . . .

Newspaper Wars in Britain

Rupert Murdoch controls print and broadcast media around the world: in Australia, Asia, Europe, and North America. His company now owns the *Times,* once the newspaper considered the voice of the British establishment. In 1993, he began a tactical war of price cuts. The *Times* cut its price from the equivalent of about 70 cents to 45 cents. As a result, it gained circulation at the expense of other full-size newspapers, especially the *Daily Telegraph,* the biggest seller, at around one million copies a day.

In June 1994, the *Daily Telegraph* dropped its price to 35 cents. On July 31, 1994, the *Independent* joined the price war, slashing its price to 45 cents from about 75 cents in an attempt to keep pace with its price-cutting rivals. The *Independent*'s daily circulation had sunk to 275,000, well below its peak of 400,000, compared with more than 500,000 copies at the *Times* and 400,000 at the *Guardian.* Murdoch promptly cut the *Times* to 35 cents. At these prices, the newspapers began losing millions—one guess is $1.8 million a month for the *Times.* But Murdoch can cover that from his empire's profits until perhaps his rivals collapse. An official board is now looking into charges of predatory pricing, a pricing strategy intended to drive out competitors.

Sources: Anthony Lewis, "Slipping Down the Tabloid Slope," *New York Times,* July 8, 1994; Reuters, "A Price War Grows Hotter," *New York Times,* August 3, 1994.

dustries in which the products are standardized and little chance exists to differentiate the products of one firm from those of another (for example, steel, generic chemicals, pharmaceuticals, gypsum wall board, and low-end copier machines). The aggregate production decisions of all the firms determine prices in such industries. Or, if there are a few dominating firms, their decisions influence the prices.

A small firm, or a firm with a negligible market share in this industry, behaves as a price-taker firm. It takes the industry prices for its products as given and then decides how many units of each product it should produce and sell. If the small firm demands a higher price for any of its products, it risks losing its customers to other competing firms in the industry unless it can successfully differentiate its products by offering special features or services. Also, if the small firm seeks to increase its market share by asking a price lower than the industry prices, it risks a retaliatory reduction in prices from its competitors. Lowering the price might result in a price war that would make the firm, and the entire industry, worse off than it would have been if the firm complied with industry prices. But this action is particularly painful to smaller firms, who have fewer resources to fall back on should an unprofitable price war break out.

Given industry prices, a price-taker firm should produce and sell as much as it can of all products whose costs are less than their prices. This may appear to be a simple decision rule, but there are two important considerations of importance to management accounting that complicate matters. First, the management accountant must decide what costs are relevant to the short-term product-mix decision. Should the management accountant include all of the product costs identified in Chapter 3 or Chapter 5, or should he or she consider only those costs that vary in the short term? Second, the management accountant must recognize that in the short term managers may not have much flexibility to alter the capacities of some of the firm's activity resources. For instance, the available equipment capacity may limit the ability of a firm to produce and sell more of products whose costs are less than their prices.

Consider Texcel Company, which sells ready-made garments to discount stores, such as KMart and Wal-Mart. Texcel has located its manufacturing plant in Jamaica, a Caribbean island, to take advantage of lower wages.

The plant manufactures five types of garments: Exhibit 7-2 presents budgeted production for the third quarter of 1997. The exhibit also displays the minimum sales quantities of each type of garment that must be supplied under

EXHIBIT 7-2
Texcel Company
Budgeted Production in Quantities for 1997, Quarter 3

Garment Type	Budgeted Production	Minimum Sales	Maximum Sales
Shirts	12,000	6,000	14,000
Dresses	5,000	2,000	8,000
Skirts	10,000	6,000	16,000
Blouses	15,000	5,000	15,000
Trousers	8,000	4,000	9,000
Total units	50,000	23,000	62,000

long-term contracts with various retail stores. The sales manager has estimated the maximum sales quantities shown in the last column. His estimates are based on his assessment of the number of orders that can be obtained for delivery in the third quarter of 1997.

Exhibit 7-3 shows unit costs for the five products. Direct material costs are based on estimated materials requirements and their estimated prices. Cutting, stitching, and packing workers are paid on a piece-rate basis. For instance, column two, shirts, shows that workers are paid $1.00 for cutting, $0.80 for stitching, and $0.05 for packing one shirt. Inspection labor costs total $7500 per quarter and are assigned to products at the rate of $0.15 per garment. Support activity costs total $10,000 each quarter and are assigned to the 50,000 units budgeted for production at the rate of $0.20 per unit.

Production is limited by the 23,800 machine-hour capacity of the garment manufacturing machines. Exhibit 7-4 displays the number of machine hours required to manufacture each garment. Note the considerable differences in the required machine time, ranging from 0.4 hour for one shirt or blouse to 0.8 hour for one dress. The planned production for the third quarter of 1997 seeks to utilize all of the 23,800 machine hours available at present.

OBJECTIVE 7.1

Understand the way a firm chooses its product mix in the short term in response to prices set in the market for its products.

The objective here is to evaluate the profitability of the different products and to decide the production levels for the five products that will maximize the profits for the Texcel Company for the third quarter of 1997. Here Texcel is contemplating short-term adjustments to its product mix. Therefore, first it is necessary to determine what costs will vary with production levels in this period and, then, what costs will remain fixed when there is a change in the production mix.

Clearly, the costs of direct materials and the direct labor that is compensated on a piece-rate basis vary with the quantity of each garment produced. Inspectors

EXHIBIT 7-3
Texcel Company
Product Costs per Unit

	Shirts	Dresses	Skirts	Blouses	Trousers
Direct materials:					
Textile	$1.80	$6.00	$4.00	$2.00	$4.50
Supplies	0.20	0.90	0.60	0.40	0.60
Direct labor:					
Cutting	**1.00**	1.50	1.00	1.00	1.00
Stitching	**0.80**	1.80	1.00	0.80	1.00
Inspection	**0.15**	0.15	0.15	0.15	0.15
Packing	**0.05**	0.05	0.05	0.05	0.05
Manufacturing support:					
Utilities	0.03	0.03	0.03	0.03	0.03
Plant administration	0.04	0.04	0.04	0.04	0.04
Machine maintenance	0.02	0.02	0.02	0.02	0.02
Machine depreciation	0.04	0.04	0.04	0.04	0.04
Facility maintenance	0.04	0.04	0.04	0.04	0.04
Facility depreciation	0.03	0.03	0.03	0.03	0.03
Totals	$4.20	$10.60	$7.00	$4.60	$7.50

EXHIBIT 7-4
Texcel Company
Machine-Hour Requirements

Garment Type	Machine Hours per Unit	Production in Units	Total Machine Hours Required
Shirts	0.4	12,000	4,800
Dresses	0.8	5,000	4,000
Skirts	0.5	10,000	5,000
Blouses	0.4	15,000	6,000
Trousers	0.5	8,000	4,000
Totals		50,000	23,800

are paid a monthly fixed salary, but they are employed as required to support the production of different garments. If production increases, Texcel may have to hire more inspectors. Therefore, inspection labor costs also vary with the quantity of production of different garments. This situation occurs because management has the flexibility to adjust the level of the inspection activity resource during the period for which the product-mix decision is made.

In contrast, the costs of utilities, plant administration, maintenance, and depreciation for the machinery and plant facility will not change with a change in

---

This plant works at full capacity to manufacture different apparel in time for the busy sales season. Since the plant capacity cannot be increased readily at short notice, the company evaluates the profitability of different products in the rank order of their contribution per machine hour. *Courtesy* Bill Gallery/Stock, Boston

the product mix because the plant is operating at its full capacity. This analysis assumes that all of these support activity costs are fixed.

The contribution from each of the garments to the firm's profits is determined by subtracting the variable costs from the price of the product. Exhibit 7-5 displays the contribution per unit for the five products. All five products have a positive contribution margin. Therefore, if the capacity were unlimited, Texcel could produce garments to fill the maximum demand for them. Texcel's capacity, however, is constrained, and therefore the company must decide how best to deploy this limited resource.

The total budgeted contribution of $141,600 ($12,000 + $24,000 + $22,000 + $54,000 + $29,600) for the budgeted production is obtained by multiplying the contribution per unit and the budgeted production quantity for each product and adding them together. (See Exhibit 7-5.) The budgeted profit is $131,600 ($141,600 − $10,000 fixed costs).

Notice that the *contribution per unit*, or price per unit less variable costs per unit, is the highest for dresses ($4.80). Does that mean that dresses are the most profitable product and that Texcel should produce as many dresses as it can possibly sell?

The answer is *no*, because, in this case, *production is limited by the available machine capacity.* The capacity is fixed in the short term, so Texcel must plan production to maximize the contribution to profit earned on every available machine hour used. Therefore, Texcel should rank order the products not by their contribution per unit, but by their *contribution per machine hour.*

Contribution per machine hour is obtained by dividing the contribution per unit by the number of machine hours per unit. Notice in Exhibit 7-5 that blouses have the highest contribution per machine hour ($9.00); therefore, Texcel should produce a total of 15,000 blouses, the maximum quantity that it can sell in the third quarter of 1997. (See Exhibit 7-2.) Trousers have the next highest contribution per

EXHIBIT 7-5
Texcel Company
Contribution Margins

Garment Type	Shirts	Dresses	Skirts	Blouses	Trousers
Price per unit	$5.00	$15.20	$9.00	$8.00	$11.00
Variable costs per unit:					
Textiles	$1.80	$ 6.00	$4.00	$2.00	$4.50
Supplies	0.20	0.90	0.60	0.40	0.60
Cutting labor	1.00	1.50	1.00	1.00	1.00
Stitching labor	0.80	1.80	1.00	0.80	1.00
Inspection labor	0.15	0.15	0.15	0.15	0.15
Packing labor	0.05	0.05	0.05	0.05	0.05
Total variable costs	$4.00	$10.40	$6.80	$4.40	$7.30
Contribution per unit	$1.00	$4.80	$2.20	$3.60	$3.70
Machine hours per unit	0.4	0.8	0.5	0.4	0.5
Contribution per machine hour	$2.50	$6.00	$4.40	$9.00	$7.40
Budgeted production	12,000	5,000	10,000	15,000	8,000
Total budgeted contributions	$12,000	$24,000	$22,000	$54,000	$29,600

machine hour ($7.40), so Texcel should produce a total of 9000 trousers, the maximum it can sell in this quarter. Texcel then should decide which products to make by rank-ordering the products by contribution per machine hour and making the most profitable products up to the maximum sales potential until it exhausts the entire available machine capacity after reserving capacity for the minimum sales levels.

Exhibit 7-6 displays the production quantities that maximize profits in the short term. The minimum production for the five products required under existing sales contracts requires a total of 11,000 machine hours. (See column 3, Exhibit 7-6.) This leaves a balance of 12,800 machine hours of capacity (23,800 − 11,000), which is sufficient to produce the maximum quantities of blouses, trousers, and dresses that Texcel can sell. These three products rank the highest in terms of their contribution per machine hour. The remaining capacity of 1500 machine hours [12,800 − (4,000 + 2,500 + 4,800)] is not adequate to produce the maximum possible quantity of skirts, the next highest ranked product. This remaining capacity is sufficient for the production of only 3000 (1500 ÷ 0.5) additional skirts. No machine capacity remains for the production of any additional shirts, the product with the lowest contribution per machine hour.

To summarize, the available machine capacity should be allocated to the five garments shown in the final production plan in Exhibit 7-7. This production plan yields a profit of $141,500, which is $9900 (about 7.5%) more than the $131,600 profit ($141,600 − $10,000) that Texcel would earn with the original production plan.

This example illustrates the basic principle used to make short-term product mix decisions when prices will be unaffected by the quantities sold. The contribution margin *per unit of the constrained resource*, which is machine hours in this example, is the criterion used to decide which products are most profitable to produce and sell at the prevailing prices.

The Impact of Opportunity Costs

Consider next a variation of the problem we have analyzed so far. Suppose that a new customer that Texcel did not include in its earlier sales forecasts wishes to place an order for 2000 shirts and is willing to pay a price higher than $5 each for

EXHIBIT 7-6
Texcel Company
Production Quantities Required to Maximize Profits

Garment Type	Minimum Quantity	Machine Hours Required		Additional Quantity	Machine Hours Required
Blouses	5,000	2,000	5,000 × 0.4	10,000	4,000
Trousers	4,000	2,000	4,000 × 0.5	5,000	2,500
Dresses	2,000	1,600	2,000 × 0.8	6,000	4,800
Skirts	6,000	3,000	6,000 × 0.5	3,000	1,500
Shirts	6,000	2,400	6,000 × 0.4	0	0
Totals	23,000	11,000			12,800

CONSIDER THIS . . .

Bidding on Business Forms

FMI Forms Manufacturers, a medium-sized printing company that produces business forms, was operating at full capacity, but it was continually "in the red," or losing money. Until the late 1980s, FMI bid on jobs without a reliable analysis of its cost structure. The direct costs considered for a job were the material or paper used in the printing process. FMI assigned support costs to jobs in proportion to their direct costs.

FMI is a machine-intensive operation. Nine presses are available to print the forms. The company uses six collators to combine parts of forms, gluing, crimping, and punching holes. The resources demanded by a job depend on the type and amount of paper used and the composition and the construction of the form. All jobs are constrained by the time necessary on a press and on a collator capable of producing forms at the required size.

Now FMI determines a separate support rate for each machine. Costs of machine operator, support personnel, and supplies are identified directly with presses and collators. Other support costs, including supervision, office salaries, and insurance, are allocated to machines based on their processing capacity (number of feet of form per minute) weighted by the maximum paper width and complexity (number of colors and stations) that they are capable of handling. This allocation is made at the beginning of each fiscal year using the previous year as a base from which to project current-year costs. Once the yearly costs are allocated to each machine, cost per hour is determined for each press and collator assuming normal operations at 80% of full capacity.

When FMI receives a request for a bid on a particular job, the company turns to computerized estimating software. It determines direct costs based on the type and quantity of paper. Then it identifies the least expensive press and collator that are mechanically capable of handling the specifications for the business form ordered. The estimated time to complete the job is multiplied by the cost per hour for the machines identified. The bid is completed by adding a standard markup to the total press, collator, and direct material costs. A higher markup is used for rush jobs and jobs requiring special features, such as nonstandard perforations, to cover the additional costs of errors and remakes.

Source: Jacci L. Rodgers, S. Mark Comstock, and Karl Pritz, "Customize Your Costing System," *Management Accounting*, May 1993, pp. 31–32.

EXHIBIT 7-7
Texcel Company
Final Production Plan

Garment Type	Production Quantity Exhibit 7-6: Minimum/ Additional Quantities	Total Machine Hours Exhibit 7-4		Total Contribution Exhibit 7-5: Contribution per Unit	
Blouses	15,000	6,000	15,000 × 0.4	$ 54,000	15,000 × $3.60
Trousers	9,000	4,500	9,000 × 0.5	33,300	9,000 × $3.70
Dresses	8,000	6,400	8,000 × 0.8	38,400	8,000 × $4.80
Skirts	9,000	4,500	9,000 × 0.5	19,800	9,000 × $2.20
Shirts	6,000	2,400	6,000 × 0.4	6,000	6,000 × $1.00
Totals	47,000	23,800		$151,500	
Less: Fixed Costs				10,000	
Profit				$141,500	

this order. How high must the price be to make it profitable for Texcel to accept this special order?

If Texcel produces more shirts, its out-of-pocket costs will increase in the short term by the amount of the variable costs of the 2000 shirts. But a simple comparison of the price with the variable costs shown in Exhibit 7-5 is not adequate for this decision. Because the production capacity is limited, Texcel must cut back the production of some other garment to enable it to produce 2000 additional shirts. Giving up the production of some profitable product results in an **opportunity cost,** which equals the lost profit on the garments that Texcel can no longer make.

Opportunity costs
The amount of lost profit when the opportunity afforded by one alternative is sacrificed to pursue another alternative.

Each shirt requires 0.4 machine hours so the new order for 2000 shirts requires a total of 800 machine hours. (See Exhibit 7-4.) To find the capacity of 800 machine hours required to produce the additional shirts, Texcel must forgo a part of the production of some other garment. How should Texcel decide which garment's production to sacrifice? Clearly, it should make the decision that minimizes the opportunity cost. Therefore, Texcel should sacrifice the product currently being produced that has the *lowest* contribution margin per unit of the constrained resources.

We know from our earlier ranking of the products that of all the products whose production exceeds the minimum required, skirts have the lowest contribution per machine hour. (See Exhibit 7-5.) Texcel must sacrifice 800 machine hours for the production of skirts. Because each skirt requires 0.5 machine hours, Texcel must give up producing 1600 skirts. Each skirt contributes $2.20, so cutting back the production of 1600 skirts causes a sacrifice of $3520 in profits ($2.20 × 1,600).

There is an alternative way to check that the opportunity cost is $3520. The contribution margin per machine hour is $4.40 for skirts, and a cutback of 800 machine hours of production of skirts results in a sacrifice of $3520 of profits ($4.40 × 800).

The cost implications of producing an additional order of 2000 shirts are now clear.

TEXCEL COMPANY
COSTS OF PRODUCING 2000 SHIRTS

Cost	Per Unit	Total
Variable cost	$4.00	$ 8,000
Opportunity cost	1.76	3,520
Total	$5.76	$11,520

Incremental costs (or revenues) are defined as the amount by which costs (or revenues) increase if one particular decision is made instead of another. Therefore, if Texcel does not charge a price of at least $5.76 per shirt, the incremental costs, including opportunity costs, will exceed the incremental revenues from this order, and Texcel would be worse off as a result. The lowest price that should be acceptable to Texcel is $11,520 for the order, or $5.76 per shirt.

Also notice that if the price of a shirt is $5.76, the contribution margin per machine hour is $4.40 [($5.76 − $4.00) ÷ 0.4], the same as that for skirts, whose production is cut back. The basic principle to realize here is that Texcel must earn at least as much *contribution margin per machine hour* on the new order as it must sacrifice on the alternative that it must give up.

SHORT-TERM PRICING DECISIONS

So far, we have examined the way managers should adjust their product mix in the short term when the marketplace has determined what prices they can charge for their products. For these types of firms, which appear in quadrant 1 of Exhibit 7-1 where the firm is a price taker, the relevant costs for the product-mix decision are the short-run variable cost plus any opportunity cost of foregone alternatives.

In many businesses, potential customers request that suppliers bid a price for an order before they decide on the supplier with whom they will place the order. In this section, we examine the relationship between costs and prices bid by a supplier for special orders that do not involve long-term relationships with the customer.

Consider Chaney Tools and Dies Company in Cleveland, Ohio. Chaney manufactures customized steel tools and dies for a wide variety of manufacturing businesses. A new customer, Hamilton Industries of Ontario, has asked for a bid for a set of customized tools.

Chapter 5 showed the way to prepare and use the information on a job bid sheet. Based on the tool design, production engineers determine the routing through different production departments and estimate the quantity of different materials required for the order and the number of labor hours required in each department. Then Chaney uses this information along with materials prices and labor wage rates to estimate the direct materials and direct labor costs displayed in Exhibit 7-8. Support activity costs are assigned to the job based on activity drivers and the corresponding activity cost driver rates as described in Chapter 6.

The full costs for the job—that is, the sum of all direct materials, direct labor, and support activity costs—are estimated to be $28,500, consisting of $8400 of direct materials, $9900 of direct labor, and $10,200 of support costs. Chaney Tools usually determines the bid price for regular customers by marking up 40% over the full costs. If Hamilton Industries were a regular customer, the bid price would have been $39,900 (1.40 × $28,500). But for this special order from a new customer, what is the minimum acceptable price?

We now consider two distinct cases. First, we examine Chaney's pricing decision when there is surplus machine capacity available in the short term to complete the production for the job. Then we examine the decision when the existing demand for Chaney's services is sufficient to fill all available capacity and the only way to manufacture the customized tools for Hamilton Industries is by working overtime or adding an extra shift.

Available Surplus Capacity

Chaney will incur direct material costs of $8400 to produce customized tools for Hamilton Industries. Chaney pays direct production labor on an hourly basis; therefore, these costs will increase by $9900 if the company accepts the Hamilton order. In addition, batch-related costs will *increase* by $3700 as a new production batch is needed for the customized tools. The costs of supervision and facility-sustaining support activities, however, will not increase if additional capacity of these resources is available to meet the production needs of the Hamilton Industries order.

Chaney's decision involves whether to accept the Hamilton Industries order. The alternative is to reject it. The incremental costs in this case include these:

CHANEY'S INCREMENTAL COSTS

Direct material	$ 8,400
Direct labor	9,900
Batch-related support activities	3,700
Total incremental costs	$22,000

The price that Chaney should charge Hamilton Industries must cover these incremental costs for the order to be profitable for Chaney. In other words, the minimum acceptable price is $22,000 *when surplus production capacity is available.* This is the price at which Chaney will break even on the Hamilton Industries order. In practice, Chaney will add a profit margin above incremental costs, and the bid price will be higher than $22,000 depending on competitive and demand conditions. In summary, when excess capacity exists, the *minimum* acceptable

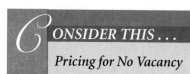

ONSIDER THIS . . .

Pricing for No Vacancy

Dismissed by the Walt Disney Company in 1972, Harris Rosen is now one of the most successful independent hotel owners anywhere. A millionaire 100 times over, Harris owns two Quality Inns, a Comfort Inn, the Clarion Plaza, the Omni, and the Rodeway, accounting for 4850 of the Orlando area's 84,400 hotel rooms.

While the average annual occupancy rate in the Orlando area has not exceeded 78.8% in the last decade, Harris's hotels have averaged 96% over that period. The secret behind Harris's ability to fill hotel rooms is fairly simple. Much to his competitors' dismay, he openly cuts prices. When it appears Harris's properties may not fill up, electronic message boards begin flashing $29.95.

He likens this fine-tuning to the airlines' practice of yield management—lowering fares at various times on seats that may otherwise remain unsold. Also used by cruise ships, the technique has not yet caught on in the hotel industry where many operators fret that cutting prices at least openly may tarnish the polished image of their chains. However, if hotel management companies that dominate the industry do not have the foresight to follow his example, Harris maintains that is their problem. "Most of them would rather wind up with empty rooms than drop prices in order to preserve the sanctity of their average daily rates," he scoffs.

Each night at 11 P.M. Harris calls the front desk at each property to see if the hotel is sold out—and if not, why not. In the morning, he is on the phone with the night auditors, recapping the previous day's occupancy rates, average room rates, and food and beverage revenues. Then he discusses the coming day's room rates, that is, the starting rates.

Harris also fills rooms by honoring the rates of the lower-price hotels that send him walk-in customers they cannot accommodate. He also nurtures the group and bus-tour business all year around contrary to the conventional wisdom in the industry, which says to ignore that segment when business is up because it is low profit. Another strategy leading to his success was building the Omni and the Clarion on either side of the Orlando Convention Center, which attracts 2.1 million people a year. Because convention business is usually booked years in advance, the hotels' proximity to the center gives them a buffer against swings in the economic cycle.

Harris says he has so much leeway to move prices because his company's debt is "a minuscule 5% to 10% of the value of its properties, so we don't need to keep rates high to pay off the interest."

Source: Edwin McDowell, "His Goal: No Room at the Inns," *New York Times*, November 23, 1995, pp. C1, C8.

Significant overcapacity in the industry caused major price reductions in steel during the 1980s. Intense competition forced mill closings as the industry eliminated underused and inefficient facilities and caused significant upgrading to improve the cost performance of the remaining mills. This steel strip mill at Weirton Steel eliminated several steps in the old process of converting a steel slab into strip steel. The reduction in the industry's excess capacity and improvements in processing have lowered the industry's cost structure and improved its profit performance. *Courtesy* Barton Denmarsh Esteban, Inc.

price must at least cover the incremental costs that the company will incur to produce and deliver the order.

No Available Surplus Capacity

OBJECTIVE 7.2

Explain the way a firm adjusts its prices in the short term depending on whether capacity is limited.

If surplus machine capacity is not available, Chaney will have to incur additional costs to acquire the necessary capacity. Chaney often meets such short-term capacity requirements by operating its plant overtime. When this occurs, Chaney pays supervisors overtime wages and incurs additional expenditures for heating, lighting, cleaning, and security. In addition, more machine maintenance and plant engineering activities will be necessary, as past experience has shown that the incidence of machine breakdowns increases during the overtime shift. Under its machinery leasing contract, Chaney also incurs additional rental costs for the extra use of machines when it adds an overtime shift.

The estimates of the amounts of incremental supervision costs (including overtime premium) for the Hamilton order is $5100 and the incremental facility-sustaining costs are $5400. Thus, the total costs are $10,500 ($5100 + $5400) if overtime is required to manufacture customized tools for Hamilton Industries. Therefore, the minimum acceptable price in this case is $32,500 ($22,000 + $10,500). The actual price will depend on the amount of markup over the incremental costs charged by the Chaney Tools and Dies Company.

The principle illustrated here is the same as that described in the previous case. The minimum acceptable price must cover all incremental costs, but when the firm must acquire additional capacity to satisfy the order, there are more incremental costs involved in the decision to accept or reject the order.

RELEVANT COSTS. **Relevant costs** (or revenues) are the costs (or revenues) that firms must consider when deciding among alternative decisions. In deciding whether to accept the Hamilton Industries order or what price to charge for the special order, Chaney must consider the appropriate incremental costs depending on whether surplus production capacity is available. The incremental costs are the relevant costs for such short-run decisions.

Relevant costs/revenues
The costs/revenues that differ across alternatives and therefore must be considered in deciding which alternative is the best.

A MIDCHAPTER REVIEW PROBLEM

The following problem and its solution illustrate the application of the basic principles for short-term pricing decisions discussed so far. It is useful to review these materials before moving on next to an analysis of long-term pricing and product-mix decisions.

Prime Printer, Inc., is a corporation based in Eagan, Minnesota, that sells high-quality printers in the Midwest regional market. It manufactures two products, L8011 and L8033, for which the following information is available:

PRIME PRINTER, INC.
COST INFORMATION ON TWO PRINTERS

	PRODUCT	
Item	*L8011*	*L8033*
Cost per unit:		
Direct materials	$ 300	$ 375
Direct labor	400	500
Variable support	500	625
Fixed support	400	500
Total cost per unit	$1600	$2000
Price	$2000	$2500
Units sold	400 units	200 units

The average wage rate including fringe benefits is $20 per hour. The plant has a capacity of 14,000 direct labor hours, but current production uses only 13,000 direct labor hours of capacity.

REQUIRED

(a) A new customer has offered to buy 40 units of L8033 if its price is lowered to $2000 per unit. How many direct labor *hours* will be required to produce 40 units of L8033? How much will Prime Printer's profit increase or decrease if it accepts this proposal? All other prices will remain as before.

(b) Suppose the customer has offered, instead, to buy 60 units of L8033 at $2000 per unit. How much will the profits increase or decrease if Prime Printer accepts this proposal? Assume that the company cannot increase its production capacity to meet the extra demand.

(c) Answer the question in (b) above, assuming, instead, that the plant can work overtime. Direct labor costs for the overtime production increase only to $30 per hour. Variable support costs for overtime production are 50% more than for normal production.

SOLUTION

(a) DLH per Unit $= \dfrac{\$500}{\$20} \quad \dfrac{\text{direct labor cost}}{\text{wage rate}}$

$= 25\ DLH$

The new order requires 1000 DLH (40 × 25), so the existing capacity is adequate.

$$Contribution\ Margin\ per\ Unit = \$2000 - (375 + 500 + 625)$$
$$= \$500$$

$$Change\ in\ Profit = 40\ \text{units} \times \$500\ \text{contribution margin}$$
$$= \$20{,}000\ \text{increase}$$

(b)

Item	L8011		L8033	
Sales price		$2000		$2500
Variable cost:				
Direct materials	$300		$375	
Direct labor	400		500	
Variable support	500	1200	625	1500
Contribution margin per unit		$ 800		$1000
DLH per unit		20		25
Contribution per DLH		$40 per DLH		$40 per DLH

The new order requires a total of 1500 DLH (25 × 60), but there are only 1000 DLH (14,000 − 13,000) available. This will leave capacity short for 500 DLH (1500 − 1000). Therefore, the change in profit is this.

$$Change\ in\ Profit = Total\ Contribution\ Margin - Opportunity\ Cost$$
$$= (60\ \text{units} \times \$500\ \text{contribution per unit})$$
$$- (500\ DLH \times \$40\ \text{contribution per } DLH)$$
$$= \$30{,}000 - \$20{,}000$$
$$= \$10{,}000\ \text{increase}$$

(c) If the plant is worked overtime to manufacture L8033 for the special order, the contribution margin during overtime work is negative $62.50 as computed below:

Item	Cost	Computation
Direct materials	$375.00	1 × $375
Direct labor	750.00	1.5 × $500
Variable support	937.50	1.5 × $625
Total variable costs	$2062.50	
Sales price	2000.00	
Contribution margin	$ (62.50)	

Therefore, the change in profit from accepting the special order and working the plant overtime is a net increase of $18,750 as detailed below:

Contribution Margin	Cost	Computation
Regular hours	$20,000	40 × $500
Overtime hours	(1,250)	20 × $62.50
Total increase	$18,750	

LONG-TERM PRICING DECISIONS

Let us consider next price-setter firms making long-term pricing decisions as indicated in quadrant 3 of Exhibit 7-1. You may have noticed that the relevant costs for the short-term special order pricing decision differ from the ***full costs*** of the job reported in Exhibit 7-8. Full costs include the direct materials, direct labor,

Full costs
Sum of all costs (direct materials, direct labor, and support) assigned to a product.

Most of the cost of providing guest accommodations in a hotel are fixed—a hotel's incremental costs are tied mainly to linen services. Therefore, during off-season in resort areas, hotels often cut their prices significantly to attract customers. Even at these lower prices, a hotel can cover its incremental costs and provide a contribution toward covering fixed costs. Hotels that have peak and off-peak periods plan to recover most of their fixed costs through the prices they charge peak-use customers.
Courtesy Spencer Grant/PhotoResearchers, Inc.

EXHIBIT 7-8
Chaney Tools and Dies Company
Job Cost Estimate

Direct materials:		
Steel		$ 8,400
Direct labor:		
Lathe	$2,600	
Griding	3,200	
Machining	4,100	9,900
Manufacturing support:		
Supervision	$3,400	
Batch-related	3,700	
Facility-sustaining	3,100	10,200
Total costs		$28,500
Markup (40%)		11,400
Bid price		$39,900

and support activity costs assigned based on normal activity cost driver rates. Is there any benefit to reporting this information about full costs to managers who are responsible for the firm's pricing decisions?

In fact, most firms rely on full-cost information reports when setting prices.[1] Typically, the accounting department provides cost reports to the marketing department, which then adds appropriate markups to the costs to determine benchmark or target prices for all products normally sold by the firm.

There is economic justification for reliance on full costs for pricing decisions in three types of circumstances:

CONSIDER THIS . . .

Hefty Increase in San Diego's Trash Fees

Cities in California's San Diego County, in a sign of growing distress mirrored nationwide among municipal sanitation systems, are threatened with a hefty five-fold increase in trash-dumping fees unless they sign up for a long-term commitment. Not anticipating a glut of dump space that has developed in many regions in the U.S., San Diego County built a $134 million recycling plant, raising dumping fees at county landfills to pay for it.

Cities in the county, excluding San Diego, generate about 1.1 million tons of trash a year. If all of that trash goes to county disposal sites, costs are covered at $55 a ton. But cities have no obligation to dump there, and some are finding cheaper alternatives in Los Angeles County and even as far away as Utah.

The less trash the county gets, the higher the per-ton fee it must charge to cover its costs. The county now proposes to charge cities based on how long they commit to bring their trash to its facilities: $58.06 a ton for 20 year commitments; $67.32 for 10 years; $87.79 for 5 years; and $235.44 a ton without a long-term commitment.

Source: Jeff Bailey, "California Cities Face Heftier Trash Fees," *Wall Street Journal,* July 27, 1994, p. A2.

[1] Lawrence Gordon, Robert Cooper, Haim Falk, and Danny Miller, *The Pricing Decision,* New York: National Association of Accountants, 1981, p. 23; Rajiv D. Banker and John S. Hughes, "Product Costing and Pricing," *The Accounting Review,* July 1994, pp. 479–494.

1. Many contracts for the development and production of customized products and many contracts with governmental agencies specify that prices should equal full costs plus a markup. Prices set in regulated industries, such as electric utilities, also are based on full costs.

2. When a firm enters into a long-term contractual relationship with a customer to supply a product, it has great flexibility in adjusting the level of commitment for all activity resources. Therefore, most activity costs will depend on the production decisions under the long-term contract, and full costs are relevant for the long-term pricing decision.

3. The third situation is representative of many industries. Most firms make short-term adjustments in prices, often through offering discounts from list prices instead of rigidly employing a fixed price based on full costs. When demand for their products is low, the firms recognize the greater likelihood of a surplus capacity in the short term. Accordingly, they adjust the prices of their products downward to acquire additional business based on the lower incremental costs when surplus capacity is available. Conversely, when demand for their products is high, they recognize the greater likelihood that the existing capacity of activity resources is inadequate to satisfy all of the demand. Accordingly, they adjust the prices upward based on the higher incremental costs when capacity is fully utilized. Also, the higher prices serve to ration the available capacity to the highest profit opportunity.

   Because demand conditions fluctuate over time, prices also fluctuate over time with the demand conditions. For instance, demand is low on weekends in the hotel industry compared to weekdays. Therefore, most hotels offer special weekend rates that are considerably lower than their weekday rates. Many amusement parks offer lower prices on weekdays when demand is expected to be low. Airfares between New York and London are higher in summer, when the demand is higher, than in winter, when the demand is

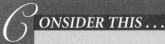

CONSIDER THIS . . .

Full Cost-Based Pricing Continues to Be Popular

A 1983 survey of 505 of the largest (Fortune 1000) companies by Govindarajan and Anthony found that over 82% of the companies price their products based on their full costs. Only 17% of the respondents indicated that they rely on variable costs for their product-pricing decisions. This survey also learned that about half of both full cost- and variable cost-based pricing companies relied only on manufacturing costs for their pricing decisions. The other half based their prices on all manufacturing and nonmanufacturing costs.

Eleven years later, Shim and Sudit conducted a similar survey of 141 companies and detected a pattern of reliance on cost data for pricing decisions similar to the earlier survey. The more recent survey

included an additional choice for the responding companies, allowing them to indicate that their pricing decisions were based on market forces and not on costs. This survey found that about 70% of the companies used full cost-based pricing, 12% used variable cost-based pricing, and only 18% used market-based pricing. About half of both full cost- and variable cost-based pricing companies continued to rely only on manufacturing costs instead of all costs for their pricing decisions.

Sources: V. Govindarajan and R. N. Anthony, "How Firms Use Cost Data in Pricing Decisions," *Management Accounting,* July 1983, pp. 30–37; E. Shim and E. F. Sudit, "How Manufacturers Price Products," *Management Accounting,* February 1994, pp. 37–39.

lower. Also, long distance telephone rates are lower in the evenings and on the weekends when the demand is lower.

Although the fluctuating short-term prices are based on the appropriate incremental costs, over the long term, their average tends to equal the price based on the full costs that will be recovered in a long-term contract. (See Exhibit 7-9.) In other words, the price determined by adding on a markup to the full costs of a product serves as a benchmark or target price from which the firm can adjust prices up or down depending on demand conditions. Most firms use full cost-based prices as target prices, giving sales managers limited authority to modify prices as required by the prevailing competitive conditions.

We have not discussed the way to determine the amount of markup. We have already seen that prices depend on demand conditions. Markups increase with the *strength of demand*. If more customers demand more of a product, the firm is able to command a higher markup for the product. Markups also depend on the *elasticity of demand*. Demand is said to be elastic if customers are very sensitive to the price, that is, when a small increase in the price results in a large decrease in the demand. Markups are lower when demand is more elastic. Markups also decrease with increases in the *intensity of competition*. If competition is intense, it is more difficult for a firm to sustain a price much higher than its incremental costs.[2] See Appendix 7-1 for a formal economic analysis of the pricing decision.

To see how demand elasticity affects the pricing decision, consider the decision by Jim and Barry's Ice Cream Company, mentioned in previous chapters, to

When oil companies lease or buy off-shore drilling platforms, like this one operated by Oryx Energy Company, the decision reflects planners' beliefs about the long-term trend of the prices of petroleum products and the trend in the cost of alternative sources of crude oil. Oryx Energy Company believed that the average long-term price of oil products could support the recovery of the cost of its commitment to this drilling platform, or it would not be operating it. *Courtesy* Oryx Energy Co.

---

[2] For achieving a targeted return on investment, a firm may use higher markups for the more capital-intensive production processes.

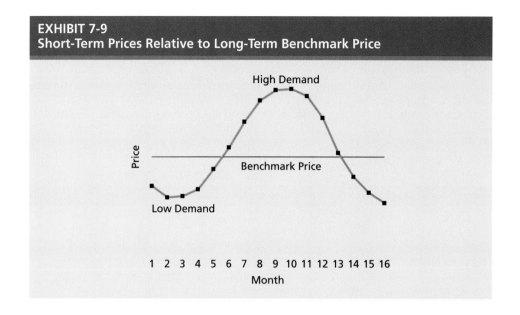

EXHIBIT 7-9
Short-Term Prices Relative to Long-Term Benchmark Price

increase ice cream prices from $2.40 per gallon to $2.50 per gallon. When prices increase, they expect the demand to decline from 80,000 gallons to 75,000 gallons. The incremental cost is $1.60 per gallon of ice cream. How much will the profits increase because of this price increase?

Contribution to profits from each gallon of ice cream increases from $0.80 ($2.40 − $1.60) to $0.90 ($2.50 − $1.60) with the increase in the price. The price increase has two effects on profits: (1) It increases the contribution for the units sold (called the "income effect" by economists), but (2) it also decreases the number of units sold and, therefore, the contribution from each unit is lost (called the "substitution effect" by economists). In this case, the increase in contribution is $0.10 per gallon ($0.90 − $0.80), or $7500 ($0.10 × 75,000) for the 75,000 gallons of expected sales after the price increase. The decrease in contribution is $4000 ($0.80 × 5000) because of the 5000-gallon decline in sales (80,000 − 75,000) of ice cream, which had a contribution margin of $0.80 per gallon prior to the price increase. Therefore, the net impact of the price increase on profits is an increase of $3500 ($7500 − $4000).

If the demand were more elastic and sales were expected to decline by 10,000 gallons (to 70,000 gallons instead of 75,000 gallons), the higher price markup would not be advisable. Then, the increase in contribution of $7000 ($0.10 × 70,000) would be more than offset by the decline of $8000 ($0.80 × 10,000) due to the sharp decrease in sales. The price increase, therefore, would result in a net decrease of $1000 ($7000 − $8000) in profits.

This example illustrates the important point that when demand is relatively inelastic, profits will usually increase with an increase in prices. When demand is elastic, however, there are usually lower price markups and, therefore, lower profits.

Firms often lower markups for strategic reasons. A firm may choose a low markup for a new product to penetrate the market and win over market share from an established product of a competing firm. In contrast to this **penetration pricing strategy,** firms sometimes employ a **skimming price strategy,** as in

Penetration pricing strategy
Charging a lower price initially to win over market share from an established product of a competing firm.

Skimming price strategy
Charging a higher price initially from customers willing to pay more for the privilege of possessing a new product.

CONSIDER THIS . . .

Pricing in Pharmaceutical Companies

The recent focus on health-care reform makes the accounting for and pricing of pharmaceutical products more critical than ever. An error in judgment or a miscalculation when initial prices are set could have a strong impact on the company producing the pharmaceuticals for many years.

The pharmaceutical company's goals for its pricing strategy are to recoup its research and development investment, earn money for future projects, and earn a fair return for its investors. For a pharmaceutical company, research and development of new products will keep the company a going concern. Without it, the company would cease to exist.

It can cost a company on average $275 million to develop a new drug, and that process can take 10 to 15 years. The odds of a company's laboratory developing a breakthrough drug are one in 1000. In addition, only three of every ten drugs that get to market recover the investment a company has made in them. With these statistics, the importance of pricing strategy cannot be overemphasized. So how does the company determine the price of a drug? Before any project starts, the company produces a projected cash flow analysis. This analysis is repeated with updated data when the product is ready to be introduced to the market. Included in the calculations are the costs to manufacture and distribute the product. In addition, the company's strategy probably includes a markup objective for its products to cover the other costs of operation, such as general selling and administration, and additional funds for research projects.

Pricing is affected by the nature of the product and market conditions. A patented breakthrough product will be priced at a premium. This strategy enables the company to recoup the higher research costs. Once a patent expires (after 17 years, which includes the time spent in research and development) and open competition and substitution of generic drugs evolve, prices will decrease in response to basic supply and demand economics.

Improvements that give a drug a therapeutic advantage may create market conditions that allow for the product to be priced above the competition. Careful analysis of the competition and current market conditions will be critical to setting the price. A price too high could discourage consumers from purchasing the product. A price too low could hinder the recovery of the investment it took to bring the product to market. New and improved products such as Merck's Vasotec will be priced in the middle of the range. Originally approved as an antihypertensive, Vasotec is now used for treating congestive heart failure. A new and improved product, such as a new dosage amount in the form of sustained release tablets, can also be priced above the competition.

At the other end of the scale are the "me, too" products and the products that have generic competition. Open market conditions will force lower prices and lead to even pricing among the competition. A high price will not generate the sales when a lower-priced product with equal qualities is available. Lower prices can be charged because there are no extensive outlays for basic research to discover new compounds that will lead to new products.

Source: Marjorie E. Holmes, "Research RX: Is Health Care Reform a Bitter Pill for the Pharmaceutical Industry?" *Management Accounting,* November 1993, pp. 40-42. Reprinted from *Management Accounting.* Copyright by Institute of Management Accountants, Montvale, NJ.

the audio and video equipment industry, to charge a higher price initially from customers who are willing to pay more for the privilege of possessing the latest technological innovations.

LONG-TERM PRODUCT-MIX DECISIONS

We now turn to quadrant 4 in Exhibit 7-1 that represents a price-taker firm that is making long-term product-mix decisions. Decisions to add a new product or to drop an existing product from the portfolio of products usually have significant

Companies such as Aluminum Company of America produce thousands of specialty products for their customers.
Most multiproduct companies try to understand which
products are making money and which are losing money
so they can decide whether a product's long-term price
can sustain the costs of making that product. In deciding
to drop a product because its price cannot cover its costs,
a company must consider whether it can eliminate the
unit, batch, product, and facility costs associated with the
product. © Steve Krongard for Alcoa

long-term implications for the cost structure of a firm. Product-sustaining costs,
such as product design and engineering, vendor and purchasing costs, part maintenance, and dedicated sales force costs, are relevant costs for such decisions.
Batch-related costs, such as setups, materials handling, and first-item inspection
(where there is inspection of only the first few items in each batch), are also likely
to change if there is a change in the product mix in favor of or against products
manufactured in large batches. Bear in mind, however, that managers cannot easily change the amount of resources committed for many product-sustaining and
several batch-related activities in the short run. The cost consequences from either introducing a new product or deleting an existing product evolve over time
because both decisions require careful implementation plans stretching over several periods. As a result, managers use the full costs of products that incorporate
the cost of using various activity resources to produce and sustain the product. Recall that such activity resources include the number of setup staff, the number of
product and process engineers, or the number of quality inspectors. Managers use
full costs since, in the long term, the firm is able to adjust the capacity of activity
resources to match the resource levels demanded by the product quantities and
mix.

Comparing product costs with their market prices reveals which products
are not profitable in the long term when firms can adjust activity resource capacities to match production requirements. If some products have full costs that exceed the market prices, the firm must consider several options. While dropping
these products appears to be an obvious option, it may be important to maintain a
full product line to make it possible for customers to enjoy one-stop shopping for
their orders. But a comparison of the prices with costs provides a valuable signal
to managers because it indicates the *net* cost of a strategy to offer a full product
line.

$\mathcal{C}$ONSIDER THIS . . .

Target Costing at a Textile Manufacturer

Culp, Inc., a North Carolina–based $260 million textile manufacturer for the home furnishings industry, recently installed a new target costing system. *Target costing* is a strategic cost management technique developed in several Japanese companies that some American firms are now implementing. Target costing seeks to reduce a product's cost over its life cycle with a commitment to continuous cost reduction.

Target cost is the price customers are willing to pay for a product less the desired profit on the product. It is the cost at which a product must be produced in the long run to attain profitability targets. Target costing takes the selling price as a given based on the realization that customers do not care about the manufacturer's costs—only their own costs, which of course is the manufacturer's selling price. Thus, it reverses traditional American pricing strategy, which sets the selling price by taking the product cost as a given and adds the desired profit margin to the cost.

Having already implemented an activity-based costing system, Culp managers learned much about the activities that generated costs. Understanding the nature of cost buildup revealed that manufacturing costs resulted from the product and process characteristics, which are driven in turn by the product design. Managers soon realized that well over four-fifths of Culp's costs were built into the product at the design stage and could not be reduced without a new design. Therefore, Culp managers decided to implement target costing at the design stage.

In the decorative furnishings business, a product's potential selling price is easily determined by market forces that consider the "look" of the product. Therefore, the emphasis is on lowering costs to meet customer demand. Design is a critical part of the value chain in this business, with new products and new applications for new markets being constantly designed. Cost management teams work closely with design teams now to develop designs that facilitate manufacturability and lead to greater profitability.

Source: J. M. Brausch, "Target Costing for Profit Enhancement," *Management Accounting,* November 1994, pp. 45–49.

Managers also may consider other options such as re-engineering or re-designing unprofitable products to eliminate or reduce costly activities and bring their costs in line with market prices. For example, they could improve the production processes to reduce setup times and streamline material and product flows. They also may want to explore the market conditions more carefully to differentiate their products further to raise the prices and bring them in line with the costs. Firms also can offer customers incentives, such as quantity discounts, to increase order sizes and thereby reduce total batch-related costs. If these steps fail, and if the marketing strategy of offering such a full product line cannot justify the high net cost of such products, managers must consider a plan to phase out the products from their line and to shift customers, instead, to alternative substitute products still retained in the company's product line.

A caveat is in order, however. Dropping products will help improve profitability *only* if the managers (1) eliminate the activity resources not required any longer to support the discontinued product or (2) redeploy the resources from the eliminated products to produce more of the profitable products that the firm continues to offer. Costs result from commitments to supply activity resources. Therefore, they do not disappear automatically with the dropping of unprofitable products. Only when companies eliminate or redeploy the resources themselves will actual expenses decrease.

In summary, capacity constraints are likely to be less of a concern for product-mix decisions that have long-term impacts because firms can adjust the level of resources committed to most activities in the long run. As a result, a comparison of the price of a product with its activity-based costs provides a valuable evaluation of its long-run profitability.

Precision Springs Revisited

Should Precision Springs slash the price of its 0.25-inch springs from $3.63 per pound to $2.48 per pound to obtain business from a reputable customer, the Genair Corporation? Should it make a counter offer of $2.70 instead to cover all of its variable manufacturing and selling costs even though full costs amount to $2.79 per pound? How would Genair cover the related costs if the selling price covers only the variable costs? These were some of the questions raised by Bob Smith to his controller and marketing manager.

The concepts discussed in this chapter help us to answer these questions. Fixed costs, such as product-sustaining or facility-sustaining costs, can be ignored, and variable costs alone are relevant only for analyzing a short-term pricing decision for a period that is too short to adjust such activity resources. For long-term pricing decisions, the costs of many more resources are relevant because firms can adjust the supply of most resources over the long term. If firms set prices to cover only short-term variable costs, they cannot survive in the long term because the existence of costs associated with committed resources will lead to continued losses over the long term.

A case for a lower price for Genair could be made as a part of a penetration pricing strategy. However, Precision Springs also must consider the reaction of both its existing customers, who may demand a lower price themselves when they learn that Precision Springs discounts its regular prices for some customers, and its competitors, who may cut prices to respond to Precision's discounting.

A Summary Example

We turn now to a numerical example that illustrates some important points discussed in this chapter. Faxtronics, Inc., is a Minnesota-based company that manufactures and sells two models (FM101 and FM102) of high-quality fax modem devices for which the following information is available:

	COSTS PER UNIT	
Item	*FM101*	*FM102*
Direct materials	$120	$160
Direct labor ($20 per hour)	50	80
Variable support ($5 per machine hour)	20	40
Fixed support	20	20
Total costs per unit	$210	$300
Price per unit	$260	$400

Demand for the two models of fax modem devices has grown rapidly in recent years, and Faxtronics can no longer meet the demand with its current production capacity. At present, the monthly demand is 8000 units for FM101 and 5000 units for FM102. Monthly capacity is limited to 60,000 machine hours.

(a) Determine the contribution margin per unit for each of the two products.
(b) Determine the product mix that maximizes profits.
(c) Suppose Faxtronics has received a special order from a new customer willing to buy 2000 units of FM101 at $300 each. What is the opportunity cost associated with this order?
(d) Should Faxtronics accept this order?

The solution to the review problem follows:

(a) Contribution margin per unit:

Item	FM101		FM102	
Selling price per unit		$260		$400
Variable costs per unit				
Direct materials	$120		$160	
Direct labor	50		80	
Variable support	20		40	
Total variable costs per unit		190		280
Contribution margin per unit		$ 70		$120

(b) Contribution margin per unit of the scarce resource:

Item	FM101	FM102
Contribution margin per unit of product	$70	$120
Number of machine hours per unit	4 (20 ÷ 5)	8 (40 ÷ 5)
Contribution margin per machine hour	$17.50	$15.00

With capacity fully utilized, FM101 is a more profitable product because it has a higher contribution margin per unit of the scarce resource (machine hours) than FM102. Therefore, Faxtronic should first satisfy all the demand for FM101 and then use the remaining machine hours of capacity to manufacture FM102. The optimal production plan is as follows:

8000 units of FM101
3500 units of FM102 [60,000 − (8,000 × 4)] ÷ 8

(c) Faxtronics has no surplus capacity available for the production of an additional 2000 units of FM101, which requires 8000 (2000 × 4) machine hours. Because FM102 has the lowest contribution margin per machine hour, Faxtronics can make available the capacity (8000 machine hours) necessary for the special order by reducing the production of FM102 by 1000 units (8,000 ÷ 8). The contribution margin for these 1000 units of FM102 is $120 per unit. Therefore, the opportunity cost to make 2000 additional units of FM101 is $120 × 1,000 = $120,000.

How should you decide whether to accept a special order from a new customer for 2000 units of this fax modem machine? *Courtesy Michael Simpson/FPG International*

(d)

Special Order Costs	Amount	Calculation
Variable cost	$380,000	$190 × 2,000
Opportunity cost	120,000	
Relevant cost	$500,000	
Relevant cost per unit	$250	$500,000 ÷ 2,000

Therefore, Faxtronics should accept this order because the price of $300 is higher than the relevant cost of $250 per unit. Faxtronics will enjoy increased profits by $100,000 [($300 − $250) × 2000] by accepting the special order.

SUMMARY

An important function of management accountants is to provide managers with appropriate cost information to assist them in their pricing and product-mix decisions. The manner in which they use cost information in making these decisions depends on whether the firm is a major player or minor player in its industry. If the firm is a major player, it would be able to influence the setting of prices. If it is a minor player, the firm would take the industry prices as given and adjust its product mix in response to the prices it could charge. The role of cost information also depends on the time frame involved in the decision. Facility-sustaining costs are frequently relevant for long-term decisions, but less often for short-term decisions.

Short-term prices are based on incremental costs that depend on the availability of activity resource capacity. If the capacity is likely to be fully utilized, then the incremental costs of overtime and other means to obtain the additional required capacity are also relevant for the pricing decision. If the firm commits to a price under a long-term contract, the normal costs of all activity resources used in the manufacture and selling of a product are relevant. Interestingly, a long-term price also can serve as a benchmark price around which actual prices may fluctuate when the firm can make short term price adjustments, depending on the demand conditions prevailing at that point in time.

Short-term product-mix decisions also require information on incremental costs that vary in the short term. If the capacity is limited for the short term, managers should use the contribution per unit of the limited capacity as the criterion to rank order the products in the production plan. For long-term product-mix decisions, managers rely on the full costs of products, which reflect the usage of the different activity resources required to design, sustain, produce, and sell the products.

Thus, the nature of the cost information required for pricing and product-mix decisions depends on the time frame considered. Regardless of whether the firm is a *price setter* or a *price taker*, full cost information is more useful for long-term decisions. Short-term adjustments require information on costs that vary in the short run.

KEY TERMS

full costs, p. 321	penetration pricing strategy, p. 325
incremental cost per unit, p. 305	price setter, p. 307
incremental costs/revenues, p. 305	price taker, p. 307
marginal revenue/cost, p. 333	relevant costs/revenues, p. 319
opportunity cost, p. 315	skimming pricing strategy, p. 325

APPENDIX 7-1

Economic Analysis of the Pricing Decision

Quantity Decision

In this chapter, we considered a firm's decision about setting its products' *prices* to maximize its profits or, more broadly, pursuing a strategic goal such as market penetration that would maximize its long-term profits. In contrast, introductory textbooks in economics usually analyze the profit maximization decision by a firm in terms of the choice of a *quantity* to produce. In turn, the quantity choice determines the price of the product in the marketplace.

We first briefly discuss this economic analysis of the quantity choice before examining the pricing decision. We present the quantity choice in terms of equating marginal revenue and marginal cost. **Marginal revenue** is defined as the increase in revenue corresponding to a unit increase in the quantity produced and sold. **Marginal cost** is defined as the increase in cost for a unit increase in the quantity produced and sold. If marginal revenue is greater than marginal cost, then increasing the quantity by one unit will increase profit. If marginal revenue is less than the marginal cost, then it is possible to increase profit by decreasing production. Therefore, profit is maximized by choosing the production quantity where marginal revenue equals marginal cost.

Exhibit 7-10 depicts marginal analysis. The marginal revenue curve is decreasing because additional sales quantity is generated only by lowering prices to all buyers. The average revenue curve represents the price itself because average

Marginal revenue (cost) The increase in revenue (cost) for a unit increase in the quantity produced and sold.

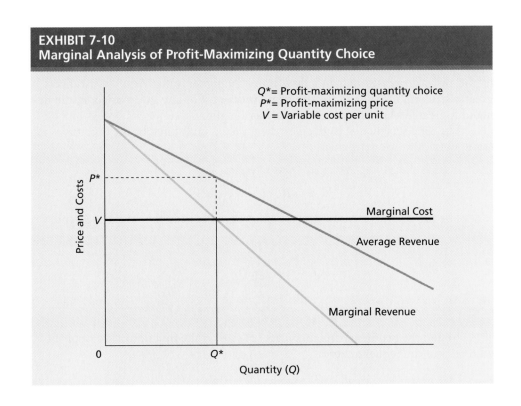

EXHIBIT 7-10
Marginal Analysis of Profit-Maximizing Quantity Choice

Q^* = Profit-maximizing quantity choice
P^* = Profit-maximizing price
V = Variable cost per unit

revenue equals total revenue divided by quantity. To obtain total revenue, it is necessary to multiply the price by the quantity. Marginal cost is depicted by a horizontal line because total cost is assumed to increase at a constant rate equal to the variable cost per unit. To determine the profit-maximizing quantity, look for the intersection of the marginal revenue and marginal cost curves because marginal revenue equals marginal cost at the point of intersection. The profit-maximizing price is the average revenue corresponding to the profit-maximizing quantity.

In this analysis, the firm chooses the quantity level, and the market demand conditions determine the corresponding price. Consider next a firm that must choose a price, not a quantity, to announce to its customers. Customers then react to the price announced and determine the quantity that they demand. In such a case the analysis of the firm's pricing decision cannot be represented graphically as conveniently as in the analysis of the quantity decision discussed above. Therefore, we shall use instead differential calculus to analyze the firm's pricing decision.

Pricing Decision

As discussed in Chapter 4, the total cost, C, expressed in terms of its fixed and variable cost components are:

$$C = f + vQ$$

where f is the fixed cost, v is the variable cost per unit, and Q is the quantity produced in units. Quantity produced is assumed to be the same as quantity demanded. The demand, Q, is represented as a decreasing linear function of the price P:

$$Q = a - bP$$

In general, we may have nonlinear demand functions, but the linear form provides a convenient characterization for our analysis. A higher value of $b > 0$ represents a demand function that is more sensitive (elastic) to price. An increase of a dollar in the price decreases demand by b units. A higher value of $a > 0$ reflects a greater strength of demand for the firm's product. For any given price, P, the demand is greater when the parameter, a, has a higher value.

The total revenue, R, is given by the price, P, multiplied by the quantity sold, Q. Algebraically, we write this:

$$R = PQ = P(a - bP)$$
$$= aP - bP^2.$$

The profit, Π, is measured as the difference between the revenue, R, and the cost, C:

$$\Pi = R - C$$
$$= PQ - (f + vQ)$$
$$= P(a - bP) - f - v(a - bP)$$
$$= aP - bP^2 - f - va + vbP$$

To find the profit-maximizing price, P^*, we set the first derivative of profit Π with respect to P equal to zero:

$$d\Pi/dP = a - 2bP + vb = 0$$

This equation implies:

$$P^* = \frac{a + vb}{2b} = \frac{a}{2b} + \frac{v}{2}$$

Long-Term Benchmark Prices

This simple economic analysis suggests that the price depends only on v, the variable cost per unit. Fixed costs are not relevant for the pricing decision. A more complex analysis (not described here) that considers simultaneously the pricing decision along with the long-term decisions of the firm to commit resources to facility-sustaining, product-sustaining, and other activity capacities indicates that the costs of these committed resources do play a role in the pricing decision.[3] The costs of these committed activity resources appear to be fixed costs in the short term, but they can be changed in the long term. The prices that a firm sets and adjusts in the short term based on changing demand conditions fluctuate around a long-term benchmark price, P^L, that reflects the unit costs of the activity resource capacities:

> **OBJECTIVE 7.4**
>
> Discuss the way a firm determines a long-term benchmark price to guide its pricing strategy.

$$P^L = \frac{a}{2b} + \frac{v + m}{2}$$

Here $m = f \div X$ is the cost per unit of normal capacity, X, of facility-sustaining activities. In this case, the degree of price fluctuations around the benchmark price increases with the proportion of fixed costs. As a result, prices appear more volatile in capital intensive industries, such as airlines, hotels and petroleum refining, where a large proportion of costs are for facility-sustaining activities.

Competitive Analysis

How does the pricing decision change when other firms compete in the same industry with products that are similar but not identical to each other? In such a situation, some customers may switch their demand to a competing supplier firm if the competitor reduces its price. Therefore, a firm's pricing decision must consider the prices that may be set by its competitors.

We consider two firms, A and B, and represent the demand, Q_A, for firm A's product as a function of its own price, P_A, and the price, P_B, set by its competitor:

$$Q_A = a - bP_A + eP_B$$

The demand for firm A's product falls by b units for each dollar increase in its own price, but increases by e units for each dollar increase in the competitor's price because firm A gains some of the market demand that firm B loses.

The profit, P_A, for firm A is represented by the following:

$$\begin{aligned} \Pi_A &= P_A Q_A - (f + vQ_A) \\ &= P_A(a - bP_A + eP_B) - f - v(a - bP_A + eP_B) \end{aligned}$$

Profit maximization requires this:

$$d\Pi_A / dP_A = a - 2bP_A + eP_B + vb = 0$$

---

[3] Rajiv D. Banker and John S. Hughes, "Product Costing and Pricing," *The Accounting Review*, July 1994, pp. 479–494.

Therefore, the profit-maximizing price P_A^O given the other firm's price P_B is this:

$$P_A^O = (a + vb + eP_B) \div 2b$$

The pricing decision thus depends on what the competitor's price is expected to be. If the firm expects its competitor to behave as it does and expects it to choose the same price as its own, then we set $P_A = P_B = P^*$ in the equation $a - 2bP_A + eP_B + vb = 0$ to obtain this:

$$a - 2bP^* + eP^* + vb = 0$$

$$P^* = \frac{a + vb}{2b - e}$$

We refer to this price as the equilibrium price because no firm can increase its profits by choosing a different price provided the other firm maintains the same price P^*. This analysis is based on a concept called Nash equilibrium for which its discoverer, John Nash, won the 1994 Nobel Prize in Economics.

QUESTIONS

7-1 "Prices must cover both variable and fixed costs of production." Do you agree with this statement? Explain.

7-2 Why is the evaluation of *short-term pricing* and product-mix decisions different from the evaluation of *long-term pricing* and product-mix decisions?

7-3 What distinguishes a *commodity-type business* from other businesses?

7-4 What two considerations complicate short-term product-mix decisions?

7-5 What firms are likely to behave as *price-taker* firms?

7-6 What firms are likely to behave as *price-setter* firms?

7-7 "When production capacity is constrained, determine what products to make by ranking them in order of their *contribution per unit.*" Do you agree with this statement? Explain.

7-8 "When production capacity is limited and it is possible to obtain additional customer orders, then a firm must consider its *opportunity costs* to evaluate the profitability of these new orders." Do you agree with this statement? What are the opportunity costs in this context?

7-9 What additional costs should a firm consider when making a short-term pricing decision when surplus production capacity is not available and it must employ overtime, extra shifts, subcontracting, or other means to augment the limited capacity?

7-10 Should a firm consider facility-sustaining costs in making a short-run pricing decision? Give two examples to illustrate your answer.

7-11 Describe three situations in which there is economic justification for using full costs for pricing decisions.

7-12 How do price markups over costs relate to the strength of demand, the elasticity of demand, and the intensity of competition?

7-13 Why do short-run prices fluctuate over time?

7-14 What strategic reasons may influence the level of markups?

7-15 What options should firms consider when long-run market prices are below full costs?

7-16 Why is full-cost information useful for long-run product-mix decisions?

EXERCISES

7-17 *Special order pricing*   Bibi Company manufactures and sells a single product, Beta. Because of an economic recession, Bibi is experiencing idle capacity sufficient to manufacture an additional 10,000 units of Beta. Variable costs are $70 per unit, and fixed costs total $200,000 per month. A Swedish manufacturer has offered $75 per unit for 8000 units of Beta. This special order will not require any additional selling expenses. Should Bibi accept this special order? What will the impact on Bibi's operating income be if it accepts this special order?

7-18 *Special order pricing* Shorewood Shoes Company makes and sells a variety of leather shoes for children. For its current mix of different models and sizes, the average selling price and costs per pair of shoes are as follows:

Item	Amount
Price	$20
Costs:	
Direct materials	$ 6
Direct labor	4
Variable manufacturing support	2
Variable selling support	1
Fixed support	3
Total costs	$16

Shoes are manufactured in batch sizes of 100 pairs. Each batch requires five machine hours to manufacture. The plant has a total capacity of 4000 machine hours per month, but current month production consumes only about 80% of the capacity.

A discount store has approached Shorewood to buy 10,000 pairs of shoes. It has requested that the shoes bear its own private label. Embossing the private label will cost Shorewood an additional $0.50 per pair. However, there will be no variable selling cost for this special order.

Determine the minimum price that Shorewood Shoes should charge for this order.

7-19 *Product-mix decision* Charlotte Company produces two types of floppy disks: standard and high density. The selling price and variable costs per box of 10 disks of each product are as follows:

Item	Standard	High Density
Selling price per box	$7.00	$10.00
Variable costs:		
Direct materials	$2.00	$ 3.00
Direct labor	1.50	2.50
Support	0.50	0.50

Because of a strike in the plant of one of its principal competitors, the demand for Charlotte's disks exceeds its capacity at present. The direct labor rate is $10 per hour, and only 4000 hours of labor time are available each week.

REQUIRED

(a) Determine the contribution margin per direct labor hour for each product.
(b) Which product should Charlotte's sales force promote? Explain.

7-20 *Product-mix decision* Boyd Wood Company makes a regular and a deluxe grade of wood floors. Regular grade is sold at $16 per square yard, and the deluxe grade is sold at $25 per square yard. The variable cost of making the regular grade is $10 per square yard. It costs an extra $5 per square yard to make the deluxe grade. It takes 15 labor hours to make 100 square yards of the regular grade and 20 labor hours to make 100 square yards of the deluxe grade. There are 4600 hours of labor time available for production each week. The maximum weekly sales for the regular and the deluxe model are 30,000 and 8000 square yards, respectively. Fixed production costs total $600,000 per year. All selling costs are fixed. What is the optimal production level in number of square yards for each product?

7-21 *Export order* Berry Company produces and sells 30,000 cases of fruit preserves each year. The following information reflects a breakdown of its costs:

Cost Item	Costs per Case	Total Costs
Variable production costs	$16	$480,000
Fixed production costs	8	240,000
Variable selling costs	5	150,000
Fixed selling and administrative costs	3	90,000
Total costs	$32	$960,000

Berry marks up its prices 40% over full costs. It has surplus capacity to produce 15,000 more cases. A French supermarket company has offered to purchase 10,000 cases of the product at a special price of $40 per case. Berry will incur additional shipping and selling costs of $3 per case to complete this order. What will be the effect on Berry's operating income if it accepts this order?

7-22 *Extra shift decision*   The manufacturing capacity of Ritter Rotator Company's plant facility is 60,000 rotators per quarter. Operating results for the first quarter of 1997 are as follows:

Sales (36,000 units @ $10)	$360,000
Variable manufacturing and selling costs	198,000
Contribution margin	$162,000
Fixed costs	99,000
Operating income	63,000

A foreign distributor has offered to buy 30,000 units at $9 per unit during the second quarter of 1997. Domestic demand is expected to remain the same as in the first quarter.

REQUIRED

(a) Determine the impact on operating income if Ritter accepts this order.

(b) Assume that Ritter decides to run an extra shift so that it can accept the foreign order without forgoing sales to its regular domestic customers. The proposed extra shift would increase capacity by 25% and increase fixed costs by $25,000. Determine the impact on operating income if Ritter operates the extra shift and accepts the export order.

7-23 *Export order*   Delta Screens Corporation is currently operating at 60% of capacity and producing 6000 screens annually. Delta recently received an offer from a company in Germany to purchase 2000 screens at $500 per unit. Delta has not previously sold products in Germany. Budgeted production costs for 6000 and 8000 screens follow:

	NUMBER OF UNITS PRODUCED	
Costs	6,000	8,000
Direct materials	$ 750,000	$1,000,000
Direct labor	750,000	1,000,000
Support	2,100,000	2,400,000
Total costs	$3,600,000	$4,400,000
Full cost per unit	$600	$550

Delta has been selling its product at a markup of 10% above full cost. Delta's marketing manager believes that although the price offered by the German customer is lower than current prices, Delta should accept the order to gain a foothold in the German market. The production manager, however, believes that Delta should reject the order because the unit cost is higher than the price offered.

REQUIRED

(a) Explain what causes the apparent decrease in cost from $600 per unit to $550 per unit when production increases from 6000 to 8000 units.

(b) If the president of Delta Screens Corporation calls on you to resolve the difference in opinions, what will you recommend? Why?

7-24 ***Pricing and impact on demand***   Columbia Bicycle Company manufactures and sells 12 different models of bicycles. Columbia is contemplating a 5% price cut across the board for all 12 models. It expects the price cut to result in an 8% increase in the number of units sold of models M124, M126, M128, W124, W126, and W128. Columbia expects the other six models B112, B116, B120, and G112, G116, G120 to experience a 4% increase in the number of units sold.

The following are the sales prices, variable costs, and sales volume (units) at present. You are required to assess the impact of the price cut on Columbia's profits.

Model	Sales Price	Variable Costs	Sales Volume
B112	$ 60	$30	3,000
B116	70	33	4,500
B120	80	36	5,000
G112	60	30	4,000
G116	70	33	4,000
G120	80	36	4,000
M124	100	42	5,000
M126	120	46	5,000
M128	140	50	10,000
W124	100	42	6,000
W126	120	46	7,000
W128	140	40	6,000

7-25 ***Pricing and impact on demand***   Andrea Kimball has recently acquired a franchise of a well-known fast-food restaurant chain. She is considering a special promotion for a week during which there would be a $0.40 reduction in hamburger prices from the regular price of $1.09 to $0.69. Local advertising expenses for this special promotion will amount to $4500. Andrea expects the promotion to increase sales of hamburgers by 20% and french fries by 12%, but she expects the sales of chicken sandwiches to decline by 8%. Some customers, who may have otherwise ordered a chicken sandwich, now will order a hamburger because of its attractive low price. The following data have been compiled for sales prices, variable costs, and weekly sales volumes:

Product	Sales Price	Variable Costs	Sales Volume
Hamburgers	$1.09	$0.51	20,000
Chicken sandwiches	1.29	0.63	10,000
French fries	0.89	0.37	20,000

Evaluate the expected impact of the special promotion on sales and profits. Should Andrea go ahead with this special promotion? What other considerations are relevant in this decision?

■ PROBLEMS

Fundamental Problems

7-26 *Appendix* Carver Company has a demand function given by this equation:

$$Q = 400 - (5 \times P)$$

Its cost function is this equation where:

$P =$ price
$Q =$ quantity produced and sold

$$C = 2000 + (20 \times Q)$$

Determine the optimal price and the corresponding demand quantity and product's unit cost.

7-27 *Product-mix and overtime decisions* Excel Corporation manufactures three products at its plant. The plant capacity is limited to 120,000 machine hours per year on a single-shift basis. Direct material and direct labor costs are variable. The following data are available for planning purposes:

Product	Total Unit Demand for Next Year	Sales Price	Direct Materials	Direct Labor	Variable Support	Machine Hours
XL1	200,000	$10.00	$4.00	$2.00	$2.00	0.20
XL2	200,000	14.00	4.50	3.00	3.00	0.35
XL3	200,000	12.00	5.00	2.50	2.50	0.25

REQUIRED

(a) Given the capacity constraint, determine the production levels for the three products that will maximize profits.
(b) If the company authorizes overtime, direct labor cost per unit will be higher by 50% due to overtime premium. Materials cost and variable support cost per unit will be the same for overtime production as regular production. Is it worthwhile operating overtime?

7-28 *Capacity and pricing decision* Hudson Hydronics, Inc., is a corporation based in Troy, New York, that sells high-quality hydronic control devices. It manufactures two products, HCD1 and HCD2, for which the following information is available:

Costs per Unit	HCD1	HCD2
Direct materials	$ 60	$ 75
Direct labor	80	100
Variable support	100	125
Fixed support	80	100
Total costs per unit	$320	$400
Price	$400	$500
Units sold	2000 units	1200 units

The average wage rate including fringe benefits is $20 per hour. The plant has a capacity of 15,000 direct labor hours, but current production uses only 14,000 direct labor hours of capacity.

REQUIRED

(a) A new customer has offered to buy 200 units of HCD2 if Hudson lowers its price to $400 per unit. How many direct labor *hours* will be required to produce 200 units of HCD2? How much will Hudson Hydronics' profit increase or decrease if it accepts this proposal? (All other prices will remain as before.)

(b) Suppose the customer has offered instead to buy 300 units of HCD2 at $400 per unit. How much will the profits increase or decrease if Hudson accepts this proposal? Assume that the company cannot increase its production capacity to meet the extra demand.

(c) Answer the question in (b) above, assuming instead that the plant can work overtime. Direct labor costs for the *overtime* production increase to only $30 per hour. Variable support costs for overtime production are 50% more than for normal production.

7-29 *Product costing and product mix*   The Emerson Electric Company estimates the following variable manufacturing support costs for 1997 for its plant in Minnetonka, Minnesota.

Cost Pool	Amount	Activity Cost Drivers		Rate
Machine operations/				
maintenance	$ 48,000	12,000	Machine hours	$ 4.00
Supervision	45,000	$225,000	Direct labor dollars	0.20
Materials handling	75,000	100,000	Pounds	0.75
Quality control	66,000	550	Number of inspections	120.00
Machine setups	75,000	250	Production runs	300.00
Total	$309,000			

Emerson's Minnetonka plant manufactures three products: A, B, and C. Cost and production data per unit are as follows:

Item	Product A	Product B	Product C
Direct materials	$12.00	$15.00	$18.00
Direct labor	$9.00	$15.00	$20.00
Machine hours	0.4	0.7	0.9
Pounds	4.0	5.0	7.0
Number of inspections	0.02	0.02	0.05
Number of production runs	0.01	0.01	0.02
Sales price	$40.00	$57.00	$78.00
Maximum demand	12,000 units	12,000 units	6,000 units
Actual production in 1995	10,000 units	5,000 units	5,000 units

REQUIRED

(a) Determine the product costs using an activity-based costing system.

(b) At present, production capacity is limited to 12,000 machine hours and capacity cannot be expanded in the next two years. Determine the optimal production levels for 1997 that will maximize profits. Present your reasoning with detailed steps. List the specific assumptions that you need to make about fixed manufacturing, fixed selling, and variable selling costs.

(c) Suppose Emerson can work its plant overtime for no more than 4000 additional machine hours. Overtime premium will add 50% to direct labor costs and 30% to variable manufacturing support costs. Determine the optimal production levels for 1997 under overtime. How many machine hours of overtime should Emerson work?

7-30 *Capacity and product-mix decision* Barney Toy Company manufactures large and small stuffed animals. It has a long-term contract with a large chain of discount stores to sell 3000 large and 6000 small stuffed animals each month. The following cost information is available for large and small stuffed animals:

Item	Large	Small
Price per unit	$32	$21
Variable costs per unit:		
Direct material	$12	$10
Direct labor	6	2
Support	2	1
Fixed costs per unit	3	3
Total unit costs	$23	$16
Estimated demand (inclusive of long-term contract)	15,000	25,000

Production occurs in batches of 100 large or 200 small stuffed animals. Each batch takes a total of 10 machine hours to manufacture. The total machine hour capacity of 3,000 machine hours cannot be increased for at least a year.

REQUIRED

(a) Determine the contribution margin per unit for each of the two sizes of stuffed animals.

(b) Determine which size is more profitable to produce. How many units should Barney produce of each size?

Because of an unexpected high demand for stuffed dinosaurs, the discount store chain has requested an additional order of 5000 large stuffed dinosaurs. It is willing to pay $37 for this special order.

(c) Determine the opportunity cost associated with this order.

(d) Should Barney Toy Company accept this order? Explain.

Suppose that the company can subcontract the production of up to 10,000 small stuffed animals to an outside supplier at a cost of $22 per animal.

(e) How many units of each size should Barney produce, subcontract, and sell? What other qualitative factors should Barney consider?

7-31 *Capacity and product-mix decision* Chang Company makes two types of wood doors: standard and deluxe. The doors are manufactured in a plant consisting of three departments: cutting, assembly, and finishing. Both labor and machine time are spent on the two products as they are worked on in each department.

In planning the production schedule for the next month, management is confronted with the fact that there is a labor shortage, and some machines must be shut down for major maintenance and repair. The following information pertains to the estimated levels of capacity of direct labor hours and machine hours available next month in the three departments:

	DEPARTMENT		
Capacity Available	Cutting	Assembly	Finishing
Machine hours	40,000	40,000	15,000
Labor hours	8,000	17,500	8,000

Direct labor and machine hours required per unit of each product are as follows:

| | DEPARTMENTS | | |
Product Hours	Cutting	Assembly	Finishing
Standard:			
Direct labor hours	0.5	1	0.5
Machine hours	2	2	1
Deluxe:			
Direct labor hours	1	1.5	0.5
Machine hours	3	3	1.5

The estimated demand for the next month is 10,000 units of standard doors and 5000 units of deluxe doors. Unit cost and price information are as follows:

Item	Standard Doors	Deluxe Doors
Unit selling price	$150	$200
Unit costs:		
Direct materials	$60	$80
Direct labor	40	60
Variable support	10	15
Fixed support	10	5

Average wage rate is $20 per hour. Direct labor and machine availability in individual departments cannot be switched from one department to another.

REQUIRED

(a) Determine whether the direct labor hour and machine-hour capacities are adequate to meet the next month's demand.

(b) How many units of each product should the company produce to maximize its profits?

(c) Suggest alternatives the company might consider to satisfy all its customers' demands.

7-32 *Product-mix decision* Anticipating a shortage of raw material supplies for the next month, Alphonso Company has to make a product-mix decision. The following unit cost information is available for products A1 and A2:

| | PRODUCT | |
Item	A1	A2
Selling price	$30.00	$31.00
Direct materials cost ($4 per lb)	$12.00	$8.00
Direct labor cost ($10 per hr.)	5.00	10.00
Variable support cost	2.50	5.00

The maximum sales for A1 and A2 are estimated to be 4000 and 8000 units, respectively. Only 25,000 pounds of the raw material will be available next month. Determine the optimal product mix.

7-33 *Product-mix and overtime decisions* Alphabet Company manufactures two products, A and B. Information on the two products is given below:

Item	Product A	Product B
Selling price	$165	$120
Variable costs:		
Materials	$20	$15
Labor ($10 per hr.)	30	20
Support	10	5

Total demand is 400 units for Product A and 600 units for Product B. Total capacity is 2100 direct labor hours.

REQUIRED

(a) What product mix should Alphabet Company choose?
(b) Suppose Alphabet Company can increase capacity by working its plant overtime, which will increase direct labor costs 50% and support costs 40%. What are the optimal production levels for the two products?

Challenging Problems

7-34 *Bid price* (Adapted from CMA June 1991) Marcus Fibers, Inc. specializes in the manufacture of synthetic fibers that the company uses in many products such as blankets, coats, and uniforms for police and firefighters. Marcus has been in business since 1975 and has been profitable each year since 1983. The company uses a standard cost system and applies manufacturing support costs on the basis of direct labor hours.

Marcus has recently received a request to bid on the manufacture of 800,000 blankets scheduled for delivery to several military bases. The bid must be stated at full cost per unit plus a return on full cost of no more than 9% after income taxes. Full cost has been defined as including all variable costs of manufacturing the product, a reasonable amount of fixed support costs, and reasonable incremental administrative costs associated with the manufacture and sale of the product. The contractor has indicated that bids in excess of $25 per blanket are not likely to be considered.

In order to prepare the bid for the 800,000 blankets, Andrea Lightner, cost accountant, has gathered the information presented below about the costs associated with the production of the blanket:

Costs	Amount
Raw materials	$1.50 per pound of fibers
Direct labor	$7.00 per hour
Direct machine costs*	$10.00 per blanket
Variable support	$3.00 per direct labor hour
Fixed support	$8.00 per direct labor hour
Incremental administrative costs	$2500 per 1000 blankets
Special fee**	$0.50 per blanket
Material usage	6 pounds per blanket
Production rate	4 blankets per direct labor hour
Effective tax rate	40%

*Direct machine costs consist of items such as special lubricants, replacement of needles used in stitching, and maintenance costs. These costs are not included in manufacturing support.

**Marcus recently developed a new blanket fiber at a cost of $750,000. In an effort to recover this cost, Marcus has instituted a policy of adding a $0.50 fee to the cost of each blanket using the new fiber. To date the company has recovered $125,000. Andrea knows that this fee does not fit within the definition of full cost as it is not a cost of manufacturing the product.

REQUIRED

(a) Calculate the minimum price per blanket that Marcus Fibers, Inc. could bid without reducing the company's net income.
(b) Using the full cost criterion and the maximum allowable return specified, calculate Marcus Fibers, Inc.'s bid price per blanket.
(c) Without prejudice to your answer to requirement (b) above, assume that the price per blanket that Marcus Fibers, Inc. calculated using the cost-plus criterion specified is greater than the maximum bid of $25 per blanket allowed. Discuss the factors that Marcus Fibers, Inc. should consider before deciding whether to submit a bid at the maximum acceptable price of $25 per blanket.

7-35 *Product-mix and special order decisions*   Holmes Manufacturing Company produces three models of aquastatic controls: A17, B23, and XLT—all of which use the same basic component. The basic components are produced in department A. For model A17, the basic components are finished in department C. For both models B23 and XLT, the basic components undergo further modification in department B before being assembled in department C. Since the modifications for B23 and XLT require similar machines and labor skills, the available capacity of department B can be used for either product.

COST PER UNIT OF THE BASIC COMPONENT

Cost	Amount
Direct materials cost	$3.80
Direct labor cost	10.00
Fixed support (allocated based on direct labor hours)	15.00
Total cost per unit	$28.80
Current production volume	4000

PRODUCT COSTS PER UNIT

Item	A17	B23	XLT
Selling price per unit	$75.00	$120.00	$160.00
Basic component costs	$28.80	$28.80	$28.80
Direct materials costs	0	$6.00	$4.50
Direct labor costs	$9.00	$20.00	$31.00
Modification hours (department B)	0	0.5 hour	0.75 hour
Finishing hours (department C)	0.3 hour	0.3 hour	0.3 hour
Fixed support (allocated based on direct labor hours)	$9.00	$20.00	$31.00
Total cost per unit	$46.80	$74.80	$95.30
Current production volume	2000	1200	800

REQUIRED

(a) A foreign distributor has asked Holmes to bid on a special order of 1000 units of the basic component. There would be a special shipping charge of $3200. The Holmes plant has excess capacity to manufacture more than 1000 basic components and this order would not affect sales of the other products. Determine the minimum price that Holmes could offer.

(b) Determine the contribution margin per unit for each of the three products.

(c) Suppose there is excess demand for all three products and the plant is currently operating at capacity. The only change that can be made is shifting workers between department B and department C. Personnel in those two departments are able to work in either area with no loss in efficiency. Determine the optimal monthly production mix of the three products. Check whether your answer changes if the price of model B23 is $140.

7-36 *Special order decision*   Kirby Company manufactures leather briefcases sold to wholesalers for $37.95. The plant capacity for manufacturing this product is 750,000 units annually, but normal volume is 500,000 units. The unit and total costs at normal volume follow:

Type of Cost	Unit Costs	Total Costs
Direct materials	$9.80	$ 4,900,000
Direct labor	4.50	2,250,000
Manufacturing support	12.00	6,000,000
Selling and administrative	6.70	3,350,000
Total Costs	$33.00	$16,500,000

Manufacturing support and selling and administrative costs include both variable and fixed costs; fixed manufacturing support costs for the current year are budgeted at $4,500,000; and fixed selling and administrative costs are $2,100,000.

The company has been approached by a prospective customer who has offered to purchase 100,000 briefcases at $25.00 each. The customer wants the product packaged in large cartons rather than the normal individual containers, and will pick them up in its own trucks. Accordingly, the variable selling and administrative costs will be lower by 60% for this order.

REQUIRED

Determine whether Kirby Company should accept this special order.

7-37 *Special order pricing, product-mix decisions*   (Adapted from CMA May 1989) Purex Company produces and sells a single product called Kleen. Annual production capacity is 100,000 machine hours. It takes one machine hour to produce a unit of Kleen. Annual demand for Kleen is expected to remain at 80,000 units. The selling price is expected to remain at $10 per unit. Cost data for producing and selling Kleen are as follows:

Variable costs per unit:	
Direct materials	$ 1.50
Direct labor	2.50
Variable manufacturing support	0.80
Variable selling and distribution	2.00
Fixed costs per year:	
Fixed manufacturing support	$100,000.00
Fixed selling and distribution	50,000.00

REQUIRED

(a) Purex Company has an inventory of 2000 units of Kleen that were partially damaged in storage. It can sell these units through regular channels at reduced prices. These 2000 units will be valueless unless sold this way. Sale of these units will not affect regular sales of Kleen. Compute the relevant unit cost for determining the minimum selling price for these units.

(b) Ajax Company has offered to make and ship 25,000 units of Kleen directly to Purex Company's customers. If Purex Company accepts this offer, it will continue to produce and ship the remaining 55,000 units. Purex's fixed manufacturing support costs will decrease to $90,000. Its fixed selling and distribution costs will remain unchanged. Variable selling and distribution costs will decrease to $0.80 per unit for the 25,000 units produced and shipped by Ajax Company. Determine the maximum amount per unit that Purex Company should pay Ajax Company for producing and shipping the 25,000 units.

(c) Purex Company has received a one-time special order for 5000 units of Kleen. Acceptance of this order will not affect the regular sales of 80,000 units. Variable selling costs for each of these 5000 units will be $1.00. Determine the minimum acceptable price for Purex Company for accepting this special order.

(d) Purex Company can use its current facilities to manufacture a product called Shine. Annual production capacity of Shine, which takes 2.5 machine hours per unit to produce, is 50,000 units. The marketing department estimates that 50,000 units of Shine can be sold each year at $16 per unit. Sale of Shine will not affect the demand for Kleen. Cost data for producing and selling Shine are as follows:

Variable costs per unit:	
Direct materials	$2.50
Direct labor	4.00
Variable manufacturing support	1.20
Variable selling and distribution	3.30
Fixed costs per year:	
Fixed manufacturing support	$100,000.00
Fixed selling and distribution	50,000.00

Determine the product mix that will maximize Purex Company's profit.

7-38 Product-mix and overtime decisions   Refer to the data for Crimson Components Company presented in Problem 6-40. The following additional information is available:

■ The company believes that it cannot change its selling prices.

■ All manufacturing support costs described in Problem 6-40 are variable costs.

■ All nonmanufacturing costs are fixed.

■ The plant has a capacity of 80,000 casting department *machine hours* and 120,000 machining department *machine hours* on a single-shift basis.

■ Estimated demand for the next year is 600,000 units of R361 and 800,000 units of R572.

REQUIRED

(a) Determine the total casting department machine hours and machining department machine hours required to produce all of the estimated demand for the next year. In which department is the capacity inadequate to meet estimated demand?

(b) Determine the contribution margins for the two products based on your analysis for requirement (b) in Problem 6-40.

(c) Determine the contribution per machine hour for the department(s) in which capacity is inadequate. Given the capacity constraint(s), determine the production levels for the two products that will maximize profits.

(d) Either or both of the casting and machining departments can be worked overtime. Direct labor cost per unit would be higher by 50% due to overtime premium. Manufacturing support costs per unit would be the same for overtime production as normal production. Is it worthwhile operating either department overtime? Explain.

7-39 Product-mix tent special order decisions   Orion Outdoors Company produces a standard model and a high-quality deluxe model lightweight tent. Orion's workforce is organized into production teams responsible for cutting, stitching, and inspection activities. Orion has determined that its labor and support costs depend on the number of direct labor hours (cutting, stitching, and inspection), number of batches, and number of shipments. Production information is as follows:

Item	Standard Model	Deluxe Model
Direct labor time (cutting and stitching) per tent	10 min.	15 min.
Average batch size	60 tents	30 tents
Direct labor inspection time per batch	2 hrs.	2.5 hrs.
Average size per shipment	60 tents	10 tents
Selling price per tent	$10	$20
Materials costs per tent	$5	$11

Demand for standard and deluxe models is expected to be 6000 and 3000 tents, respectively. Direct labor time available for cutting, stitching, and inspection activities is 2000 hours. The labor cost is $12 per hour, including fringe benefits and shipping cost is $15 per shipment. Orion produces to demand and maintains no inventory on hand.

REQUIRED

(a) Determine the production quantities for the two models that will maximize profits. Assume in this case that it is not possible to change the number of available labor hours.

(b) Suppose next that labor time available for cutting, stitching, and inspection can be increased as needed. The sales manager has received an offer from Northlands Retail Company for 2000 deluxe model tents at a price of $18.50 each. This order will be produced and shipped in batch sizes of 50 tents. Inspections for this order of deluxe model batches will take 2.5 hours per batch.

Should Alphabet Company accept this order? What other qualitative factors should the company also consider?

7-40 *Appendix* Colway Company estimates the relation between the demand for its products and the price it sets, in terms of this equation where:

$$Q = \text{the quantity demanded}$$
$$P = \text{the price of the product}$$
$$Q = a - bP$$

The marketing manager, Trisha Colway, conducted a market research study in fall 1997 that indicated that $b = 500$ and $a = 8400$ on average for the first quarter of 1998.

Capacity costs are $m = \$3.00$ per unit and variable costs are $v = \$8.10$ per unit. If committed capacity is exceeded, the variable costs increase to $w = \$12.70$ per unit.

Trisha determined that the long-term benchmark price is given by this:

$$P^L = \frac{a}{2b} + \frac{v + m}{2}$$

$$= \frac{8400}{2 \times 500} + \frac{\$8.10 + \$3.00}{2}$$

$$= \$13.95$$

Trisha also set the capacity level at $X = 2150$ units.

Colway Company keeps track of demand conditions throughout the quarter. It announces a new price for each week in the Sunday-morning newspaper based on the most current information it has on demand conditions. The following are the estimates of the demand parameter for each of the 13 weeks in the first quarter of 1998.

Week t	Current Estimate of a_t	Weekly Price P_t
1	8200	$12.25
2	8350	?
3	8600	?
4	8500	?
5	8400	?
6	8850	?
7	8300	?
8	8050	?
9	8200	?
10	8800	?
11	8350	?
12	7950	?
13	8650	?

The estimate of b remained at $b = 500$ for all 13 weeks. The short-term (weekly) price is set at this if the capacity is *not* exceeded by the realized demand:

$$P_t^* = \frac{a_1}{2b} + \frac{v}{b}$$

It is set at this if the capacity *is* exceeded

$$P_t^* = \frac{a_t}{2b} + \frac{w}{2}$$

Note that if the price is set at this:

$$P_t^* = \frac{a_t}{2b} + \frac{v}{2}$$

the resultant demand will not exceed the capacity $X = 2150$ only if this occurs:

$$Q = a_t - bP_t = a_t - 500\left(\frac{a_t}{1000} + \frac{8.10}{2}\right) = \frac{a_t}{2} - 2025$$

is less than $X = 2150$, that is, if $a_t < 8350$.
Similarly, if the price is set at this:

$$P_t^* = \frac{a_t}{2b} + \frac{w}{2}$$

the resultant demand will exceed the capacity $X = 2150$ only if $a_t > 10{,}650$.

REQUIRED

(a) You are required to determine these weekly prices, plot them on a graph for each of the 13 weeks and compare them with the long-term benchmark price. What is the average of the weekly prices?

(b) Determine the total profit over the 13-week period. Repeat the same exercise after setting the capacity (X) at different levels ($X = 1750, 1950, 2350, 2550$). Plot the total profit on a graph against different levels of capacity that you select.

7-41 *Special order pricing* (Adapted from CMA December 1988) The Sommers Company, located in southern Wisconsin, manufactures a variety of industrial valves and pipe fittings that are sold to customers in nearby states. Currently, the company is operating at about 70% capacity and is earning a satisfactory return on investment.

Management has been approached by Glasgow Industries Ltd. of Scotland with an offer to buy 120,000 units of a pressure valve. Glasgow Industries manufactures a valve that is almost identical to Sommers' pressure valve. However, a fire in Glasgow Industries' valve plant has shut down its manufacturing operations. Glasgow needs the 120,000 valves over the next four months to meet commitments to its regular customers. The company is prepared to pay $19 each for the valves, FOB shipping point, that is, freight and transportation insurance expenses are paid by the buyer, Glasgow Industries Ltd.

Sommers' product cost, based on current attainable standards, for the pressure valve is this:

Direct materials	$ 5.00
Direct labor	6.00
Manufacturing support	9.00
Total cost	$ 20.00

Manufacturing support costs are applied to production at the rate of $18 per standard direct labor hour. This rate is made up of the following components:

Variable manufacturing support	$ 6.00
Fixed manufacturing support	12.00
Cost driver rate	$18.00

Additional costs incurred in connection with sales of the pressure valve include sales commissions of 5% and freight expense of $1 per unit. However, the company does not pay sales commissions on special orders that come directly to management.

In determining selling prices, Sommers adds a 40% markup to product cost. This provides a $28 suggested selling price for the pressure valve. The marketing department, however, has set the current selling price at $27 in order to maintain the company's market share.

Production management believes that it can handle the Glasgow Industries order without disrupting its scheduled production. The order would, however, require additional fixed manufacturing support costs of $12,000 per month in the form of supervision and clerical costs.

If management accepts the order, 30,000 pressure valves will be manufactured and shipped to Glasgow Industries each month for the next four months. Shipments will be made in weekly consignments, FOB shipping point.

REQUIRED

(a) Determine how many additional direct labor hours would be required each month to fill the Glasgow Industries order.
(b) Evaluate the impact of accepting the Glasgow Industries order on Sommers' profit.
(c) Calculate the minimum unit price that Sommers' management could accept for the Glasgow Industries order without reducing its profits.
(d) Identify the factors, other than price, that Sommers Company should consider before accepting the Glasgow Industries order.

7-42 *Product-mix decisions*   (Adapted from CMA December 1991) Bakker Industries sells three products (Products 611, 613, and 615) that it manufactures in a factory consisting of four departments (departments 1 through 4). Both labor and machine time are applied to the products in each of the four departments. The machine processing and labor skills required in each department are such that neither machines nor labor can be switched from one department to another.

Bakker's management is planning its production schedule for the next several months. There are labor shortages in the community. Some of the machines will be out of service for extensive overhauling. Available machine and labor time by department for each of the next six months is listed below.

	DEPARTMENT			
Monthly Capacity Availability	**1**	**2**	**3**	**4**
Normal machine capacity in machine hours	3500	3500	3000	3500
Capacity of machines being repaired in machine hours	(500)	(400)	(300)	(200)
Available machine capacity in machine hours	3000	3100	2700	3300
Labor capacity in direct labor hours	4000	4500	3500	3000
Available labor in direct labor hours	3700	4500	2750	2600

LABOR AND MACHINE SPECIFICATIONS PER UNIT OF PRODUCT

		DEPARTMENT			
Product	Labor and Machine Time	1	2	3	4
611	Direct labor hours	2	3	3	1
	Machine hours	2	1	2	2
613	Direct labor hours	1	2	0	2
	Machine hours	1	1	0	2
615	Direct labor hours	2	2	1	1
	Machine hours	2	2	1	1

The sales department's forecast of product demand over the next six months is presented below.

Product	Monthly Sales Volume
611	500 units
613	400 units
615	1000 units

Bakker's inventory levels will not be increased or decreased during the next 6 months. The unit price and cost data valid for the next six months are presented below.

	PRODUCT		
Item	611	613	615
Unit costs:			
Direct material	$ 7	$ 13	$ 17
Direct labor			
Department 1	12	6	12
Department 2	21	14	14
Department 3	24	0	16
Department 4	9	18	9
Variable support	27	20	25
Fixed support	15	10	32
Variable selling	3	2	4
Unit selling price	$196	$123	$167

REQUIRED

(a) Determine whether the monthly sales demand for the three products can be met by Bakker Industries' factory. Use the monthly requirement by department for machine hours and direct labor hours for the production of products 611, 613, and 615 in your calculations.

(b) What monthly production schedule should Bakker Industries select in order to maximize its dollar profits? Support the schedule with appropriate calculations, and present a schedule of the contribution to profit that would be generated by the production schedule selected.

(c) What other alternatives might Bakker Industries consider to be able to supply its customers all the products they demand?

7-43 *Product-mix decision*   (Adapted from CMA June 1990) Sportway, Inc. is a wholesale distributor supplying a wide range of moderately priced sporting equipment to large chain stores. About 60% of Sportway's products are purchased from other companies while the remainder of the products are manufactured by Sportway. The company has a plastics department that is currently manufacturing molded fishing tackle boxes.

Sportway is able to manufacture and sell 8,000 tackle boxes annually, making full use of its direct labor capacity at available work stations. Presented below are the selling price and costs associated with Sportway's tackle boxes.

Selling price per box		$86.00
Costs per box:		
Molded plastic	$ 8.00	
Hinges, latches, handle	9.00	
Direct labor ($15/hour)	18.75	
Manufacturing support	12.50	
Selling and administrative	17.00	65.25
Profit per box		$20.75

Because Sportway believes it could sell 12,000 tackle boxes if it had sufficient manufacturing capacity, the company has looked into the possibility of purchasing the tackle boxes for distribution. Maple Products, a steady supplier of quality products, would be able to provide up to 9000 tackle boxes per year at a price of $68 per box delivered to Sportway's facility.

Bart Johnson, Sportway's product manager, has suggested that the company could make better use of its Plastics Department by manufacturing skateboards. To support his position, Johnson has a market study that indicates an expanding market for skateboards and a need for additional suppliers. Johnson believes that Sportway could expect to sell 17,500 skateboards annually at a price of $45.00 per skateboard. Johnson's estimate of the costs to manufacture the skateboards is presented below.

Selling price per skateboard		$45.00
Costs per skateboard:		
Molded plastic	$5.50	
Wheels, hardware	7.00	
Direct labor ($15 per hour)	7.50	
Manufacturing support	5.00	
Selling and administrative costs	9.00	34.00
Profit per skateboard		$11.00

In the plastics department, Sportway uses direct labor hours as the cost driver for manufacturing support costs. Included in the manufacturing support for the current year is $50,000 of factory-wide, fixed manufacturing support that has been allocated to the plastics department. For each unit of product that Sportway sells, regardless of whether the product has been purchased or is manufactured by Sportway, there is an allocated $6 fixed support cost per unit for distribution that is included in the selling and administrative cost for all products. Total selling and administrative costs for the purchased tackle boxes would be $10 per unit.

REQUIRED

In order to maximize the company's profitability, prepare an analysis based on the data presented that will show which product or products Sportway, Inc. should manufacture and/or purchase and will show the associated financial impact. Support your answer with appropriate calculations.

7-44 *Process or sell decision*   The Troy Company manufactures electronic subcomponents that can be sold at the end of process A or can be processed further in process B and sold as special parts for a variety of electronic appliances. The entire output of

Process A can be sold at a market price of $2 per unit. The output of process B had been sold at a price of $5.50 for the past three years, but the price has recently fallen to $5.10 on most orders.

Based on an analysis of the product markets and costs, Toni Tobin, the vice-president of marketing, thinks that process B output should be dropped whenever its price falls below $4.50 per unit. The total available capacity is interchangeable between process A and process B. She recommends that with present prices, all sales should be process B output. Her analysis is summarized below:

Output of Process A		
Selling price, after deducting relevant selling costs		$2.00
Costs:		
Direct materials	$1.00	
Direct labor	0.20	
Manufacturing support	0.60	
Cost per unit		1.80
Operating profit		$0.20

Output of Process B		
Selling price, after deducting relevant selling costs		$ 5.10
Transferred-in variable cost from process A	$1.20	
Additional direct materials	1.50	
Direct labor	0.40	
Manufacturing support for additional processing	1.20	
Cost per unit		4.30
Operating profit		$ 0.80

Direct materials and direct labor costs are variable. All manufacturing support costs are fixed and allocated to units produced based on hours of capacity.

The total hours of capacity available are 600,000. A batch of 60 units requires one hour for process A and two hours of additional processing for process B.

REQUIRED

(a) If the price of process B output for the next year is likely to be $5.10, should all sales be only the output of process B?
(b) What is the lowest acceptable price for process B output to make it as profitable as process A output?
(c) Suppose 50% of the manufacturing support costs are variable. Do your answers to (a) and (b) above change? If so, how?

■ CASES

7-45 *Product-mix decision*   Aramis Aromatics Company produces and sells its product AA100 to well-known cosmetics companies for $940 per ton. The marketing manager is considering the possibility of refining AA100 further into finer perfumes before selling them to the cosmetics companies. Product AA101 is expected to command a price of $1500 per ton, and AA102 a price of $1700 per ton. The maximum expected demand is 400 tons for AA101 and 100 tons for AA102.

The annual plant capacity of 2400 hours is fully utilized *at present* to manufacture 600 tons of AA100. The marketing manager proposed that Aramis sell 300 tons of AA100, 100 tons of AA101, and 75 tons of AA102 in the next year. It requires four hours of capacity to make one ton of AA100, two hours to refine AA100 further into AA101, and four hours to refine AA100 into AA102 instead. The plant accountant has prepared the following cost sheet for the three products:

	COSTS PER TON		
Cost Item	**AA100**	**AA101**	**AA102**
Direct materials:			
Chemicals and fragrance	$560	$ 400	$ 470
AA100	0	800	800
Direct labor	60	30	60
Manufacturing support:			
Variable	60	30	60
Fixed	120	60	120
Total manufacturing costs	$800	$1320	$1510
Selling support:			
Variable	20	30	30
Fixed	10	10	10
	$830	$1360	$1550
Proposed sales level	300 tons	100 tons	75 tons
Maximum demand	600 tons	400 tons	100 tons

REQUIRED

(a) Determine the contribution margin for each product.

(b) Determine the production levels for the three products under the present constraint on plant capacity that will maximize total contribution.

(c) Suppose a customer, Cosmos Cosmetics Company, is very interested in the new product AA101. It has offered to sign a long-term contract for 400 tons of AA101. It is also willing to pay a higher price if the entire plant capacity is dedicated to the production of AA101. What is the minimum price for AA101 at which it becomes worthwhile for Aramis to dedicate its entire capacity to the production of AA101?

(d) Suppose, instead, that the price of AA101 is $1500 per ton and that the capacity can be increased temporarily by 600 hours if the plant is operated overtime. Overtime premium payments to workers and supervisors will increase direct labor and variable manufacturing support costs by 50% for all products. All other costs will remain unchanged. Is it worthwhile operating the plant overtime? If the plant is operated overtime for 600 hours, what are the optimal production levels for the three products?

7-46 *Pricing decision*   Refer to the data for Sweditrak Corporation presented in Case 6-45. The following additional information is now available.

The production volume budgeted for each product in weeks 47 to 52 is the same as the volume level in week 46. In early December, the company is considering contracting with a French company to *produce* 400 units of the deluxe model on a four-week trial basis for $200 per unit. Accepting this offer would restrict Sweditrak's own deluxe production to 50 units per week.

REQUIRED

(a) Is it profitable for Sweditrak to accept this offer? What other qualitative factors should Sweditrack also consider in evaluating this offer?

Suppose that Sweditrak is pleased with the quality of the trial shipment and the French company is willing to commit to produce 400 units of the deluxe model each week for the next three years and charge $200 per unit. Sweditrak expects the domestic demand for its two models to remain stable at 450 units per week for the next three years. During this three-year time period, Sweditrak can adjust the capacity of each department to any desired levels. Capacity changes will result in proportional changes in fixed costs.

(b) What are the relevant costs for this long-term decision?

(c) Will it be profitable for Sweditrak to accept the long-term offer?

7-47 ***Pricing Experiment*** This is a pricing experiment in which you will work with a team using cost accounting information in pricing decisions. Each team represents one firm in a market. Each market is completely independent of other markets. Your market has four firms that use similar production technology to produce two types of hiking boots: a lightweight model (*LT*) and a mountaineering model (*MT*). Each firm faces the same demand curves where P is your price and $P1$, $P2$, and $P3$ are the other three firms' prices:

$$Demand\ for\ LT = 19919 - 500 \times P + 84 \times (P1 + P2 + P3)$$

$$Demand\ for\ MT = 6632 - 109 \times P + 18 \times (P1 + P2 + P3)$$

Notice that if you increase your price, your demand will fall. If, however, your competitors raise their prices, you will gain some of the market share they lose.

Your instructor will provide you a confidential cost report that you should use in your pricing decisions. No cost data should be shared with other teams.

There will be five periods in this pricing experiment. For each period, your firm must submit the prices at which you are prepared to sell each type of boot. Your firm operates on a just-in-time basis and produces to order. Hence, there are no inventory or production-quantity decisions to be made.

The market share you obtain or the profit you make in any one period will *not* in any form affect your performance in subsequent periods. Your parent company has committed to remain in this market for all five periods. However, your parent company expects you to maximize profits in each period.

You should come to the experiment session with your first set of prices. The prices should be specified in whole dollars only (no cents). Once you have decided on prices, enter the prices on the pricing sheet below and submit it to the instructor. The instructor will determine the quantities sold for each firm and return the pricing sheet to you with a market report (next page) containing the following information: what

PRICING SHEET					
FIRM:_____		MARKET:_____			
	Period 1	Period 2	Period 3	Period 4	Period 5
LT—Price					
MT—Price					

each firm sold, what prices each firm charged, and what the actual net income was for each firm. Then you will need to decide on prices for the next period.

	MARKET REPORT				

MARKET:_____   PRICE:_____

Firm	Lightweight Boots		Mountaineering Boots		Net Income
	Price	Quantity	Price	Quantity	

Prior to the experiment session, your team should spend two to three hours understanding the cost and demand structure and thinking about how to set prices. You should also devise a strategy to adjust prices if necessary based on what you observe about your competitors' decisions and about your own and your competitors' performance in each period. Remember the purpose of this experiment is to learn about pricing in a competitive setting.

After participating in the experiment you are required to prepare a report of no more than four typed and double-spaced pages that describe how you determined your costs and pricing rules and how competition affected your pricing. Your report must also include a statement of budget versus actual in the format shown below, together with detailed calculations of the costs of your two products.

STATEMENT OF BUDGET VERSUS ACTUAL

FIRM:_____   MARKET:_____

	Period 1	Period 2	Period 3	Period 4	Period 5	Total
Number of LT sold						
Price—LT						
Revenues—LT						
Number of MT sold						
Price—MT						
Revenues—MT						
Total revenues						
Estimated costs—LT						
Estimated costs—MT						
Total costs						
Estimated net income						
Actual net income						
Variance between actual and estimated net income						

PROCESS AND ACTIVITY DECISIONS

TOBOR TOY COMPANY

***Courtesy* Mark Young**

For 45 years, the Tobor Toy Company had been producing high-quality plastic toys for children. The company's best-selling toy was a very expensive mechanical toy robot that performed many functions and had a number of unique features; it commanded a 30% market share. In early 1996, however, Tobor experienced a large drop in sales and market share. After some investigation, this was attributed to a significant decrease in the quality of the product as well as general delays in getting the product to customers. Customers complained that the toy robots failed to perform many of their functions and simply stopped working after several days. The number of returns was astronomical.

Top management decided that the quality of the toy robot needed to be improved dramatically so that the company could regain its reputation and market share. Rumors began to surface that the quality problem was due to deterioration of equipment and an out-of-date production process. Also, morale among the workers was poor. Thomas Archer, senior manager of manufacturing, was asked to conduct a thorough investigation and arrive at recommendations for change and improvement.

After several weeks of study, Thomas and a cross-functional team of management personnel documented numerous shop floor problems:

1. A disorganized, sloppy production system in which piles of work in process and raw materials inventory were scattered all over the shop floor
2. A lengthy and complex flow of production
3. The use of outdated machinery

In addition, the quality of the computer chip that allowed the robot to perform its many functions was found to be highly variable; some workers seemed to be working hard, but many others were constantly idle; and there were as many defective robots sent back for rework as acceptable ones. Thomas, who had been studying the just-in-time (JIT) manufacturing philosophy, believed that the Tobor company could benefit greatly from implementing JIT. The JIT system seemed to have many advantages, such as streamlining the production process and improving facilities layout, eliminating waste, reducing raw and work-in-process inventories, and generally creating an environment in which producing quality products was rewarded. Further, costs would be easier to control if the company had a well-designed and well-understood production process. Thomas's report to top management raised a number of questions.

1. Should many of the existing machines, including the major injection molding machine, be replaced?
2. What should the company do about the local vendor who produced the faulty computer chips?
3. Would it make sense to implement an entirely new production process such as JIT?

After a month of study, top management decided to implement the JIT approach. The cost of implementation and worker training amounted to $300,000. Management was adamant that Thomas and his team carefully monitor the quality of products and the changes in the amount of rework, which the company classified as major or minor. After the first year, Thomas plotted a graph of the rates of major rework, which required scrapping the robot, and minor rework, which included repairs, such as realignment of parts and gears, as shown in Exhibit 8-1. Within the year major rework had declined by about 2.5%, while the minor rework rate showed a larger decrease of 6.6%.

Thomas felt that improvement in yield rates should improve cycle time efficiency. Cycle time was the time it took to produce the robot from start to finish. On average, he found that average cycle time had decreased from 16.4 days to 7.2 days and that the work-in-process inventory had decreased from $1,774,000 to $818,000, or $956,000.

Thomas knew that the transition to a full JIT system would take some time, but he also wondered what the bottom line effect on company profits would be for the year. Would the benefits of less rework, yield increases, and cycle time and inventory reductions be sufficient to offset the $300,000 implementation cost?

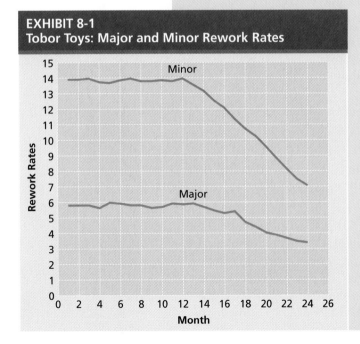

EXHIBIT 8-1
Tobor Toys: Major and Minor Rework Rates

EVALUATION OF MONETARY IMPLICATIONS

Managers must evaluate the monetary implications of decisions that require determining tradeoffs between the costs and benefits of different alternatives. Monetary implications are important when considering decisions such as whether to redesign an entire production process or replace existing machines or whether to buy components from outside subcontractors or make the components in house. Financial information about the different types of costs forms the basis of evaluating an organization's activities and processes as in the case of the Tobor Toy Company.

SUNK COSTS ARE NOT RELEVANT

The costs and revenues that are *relevant* for decision making depend on the decision context and the alternatives available. When choosing among different alternatives, managers should concentrate only on the costs and revenues that differ across the decision alternatives; these are the relevant revenues and costs. The costs that remain the same regardless of the alternative chosen are not considered relevant for the decision.

One category of costs that often causes confusion for decision makers is costs incurred in the past, or **sunk costs**. These are the costs of resources that already have been committed and regardless of a decision cannot be changed by any current action or decision. Because sunk costs cannot be influenced by whatever alternative the manager chooses, they are not relevant to the evaluation of alternatives.

Sunk costs
Costs of resources that have already been committed and, regardless of what decision managers make, cannot be changed by any current action or decision.

Relevant Costs for the Replacement of a Machine

Consider the following situation. Bonner Company purchased a new drilling machine for $180,000 from Newtech Corporation on July 1, 1996, paying $30,000 in cash and financing the remaining $150,000 of the price with a bank loan. The loan requires a monthly payment of $5200 for the next 36 months.

On July 27, 1996, a sales representative of another supplier of drilling machines approached Bonner Company with a newly designed machine that had only recently been introduced to the market. Precision Machinery Company, the supplier of the new machine, offered special financing arrangements. It agreed to pay $50,000 for the old Newtech machine. The trade-in of the old machine would serve as the down payment of $50,000 required for the new Precision machine. In addition, Precision would require monthly payments of $6000 for the next 35 months.

The new Precision design relied on an innovative use of computer chips that would reduce the labor required to operate a drilling machine. Bonner estimated that direct labor costs would decrease by $4400 per month on the average if it purchased the Precision machine. In addition, the new machine would decrease maintenance costs by $800 per month because it had fewer moving parts than Bonner's current machines. The greater reliability of the machine would also allow Bonner to reduce materials scrap cost by $1000 per month. Should Bonner dispose of the Newtech machine it had just purchased on July 1 and buy the new machine from Precision Corporation? What costs are relevant for this decision?

OBJECTIVE 8.1

Understand why sunk costs are not relevant costs.

Analysis of Relevant Costs

If Bonner buys the new machine from Precision, it would still be responsible for the monthly payments of $5200 committed to Newtech on July 1. Therefore, the $30,000 that Bonner paid in cash for the Newtech machine and the $5200 committed to pay each month for the next 36 months are all sunk costs. Bonner already has committed these resources, and whether it decides to buy the new machine from Precision or not, it cannot avoid any of these costs. *None of these sunk costs are relevant for the decision.*

What costs are relevant regarding whether to purchase the new Precision machine? The 35 monthly payments of $6000 and the down payment of $50,000 are relevant costs because they depend on Bonner's decision. In addition, labor, materials, and machine maintenance costs will be affected if Bonner acquires the new Precision machine. The expected monthly savings of $4400 in labor costs, $1000 in materials costs, and $800 in machine maintenance costs are relevant. The revenue of $50,000 expected on the trade-in of the old machine is also relevant because the old machine will be disposed of only if Bonner decides to acquire the Precision machine.

Exhibit 8-2 summarizes the relevant costs and revenues of this decision. In a comparison of the cost increases/cash outflows to cost savings/cash inflows, the down payment required for the new Precision machine is matched by the expected trade-in value of the Newtech machine. Furthermore, the expected savings in labor, materials, and machine maintenance costs each month ($6200) are more than the monthly lease payments for the new Precision machine ($6000). Thus, it is apparent that Bonner Company will be better off trading in the Newtech machine and replacing it with the Precision machine.

Comparisons of Cash Flows at Different Points in Time

How should Bonner evaluate this decision if the comparisons of both the immediate cash flows (down payment versus *disposal value*) and the recurrent cash flows (monthly lease payments versus monthly cost savings) did *not* favor purchasing the Precision machine? Cash flows at different points in time cannot be compared di-

---

EXHIBIT 8-2
Bonner Company: Relevant Costs and Revenues

Cost Increases and Cash Outflows		Cost Savings and Cash Inflows	
1. Down payment on the new Precision machine	$50,000	1. Disposal of the old Newtech machine	$50,000
2. Monthly lease payments on the Precision machine	$6,000	2. Monthly cost savings Labor Materials Maintenance	$ 4,400 1,000 800 $ 6,200

CONSIDER THIS...

Throwing Good Money after Bad

Suppose you are a bank loan officer. A customer with a good credit history comes to you and asks for a $50,000 business startup loan. After careful review of the application, you personally take the initiative to approve the loan. Six months later, the customer shows up in your office and says: "I have some bad news, and I have some good news. The bad news is that the company is having problems. Without additional help we will not survive, in which case you will lose the $50,000. The good news is that I am confident that if you lend us an additional $50,000, we can turn the whole thing around." Do you lend the additional $50,000?

This example, from an article by Professor Dipanker Ghosh, illustrates a current decision that a person faces because of a previous decision. According to the concept of sunk cost, any resources used earlier should not be considered when making future-oriented decisions. Despite this concept, many decision makers continue to pour resources into a highly uncertain project or "throw good money after bad" and escalate their resource commitments.

One of the principal reasons for escalation behavior lies with the characteristics of individual decision makers. For instance, from a psychological standpoint some individuals feel a need to justify a losing project by increasing their commitment in the hope of turning a situation around. These individuals are seeking their own or external justification for their decisions. Other individuals are susceptible to "selective perception" in which they use all available positive information to continue to justify a project but fail to process any negative information that may lead to termination. Still others are affected by whether information is viewed in terms of gains or losses. This concept is known as "framing." When information is framed in terms of gains (for example, the glass is half full), individuals tend to be risk averse; when information is framed in terms of losses (for example, the glass is half empty), individuals tend to be risk seeking. Others engage in "impression management" and resist abandoning a losing project because they believe that giving the project up will diminish their reputation in the eyes of coworkers and superiors.

There are several ways to reduce escalation behavior. First, the performance evaluation system should focus on managers' decision processes rather than decision outcomes. This approach recognizes that a good decision may not lead to a good outcome and can reduce the pressure of justification and decrease the tendency for escalation by allowing managers to terminate a losing project. Both selective perception and framing can be overcome through training in how to evaluate information. Further, the management accountant can play a critical role in helping decision makers by providing information in reports that are clear, precise, timely, and useful. Finally, impression management can be overcome by aligning the outcomes of decisions with the appropriate organizational rewards such as financial compensation, promotions, etc.

Source: Dipanker Ghosh, "Throwing Good Money after Bad," *Management Accounting,* July 1995, pp. 51–54.

rectly because of the time value of money that requires interest to be paid on bank deposits or borrowings from financial institutions. Chapter 10 addresses the problem of evaluating and aggregating multiperiod implications of managerial decisions in more detail.

Summary of Relevant Costs

The ability to identify the costs and revenues relevant for the evaluation of alternatives is critical at this stage. Equally important is the ability to recognize that some costs and revenues are not relevant in such evaluations. Neither the payments that Bonner has already made on the Newtech machine nor the remaining monthly payments that it committed to make is relevant for this evaluation. Rather both payments are sunk costs because neither alternative available to Bonner can change the cash flows already made or those committed to be made in the future.

Assuming Responsibility for Decisions

The correct decision for Bonner Company on a technical level is to dispose of the machine and replace it. However, not all managers would make this decision because of concern about their reputations within their organizations. By reversing a major decision made just a month earlier a manager might make it appear as if the earlier decision was made in error. In many circumstances, by maintaining the original course of action the manager does not have to reveal that there is a better decision that could be made.

Three other factors can enter into the decision facing Bonner Company. First, if the manager does not purchase the new machine, it may be viewed as suboptimal behavior, that is, allowing lower productivity or performance by using the old machine rather than improving performance with the new machine. Ultimately by not making the correct decision now, the manager may incur the effects of a bad decision in later periods. Another factor to consider is that if the manager admits that she made an error in purchasing the old machine she might garner more respect from her colleagues by being willing to admit that she made a mistake. Finally, many decision makers have a difficult time distinguishing sunk cost business decisions from personal sunk cost decisions. In contrast to business decisions the associated costs of previous life decisions can evoke a complex set of personal feelings. As an example, the decision to end a personal friendship or relationship is probably much more complex than replacing a business asset because the personal decision takes into account one's history with an individual with all of its ups and downs. Unlike the business regarding the machines, one does not end a friendship simply because a new friend materializes. Thus, identifying what is relevant and disentangling personal responses when dealing with business decisions are critical tasks for any business decision maker.

OBJECTIVE 8.2

Analyze make-or-buy decisions.

MAKE-OR-BUY DECISIONS

Make-or-buy decision
Decision either to make a part or component in-house or to purchase it from an outside supplier.

Management accountants often supply information about relevant costs and revenues to help managers make special one-time decisions. An example of such a decision that many managers have had to make in recent years is a **make-or-buy decision**. As managers have attempted to reduce costs and increase the competitiveness of their products, they have faced decisions about whether their companies should manufacture some parts and components for their products in-house at their own plant or whether they should subcontract with another company to supply these parts and components. Such make-or-buy decisions illustrate how to identify relevant costs and revenues.

Consider the decision faced by Mark Meador, production manager at Kentucky Motors, Inc. The company manufactures about 15% of the lamps required for its automobiles in its own plant near Dayton, Ohio. As a part of overall corporate efforts to reduce costs, Mark wants to evaluate the possibility of **outsourcing** all the lamps, that is, buying them from an outside supplier instead of manufacturing some of them in-house. He obtains firm quotes from several suppliers for the four types of lamps the company manufactures in-house: standard rear lamps, standard front lamps, multicolored rear lamps, and curved side and rear lamps.

Exhibit 8-3 displays details of the two lowest quotes from outside suppliers for a representative lamp for each of the four product lines manufactured in-house. Apparently, the lowest outside bids for each of the four products are lower than the total in-house manufacturing costs of each lamp. Should Mark accept the outside bids and terminate the in-house production of these products? What costs must Mark identify and consider when making this decision?

Outsourcing
Purchasing a product, part, or component from an outside supplier instead of manufacturing it in-house.

Avoidable Costs

To answer these questions, the decision maker must identify what costs are relevant for the decision. The concept of avoidable costs is useful for Mark to consider. **Avoidable costs** are the costs eliminated when a part, a product, a product line, or a business segment is discontinued.

The alternatives are whether to manufacture each lamp in house or to outsource its production. If Mark Meador decides to outsource a product, Kentucky Motors can avoid certain production costs. If the company purchases the standard rear lamp SR214 directly from the lowest bidder, it must pay $2,952,000 ($82 × 36,000). Doing so, the company saves $1,296,000 of direct material costs ($36 × 36,000). Also, it could reduce direct labor and supervisory costs and other resources

Avoidable costs
Costs that are eliminated when a part, a product, a product line, or a business segment is discontinued.

EXHIBIT 8-3
Kentucky Motors, Inc.: Product Costs per Unit and Outside Quotes for Four Representative Products

Product Line	Standard Rear Lamp	Standard Front Halogen Lamp	Multicolored Rear Lamp	Curved Side and Rear Lamp
Dimensions	20 cm × 6 cm	14 cm × 4 cm	14 cm × 4 cm	18 cm × 4 cm
Product number	SR214	SF120	MR314	CS418
Product costs per unit:				
Direct materials	$36	$ 49	$ 56	$ 58
Direct labor	22	25	24	28
Unit-related overhead	14	16	18	20
Batch-related overhead	10	16	19	22
Product-sustaining overhead	6	12	14	19
Facility-sustaining overhead	8	10	11	14
Total manufacturing costs	$96	$128	$142	$161
Bids from outside suppliers:				
Lowest	$82	$109	$140	$156
Second-lowest	$88	$116	$147	$164
Annual production (units)	36,000	48,500	6,800	8,700

CONSIDER THIS . . .

Target Costing for Make-or-Buy Decisions at Teijin Seiki Co., Ltd.

Teijin Seiki Co., Ltd., is a diversified manufacturer of machines and machine components for industries such as heavy equipment, textile, aerospace, robotics, and printing. It has plants in several locations around Japan. Its textile machinery division introduced a flexible manufacturing system (FMS) in its main factory with the expectation that it would achieve high quality, low costs, and quick delivery. However, unexpected confusions arose from the product cost calculations.

Consider a part that was shifted to in-house production to take advantage of the FMS. This work takes outside suppliers 20 hours to process but only 10 hours in-house. With an $80 direct labor hour in-house conversion cost (direct labor plus manufacturing overhead) rate, in-house production cost was estimated as $800 ($80 × 10 hours). But outside suppliers charged only $35 per hour for conversion costs, and therefore, outside costs worked out to $700 ($35 × 20 hours). Production people who introduced FMS were frustrated by this cost analysis that showed that farming the work out was more economical than doing it in-house even though FMS

processing time was one-half that of outside suppliers.

Management considered an alternative—to include only variable costs in the in-house conversion cost rate. However, this proposal was rejected because management felt that in the long term all fixed costs should be recovered in product costs. Makoto Kawada, the general manager in charge of the Office of Technology Development for Teijin Seiki Co., Ltd., and his colleagues worked out an ingenious solution based on target costs: When outside suppliers can make a part at a conversion cost rate of $35 per hours, Teijin Seiki must do in-house work at the same rate to stay competitive. The $35 hourly rate is the *target cost* representing the baseline to be achieved through a cost-reduction program. The conversion cost under this target costing method is $350 ($35 × 10 hours), and the $450 residual ($800 − $350) is a "competitive variance" viewed as nothing less than waste to be eliminated.

Source: Makoto Kawada and Daniel Johnson, "Strategic Management Accounting—Why and How," *Management Accounting*, August 1993, pp. 22–38.

contributing to unit-related overhead costs. As a result, the company can avoid incurring $792,000 of direct labor costs ($22 × 36,000) and $504,000 of unit-related overhead costs ($14 × 36,000). In addition, with a suitable contraction or redeployment of resources, Kentucky Motors also can avoid $360,000 of batch-related ($10 × 36,000) overhead costs and $216,000 of product-sustaining ($6 × 36,000) overhead costs.

To decide whether facility-sustaining overhead costs also are avoidable requires further consideration. Kentucky Motors cannot dispose of the part of the plant facility used to support the production of SR214 because most of the facility-sustaining overhead costs represent prorated costs of common facilities. The common facilities represent indivisible resources, such as those pertaining to building space and machines, that cannot be eliminated without disposing of the entire machine or building. Therefore, facility-sustaining overhead costs are unavoidable, or fixed, with respect to a decision to outsource product SR214.

It is sometimes possible to find an alternative use for the part of the facilities made available by not producing a product. Mark considered the possibility of shifting the other production lines manufactured in the same rented facility to the Dayton plant. In this way, Kentucky Motors can save the facility-sustaining costs for the rental facility by terminating its lease there. Such indirect savings in facility-sustaining costs for the organization, therefore, are relevant for the decision to outsource product SR214 because the cost savings can arise only if SR214 is outsourced. On further inquiry, however, Mark determined that it would be technically infeasible to transfer the manufacture of the other product lines to the Dayton plant.

To summarize the analysis so far, if product SR214 is outsourced, Kentucky Motors can avoid $3,168,000 of manufacturing costs. This is $216,000 more than the total price of $2,952,000 that Kentucky Motors has to pay the outside supplier.

Avoidable production costs	
Direct material costs	$1,296,000
Direct labor costs	792,000
Unit-related overhead costs	504,000
Batch-related overhead costs	360,000
Product sustaining overhead costs	216,000
	$3,168,000
Cost to outside supplier	2,952,000
Increase in profits from outsourcing	$ 216,000

Alternatively, notice that avoidable costs average $88 per unit in comparison with the lowest bid of $82 per unit to outsource product SR214.

$$\$36 + \$22 + \$14 + \$10 + \$6 = \$88$$

Therefore, Kentucky Motors stands to gain $6 per unit, or $216,000 overall.

$$\$36,000 \times \$6 = \$216,000$$

Qualitative Factors

OBJECTIVE 8.3

Understand the influence of qualitative factors on the quantitative analysis of decisions.

Are these quantitative estimates of costs and revenues the only relevant considerations before Mark decides to outsource SR214? In fact, for most such decisions several other factors, which are more qualitative in nature, need to be considered.

A question naturally arises about the permanence of the lower price. Has this supplier chosen to "low-ball" the price to get a "foot in the door"? If so, after Kentucky Motors discontinues the production of SR214 at its Dayton plant, will the supplier raise the prices for subsequent orders? This question raises the important point that the reputation of the selected outside supplier is a central part of making the decision. Even more important is the reliability of the supplier in meeting the required quality standards and in making deliveries on time. Poor performance on either of these dimensions can result in considerable costs elsewhere for the organization, especially if the component outsourced is critical for the final product. The same type of qualitative considerations are also important when Tobor Toy Company considers the poor-quality computer chip that it has been receiving from its supplier. Lack of availability of the component or a high reject rate for a component can lead to idling of assembly lines as well as unnecessary delays in meeting customer delivery schedules. In addition, such factors create customer dissatisfaction due to faulty products. Therefore, many companies have adopted the practice of certifying a small set of suppliers who are reliable

Certified supplier
A specially selected supplier who is assured a high level of business for conforming to high standards for quality and delivery schedules.

consistently and, therefore, dependable in terms of supplying quality items as needed. Companies provide these **certified suppliers** with incentives, such as quick payments and guaranteed total purchase volumes, so that they will comply with strict quality and delivery schedules.

In many industries, technological innovation is an important determinant of competitive advantage. For example, Teijin Electronics Corporation has identified several different technologies as being critical for its businesses in the next 20 years. It relies on certified suppliers for many of the components for its products, but it has a corporate policy to produce in-house all components that use one of its critical technologies. This policy enables Teijin's research and development staff to experiment, learn, innovate, and implement these critical technologies in-house so that it can retain its leadership and control over innovations in these important areas.

*F*ACILITIES LAYOUT SYSTEMS

OBJECTIVE 8.4

Describe the different types of facilities layouts.

Decisions involving the replacement of a single or several machines often cannot be made without considering the entire production process. This section covers the larger issues relating to facilities design. The three most common designs are (1) process layouts, (2) product layouts, and (3) cellular manufacturing.

The goal for most organizations today is to make their operations run smoothly and quickly with the least amount of error possible. One key issue for most manufacturing organizations in doing this is how to reduce inventories and the cycle time of production.

Process Layouts

Process layout
Organization system in which all similar equipment or functions are grouped together.

To understand why inventories pile up in conventional processing systems thereby increasing cycle time, it is important to understand the conventional way that facilities, whether they are factories or offices, are organized. In a **process layout**, all similar equipment or functions are grouped together. For example, at most universities the offices of staff in the same department or faculty are located close together. Most large automobile service stations are organized so that mufflers are fixed in one area, wheel alignments in another, body work and painting in another, and mechanical work in still another area. In most printing shops similar machines are grouped together. Such process layouts exist in organizations in which production is done in small batches of unique products. In a process layout, the product is moved from area to area as it sequences through various processing stages. In addition to long production paths, process layouts also lead to high inventory levels because it is necessary to store work in process in each area while it awaits the next operation. Often a product can travel for several miles within a factory as it is transformed from raw materials to finished goods.

In a process layout, which most organizations use, work in process follows a serpentine path, usually in batches, through the factories and offices that create it. Along this path employees at processing stations perform an activity as the good or service passes. For example, the process associated with a loan application at a bank may occur as follows. The customer goes to the bank—a moving activity. The bank takes the loan application from the customer—a processing activity.

Loan applications are accumulated—a storage activity—and passed to a loan officer—a moving activity—for approval—both a processing activity and an inspection activity. Loans that violate standard loan guidelines are accumulated—a storage activity—and then passed—a moving activity—to a regional supervisor for approval—a processing activity. The customer is contacted when a decision has been made—a processing activity—and if the loan is approved, the loan proceeds are deposited in the customer's account—a processing activity.

In most banks, work in process piles up at each of the processing points, or stations. Loan applications may be piled on the bank teller's desk, the loan officer's desk, and the regional supervisor's desk. Work-in-process inventory, such as bank loan applications, accumulates at processing stations in a conventional organization for three reasons.

1. Handling work in batches is the most obvious cause of work-in-process inventory in a process layout system. Organizations use batches to reduce setting up, moving, and handling costs. But batch processing increases the inventory levels in the system because at each processing station all the items in the batch must wait while the designated employees process the entire batch before moving all the parts in the batch to the next station.

2. If the rate at which each processing area handles work is unbalanced—because one area is slower or has stopped working due to problems with equipment, materials, or people—work piles up at the slowest processing station. Such scheduling delays create another reason that inventory levels increase in a process layout system.

3. Since supervisors evaluate many processing area managers on their ability to meet production quotas, processing station managers try to avoid the risk of having their facility idle. Many managers deliberately maintain large stocks of incoming work in process so that they can continue to work even if the processing area that feeds them is shut down. Similarly, to avoid idling the next processing station and suffering the resulting recriminations, managers may store finished work to continue to supply stations further down the line when their stations are shut down because of problems.

Some organizations have developed innovative approaches to eliminate many of the costs relating to moving and storing; these are significant nonvalue-added costs associated with process layout systems. Exhibit 8-4 illustrates the system that Gannett Corporation, the United States' largest newspaper publisher, has developed. Gannett uses computers and electronic communication in its electronic pagination process to eliminate the physical movement of work in process. By eliminating the physical movement of work, the company reduces both cycle time and costs.

Product Layouts

In a **product layout**, equipment is organized to accommodate the production of a specific product, for example, an automobile assembly line or a packaging line for cereal or milk. Product layouts exist primarily in companies with high-volume products. In a product layout, the product moves along an assembly line and the

Product layout
Organization of equipment or functions to accommodate the production of a specific product.

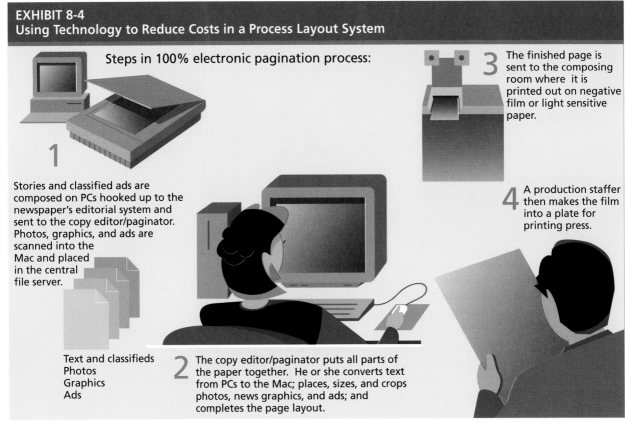

EXHIBIT 8-4
Using Technology to Reduce Costs in a Process Layout System

Steps in 100% electronic pagination process:

1 Stories and classified ads are composed on PCs hooked up to the newspaper's editorial system and sent to the copy editor/paginator. Photos, graphics, and ads are scanned into the Mac and placed in the central file server.

Text and classifieds
Photos
Graphics
Ads

2 The copy editor/paginator puts all parts of the paper together. He or she converts text from PCs to the Mac; places, sizes, and crops photos, news graphics, and ads; and completes the page layout.

3 The finished page is sent to the composing room where it is printed out on negative film or light sensitive paper.

4 A production staffer then makes the film into a plate for printing press.

Source: Jennifer McDonald, Gannet News Service.

parts to be added to it are stored along the line. For example, in large cities specialized hospitals, such as clinics that focus on hearing problems, justify having a product layout because of the resulting volume of specialized patients. For such assembly line processes, placement of equipment or processing units is made to reduce the distance that products or patients must travel.

Product layout systems planners can often arrange for raw materials and purchased parts to be delivered directly to the production line where and when they are needed. Suppose that an assembly line is scheduled to handle 600 cars on a given day. The purchasing group knows that these 600 automobiles require 2400 regular tires and 600 spare tires. Under ideal conditions, the purchasing group will arrange delivery of small batches of these tires to the assembly line as they are needed. However, because each batch of tires from the supplier incurs some batch-related ordering, transportation, and delivery costs, planners may arrange for a few days' worth of tires to be delivered at a time.

Consider the work in process in a cafeteria setting. People pass by containers of food and take what they want. Employees organize the food preparation activities so that the containers are refilled just as they are emptied—not one unit at a time. For example, the cook does not make and replace one bowl of soup at a time because batch-related setup costs of making soup in this fashion will be prohibitively expensive. Reducing setup costs, however, allows the reduction of batch sizes (the size of the containers) along the line. This reduces the level of inventory in the system and, therefore, costs. It also improves quality while increasing customer satisfaction. The ultimate goal is to reduce setup costs to zero and to reduce processing time to as close as possible to zero so that it is possible to produce and deliver individual products just as they are needed.

Cellular Manufacturing

A third approach to facilities layout is a hybrid approach often called cellular manufacturing. **Cellular manufacturing** refers to the organization of a plant into a number of cells so that within each cell all machines required to manufacture a group of similar products are arranged in close proximity to each other. As Exhibit 8-5 illustrates, the shape of a cell is often a U shape, which allows workers convenient accessibility to required parts. The machines in a cell manufacturing layout are usually flexible and can be adjusted easily or even automatically to make different products. Often the number of employees needed to produce a product can be reduced due to a new work design. Also, the U shape provides better visual control because employees can observe more directly what their coworkers are doing.

Glendale Electric Corporation is a leader in the manufacture of small electrical appliances for household and industrial use. It produces a variety of electrical valve controls at its plant in Encino, California. Until recently, the plant was organized into five production departments: casting, machining, assembly, inspection, and packing. Now the plant layout has been reorganized to streamline production flows and enable cellular manufacturing.

The plant manufactured 128 different products that have been grouped into eight product lines for accounting purposes based on common product features and production processes. Under the old plant layout, the 128 products followed a similar sequence of steps in the manufacturing process. (See Exhibit 8-6.) Manufacturing of panels for valve controls occurred in large batches in the casting department. Then the manufactured panels were stored in a large work-in-process storage area located near the machining department, where they remained until

Cellular manufacturing Organization of the plant into a number of cells so that within each cell, all machines required to manufacture a group of similar products are arranged sequentially in close proximity to each other.

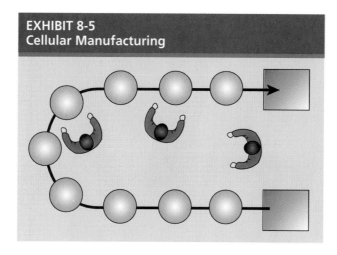

EXHIBIT 8-5
Cellular Manufacturing

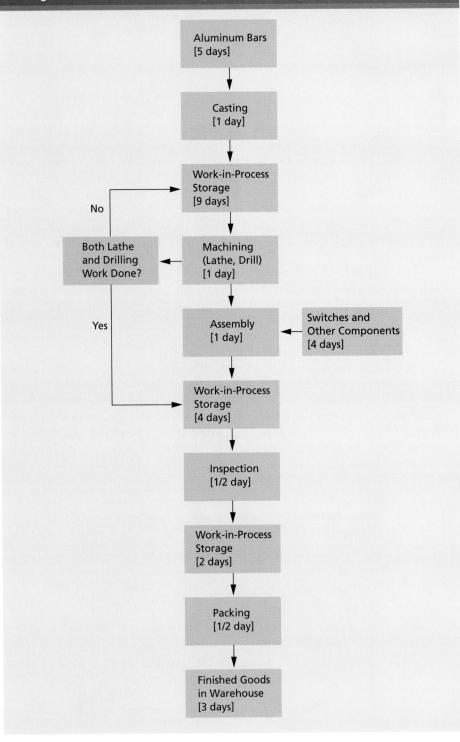

EXHIBIT 8-6
Glendale Electric Corporation: Production Flows and Average Time under Old Plant Layout

the lathes and drilling machines were free. After machining, the panels were stored until they were requisitioned for assembly, where switches and other components received from outside suppliers were placed onto each panel. Another storage area located near the assembly department was used for work in process awaiting inspection or packing, which occurred before they were packed for shipping. Finally, the packed valve control panels were stored in the finished goods warehouse until they were shipped to distributors and other customers.

This production flow required storage of work-in-process inventory for a long time, and at several times before the beginning of the next production stage. As mentioned previously, manufacturing cycle time is measured as the time from the receipt of the raw materials from the supplier to the point of delivery of the finished goods to the distributors and customers. At Glendale, this required 27 days (5 + 1 + 9 + 1 + 1 + 4 + 1/2 + 2 + 1/2 + 3) under the old plant layout. The four days that switches and other components were kept as inventory were not added to the **processing time,** the time expended for the product to be made, because the time spent in inventory represented parallel time with other production activities, such as work-in-process storage and machining. Therefore, the storage requirements for switches and other components did not prolong the time for the total production activity in the plant.

Processing time
Time expended in making a product.

This picture shows a manufacturing cell in an ITW DeVilbiss factory that makes air-spray equipment. The cellular approach to manufacturing minimizes the amount of work in process moving and handling by locating the equipment needed to make a product in a single area in the factory. Cellular manufacturing helps the company to improve quality, reduce cycle times, and reduce costs. The bins in the right foreground, called *KanBan bins*, indicate which parts are needed by the assembly cell. Work in this machining cell is triggered by the return of empty bins from the assembly cell. *Courtesy* ITW.

Manufacturing cycle efficiency (MCE)
Method of assessing process efficiency based on the relationship between actual processing time and total cycle time.

Organizations often are concerned about how efficient their manufacturing process is. One widely used measure for assessing process efficiency is known as **manufacturing cycle efficiency (MCE)** and is calculated as follows:

$$MCE = \frac{Processing\ time}{Processing\ time\ +\ Moving\ time\ +\ Storage\ time\ +\ Inspection\ time}$$

Notice that of the 27 days required for the manufacturing cycle, only 4 days are spent on actual processing time [(1 casting) + (1 purchasing) + (1 assembly) + (1/2 inspection) + (1/2 packing)]. The other 23 days are spent in non-value-added activities such as moving, storage, and inspecting. The amount of time materials spend in inventory can be as many as 23 days. The MCE formula reveals that processing time equals 15% (4 ÷ 27) of total cycle time. These results are representative of many other plants that manufacture products from mechanical or electronic components.

INVENTORY COSTS AND PROCESSING TIME

Inventory and Processing Time

Not only does batch production create inventory costs, but it also creates the delays associated with storing and moving inventory; this increases cycle times, thereby reducing service to customers. These delays can happen at any stage of the production cycle even before manufacturing begins. For example, because of high setup costs, a manufacturer may require that a product be manufactured in some minimum batch size. If a customer order is less than the minimum batch size and if the order cannot be filled from existing finished goods inventory, then the customer must wait until enough orders have accumulated to meet the minimum batch size requirement. For example, it may take a loan officer only five minutes to read and approve a loan application. However, the application may wait for several hours or even several days to reach the loan officer because it is too expensive to have a clerk running back and forth with each loan application.

Inventory-Related Costs

Demands for inventory lead to huge costs in organizations, including the cost of moving, handling, and storing the work in process, in addition to costs due to obsolescence or damage. Many organizations have found that factory layouts and inefficiencies that create the need to hold work in process inventory also hide other problems leading to excessive costs of rework.

For example, in batch operations, workers near the end of a process—downstream—often find problems due to the way that workers earlier in the process—upstream—have done their jobs. Work completed in batches often produces items that are defective and require rework. However, when work is performed continuously on one item at a time, workers downstream can identify an upstream problem almost immediately and correct the problem before it leads to the production of more defective parts.

REORGANIZATION.   A primary objective of the reorganization of the Glendale plant layout was to reduce the production cycle time. Thus, the plant was reorganized into eight manufacturing cells (corresponding to the eight product lines) in addition to the casting department. Each cell focused on the manufacture of similar products belonging to the same product line.

Exhibit 8-7 depicts the production flows under the new plant layout. While the casting department remains a separate department, the other four operations—machining, assembly, inspection, and packing—are now located in close proximity to each other in manufacturing cells. Aluminum panels received from the casting department are lathe-machined, drilled, and assembled in the manufacturing cells. Workers in the cells also are responsible for inspection and packing operations.

Glendale Electric also made a transition toward just-in-time production to be concurrent with the change in the plant layout. This required that there were no work-in-process inventories among the various stages of operations in the manufacturing cells because panel production flowed immediately from lathe to drilling to assembly to inspection to packing operations. In addition, the required plan eliminated time between operations because production was pulled from one stage to the next based on orders for the finished product.

When comparing Exhibits 8-6 and 8-7, notice that Glendale Electric Corporation did not reduce the amount of time spent on actual manufacturing when it changed the plant layout. The time spent on manufacturing operations after the change (see Exhibit 8-7) is the same as the time spent before the change. (See Exhibit 8-6.) However, the cycle time is reduced substantially in the new plant layout from 27 days to only 12 days. Thus, MCE changes from 15% to 33% (4 ÷ 12). This is a significant improvement in efficiency over the previous layout. The improvement is due to eliminating the need for work-in-process inventory among many of the manufacturing operations.

ANALYSIS OF RELEVANT COSTS AND BENEFITS.   Has this change helped improve the profitability of the Encino plant? Ellen Glaze, the Encino

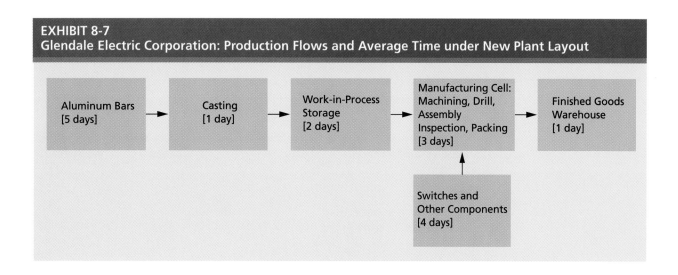

EXHIBIT 8-7
Glendale Electric Corporation: Production Flows and Average Time under New Plant Layout

plant controller, identified the following costs associated with the implementation of the changes in the plant layout:

Moving machines and reinstallation	$ 600,000
Training workers for cellular manufacturing	+400,000
Total costs	$1,000,000

Ellen also identified two types of benefits resulting from the plant reorganization: (1) an increase in sales because of the decrease in production cycle time and (2) a reduction in inventory-related costs because of the decrease in the amount and handling of work-in-process inventory. Ellen interviewed several production and sales managers to assess the extent of these benefits. She began with Dan Elnorte, a senior sales manager with 17 years of experience at Glendale.

Ellen Glaze: Has the reduction in production cycle time increased sales?

Dan Elnorte: Yes, we have been able to win over many customers from our competitors because we can now quote a much shorter delivery lead time to them. Also, we have been able to retain some of our own customers because we have cut our delivery lead time. We commissioned a market research study to ascertain the impact that reduction in delivery lead time has had on our sales. On the basis of this study, our best estimate is that an increase of $880,000 in sales this year can be attributed to the change in our production cycle time. Details of estimated sales increases for individual products are also provided in this study. I think you'll find it interesting.

Ellen next turned to her assistant, Hans Selto, to collect the information necessary to assess the impact of the sales increase on Glendale profits. Ellen asked Hans to determine the contribution margin for the Encino plant's products. He returned the next day with several detailed cost accounting reports.

Hans Selto: I've prepared a detailed analysis of the incremental costs for all our products. Here is a summary that gives the totals for all 128 products. (See Exhibit 8-8.) I began with the estimate of the increase in sales for each of the 128 products. Here is an example for Product TL32. (See Exhibit 8-9.) I multiplied the 800-unit sales increase by the direct materials cost of $7 per

EXHIBIT 8-8
Glendale Electric Company Impact of Increase in Sales on Profits

Increase in sales revenue		$880,000
Increase in costs:		
Direct materials	$245,000	
Direct labor	140,000	
Unit-related overhead	108,000	
Batch-related overhead	86,000	579,000
Net increase in profit		$301,000

EXHIBIT 8-9
Glendale Electric Company
Profit Impact of Increase in Sales of Product TL32

Increase in sales	(800 units × $29 price per unit)		$23,200
Increase in costs:			
Direct materials	(800 units × $7 cost per unit)	$5,600	
Direct labor	(800 units × $4 cost per unit)	3,200	
Unit-related overhead	(800 units × $3 overhead per unit)	2,400	
Batch-related overhead	(800/100 batches × $250 overhead per batch)	2,000	13,200
Net increase in profit			$10,000

unit, direct labor cost of $4 per unit, and unit-related overhead of $3 per unit. I also determined that eight additional batches are required for the increased production by using the fact that TL32 is manufactured in batch size of 100 units.

None of the product-sustaining or facility-sustaining overhead should increase because there are no new products added by increases in the size of the plant and no additions to plant machinery. The $10,000 increase in profit is obtained by calculating the difference between the $23,200 increase in sales revenue and the $13,200 increase in costs The summary in Exhibit 8-8 displays the totals of similar revenue and cost numbers across all of our 128 products.

Ellen Glaze: Thanks, Hans, for all your effort. I see that our best estimate is that the increase in sales because of the lower production cycle time has led to an overall increase of $301,000 in profit this year.

Ellen next met with Doreen Young, production and inventory manager at the Encino plant, to find out how the reduction in the level of work-in-process inventory affected the consumption of support activity resources.

Ellen Glaze: Has the change in the plant layout led to changes in the handling and storage of work-in-process inventory?

Doreen Young: Yes, we have been able to make many changes. We do not need a materials handling crew to move work-in-process inventory from lathes to drilling machines to storage areas on the shop floor. Moreover, we do not need to move and store work-in-process inventory between the assembly, inspection, and packing stages either. We did not reduce the number of materials handling workers immediately, but as work patterns stabilized a few weeks after the change in the plant layout, we reduced our materials handling crew from 14 to only 8 workers.

Ellen Glaze: Were there any other changes in the workload of people performing these support activities?

Doreen Young: With an almost 70% reduction in work-in-process inventory (down from $2,270,000 to $690,000), we had a corresponding decrease in inventory-related transactions. We did not require as much recordkeeping for the movement of materials into and out of storage. We expect to be able to reduce our shop-floor-stores staff by about 75%, from four to only one worker. So far we have reassigned only one worker, but two more will be reassigned to other production-related tasks next week.

Ellen Glaze: So far we have talked about personnel. Were any other resources freed up as a result of the reduction in work-in-process inventory?

Doreen Young: Yes, we need only one-third of the storage space we used earlier for work-in-process inventory. The extra space is idle at present, however, because we haven't yet found an alternative use for it. I don't believe there was any proposal to use that extra space in the three-year facilities plan prepared last month, but eventually as production activity expands we should be able to place new manufacturing cells in the space formerly used to store work-in-process inventory.

Ellen Glaze: But you don't expect any immediate benefit to arise from the availability of the extra storage space?

Doreen Young: Yes, that's correct. But there is one more benefit that you shouldn't forget. When some panels are produced in large batches and stored awaiting the next stage of processing, we always find that some of them get damaged in handling, and at times some of them become obsolete because the customer no longer requires them. The change to just-in-time production in the manufacturing cells and the elimination of much of our work-in-process inventory have resulted in a reduction in materials scrap and obsolescence cost from 0.32% of materials cost to only 0.12%.

Ellen Glaze: Thank you, Doreen. The information you have provided will be very useful in evaluating the impact of the change in the plant layout.

Ellen and Hans sat down in Ellen's office to analyze the information that they had collected so far. Facility-sustaining costs pertaining to plant space included building depreciation, insurance, heating, lighting, janitorial services, building upkeep, and maintenance. The overhead rate for this activity was $108 per square foot. However, Ellen and Hans decided that the costs associated with the extra storage space were at present a sunk cost with no cost savings yet realized from freeing up this space.

A check of the materials handling activity costs indicated that the annual wages of workers in this grade averaged $21,000, with 35% more, or $7350 ($21,000 × 0.35), added to this for fringe benefits. The total materials handling cost savings, therefore, was $170,100 ($28,350 × 6) because the crew size was reduced by six workers. In a similar fashion, Hans determined that the annual wages of stores personnel averaged $26,400. With a 35% fringe benefit rate and an expected reduction of three workers, the total annual cost savings was $106,920 ($26,400 × 1.35 × 3). There can be significant costs involved in financing inventories. Ellen estimated the interest rate on bank loans to finance the investment in inventories to be 12% per year. The work-in-process inventory was reduced by $1,580,000 ($2,270,000 − $690,000). This reduced cost of inventory financing correspondingly by $189,600 ($1,580,000 × 0.12).

Finally, Ellen determined that the total annual materials cost was $31,000,000. If the rate of materials, scrap and obsolescence had remained at the previous 0.32% of materials cost, this loss would have been $99,200 ($31,000,000 × 0.0032). But because of the reduction in the rate to 0.12%, the cost of materials scrap and ob-solescence was reduced to only $37,200 ($31,000,000 × 0.0012). This represents a cost savings of $62,000 ($99,200 − $37,200).

SUMMARY OF COSTS AND BENEFITS.   Ellen then summarized the infor-mation on cost savings resulting from the change in the plant layout. (See Exhibit 8-10.) She estimated that annual benefits were $829,620. In comparison, the one-time costs of implementing the change were only $1,000,000. If benefits from the changed layout continue to accrue at the same rate for at least the next three months, the total benefits would exceed the amount that Glendale invested in the project.

$$\$829,620 \times \tfrac{15}{12} = \$1,037,025$$

In other words, the investment would be paid off in only 1.25 years with the ben-efits resulting from the investment.

The Glendale case study introduces several important concepts. We have identified several different ways in which new manufacturing practices can im-prove a plant's profitability. In particular, we have seen that financing is a principal inventory-related cost. It is important to consider this cost, although financing costs are often not emphasized in many traditional cost accounting systems. Streamlining manufacturing processes also reduces the demand placed on many support-activity resources. Activity analysis, therefore, is useful for assessing the potential cost savings that can be realized from more efficient product flows.

Many new manufacturing practices are designed to promote continuous im-provement in manufacturing performance by enabling workers to learn and inno-vate. Changing to a manufacturing cell layout often results in improvements in production yield rates and, consequently, improvements in overall plant produc-tivity. Although the managers at Glendale did not consider this possibility, it is often the most important benefit from the implementation of new manufacturing practices.

EXHIBIT 8-10
Glendale Electric Corporation: Annual Benefits Resulting from the Change in Plant Layout

Contribution from increased sales:			
Sales increase	(Exhibit 8–8)	$880,000	
Incremental manufacturing costs	(Exhibit 8–8)	(579,000)	$301,000
Cost savings from work-in-process inventory reduction:			
Cost of financing investment in work-in-process inventory		$189,600	
Cost of materials handling labor		170,100	
Cost of stores labor		106,920	
Cost of materials scrap and obsolescence		62,000	528,620
Total benefits			$829,620

CONSIDER THIS . . .

Quest for Quality: Working on Rework

Tennant Company, based in Golden Valley, Minnesota, is a worldwide leader in the manufacture of industrial sweeper and scrubber machines. It is also recognized as a leader in the quality improvement programs being adopted increasingly by U.S. manufacturers.

In planning its manufacturing capacity over a decade ago, Tennant management counted 20 rework mechanics in manufacturing, 1 rework person in sheet metal, a rework station in welding, and a touch-up paint booth in assembly. Rework tied up almost 10,000 square feet of manufacturing floor space. Why such a large amount? It was the custom for every assembled sweeper and scrubber machine to routinely go through rework. It was not uncommon to have 50 to 100 machines waiting in line to be checked and have defective parts replaced. The managers realized that if this continued they would soon need a football field for the waiting machines and there would be no space left for manufacturing at current plants.

At about this time, the quality guru Phil Cosby, famous for his claim that "quality is free," visited the Tennant Company. "Build the machines right *the first*

time," he advised. "That will cut the need for rework machines in half." Thus began Tennant Company's quest for quality.

Tom Peters, the well-known management consultant and author of *In Search of Excellence*, describes Tennant's success story as "one of passionate commitment, persistence, wholesale people involvement—and sound management systems and problem-solving techniques. The results so far . . . are compelling. Manufacturing rework dropped from 33,000 hours to 4,800 hours between 1980 and 1988." Rework mechanics were reassigned to assembly lines, the final test area, or engineering. Their experience was valuable in solving quality-related problems and in reducing first-pass defect rates by over 50%. Almost 8,000 square feet of floor space was freed for production. Also, production cycle time was reduced with the number of orders shipped within 24 hours increasing from 47% to 75%.

Source: R. L. Hale, D. R. Hoelscher, and R. E. Kowak, *Quest for Quality*, Tennant Company, 1989.

JUST-IN-TIME MANUFACTURING

Just-in-time manufacturing
Making a good or providing a service only when the customer who may be internal or external requires it.

A **just-in-time manufacturing** system requires making a good or service only when the customer, internal or external, requires it. Just-in-time production requires a product layout with a continuous flow, that is, one with no delays, once production starts. This means that there must be a substantial reduction in setup costs in order to eliminate the need to produce in batches; therefore, processing systems must be reliable.

Product and cellular manufacturing layouts reduce costs and quality problems associated with conventional manufacturing and facilities layouts. These additional examples illustrate just-in-time (JIT) manufacturing approaches that companies have been using successfully in their operations.

OBJECTIVE 8.5

Explain the purpose of just-in-time manufacturing systems.

Implications of Just-in-Time Manufacturing

Just-in-time manufacturing is simple in theory but hard to achieve in practice. Some organizations are hesitant about implementing it because with no work-in-process inventory a problem anywhere in the system can stop all production. For

CONSIDER THIS . . .

Seeing the Big Picture: Manufacturing, Marketing, and Distribution Activities and the Average Cost of a Compact Disk

While we have focused in this chapter on process and activity decisions related to manufacturing, marketing and distribution activities also need to be scrutinized and improved as their costs are significant in determining product costs. The methods used to reduce cycle time in manufacturing can be applied to both marketing and distribution activities. Further, in the illustration below detailing the breakdown of the average wholesale price of a compact disk (CD), there are a number of other types of costs that need to be managed including record company overhead, recording costs, artist and copyright fees, and so forth. Thus, seeing and managing the "big picture" of the cost of a CD involves an understanding of many organizational functions.

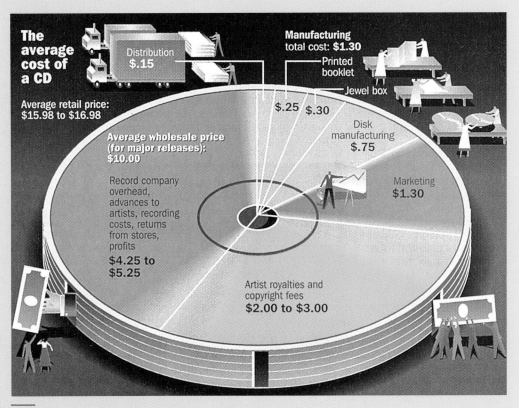

Source: *U.S. News and World Report*, September 25, 1995, p. 68.

this reason, organizations that use just-in-time manufacturing must eliminate all the sources of failure in the system. The production process must be redesigned so that it is not prohibitively expensive to process one or a small number of items at a time. This usually means reducing the distance over which work in process has to travel and using very flexible people and equipment that can handle all types of jobs. Production people must be better trained so that they can carry out their activities without mistakes. Suppliers must be able to produce and deliver defect-free materials or components just when they are required, and equipment must be maintained so that machine failures are eliminated.

The lending process at the bank is an example of how information technology facilitates just-in-time production in service companies. For instance, one way to reduce the batch cost of handling loan applications is to process them on a computer so that a loan application can be moved instantly over any distance. The bank clerk may receive information required to put the loan application on a computer, or customers with computing capabilities may submit loan applications electronically, eliminating the need for them to physically come into the bank.

The loan application can be processed by a computer program that scans consumer credit databases to immediately reject or flag applications by customers who have credit problems. Simple loan applications can be approved on the spot, depending on verification of the client's claims. This improves service and reduces the amount of loan officer time spent approving applications. Complex loan applications can be called out of the database instantly by loan officers many miles away. At that point, applications can be reviewed and approved almost as quickly as simple loan applications. By moving away from a physical (paper) loan application required to move among people performing different tasks, the electronic process can prove to be more efficient and faster. Moreover, by eliminating the need to batch loan applications for approval, a centrally located loan officer can be provided with a constant stream of loan applications from many branches. In this way, customers can have their loan applications approved or disapproved shortly after submission. Overall, the bank can be much more responsive to its customers if it uses electronic loan application processing.

Consider how just-in-time manufacturing can be used at a fast food restaurant. Some fast-food restaurants use a just-in-time, continuous-flow product layout, while others use batch production in a process layout. In fact, some fast-food restaurants combine both approaches into these hybrid systems that use a batch approach to production and keep inventories at predefined levels. For example, the restaurant may use racks or bins to hold food ready to be sold to the customer and have employees start another batch of production when the existing inventory falls below a line drawn on the bin or rack. At off-peak times, the restaurant may produce to order.

The motivation to use the just-in-time approach is to improve the quality of the food and to reduce waste by eliminating the need to throw out food that has been waiting around too long. The motivation to use batch production is to sustain a certain level of inventory to reduce the time the customer has to wait for an order. As processing time and setup costs drop, the organization can move closer to just-in-time manufacturing and reduce the waste and quality problems that arise with batch production.

Just-in-Time Manufacturing and Management Accounting

Just-in-time manufacturing has two major implications for management accounting. *First*, management accounting must support the move to just-in-time manufacturing by monitoring, identifying, and communicating to decision makers the sources of delay, error, and waste in the system. Important measures of a JIT system's reliability would include these factors of manufacturing cycle effectiveness:

1. Defect rates
2. Cycle times
3. Percent of time that deliveries are on time
4. Order accuracy
5. Actual production as a percent of planned production
6. Actual machine time available compared to planned machine time available

Conventional production systems emphasize labor and machine utilization ratios that encourage large batch sizes and production that generates inventory quantities that lead to long manufacturing cycle times. Therefore, conventional labor and machine productivity ratios are inconsistent with the just-in-time production philosophy, in which operators are expected to produce only what is requested when it is requested and on time. *Second,* the clerical process of management accounting is simplified by just-in-time manufacturing because there are fewer inventories to monitor and report.

*T*OBOR TOY COMPANY REVISITED

Tobor Toy Company succeeded in decreasing its major rework rate from 5.8% to 3.3% and its minor rework rate from 13.6% to 7.0%. Major rework required scrapping the robot. Minor rework required correcting the alignment of robot body parts, or fixing the ways that the gears were functioning, and conducting this work in a specially designated rework area.

As a result of the improvements in the rework rates, average production cycle time was reduced by 9.2 days, from 16.4 days to 7.2 days. Average work-in-process inventory was reduced from $1,774,000 to $818,000. The task before Thomas Archer, Tobor Toy's senior manufacturing manager, was to prepare a report for his chief executive officer detailing how these improvements had affected the company's profits.

> **OBJECTIVE 8.6**
>
> Describe the cost savings resulting from reductions in inventories, reduction in production cycle time, production yield improvements, and reductions in rework and defect rates.

Production Flows

Thomas began by obtaining the production flowchart shown in Exhibit 8-11. In the first step, the arms and legs of the robot were produced via an injection-molding process in plastic. To accomplish this, metal molds were designed for each component. A measured amount of polypropylene in the form of granules was fed into a horizontal heated cylinder where it was forced into a closed cold mold by a plunger. The liquid plastic entered the mold by means of a channel that led directly into the mold. Runners fed off the channel and moved the liquid plastic to each individual cavity. On cooling, the plastic took the shape of the mold. The process was designed so that each channel produces enough components for 60 robots.

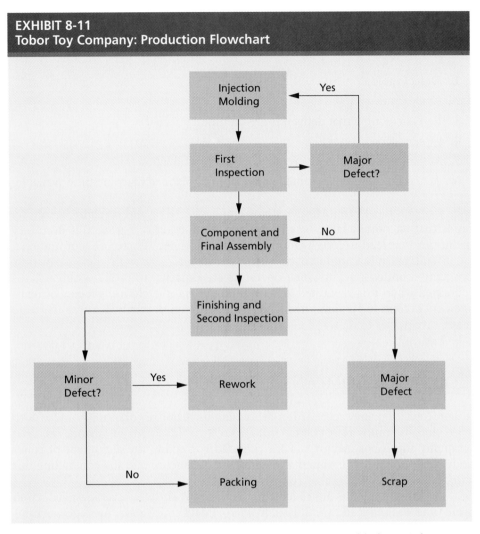

EXHIBIT 8-11
Tobor Toy Company: Production Flowchart

Workers assembled the various components on an assembly line. Other components, such as the computer chip, nylon gears, wheels, and other parts were added as the production process proceeded. At the end of the process, defective robots were rejected and returned for rework or scrapping depending on the defect.

Several finishing operations and inspections were performed next. Any excess plastic, or flashing, from the molding process was eliminated. The toy robot was then polished so that it had a high gloss. As this process was occurring, each robot was inspected. A separate rework area was set aside for workers who were responsible for correcting the defects and inspecting the reworked robots to ensure that no defects remained. Robots that passed inspection, either before or after rework, were packed and became available for shipment to customers.

Effects on Work-in-Process Inventory

Thomas next turned his attention to records for work-in-process inventory. He had already found that the average work-in-process inventory decreased by $956,000 after the implementation of the JIT system. He determined from meetings with production personnel that work-in-process inventory was maintained between each pair of successive process stages because each batch of robots had to await the completion of the work on the preceding batch of robots. Thomas could not find any more detailed records to identify the change in work-in-process inventory among specific stages of the production process. Work-in-process inventory, however, was known to be influenced directly by the number of major and minor defects. When defect rates were high, inventory of rejected robots would build up, awaiting rework or scrap. More importantly, production supervisors sought to accumulate a large inventory of work in process in stages occurring after the two inspection stages to enable them to keep busy even when many robots were rejected. Therefore, production managers attributed the reduction in the work-in-process inventory entirely to improvements in the defect rates.

Impact on Production Costs

An important part of Thomas's analysis was an assessment of the impact that the improvement in defect rates had on production costs. Direct material costs included the cost of the plastic content and the cost of the gears and computer chip in the robot. The average cost of this type of chip in a robot was $58.

Thomas also collected information on direct labor, unit-related overhead, and batch-related overhead costs for each stage of the production process. Exhibit 8-12 includes these costs presented on a unit (robot) basis. Unit-related overhead costs include labor supervision, plastic, gears, chips, and power costs. Batch-related costs for each batch of 60 robots is presented on a unit basis. Batch-related costs include materials handling and setup of molds.

Thomas excluded product-sustaining and facility-sustaining costs from the analysis. There were no new product introductions or deletions as a consequence of the implementation of the JIT system. The installed plant machine capacity was already greater than its maximum use in recent years, and reductions in defect rates increased the surplus capacity even for the Tobor plant. The company had yet to find new products or new markets that could use this excess capacity; that is, it remained as a sunk cost.

EXHIBIT 8-12
Tobor Toy Company: Incremental Conversion
Costs per Robot by Production Stage

	Injection Molding	First Inspection	Component and Final Assembly	Finishing and Second Inspection	Packing
Direct Labor (Including Fringe Benefits)	$14	$10	$20	$8	$6
United-Related Overhead	6	2	12	2	2
Batch-Related Overhead	8	1	2	1	8
Total Costs	$28	$13	$34	$11	$16

This employee was part of an employee involvement group at a Ford Motor Corporation truck plant that discovered that paint marks and smudges were being caused by paint-booth gloves that were too large and cumbersome. This discovery led to the design and use of the less cumbersome gloves, which reduced the rework cost associated with repainting the damaged parts. *Courtesy* Ford Motor Corporation.

Cost of Rework

What is the cost of a major defect detected during the *first inspection* following the injection molding stage? Because a robot with a major defect cannot be processed further, all the incremental conversion costs already incurred on the robot are wasted and all operations must be repeated, therefore incurring the same incremental conversion costs again. Thomas summarized the costs associated with the correction of a major defect as displayed in Exhibit 8-13 and found that they cost $42 per robot.

This estimation includes unit- and batch-related overhead costs because more of these costs would be incurred when all of the mold-making, casting, and first-inspection operations were repeated to rectify the major defect. Because of

EXHIBIT 8-13 Tobor Toy Company: Cost per Unit (Robot) for the Correction of a Major Defect	
Type of Cost	**Amount**
Conversion costs for injection molding:	
Direct labor	$14
Unit-related overhead	9
Batch-related overhead	5
Costs of first inspection:	
Direct labor	10
Unit-related overhead	3
Batch-related overhead	1
Total Costs	$42

the excess capacity situation at the plant, product- and facility-sustaining overhead costs would not increase when repeating production operations. Therefore, they were not relevant for this analysis. However, if the plant and machine capacity had already been fully utilized and there was no slack to accommodate these repeated operations, the incremental costs of acquiring the additional capacity would be a factor to consider in this analysis.

Thomas found it somewhat easier to assess the costs of correcting minor defects, which are detected at the second inspection and do not require the rejection of the entire robot. Instead such minor defects require additional rework operations. Therefore, the incremental costs of correcting minor defects are the rework costs. Thomas determined that the cost of rework per robot comprised the following costs:

Direct rework labor	$24
Unit-related overhead	+12
Total cost	$36

Because each robot is reworked independently of the batch in which it was produced, Thomas determined that there were no batch-related overhead costs. Product- and facility-sustaining overhead costs also were not relevant because of the excess capacity situation.

Tobor manufactures and sells 180,000 robots each year. Before implementation of the JIT system, on average, 10,440 major defects (180,000 × 0.058) and 24,480 minor defects (180,000 × 0.136) occurred each year. Now, only 5940 major defects (180,000 × 0.033) and 12,600 minor defects (180,000 × 0.070) occur, representing a reduction of 4500 and 11,880 defects, respectively. Therefore, the savings in the cost of correcting major and minor defects because of the JIT system are $189,000 for major rework ($42 × 4500) and $427,680 ($11,880 × 36) for minor rework.

	Major defects	*Minor defects*
Before JIT	10,440	24,480
After JIT	5,940	12,600
Reduction	4,500	11,880
Cost per correction	× $42	× $36
JIT cost reduction	$189,000	$427,680

Cost of Carrying Work-in-Process Inventory

Thomas turned next to the problem of evaluating the cost savings resulting from the reduction in the amount of work-in-process inventory. Interest rates on bank loans to finance the investment in inventories averaged 12.5% per year. With a reduction of $956,000 in work-in-process inventory (1,774,000 − $818,000), the cost of financing also decreased by $119,500 (956,000 × 0.125).

In addition, Thomas estimated that batch-related overhead costs for various production stages included a total cost of $30 per batch (of 60 robots) that pertained to activities such as work in process, inventory handling, and storage. With the 53.89% reduction in work-in-process inventory [100 × (956,000 ÷ 1,774,000)], Thomas expected these related costs also to decrease by about 30%, or equivalently by about $9 per batch ($30 × 0.30). With an annual production of 180,000 robots in 3000 batches (180,000 ÷ 60), Thomas expected a decrease of $27,000 in the costs of work-in-process inventory handling and storage costs ($9 × 3000). As in the case of Glendale Electric Corporation, however, Thomas's estimate of $27,000 represented the reduction in the demand for these activities because of the reduction in work-in-process inventory. Over time, these costs should decrease by this amount. But for the reduction to actually occur, the plant management must identify the personnel and other resources committed to this activity and eliminate the resources not required because of the reduction in the demand for them.

Benefits from Increased Sales

Thomas finally decided to evaluate whether the reduction in the production cycle time had resulted in any gains in sales. For this purpose, he met with the marketing manager, Paul Genus. Paul pointed out that annual sales had remained stable

Customer complaints that paper rolls supplied by Consolidated Papers were breaking in their printing presses led a group of employees at Consolidated Papers to identify the cause. The employees discovered that the breakage occurred because of slight tears at the edges of the paper created when the paper was being trimmed to width during its production. The solution was to design a simple device that held the paper tightly while it was being slit. The cost of this investigation and the device designed to eliminate the problem was justified on the grounds that failing to solve the problem would have cost the company far more in lost sales. *Courtesy* **Consolidated Papers, Inc.**

at around 180,000 robots for the past three years. However, he believed that the improvement in the production cycle time did have an impact on sales. Because of the increased competition in the robot market, Paul had expected to lose sales of about 2000 robots. But the reduction of 6.5 days in the production cycle time had permitted him to respond more aggressively to market demand by offering the robots to customers with a much shorter lead time. As a result, Tobor had not lost any market share in this market segment. Paul believed that the shorter production cycle time led to maintaining sales of about 2000 robots that otherwise would have been lost.

Thomas determined that the average net selling price (the net of sales commission and shipping costs) for these 2000 robots was $400. Exhibit 8-14 presents his list of the incremental costs for the production of these robots.

Notice in Exhibit 8-14 that rework costs are prorated over the good units of production. For instance, incremental costs for major rework are $42 for each robot that requires rework. For every 1000 robots an average of 33 robots (1000 $\times$ 3.3%) now require major rework. Therefore, the company obtains 967 good robots (1000 $-$ 33). The total incremental major rework cost for 33 robots is $1386 ($42 $\times$ 33), which is borne by the 967 good robots at the rate of $1.43 (1386 $\div$ 967) per good robot.

The contribution margin is estimated to be $54 per robot, or $108,000 in total for the 2000 robots ($54 $\times$ 2000). Without the JIT system and the consequent reduction in cycle time, this contribution from sales would have been lost. This benefit is attributable to the program being evaluated, like the contribution margin on the sales increase in the case study of the plant layout changes at Glendale Electric Corporation.

EXHIBIT 8-14
Tobor Toy Company: Incremental Costs of Production per Robot

Type of Cost	Cost per Robot
Direct materials:	
Chip	$58.00
All others	32.00
Incremental conversion costs:	
Injection molding	28.00
First inspection	13.00
Component and final assembly	34.00
Second inspection	11.00
Packing	16.00
Prorated rework costs:	
Major defects*	1.40
Minor defects†	2.70
Total incremental costs	$196.10
Average net sales price	$250.00
Contribution margin per robot	$53.90

* $\frac{3.3}{100 - 3.3} \times \$42 = \$1.43$

† $\frac{7}{100 - 7} \times \$36 = \$2.71$

> **EXHIBIT 8-15**
> **Tobor Toy Company: Summary of Annual Benefits Resulting from the JIT System**
>
> | | | |
> |---|---:|---:|
> | Reduction in rework costs: | | |
> | Major rework | $189,000 | |
> | Minor rework | 427,680 | $616,680 |
> | Reduction in work-in-process inventory-related costs: | | |
> | Financing costs | $107,000 | |
> | Inventory handling and storage activity costs | 27,000 | 134,000 |
> | Contribution from sales increases resulting from | | 108,000 |
> | improved production cycle time | | $858,680 |

Summary of Costs and Benefits

Exhibit 8-15 displays Thomas's summary of the benefits from the quality-improvement program. Total estimated annual benefits of $858,680 are much greater than the one-time costs of $300,000 spent on the JIT system and worker training discussed in the opening vignette to this chapter.

A SUMMARY EXAMPLE

VoiceTek Corporation is a major producer of telephone products. The corporation is considering introducing a videophone that will be targeted for the business market. The proposed price is $1000 per unit. The following cost information is based on the expected annual sales level of 60,000 units for the new product:

$18,000,000	direct material cost
12,000,000	direct labor costs
6,000,000	variable manufacturing overhead
10,000,000	fixed manufacturing overhead

The average inventory levels for the videophone are estimated to be as follows:

Direct material	2 months of production
Work-in-process	2 months of production
(100% complete for materials and 50% for labor and variable manufacturing overhead)	
Finished goods	1 month of production

Annual inventory carrying costs, not included in these variable costs, are estimated to be 10%. In addition, the marketing manager estimates that the total sales revenue of the existing products will be reduced by $12,000,000 once the videophone is on the market. The average contribution margin ratio for the existing products is 30%.

(a) Compute the relevant costs (revenues) for the videophone.

(b) Should VoiceTek introduce the new product?

(c) Determine the breakeven point in units for the videophone.

The following information presents the solution to this problem.

(a) Selling price per unit $1000

   Less:
   Variable cost per unit
      Direct materials
         $18,000,000 ÷ 60,000 = $300
      Direct labor
         $12,000,000 ÷ 60,000 = $200
      Overhead
         $6,000,000 ÷ 60,000 = $100

      Total $600

$$\frac{-600}{}$$

   Contribution margin per unit $400

   Inventory carrying value
      Direct materials
         $300 × 60,000 units × $\frac{2}{12}$ = $3,000,000

      Work in process
         {$300 + [(200 + 100) × 50%]} × 60,000 × $\frac{2}{12}$ = $4,500,000

      Finished goods
         ($300 + 200 + 100) × 60,000 × $\frac{1}{12}$ = $3,000,000

      Inventory carrying cost
         ($3,000,000 + $4,500,000 + $3,000,000) × 10% = $1,050,000

   Relevant costs
      Increase in contribution margin for sale of videophone
         $400 × 60,000 = $24,000,000
      Decrease in contribution margin from cannibalization of existing sales
         $12,000,000 × 30% = $3,600,000
      Additional inventory carrying costs
         $1,050,000
      Increase in fixed manufacturing overhead
         $10,000,000

(b) Increase in VoiceTek's operating profit
         $24,000,000 − $3,600,000 − $1,050,000 − $10,000,000 = $9,350,000

   Therefore, VoiceTek should introduce the videophone.

(c) Let X be the breakeven point in units.

$$\$400 \times X = \$10,000,000 + \$3,600,000 + (\$300 \times X \times \frac{2}{12} + 450$$
$$\times X \times \frac{2}{12} + \$600 \times X \times \frac{1}{12}) \times 0.1$$
$$\$382.5X = \$13,600,000$$
$$X = 35,556 \text{ units}$$

SUMMARY

An important component of the management accountant's responsibility is to evaluate the impact of managerial decisions and actions that affect the organization's activities and processes. To support decision making, it is necessary to identify different alternatives available to managers as well as to evaluate how costs and revenues differ across alternative actions. Relevant costs and revenues are those costs and revenues that differ across the alternative choices available to managers. As a general rule, sunk costs are not relevant costs.

Management accountants must also be able to evaluate the financial impact of recent activity and process decisions, such as improved plant layouts that streamline production operations. Different types of costs and other financial information are required to assist in the evaluation of various decisions affecting an organization's activities and processes. Finally, detailed evaluations of implemented actions may shed light on ways to increase the benefits derived from them.

The JIT manufacturing system has many positive effects on the levels of work-in-process inventory, the cost of support activities of handling and storing work-in-process inventory, and the amounts of major and minor rework. Further, it reduces cycle times so that there are shorter lead times to fulfilling customer orders. All these changes have a very tangible bottom-line effect.

KEY TERMS

avoidable costs, p. 365

cellular manufacturing, p. 371

certified supplier, p. 368

just-in-time manufacturing, p. 380

make-or-buy decision, p. 364

manufacturing cycle efficiency
  (MCE),   p. 374

outsourcing, p. 365

process layout, p. 368

processing time, p. 373

product layout, p. 369

sunk costs, p. 361

■ QUESTIONS

8-1 Why should decision makers focus only on the relevant costs for decision making?

8-2 Are sunk costs relevant? Explain.

8-3 Are direct materials and direct labor costs always relevant? Explain with examples.

8-4 When are (1) product-sustaining and (2) facility-sustaining costs relevant? Give examples of each case.

8-5 Why can't we directly compare cash flows at different points in time?

8-6 What behavioral factors may influence some managers to consider sunk costs as being relevant in their decisions?

8-7 Are avoidable costs relevant? Explain.

8-8 Give two examples of costs and decision contexts in which the costs are not relevant for a short-term context but are relevant for a long-term context.

8-9 Why are facility-sustaining support costs often not relevant for make-or-buy decisions? Give an example when facility-sustaining support costs are relevant for a make-or-buy decision.

8-10 What qualitative considerations are relevant in a make-or-buy decision?

8-11 What are the opportunity costs that are relevant in a make-or-buy decision?

8-12 What is the difference between process and product layout systems?

8-13 What is cellular manufacturing?

8-14 How is a just-in-time manufacturing different from a conventional manufacturing system?

8-15 What creates the need to maintain work-in-process inventory? Why is work-in-process inventory likely to decrease on the implementation of (a) cellular manufacturing, (b) just-in-time production, and (c) quality-improvement programs?

8-16 Why are production cycle time and the level of work-in-process inventory positively related?

8-17 List two types of costs incurred when implementing a cellular manufacturing layout.

8-18 What are two types of financial benefits resulting from a shift to cellular manufacturing, just-in-time production, or continuous-quality improvements?

8-19 What is the additional cost of replacing one unit of a product rejected at inspection and scrapped?

8-20 What is the additional cost if a unit rejected at inspection can be reworked to meet quality standards by performing some additional operations?

8-21 What costs and revenues are relevant in evaluating the profit impact of an increase in sales?

8-22 "Design an accounting system that routinely reports only relevant costs," advised a management consultant. Is this good advice? Explain.

■ EXERCISES

8-23 *Relevant costs* Don Baxter's five-year-old Camaro requires repairs estimated at $5400 to make it roadworthy again. His friend, Mike Blue, suggested that he buy a five-year-old Chevette instead for $5400 cash. Mike estimated the following costs for the two cars:

Costs	Camaro	Chevette
Acquisition cost	$24,000	$5,400
Repairs	5,400	0
Annual operating costs:		
Gas, maintenance, insurance	2,900	1,800

REQUIRED

(a) What costs are relevant and what costs are not relevant for this decision? Why?

(b) What should Don do? Explain.

(c) What quantitative and qualitative factors are relevant for his decision? Why?

8-24 *Relevant costs* Gilmark Company has 10,000 obsolete lamps carried in inventory at a cost of $12 each. They can be sold as they are for $4 each. They can be reworked, however, at a total cost $55,000 and sold for $10 each. Determine whether it is worthwhile to rework these lamps.

8-25 *Sunk costs* Ideal Company's plant manager is considering buying a new grinding machine to replace an old grinding machine or overhauling the old one to ensure compliance with the plant's high quality standards. The following data are available:

Old grinding machine	
Original cost	$50,000
Accumulated depreciation	40,000
Annual operating costs	18,000
Current salvage value	4,000
Salvage value at the end of 5 years	0
New grinding machine	
Cost	$70,000
Annual operating costs	13,000
Salvage value at the end of 5 years	0
Overhaul of old grinding machine	
Cost of overhaul	$25,000
Annual operating costs after overhaul	14,000
Salvage value at the end of 5 years	0

REQUIRED

(a) What costs should the decision maker consider as sunk costs?
(b) List all relevant costs and when they are incurred.
(c) What should the plant manager do? Why?

8-26 *Make versus buy* The assembly division of Cassandra Resolution, Inc., is bidding on an order of 1000 TV sets. The division is very anxious to get this order since it has a substantial amount of unused plant capacity. The variable cost for each TV set is $600 in addition to the cost of the picture tube. The divisional purchasing manager has received two bids for the tube. One is from Cassandra Resolution's picture tube division. This bid is for $55 per picture tube, although its variable cost is only $42 per tube. The other is from an outside vendor for $65 per unit. Cassandra Resolution's picture tube division has sufficient unused capacity for this order.

REQUIRED

(a) Determine the relevant costs for this order for the assembly division under both internal and outsourcing arrangements.

(b) Determine the relevant costs for this order for Cassandra Resolution as a company under each of the sourcing arrangements.

8-27 *Make versus buy* Kane Company is considering outsourcing a key component. A reliable supplier has quoted a price of $64.50 per unit. The following costs of the component when manufactured in-house are expressed on a per-unit basis.

Direct materials	$23.40
Direct labor	16.10
Unit-related overhead	14.70
Batch-related overhead	9.80
Product-sustaining overhead	22.20
Facility-sustaining overhead	6.90
	$93.10

REQUIRED

(a) What assumptions need to be made about the behavior of overhead costs for Kane?

(b) Should Kane Company outsource the component?

(c) What other factors are relevant for this decision?

8-28 *Cellular manufacturing and cost savings* Laver Company is considering reorganizing its plant into manufacturing cells. The following estimates have been prepared to assess the potential benefits from the change:

Category	Before the Change	After the Change
Production cycle time	68 days	32 days
Work-in-process inventory	$160,000	$105,000
Total sales	$1,260,000	$1,690,000
Costs as percent of sales:		
Direct materials	30%	26%
Direct labor	22%	21%
Variable overhead	28%	22%
Fixed overhead	12%	8%

Inventory financing costs are 12% per year. Estimate the total benefits likely to result from the switch to cellular manufacturing operations.

8-29 *Quality improvement programs and cost savings* Pyro Valves Company manufactures brass valves meeting precise specification standards. All finished valves are inspected before packing and shipping to customers. Rejected valves are returned to the initial production stage to be melted and recast. As a result of a quality-improvement program, the reject rate has decreased from 6.4% to 5.1%. The following unit cost data are available:

Costs	Casting	Finishing	Inspection	Packing	Total
Direct materials	$225	$ 12	$ 0	$ 8	$ 245
Direct labor	84	121	24	16	245
Variable overhead	122	164	30	20	336
Fixed overhead	63	89	16	10	178
	$494	$386	$70	$54	$1,004

Improvements in reject rates have also led to a decrease in work-in-process inventory from $386,000 to $270,000. Inventory carrying costs are estimated to be 15% per year. Estimate the annual cost savings as a result of the quality improvement, assuming that Pyro sells 10,000 valves each year.

8-30 *Relevant costs in the make versus buy decision*   Premier Company manufactures gear model G37 used in several of its farm-equipment products. Annual production volume of G37 is 20,000 units. Unit costs for G37 are as follows:

Direct materials costs	$ 55
Direct labor costs	30
Variable overhead costs	25
Fixed overhead costs	15
	$125

Alternatively, Premier can also purchase gear model G37 from an outside supplier for $120 per unit. If G37 is outsourced, Premier can use the facility where G37 is currently manufactured for production of another gear—model G49. This would save Premier $113,000 in facility rental and other costs presently incurred. Should Premier make or buy G37?

8-31 *Relevant costs and revenues*   Joyce Printers, Inc., is considering replacing its current printing machines with newer, faster, and more efficient printing technology. The following data have been compiled:

Category	Existing Machines	New Machines
Original cost	$80,000	$120,000
Annual operating costs	$50,000	$30,000
Remaining useful life	5 years	5 years
Salvage value after 5 years	$5,000	$10,000

The existing machines can be disposed of now for $40,000. Keeping them will cost $20,000 for repair and upgrading. Should Joyce Printers keep the existing printing machines? Explain.

8-32 *Relevant costs for decision making*   Kentucky Motors has manufactured compressor parts at its plant in Pitcairn, Indiana, for the last 18 years. An outside supplier, Superior Compressor Company, has offered to supply compressor model A238 at a price of $200 per unit. Unit manufacturing costs for A238 are as follows:

Direct materials	$ 80
Direct labor	60
Unit-related overhead	26
Batch-related overhead	22
Product-sustaining overhead	8
Facility-sustaining overhead	17
	$213

REQUIRED

    (a) Should Superior Compressor's offer be accepted if the plant is presently operating below capacity?

    (b) What is the maximum acceptable purchase price if the plant facilities are fully utilized at present and if any additional available capacity can be deployed for the production of other compressors?

8-33 *Facilities layout* How would you classify the layout of a large grocery store? Why do you think it is laid out this way? Can you think of any way to improve the layout of a conventional grocery store? Explain your reasoning. (Hint: Think about JIT, Cycle time, etc.)

■ PROBLEMS

Fundamental Problems

8-34 *Relevant costs and revenues: changes in facilities layout* To facilitate a move toward JIT production, SMY Company is considering a change in its plant layout. The plant controller, Anita West, has been asked to evaluate the costs and benefits of the change in plant layout. After meeting with production and marketing managers, Anita has compiled the following estimates:

■ Machine moving and reinstallation will cost $100,000.

■ Total sales will increase by 20% to $1,200,000 because of a decrease in production cycle time required under the new plant layout. Average contribution margin is 31% of sales.

■ Inventory-related costs will decrease by 25% because of expected decrease in work-in-process inventory. Presumably, the annual average carrying value of work-in-process inventory is $200,000. The annual inventory financing cost is 15%.

Should SMY implement the proposed change in plant layout? Support your answer.

8-35 *Relevant costs in the make versus buy decision* O'Connor Appliance Company manufactures 12,000 units of part BYKA4 annually. The part is used in the production of one of its principal products. The following unit cost information is available on part BYKA4.

Direct materials	$11
Direct labor	9
Unit-related overhead	4
Batch-related overhead	5
Product-sustaining overhead	2
Facility-sustaining overhead	2
Allocated corporate overhead	5
	$38

A potential supplier has offered to manufacture this part for O'Connor Appliance for $30 per unit. If O'Connor Appliance outsources the production of part BYKA4, 50% of batch-related and 80% of product-sustaining activity resources can be eliminated. Furthermore, the production facility now being used to produce this part can be used for a fast-growing new product line that would otherwise require the use of a neighboring facility at a rental cost of $20,000 per year. Should O'Connor Appliance purchase part BYKA4 from the outside supplier? What costs are relevant for this decision? What additional factors should O'Connor consider?

8-36 *Relevant costs: replacement decision* Anderson Department Stores is considering the replacement of the existing elevator system at its downtown store. A new system has been proposed that runs faster than the existing system, experiences few break-downs and, as a result, promises considerable savings in operating costs. Information on the existing system and the proposed new system follow:

Category	Existing System	New System
Original cost	$300,000	$875,000
Remaining life	6 years	6 years
Annual cash operating costs	$150,000	$8,000
Salvage value at present	$100,000	$0
Salvage value in 6 years	$25,000	$100,000

REQUIRED

(a) What costs are not relevant for this decision?
(b) What are the relevant costs?

8-37 *Incremental revenues and costs*   Genis Battery Company is considering accepting a special order for 50,000 batteries that it received from a discount retail store. The order specified a price of $4.00 per unit, which reflects a discount of $0.50 per unit relative to the company's regular price of $4.50 per unit. Genis' accounting department has pre-pared the following analysis to show the cost savings resulting from additional sales:

Costs	Cost per Unit without the Additional Sales (100,000 units)	Cost per Unit with the Additional Sales (150,000 units)
Variable	$3.30	$3.30
Fixed	0.90	0.60
	$4.20	$3.90

No additional fixed costs will be incurred for this order because the company has sur-plus capacity. Because the average cost per unit will be reduced from $4.20 to $3.90, Genis' president believes that a reduction in the price to $4.00 is justified for this order.

REQUIRED

(a) Should the order for the 50,000 units at a price of $4 be accepted? What will be the impact on Genis's operating income?
(b) Is the accounting department's analysis the best way to evaluate this decision? If not, what alternative method can you suggest?
(c) What other considerations are important in this case? Why?

8-38 *Relevant costs: replacement decision*   Syd Young, the production manager at Fuchow Company, purchased a cutting machine for the company last year. Six months after the purchase of the cutting machine, Syd learned about a new cutting machine that is more reliable than the machine that he purchased. The following information is avail-able for the two machines:

Category	Old Machine	New Machine
Acquisition cost	$300,000	$360,000
Remaining life	4 years	4 years
Disposal value now	$100,000	$0
Salvage value at the end of 4 years	$4,000	$6,000

Annual operating costs for the old machine are $140,000. The new machine will de-crease annual operating costs by $60,000. These amounts do not include any charges for depreciation. Fuchow Company uses the straight-line depreciation method. These estimates of operating costs exclude rework costs. The new machine will also result in a reduction in the defect rate from the current 5% to 2.5%. All defective units are re-worked at a cost of $1 per unit. The company, on average, produces on average 100,000 units annually.

REQUIRED

(a) Should Syd Young replace the old machine with the new machine? Explain, list-ing all relevant costs.
(b) What costs should be considered as sunk costs for this decision?
(c) What other factors may affect Young's decision?

8-39 *Cycle time efficiency and JIT*   Walker Brothers Company is considering installing a JIT manufacturing system in the hope that it will improve their overall manufacturing cycle efficiency. Data from the traditional system and estimates for the JIT system are presented below for their Nosun Product:

Time Category	Traditional System	JIT System
Storage	4 hours	1 hour
Inspection	40 minutes	5 minutes
Moving	80 minutes	20 minutes
Processing	2 hours	75 minutes

REQUIRED

(a) Calculate manufacturing-cycle efficiency under the traditional and JIT systems for the Nosun Product.
(b) Strictly based on your MCE calculations above, should Walker Brothers imple-ment the JIT system? Explain.

8-40 *JIT and cellular manufacturing*   You are a manufacturing manager faced with the decision to improve manufacturing operations and efficiency. You have been studying both cellular manufacturing and just-in-time manufacturing systems. Your boss ex-pects you to prepare a report covering the costs and benefits of each approach.

REQUIRED

(a) Write a detailed memorandum discussing the costs and benefits of cellular manu-facturing versus JIT.
(b) Which approach do you favor from (1) a customer's perspective and (2) from management's perspective? Explain.

Challenging Problems

8-41 *Relevant costs: replacement decision*   Rossman Instruments, Inc., is considering leas-ing new state-of-the-art machinery at an annual cost of $900,000. The new machinery has a four-year expected life. It will replace existing machinery leased one year earlier at an annual lease cost of $490,000 committed for five years. Early termination of this lease contract will incur a $280,000 penalty. There are no other fixed costs.

The new machinery is expected to decrease variable product costs from $42 to $32 per unit because of improved-materials yield, faster machine speed, and lower direct labor, supervision, materials handling, and quality-inspection requirements. The sales price will remain at $56. Improvements in quality, production cycle time, and customer responsiveness are expected to increase annual sales from 36,000 units to 48,000 units.

The variable product costs stated earlier exclude the inventory-carrying costs. Because the new machinery is expected to affect inventory levels, the following estimates are also provided. The enhanced speed and accuracy of the new machinery are expected to decrease production cycle time by half, and consequently, lead to a decrease in work-in-process inventory level from three months to just one and one-half months of production. Increased flexibility with these new machines is expected to allow a reduction in finished goods inventory from two months of production to just one month. Improved yield rates and greater machine reliability will enable a reduction in raw materials inventory from four months of production to just one and one-half months. Annual inventory carrying cost is 20% of inventory value.

Category	Old Machine	New Machine
Average per unit cost of raw materials inventory	$12	$11
Average per unit cost of work-in-process inventory	25	20
Average per unit cost of finished-goods inventory	38	28
Selling cost per unit sold	4	4
Variable product cost per unit produced	42	32

REQUIRED

(a) Determine the total value of annual benefits from the new machinery. Include changes in inventory carrying costs.
(b) Should Rossman replace its existing machinery with the new machinery? Present your reasoning with detailed steps identifying relevant costs and revenues.
(c) Discuss whether a manager evaluated on the basis of Rossman's net income will have the incentive to make the right decision as evaluated in (b) above.

8-42 *Relevant costs: dropping a product* Merchant Company manufactures and sells three models of electronic printers. Ken Gail, president of the company, is considering dropping model JT484 from its product line because the company has experienced losses for this product over the last three quarters. The following product-level operating data have been compiled for the most recent quarter:

Category	Total	JT284	JT384	JT484
Sales	$1,000,000	$500,000	$200,000	$300,000
Variable costs	600,000	300,000	100,000	200,000
Contribution margin	$ 400,000	$200,000	$100,000	$100,000
Fixed costs:				
Rent	$ 50,000	$ 25,000	$ 10,000	$ 15,000
Depreciation	60,000	30,000	12,000	18,000
Utilities	40,000	20,000	5,000	15,000
Supervision	50,000	15,000	5,000	30,000
Maintenance	30,000	15,000	6,000	9,000
Administrative	100,000	30,000	20,000	50,000
Total fixed costs	$ 330,000	$135,000	$ 58,000	$137,000
Operating income loss	$ 70,000	$ 65,000	$ 42,000	($37,000)

In addition, the following information is also available:

■ Factory rent and depreciation will not be affected by a decision to drop model JT484.

■ Quarterly utility bills will be reduced from $40,000 to $31,000 if JT484 is dropped.

- Supervision costs for JT484 can be eliminated if dropped.
- The maintenance department will be able to reduce quarterly costs by $7000 if JT484 is dropped.
- Elimination of JT484 will make it possible to eliminate two administrative staff positions with combined salaries of $30,000 per quarter.

REQUIRED

(a) Should Merchant Company eliminate JT484?
(b) Merchant's sales manager believes that it is important to continue to produce JT484 to maintain a full product line. He expects the elimination of JT484 will reduce sales of the remaining two products by 5% each. Will this information change your answer to (a)? Explain.

8-43 *Relevant costs: introducing a new product* Macready Company is considering introducing a new model of personal compact disk players at a price of $105 per unit. Its controller has compiled the following incremental cost information based on an estimate of 120,000 units of sales annually for the new product:

Direct materials cost	$3,600,000
Direct labor cost	$2,400,000
Variable manufacturing overhead	$1,200,000
Sales commission	10% of sales
Fixed cost	$2,000,000

The average inventory levels for the new product are estimated as follows:

Raw materials	2 months of production
Work in progress (100% complete for materials and 50% complete for labor and variable manufacturing overhead)	1 month of production
Finished goods	2 months of production

Annual inventory carrying costs not included in the variable-manufacturing overhead listed earlier are estimated to be 12% of inventory value. In addition, the sales manager expects the introduction of the new model to result in a reduction in sales of the existing model from 300,000 to 240,000 units. The contribution margin for the old product is $20 per unit.

REQUIRED

(a) Determine the total impact on Macready's profit from the introduction of the new product.
(b) Should Macready introduce the new product? Explain.
(c) Determine the breakeven point (in units) for the new product. Assume that sales of the old product decrease by one unit for every two-unit increase in the sales of the new product.

8-44 *Cellular manufacturing and cycle time efficiency* Ray Brown's company, Whisper Voice Systems, is trying to increase its manufacturing cycle efficiency (MCE). Because Ray has a very limited budget, he has been searching for a way to increase his MCE by using cellular manufacturing. One of Ray's manufacturing managers, Maria Lopez, has been studying cellular manufacturing and claims that with minimal cost that includes downtime in the operation she can rearrange existing machinery and workers and improve MCE. Ray is quite skeptical about this and decides to allow Maria to rearrange a small part of his operation. In order for Ray to be satisfied, he has stated that MCE must increase by 12%. MCE data before and after the rearrangement are presented below.

Time Category	Before Rearrangement	After Rearrangement
Inspection	30 minutes	15 minutes
Moving	45 minutes	10 minutes
Processing	70 minutes	30 minutes
Storage	55 minutes	20 minutes

REQUIRED

(a) Does the change in MCE meet Ray's requirement? Why or why not?

8-45 *Facilities layout*   One aspect of facilities layout for McDonald's is that when customers come into the building they can line up in one of several lines and wait to be served. In contrast, at Wendy's customers are asked to stand in one line that snakes around the front of the counter and wait for a single server.

REQUIRED

(a) What is the rationale for each approach?
(b) Which approach do you favor from (1) a customer's perspective and (2) from management's perspective? Explain.

■ CASE

8-46 *Relevant costs and revenues; marketing channels*   Diamond Bicycle Company manufactures and sells bicycles nationwide through marketing channels ranging from sporting goods stores to specialty bicycle shops. Diamond's average selling price to its distributors is $185 per bicycle. The bicycles are retailed to customers for $349.

After several years of high sales, Diamond's sales have slumped to 160,000 bicycles per year in the last three years, which is only 70% of its manufacturing capacity. Diamond expects the demand for its products to remain the same in the next few years.

Premier Stores, a nationwide chain of discount retail stores, has recently approached Diamond to manufacture bicycles for Premier to sell. Premier has offered to purchase 40,000 bicycles annually for a three-year period at $125 per bicycle. It is not willing to pay a higher price because it plans to retail the bicycles at only $200. Diamond has not previously sold bicycles through any marketing channel other than specialty stores.

Mike Diamond is the chief executive officer of Diamond Bicycle. Although Premier's offer is well below Diamond's normal price, Mike is interested in the offer because Diamond has considerable surplus capacity. He has been supplied with the following variable product cost information:

Direct material costs	$50
Direct labor costs	30
Variable manufacturing overhead costs	25
	$105

The direct materials includes $2 for embossing Premier's private label on the bicycle.

Fixed overhead costs total $2,000,000 annually. Diamond also pays a 10% commission on sales to its sales staff but will not need to pay any salesperson for the special sale to Premier. Average inventory levels for Premier's offer are estimated to be as follows:

Type of Inventory	Inventory Level
Raw materials	1 month of supplies
Work in process	1.5 months of supplies (100% complete for materials and 50% complete for other variable manufacturing costs)
Finished goods	0.5 month of supplies

Annual inventory carrying cost is estimated to be 10% of the inventory carrying value. Premier's offer requires Diamond to deliver bicycles to Premier's regional warehouse so that Premier can have ready access to an inventory of bicycles to meet fluctuating market demand. Diamond estimated that about 5% of Diamond's present sales will be lost if Premier's offer is accepted because some customers will comparison-shop and find the same quality bicycle available at a lower price in Premier stores.

REQUIRED

(a) Should Mike Diamond accept Premier's offer?
(b) What strategic and other factors should be considered before Mike makes a final decision?

9

BUDGETING: RESOURCE ALLOCATION TO ACHIEVE ORGANIZATIONAL OBJECTIVES

THE LEGAL SERVICES DEPARTMENT

© Dawson Jones/Stock Boston, Inc.

Fred Powell, the manager of a government department known as the Legal Services Department, was feeling a great deal of pressure. His department provides legal advice to other government departments and agencies. Although unable to increase taxes, the government was facing increasing pressures to reduce its deficit while also engaging in continuing rounds of budget cuts. Last year all departments had their allocations cut by 7%; this year it was 5%. Fred expected the trend to continue.

In the face of these funding cuts, the Legal Services Department was experiencing continuous increases in the demand for legal services. The funding cuts, combined with the increasing pressure on the remaining resources, were creating enormous pressures in the Legal Services Department. These pressures were now prompting resignations within the department, and because of the job stress created by chronic underfunding, Fred was starting to lose long-term employees whom he valued. He knew he had to do something but wondered if he was powerless in a world in which he controlled neither the allocations of funds nor the rate of demand on his department.

Like most managers, Fred Powell found himself in a position that required a systematic and comprehensive approach to planning.

DETERMINING THE LEVELS OF COMMITTED AND FLEXIBLE RESOURCES

Thus far we have discussed costs as they relate to short- and long-term decisions. Those that varied with the activity level in the firm were referred to as variable, or *flexible*, costs, while those that did not change with changes in activity levels were referred to as fixed, or *committed*, costs. In many business decisions, especially those made in the short term, committed costs are usually thought of as given and thus most relevant costs are flexible costs. In an ideal situation, the supply of committed resources is determined based on the demands for the services provided for projected levels of product volumes and mix. The budgeting process also illustrates that some resources, once acquired, cannot be disposed of easily if demand is less than expected. In this chapter, we discuss the budgeting process—the process that determines the level of most committed costs. The evaluation of these longer-term resources will be discussed in Chapter 10 on Capital Budgeting.

THE BUDGETING PROCESS

OBJECTIVE 9.1

Understand the primary role of budgets and budgeting in organizations.

At one time or another, most members of households have developed a financial plan that guides them in allocating their resources over a specific period of time. Usually, the plan reflects spending priorities and demands, including specific categories in which money will be spent such as the mortgage, utilities, property taxes, and essential items like food and clothing. Family budgets often are the result of negotiations between parents, children, and others reflecting their different needs and objectives. For instance, money left over after required spending on food, clothing, medicine, insurance, and housing may go into savings or be used for other purposes; one parent may want to use most of the remaining disposable income for a trip abroad, while the other may want to use the money to paint the house. Within the same household, a teenager may ask the parents for help in financing the purchase of a used car. The family budget is a planning tool, but it is also serves as control on the behavior of family members by setting limits on what can be spent within each budget category. Without a budget, families have no way of knowing how much and where their money is being spent. Such a situation can easily lead a family into unexpected debt and severe financial difficulties.

Budgets play a similar planning and control role for managers within business units and are a central part of the design and operation of management accounting systems. Exhibit 9-1 shows the central role played by budgets and the relationship between planning and control. Note that there are distinct but linked steps for each function—three for planning and two for control.

As in a household, budgets in organizations reflect in quantitative terms how to allocate financial resources to each organizational subunit based on its activities and short-run objectives. For example, a branch manager of a bank may want to increase local market share, which may require a larger spending budget from the previous year in order to increase the amount of local advertising, implement a training program among the staff to increase its efforts to improve customer service, and renovate the building to make it more appealing to customers. Thus, a **budget** is a quantitative expression of the money inflows and outflows to determine whether a financial plan will meet organizational objectives. **Budgeting** is the process of preparing budgets.

Budget
A quantitative expression of the money inflows and outflows to determine whether a financial plan will meet organizational goals.

Budgeting
The process of preparing budgets.

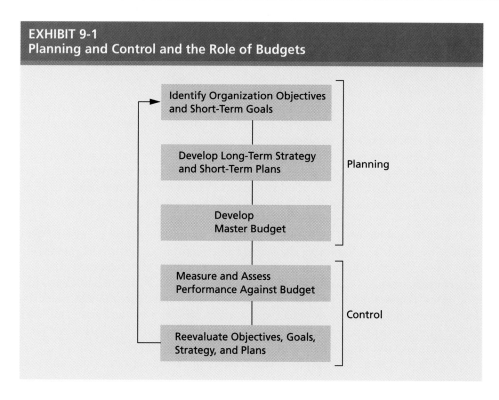

EXHIBIT 9-1
Planning and Control and the Role of Budgets

Budgets also provide a means to *communicate* the organization's short-term goals to its members. Budgeting activities of organization units can reflect how well unit managers understand the organization's goals and provide an opportunity for the organization's senior planners to correct misperceptions about the organization's goals. For example, suppose that an organization recognized quality as a critical success factor and wanted to promote quality awareness. If a department prepared a budget that reflected no expenditures on employee quality training, a senior planner would recognize that the importance of quality training had not been communicated properly.

Budgeting also serves to coordinate the organization's many activities. For example, budgets show the effect of sales levels on acquisition, production, and administrative activities and on the number of employees that need to be hired to serve customers. Therefore, budgeting is a tool that forces coordination of the organization's activities and helps identify coordination problems. Suppose, for example, that the sales force plans to significantly expand sales. By comparing selling plans with manufacturing capacity, planners may discover that the manufacturing operations are unable to support the planned level of sales. High-speed computers are invaluable in this coordination role because they allow planners to simulate easily the impact of different decisions on the organization's financial, human, and physical resources. Simulation, or what-if, analysis helps managers choose a course of action among many alternatives by identifying a decision's consequences in a complex system with many interdependencies.

By considering interrelationships among operating issues, budgeting can provide an indication of potential problems and can serve as a tool to help provide solutions to these problems. For example, organizations such as canneries that engage in seasonal production must invest large amounts of cash in inventory during the canning season. Then during the year the organization sells its inventory and recovers cash. Budgeting reflects this cycle and provides information to help the organization plan the borrowing needed to finance the inventory buildup early in this cycle. If budget planning indicates that the organization's sales potential exceeds its manufacturing potential, the organization can develop a plan to put more capacity in place or to reduce planned sales. The ability to identify potential problems early is important as it usually takes organizations several months to several years to put new capacity in place.

Budgets are prepared for specific time periods to allow managers to compare actual results for the period with planned results. Differences between actual results and the budget plan are called **variances.** Variances provide a signal that operations did not go as planned. Variances are a part of a larger control system for monitoring results. Supervisory staff often use variances as an overall check on how well the people who are managing the day-to-day operations are discharging their responsibilities. Variances also show the effectiveness of the control systems that operations people are using and the organization's effectiveness relative to other organizations. Other types of information, such as trends in actual production rates, numbers of defects and yields, and cycle times, provide additional information to help employees detect and correct problems as they arise and learn about and improve operations. We will develop the role of information for feedback, learning, and improvement in more detail in Chapter 11.

Variance
The difference between actual results and the budget plan.

Budgeting generally requires three types of resources over different time periods:

1. Flexible resources that give rise to variable costs. These can be acquired or disposed of in the short term.
2. Intermediate-term committed resources that give rise to fixed costs.
3. Long-term committed resources that give rise to fixed costs.

In the next section we will discuss the overall framework for budgeting in organizations. The discussion will begin with the budgeting process and lead to formulation of the overall master budget. The master budget will then be broken down into the two major types of budgets:

1. Operating budgets summarize activities such as sales, purchasing, and production.
2. Financial budgets, such as balance sheets, income statements, and cash flow statements, identify the expected financial consequences of the activities summarized in the operating budgets.

A comprehensive example of the budgeting process using this framework will be presented. After this, we will turn to the behavioral and organizational aspects of budgeting. Budgets are critical to many people in organizations. Therefore, we need to understand behavioral issues that arise from the participants in the budget setting process, and the kinds of games (such as distortion and manipulation) that people sometimes play with budgets.

OBJECTIVE 9.2
Explain the importance of each element of the budgeting process.

Exhibit 9-2 summarizes many different components of the budgeting process. The dotted lines from the projected financial statements (box 12) and statement of expected cash flows (box 11) to organization goals (box 1) shows how the estimated *financial consequences*[1] from the organization's tentative budgets can in-

[1] Operating decisions have many nonfinancial consequences, such as quality and service to customers, that budgets ignore (other than in their effects on sales and costs).

These employees at Bethlehem Steel's Sparrows Point Plant are part of the teams responsible for making many of Bethlehem Steel's important products, including coated sheet steel, tin plate, and steel plate. Producing many products under one roof requires planning and budgeting systems to organize and coordinate all the activities associated with making these products. *Courtesy* Bethlehem Steel

fluence the organization's plans and objectives. The dotted lines illustrate an iterative process in which planners compare projected financial results with the organization's financial goals. If initial budgets prove infeasible or unacceptable, planners repeat the budgeting cycle with a new set of decisions until the results are both feasible and financially acceptable.

The budgeting process describes the broad activities performed during the budget period. Planners can select any budget period but usually choose one year. We will assume a one-year cycle in the following discussion.

MASTER BUDGET OUTPUTS

Developing the **master budget** in Exhibit 9-1 (third box) includes two sets of outputs from Exhibit 9-2: the plans or operating budgets that operating personnel use to guide operations [sales plan (box 2), capital spending plan (box 3), production plan (box 5), production capacity (box 6), materials purchasing plan (box 7), labor hiring and training plan (box 8), and the administrative and discretionary spending plan (box 9) in Exhibit 9-2][2] and the expected or projected financial results. Planners usually present the projected financial results, or **financial budgets,** in three forms:

1. A statement of expected cash flows (box 11)
2. The projected balance sheet (box 12)
3. The projected income statement (box 12).

[2] Boxes 1 and 4 in Exhibit 9-2 are derived from the organization's goals and plans, which are shown as the first two boxes in Exhibit 9-1.

Master budget
The budget that encompasses all operating and financial budgets.

Financial budgets
Budgets that summarize the expected financial results from the chosen operating plans.

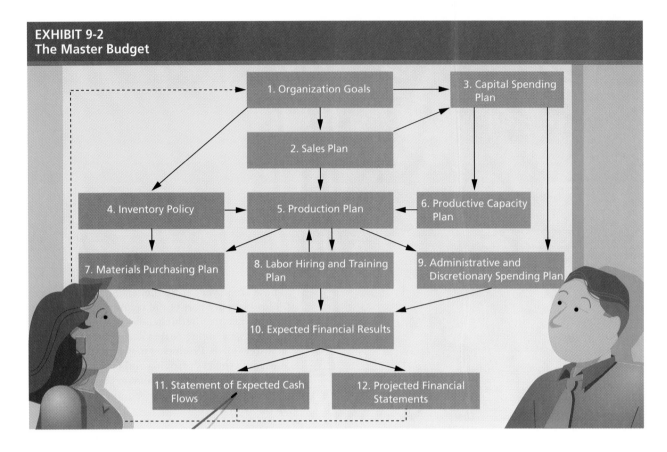

EXHIBIT 9-2
The Master Budget

The projected balance sheet and projected income statement are generally called **pro forma** financial statements.

Pro forma statement
A forecasted or estimated statement.

Operating Budgets

Sales plan
A document that summarizes planned sales for each product.

Operating budgets typically consist of these six operating plans (shown in Exhibit 9-2):

Capital spending plan
An operating plan that specifies when long-term capital expenditures such as acquisitions for buildings and special-purpose equipment must be made to meet objectives.

1. The **sales plan** (box 2) identifies the planned level of sales for each product.
2. The **capital spending plan** (box 3) specifies the long-term capital investments, such as buildings and equipment, that must be made to meet activity objectives.
3. The **production plan** (box 5) schedules all required production.[3]
4. The **materials purchasing plan** (box 7), schedules all required purchasing activities.

Production plan
An operating plan that identifies all required production.

5. The **labor hiring and training plan** (box 8) specifies the number of people the organization must hire or release to achieve its activity objectives, as well as all hiring and training policies.

Materials purchasing plan
An operating plan that schedules purchasing activities.

[3] Box 6 indicates the productive capacity plan, which reflects capacity at the start of the period, plus or minus any additions or deletions made during the period.

6. The **administrative and discretionary spending plan** (box 9), includes administration, staffing, research and development, and advertising.

Operating budgets specify the expected requirements and results of any selling, capital spending, manufacturing, purchasing, labor management, and administrative activities during the planning period. Operations personnel use these plans to guide and coordinate the level of various activities during the planning period. Exhibit 9-3 illustrates information to be used to determine operating budgets in the future.

Financial Budgets

Planners prepare the projected balance sheet and income statement to evaluate the financial consequences of proposed decisions. Financial analysts use the statement of projected cash flows in two ways:

1. To plan when excess cash will be generated so that they can undertake short-term investments.

2. To organize how to meet any cash shortages.

Exhibit 9-4 illustrates the manufacturing of high volumes of high quality, low-cost glass bottles by the Ball Corporation glass plant. While the product layout appears straightforward, planners need operating and financial budgets to estimate the operating and financial consequences of their operating plans. These

Labor hiring and training plan
An operating plan that schedules the hiring, releasing, and training of people that the organization must have to achieve its activity objectives.

Administrative and discretionary spending plan
An operating plan that summarizes administrative and discretionary expenditures.

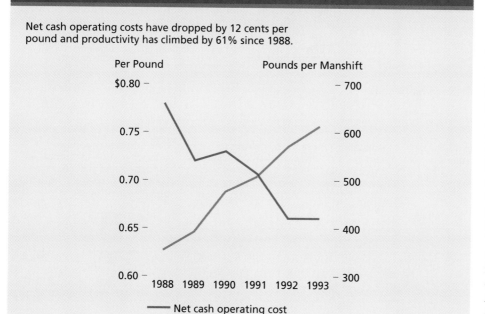

EXHIBIT 9-3
Combining Operating and Financial Data

Net cash operating costs have dropped by 12 cents per pound and productivity has climbed by 61% since 1988.

— Net cash operating cost
— Productivity

Although operating budgets and financial budgets focus on different types of information, the numbers are interrelated. Exhibit 9-3, prepared by Magma Copper Company, shows how cost per pound of copper fell while pounds of copper produced per person shift increased between 1988 and 1993. This relationship and these trends would be reflected in the labor and cost budgets prepared by Magma Copper planners. *Source:* Magma Copper Company promotional brochure.

EXHIBIT 9-4
Inside a Ball Glass Plant

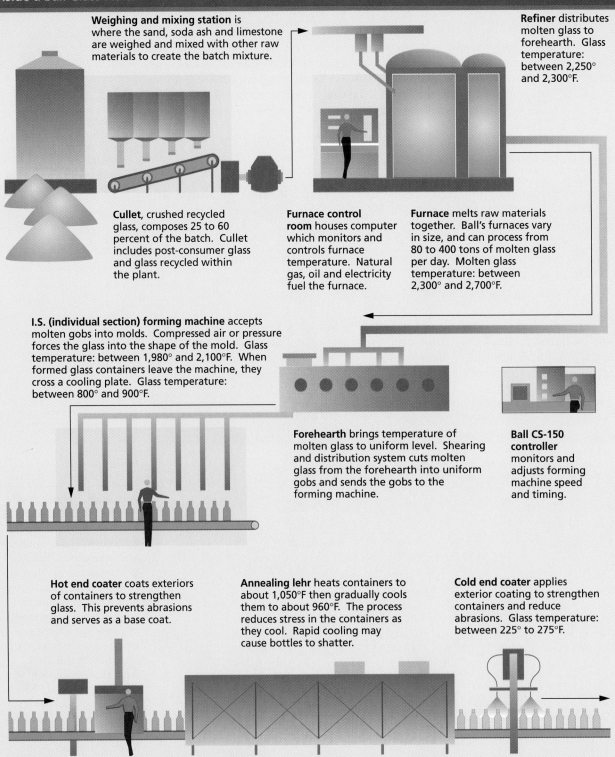

Weighing and mixing station is where the sand, soda ash and limestone are weighed and mixed with other raw materials to create the batch mixture.

Refiner distributes molten glass to forehearth. Glass temperature: between 2,250° and 2,300°F.

Cullet, crushed recycled glass, composes 25 to 60 percent of the batch. Cullet includes post-consumer glass and glass recycled within the plant.

Furnace control room houses computer which monitors and controls furnace temperature. Natural gas, oil and electricity fuel the furnace.

Furnace melts raw materials together. Ball's furnaces vary in size, and can process from 80 to 400 tons of molten glass per day. Molten glass temperature: between 2,300° and 2,700°F.

I.S. (individual section) forming machine accepts molten gobs into molds. Compressed air or pressure forces the glass into the shape of the mold. Glass temperature: between 1,980° and 2,100°F. When formed glass containers leave the machine, they cross a cooling plate. Glass temperature: between 800° and 900°F.

Forehearth brings temperature of molten glass to uniform level. Shearing and distribution system cuts molten glass from the forehearth into uniform gobs and sends the gobs to the forming machine.

Ball CS-150 controller monitors and adjusts forming machine speed and timing.

Hot end coater coats exteriors of containers to strengthen glass. This prevents abrasions and serves as a base coat.

Annealing lehr heats containers to about 1,050°F then gradually cools them to about 960°F. The process reduces stress in the containers as they cool. Rapid cooling may cause bottles to shatter.

Cold end coater applies exterior coating to strengthen containers and reduce abrasions. Glass temperature: between 225° to 275°F.

This diagram of a Ball Corporation glass plant shows a product layout designed to produce high volumes of high-quality, low-cost glass bottles. Planners need operating and financial budgets to estimate the operating and financial consequences of their operating plans and to evaluate the implications, both operating and financial, of changing plans. *Courtesy* Ball Corporation

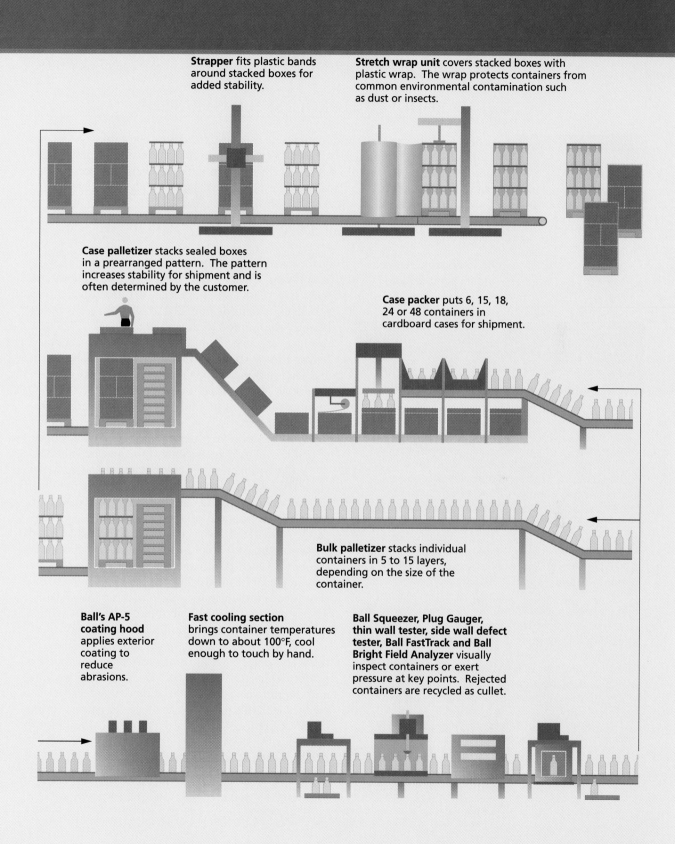

Strapper fits plastic bands around stacked boxes for added stability.

Stretch wrap unit covers stacked boxes with plastic wrap. The wrap protects containers from common environmental contamination such as dust or insects.

Case palletizer stacks sealed boxes in a prearranged pattern. The pattern increases stability for shipment and is often determined by the customer.

Case packer puts 6, 15, 18, 24 or 48 containers in cardboard cases for shipment.

Bulk palletizer stacks individual containers in 5 to 15 layers, depending on the size of the container.

Ball's AP-5 coating hood applies exterior coating to reduce abrasions.

Fast cooling section brings container temperatures down to about 100°F, cool enough to touch by hand.

Ball Squeezer, Plug Gauger, thin wall tester, side wall defect tester, Ball FastTrack and Ball Bright Field Analyzer visually inspect containers or exert pressure at key points. Rejected containers are recycled as cullet.

413

budgets are also used to evaluate the implications if specific aspects of the operating budget, such as the sales, production, and materials purchasing plans, change.

THE BUDGETING PROCESS ILLUSTRATED

OBJECTIVE 9.4

Understand the way that organizations effectively use and interpret budgets.

The budgeting process can sometimes be frustrating and time consuming. Some organizations invest thousands of hours over many months to prepare the master budget documents just described. We will illustrate an entire budgeting process with a simplified but still comprehensive exercise that covers many budgeting elements.[4]

Ontario Tole Art, Buoy Division

Ontario Tole Art sells high quality wooden and metal objects, both new and antique, painted by the owner, Gael Foster. Until recently each object was unique and Gael did all the work by herself. Two years ago, however, Gael developed a new product line that she intended to sell in larger volumes because she wanted to expand her business. The new products are two models of painted fishing buoys— Santa, a buoy painted to look like Father Christmas, and Danny Buoy, a buoy painted to look like an Irish fisherman. Gael set up a new operation for this new product called Ontario Tole Art, Buoy Division (hereafter called Ontario Tole Art). Gael did the planning for this operation and hired a manager, Julius Lopes, to handle the daily operations of the new business.

The production process begins when Gael purchases, for $2.25 each, a used fishing buoy from local fishers. An artist sands the used buoys to remove old paint and debris and applies a base coat of primer paint. When the base coat is dry, the artist hand paints the image of the Santa or the fisherman onto the buoy. Once the image dries, the artist applies a finishing coat of varnish. When the varnish dries, the artist wraps the finished buoy in packing material and inserts it into a specially designed mailing container that Ontario Tole Art ships directly to the customer.

Ontario Tole Art has two types of customers, retail and dealer. Retail orders arrive by mail and are prepaid. The retail price per unit, including packing and shipping charges, is $80. If there is any excess capacity, Gael sells to dealers at the lower per unit price of $55. Gael loses dealer orders that she does not fill immediately because dealers will buy alternative products from other producers.

CONSIDER THIS . . .

Budgeting in Government

In profit-seeking organizations, revenues and expenditures are interrelated; organizations spend money to earn revenues. In many cases, there is a physical relationship between the amount of money spent (on things such as raw materials) and the amount of revenue. In government organizations, however, revenues and expenditures are independent. Governments develop revenue budgets, which are estimates of the amount of money that they will raise or will be allocated. Legislatures approve expenditure budgets, which provide public servants with the authority to spend government revenues on specific projects. Occasionally governments pass laws (often called *balanced-budget requirements*) limiting government expenditures to the amount of revenues raised, but revenues and expenditures are separate. For most governments, controlling government expenditures means ensuring that authorized government spending has not been exceeded by actual spending rather than assessing whether the programs on which money was spent accomplished their objectives.

Source: Stanley C. Beiner, "Budgeting in Not-for-Profit Organizations," *CMA Magazine,* November-December 1987, pp. 20–27.

---

[4] To understand the budgeting process, you must go through an actual budgeting experience with a real company. The example that follows is a compromise between what people really face in practice and what is reasonable for you to consider as you study budgeting. This example considers most budgeting elements. The additional challenge in practice is to estimate and assimilate much more information into the budgeting process.

Courtesy **Anthony Atkinson**

Sales to dealers are on account; stated terms call for the dealers to pay the full amount of the invoice within 30 days of billing. Receipts from dealers, however, are often delinquent. Typically only 30% of dealers pay in the month following the sale; 45% pay in the second month following the sale, 20% in the third month following the sale, and 5% of dealer sales are never collected.

Ontario Tole Art hires local area artists to paint the buoys. Due to local employment conditions, Ontario Tole Art must hire artists for periods of three months. The artists receive a fixed monthly salary of $2000 and work up to a maximum of 160 hours per month. The Ontario Tole Art manager makes staffing decisions at the start of each quarter, beginning January 1. The total time to sand, base coat, paint, and pack each buoy is 0.8 labor hour.

Paint costs $3.15 for each buoy. Other manufacturing costs, including sandpaper, brushes, varnish, and other shop supplies, amounts to $2.75 per buoy. Packing materials cost $1.95 per buoy and shipping by courier costs $7.50 per buoy.

Ontario Tole Art rents space in a local industrial mall where the employees work on the buoys. The one-year lease stipulates that rent is to be paid quarterly in advance. Ontario Tole Art can rent shops of several sizes that would provide the following monthly capacities in buoys: 600, 800, 1000, and 1200. The quarterly rents for each of these units are $3600, $4800, $6000, and $7200, respectively. All production takes place to order, and Ontario Tole Art acquires supplies only as needed.

Shop Space Type	Shop Capacity (Number of Buoys)	Quarterly Rent
A	600	$3600
B	800	4800
C	1000	6000
D	1200	7200

Insurance, heating, lighting, and business taxes cost $20,000 per year and advertising expenses amount to $40,000 per year. Julius, the manager of Ontario Tole Art, receives $30,000 per year to supervise the operation, manage the raw materials acquisitions, handle all the order taking and billing, and do the accounting. All operating expenses are incurred and paid in equal monthly installments.

Realized sales for October, November, and December of 1996 and forecasted demand for 1997 appear in Exhibit 9-5. Based on this **demand forecast,**[5] Gael and her manager have decided to rent an 800-capacity unit for 1997 and to hire two painters in the first quarter, two painters in the second quarter, one painter in the third quarter, and three painters in the fourth quarter.

Gael plans to withdraw $20,000 from the company at the start of each six-month period for a total of $40,000 per year as her compensation for functioning as owner and planner. She also wants to maintain all the firm's cash in a bank account for her business only with a minimum cash balance of $5000. (See Exhibit 9-6.) She has arranged a $50,000 **line of credit** with her bank to provide her with short-term funds for the company. At the start of each month, the bank charges interest at the rate of 1% on the balance of the line of credit as of the end of the previous month. The bank pays interest at the rate of 0.6% on any cash in excess of $5000 held in the account. The bank pays interest on the first day of each month based on the balance in the account at the end of the previous month.

Demand forecast
An estimate of the market demand, or sales potential, for a product under specified conditions.

Line of credit
A short-term financing arrangement, with a pre-specified limit, between an organization and a financial institution.

EXHIBIT 9-5
Ontario Tole Art
Forecasted Unit Demand 1996–1997

| | | TYPE OF DEMAND | | |
Month	Retail	Dealer	Total
October 1996*	275	510	785
November 1996*	420	425	845
December 1996*	675	175	850
January 1997	100	375	475
February 1997	105	400	505
March 1997	95	425	520
April 1997	115	350	465
May 1997	75	300	375
June 1997	60	250	310
July 1997	50	300	350
August 1997	55	325	380
September 1997	75	300	375
October 1997	150	300	450
November 1997	290	350	640
December 1997	350	400	750

*Actual

[5] We distinguish between a demand forecast, which is an estimate of the sales potential in a given market, and a sales plan, which is a forecast of the sales sought and planned in that market. Clearly, the numbers in the sales plan cannot exceed the numbers in the demand forecast.

EXHIBIT 9-6
Ontario Tole Art
Proposed Balance Sheet, January 1, 1997

Cash	$ 5,000	Owner's equity	$34,948
Accounts receivable	29,948		
Total assets	$34,948	Total liabilities and Owner's equity	$34,948

Demand Forecast

An organization's goals provide the starting point and the framework for evaluating the budgeting process. (See box 1, Exhibit 9-2.) For example, at Ontario Tole Art, the goals are to produce high quality products and to expand the business. To assess the plan's acceptability, Gael compares the projected financial results from the tentative operating plan to the organization's financial goals.

As shown in Exhibit 9-5, the budgeting process is influenced strongly by the demand forecast, an estimate of sales demand at a specified selling price. Organizations develop demand forecasts in many ways. Some use sophisticated market surveys conducted either by outside experts or by their own sales staff. Other organizations use statistical models that generate demand forecasts from trends and forecasts of economic activity in the economy and the relation of past sales patterns to this economic activity. Other companies simply assume that demand will either grow or decline by some estimated rate over previous demand levels.

Regardless of the approach used to develop the demand forecast, the organization must prepare a sales plan for each key line of goods or services. The sales plans provide the basis for other plans to acquire the required factors of production, such as labor, materials, production capacity, and cash. Production plans are sensitive to the sales plan; therefore, most organizations develop budgets on computers so that planners can readily explore the effects of changes in the sales plan on production plans.

Choosing the amount of detail to present in the budget involves making trade offs. A greater level of detail in the forecast improves the ability of the budgeting process to identify potential bottlenecks and problems by specifying the exact timing of production flows in the organization. On the other hand, forecasting and planning in great detail for each unique item in organizations with thousands of products of production is prohibitively expensive and overwhelming to compute. Therefore, most organizations strike a balance that reflects the judgment of production planners between the need for detail and the cost and practicality of detailed scheduling. Planners do this by grouping products into pools of products so that each product in a given pool places roughly equivalent demands on the organization's resources.

Because Ontario Tole Art has only one basic product, a painted buoy with only two variations, its budget can be very detailed and comprehensive. Organizations with many products and services may choose, however, to budget at a more aggregated level such as by product line.

The Production Plan

Planners match the completed sales plan with the organization's inventory policy and capacity level to determine a production plan. (See box 5, Exhibit 9-2.) The plan identifies the intended production during each subperiod of the annual budget. Budget subperiods may be daily, weekly, or monthly.

Planners use the inventory policy (box 4, Exhibit 9-2) along with the sales plan (box 2, Exhibit 9-2) to develop the production plan (box 5, Exhibit 9-2). Therefore, the inventory policy is critical and has a unique role in shaping the production plan. Some organizations use a policy of producing goods for inventory and attempt to keep a predetermined, or *target*, number of units in inventory at all times. This inventory policy often reflects a *level* production strategy that is characteristic of an organization with highly skilled employees or equipment dedicated to producing a single product.[6] In these organizations, monthly sales draw down the inventory levels, and the production plan for each month attempts to restore inventory levels to their predetermined target levels.

Other organizations have an inventory policy of producing for planned sales in the next budget subperiod. Organizations moving toward a just-in-time inventory policy often produce goods to meet the next subperiod's demand as an intermediate step on the path to moving to a full just-in-time inventory system. Each subperiod becomes shorter and shorter until the organization achieves just-in-time production. In this setting, the inventory target is the level of next week or next month's planned sales, and the scheduled production is the amount required to meet the inventory target. Implementing a just-in-time inventory policy requires flexibility among employees, equipment, and suppliers and a well-designed production process. In organizations using this strategy, demand drives the production plan directly; that is, the production in each period equals the next period's planned sales. This is the inventory policy that Ontario Tole Art uses. (See box 4, Exhibit 9-2.)

Aggregate Planning

Throughout the production planning process, planners or users of computers with planning software compare the production plan implied jointly by the sales and inventory plans to the amount of available productive capacity. This comparison assesses the feasibility of the proposed production plan. Planners call this **aggregate planning.**

Aggregate planning
An approximate determination of whether the organization has the capacity to undertake a proposed production plan.

Aggregate planning does not attempt to develop a detailed production schedule that people use to guide daily production in the organization. Rather, aggregate planning determines whether the proposed production plan can be achieved by the production capacity the organization either has in place or can put in place during the planning period. Even planning at this aggregate level can be complicated because planners may need to consider ways to modify existing facilities that would otherwise constrain planned procedures. For instance, one type of modification suggested in the previous chapter would be to rearrange existing facilities into work cells.

---

[6] A level production strategy reflects a lack of flexibility. Highly skilled production workers cannot be used to do various jobs in the organization. Therefore, they must be kept busy at one job. Similarly, dedicated equipment that can be used for only one job must be kept busy to justify its expense.

Developing the Spending Plans

Once planners have identified a feasible production plan, they can make tentative resource commitments. The purchasing group prepares a materials purchasing plan to acquire the raw materials and supplies that the production plan requires. (See box 7, Exhibit 9-2.) Materials purchasing plans are driven by the cycle of the organization's and the suppliers' production plans. These plans notify suppliers of the quantity of materials they should supply and the timing of those deliveries. Because sales and production plans change during the year, the organization and its suppliers should be able to quickly adjust their plans based on information received during the operating period. However, at some point, the budget planning subinterval production and purchasing plans are committed for that subperiod. For most organizations, this commitment point occurs anywhere from one day to one quarter before the anticipated production date.

The personnel and production groups prepare the labor hiring and training plan. (See box 8, Exhibit 9-2.) This plan works backward from the date when the personnel are needed in order to develop hiring and training schedules that will ensure the availability of needed personnel. This plan can include both expansion and contraction activities. In the case of contraction, the organization uses retraining plans to redeploy employees to other parts of the organization or develops plans to discharge employees from the organization. In the case of employees who lose their employment, discharge plans may include retraining and other activities to help them find new jobs. Because discharging employees reflects moral, ethical, and legal issues and may involve high severance costs, most organizations attempt to avoid this action unless no other use can be found for the employees.

Staff and other groups prepare an administrative and discretionary spending plan, which summarizes the proposed expenditures on activities such as those for research and development, advertising, and training. (See box 9, Exhibit 9-2.) Discretionary expenditures provide the infrastructure required by the emerging production and sales plan. The term discretionary is used because the amount spent is not driven by actual sales and production levels. Rather, the senior managers in the organization determine the amount of **discretionary expenditures.** Once determined, however, the amount to be spent on discretionary activities becomes fixed for the period because it is unaffected by product volume and mix.

For example, if a fast-food restaurant plans to make 3000 hamburgers during some planning interval, it knows the quantity of materials that it will use because there is a physical relationship, or **engineered expenditure,** between ingredients such as meat, buns, condiments, and packages and the number of hamburgers made. However, no direct physical, or engineered, relationship exists between the number of hamburgers sold and the discretionary amounts spent on advertising and employee training.

Finally, the appropriate authority in the organization approves the **capital spending plan** for putting new productive capacity in place. (See box 3, Exhibit 9-2.) Because capital spending projects usually involve time horizons longer than the period of the operating budgets, the capital spending plan is driven by a long-term planning process rather than the one-year cycle of the operating budget. The spending plans for material, labor, and support resources are based on a forecast of the activities the organization must complete to achieve the production targets identified in its production plan. As the planning period unfolds and time reveals the actual production requirements, production planners make

Discretionary expenditure
An expenditure whose cost has no direct relationship between the level of spending on an activity and active production levels.

Engineered expenditure
An expenditure whose short-term cost is directly determined by the proposed level of activity.

commitments to detailed production schedules and the required related purchasing requirements.

Choosing the Capacity Levels

At Ontario Tole Art these three types of resources determine the monthly production capacity:

1. **Flexible resources that the organization can acquire in the short term.** Paint and packing supplies are examples. If suppliers either do not deliver these resources or if they deliver unacceptable products, production may be disrupted. This problem was not identified as an issue for Ontario Tole Art, but it is a practical concern for many organizations. Organizations spend a great deal of time and money developing supplier relationships so that they will receive zero-defect materials and purchased parts just when needed.

2. **Committed resources that the organization must acquire for items for the intermediate term.** Between July 1 and September 30, Ontario Tole Art plans to employ one painter. Because each painter works 160 hours per month and because each buoy requires 0.8 hours to complete, the monthly capacity provided by intermediate-term activity decisions between July 1 and September 30 is 200 (160/0.8) units.

3. **Committed resources that the organization must acquire for the long term.** Gael plans to rent a shop that provides a monthly capacity of 800 units. Gael requires a simple setting with a relatively short commitment period. Other organizations may take several years to acquire long-term capacity that may last for 10 years or more, whose cost is justified only if it is used that long. Consider the amount of time an oil company takes to build an oil refinery or the time that a municipality needs to build a hospital. Committed resources are expensive and are called *committed* because the cost is the same whether the facility is used or not and the level of capacity and capacity-related costs are very difficult to change in the short term. Therefore, committed resources impose risk on the organization.

As summarized in Exhibit 9-7, the nature of the resources defines whether they are short term, intermediate term, or long term. Many organizations develop sophisticated approaches for choosing a production plan that balances the use of short-term, intermediate-term, and long-term capacity to minimize the waste of resources.

For example, the size and the number of service areas in a bank represent the capacity available for use during any period provided by long-term building decisions. The level of long-term capacity chosen reflects the organization's assessment of its long-term growth trend.

For Ontario Tole Art, which is renting capacity, long-term capacity is defined by the lease stipulations, which equals one year. If Ontario Tole Art were building this capacity, long-term capacity would be defined by the time needed to plan and build the facility.

The number of full-time staff employed by a bank determines the long-term capacity available for the intermediate term. For example, if the plan were to acquire capacity that the organization could use increasingly as sales grew, the in-

EXHIBIT 9-7
Summary of Capacity Types and Commitment Time

Term	Type of Capacity Acquired	Examples
Flexible resources required in short term (less than several weeks)	Provides the ability to use existing capacity	Raw materials, supplies, casual labor
Committed resources acquired for the intermediate term (several weeks to six months)	General-purpose capacity that is transferrable between organizations given time	People, general purpose equipment, specialty raw materials
Committed resources acquired for the long-term (more than six months)	Special purpose capacity is customized for the organization's use	Buildings, special purpose equipment

termediate-term capacity decisions would put other elements that require intermediate-term commitments in place. These would include defining the number of people and banking equipment necessary that allow the bank to use its long-term capacity. The intermediate-term capacity decision reflects the longer of the time needed to put intermediate-term capacity in place or the contracting period contract for intermediate-term capacity. For Ontario Tole Art this is the contracting period for artists, which is three months.

This clean room facility at LSI Logic Corporation has many types of costs. The room itself reflects a cost of capacity acquired for the long term. The cost of hiring and training the people who work in the room reflects a cost of capacity acquired for the intermediate term. The cost of the power used is a short-term cost acquired only when the power is required. *Courtesy* **LSI Logic**

Finally, the number of part-time or temporary staff employed by a bank determines its capacity on a day-to-day basis. Such short-term capacity decisions reflect the cyclical demands that the bank may face daily, weekly, monthly, or annually. The short-term capacity decision reflects the time needed to put short-term capacity in place. For Ontario Tole Art, this is the time period that suppliers require for delivery, which is assumed to be virtually instantaneous. However, if Ontario Tole Art had to order and wait for supplies, it would become very important to plan their acquisitions so that in the very short term Ontario Tole Art would not have to stop production while it waited for supplies to arrive. In this sense, supplies provide the short-run capacity to use longer-term capacity.

This discussion raises the question of how production planners choose capacity levels. Organizations use many different approaches to plan capacity. The process Ontario Tole Art used was to choose a level of shop capacity (one of 600, 800, 1000, or 1200) and then to hire the number of painters in each quarter that, given the forecasted demand and chosen shop capacity, provided the highest level of expected profits.

We can classify the resource-consuming activities for Ontario Tole Art into three groups, which are typical of all organizations:

1. Activities that create the need for resources and, therefore, resource expenditures in the *short term*. For Ontario Tole Art, these short-term activities include the acquisition, preparation, painting, packing, and shipping of buoys. Acquiring the resources for these short-term activities requires expenditures that vary directly with the production levels because the inventory policy is to produce only to order.

2. Activities undertaken to acquire capacity for the *intermediate term*. For Ontario Tole Art, this is the quarterly acquisition of painting capacity, that is, hiring the painters to paint the buoys.

3. Activities undertaken to acquire capacity that must be acquired for the *long term*. For Ontario Tole Art, this includes the annual choice of the level of shop capacity, level of advertising, the manager and manager's salary, and expenditures for items such as insurance and heat.

Planners classify activities by type because they plan, budget, and control short-, intermediate-, and long-term expenditures differently. Analysts evaluate short-term activities using efficiency and effectiveness considerations and ask questions such as the following:

1. Is this expenditure necessary to add value to the product from the customer's perspective?

2. Can the organization improve the execution of this activity?

3. Would changing how this activity is done provide more customer satisfaction?

Analysts evaluate intermediate- and long-term activities by using efficiency and effectiveness considerations and ask questions such as these:

1. Are alternative forms of capacity available that are less expensive?

2. Is this the best approach to achieve our goals?

3. How can we improve the capacity selection decision to make capacity less expensive or more flexible?

Choosing the capacity plan— making the commitments to acquire intermediate-term and long-term capacity—commits the intermediate-term and long-term expenditures. Choosing the production plan, that is, choosing the level of the short-term activities, fixes the short-term expenditures that the master budget summarizes.

Handling Infeasible Production Plans

Although the relationships between planning and production at Ontario Tole Art are simple, the company's planning process reflects how planners use forecasted demand to plan activity levels and provide required capacity. If planners find the tentative production plan infeasible because of resource or capacity constraints, they have to make provisions to acquire more capacity or reduce the planned level of production. For example, if the labor market is tight and Ontario Tole Art can hire only two artists between January and June, Gael would have to revise her capacity and production plans to reflect this constraint.

Interpreting the Production Plan

Exhibit 9-8 summarizes the production plan that Ontario Tole Art has developed for 1997. The three elements that drive planning are (1) demand, which is what people are willing to buy at the stated price; (2) the capacity levels chosen; and (3) production output. Ontario Tole Art makes no products until it receives an order. Therefore, *production is the minimum of demand and capacity.* In equation form, we may write this:

$$Production = Minimum\ (Total\ Demand,\ Production\ Capacity)$$

At Ontario Tole Art these equations apply:

$$Production\ capacity = Minimum\ (Shop\ Capacity,\ Painting\ Capacity,\ Supplies\ Capacity)$$

$$Total\ Demand = Retail\ Demand + Dealer\ Demand$$

EXHIBIT 9-8
Ontario Tole Art: Demand and Sales Data, Number of Units, 1997

	Jan.	Feb.	March	April	May	June	July	Aug.	Sept.	Oct.	Nov.	Dec.
Retail demand	100	105	95	115	75	60	50	**55**	75	150	290	350
Dealer demand	375	400	425	350	300	250	300	**325**	300	300	350	400
Total demand	475	505	520	465	375	310	350	**380**	375	450	640	750
Shop capacity	800	800	800	800	800	800	800	**800**	800	800	800	800
Painting capacity	400	400	400	400	400	400	200	**200**	200	600	600	600
Production capacity	400	400	400	400	375	310	200	**200**	200	450	600	600
Retail units made and sold	100	105	95	115	75	60	50	**55**	75	150	290	350
Dealer units made and sold	300	295	305	285	300	250	150	**145**	125	300	310	250
Total units made and sold	400	400	400	400	375	310	200	**200**	200	450	600	600

In Ontario Tole Art's case, the production capacity is the minimum of the long-term capacity (the productive capacity of the shop), the intermediate-term capacity (the painting capacity provided by hiring artists), and the short-term capacity (the capacity provided by the short-term acquisition of materials.)[7] For example, in August the retail demand is 55 units and the dealer demand is 325 units, totaling 380 units. The shop capacity is 800 units and the painting capacity is 200 units. Therefore, production capacity, which is the minimum of the shop capacity and painting capacity, is 200 units. Planned production and sales of 200 units represents the minimum of total demand (380 units) and production capacity (200 units).

The Financial Plans

Once the planners have developed the production, staffing, and capacity plans, they can prepare a financial summary of the tentative operating plans. The financial results for Ontario Tole Art implied by the production plan developed in Exhibit 9-8 appear in the following exhibits. Exhibit 9-9 presents the cash flows expected from the production and sales plan. Exhibit 9-10 and Exhibit 9-11 summarize the projected balance sheet and income statement, respectively, expected as a result of the production and sales plans. (These are examples of the elements of boxes 11 and 12 in Exhibit 9-2.) Planners use the projected balance sheet as an overall evaluation of the net effect of operating and financing decisions during the budget period and the income statement as an overall test of the profitability of their proposed activities.[8]

Understanding the Cash Flow Statement

The cash flow statement in Exhibit 9-9 is organized into three sections:

1. Cash inflows from retail cash sales and collections of dealer receivables
2. Cash outflows for flexible resources that are acquired and consumed in the short term (buoys, paint, other supplies, packing, and shipping) and cash outflows for committed resources that are acquired and consumed in the intermediate term and long term (painters, shop rent, manager's salary, other shop costs, interest paid, and advertising costs)
3. Results of financing operations

In each month, the format of the cash flow statement is as follows:

$$Cash\ Inflows\ -\ Cash\ Outflows\ =\ Net\ Cash\ Flow$$

In January, for example, ending cash was found as follows:

$$Net\ Cash\ Flows\ +\ Opening\ Cash\ +\ Effects\ of\ Financing\ Operations\ =\ Ending\ Cash$$
$$\$3676\ +\ \$5000\ +\ [(\$20,000)\ +\ \$16,324]\ =\ \$5000$$

---

[7] In this example we assume that there is instantaneous supply; therefore, in this situation, short-term capacity is equal to intermediate-term capacity.

[8] Note that when taxes are considered, an income statement is needed to estimate taxes that must be paid (in cash) to feedback to the cash flow plan.

EXHIBIT 9-9
Ontario Tole Art
Cash Flow and Financing Data—1997

CASH INFLOWS	Jan.	Feb.	March	April	May	June	July	Aug.	Sept.	Oct.	Nov.	Dec.
Retail sales	$ 8,000	$ 8,400	$ 7,600	$ 9,200	$ 6,000	$ 4,800	$ 4,000	$ 4,400	$ 6,000	$12,000	$23,200	$28,000
Dealer collections— 1 Month	2,887	4,950	4,868	5,033	4,703	4,950	4,125	2,475	2,392	2,062	4,950	5,115
Dealer collections— 2 Months	10,519	4,331	7,425	7,301	7,549	7,054	7,425	6,188	3,713	3,589	3,094	7,425
Dealer collections— 3 Months	5,610	4,675	1,925	3,300	3,245	3,355	3,135	3,300	2,750	1,650	1,595	1,375
Total	$27,016	$22,356	$21,818	$24,834	$21,497	$20,159	$18,685	$16,363	$14,855	$19,301	$32,839	$41,915
CASH OUTFLOWS												
Flexible Resources:												
Buoys	$ 900	$ 900	$ 900	$ 900	$ 844	$ 698	$ 450	$ 450	$ 450	$ 1,013	$ 1,350	$ 1,350
Paint costs	1,260	1,260	1,260	1,260	1,181	977	630	630	630	1,418	1,890	1,890
Other supplies costs	1,100	1,100	1,100	1,100	1,031	853	550	550	550	1,238	1,650	1,650
Packing costs	780	780	780	780	731	605	390	390	390	878	1,170	1,170
Shipping costs	3,000	3,000	3,000	3,000	2,813	2,325	1,500	1,500	1,500	3,375	4,500	4,500
Committed Resources:												
Painters' salaries	$ 4,000	$ 4,000	$ 4,000	$ 4,000	$ 4,000	$ 4,000	$ 2,000	$ 2,000	$ 2,000	$ 6,000	$ 6,000	$ 6,000
Shop rent	4,800	0	0	4,800	0	0	4,800	0	0	4,800	0	0
Manager's salary	2,500	2,500	2,500	2,500	2,500	2,500	2,500	2,500	2,500	2,500	2,500	2,500
Other shop costs	1,667	1,667	1,667	1,667	1,667	1,667	1,667	1,667	1,667	1,667	1,667	1,667
Interest paid (received)	0	163	127	95	81	48	17	208	177	160	231	145
Advertising costs	3,333	3,333	3,333	3,333	3,333	3,333	3,333	3,333	3,333	3,333	3,333	3,333
Total	$23,340	$18,703	$18,667	$23,435	$18,181	$17,006	$17,837	$13,228	$13,197	$26,382	$24,291	$24,205
Net cash flow this month	$ 3,676	$ 3,653	$ 3,151	$ 1,399	$ 3,316	$ 3,153	$ 848	$ 3,135	$ 1,658	−$7,081	$ 8,548	$17,710
FINANCING OPERATIONS												
Opening cash	5,000	5,000	5,000	5,000	5,000	5,000	5,000	5,000	5,000	5,000	5,000	5,000
Cash invested (withdrawn)	−20,000	0	0	0	0	0	−20,000	0	0	0	0	0
Cash available	−11,324	8,653	8,151	6,399	8,315	8,155	−14,152	8,134	6,658	−2,079	13,548	22,710
Opening loan	0	16,324	12,671	9,520	8,121	4,806	1,652	20,803	17,669	16,010	23,089	14,541
Borrowing made	16,324	0	0	0	0	0	19,152	0	0	7,079	0	0
Borrowing repaid	0	3,653	3,151	1,399	3,315	3,155	0	3,134	1,658	0	8,548	14,541
Ending loan	16,324	12,671	9,520	8,121	4,806	1,652	20,803	17,669	16,010	23,089	14,541	0
Ending cash	5,000	5,000	5,000	5,000	5,000	5,000	5,000	5,000	5,000	5,000	5,000	8,168

EXHIBIT 9-10
Ontario Tole Art
Projected Balance Sheet
December 31, 1997

Cash	$ 8,168	Owner's equity	$35,613
Accounts receivable	27,445		
Total assets	$35,613	Total liabilities and owner's equity	$35,613

To help you to understand the derivation of the numbers in Ontario Tole Art's cash flow statement, let's look closely at the numbers for July.

CASH INFLOWS SECTION.   Recall that the pattern of collections at Ontario Tole Art is as follows:

1. Retail orders are paid for with the order at a retail price per unit of $80.

2. Sales to dealers for $55 per unit are on account with a typical collection pattern being 30% in the month following the sale, 45% in the second month following the sale, 20% in the third month following the sale, and 5% never collected.

Therefore, in July, Ontario Tole Art will collect (1) all the retail sales for July, (2) 30% of the dealer sales from June, (3) 45% of the dealer sales from May, and (4) 20% of the dealer sales from April. Exhibit 9-12 summarizes these July collections.

EXHIBIT 9-11
Ontario Tole Art
Projected Income Statement
For the Year Ended December 31, 1997

Revenue		$279,134
Flexible resource expenses		
Buoys	$10,205	
Paint	14,286	
Other supplies	12,472	
Packing	8,844	
Shipping	34,013	79,820
Contribution margin		$199,314
Committed resource expenses		
Painters' salaries	$48,000	
Shop rent	19,200	
Other shop costs	20,004	
Manager's salary	30,000	117,204
Other expenses		
Advertising	$40,000	
Interest paid	1,452	41,452
Net income		$ 40,658

EXHIBIT 9-12
Ontario Tole Art
Summary of Cash Collections in July, 1997

Item	Calculation	
Retail sales from July (see Exhibit 9-8)		$ 4,000
30% of June dealer sales*	30% × 250 × $55 =	4,125
45% of May dealer sales	45% × 300 × $55 =	7,425
20% of April dealer sales	20% × 285 × $55 =	3,135
Total		$18,685

*Sales equals units sold multiplied by the selling price of $55 per unit.

CASH OUTFLOWS SECTION.   Exhibit 9-13 summarizes the cash outflow numbers for July. Note that for expenditures on flexible resources that are acquired in the short-term, this equation applies:

$$Cash\ Outflows\ =\ Units\ Purchased\ \times\ Price\ per\ Unit\ of\ Flexible\ Resource$$

For expenditures on committed resources, that is, resources acquired in the intermediate term or long term, this equation applies:

$$Cash\ Outflows\ =\ Monthly\ Expenditure\ for\ Committed\ Resource$$

FINANCING SECTION.   The financing section of the cash flow statement summarizes the effects on cash of transactions that are not a part of the normal operating activities. This section includes the effects of issuing or retiring stock or debt and buying or selling capital assets. Exhibit 9-14 shows a common format used in the financing section of the cash flow statement with the corresponding

EXHIBIT 9-13
Ontario Tole Art
Cash Outflow Calculations for July, 1997

Item	Amount	Formula	Calculation
Flexible Resources:			
Buoy cost	$ 450	July production × Price per buoy	200 × $2.25
Paint cost	630	July production × Paint cost per buoy	200 × $3.15
Other supplies cost	550	July production × Other supplies cost per buoy	200 × $2.75
Packing costs	390	July sales × Packing cost per buoy	200 × $1.95
Shipping costs	1,500	July sales × Shipping cost per buoy	200 × $7.50
Committed Resources:			
Painters' salaries	2,000	Number of painters in July × Monthly salary	1 × $2,000
Shop rent	4,800	Units of capacity × Capacity cost per unit	800 × $6
Manager's salary	2,500	Annual salary ÷ 12	$30,000 ÷ 12
Other shop costs	1,667	Annual other costs ÷ 12	$20,000 ÷ 12
Interest paid	17	June ending loan balance × 1%	$ 1,652 × 1%
Advertising costs	3,333	Annual advertising ÷ 12	$40,000 ÷ 12

numbers for July. Note that the format of the financing section of the cash flow statement is as follows:

Cash Flows This Period + Opening Balance ± Changes = Closing Balance

The major sources and uses of cash in most organizations are operations, investments or withdrawals by the owner in an unincorporated organization, long-term financing activities related to issuing or retiring stock or debt, and short-term financing activities.

Short-term financing usually involves obtaining a line of credit with a financial institution. The line of credit may be secured or unsecured. The line of credit allows a company to borrow up to a specified amount at any time and may be secured or unsecured. The line of credit is secured if the organization has pledged an asset that the financial institution can seize if the borrower defaults on the line of credit provisions. The financial institution sets a limit on the line of credit, and the borrower (Ontario Tole Art) pays interest periodically, such as monthly, on the outstanding balance borrowed. See the ending loan row in Exhibit 9-9, and note that Ontario Tole Art's line of credit balance varies between zero and $23,089 during the year, well within the limit of $50,000 that Gael negotiated with the bank.

Note that the format of the financing section of the cash flow statement in Exhibit 9-9 for Ontario Tole Art does not follow the format used in Exhibit 9-14. The financing section of Ontario Tole Art's cash flow statement provides information about the line of credit balance. Many organizations include line-of-credit information in the cash flow statement because financial statement readers should be aware of the limits that can potentially constrain operations.

Using the Financial Plans

Ontario Tole Art's cash flow statement, shown in Exhibit 9-9, provides several types of useful information. First, it contains a short-term financing plan that suggests that, if events unfold as expected, Ontario Tole Art's cash balance increases only modestly during the year because of the $40,000 withdrawal that Gael will make from the business. Therefore, the company will use its line of credit agreement heavily. It will be borrowing from the bank for 11 of the 12 months in the year.

EXHIBIT 9-14
Format of Financing Section of Cash Flow Statement

	Net cash flow from operations	848
+	Opening cash	+ 5,000
±	Cash invested or withdrawn*	−20,000
±	Cash provided or used in issuing or retiring stock or debt	0
=	Cash available before short-term financing	−14,152
±	Cash used or provided by short-term financing	19,152
=	Ending cash	5,000

*In the case of a private business such as Ontario Tole Art, this refers to the capital transactions by the owner.

Organizations can raise money from outsiders by borrowing from banks, issuing debt, or selling shares of equity. A cash flow forecast helps an organization identify if and when it will require external financing. The cash flow forecast also shows whether any projected cash shortage will be temporary or cyclical, which can be met by a line-of-credit arrangement, or whether it will be permanent, which would require a long-term loan from a bank, further investment by the current owners, or investment by new owners. Based on the information provided by the cash flow forecast, organizations can plan the appropriate mix of external financing to minimize the long-run cost of capital.

The projected income statement and balance sheet provide a general assessment of the operating efficiencies at Ontario Tole Art. If Gael believes that these projected results are unacceptable, she must take steps to change the organization processes that create the unacceptable results. For example, if the employees consistently use more quantities of any factor of production than competitors use, such as paint, labor, or capacity, Gael should attempt to modify procedures and therefore resource use to be able to compete profitably with its competitors.

Suppose that Julius has studied the projected financial results in the initial budget plans and has decided that the 14.6% profit margin on sales ($40,658 ÷ $279,134 from Exhibit 9-11) is too low. Julius has reached this conclusion because Ontario Tole Art is in the craft industry in which competitors often duplicate attractive products quickly resulting in short periods of product profitability. After determining that this profit margin on sales is too low, the manager may develop a marketing program to improve the cost/revenue performance at Ontario Tole Art.

Using the Projected Results

The operating budgets, like the production plan, hiring plan, capital spending plan, and purchasing plan for materials and supplies, provide a framework for developing expectations about activity levels in the upcoming period. Planners also use the operating budgets to test the feasibility of production plans. As the period unfolds, production and operations schedulers will make more accurate forecasts and base their production commitments on them. Thus, planners use the budget information to accomplish the following:

1. **Identify broad resource requirements.** This helps develop plans to put needed resources in place. For example, Julius can use the activity forecast to plan when the organization will have to hire and train temporary help.

2. **Identify potential problems.** This helps avoid problems or deal with them systematically. For example, Julius can use the statement of operating cash flows to identify when the business will need short-term financing from its bank. This will help the manager negotiate with a bank lending officer for a line of credit that is both competitive and responsive to Ontario Tole Art's needs. The forecasted cash flows also will identify when the buoy business will generate cash that Gael can invest in other business opportunities.

3. **Compare projected operating and financial results.** These are compared with those of competitors as a general test of the efficiency of the organization's operating processes. For example, the differences between planned and actual costs at Ontario Tole Art will focus Julius's attention on under-

standing whether the plans were unrealistic or whether the execution of a sound business plan was flawed. This signals the need for improved planning, better execution, or both.

WHAT-IF ANALYSIS

The budgeting process also allows management to consider alternative strategies. If planners use the computer for the budgeting process, they can use the budgeting framework to explore the effects of alternative marketing, production, and selling strategies. Julius may consider raising prices, opening a retail outlet, or using different employment strategies. Alternative proposals take the form of "what-if"[9] questions in a process called **what-if analysis.**

What-if analysis
A strategy that uses a model to predict the results of varying a model's key parameters or estimates.

Julius may ask: "What if I decrease prices on my retail products by 5% and sales increase by 10%? Is that desirable?" The answer is that Ontario Tole Art profits will fall from $40,658 to $37,695.[10] Therefore, this proposed price adjustment is undesirable.

Julius may also wonder: "What if I opened a retail outlet? Suppose that retail sales would increase by 50% if Ontario Tole Art opened a retail outlet that would cost $40,000 per year to operate (including all costs). The retail outlet orders would be shipped by courier to the customer's address. Would this change be desirable?" If Ontario Tole Art follows this strategy, profits will increase to $46,586, which seems to be an improvement over the currently projected profit of $40,658. However, Julius may not want to address the problems associated with operating a retail store for an incremental profit increase of only $5,928 ($46,586 − $40,658).

The structure and information required to prepare the master budget can be used very easily to provide the basis for what-if analysis. (It took only several seconds to answer Julius' questions using the spreadsheet developed to prepare the Ontario Tole Art's cash flow forecast).

Evaluating Decision-Making Alternatives

Suppose that Julius is considering renting a machine to automatically sand the buoys and apply the primer coat. The capacity of the machine is 1300 buoys per month. This machine will reduce the painting time per buoy from 0.8 hours to 0.5 hours but will increase annual shop costs from $20,000 to $35,000. The reduction in painting time per buoy enables Ontario Tole Art to reduce the number of painters needed for any level of scheduled production.

Exhibit 9-15 shows the revised pro forma income statement reflecting the rental of the sanding and priming machine.[11] Renting this machine will increase

---

[9] What-if analysis is undertaken using computer spreadsheet software. Your instructor may have the spreadsheet that was used to prepare the cash flow budget in this chapter and to undertake the what-if analysis reported in the text. If so, you might use it to do your own what-if analysis.

[10] This revised profit number was found by inserting the revised price and demand schedule in the spreadsheet that was used to prepare the original budget figures. The detailed calculations used to develop these numbers are laborious and are not repeated here. If you wish, you can obtain the spreadsheet that was used to develop these numbers and verify that they are correct and also experiment with alternative possibilities.

[11] Again these numbers were found by inserting the change in the spreadsheet used to develop Ontario Tole Art's budget; the calculations are too laborious to reproduce here.

projected net income from the original level of $40,658 to $45,484, a 12% increase of $4826.

Sensitivity Analysis

What-if analysis is only as good as the model it uses. The model must be complete, it must reflect relationships accurately, and it must use reasonable estimates. If the model is complete and reflects capacity, cost, and revenue relationships accurately, the remaining issue is the accuracy of the data used. For this reason, planners test planning models by varying key estimates.

For example, suppose that one machine represents a bottleneck resource for manufacturing operations. Then the productivity, or output per hour, of that machine is a key estimate for the production plan. The production planner could test the effect of errors in the estimate of the machine's productivity on the production plan by varying the productivity number by 10% or 20% above and below the estimate used in the planning budget.

If forecasting errors on an estimate used in the production plan have a dramatic effect on the plan,

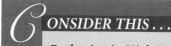

CONSIDER THIS ...

Budgeting in High-Technology Organizations

Photon Technology International, Inc., is a manufacturer of high-technology equipment used for medical research and diagnostic purposes. Like most growing companies, Photon Technology needed large amounts of cash to finance inventories, investments in capital assets, and accounts receivable. In addition, as a high-technology company, it needed to make large investments in research and development. In response to continuing liquidity problems, Chuck Grant, the chief operating officer, introduced a budgeting cycle. The budgeting cycle allowed the company to identify and anticipate its cash requirements and plan to meet them systematically. Photon undertook three what-if scenarios to develop contingency plans to meet its cash requirements under best-case, worst-case, and most likely situations affecting cash flows.

Source: Janine S. Pouliot, "High-Tech Budgeting," *Management Accounting,* May 1991, pp. 30–31.

EXHIBIT 9-15
Ontario Tole Art
Sanding/Priming Machine Option
Projected Income Statement
For the Year Ended December 31, 1997

Revenue		$282,530
Flexible resource expenses		
Buoys	$10,350	
Paint	14,490	
Other supplies	12,650	
Packing	8,970	
Shipping	34,500	80,960
Contribution margin		$201,570
Committed resource expenses		
Painter's salaries	$30,000	
Shop rent	19,200	
Other shop costs	35,000	
Manager's salary	30,000	114,200
Other expenses		
Advertising	$40,000	
Interest paid	1,886	41,886
Net income		$ 45,484

These consultants are involved in planning how they will staff their operation for the coming year. Planning of this type is critical, because consulting organizations constantly try to provide clients with the highest possible level of service while also monitoring service costs. *Courtesy* **Jim Pickerell/The Image Works**

Sensitivity analysis
An analytical tool that involves selectively varying key estimates of a plan or budget.

we say that the model is *sensitive* to that estimate. If the consequences from a bad estimate are severe, planners may want to invest time and resources to improve the accuracy of their estimates. **Sensitivity analysis** is the process of selectively varying a plan's or a budget's key estimates. Such sensitivity analysis allows planners to identify the estimates that are most critical for the decisions based on that model.

For example, the labor that Ontario Tole Art needs to make each product is an important parameter in its planning budget. Small changes in this parameter, which is the key productive resource, produce large changes in the profit figure. If Ontario Tole Art can develop a process or redesign the product so that labor time needed to make a buoy would be reduced by 10%, from 0.8 to 0.72 hours per buoy, projected profit would rise from $40,658 to $53,255, a 31% increase.[12] This is a signal to Julius that designing and running the manufacturing process so that the artists can work as efficiently as possible are keys to the success of the business.

COMPARING PLANNED AND ACTUAL RESULTS

Organizations often find it useful for the purpose of understanding results to compare expected, or projected, results in the master budget with actual results. Chapter 5 indicated how organizations can use differences, or variances, between the planned and actual level of costs as a warning signal to trigger a more detailed investigation of the circumstances that led to the variances. In Chapter 11 we will discuss the concept of control, which is the umbrella concept that includes variance analysis.

THE ROLE OF BUDGETING IN SERVICE AND NOT-FOR-PROFIT ORGANIZATIONS

OBJECTIVE 9.6

Define the role of budgets in service and not-for-profit organizations.

To this point, we have discussed the role of budgeting in manufacturing organizations. Budgeting serves a slightly different but equally relevant role in natural resource companies, service organizations, and not-for-profit (NFP) organizations

---

[12] Once again, these numbers were developed by making the appropriate changes in the spreadsheet used to develop the original budget numbers for Ontario Tole Art.

such as charitable organizations and government agencies. As in manufacturing organizations, budgeting helps nonmanufacturing organizations perform their planning function by coordinating and formalizing responsibilities and relationships and communicating the expected plans. Exhibit 9-16 summarizes the main focus of the budgeting process in manufacturing, natural resource, service, and NFP organizations.

In the natural resources sector, the key focus is on balancing demand with the availability of natural resources, such as minerals, fish, or wood. Because the natural resource supply often constrains sales, success requires managing the resource base effectively to match resource supply with potential demand.

In the service sector, the key focus is on balancing demand and the organization's ability to provide services, which is determined by the number and mix of skills in the organization. Although the service sector frequently uses machines to deliver products to customers, most operations remain labor paced; that is, they operate at a pace dictated by their human operators. Therefore, people rather than machines usually represent the capacity constraint in the service sector. A key issue in planning in the service sector is to consider the time needed to put skilled new people in place as sales increase. Planning is critical in high-skill organizations, such as in a consulting business because people capacity is expensive and services cannot be inventoried when demand falls below capacity.

In NFP organizations, the traditional focus of budgeting has been to balance revenues raised by taxes or donations with spending demands. Government agencies call planned cash outflows, or spending plans, **appropriations.** Appropriations set limits on a government agency's spending. Governments worldwide are facing increased pressures to eliminate deficits without raising tax revenues. Therefore, many governments are looking for ways to eliminate unnecessary expenditures and to make necessary expenditures more efficient rather than just ensuring that government agencies do not spend more than they have been authorized to do. Thus, as part of the planning process, these agencies must establish priorities for their expenditures and improve the productivity with which they deliver services to constituents.

Appropriation
An authorized spending limit in a government department.

PERIODIC AND CONTINUAL BUDGETING

The basic budgeting process described in this chapter involves many organizational design decisions, such as the periodicity of the budget process, the basic budget spending assumptions, and the degree of top-management control.

The budget process described for Ontario Tole Art is performed on an annual or **periodic budget** cycle. Gael, the owner, prepares budgets periodically for

Periodic budget
A budget that is prepared for a specified period of time, usually 1 year.

EXHIBIT 9-16
Focus of Budgeting in Different Organizations

Organization Type	Main Focus of Budgeting Process
Manufacturing	Sales and manufacturing activities
Natural resource	Sales, resource availability, and acquisition
Service	Sales activities and staffing requirements
NFP	Raising revenues and controlling expenditures

Ethics in Budgeting

Ivan Kilpatrick, a former vice-president of Bombardier, Inc., a large Canadian manufacturer of specialty vehicles, has a complaint. He claims that many management accountants, under pressure from senior executives, knowingly prepare budgets that overstate revenues and understate expenses. As evidence to support his assertion, Mr. Kilpatrick observed that profit variances are almost always unfavorable rather than being unfavorable about 50% of the time, which is what would be expected if the estimates were unbiased. Mr. Kilpatrick observed, "Accountants must remember that we are members of a profession, and we should speak out against the nonsense of fantasy forecasts."

Source: Ivan Kilpatrick, "It's Time to Face the Music on Budgets," *CMA Magazine,* March 1994, p. 6.

each planning period. Although planners may update or revise the budgets during the period, periodic budgeting is typically performed once per budget period.

In **continual budgeting,** as one budget period, usually a month or a quarter, passes, planners delete that budget period from the master budget and add another budget period in its place. Therefore, if Ontario Tole Art used continual budgeting with a one-year cycle, Julius would drop one month from the beginning of the budget period and add one month to the end of the budget period as each month passes. For example, at the end of February 1997, Julius would drop February from the budget and add February 1998.

The length of the budget period used in continual budgeting reflects the competitive forces, skill requirements, and technology changes that the organization faces. The budget period must be long enough for the organization to anticipate important environmental changes and adapt to them and yet short enough to ensure that estimates for the end of the period will be reasonable and realistic.

Continual budgeting
A budgeting process that plans for a specified period of time, usually one year, and is organized into budget subintervals, usually a month or a quarter.

Advocates of periodic budgeting argue that continual budgeting takes too much time and effort and that periodic budgeting provides virtually the same benefits at a smaller cost. Advocates of continual budgeting argue that it keeps the organization planning, assessing, and thinking strategically year-round rather than just once a year at budget time.

CONTROLLING DISCRETIONARY EXPENDITURES

Organizations use three general approaches to budget discretionary expenditures for items such as spending on R&D:

1. incremental budgeting
2. zero-based budgeting (ZBB)
3. project funding

Each has important differences, which explains why all three are used in practice.

Incremental budgeting
An approach to developing appropriations for discretionary expenditures that assumes that the starting point for each discretionary expenditure item is the amount spent on it in the previous year.

Incremental Budgeting

Incremental budgeting bases a period's expenditure level for a discretionary item on the amount spent for that item during the previous period. For example, if the total budget for discretionary items increases by 10%, each discretionary item is allowed to increase 10%. This basic model has variations, for example, if the total spending on all discretionary items is allowed to increase by 10%, all discretionary spending may experience an across-the-board increase of 5% and the remaining 5% increase in total spending may be allocated to discretionary items based on merit or need.

Some people have criticized incremental budgeting because it does not require justifications of the organization's goals for discretionary expenditures. Incremental budgeting includes no provision to reduce or eliminate expenditures as the organization changes nor does it have a mechanism to provide disproportionate support to discretionary items that will yield substantial benefits.

Zero-Based Budgeting

Zero-based budgeting (ZBB) requires that proponents of discretionary expenditures continually justify every expenditure. For each planning period, the starting point for each budget line item is zero. Zero-based budgeting arose, in part, to combat indiscriminate incremental budgets since that approach can require very little thought and result in misallocation of resources.

Under zero-based budgeting, planners allocate the organization's scarce resources to the spending proposals they think will best achieve the organization's goals. While seemingly logical, the zero-based approach to planning discretionary expenditures is controversial. This approach has been used primarily to assess most government expenditures, but in profit-seeking organizations it has been applied only to discretionary expenditures such as research and development, advertising, and employee training.

Traditionally, zero-based budgeting ideas do not apply to engineered costs (short-term costs that have an identifiable relationship with some activity level). Engineered costs are controlled by measuring and using reports of the amounts of resources consumed by operating activities and by the cost variances described earlier. But even for engineered costs, ZBB could be effective when combined with the *re-engineering* approach. For example, re-engineering a product or process involves developing a vision of how a product should perform or how a process should work independently of current conditions. It is possible to use ZBB as a tool to provide baseline costs to new products or processes.

Zero-based budgeting
An approach to developing appropriations for discretionary expenditures that assumes that the starting point for each discretionary expenditure is zero.

Project Funding

Critics of zero-based budgeting have observed that it is very expensive because it requires so much employee time to prepare. These critics have proposed an intermediate solution between the two extremes of zero-based budgeting and incremental budgeting to mitigate the disadvantages of each. The intermediate solution is called **project funding**, which is a proposal for discretionary expenditures with a specific time horizon or sunset provision.[13]

People proposing discretionary expenditures state their request in terms of a project proposal that includes how long the project will last and how much money it will require each period during the project's life. Planners approve no discretionary spending for projects that have indeterminate lengths or spending amounts. If the planners approve the project, they agree to provide the level of

Project funding
An approach to developing appropriations for discretionary expenditures that organizes appropriations into a package with a focus on achieving some defined output.

---

[13] Projects with indefinite lives are sometimes called programs.

After Hurricane Andrew hit the south Florida and Louisiana coasts in 1992, Shell Oil
Company established this aid center in Homestead, Florida. Shell funded this discretionary spending as a project. *Courtesy* Shell Oil Company

support requested in the plan. Requests to extend or modify the project must be
approved separately. The advantage of providing sunset provisions is that they
strike an intermediate balance between the high cost resulting from the need for
the close scrutiny and continual justification provided by zero-based budgeting
and the much lower cost of incremental budgeting.

MANAGING THE BUDGETING PROCESS

Who should manage and oversee the budgeting process? Many organizations use
a budget team, headed by the organization's budget director, sometimes the controller, to coordinate the budgeting process. The budget team usually reports to a
budget committee, which generally includes the chief executive officer, the chief
operating officer, and the senior executive vice-presidents. The composition of
the budget committee reflects the role of the budget as a key planning document
that reflects and relates to the organization's strategy and objectives. The danger
of using a budget committee is that it may signal to other employees that budgeting is something that is relevant only for senior management. Senior management
must take steps to ensure that the organization members affected by the budget
do not perceive it and the budgeting process as something beyond their control or
responsibility.

OBJECTIVE 9.7

Evaluate the behavioral
effects of budgeting
on an organization's
employees.

BEHAVIORAL ASPECTS OF BUDGETING

Since people are involved in the entire process, budgets often do not develop in a
smooth, frictionless manner. How do people try to affect the budget and, in turn,

how do budgets affect people's behavior? These questions have led social scientists to engage in extensive study about the human factors involved in budgeting.

Regardless of whether you are developing a family budget, a budget for a small company like Ontario Tole Art, or a budget for a major multinational company, you should be aware that the ways that people interact with budgets are essentially the same. In this section, we will discuss two interrelated behavioral issues in budgeting:

1. **Designing the Budget Process.** How should budgets be determined, who should be involved in the budgeting process, and at what level of difficulty should the budget be set to have the greatest positive influence on people's motivation and performance?

2. **Influencing the Budget Process.** How do people try to influence or manipulate the budget to their own ends?

Designing the Budget Process

Where do the data come from that planners use to prepare the master budget and supporting plans? How should budgets be determined and who should be involved in the budgeting process?

The three most common methods of setting budgets are known as authoritarian, participation, and consultation. **Authoritative budgeting** occurs when a superior simply tells subordinates what their budget will be. The benefit to the organization is that the process is straightforward and efficient—it allows superiors to assign budgets and promotes overall coordination among subunits in the organization because it is done from a single perspective. Managers who want to impose a budget in a top-down manner often desire control and have authoritarian aspects to their personalities. One disadvantage of imposing budgets is that superiors may have no clear idea what the appropriate target levels within the budget should be. Targets are the goals related to each part of the budget. In this instance, the superior indicates what the goals of subordinates will be. Under authoritative budgeting, a subordinate who has high aspirations for the coming year regarding new goals may now become frustrated and debilitated. A second problem is the lack of motivation and commitment to the budgeted goals because of the lack of employee participation in establishing the budget. Worse yet, if the superior sets high goals and only provides a small budget for resource spending, motivation can decrease significantly and individuals and the organization can fail to attain their goals.

Research shows that the most motivating types of budgets are those that are *tight*—those with targets that are perceived as ambitious but attainable. Recently, companies such as Boeing and General Electric have implemented what are known as **stretch targets.** In the past, both these companies used an incremental approach in which targets from the previous year were increased slightly. Stretch targets exceed previous targets by a significant amount and usually require an enormous increase in a goal over the next budgeting period. **Stretch budgeting** means that the organization will attempt to reach much higher goals with the current budget. The rationale for this approach is that stretch targets really push an organization to its limits. The theory behind this type of budgeting is that only in this manner will companies completely reevaluate the ways in which they develop

Authoritative budgeting
A top-down approach to budgeting in which a superior tells a subordinate what the budget will be.

Stretch targets
Those targets that represent significant increases in the targeted amount, or goal, above the existing targets or goals.

Stretch budgeting
An approach to budgeting in which an organization attempts to achieve much higher goals than normal with the current budget.

3M's Scotch-Brite soap pads set a record from the idea stage to being brought to market based on the stretch target concept. The product is made from recycled plastic beverage bottles and will not rust or splinter. In the first 18 months of being introduced, the product garnered 22% of the $100-million-a-year U.S. market from Brillo and SOS. *Courtesy* Chris Corsmeier Photography

Participative budgeting
A method of budgeting in which superiors and subordinates jointly set the budget.

and produce products and services. While some employees thrive in this type of environment, the pace of work and difficulty of achieving stretch targets can frustrate many and cause others to quit their jobs. Further, while employees may be able to push themselves very hard to meet the stretch target in the short run, they may not be able to sustain an enormously high level of effort in every subsequent period. Organizations need to make sure that they provide resources and a plan so that employees believe that stretch targets are achievable.

Participative budgeting is a method of budget setting that involves a *joint decision-making process* in which all parties agree about setting the budget targets. Allowing employees to participate in decision making provides an opportunity for them to use their private or specific information to jointly set their goals and negotiate the level of their budget. Participation has many benefits for employees, such as greater feelings of commitment to the budget and, therefore, a higher level of motivation to attain goals and keep within the budget. Research on participative budgeting has shown that employees generally feel greater job satisfaction, and higher morale, due primarily to greater control over their jobs. In some instances, higher levels of performance can result. Allowing participation has an additional benefit for management because participation often induces subordinates to reveal what is called their *private information* about how well they can perform their jobs

---

CONSIDER THIS . . .

Five Ways to Manage People Facing Stretch Targets

In an interview with *Fortune,* Steve Kerr, described as the "Chief Learning Officer" at General Electric, states that "Most organizations don't have a clue about how to manage stretch goals." He offers the following advice:

1. By definition, stretch goals are very difficult to meet. Don't punish people for not hitting them.
2. Don't set goals that stretch your employees crazily.
3. Understand that stretch targets can unexpectedly affect other parts of the organization.
4. Don't give tough stretch goals to those people already pushing themselves to the limit.
5. Share the wealth generated by reaching stretch goals.

Source: Strat Sherman, "Stretch Goals: The Dark Side of Asking for Miracles," *Fortune,* November 13, 1995, pp. 231–232.

or to introduce new ideas that may help improve existing processes. As a result of discussing the budget jointly, subordinates indirectly reveal this information and their level of aspiration to management. This allows the private information of the subordinate to become incorporated into the planning process.

The third method of setting the budget is called **consultative budgeting.** Consultative budgeting occurs when managers ask subordinates to discuss their ideas about the budget, but no joint decision making occurs. Instead, the superior solicits the subordinates' ideas but determines the final budget alone. For many large organizations in which complete participation is impractical, consultation is the norm. A variant of the consultative form of budgeting may occur when the subordinate believes that his or her input will be used directly in setting the budget, even though his or her superior really has no intention of considering the subordinate's input. This process is called **pseudo-participation** and can have a very strong debilitating effect on subordinates if they find out that the superior was insincere.

Influencing the Budget Process

Clearly, the budgeting process is not a simple mechanical process. The budgeting process highlights the need for interactions involving resource allocation, organizational goals, and human motivation and performance. As with families, budgets in large organizations represent the outcomes of negotiations among individuals. Some individuals will do all that they can to increase the size of their budget because they believe that the size of one's budget is a symbol of power and control in organizations.

While the budget is used as a tool for planning, coordinating, and resource allocation, it is also used to measure performance and ultimately to control and influence behavior. In addition, many managers have their incentive compensation tied directly to budget and goal attainment. When incentives and compensation are tied to the budget, some managers engage in behavior that is dysfunctional to their organizations. Managers have been known to play **budgeting games** in which they attempt to manipulate information and targets to achieve as high a bonus as possible. One well-known way that managers engage in budgeting games is through the participation process.

Participation provides employees the opportunity to affect their budgets in ways that may not always be in the best interests of the organization. For instance, subordinates might ask for excess resources above and beyond what they need to accomplish their budget objectives. This results in a misallocation of resources for the organization as a whole. Another risk is that subordinates will distort information by claiming that they are not as efficient or effective at what they do as they appear, thereby attempting to lower management's expectations of their performance. Subordinates may want some additional cushion in performance requirements in case there is an unforeseen change in the work environment that detrimentally affects resources or impairs their ability to meet the budget. If subordinates succeed in this type of negotiation, they will find it easy to meet or exceed their budgeted objectives. Again the organization suffers as it is not obtaining the most accurate information that is available to assess, and thereby improve, its operations. Both of these acts—requiring excess resources and distorting performance information—fall under the heading of creating **budget slack.**

Consultative budgeting
A budgeting process in which a subordinate is asked to discuss ideas about the budget, but no joint decision making occurs.

Pseudo-participation
An approach to budgeting in which a subordinate believes he or she will have an influence on the budget process but actually does not have any effect.

Budget games
Attempts by managers to manipulate information and targets to achieve their budgets and to attain high bonuses.

Budget slack
The result of subordinates either (1) building excess resources above and beyond what they need to achieve their budget objectives or (2) distorting information about their ability to achieve a budget.

*C*ONSIDER THIS . . .

"Oh the (Budgeting) Games People Play Now, Every Night and Every Day Now, Never Meaning What They Say, Never Saying What They Mean" (with apologies to Joe South; Capitol Records, 1969)

In this humorous article, Sigmund Ginsburg describes the nine classic types of approaches that managers use in negotiating their budgets. Do you recognize any of these characters?

- **The Gardener** is known for "watering" his budget so that all the bushes and trees grow many new shoots. Each shoot represents something he doesn't really desire such as a new coffee machine or a training seminar for his staff. At budget time, the gardener makes slick presentations that justify his requests; however, by that time the garden has grown into a jungle. Trying to cut his budget is exhausting and that is how the gardener always fares well with his budget.

- **The Duck Hunter** knows how to use decoys well. She peppers her budget with ducks, some of which are real and some of which are decoys. The decoys are often an expensive new project presented in very complex terms. The duck hunter's strategy is to focus your attention on the details relating to the decoy so that you will not notice her real programs. She will try to get you so intrigued with the decoys that you could spend an entire day discussing them and not the real issues.

- **The Entrepreneur's** song is "I need the right kind of investment and management support for my new idea." The entrepreneur is flamboyant, gutsy, and innovative. He uses graphs and charts to illustrate how with very little money he will make the company a fortune. The problem is that many of the entrepreneur's ideas are untested. If he fails, he will simply tell you that he was implementing a high-risk proposition.

- **The Gambler** has a perfect poker face when it comes to negotiations. His air is that of an old-time riverboat confidence man. He needs his budget to achieve a big score and he is willing to take enormous risks to win. His threat is "Cut my budget and I'll resign." He's hoping that you won't call his bluff.

- **The Surgeon** enters your office looking very grim. She has just performed a major operation on her budget. You can almost see the bloodstains on her gown. She laments that the patient cannot take any more as she has cut everything to the bare bone. Any more surgery will damage the vital organs.

When you suggest that she cut some more, she tells you that she won't take responsibility if her department cannot meet its objectives.

- **The Good Soldier** is a true company person and follows all company policies and believes in all company objectives. She claims to have adhered strictly to your orders regarding a bare bones budget. As she is turning over her battle plan to you, she states that she will leave it up to you to make any changes. Since every officer needs a good soldier to depend on, you may feel that you should trust her judgment and give her the money. If you do, you may find that with her experience she has successfully padded the budget.

- **The Drowning Man** makes his budget presentation as if it were his last. "We are going down for the last time." He requests more money so that he and his employees can keep their heads above water. Using guilt, the drowning man wants you to feel that you have always underfunded him. Now is the time to help him he cries. Faced with such a plea, you have to decide whether now is the time to fund him.

- **The Savior** approaches you and says, "I'm not here to talk about saving some funds for my department, I'm here to talk about saving the entire firm." Speaking in an impassioned manner, the savior says that his department needs a great deal of money not only to achieve its objectives but to carry the entire company. It appears that he is willing to take on the weight of the company; however, he is also implying that if you don't fund him, the company's future is at stake. Do you believe him?

- **The Honest Guy** is a very rare animal indeed. This is someone who really means what he says. His budget seems to be accurate and realistic. He does not dwell on past accomplishments and discusses his department's problems in a straightforward manner. He guarantees that there is no fat in his budget. In dealing with the honest guy, you have to follow your instincts and give him his budget. If you cut him arbitrarily, he may turn into the drowning man—something you certainly do not want to happen.

Source: Sigmund G. Ginsburg, "Negotiating Budgets: Games People Play," *INC.*, September 1981, pp. 89–91.

Consider a manager who is worried that a supplier will be unwilling to sell raw materials at an historically budgeted price. The manager may decide to increase the amount requested for purchasing raw materials, which would build slack into this budget line item. The request leads to assigning excess resources for this purpose and hence fewer resources for other purposes. Other distortions can arise from arbitrary increases in resource requests because the resulting established standard costs for products will be incorrect. Further, subordinates are also concerned about standards or budgets that are too difficult to attain; if their bonuses are based on attaining a budget, they will opt for an easier budget. To counter the problem of low target-setting, management may design an incentive system that provides higher levels of bonuses based on attaining higher targets.

Budgeting games can never be eliminated, although some organizations have devised methods to decrease the amount of budget slack. They can use an iterative process to formulate the budget, for example, developing a very lengthy budgeting cycle that may last as long as a year. Then subordinate managers submit a preliminary budget, which is modified by senior management and then sent back to subordinate managers for modification. The modifications usually require justification for each line item in painful detail. This process continues for several iterations until senior management becomes convinced that they have eliminated as much slack as possible out of the subordinate manager's budget. The other benefit to this process is that by the time the budget is agreed upon, both parties have developed a strong commitment to the budget. This commitment gives them confidence that they can achieve their goals for the coming year.

THE LEGAL SERVICES DEPARTMENT REVISITED

Faced with the certainty that funding matters would get worse and not better, Fred Powell identified the need for developing a budgeting system. He started by asking funding planners who develop government spending allocations to provide funding estimates for the next two or three years. Fred also identified the range of legal services that his department was offering and the approximate cost to perform each service. Then he organized services into three groups: (1) those that were required by law, (2) those that were discretionary but critical, and (3) those that were not critical. He identified the quantity of each service needed as well as the cost of providing it and compared the totals with estimates of expected funding.

During this process, Fred discovered two things. First, the cost of some of the activities that his staff was undertaking seemed to be higher than comparable costs quoted for similar work by outsiders. He discovered that most of these services involved court situations in which his staff was relatively inexperienced. These situations required much longer preparation times than that used by outsiders who specialized in these matters. Second, most of the growth in demand for services was coming from services that were required by law and were the result of changes in legislation.

Fred and his supervisor approached a government committee with this information and explained to them the consequences in terms of work and cost of the changes in the legislation. They reached an agreement that allowed Fred to contract with outside organizations that could provide certain specialty legal services more efficiently and to divide the budget into two components—the committed component and the discretionary component. The committee agreed to provide ongoing support to set priorities for legal services. This allowed Fred, given the budget allocation and the committed amount of work, to identify which discretionary services would be accomplished and which would be rejected due to lack of funding.

SUMMARY

A budget is a quantitative expression of the money inflows and outflows used to determine whether a financial plan will meet organizational goals. A budget supports the management roles of planning and control by providing the means to express plans and the foundation for control activities. In many short-term decisions, only flexible costs are relevant, while committed costs are thought of as given. In this chapter, we discussed the budgeting that determines the level of committed costs. In an ideal situation, the supply of committed resources is determined based on the demands for the services the resources provide for projected levels of product volumes and mix.

The budgeting process forces the organization to do the following:

1. Identify its long-term objectives and short-term goals and be specific in setting goals and evaluating performance relative to those goals.
2. Recognize the need to view the organization as a system of interacting components that must be coordinated.
3. Communicate the organization's goals to all organization members and involve them in the budgeting process.
4. Anticipate problems, thereby handling them proactively rather than reactively.

The master budget is the set of operating and financial plans that summarize the organization's activities for the upcoming budget period, which is usually one year. The financial plans developed in the master budget include a projected or pro forma cash flow statement, balance sheet, and income statement. Planners use the projected balance sheet and income statement to evaluate the financial consequences of a proposed short-term business plan. Financial managers use the statement of projected cash flows to plan when the business will generate excess cash to help plan short-term investments or ways to meet their cash shortages in the least expensive manner.

The chapter presented a detailed master budgeting exercise and developed the financial plans for a set of given operating plans. Organizations make financial commitments when they acquire special-purpose facilities or capacity in the long term and general-purpose facilities or capacity in the intermediate term. In the short term, organizations acquire other resources, such as materials and casual labor, as needed, allowing them to use longer-term capacity to produce products and services.

The insights of what-if analysis, a modeling exercise that explores the operating and financial consequences of varying a proposed plan, allows decision makers to plan effectively. In addition, sensitivity analysis explores the sensitivity of operating decisions and financial results to the estimates used in the planning model.

The source of information used in budgeting models is important in two ways. First, the information source should be credible and reliable. Second, the potential use of planning information for control can create a potential behavioral conflict. Budgeting in nonmanufacturing environments, such as the natural resource sector, the service sector, and the nonprofit sector, were discussed. The chapter also described incremental budgeting and compared it with zero-based budgeting, which bases the appropriations in the current budget on those in the previous budget. Finally, there are important behavioral considerations regarding the budgeting process, such as who should be involved with the process, the concept of budget slack, and stretch budgets and commitment.

KEY TERMS

administrative and discretionary
   spending plan, p. 411

aggregate planning, p. 418

appropriation, p. 433

authoritative budgeting, p. 437

budget, p. 406

budget games, p. 439

budgeting, p. 406

budget slack, p. 439

capital spending plan, p. 410

consultative budgeting, p. 439

continual budgeting, p. 434

demand forecast, p. 417

discretionary expenditure, p. 419

engineered expenditure, p. 419

financial budgets, p. 409

incremental budgeting, p. 434

labor hiring and training plan,   p. 411

line of credit, p. 428

master budget, p. 409

materials purchasing plan, p. 410

participative budgeting, p. 438

periodic budget, p. 433

production plan, p. 410

pro forma statement, p. 410

project funding, p. 435

pseudo-participation, p. 439

sales plan, p. 410

sensitivity analysis, p. 432

stretch budgeting, p. 437

stretch targets, p. 437

variance, p. 408

what-if-analysis, p. 430

zero-based budgeting, p. 435

ASSIGNMENT MATERIAL

■ QUESTIONS

9-1   What is a budget?

9-2   What is the difference between flexible and committed resources?

9-3   What role do budgets play in determining the level of flexible and committed resources?

9-4   A student develops a spending plan for a school semester. Is this budgeting? Why?

9-5   How does a family's budget differ from a budget developed for an organization?

9-6   What is a demand forecast and why is it relevant in budgeting?

9-7   Is employee training an example of a discretionary expenditure? Why?

9-8   What is a line of credit? How is it useful to a small organization?

9-9   Using the notion of aggregate planning, what problems would municipal authorities face when planning transportation for people attending a rock concert in the city's center?

9-10   What is an appropriation? Give an example of one in a university.

9-11   What does a capital spending plan do?

9-12   What is an example of a committed expenditure?

9-13   Are food costs in a university residence cafeteria an engineered cost or a committed cost? Briefly explain.

9-14   What is the difference between operating and financial budgets?

9-15   What is a production plan? Give an example of one in a courier company.

9-16   What is a variance? How is a warning light in a car that indicates that the oil pressure is low like a variance?

9-17   What do you think is the most significant committed resource in terms of dollar expenditures in a university?

9-18   What are the similarities and differences between what-if and sensitivity analysis?

9-19   Are materials always a flexible resource? Why?

9-20   You are planning your expenses for the upcoming school semester. You assume that this year's expenditures will equal last year's plus 2%. What approach to budgeting are you using?

9-21   You are willing to donate to worthy organizations. However, you believe strongly that each request for a donation should be evaluated based on its own merits. You would not feel bad in any year if you donated nothing. What approach to budgeting are you using?

9-22   What is the relationship between a demand forecast and a sales plan?

9-23   Would a labor hiring and training plan be more important in a university or a municipal government office that hires casual workers to do unskilled work? Why?

9-24   What is a periodic budget?

9-25   What are the two interrelated behavioral issues in budgeting?

9-26   What are the three methods of setting the budget?

9-27 What is the most motivating type of budget?

9-28 What is budget slack?

9-29 What is a stretch target?

■ EXERCISES

9-30 *Budgeting process*   The text mentioned that budgeting is often an iterative process. If the results of a plan are unacceptable, it is changed to find better results. Does this suggest anything to you about the process of planning?

9-31 *Budgeting information*   Consider a company that sells prescription drugs. It has salespeople who visit doctors and hospitals to encourage physicians to prescribe its drugs. The company sells to drugstores. Salespeople are evaluated based on the sales in their territory. Their income is a salary plus a bonus if actual sales exceed planned sales. To plan operations, this company needs to develop estimates of total sales. Where should it get this information?

9-32 *Budgeting and planning*   Some people say that "budgets are great for planning but not for control." What do you think they mean by that? Do you agree with this sentiment? Explain.

9-33 *Budgeting: types of resources in a university*   For a university, identify a cost that you think is controllable in the short term and explain why you think it is. Identify a cost that you think is controllable in the intermediate term and explain why you think it is. Identify a cost that you think is controllable in the long term and explain why you think it is. What does this cost structure imply about the university's flexibility in responding to changing student demands and enrollment?

9-34 *Financial budgets*   Many managers consider the pro forma financial statements to be the most important product of the master budgeting process. Why do you think they believe this?

9-35 *Financial budgets: cash flows*   Monthly cash budgets, of inflows and outflows, are an important part of the budgeting process in most organizations. In the course of preparing a cash budget, the organization must estimate its cash inflows from credit sales. Suppose that in response to projected cash shortfalls the organization decides to speed up its collections of credit sales. What effect can this have on the organization?

9-36 *Consulting company: types of resources*   Budgeting allows an organization to identify broad resource requirements so that it can develop plans to put needed resources in place. Use an example to illustrate why this might be valuable in a consulting company that provides advice to clients.

9-37 *Canning company: budgeting process*   Budgeting allows an organization to identify potential problems so that plans can be developed to avoid these problems or to deal with them systematically. Give an example of how budgeting might serve this role in a company that buys vegetables and cans them.

9-38 *Machine shop: comparing financial and operational results*   Budgeting allows an organization to compare its projected operating and financial results with those of competitors as a general test of the efficiency of the organization's operating processes. Explain how this might be valuable for a machine shop that does custom machining work for its customers.

9-39 *Sensitivity analysis*   Sensitivity analysis is an important component of any budgeting exercise. Which estimates do you think will be most crucial in developing a master budget? Why?

9-40 *Sensitivity analysis: cost cutting*   A university faced with a deficit reacts by cutting resource allocations to all faculties and departments by 8%. Do you think this is a good approach to budgeting? Why?

9-41 *Method of setting the budget*   How does participation in the budgeting process differ from consultation?

9-42 *Budget slack*   What are the pros and cons of building slack into the budget from (a) the point of view of the employee building in slack and (b) from a senior manager's point of view?

9-43 *Budgeting games*   What are budgeting games, and why do employees engage in them?

■ PROBLEMS

Fundamental Problems

9-44 *Operating budgets: production plan*   Borders Manufacturing is developing a sales and production plan as part of its master budgeting process. Projected monthly sales, which occur uniformly during each month, for the upcoming year follow:

BORDERS MANUFACTURING

Projected Monthly Sales

Month	Unit Sales
January	8742
February	9415
March	7120
April	8181
May	7942
June	9681
July	2511
August	2768
September	2768
October	2283
November	1542
December	1980
January	8725

Production for each month equals one-half of the current month's sales plus one-half of the next month's projected sales. Develop the production plan for Borders Manufacturing for the upcoming year.

9-45 *Operating budgets: labor hiring and production plan*   Mira Vista Planters provides reforestation services to large paper products companies. It must hire one planter for every 10,000 trees that it has contracted to plant each month. An employee must receive one week of evaluation and training before being profitably employed. For every five prospective employees who enter training, three are deemed suitable for employment. When cutbacks occur, employees are laid off on the first day of the month. Every employee laid off receives severance pay equal to one week's salary, which is on average $400, regardless of how long the layoff will last. Laid-off employees inevitably drift away and new hires must be trained.

The company has been offered the following contracts for the upcoming year. Each monthly contract is offered on an accept or reject basis, that is, if a monthly contract is accepted, it must be completed in full. Partial completion is not acceptable. The revenue per tree planted is $0.20.

MIRA VISTA PLANTERS
Monthly Tree Planting Contracts

Month	Trees
January	8,692
February	5,765
March	8,134
April	34,400
May	558,729
June	832,251
July	1,286,700
August	895,449
September	733,094
October	203,525
November	29,410
December	9,827

Prepare a labor plan for the upcoming year, indicating the following for each month:
(a) Whether you feel the company should accept or reject the proposed planting contract.
(b) How many people will be hired for training. (Recall that an employee is not available for planting during the week of training and that only three of the five employees accepted for training can be hired.)
(c) How many people will be laid off. The organization will have two trained employees on January 1.

9-46 *Operating budgets: materials purchasing plan*   Pasadena Chemical Company manufactures a wide range of chemical compounds. One of the most difficult compounds is a cleaning solvent made from an expensive and volatile raw material called *tetrax* that is often in short supply. The company uses one liter of tetrax for every 100 liters of cleaning solvent that it makes.

Tetrax costs $560 per liter and must be stored in space leased in a special warehouse. The storage cost including all related costs is $2 per liter per day stored. The chemical is unstable and on average the loss is 1% of the volume stored per day. The cleaning compound can also be made from *monax*, which costs $1000 per liter. Because of the prohibitive cost of monax, however, Pasadena avoids using it unless it is absolutely necessary.

The three existing tetrax suppliers have been unreliable. For this reason, Pasadena has refused to begin production of the cleaning compound. Recently, a new supplier joined the field and guarantees the supply of tetrax under three conditions. Customers must be prepared to take weekly deliveries of tetrax, the weekly order must be for precisely the same quantity each week, and the contract must cover one year. If these conditions are met, the supplier will replace any undelivered tetrax with monax.

Because the cleaning compound itself is also volatile, users demand the product when they are ready for it and no sooner. Suppliers carefully estimate the amount of cleaner they require and will not accept less than the ordered amount.

The contracted cleaning compound sales for next year follow:

PASADENA CHEMICAL COMPANY
CLEANING SOLVENT PRODUCT

Month	Unit Sales	Month	Unit Sales
January	41,203	July	41,889
February	48,077	August	42,107
March	53,646	September	47,488
April	60,038	October	49,638
May	46,332	November	49,942
June	50,508	December	37,593

REQUIRED

(a) Set up a spreadsheet for this problem. The spreadsheet should allow you to compute the total cost of a contract with the new supplier. This total cost includes purchase price, storage cost, and the cost, if necessary, of any monax that would be purchased. The spreadsheet should be set up to allow you to vary the purchase quantity of tetrax easily. To simplify the problem, make the following assumptions:

- The loss each month is 1% times the number of days times the sum of (1) the average of the opening and ending inventory (before the loss) and (2) one-half the batch size.

- The cost of carrying inventory each month is 2 times the number of days times the sum of (1) the average of opening and closing inventory (after the loss) and (2) one-half the batch size.

- Production takes place 7 days per week.

- January, March, July, and November have 5 weeks; the rest of the months of the year have 4 weeks.

(b) What is the best weekly quantity to contract for purchase from the new supplier?

9-47 *Operating budgets: labor hiring plan* Strathfield Motel is planning its operations for the upcoming tourist season. The motel has 60 units and the following table presents the average number of daily rentals expected for each of the 12 weeks of the tourist season.

STRATHFIELD MOTEL
AVERAGE NUMBER OF DAILY RENTALS

Week	Average Units Rented	Week	Average Units Rented
1	46	7	55
2	48	8	55
3	54	9	50
4	60	10	45
5	60	11	37
6	60	12	30

The motel hires housekeeping staff on a weekly basis. Each person can clean 15 rooms per day. Employees must be hired for the entire week at a wage of $400 per employee per week. Because of the motel's location in a medium-sized city there are always trained people available to work on short notice.

The motel does not own its linen and towels but rents them from a rental agency in a nearby city. The rental contract must be signed for a four-week period and for a fixed amount of linen and towels. Therefore, the motel must sign three contracts for the 12-week tourist season. The contract provides the linen required for each room for $3 per night.

Prepare a weekly budget for the hotel showing the following:

(a) The number of housekeeping staff to employ

(b) The number of linen and towel units to contract

9-48 *Financial budgets: expense budget*   During the school year, the Homebush School band arranges concert dates in many communities. Because only part of the school's travel expenses are covered by the concert admission fees, the band raises money in the local community through events such as car washes to help defray its operating expenses.

To estimate its expenses for the upcoming year, the band's manager has estimated the number of concert dates for each of the school months, September through May. For each concert, the manager estimates hotel costs of $900, food costs of $480, bus rental costs of $600, and other costs of $200.

The following table presents the number of planned concerts during the upcoming year.

**HOMEBUSH SCHOOL BAND
SCHEDULED CONCERTS**

Month	Scheduled Concerts	Month	Scheduled Concerts
September	3	February	4
October	4	March	2
November	5	April	5
December	8	May	7
January	3		

Prepare a monthly schedule estimating the band's travel expenses.

9-49 *Methods of setting budgets*   Budgets are usually set through one of three methods—participation, authority, or consultation.

REQUIRED

Write an essay stating the circumstances under which each method is most appropriate. If you disagree with a particular method, justify your answer.

9-50 *Methods of setting budgets*   Megan Espanoza, manager of the Wells Division of Mars, Inc., a large credit card company, recently received a memorandum about the budgeting process for 1997. For the coming year, senior management at Mars would follow a new procedure regarding the budget-setting process. The process would work in the following manner. Megan and the other division managers would each submit a budget proposal outlining their operating plans and financial requirements. Management would then study the proposals and determine the budget for each division.

REQUIRED

(a) What is this form of budgeting called?

(b) What are the pros and cons of this approach? Explain.

Challenging Problems

9-51 *Operating budgets: materials purchasing plan*   Worthington Company makes cash (20% of total sales), credit card (50% of total sales), and account sales (30% of total sales). Credit card sales are collected in the month following the sale, net of a 3% credit card fee. This means that if the sale is $100, the credit card company's fee is $3, and Worthington receives $97. Account sales are collected as follows: 40% in the first month following the sale, 50% in the second month following the sale, 8% in the third month following the sale, and 2% never collected.

The following table identifies the projected sales for the next year.

WORTHINGTON COMPANY
PROJECTED SALES

Month	Sales	Month	Sales
January	12,369,348	July	21,747,839
February	15,936,293	August	14,908,534
March	13,294,309	September	11,984,398
April	19,373,689	October	18,894,535
May	20,957,566	November	21,983,545
June	18,874,717	December	20,408,367

If the collections from these sales are the only cash inflows in Worthington Company, prepare a statement showing the cash expected each month.

9-52 *Operating budgets: materials purchasing plan*   Masefield Dairy is preparing a third-quarter budget (July, August, and September) for its ice cream products. It produces five brands of ice cream, and each uses a different mix of ingredients. Its suppliers deliver ingredients just in time provided that they are given 2 months' notice. The following table indicates the units of each type of ingredient required per unit of each product.

MASEFIELD DAIRY
REQUIRED INGREDIENTS

			Product		
Ingredients	A	B	C	D	E
Ice cream	1	2	1	1	1
Ingredient 1	2	0	3	1	4
Ingredient 2	0	1	2	4	0
Ingredient 3	1	3	0	2	2
Ingredient 4	0	2	1	0	2
Ingredient 5	3	1	3	0	1

The following table summarizes the estimated unit sales for each product in each of the months in the third quarter.

MASEFIELD DAIRY
ESTIMATED UNIT SALES

Product	July	August	September
A	194,675	162,033	129,857
B	104,856	98,375	76,495
C	209,855	194,575	170,654
D	97,576	75,766	55,966
E	47,867	39,575	20,958

Prepare a monthly purchases budget for the ice cream ingredients.

9-53 *Financial budgets: wages and expense budgets*   Nathaniel's Motor Shop does major repair work on automobile engines. The major cost in the shop is the wages of the mechanics. The shop employs nine mechanics who are paid $750 for working a 40-hour week. The work week consists of five days of eight hours. Employees actually work seven hours each day, because they are given one hour of breaks each day. They are highly skilled and valued by their employer so these mechanics are paid whether or not there is work available for them to do. They are also paid $30 for every overtime hour or partial overtime hour that they work.

The machine shop industry estimates that for every mechanic hour actually worked in a shop like this, the employee consumes about $25 of variable overhead items, such as lubricants, tool parts, and electricity.

The motor shop has estimated that the following work will be available each week during the next 10 weeks.

NATHANIEL'S MOTOR SHOP
ESTIMATED WORK

Week	Hours of Work	Week	Hours of Work
1	255	6	280
2	330	7	260
3	300	8	300
4	285	9	340
5	325	10	355

Develop a weekly budget of mechanic wages and variable overhead costs.

9-54 *Financial budgets: cash outflows*   Country Club Road Nurseries grows and sells garden plants. The nursery is active between January and October each year. During January, the potting tables and equipment are prepared. The potting and seeding are done in February. In March and April, the plants are cultivated, watered, and fertilized. May and June are the peak selling months. July, August, and September are the peak months for visiting customers in their homes to provide them with advice and help solve their problems. During October, the equipment and buildings are secured for the winter months, and in November and December, full-time employees take their paid holidays and the business is closed.

The nursery employs 15 full-time staff and, depending on the season, up to 20 part-time staff. The full-time staff are paid an average wage of $2700 per month and work 160 hours per month.

The part-time staff are paid $10 per hour. Because the nursery relies on local students for part-time work, there is no shortage of trained people willing to work the hours that are available. The ratio of full-time employee hours worked to part-time employee hours worked is as follows: January, 5:1; February, 5:1; March, 3:1; April, 3:1; May, 1:1; June, 1:1; July, 1:1; August, 1:1; September, 2:1; and October, 4:1. Because part-time students are mainly used for moving and selling activities, their work creates very little incremental overhead costs.

Fixed costs, other than wages, associated with this operation are about $55,000 per month. The cost drivers in this operation are the activities that the full-time employees undertake. These cost drivers are proportional to the hours worked by the full-time employees. The variable costs depend on the season and reflect the common employee activities during that season. Average variable costs per employee hour worked are as follows: January, $15; February, $15; March, $15; April, $15; May, $5; June, $5; July, $20; August, $20; September, $20; and October, $10. These variable costs include both overhead items, such as power and water, and direct items such as soil and pots. Assume that all expenses are paid in the month that they are incurred.

Based on the information provided, prepare a cash outflow statement for the upcoming year.

9-55 *Operating budgets: labor hiring plan*   Shadyside Insurance Company manages a medical insurance program for its clients. Employees of client firms submit claims for reimbursement of medical expenses. Shadyside processes these claims, checks them to ensure that they are covered by the claimant's policy, notes whether the claimant has reached any limit on coverage, computes any deductible, and issues a check for the claimant's refund.

Three types of clerks work in the claims processing department: supervisors, senior clerks, and junior clerks. The supervisors are paid $42,000 per year, the senior clerks are paid $37,000 per year, and the junior clerks are paid $32,000 per year. For every 150,000 claims processed per year, Shadyside plans to use one supervisor, six junior clerks, and two senior clerks.

In 1994 the company processed 2,000,000 medical claims and employed 14 supervisors, 30 senior clerks, and 83 junior clerks.

REQUIRED

(a) Compute the excess costs or cost savings relating to the claims processing staff.

(b) How would you interpret these results? What additional information would you ask for if you were making a determination of the clerical group's processing efficiencies?

9-56 *Budgeting: Motivational Issues*   Manoil Electronics manufactures and sells electronic components to electronics stores. The controller is preparing her annual budget and has asked the sales group to prepare sales estimates. All members of the sales force have been asked to estimate sales in their territory for each of the organization's 10 major products.

The marketing group is paid a salary and a commission based on sales in excess of some target level. You have discovered that the sales manager uses the sales estimates to develop the target levels at which commissions begin. Specifically, the sales manager takes the sales estimate, adds 10%, and the result becomes the sales hurdle level. If sales are less than the hurdle level, no commissions are paid. If sales are above the hurdle level, commissions are paid at varying rates.

REQUIRED

(a) What is the motivation of the sales force if they know the relationship between their estimate and the target level of sales?

(b) What is the likely consequence of basing the organization's budgets on these estimates?

(c) If you were the controller in this situation and were responsible for both the reward system and the budgeting system, what would you do?

9-57 *Budget slack*   Mike Shields was having dinner with one of his friends at a restaurant in Memphis. His friend, Woody Brooks, a local manager of an express mail service told Mike that he consistently overstated the amount of resources needed in his budget requests for his division. He also told Mike that year after year he was able to obtain the budget requested. When Mike asked him why he did this, Woody replied, "It's a dog-eat-dog world out there. If I'm going to succeed and move up the ladder, I've got to perform well. Having those extra resources really helps!"

REQUIRED

Write an essay discussing Woody's point of view related to budgeting. Is he justified in his approach? Please explain.

■ CASES

9-58 *Budgeting: Motivational Issues*   Nate Young is the dean of a business school. The university is under strong financial pressures, and the university president has asked all the deans to cut costs. Nate is wondering how he should respond to this request.

The university receives its operating funds from three sources: (1) tuition (60%), (2) government grants (25%), and (3) gifts and endowment income (15%). The money flows into the university's general operating fund. A management committee consisting of the university president, the three vice presidents, and the nine deans allocates funds to the individual schools. The university's charter requires that it operate with a balanced budget.

The initial allocation of funds reflects (1) committed costs that cannot be avoided, primarily the employment costs of tenured faculty and (2) committed costs relating to overhead items, such as staff, building maintenance, and other operations costs. The balance of funds is allocated to discretionary activities, such as scholarships, program changes or additions, and sports.

The various deans compare their respective funding levels. The basis of comparison is to divide total university expenditures by the number of full-time students to get an average cost per student. Then the average cost per student is multiplied by the number of full-time students to get the target funding for each school. On average, the actual funding for the business school has been about 70% of the target funding, which is the second lowest in the university. (The lowest is the arts faculty.)

Because of the rapid growth of committed and administrative costs, the amount of funds allocated to discretionary activities has been declining from a historic level of about 10%. This year, the projected revenues will not even cover the projected committed costs. In response to this development, the president has called on all deans to "do your best to reduce the level of expenditures."

The president's request has been met with skepticism by many deans, who are notorious for digging in their heels, ignoring requests for spending cuts, and then being bailed out by funds released from other activities or raised to meet the budget shortfall. Many deans believe that the departments that sacrificed and reduced their budgets would only create funds that would be used by the university to support other schools that had made little or no effort to reduce their budgets. Then these schools would be asked to make even more cuts to make up for the lack of cuts in schools that made little progress in cost reduction. On the other hand, the deans also believe that if there were no reaction to the president's initial request for cost reductions, arbitrary cutbacks would be imposed on the individual schools.

In response to this situation, Nate is wondering what to do. He knows that by increasing class sizes slightly, using some part-time instructors, and eliminating some optional courses that seldom attract many students, he can trim about $800,000 from his operating budget of $11,000,000. However, making these changes would create hardships for both the students and faculty in the business school and, given the historic relationship of the school's average funding to its target funding, Nate is wondering whether the business school should be asked to make additional sacrifices.

Nate knows that he has several alternatives:

- ■ Do nothing, arguing that the business school is already cost effective relative to others and it is the time for others to reduce their cost structures.

- ■ Make the cuts that he has identified but stretch them out over a number of years and stop making them if other schools are not doing their share in cutting costs.

- ■ Make the cuts unilaterally and advise the administration that the business school budget can be reduced by about $800,000.

Explain what you would do if you were Nate and why. Your explanation should include your analysis of the motivation of all schools to cut costs in an environment that traditionally has taken advantage of those that cooperate.

9-59 *Budgeting: comprehensive problem*   Judd's Reproductions makes reproductions of antique tables and chairs and sells them through three sales outlets. The product line consists of two styles of tables, three styles of cabinets, and two styles of chairs. Although customers often ask Judd Molinari, the owner/manager of Judd's Reproductions, to make other products, he does not intend to expand the product line.

The planning group at Judd's Reproductions prepares a master budget for each fiscal year, which corresponds to the calendar year. It is December 1996, and the planners are completing the master budget for 1997.

Unit prices are $200, $900, and $1800, respectively, for the chairs, tables, and cabinets. Customers pay (1) by cash and receive a 5% discount, (2) by credit card (the credit card company takes 3% of the revenue as its fee and remits the balance in the month following the month of sale), or (3) on account (only exporters buy on account). The distribution of cash, credit card, and exporter sales is 25%, 35%, and 40%. Of the credit sales to exporters, Judd's Reproductions collects 30% in the month following the sale, 50% in the second month following the sale, 17% in the third month following the sale, and 3% go uncollected. Judd's Reproductions recognizes the expense of cash discounts, credit card fees, and bad debts in the month of the sale.

Judd's employs 40 people who work in the following areas: 15 in administration, sales, and shipping; 2 in manufacturing supervision (director and a scheduler); 9 in manufacturing fabrication and assembly (carpenters); and 14 in manufacturing, finishing, and other (helpers, cleaners, and maintenance crew).

The carpenter hours required to make the parts for and assemble a chair, table, or cabinet are 0.4, 2.5, and 6, respectively. Production personnel have organized the work so that each carpenter hour worked requires 1.5 helper hours. Therefore, production planners maintain a ratio on average of 1.5 helpers for every carpenter. The company pays carpenters and helpers $24 and $14 per hour, respectively (including all benefits).

Judd's Reproductions guarantees all employees their pay regardless of the hours of work available. When the employees are not doing their regular jobs, they undertake maintenance, training, community service, and customer relations activities. Judd's pays each employee weekly for that week's work. If an employee works 172 hours or less during the month, Judd's pays the employee the product of his hourly rate and 172. The company pays 150% of the normal hourly rate for every hour over 172 that the employee works during the month. Planners add new carpenters if the projected total monthly overtime is more than 5% of the total regular carpenter hours available. Judd's has a policy of no employee layoffs. Any required hiring is done on the first day of each month.

Judd's Reproductions rents a converted warehouse as a factory; it costs $600,000 per year. The company pays rent quarterly beginning January 1 of each year. Judd's pays other fixed manufacturing costs, which include manufacturing supervision salaries and which amount to $480,000, in equal monthly amounts.

The capital investment policy is to purchase, each January and July, $5000 of machinery and equipment per carpenter employed during that month. Judd's recognizes depreciation at the rate of 10% of the year-end balance of the Machinery and Equipment account. Statistical studies of cost behavior have determined that supplies, variable overhead, and maintenance costs vary with the number of carpenter hours worked and are $5, $20, and $15, per hour, respectively.

The units of wood required for chairs, tables, and cabinets are 1, 8, and 15, respectively. Each unit of wood costs $30. The inventory policy is to make products in the month they will be sold. Two suppliers deliver raw materials and supplies as required.

The company pays for all materials, supplies, variable overhead, and maintenance items on receipt.

Annual administration salaries, fixed selling costs, and planned advertising expenditures are $300,000, $360,000, and $600,000, respectively. Judd's Reproductions makes these expenditures in equal monthly amounts. Packaging and shipping costs for chairs, tables, and cabinets are $15, $65, and $135, respectively. Variable selling costs are 6% of each product's list price. Judd's Reproductions pays packaging, shipping, and variable selling costs as incurred.

Using its line of credit, Judd's Reproductions maintains a minimum balance of $50,000. All line-of-credit transactions occur on the first day of each month. The bank charges interest on the line-of-credit account balance at the rate of 10% per year. Judd's pays interest on the first day of each month on the line-of-credit balance outstanding at the end of the previous month. On the first of each month, the bank pays interest at the rate of 3% per year on funds exceeding $50,000 in the company's Cash account at the end of the previous month.

Realized sales for October, November, and December 1996 appear in the following table:

JUDD'S REPRODUCTIONS

	Unit Sales 1996		
Item	October	November	December
Chairs	900	975	950
Tables	175	188	201
Cabinets	90	102	95

Sales staff estimates the unit demand for 1997 as follows: chairs, 1000 plus a random number uniformly distributed between 0 and 50 plus 15% of the previous month's sales of chairs; tables, 200 plus a random number uniformly distributed between 0 and 20 plus 15% of the previous month's sales; and cabinets, 100 plus a random number uniformly distributed between 0 and 10 plus 15% of the previous month's sales of cabinets. This estimation process resulted in the demand forecasts and the sales plan found in the following table.

JUDD'S REPRODUCTIONS

	Projected Unit Sales 1997		
Month	Chairs	Tables	Cabinets
January	1020	200	109
February	1191	237	120
March	1179	243	119
April	1195	250	126
May	1200	252	122
June	1204	255	125
July	1194	242	123
August	1199	253	121
September	1222	243	127
October	1219	248	126
November	1207	244	126
December	1192	255	119

Planners project Judd's Reproductions' balance sheet, at January 1, 1997, to be as follows:

JUDD'S REPRODUCTIONS

Balance Sheet, January 1, 1997

Cash	$ 50,000	Bank loan	$ 0
Accounts receivable	575,008		
Machinery (net book value)	360,000	Shareholder's equity	985,008
Total	$985,008	Total	$985,008

REQUIRED

(a) Prepare a sales forecast, staffing plan, production plan, cash flow statement, pro forma income statement, and pro forma balance sheet for 1997.

(b) The level of bad debts concerns Judd's Reproductions' controller. If Judd's insists on cash payments from exporters who would be given the cash discount, the sales staff expects that total sales to exporters in 1997 will fall by 5% (sales in 1996 will not be affected). Based on the effect of this change on profitability, is it desirable? (Round sales forecasts to the nearest unit.)

(c) Ignore the changes described in (b) above and return to the data in the original example. The sales staff is considering increasing the advertising budget from $600,000 to $900,000 and cutting prices by 5%. This should increase sales by 30% in 1997 (sales in 1996 will not be affected). Based on the effect of this change on profitability, is it desirable? (Round sales forecasts to the nearest unit.)

(d) Is there a criterion other than profitability that may be used to evaluate the desirability of the changes proposed in (b) and (c)? If yes, what is that criterion and why is it important? If no, why is profitability the sole relevant criterion?

9-60 *Budgeting and cost drivers*   Dinkum Company provides package courier services. Each afternoon its couriers pick up packages; they drive trucks operating out of local terminals. Packages are returned to the terminal and are transported to the central hub that evening. In the hub, packages are sorted during the late evening and are sent to the destination terminal overnight. The next morning couriers from the destination terminal deliver packages to the addressees.

Most of the routes that the couriers follow are fixed. Each day the couriers have both scheduled and unscheduled pickup and drop-off stops. However, studies have shown that adding an unscheduled stop to a route or picking up an additional shipment at a scheduled stop creates negligible additional costs. The key costs in terms of the courier's time, the vehicle, and the fuel costs are determined by the route itself. Therefore, most of the costs at Dinkum result from decisions that reflect the planned level of activity rather than decisions that reflect the actual volume of activity. The major exception is the sorting cost in the hubs and terminals. Because sorting labor is hired on a part-time basis as required, the sorting cost varies with the number of shipments handled.

Linda Price, the manager of the Miami terminal, is preparing an expense budget for the upcoming year. She plans to base this year's budget on the trends from the previous years. The following table shows the level of costs in the previous 2 years.

DINKUM COURIER COMPANY

Item	Activity Cost Levels		
	1995	1996	1997
Shipments handled	8,500,000	10,300,000	$11,100,000
Administrative costs	$ 300,000	$ 315,000	$ 320,000
Truck depreciation and maintenance	$ 750,000	$ 830,000	$ 850,000
Courier fuel costs	$ 600,000	$ 660,000	$ 670,000
Courier wages	$1,750,000	$ 1,810,000	$ 1,850,000
Terminal overhead costs	$ 240,000	$ 280,000	$ 260,000
Labor costs in terminal	$ 120,000	$ 150,000	$ 170,000

REQUIRED

(a) Identify what you think are the cost drivers for each of the items in this table.

(b) Given the information provided, prepare an expense budget for the upcoming year, assuming that the volume of shipments handled is expected to be 14,000,000 units.

10

CAPITAL BUDGETING

MICROSOFT WINDOWS 95

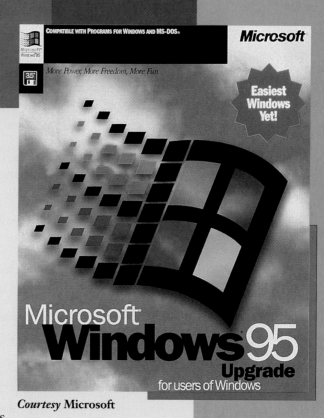

Courtesy **Microsoft**

I n August 1995, accompanied by guitar riffs and the Rolling Stones singing "Start Me Up," Microsoft Corporation, the world's largest manufacturer of software, introduced its new operating system: Windows 95. Microsoft touted Windows 95, which had been in development for at least five years, as a significant improvement in terms of both functionality and aesthetics over the operating system that it replaced.

People in the computer software industry, in particular, and in marketing, in general, admitted they had never seen anything like the marketing campaign that accompanied the launch of Windows 95. Reputed to cost between $200 and $300 million, this global marketing campaign used every advertising medium. Observers wondered whether this product's enormous development and launch costs were justified for an operating system that some industry observers said took Microsoft to where Apple's Macintosh had been five years before.

LONG-TERM (CAPITAL) ASSETS

In considering Microsoft's launch of Windows 95, reflect back to Chapters 5 and 6, which discussed the cost of assets that organizations purchase in advance and then use for several years to make goods and provide services. These long-term, or capital, assets create the committed costs known as batch-related, product-related, and process-sustaining costs. The significant investment made by Microsoft in developing and launching Windows 95 illustrates issues addressed in this chapter, including the approach that planners use to evaluate the acquisition of long-term assets that create significant cost commitments.

Cost commitments associated with long-term assets create risk for an organization because they remain even if the asset does not generate the anticipated benefits. In this sense, long-term assets reduce an organization's flexibility. Therefore, organizations approach the investment in long-term assets with considerable care.

Organizations have developed specific tools to control the acquisition and use of long-term assets for three reasons:

OBJECTIVE 10.1

Understand the nature and importance of long-term assets.

1. Unlike short-term assets whose acquisition rate can be modified quickly in response to changes in demand, organizations usually are *committed* to long-term assets for extended periods of time. This type of commitment creates the potential for either excess or scarce capacity that, in turn, creates excess costs or lost opportunities, respectively.

2. The amount of capital committed to the acquisition of capital assets is usually very *large*; therefore, acquiring long-term assets creates significant financial risks for organizations.

3. The long-term nature of capital assets creates *technological risk* for organizations.

Capital budgeting
A systematic approach to evaluating the economic desirability of a long-term investment.

Capital budgeting is a systematic approach to evaluating an investment in a long-term, or capital, asset.

When most people think of a long-term asset, they think of machinery and equipment. However, many organizations incur significant employee training costs. These expenditures should be evaluated as long-term investments. *Courtesy* **Will & Deni McIntyre/Photo Researchers Inc.**

INVESTMENT AND RETURN

By definition, a long-term asset is acquired and paid for before it generates benefits that last two or more years. The fundamental evaluation issue in dealing with a long-term asset is whether its future benefits justify its initial cost.

Investment is the monetary value of the assets that the organization gives up to acquire a long-term asset. **Return** is the increased cash flows in the future attributable to the long-term asset. Investment and return are the foundations of capital budgeting analysis.

Capital budgeting analysis focuses on whether the increased cash flows that the organization expects the asset to generate justify the investment in a long-term asset. The tools and methods used in capital budgeting focus on comparing investment and return or, more generally, the cash outflows and inflows associated with a long-term asset.

TIME VALUE OF MONEY

The most important idea in capital budgeting is the concept of the **time value of money.** Because money can earn a return, its value depends on when it is received. Like all commodities, money has a cost. The cost of using money is not an out-of-pocket cost, like the cost of buying raw materials or paying a worker. Rather, the cost of using money is the opportunity lost from being unable to invest the money in another investment alternative. For example, if you invest your cash in a stock, you forgo the opportunity to deposit it in a savings account and earn interest on it. Therefore, the basic problem in capital budgeting is that investment cash is paid out now and, in return, cash is received in the future. Therefore, in making investment decisions, it is necessary to have an equivalent basis to compare the cash flows that occur at different points of time.

Because money has a time-dated value, the most fundamental and important thing to remember in capital budgeting is that *amounts of money received at different periods of time must be converted into their value on a common date to be compared.*

Some Standard Notation

To simplify the discussion that follows, we will use the following notation throughout our discussion of capital budgeting:

Abbreviation	Meaning
n	**Number of periods** considered in the investment analysis; common period lengths are a month, a quarter, or a year
FV	**Future value,** or ending value, of the investment n periods from now
PV	**Present value,** or the value at the current moment in time, of an amount to be received n periods from now
a	**Annuity,** or equal amount, received or paid at the end of each period for n periods
r	**Rate of return** required, or expected, from an investment opportunity; the rate of interest earned on an investment

---

OBJECTIVE 10.2

Discuss the basic tools and concepts of financial analysis: investment, return, future value, present value, annuities, and required rate of return.

Investment
The monetary value of the assets that the organization gives up to acquire a long-term asset.

Return
The increased cash flows in the future attributable to the long-term asset.

Time value of money
The primary concept in capital budgeting, which states because money can earn a return, its value depends on when it is received.

Number of periods (n)
In capital-budgeting analysis, the number of periods, usually measured in months, quarters, or years, whose cash flows a proposed long-term investment will affect.

Future value (FV)
The amount to which an amount invested today will increase over a stated number of periods at a stated periodic rate of return; the ending value of an investment n periods from now at a stated rate of interest.

Annuity (a)
An investment that promises a constant amount each period for a stated number of periods—also known as an n-period annuity; the equal amount received or paid at the end of each period for n periods.

Future Value

Because of the time value of money, it is always better to have money now rather than in the future. Having $1.00 today is more valuable than receiving $1.00 in one year or five years, because the $1.00 on hand today can be invested to grow to more than $1.00 in the future.

Consider the difference between having $1.00 now and $1.00 a year from now, for example. If you have $1.00 now, you might invest it in a savings account to earn 5% interest. After one year, you will have $1.05. We call this $1.05 the future value of $1.00 in one year when the rate of return is 5%. This means that the future value is the amount that an amount invested today will be after a stated number of periods at a stated periodic rate of return. The following equation provides the formula for future value:

$$\text{Future value of investment in 1 period} = \text{Investment} \times (1 + \text{Periodic rate of return})$$
$$FV = PV \times (1 + r)$$

Suppose that Karl Nesarajah wants to borrow $10,000 to buy a used car. He plans to repay the loan in full after one year. If the rate of interest is 7% per year, Karl will have to repay $10,700 at the end of the year as the following shows:

$$
\begin{aligned}
FV &= PV \times (1 + r) \\
&= \$10,000 \times (1.07) \\
&= \$10,700
\end{aligned}
$$

In summary, future value is the amount a present sum of money will be, given a specified rate of interest and time period.

Multiple Periods

Because investment opportunities can involve multiple periods, we need to compute future value over several periods. Exhibit 10-1 shows how an initial amount

Most people must negotiate a car loan to buy a new car. Car loans involve a financial institution providing a borrower with an amount of cash that the customer uses to acquire the car. In exchange, the borrower sells the financial institution an annuity, which is a promise to pay a stated amount for a stated number of periods. *Courtesy* **Rhoda Sidney/ Stock, Boston**

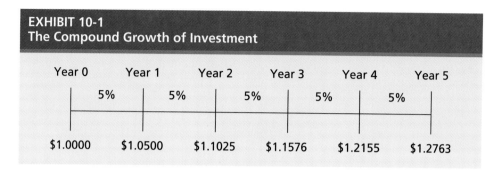

EXHIBIT 10-1
The Compound Growth of Investment

Year 0	Year 1	Year 2	Year 3	Year 4	Year 5
	5%	5%	5%	5%	5%
$1.0000	$1.0500	$1.1025	$1.1576	$1.2155	$1.2763

of $1.00 accumulates to $1.2763 over five years when the rate of return is 5% per year. The calculations shown assume the following:

1. Any interest earned is not withdrawn until the end of the fifth year; therefore, interest is earned each year on both the initial investment and the interest earned in previous periods, which financial analysts call the compounding effect of interest.
2. The rate of return is constant.

Computing Future Values for Multiple Periods

It is possible to compute the future value of an investment for multiple periods in a number of ways. Remember that these calculations assume that no interest is withdrawn until the end of the investment period.

CALCULATOR METHODS.   You can use either of these methods.

■ **Sequential Multiplication:** Multiply $1.00 by 1.05 five times to compute the future value of $1.00 in five periods when the rate of interest is 5%: $1.2763

■ **Exponents:** If your calculator can compute exponents directly, you can avoid repeated multiplication by computing $(1.05)^5$ directly.

$$\$1.00 \times 1.05 \times 1.05 \times 1.05 \times 1.05 \times 1.05 = \$1.00 \times 1.05^5$$

These calculations show that the general formula for a future value is this:

$$FV = PV \times (1 + r)^n$$

This formula is the multiperiod extension of the future value formula presented earlier.

TABLE METHOD.   Tables provide the factors needed to compute a future value. For example, the table in Exhibit 10-2 provides the future value factor for different numbers of periods and rates of return. If you look down the 5% column and find where that column intersects with the row for five periods, you will find

EXHIBIT 10-2
Future Value of $1

Period	2%	5%	7%	10%	12%	15%	17%	20%
1	1.0200	1.0500	1.0700	1.1000	1.1200	1.1500	1.1700	1.2000
2	1.0404	1.1025	1.1449	1.2100	1.2544	1.3225	1.3689	1.4400
3	1.0612	1.1576	1.2250	1.3310	1.4049	1.5209	1.6016	1.7280
4	1.0824	1.2155	1.3108	1.4641	1.5735	1.7490	1.8739	2.0736
5	1.1041	1.2763	1.4026	1.6105	1.7623	2.0114	2.1924	2.4883
6	1.1262	1.3401	1.5007	1.7716	1.9738	2.3131	2.5652	2.9860
7	1.1487	1.4071	1.6058	1.9487	2.2107	2.6600	3.0012	3.5832
8	1.1717	1.4775	1.7182	2.1436	2.4760	3.0590	3.5115	4.2998
9	1.1951	1.5513	1.8385	2.3579	2.7731	3.5179	4.1084	5.1598
10	1.2190	1.6289	1.9672	2.5937	3.1058	4.0456	4.8068	6.1917
15	1.3459	2.0789	2.7590	4.1772	5.4736	8.1371	10.5387	15.4070
20	1.4859	2.6533	3.8697	6.7275	9.6463	16.3665	23.1056	38.3376
25	1.6406	3.3864	5.4274	10.8347	17.0001	32.9190	50.6578	95.3962

the value 1.2763. Multiply this factor by the amount of the initial investment to find the future value in the required number of periods at the stated rate of return:

$$FV_{5\%,\ 5\ \text{periods}} = \$1 \times factor_{5\%,\ 5\ \text{periods}}$$
$$= \$1 \times 1.2763$$
$$= \$1.2763$$

Suppose two parents have just won $100,000 in a lottery. They decide to place $20,000 of this money in a trust fund for their newborn child's education. If the money is invested to earn 7% each year with all interest reinvested, the equation for future value computes the amount to which it will have accumulated after 15 years.

$$FV_{7\%,\ 15\ \text{periods}} = \$20,000 \times factor_{7\%,\ 15\ \text{periods}}$$
$$= \$20,000 \times 2.7590$$
$$= \$55,180$$

In the automobile-purchasing example, suppose that Karl believes that it will take three years to accumulate enough money to repay his car loan. If the required interest is 7% per year, the loan repayment in three years would be this:

$$FV_{7\%,\ 3\ \text{periods}} = \$10,000 \times factor_{7\%,\ 3\ \text{periods}}$$
$$= \$10,000 \times 1.2250$$
$$= \$12,250$$

SPREADSHEET METHOD.   Every computer spreadsheet program can compute future values and all the other financial calculations that we describe below. See the Excel spreadsheet application on the next page.

The Compound Growth of Interest

When an amount of money is invested and left to accumulate for multiple periods, the rate of growth is compounded because interest is earned on interest earned in previous periods. Exhibit 10-3 shows the nature of compound growth for various rates of interest. Note that the rate of growth is exponential; that is, growth occurs at an increasing rate.

Present Value

An investor may expect a proposed investment to generate benefits in the form of increased cash flow over many periods into the future. The investor must compare these cash flow benefits, or inflows, to the investment's costs, or outflows, in order to assess the investment. Because of the time value of money, all cash flows associated with an investment must be converted to their equivalent value at some common date to make meaningful comparisons between the project's cash inflows and outflows.

Although any point in time can be chosen as the common date for comparing inflows and outflows, the conventional choice is the point when the investment is undertaken. Analysts call this point *time zero*, or *period zero*. Therefore, conventional capital budgeting analysis converts all cash flows to their equivalent value at time zero.

Analysts call a future cash flow's value at time zero its **present value,** and the process of computing present value, **discounting.** Recall the formula for future value:

$$FV = PV \times (1 + r)^n$$

> **EXCEL SPREADSHEET APPLICATION**
>
> COMPUTING FUTURE VALUE   The Excel formula to compute the future value of a single payment is this:
>
> $$FV \times (1 + r)^{\wedge}n$$
>
> To compute the loan repayment, Karl would have to enter these numbers into a cell in an Excel spreadsheet.
>
> $$= 10000 \, ^* \, (1 + 0.07)^{\wedge}3$$

Present value (PV)
A future cash flow's value at time zero; the value at the current moment in time of an amount to be received n periods from now and given a rate of interest.

Discounting
The process of computing present value.

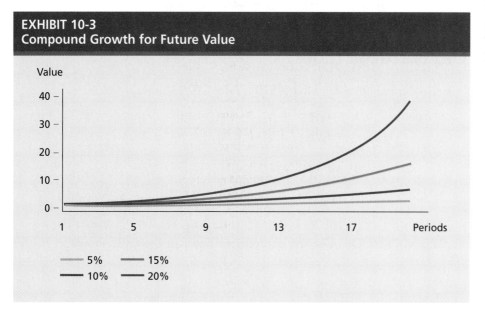

EXHIBIT 10-3
Compound Growth for Future Value

Value

40 —
30 —
20 —
10 —
0 —

1   5   9   13   17   Periods

——— 5%   ——— 15%
——— 10%   ——— 20%

Many people set aside money today to provide for future expenditures such as college education for their children or for retirement. Financial planners help investors decide how much they need to set aside to provide a future amount and the form of the investment. *Courtesy* **Bob Daemmrich/ Stock, Boston**

We can rearrange this formula to compute the present value:

$$PV = \frac{FV}{(1 + r)^n}$$

This can also be stated:

$$PV = FV \times (1 + r)^{-n}$$

Suppose that two parents want to accumulate $70,000 over 15 years for their newborn child's education. These parents have idle cash available now to make this investment, which will earn 7% annually. What amount of money must they invest now? What we have to do here is compute the present value of $70,000 with a rate of return of 7%.

Repeat any of the methods described earlier to compute the future value of a present amount of money:

CALCULATOR METHODS.   Use either of these methods.

■ Sequential Division: Divide $70,000 by 1.07 15 times.

$70,000 ÷ 1.07 ÷ 1.07 ÷ 1.07 ÷ 1.07 ÷ 1.07 ÷ 1.07 ÷ 1.07 ÷ 1.07
÷ 1.07 ÷ 1.07 ÷ 1.07 ÷ 1.07 ÷ 1.07 ÷ 1.07 ÷ 1.07

■ Exponents: Evaluate the equation directly:

$$\$70,000 \div 1.07^{15}$$

TABLE METHOD.   Use the appropriate factor in the table shown in Exhibit 10-4.

SPREADSHEET METHOD.   See the Excel spreadsheet application.

EXHIBIT 10-4
Present Value of $1

Period	2%	5%	7%	10%	12%	15%	17%	20%
1	0.9804	0.9524	0.9346	0.9091	0.8929	0.8696	0.8547	0.8333
2	0.9612	0.9070	0.8734	0.8264	0.7972	0.7561	0.7305	0.6944
3	0.9423	0.8638	0.8163	0.7513	0.7118	0.6575	0.6244	0.5787
4	0.9238	0.8227	0.7629	0.6830	0.6355	0.5718	0.5337	0.4823
5	0.9057	0.7835	0.7130	0.6209	0.5674	0.4972	0.4561	0.4019
6	0.8880	0.7462	0.6663	0.5645	0.5066	0.4323	0.3898	0.3349
7	0.8706	0.7107	0.6227	0.5132	0.4523	0.3759	0.3332	0.2791
8	0.8535	0.6768	0.5820	0.4665	0.4039	0.3269	0.2848	0.2326
9	0.8368	0.6446	0.5439	0.4241	0.3606	0.2843	0.2434	0.1938
10	0.8203	0.6139	0.5083	0.3855	0.3220	0.2472	0.2080	0.1615
15	0.7430	0.4810	**0.3624**	0.2394	0.1827	0.1229	0.0949	0.0649
20	0.6730	0.3769	0.2584	0.1486	0.1037	0.611	0.0433	0.0261
25	0.6095	0.2953	0.1842	0.0923	0.0588	0.0304	0.0197	0.0105

The table in Exhibit 10-4 shows that the factor used to compute present value when there are 15 interest periods and a periodic interest rate of 7% is 0.3624. Therefore, we can compute the present value of this investment as follows:

$$PV = \$70,000 \times factor_{7\%,\ 15\ periods}$$
$$= \$70,000 \times 0.3624$$
$$= \$25,368$$

Thus, if the rate of return is 7%, the parents must invest $25,368 today to accumulate the $70,000 they would like to give their child for the college fund.

Decay of a Present Value

Invested amounts grow at a compound rate through time because of the process of earning interest on interest. Similarly, receiving a fixed amount of cash at some future time becomes less valuable as (1) interest rates increase and (2) time period lengthens regarding when the cash is received. Exhibit 10-5 shows the nature of the loss of present value with various rates of interest and future cash receipt times. Note that present value decays at a reducing rate.

Present Value and Future Value of Annuities

Not all investments have cash outlays at time zero and provide a single benefit at some point in the

EXCEL SPREADSHEET APPLICATION

COMPUTING PRESENT VALUE   The Excel formula to compute the future value of a single payment is this:

$$FV/(1 + r)^{\wedge}n$$

Therefore, to compute the amount the parents would have to invest now you would enter

$$= 70000/(1 + 0.07)^{\wedge}15$$

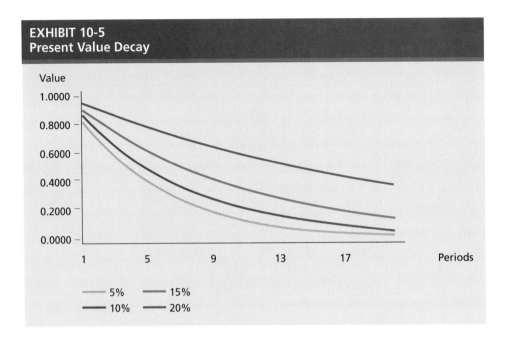

EXHIBIT 10-5
Present Value Decay

future. Most investments provide a series, or stream, of benefits over a specified period in the future. An investment that promises a constant amount each period over *n* periods is called an *n-period annuity*. For example, many lotteries are examples of an *n*-period annuity because they pay prizes in the form of an annuity that lasts, for example, for 20 years.

Formulas and financial tables that allow analysts to compute the present value of annuities directly were produced before the widespread availability of calculators and spreadsheets. Today most present value calculations are performed on calculators or computer spreadsheets that can calculate present values directly so that knowledge of the formulas and tables themselves is less important. The issue of rounding can be vexing. Because of different rounding, answers found with a regular calculator may vary slightly from those found with a spreadsheet

This person has just won the Texas Lottery. The state will pay the winner $50,000 per year for 20 years. Is this lottery prize really worth a million dollars? *Courtesy* Bob Daemmrich/Stock, Boston

program or financial calculator. Moreover, a column of figures may appear not to sum to the indicated total. This book follows the convention of using the number computed by the specialized calculation or computer. Appendix 10.1 summarizes the formulas for the present and future values of annuities.

To illustrate the notion of an annuity and its present value, suppose that you have won a lottery prize that pays $1,000,000 a year for 20 years. You are interested in selling this annuity to raise cash to purchase a business. What is the appropriate value for this annuity today, if the current rate of interest is 7%?

Using a calculator we can compute the present value of each of the 20 $1,000,000 payments and sum these present values to compute the present value of the annuity. Exhibit 10-6 shows the calculations used to find the present value of each payment in this way. Alternatively, we can use the formula shown in Appendix 10-1 to compute the present value with a single calculation. The table in Exhibit 10-7 provides the factors used to compute the present value of an annuity for various combinations of periods and interest rates.

Using this table we can compute the present value of the lottery annuity as follows:

$$PV = a \times factor_{7\%, 20 \text{ periods}}$$
$$= \$1,000,000 \times 10.594$$
$$= \$10,594,000$$

EXHIBIT 10-6
Computing the Value of an Annuity

Period	Amount	PV Factor	PV
1	$1,000,000	0.9346	$934,579.44
2	1,000,000	0.8734	873,438.73
3	1,000,000	0.8163	816,297.88
4	1,000,000	0.7629	762,895.21
5	1,000,000	0.7130	712,986.18
6	1,000,000	0.6663	666,342.22
7	1,000,000	0.6227	622,749.74
8	1,000,000	0.5820	582,009.10
9	1,000,000	0.5439	543,933.74
10	1,000,000	0.5083	508,349.29
11	1,000,000	0.4751	475,092.80
12	1,000,000	0.4440	444,011.96
13	1,000,000	0.4150	414,964.45
14	1,000,000	0.3878	387,817.24
15	1,000,000	0.3624	362,446.02
16	1,000,000	0.3387	338,734.60
17	1,000,000	0.3166	316,574.39
18	1,000,000	0.2959	295,863.92
19	1,000,000	0.2765	276,508.33
20	1,000,000	0.2584	258,419.00
Total			$10,594,014.25

EXHIBIT 10-7
Present Value of an Annuity of $1

Period	2%	5%	7%	10%	12%	15%	17%	20%
1	0.9804	0.9524	0.9346	0.9091	0.8929	0.8696	0.8547	0.8333
2	1.9416	1.8594	1.8080	1.7355	1.6901	1.6257	1.5852	1.5278
3	2.8839	2.7232	2.6242	2.4869	2.4018	2.2832	2.2096	2.1065
4	2.8077	3.5460	3.3872	3.169	3.0373	2.8550	2.7432	2.5887
5	4.7135	4.3295	4.1002	3.7908	3.6048	3.3522	3.1993	2.9906
6	5.6014	5.0757	4.7665	4.3553	4.1114	3.7845	3.5892	3.3255
7	6.4720	5.7864	5.3893	4.8684	4.5638	4.1604	3.9224	3.6046
8	7.3255	6.4632	5.9713	5.3349	4.9676	4.4873	4.2072	3.8372
9	8.1622	7.1078	6.5152	5.7590	5.3282	4.7716	4.4506	4.0310
10	8.9826	7.7217	7.0236	6.1446	5.6502	5.0188	4.6586	4.1925
15	12.8493	10.3797	9.1079	7.6061	6.8109	5.8474	5.3242	4.6755
20	16.3514	12.4622	**10.5940**	8.5136	7.4694	6.2593	5.6278	4.8696
25	19.5235	14.0939	11.6536	9.0770	7.8431	6.4641	5.7662	4.9476

Consider a bond with a face value of $1000 that pays $60 in interest every six months for 10 years, that is, $60 per period for 20 six-month periods and a lump sum of $1000 at the end of the 10th year. If an investor's required return is 5% per six-month period, what would the investor be willing to pay for this bond?

There are two components of the bond, the periodic interest payments of $60 for 20 periods and the lump-sum payment at the end of the 20th period. The following formula shows the calculation of the present value for the periodic interest payments:

$$
\begin{aligned}
PV &= a \times factor_{5\%,\ 20\ periods} \\
&= \$60 \times 12.4622 \\
&= \$747.73
\end{aligned}
$$

The following formula shows the calculation of the present value for the single lump-sum payment of $1000 after 20 periods:

$$
\begin{aligned}
PV &= FV \times factor_{5\%,\ 20\ periods} \\
&= \$1000 \times 0.3769 \\
&= \$376.90
\end{aligned}
$$

Therefore, the present value of the bond is $1124.63 ($747.73 + $376.90). The bond sells at a premium—that is, its price is greater than its redemption value of $1000—because it is paying 6% interest ($60) each period, when the market interest rate is only 5%. A bond that paid only a 4% interest ($40) each period would sell at a discount from its redemption value. You should be able to show that this discount is $124.61.

COMPUTING THE ANNUITY REQUIRED TO REPAY A LOAN

We often need to compute the annuity value that a current investment will generate. For example, if you agree to repay a loan with equal periodic payments, you are selling the lender an annuity in exchange for the face value of the loan. The factor required to compute the amount of the annuity to repay a present value is simply the inverse of the present value factor for an annuity. Exhibit 10-8 provides a table of these factors for selected periods and rates of return.

In our automobile-purchasing example, suppose Karl discovers that no one will lend him $10,000 to be repaid at the end of three years because financial institutions reduce risk by requiring periodic loan repayments. Therefore, Karl must make payments semiannually with a semiannual interest rate of

EXCEL SPREADSHEET APPLICATION

COMPUTING THE PRESENT VALUE OF AN ANNUITY
Excel has a built-in function to evaluate the present value of an annuity.

The function has this form:

$$PV(\textit{rate, number of periods, annuity})$$

Therefore, to compute the present value of the lottery annuity you would enter this:

$$= PV(0.07,20,1000000)$$

This huge shovel improves productivity in coal mining at Kerr-McGee Corporation by reducing the number of passes needed to fill a haul truck. When deciding to make the investment in this shovel, planners at Kerr-McGee had to compare its purchase price with the cost savings resulting from the productivity improvements expected from using this equipment during its lifetime. *Courtesy* Kerr-McGee

EXHIBIT 10-8
Annuity Required to Repay an Amount of $1

Period	2%	5%	7%	10%	12%	15%	17%	20%
1	1.0200	1.0500	1.0700	1.1000	1.1200	1.1500	1.1700	1.2000
2	0.5150	0.5378	0.5531	0.5762	0.5917	0.6151	0.6308	0.6545
3	0.3468	0.3672	0.3811	0.4021	0.4163	0.4380	0.4526	0.4747
4	0.2626	0.2820	0.2952	0.3155	0.3292	0.3503	0.3645	0.3863
5	0.2122	0.2310	0.2439	0.2638	0.2774	0.2983	0.3126	0.3344
6	0.1785	**0.1970**	0.2098	0.2296	0.2432	0.2642	0.2786	0.3007
7	0.1545	0.1728	0.1856	0.2054	0.2191	0.2404	0.2549	0.2774
8	0.1365	0.1547	0.1675	0.1874	0.2013	0.2229	0.2377	0.2606
9	0.1225	0.1407	0.1535	0.1736	0.1877	0.2096	0.2247	0.2481
10	0.1113	0.1295	0.1424	0.1627	0.1770	0.1993	0.2147	0.2385
15	0.0778	0.0963	0.1098	0.1315	0.1468	0.1710	0.1878	0.2139
20	0.0612	0.0802	0.944	0.1175	0.1339	0.1598	0.1777	0.2054
25	0.0512	0.0710	0.0858	0.1102	0.1275	0.1547	0.1734	0.2021

5%. Karl's required semiannual payment will be $1970 for three years, as shown in the following calculation:

$$a = PV \times factor_{5\%,\ 6\ periods}$$
$$= \$10,000 \times 0.1970$$
$$= \$1970$$

Cost of capital
The return that the organization must earn on its investments in order to meet its investors' return requirements. This is the interest rate that organizations use in their time value of money, discounting, or compounding, calculations.

Cost of Capital

The **cost of capital** is the interest rate organizations use in computing the time value of money; the cost of capital equals the return that the organization must earn on its investment to meet its investors' return requirements. From a financial perspective, when the organization expects to earn less than its cost of capital from a proposed investment, it should return the funds that otherwise would be required for the proposed investment to its providers of capital. If the organization expects to earn more than its cost of capital from a proposed investment, the investment is desirable. Any surplus earned increases the organization's wealth. The cost of capital is the benchmark that the organization uses to evaluate investment proposals. The organization's cost of capital reflects both the amount and cost of debt and equity in its financial structure and the financial market's perception of the financial risk of the organization's activities. Finance courses cover in depth the way that organizations determine their cost of capital.

EXCEL SPREADSHEET APPLICATION

COMPUTING THE ANNUITY NEEDED TO REPAY A LOAN Excel has a built-in function to compute the annuity required to repay a loan.

The function has this form:

PMT(rate, number of periods, loan)

Therefore, to compute the annuity required to repay Karl's car loan, you would enter this into a cell on in your Excel spreadsheet:

= *PMT*(0.05,6,10000)

CAPITAL BUDGETING

Capital budgeting is the collection of tools that planners use to evaluate the desirability of acquiring long-term assets. Organizations have developed many approaches to capital budgeting. Five approaches are discussed here:

1. Payback
2. Accounting rate of return
3. Internal rate of return
4. Net present value
5. Economic value added

To show how each of these methods works and alternative perspectives, we will apply each to the following investment opportunity.

Shirley's Doughnut Hole

Shirley's Doughnut Hole is considering the purchase of a new automatic doughnut cooker that would cost $70,000 and last five years. It would expand capacity and reduce operating costs, thereby allowing Shirley's to increase profits by $20,000 per year. Shirley's cost of capital is 10%; the new cooker would be sold for $10,000 at the end of five years. Is this investment worthwhile?

Payback Criterion

The **payback period,** or criterion, computes the number of periods needed to recover a project's initial investment. Shirley's initial investment of $70,000 is recovered midway between years 3 and 4, as Exhibit 10-9 shows. Therefore, the payback period for this project is 3.5 years.

    Many people consider the payback period to be a measure of the project's risk. Because the organization has unrecovered investment until it reaches the payback period, the longer the payback period, the higher the risk. Organizations

Payback period
The number of periods required to recover a project's initial investment.

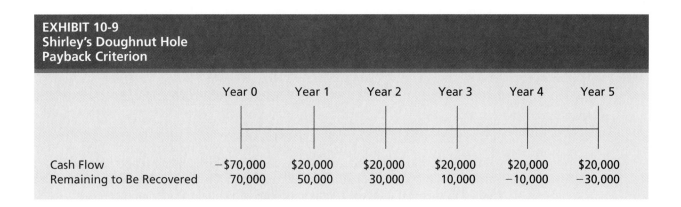

EXHIBIT 10-9
Shirley's Doughnut Hole
Payback Criterion

	Year 0	Year 1	Year 2	Year 3	Year 4	Year 5
Cash Flow	−$70,000	$20,000	$20,000	$20,000	$20,000	$20,000
Remaining to Be Recovered	70,000	50,000	30,000	10,000	−10,000	−30,000

compare a project's payback period with a criterion or target, which reflects what the organization thinks is an appropriate level of risk.

There are two problems with the payback criterion:

1. It ignores the time value of money. In the Shirley's example, suppose that the cash flows resulting from the cooker were $60,000 in the first year, $0 in the second year, $0 in the third year, $20,000 in the fourth year, and $20,000 in the fifth year. This set of cash flows has the same payback period, 3.5 years, as the original alternative. However, this alternative would clearly be more desirable because Shirley's recovers $60,000 at the end of year 1. In the first set of cash flows, Shirley's does not recover $60,000 until the end of year 3. With the time value of money, it is always preferable to receive cash earlier.

2. It ignores the cash outflows that occur after the initial investment and the cash inflows that occur after the payback period. In Shirley's suppose that there are two alternative cookers that Shirley's is considering. Cooker 1 is as described in the original example. Cooker 2's cash flows are identical to those of cooker 1 except that its disposal value is $20,000. By any standard, cooker 2 is the better deal. However, the payback method would consider the two alternatives equivalent because their payback periods are both the same: 3.5 years.

Despite these limitations, repeated surveys of practice have shown that the payback calculation is by far the most widely used approach of organizations for capital budgeting.

Accounting Rate of Return Criterion

Analysts compute the accounting rate of return by dividing the average accounting income by the average level of investment. Analysts use the accounting rate of return to approximate the return on investment, which is the ratio of the average income from an investment over the average investment level.

To compute the accounting rate of return, first accounting income must be computed. Suppose that Shirley's decides to depreciate the cooker so that the total amount of depreciation equals the cooker's historical cost less its salvage value. Using the straight-line method, which reflects equal depreciation each year, the annual depreciation is $12,000 as shown in the following equation:

$$Annual\ Depreciation = \frac{Historical\ Cost - Salvage\ Value}{Asset\ Life}$$

$$= \frac{\$70,000 - \$10,000}{5}$$

$$= \$12,000$$

Therefore, the increased annual income that Shirley's will report related to the new cooker will be $8000 ($20,000 − $12,000). Since all annual incomes are equal in this example, the average income will equal the annual income.

The average investment for the cooker will be $40,000, as shown in the following equation:

$$Average\ Investment\ =\ \frac{Initial\ Investment\ +\ Salvage\ Value}{2}$$

$$=\ \frac{\$70,000\ +\ \$10,000}{2}$$

$$=\ \$40,000$$

Therefore, the accounting rate of return for the cooker investment can be computed as follows:

$$Accounting\ Rate\ of\ Return\ =\ \frac{Average\ Income}{Average\ Investment}$$

$$=\ \frac{\$8000}{\$40,000}$$

$$=\ 20\%$$

If the accounting rate of return exceeds the criterion or target rate of return, the project is acceptable. Like the payback method, the accounting rate of return method has drawbacks because, by averaging, it does not consider the explicit timing of cash flows. However, the accounting rate of return method is an improvement over the payback method in that it considers cash flows in all periods.

Net Present Value Criterion

The **net present value** is the sum of the present values of all cash inflows and outflows associated with a project. This is the first method described that incorporates the time value of money. Here are the steps used to compute an investment's net present value:

Net present value
The sum of the present values of all the cash inflows and cash outflows associated with a project; also known as residual income and economic income.

STEP 1 Choose the appropriate period length to evaluate the investment proposal. The period length depends on the periodicity of the investment's cash flows. The most common period length used in practice is annual, although analysts also use quarterly and semiannual period lengths.

STEP 2 Identify the organization's cost of capital, and convert it to an appropriate rate of return for the period length chosen in step 1.

STEP 3 Identify the incremental cash flow in each period of the project's life.

STEP 4 Compute the present value of each period's cash flow.

STEP 5 Sum the present values of all the periodic cash inflows and outflows to determine the investment project's net present value.

STEP 6 If the project's net present value, also called *residual income*, is positive, the project is acceptable from an economic perspective.

In the case of Shirley's, the question is whether the five-year annuity of $20,000 plus the single salvage payment of $10,000 after five years justifies the initial $60,000 investment. Let's follow the six steps just mentioned to determine the net present value of this investment:

STEP 1 The period length is one year because all cash flows are stated annually. The convention in capital budgeting is to assume, unless otherwise stated, that the cash flows occur at the end of each period.

STEP 2 Shirley's stated cost of capital is 10% per year. Because the period chosen in step 1 is annual, no adjustment is necessary to the rate of return.

STEP 3 The incremental cash flows, as shown in Exhibit 10-10, are a $70,000 outflow immediately, $20,000 inflow at the end of each year for five years, and $10,000 salvage at the end of five years. It is very useful to organize the cash flows associated with a project on a time line like the one shown. This allows you to identify and consider all the project's cash flows systematically.

STEP 4 The present value of a five-year annuity of $20,000 when the organization's cost of capital is 10% is $75,816 as shown in the following equation:

$$PV = a \times factor_{10\%, \text{ 5 years}}$$
$$= \$20{,}000 \times 3.7908$$
$$= \$75{,}816$$

The present value of the $10,000 salvage in five years when Shirley's Doughnut Hole's cost of capital is 10% equals $6209:

$$PV = FV \times factor_{10\%, \text{ 5 years}}$$
$$= \$10{,}000 \times 0.6209$$
$$= \$6209$$

STEP 5 The present value of the cash inflows attributable to this investment is $82,025 ($75,816 + $6,209). Because the investment of $70,000 takes place at time zero, the present value of the total outflows is $70,000. The net present value, or residual income, of this investment project is $12,025 ($82,025 − $70,000).

STEP 6 Because the project's net present value is positive, Shirley's should purchase the cooker because it is economically desirable.

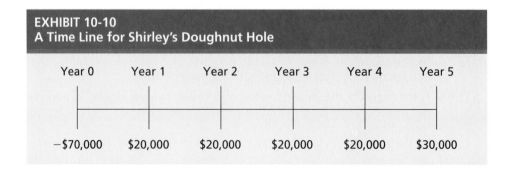

EXHIBIT 10-10
A Time Line for Shirley's Doughnut Hole

Year 0	Year 1	Year 2	Year 3	Year 4	Year 5
−$70,000	$20,000	$20,000	$20,000	$20,000	$30,000

Exhibit 10-11 summarizes the individual cash flow calculations for the new doughnut cooker investment.

Internal Rate of Return Criterion

The **internal rate of return (IRR)** is the actual rate of return expected from an investment. The IRR is the discount rate that makes the investment's net present value equal zero. If an investment's net present value is positive, its internal rate of return exceeds its cost of capital. If an investment's net present value is negative, its internal rate of return is less than its cost of capital. By trial and error, we can find that the IRR in Shirley's is 16.14% as shown in Exhibit 10-12. Because a 16.14% internal rate of return is greater than the 10% cost of capital, the project is desirable.

Because a project's net present value summarizes all its financial elements, the internal rate of return criterion need not be used when preparing capital budgets. Moreover, the internal rate of return criterion has several disadvantages.

1. It assumes that an organization can reinvest a project's intermediate cash flows at the project's internal rate of return, which is frequently an invalid assumption.

2. Using the internal rate of return criterion to evaluate proposed investments can create ambiguous results, particularly when evaluating competing projects in situations where capital shortages prevent the organization from investing in all projects with a positive net present value and when projects require significant outflows at different times during their lives.

EXCEL SPREADSHEET APPLICATION

COMPUTING AN INVESTMENT'S NET PRESENT VALUE   Excel has a built-in function to compute a project's net present value.

The function has this form:

NPV(rate, value 1, value 2, . . . , value n)

Suppose that you entered the periodic net cash flows into the following cells in an Excel spreadsheet: -70000 in cell B6, 20000 in cells B7 through B10, and 30000 in cell B11. The net present value function would be this:

NPV(0.1, B7: B11) + B6

Note that any cash flows that take place at time 0, in this case the initial investment, must be outside the range evaluated by the function.

Internal rate of return (r)
The rate of interest earned on an investment.

EXHIBIT 10-11
Shirley's Doughnut Hole: Computing Net Present Value

COST OF CAPITAL		10%	
Time	Amount	PV Factor	PV
0	($70,000.00)	1.0000	($70,000.00)
1	20,000.00	0.9091	18,181.82
2	20,000.00	0.8264	16,528.93
3	20,000.00	0.7513	15,026.30
4	20,000.00	0.6830	13,660.27
5	30,000.00	0.6209	18,627.64
Total			$12,024.95

EXHIBIT 10-12
Shirley's Doughnut Hole: Internal Rate of Return Calculation

INTERNAL RATE OF RETURN			16.14%
Time	Amount	PV Factor	PV
0	($70,000.00)	1.0000	($70,000.00)
1	20,000.00	0.8610	17,220.60
2	20,000.00	0.7414	14,827.45
3	20,000.00	0.6383	12,766.87
4	20,000.00	0.5496	10,992.66
5	30,000.00	0.4733	14,197.51
Total			$5.08

The net present-value calculation is a superior alternative to the internal rate of return criterion and requires only one additional piece of information—the organization's cost of capital—for its calculation. However, internal rate of return is pervasive in financial markets and is widely used in capital budgeting (see Exhibit 10-13).

Economic Value Added Criterion

Recently, a number of analysts and consultants have proposed the use of the economic value added as a tool to evaluate organization performance. While the economic value added criterion is not directly suitable for evaluating new investments, its insights are useful.

EXHIBIT 10-13
Criteria Used for Investment Justification (Percentage of Total Respondents)

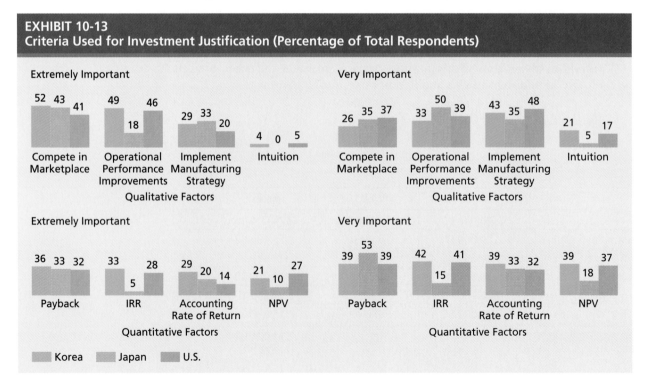

Computing economic value added begins by using accounting income calculated according to generally accepted accounting principles. Then the analyst adjusts accounting income to correct what proponents of economic value added consider to be its conservative bias.[1] For example, adjustments include capitalizing and amortizing research and development and significant product launch costs. Next the analyst computes the amount of investment in the organization and derives economic value added as follows:

$$Economic\ Value\ Added\ =\ Adjusted\ Accounting\ Income\ -\ (Cost\ of\ Capital$$
$$\times\ Investment\ Level)$$

The formula for economic value added is directly related to the net present value criterion. The major difference between the two criteria is that economic value added begins with accounting income, which includes various accruals and allocations rather than net cash flow as does net present value. This is why economic value added is more suited to evaluating an on-going investment, for example, in a product or a division, rather than evaluating a new-investment opportunity.

Effect of Taxes

OBJECTIVE 10.4

Explain the effect of taxes on investment decisions.

So far we have ignored the effect of taxes on capital budgeting. In practice, capital budgeting must consider the tax effects of potential investments. The exact effect of taxes on the capital budgeting decision depends on tax legislation, which is specific to a tax jurisdiction. In general, however, the effect of taxes is twofold:

1. Organizations must pay taxes on any net benefits provided by an investment.

2. Organizations can use the depreciation cost of a capital investment to offset some of their taxes. The rate of taxation and the way that legislation allows organizations to depreciate the acquisition cost of their long-term assets as a taxable expense varies.

Suppose that Shirley's income is taxed at the rate of 40%. To keep things simple, suppose that the relevant tax legislation allows Shirley's to claim straight-line depreciation of its net investment, which is historical cost less salvage value in long-term assets as a tax deductible expense. If Shirley's after-tax cost of capital is 7%, is the cooker project desirable?

This analysis requires converting all pretax cash flows to after-tax cash flows. In turn, this requires

EXCEL SPREADSHEET APPLICATION

COMPUTING AN INVESTMENT'S INTERNAL RATE OF RETURN Excel has a built-in function to compute a project's internal rate of return.

The function has this form:

IRR(value 1, value 2, . . . , value n, guess)

Suppose that you entered these periodic net cash flows into the following cells in an Excel spreadsheet: −70000 in cell B6, 20000 in cells B7 through B10 and 30000 in cell B11. The net present value function would be this:

IRR(B6: B11, .05)

The *guess* is your estimate of the project's internal rate of return. You can generally start with a rate like 10% or the organization's cost of capital.

---

[1] For details about these adjustments and about the economic value added method in general, see G. Bennett Stewart, III, *The Quest for Value*, HarperCollins, 1991.

The planners of Coastal Corporation considered both financial factors such as return on investment from this huge gas-processing plant and nonfinancial benefits. The plant extracts liquid hydrocarbons from the gas byproducts of nearby refineries and reduces local air pollutants by more than one ton of sulfur a day, thereby helping the refineries comply with air-quality standards. Including nonfinancial considerations in an evaluation of an investment proposal raises complex questions of how to weight these nonfinancial benefits in the overall investment decision. *Courtesy* The Coastal Corporation

knowing the amount of depreciation that will be claimed each year. Using straight-line depreciation, Shirley's Doughnut Hole will claim $12,000 depreciation each year, as noted earlier.

With this information, we can now compute the after-tax cash flows attributable to this investment. Exhibit 10-14 shows these calculations.

EXHIBIT 10-14
Net Present Value Calculations with Taxes

Time	Cash Flow	Depreciation	Tax Income	Tax @ 40%	Net Cash Flow	PV Factor	PV
0	($70,000)				($70,000)	1.0000	($70,000)
1	20,000	$12,000	$8,000	$3,200	16,800	0.9346	15,701
2	20,000	12,000	8,000	3,200	16,800	0.8734	14,674
3	20,000	12,000	8,000	3,200	16,800	0.8163	13,714
4	20,000	12,000	8,000	3,200	16,800	0.7629	12,817
5	20,000	12,000	8,000	3,200	16,800	0.7130	11,978
5	10,000	0	0	0	10,000	0.7130	7,130
Total							$6,013

Because they operate the equipment and have the most direct knowledge of the conditions under which it will be used, production-level employees are increasingly involved in capital investment decisions. These Mobil Corporation employees are discussing ways to improve the production process that makes wrapping film. *Courtesy* © Cheryl Rossum/Mobil Corp.

The investment in the cooker provides two after-tax benefits:

1. A 5-year annuity of $16,800
2. A lump-sum payment of $10,000 at the end of 5 years

Because the cooker's book value at the end of five years is $10,000, there is no gain in selling it for $10,000. Rather, its salvage value is treated as a return of capital and is not taxed. When the organization's cost of capital is 7%, the value of the five-year annuity of $16,800 is $68,883 as shown in the following equation:

$$
\begin{aligned}
PV &= a \times factor_{7\%,\ 5\ years} \\
&= \$16,800 \times 4.1002 \\
&= \$68,883
\end{aligned}
$$

The present value of the lump-sum payment of $10,000 is $7,130, as shown in the following equation:

$$
\begin{aligned}
PV &= FV \times factor_{7\%,\ 5\ years} \\
&= \$10,000 \times 0.7130 \\
&= \$7130
\end{aligned}
$$

Therefore, the present value of the incremental inflows attributable to this investment is $76,013 ($68,883 + $7,130). Since the $70,000 investment takes place at time zero, the present value of the total outflows is $70,000, and the net present value of this investment project is $6,013 ($76,013 − $70,000). Because the project's net present value is positive, it is economically desirable.

A summary example

Assume that you have the opportunity to invest in a new product that will have a 10-year life. The initial investment is $10 million in machinery and equipment, which will have a salvage value of $200,000 at the end of the 10th year. Your best judgment is that the product will increase profits by $2,500,000 in the first year and after that the incremental profits will decline by 10% per year. Your company faces a marginal tax rate of 40% and its after-tax cost of capital is 7%. Should you invest in this project?

Exhibit 10-15 summarizes the details of this problem. We will now consider this investment opportunity from the perspective of the different capital-budgeting criteria. In a given capital-budgeting situation, an organization may use several of these approaches to evaluate an investment proposal given that the different capital-budgeting criteria can rank investment opportunities differently. For example, an organization may turn down a long-lived project with a positive net present value and a long payback period because of risk considerations. Therefore, if an organization is using several capital-budgeting criteria, it must develop an individual, and therefore ad hoc, approach to determine how to make choices in situations where different criteria provide different recommendations. Because of its problematic and ad hoc nature this type of approach is not considered in the following discussion. Instead, we focus on the individual application of each criterion.

Payback Criterion

Exhibit 10-16 summarizes the information needed to compute the payback period for this project.

EXHIBIT 10-15
New Product Evaluation Example

Year	Cash Flow	Depn.	Tax Inc.	Tax @ 40%	Acc. Inc.	NCF	PV Factor	PV
0	($10,000,000)							($10,000,000)
1	$2,500,000	$980,000	$1,520,000	$608,000	$912,000	$1,892,000	0.9346	$ 1,768,224
2	2,250,000	980,000	1,270,000	508,000	762,000	1,742,000	0.8734	1,521,530
3	2,025,000	980,000	1,045,000	418,000	627,000	1,607,000	0.8163	1,311,791
4	1,822,500	980,000	842,500	337,000	505,500	1,485,500	0.7629	1,133,281
5	1,640,250	980,000	660,250	264,100	396,150	1,376,150	0.7130	981,176
6	1,476,225	980,000	496,225	198,490	297,735	1,277,735	0.6663	851,409
7	1,328,603	980,000	348,603	139,441	209,162	1,189,162	0.6227	740,550
8	1,195,742	980,000	215,742	86,297	129,445	1,109,445	0.5820	645,707
9	1,076,168	980,000	96,168	38,467	57,701	1,037,701	0.5439	564,440
10	1,168,551	980,000	(11,449)	(4,580)	193,131	1,173,131	0.5083	596,360
Total								$ 114,469

EXHIBIT 10-16
New Product Evaluation Example Payback Criterion

Year	Cash Flow	Depn.	Tax Inc.	Tax @ 40%	NCF	CUM NCF
0	($10,000,000)				($10,000,000)	($10,000,000)
1	$2,500,000	$980,000	$1,520,000	$608,000	1,892,000	(8,108,000)
2	2,250,000	980,000	1,270,000	508,000	1,742,000	(6,366,000)
3	2,025,000	980,000	1,045,000	418,000	1,607,000	(4,759,000)
4	1,822,500	980,000	842,500	337,000	1,485,500	(3,273,500)
5	1,640,250	980,000	660,250	264,100	1,376,150	(1,897,350)
6	1,476,225	980,000	496,225	198,490	1,277,735	(619,615)
7	1,328,603	980,000	348,603	139,441	1,189,162	569,547
8	1,195,742	980,000	215,742	86,297	1,109,445	1,678,992
9	1,076,168	980,000	96,168	38,467	1,037,701	2,716,693
10	1,168,551	980,000	(11,449)	(4,580)	1,173,131	3,889,823

Exhibit 10-16 shows that the investment is recovered sometime during the seventh year. The payback period value is 6.52, as shown in the following equation:

$$Payback\ Period = 6 + \frac{\$619,615}{\$619,615 + \$569,547}$$

$$= 6.52\ years$$

An organization using the payback criterion needs to decide if it is willing to accept projects with payback periods of this length. If so, the project may be accepted.

Accounting Rate of Return Criterion

From the information given in the sixth column of Exhibit 10-15, we can compute the expected average accounting income for this investment, which is $408,982. The average investment level is $4,900,000 as shown in the following equation:

$$Average\ Investment = \frac{Initial\ Investment - Salvage\ Value}{2}$$

$$= \frac{\$10,000,000 - \$200,000}{2}$$

$$= \$4,900,000$$

Therefore, the accounting rate of return is 8.35% as shown in the following equation:

$$Accounting\ Rate\ of\ Return = \frac{Average\ Accounting\ Income}{Average\ Investment}$$

$$= \frac{\$408,982}{\$4,900,000}$$

$$= 8.35\%$$

The organization needs to decide whether this accounting rate of return is acceptable.

Net Present Value Criterion

Exhibit 10-15 shows the computation of the net present value of this project, which is $114,469. Judged by the net present value criterion, this project should be accepted.

Internal Rate of Return Criterion

The internal rate of return for this project, which can be found by trial and error or by direct calculation using a spread sheet, is 7.28%. Recall that the internal rate of return is the rate of interest that makes the net present value of this project zero. Since this value exceeds the organization's after-tax cost of capital of 7%, the project would be accepted.

WHAT-IF AND SENSITIVITY ANALYSIS

OBJECTIVE 10.5

Identify the role and nature of what-if and sensitivity analysis in capital budgeting.

Capital-budgeting analysis relies on estimates of future cash flows. Because estimates are not always realized, many decision makers like to know how their estimates affect the decision they are making. In the Shirley's example, Shirley may ask, "What must the cash flows be to make this project unattractive?" Fortunately, it is easy to answer this question.

Most planners today use personal computers and electronic spreadsheets for capital budgeting. The planner can set up a computer spreadsheet so that it is possible to make changes to the estimates of the decision's key parameters. If the analysis explores the effect of a change in a parameter on an outcome, we call this investigation a **what-if analysis.** For example, the planner may ask, "What will my profits be if sales are only 90% of the plan?" A planner's investigation of the effect of a change in a parameter on a decision is called a **sensitivity analysis.** For example, the planner may ask, "How low can sales fall before this investment is unattractive?"

What-if analysis
An analysis that explores the effect of a change in a parameter on an outcome.

Sensitivity analysis
An investigation of the effect of a change in a parameter on a decision.

In the situation in which Shirley's faces taxes, suppose that the expected incremental cash flows from the operation were only 95% of what was planned, that is, $19,000 instead of $20,000. Is the cooker still an attractive investment? The answer is yes. As seen in Exhibit 10-17, the annual cash benefits need to fall below $17,556 each year before the project is economically undesirable. This is a drop of 12% from the estimated amount of $20,000, which is not a big error. Therefore, the decision is sensitive to the estimated benefits.

STRATEGIC CONSIDERATIONS

OBJECTIVE 10.6

Evaluate the effects of strategic considerations on capital budgeting.

So far, we have considered only the profits from incremental revenues or the expected cost savings offered by a long-term asset. The common benefits associated with acquiring long-term assets ignore these assets's strategic benefits, which are of increasing importance. Including strategic benefits in a capital-budgeting example is very controversial because they are difficult to estimate and, therefore, risky to include. However, strategic benefits are, in fact, likely to be no more difficult to estimate than the profits from expected sales or expected cost savings.

EXHIBIT 10-17
Net Present Value Calculations with Taxes

Time	Amount	Depreciation	Tax Income	Tax @ 40%	NCF	PV Factor	PV
0	($70,000)				($70,000)	1.0000	($70,000)
1	17,556	$12,000	$5,556	$2,222	15,334	0.9346	14,330
2	17,556	12,000	5,556	2,222	15,334	0.8734	13,393
3	17,556	12,000	5,556	2,222	15,334	0.8163	12,517
4	17,556	12,000	5,556	2,222	15,334	0.7629	11,698
5	27,556	12,000	5,556	2,222	25,334	0.7130	18,063
Total							$1

Strategic benefits reflect the enhanced revenue and profit potential that derive from some attribute of a long-term asset. Usually long-term assets provide the following strategic benefits:

1. They allow an organization to make goods or deliver a service that competitors cannot, for example, developing a patented process to make a product that competitors cannot replicate.

2. They support improving product quality by reducing the potential to make mistakes, for example, improving machining tolerances or reducing reliance on operator settings.

3. They help shorten the cycle time needed to make the product, for example, one-hour photo-developing.

Many convenience stores have purchased and installed automatic debit machines. Customers present a bank card and purchases are deducted directly from the customer's bank account. Many customers find this service convenient because they have to carry less cash. If stores install these machines, the expense involved is a cost of being in business. The failure to provide this service will lead to a loss of sales. *Courtesy* Laima Druskis/Photo Researchers Inc.

For example, Shirley's may consider investing in a new cooker that can sense when a doughnut is cooked and then eject it automatically. This cooker may offer a number of benefits.

1. It may allow Shirley to hire less-skilled and lower-paid employees to work in the Doughnut Hole.
2. By compensating for ambient factors, such as external temperature and humidity, the cooker may improve the consistency of cooking and, therefore, the quality of the doughnuts. As customers recognize the high-quality of the doughnut, they are likely to find Shirley's doughnuts more desirable. In this situation, the benefits from the automatic cooker can include increased sales and lower operating expenses if the competitors do not have this cooker. On the other hand, the automatic cooker can prevent an erosion of sales if Shirley's competitors also purchase it.

In either situation, acquiring the automatic cooker provides benefits to Shirley's that should be incorporated in the capital-budgeting analysis. Moreover, any capital-budgeting analysis needs to reflect the alternatives available to competitors and not simply assume that the status quo will continue indefinitely.

POST-IMPLEMENTATION AUDITS AND CAPITAL BUDGETING

OBJECTIVE 10.7

Understand the role of post-implementation audits in capital budgeting.

The decisions reached using capital-budgeting models rely heavily on estimates, particularly on the project's cash flows and its life. These estimates come from many sources: past experience, judgment, or the experience of others, such as competitors. When estimates are used to support proposals, recognizing the behavioral implications that lie behind them is important. For example, a production supervisor who is very anxious to have the latest production equipment may be very optimistic to the point of being reckless in forecasting the benefits of acquiring the equipment in terms of cost reduction, quality improvement, and production-time improvements. This behavior is mitigated if people understand that, once equipment is acquired, the company will compare results with the claims made in support of the equipment's acquisition and that higher costs, including depreciation, will be assigned to products or customers produced with or served by this asset.

Many organizations fail to compare the estimates made in the capital budgeting process with the actual results. This is a mistake for three reasons:

1. By comparing estimates with results, the organization's planners can identify where their estimates are wrong and try to avoid making similar mistakes in the future.
2. By assessing the skill of planners, organizations can identify and reward those who are good at making capital-budgeting decisions.
3. By not auditing the results of acquiring long-term assets, companies create an environment in which planners may be tempted to inflate their estimates of the cash benefits associated with their projects to get them approved.

After-the-fact audits can provide an important discipline to capital budgeting, which is a subjective judgmental process. Revisiting the decision to purchase a long-lived asset is called a **post-implementation audit** of the capital-budgeting decision and provides many valuable insights for decision-makers.

Post-implementation audit
Re-assessing the decision to purchase a long-lived asset.

BUDGETING OTHER SPENDING PROPOSALS

Organizations develop spending proposals for discretionary items that are not capital expenditure items, such as research and development, advertising, and training. Discretionary expenditure items that are not capital expenditures can provide benefits that will be realized for many periods into the future. However, financial accounting conventions relating to external reporting (GAAP) require that discretionary expenditure items not related to capital be expensed in the periods in which they are made, even if they provide future benefits.

Despite the financial accounting treatment of discretionary expenditures, their magnitude suggests that they should be evaluated like capital spending projects as much as possible. The approach to analyzing a discretionary expenditure is identical to that used when deciding whether to make a capital investment. Planners should estimate the discounted cash inflows (benefits) and discounted cash outflows (costs) associated with any discretionary spending project and accept the project if the net present value of the discounted cash flows is positive.

MICROSOFT WINDOWS 95 REVISITED

Estimates of the amount that Microsoft Corporation spent on launching Windows 95 vary between $200 and $300 million. Assume that the actual cost was $250 million. Suppose that Microsoft Corporation spent three times the launch cost to develop Windows 95. Therefore, the estimate is that the total long-term investment needed to develop and launch Windows 95 was $1 billion.

Imagine that the lifetime of Windows 95 is five years. This requires comparing the anticipated benefits associated with selling this product over its five-year lifetime with the initial investment of $1 billion. The sales price of Windows 95 is approximately $100. Assume that the selling price to retailers and distributors is $70 and that the profit margin on software is 80% of the selling price, making the profit margin to Microsoft Corporation $56 ($70 $\times$ 80%) for each unit sold. If variable costs in terms of after-sales technical support associated with each unit are $6, this yields a net margin of $50 on each unit sold. Finally, assume that there are future benefits beyond the five-year estimated life for Windows 95 since customers who move to Windows 95 will buy subsequent products designed for Windows 95 users. Estimate the future benefit beyond the fifth year as $250 million.

Assuming an initial investment of $1 billion, a terminal value of $250 million in five years, and an after-tax cost of capital of 10%, the present value of the $250 million in five years is $155.225 million as shown in the following equation:

$$PV = FV \times factor_{10\%, \text{ 5 years}}$$
$$= \$250,000,000 \times 0.6209$$
$$= \$155,225,000$$

The five-year annuity provided by this initial investment must provide the present value of the initial investment less the salvage value. This amount is $844,775,000 ($1,000,000,000 - $155,225,000). The amount of the annuity that recovers this net present value is $68,805,830 as shown in the following equation:

$$a = PV \times factor_{10\%, 5 \text{ years}}$$
$$= \$844,775,000 \times 0.2638$$
$$= \$222,851,645$$

Thus, Microsoft must sell about 4,457,033 ($222,851,645/$50) units of software each year for five years to make this investment worthwhile.

How is Microsoft Corporation doing? Outsiders estimate that Microsoft Corporation recorded sales in excess of one million units in the first four days following the release of Windows 95. On October 17, 1995, Microsoft announced that it had sold seven million copies during the first quarter following its introduction.

SUMMARY

This chapter introduces basic capital budgeting concepts. Capital budgeting compares the costs and benefits of a long-term, or capital, asset. The acquisition of long-term assets requires that organizations plan carefully because these assets involve long-term commitments of huge amounts of money. Therefore, organizations must proceed carefully when investing in long-term assets.

We introduced the concepts of investment and return, the present and future value of money, cost of capital, net present value, and internal rate of return as part of the capital budgeting discussion.

Because the cash flows associated with a long-term asset invariably take place at different points in time and because money has a time value, we use the concept of present value to convert all cash outflows and inflows to a common point in time so that they are comparable.

Taxes affect cash flows in two ways.

1. Taxing authorities define both the income subject to taxes and the depreciation schedule, which includes the pattern of depreciation and the period over which the depreciation can be recognized in computing taxable income.

2. Taxing authorities set the tax rate that organizations apply to taxable income in determining taxes payable.

Capital budgeting involves uncertainties relating to estimating future cash flows. This includes estimating cost savings resulting from the acquisition of an asset and the amount of increased profits resulting from the increased revenues associated with the acquisition of an asset. Planners can use what-if analysis and sensitivity analysis to investigate the effects of forecasting uncertainties on the capital-budgeting model.

Because capital budgeting compares the incremental cash inflows and incremental cash outflows attributable to the acquisition of a long-term asset, it is critical that the baseline, or status quo, position be carefully chosen. For example, if competitors are acquiring equipment to improve quality and retain customers, the capital budgeting analysis associated with acquiring that equipment must reflect the revenue and profit losses if the existing equipment is kept while competitors upgrade their equipment.

KEY TERMS

APPENDIX 10-1

Annuity Formulas

To compute the present value of an annuity, use this formula:

$$PV = a \times \left[\frac{(1 + r)^n - 1}{r \times (1 + r)^n} \right]$$

To compute the amount of an annuity that will repay a present value (loan), use this formula:

$$a = PV \times \left[\frac{r \times (1 + r)^n}{(1 + r)^n - 1} \right]$$

APPENDIX 10-2

Effective and Nominal Rates of Interest

To this point, we have assumed that the analyst, who makes investment decisions about long-term assets, has been provided with the appropriate periodic rate of return. However, investment situations often specify a rate of return for a period that differs from the period used in the investment analysis. Therefore, you must have a way of converting one periodic rate to another. To do this, we use the notion of nominal and effective rates of interest.

Financial institutions usually express the rate of interest they pay in annual terms. This means that if a financial institution promises a rate of return of 6% on investments, the 6% is the nominal, or stated, annual rate of interest. For example, the bank will say that it will pay "an annual rate of 6% computed and paid quarterly." If a financial institution pays interest quarterly when the nominal rate of interest is 6% per year, interest is paid at the rate of 1.5% (6% ÷ 4) per quarter. Therefore, the effective quarterly rate of interest is 1.5%.

Exhibit 10-18 shows that, under these conditions, $1.00 invested at the beginning of the year accumulates to $1.0614 at the end of the year (4 periods later).

Thus, the effective annual rate of interest is 6.14% rather than the nominal rate of interest of 6%. Why is this true? Periodic compounding has allowed the saver to earn interest on interest earned during the year, which yields a higher return than the nominal rate of return. This is known as the effective rate of interest.

We compute the effective annual rate of interest, r_e, where r_n is the stated, or nominal, annual rate of interest and n is the number of compounding periods per year as follows:

$$r_e = \left(1 + \frac{r_n}{n}\right)^n - 1$$

Consider the interest that a credit-card company charges on outstanding monthly balances. The nominal rate of interest is 15%. What is the effective annual rate of interest? Because interest is computed and charged monthly, the effective annual rate of interest is 16.08% as shown in the following equation:

$$r_e = \left(1 + \frac{r_n}{n}\right)^n - 1$$
$$= \left(1 + \frac{0.15}{12}\right)^{12} - 1$$
$$= (1.0125)^{12} - 1$$
$$= 0.1608$$

You should consider this when you accumulate unpaid charges on your credit card! For example, suppose that a student uses a credit card in January to buy a $500 portable stereo system. The student plans to repay the amount on June 1 upon receipt of a first paycheck from a summer job. The credit card bill arrives on February 1 but no payment is made until June 1. Therefore, the bill will accumulate interest for four months. If the stated interest rate on unpaid balances is 15% per year, or 1.25% per month, the amount that the $500 purchase will have accumulated to by June 1 is as follows:

$$FV = P \times factor_{1.5\%, \, 4 \text{ periods}}$$
$$= \$500 \times (1.0125)^4$$
$$= \$500 \times 1.0509$$
$$= \$525.47$$

This is a significant amount to consider.

EXHIBIT 10-18
Compound Growth @ 1.5% Interest

Period	Start	Interest	End
1	$1.0000	$0.0150	$1.0150
2	1.0150	0.0152	1.0302
3	1.0302	0.0155	1.0457
4	1.0457	0.0157	1.0614

ASSIGNMENT MATERIAL

■ QUESTIONS

10-1 What is the cost of capital?

10-2 What does the time value of money mean?

10-3 What is discounting?

10-4 What is present value?

10-5 What is future value?

10-6 What is the significance and role of time zero in capital budgeting?

10-7 What is net present value?

10-8 What is the defining feature of a long-term, or capital, asset?

10-9 What are inflows and outflows in capital budgeting?

10-10 What is an investment?

10-11 Give an example of an annuity.

10-12 What does return mean?

10-13 What is the discount rate?

10-14 Why are incremental cash flows important in capital budgeting?

10-15 What does the compounding effect mean?

10-16 What is internal rate of return?

10-17 How is the idea of net present value used in capital budgeting?

10-18 What is the role of future value in capital budgeting?

10-19 What is the difference between the nominal and effective rate of interest?

10-20 What does payback period mean?

10-21 Why do planners compute the present value of a sum that will be received in the future?

10-22 How would you explain the idea of internal rate of return using nonfinancial terms?

10-23 What is capital budgeting?

10-24 Why are post-implementation audits useful?

10-25 Give an example of the use of sensitivity analysis.

■ EXERCISES

10-26 *Long-term assets* What are the attributes of long-term assets? Why do organizations use capital budgeting to evaluate the acquisition of long-term assets?

10-27 *Capital budgeting objectives* What are the major objectives in capital budgeting?

10-28 *Explaining capital budgeting* How would you describe capital budgeting to someone who is intelligent but knows nothing about the time value of money or the concept of a required return on an investment?

10-29 *Quantifying intangible benefits in capital budgeting* Suppose that you work for a bank and are proposing a system that customers can access from their home computers to do their banking. Only about one-half of the estimated cost of this system can be recovered by decreased clerical time required in the banks. However, you believe that the balance of the cost will be more than made up by improved customer service that will attract more customers. How would you handle this situation in a capital budgeting exercise?

10-30 *Time value of money*   Is it always true that money now is worth more than the same amount of money received a year from now?

10-31 *Evaluating payment alternatives*   Which is a better deal: $1000 at the end of one year or $500 at the end of six months and another $500 at the end of 12 months? Why?

10-32 *Explain compounding*   Explain the notion of compounding interest using an example.

10-33 *Valuing an annuity*   You have won a lottery with an advertised prize of $1,000,000. The prize is to be paid in installments of $100,000 per year for the next 10 years. Is this prize really worth $1,000,000? Explain.

10-34 *Valuing a perpetual annuity*   Suppose that a financial instrument promises to pay you, your heirs, or their heirs, $1000 a year forever. What is the current worth of this instrument? Make any assumption that you believe you need to answer this question.

10-35 *Cost of capital determinants*   Would you expect the cost of capital to be higher for an electric utility or a genetics laboratory? Explain.

10-36 *Reconciling different lifetimes in capital budgeting*   Suppose that in a capital budgeting exercise you were considering the choice between two machines to do a job. However, one machine lasts five years and the other lasts only four years. How would you make a financial comparison between the two machines in this situation?

10-37 *Valuing a business*   You have inherited a small convenience store. How would you compute the internal rate of return from this store if you decided to keep it?

10-38 *Taxes and capital budgeting*   Describe the effect of taxes in capital budgeting.

10-39 *Sensitivity analysis and capital budgeting*   Suppose that you are advising someone who is using capital budgeting to evaluate the purchase of a clothing store. What role might sensitivity analysis play in this evaluation?

10-40 *Capital budgeting and risk*   Suppose that you are using capital budgeting to evaluate two alternative business opportunities. Both require comparable investments and have comparable average cash flows. However, the cash flows of one business appear to be more volatile than those of the other—that is, the cash flows of this opportunity vary more about its average. Is this an important consideration in capital budgeting?

■ PROBLEMS

Fundamental Problems

10-41 *Capital budgeting and sensitivity analysis*   Ritchie's Trucking hauls logs from wood lots to pulp mills and saw mills. Ritchie now operates a single truck and is considering buying a second truck. The total required investment in the truck and trailer would be $130,000. The equipment would have a five-year life and a salvage value of $20,000. Ritchie's cost of capital is 12% and Ritchie faces a marginal tax rate of 35%. You can assume that for tax purposes Ritchie will depreciate the net cost (that is, purchase price less salvage value) of the new equipment on a straight-line basis.

Adding a second truck would provide two major advantages for Ritchie. First, the new equipment would allow Ritchie to accept business that he now turns down because of a lack of capacity. Ritchie expects that the net cash flow associated with this additional business is about $25,000 per year. Second, the new equipment would allow Ritchie to reduce the cost of current operations primarily by discontinuing the practice of having to pay drivers overtime. This savings would amount to approximately $10,000.

REQUIRED

   (a) Is the investment in the new equipment justified?
   (b) What is the minimum amount of annual benefit from the investment in the new equipment that will make the project acceptable?

10-42 *Valuing a bond*   A company issues a bond with the following characteristics:

   (a) Semiannual interest payments of $45 for 10 years
   (b) A lump-sum repayment of the $1000 face value of the bond after 10 years

If the bond market requires 10% interest compounded semiannually for the debt issued by this company, what is the market price (present value) of this bond?

10-43 *Valuing zero coupon bonds*   A government issues a savings bond that will pay the holder $1000 in 10 years. (This is called a zero coupon bond.) If the bond market is now requiring 5% annual interest on government debt, what will be the issue price (present value) of this bond?

10-44 *Revaluing a bond*   Review the data in 10-43. Suppose that you purchased the bond mentioned in that question. It is now one year later and the bond market now requires 7% interest on government debt. What will you receive for this bond if you sell it today?

10-45 *Choosing an annuity*   You have been offered the following two annuities for the same price. Annuity 1 pays $50,000 per year for 10 years. Annuity 2 pays $40,000 per year for 20 years. If your cost of capital is 10%, which of these two annuities is a better deal? Why?

10-46 *Capital budgeting with strategic consideration*   Ronnie's Welding uses welding equipment mounted in the bed of a pickup truck to provide on-site welding services. The expected life of his existing equipment is five more years, after which the equipment will be worthless and scrapped for zero salvage.

Ronnie is considering replacing his existing welding equipment. The new equipment will allow him to do jobs that he must now decline and also reduce the costs of his current jobs. The new equipment should last five years, reduce the operating costs associated with existing jobs by $9000 per year, and attract new jobs that will provide incremental profits of $5000 per year. The purchase price of the new equipment is $50,000, net of what Ronnie could get from selling his old equipment. The salvage value of the new equipment would be $2000 in five years. Assume that Ronnie can borrow money at 12% and that he faces a 40% marginal tax rate. Assume that for tax purposes Ronnie will depreciate the net investment (that is purchase price less salvage value) on a straight-line basis.

   (a) Is this investment desirable?
   (b) Suppose that while he is considering this project, Ronnie discovers that the quality of the welds produced by the new machine exceeds the quality of the welds made by the old machine. Because weld quality is related to safety, Ronnie knows that this will be attractive to many of his customers. Suppose that Ronnie believes that if he buys the machine and his competitors do not, the increased profits associated with the new machine will be $8000 instead of the original estimate of $5000. Is this investment desirable?
   (c) Ronnie knows that his competitors have access to the same trade information that he does and that he cannot restrict their access to the equipment that he is considering. What do you think would happen if all these competitors purchased the equipment? What do you think would happen if only one competitor purchased the equipment?

10-47 *Net present value, payback, and accounting rate of return*   Consider the following two mutually exclusive projects, each of which requires an initial investment of $100,000 and has no salvage value. This organization, which has a cost of capital of 15%, must choose one or the other.

CASH FLOWS OF PROJECTS A AND B

Year	Project A	Project B
1	30,000	$ 0
2	30,000	20,000
3	30,000	20,000
4	30,000	50,000
5	30,000	90,000

(a) Compute the payback period of these projects. Using the payback criterion, which project is more desirable?

(b) Compute the net present value of these two projects. Using the net present value criterion, which project is more desirable?

(c) What do you think about the idea of using the payback period to adjust for risk?

(d) How do you think conventional capital budgeting adjusts for a project's risk?

(e) Assuming that straight-line depreciation is used to compute income, compute the accounting rate of return for these two projects.

(f) What do you think of the accounting rate of return criterion?

10-48 *Capital budgeting and sensitivity analysis*   Magic Mountain Enterprises runs a ski center. Its 14 downhill runs vary in difficulty from beginner to expert. To attract more customers, Maria Jasper, the owner/manager, is considering developing cross-country ski trails. The cross-country ski trails would take two years to build and would cost $1,000,000 per year to build. The trails would open for business in year 3 and would generate $500,000 per year in net cash flows. Maria has a required return of 12% on all investments.

The land on which the trails would be built is leased. The lease costs are included in the $500,000 annual net cash flow calculation. The lease will expire nine years from now, that is, after the trails have been operated for seven years. There will be no opportunity to renew the lease, and Maria will not be compensated for any of the work done building the ski trails.

(a) Compute the net present value of the decision to enter the cross-country ski business. Should the investment be made? (Ignore taxes in your analysis.)

(b) What is the minimum annual net cash flow from the cross-country ski business during the seven years of operations that would make this investment desirable?

10-49 *Allocating capital funds*   You are the general manager of a consumer products company. One of your major tasks is to approve new product proposals brought to you by the product managers who report to you. The product managers are by and large an aggressive lot who are eager to expand the product lines they supervise. These product managers are paid a wage, which is based in part on the number of products that they supervise. In addition, they receive a bonus that is based on product sales. Each year you receive between 20 and 25 new product proposals.

Each year the Appropriations Committee gives you a fund that you use to fund new product introductions. This fund is usually in the range of $60 million. On average each new product introduction costs about $10 million Therefore, you can fund between five and six new product introductions each year.

REQUIRED

(a) What effect do you think post-implementation audits, which compare managerial claims made during new product proposals with actual results, would have on new product proposals?

(b) Do you think that managers would have to be penalized for variances between planned and actual results for the post-implementation audit to have any behavioral effect? If so, how should the company structure the penalty? If not, why would penalties not be necessary?

(c) Do you think that the way managers are paid is appropriate? If so, why? If not, what changes would you suggest?

Challenging Problems

10-50 *Effective rate of interest*   Compute the effective annual rate of interest in each of the following cases:

(a) A bank promises 8% interest compounded annually.
(b) A bank promises 8% interest compounded semiannually.
(c) A bank promises 8% interest compounded quarterly.
(d) A bank promises 8% interest compounded monthly.
(e) A bank promises 8% interest compounded daily.
(f) Bonus: A bank promises 8% interest compounded continuously.

10-51 *Finding the interest rate*   You want to borrow $10,000 and repay the loan with equal monthly payments for five years. The bank has advised you that the required monthly payment will be $222.45. What is the monthly rate of interest and the effective annual rate of interest that the bank is proposing to charge you for this loan?

10-52 *Capital budgeting and sensitivity analysis*   You work for an automobile company that is considering developing a new car. The product development costs for this new car will be $500 million per year for three years. During the third year of product development, the company will incur $1 billion for manufacturing set up costs. Three years after the start of product development, the company will begin making and selling cars. Production and sales will last seven years, and each car sold will generate an incremental profit of $2,500. After seven years, the salvage value associated with the manufacturing facilities will be $200 million. The company's cost of capital is 12%. What is the minimum number of cars the company must sell during each of the seven years of the product's life to make this investment desirable? What will the minimum number of vehicles be if the company's cost of capital is 15%? (Ignore taxes when answering this question.)

10-53 *Accumulating a target level of wealth*   Carolyn Martin, who is now 30, wants to retire at age 60 with $2,500,000 in an investment account. If funds can be invested to earn 12% per year compounded annually, what equal annual amount must she invest? What will the required amount be if the funds are invested to earn 12% per year compounded semiannually?

10-54 *Accumulating a retirement fund*   Review the data in 10-53. Suppose that Carolyn decides that it is unrealistic to invest an equal annual amount in her retirement fund. Instead she decides to invest increasing amounts each year. If the amount that she invests each year is 5% more than the amount she invested in the previous year, what amount must she invest in the first year?

10-55 *Value in the face of risk*   Return to the data in 10-45. Suppose that you are 65 years old and are deciding which of these two annuities to buy. The proposal is that the annuity will cease upon your death—that is, in the event of your death, the balance of the annuity that you buy will not be paid to your heirs. Choose one of the two annuities showing the basis for your choice.

10-56 *Capital budgeting and uncertainty*   Jane Eby, the chief financial officer of Baden Discount Enterprises, is faced with choosing between two machines. A new machine is needed to replace an existing machine that makes plastic mop handles for one of the company's most popular products. Jane is not sure about the demand for these mops, but estimates that it would not be less than 20,000 units per year or more than 30,000 units per year for the next five years.

The two machines are the semiautomatic and the automatic, respectively. Relative to the semiautomatic machine, the automatic machine makes the handles more quickly and makes fewer mistakes that require rework. Thus, the total cost per unit for materials and labor for mop handles made by the automatic and semiautomatic machines is not the same. The total unit cost of material and labor for mop handles is $6 on the automatic machine and $8 on the semiautomatic machine.

The automatic and semiautomatic machines cost $500,000 and $300,000, respectively, and both would last five years. After five years of use, either machine could be scrapped for a zero salvage value. This organization has a cost of capital of 12%. (Ignore the effect of taxes when answering this question.)

How should Jane choose between the two machines in this situation? Be specific. You do not have to make a specific decision about one machine or the other, but your recommendation should tell her exactly how she should make the decision.

10-57 *Capital budgeting and inflation*   Inflation is a general increase in the price level. For example, if the annual cash flows and salvage value in Exhibit 10-14 were subject to inflation at the annual rate of 4%, the cash flows would be those shown in Exhibit 10-19. (Note that, under these conditions, the annual depreciation is now $11,566 [($70,000 − $12,167) ÷ 5].)

However, with inflation, the required rate of return must be increased so that it will provide for both the time value of money and the purchasing power loss due to inflation. In general, the required rate of return is this:

$$(1 + \text{Required rate of return}) = (1 + \text{Real rate of interest}) \times (1 + \text{Inflation rate})$$

$$\text{Required rate of return} = (1 + \text{Real rate of interest}) \times (1 + \text{Inflation rate}) - 1$$

$$\text{Required rate of return} = \text{Real rate of interest} + \text{Inflation rate} + \text{Real rate of interest} \times \text{Inflation rate}$$

where the real rate of interest is the return required in the absence of inflation.

(a) Using the appropriate required return, compute the project's net present value.
(b) Why is the net present value of the project lower under conditions of inflation than it was without inflation?

EXHIBIT 10-19
Shirley's Doughnut Hole
Inflation Effects

Time	Amount	Depreciation	Tax Income	Tax @ 40%	NCF
0	($70,000.00)				($70,000.00)
1	20,800.00	11,566.69	9,233.31	$3,693.32	17,106.68
2	21,632.00	11,566.69	10,065.31	4,026.12	17,605.88
3	22,497.28	11,566.69	10,930.59	4,372.23	18,125.05
4	23,397.17	11,566.69	11,830.48	4,732.19	18,664.98
5	36,499.59	11,566.69	12,766.36	5,106.55	31,393.04

10-58 *Changing the payment frequency* Suppose that you are buying a house and require a $200,000 mortgage. You have told the bank that you want to repay your mortgage over 30 years. The bank has indicated that, whatever payment option you consider, you will be charged an effective annual interest rate of 7% on your mortgage.

REQUIRED

What will be your payment if you are required to make:

(a) Mortgage payments once a year.
(b) Mortgage payments semiannually.
(c) Mortgage payments quarterly.
(d) Mortgage payments monthly.
(e) Mortgage payments weekly.
(f) Explain any relationship that you see in your responses to parts (a) through (e).

■ CASES

10-59 *Sensitivity and what-if analysis* Your instructor has an Excel spreadsheet for the Shirley's Doughnut Hole example used in the chapter. You will need it to answer this question. The file shows how easily capital budgeting calculations can be done on a computer. (Knowledge and judgment are required to perform capital budgeting analysis; however, the computer makes the necessary calculations easy.) This exercise shows you how quickly you can answer what-if or sensitivity analysis questions after you have set up the spreadsheet. Do not be misled by the simple nature of the problem. The procedure is the same for more complex problems.

After you retrieve this file, look at the layout of the spreadsheet. The key problem parameters are the initial investment amount in cell D4, the annual benefits in cell D5, the salvage value in cell D6, the cost of capital in cell D3, and the tax rate in cell D9. The project's net present value is shown in cell D10.

(a) Move to cell D5 and adjust the annual benefits up or down until the amount in cell D10 is zero. (This will be about $17,556.) This is the annual benefit that just makes the project desirable. Note that $17,556 is about 88% of $20,000, the estimated value of the benefit. Therefore, the decision of whether to invest in this project is quite sensitive to our estimate of the cost savings. This causes us to focus our attention on the estimate of cost savings.

(b) Put the value of $20,000 in cell D5. The net present value shown in cell D10 should be $6,013. Now move to cell D3 and experiment with the cost of capital until the net present value in cell D10 is zero. (This will be about 9.94%.) This is 42% more than the estimated required return of 7%, so we would consider the decision to invest in the cooker relatively insensitive to the estimate of the required return.

(c) Put the value of 7% (0.07) in cell D3. Again the net present value shown in cell D10 should be $6,013. Now let's look at the project life estimate. This simple spreadsheet is not set up in a way that allows us to vary the project life easily, although if you want to, it can be done fairly easily with spreadsheet macros.

(d) Suppose that you want to know if the doughnut cooker investment would be justified if the cooker lasted only four years. Delete row 28. Move to the new cell A28 and enter 4. This terminates the project after four years. However, we must adjust the depreciation so that it is taken over four years instead of five. Move to cell D8 and enter 4. This will adjust the depreciation amount. You can see that the project now has a present value of −$1401, which means that the project is undesirable. The decision to buy the cooker is very sensitive to the estimate of the cooker's life.

This simple example gives you the idea of how to use sensitivity analysis to identify what estimates are critical to the project's acceptance or rejection and where to spend more time or money improving the accuracy of estimates used in the analysis.

Suppose that the required return is 9%. If everything else in the problem remains the same, what is the minimum amount of the annual benefits that would make the project desirable?

10-60 *Evaluating an investment proposal under uncertainty* Serge Martin, general manager of the hapless Hogtown Flyers, is considering the acquisition of Mario Flanagan to bolster his team's sagging fortunes. Mario has played the last two seasons in Europe, so there would be no compensation paid to another team if he is hired. Mario, a prolific scorer, is holding out for a 10-year contract with contract demands of (1) an immediate and one-time payment of $200,000 as a signing bonus and (2) $1,000,000 in salary in the first year. Mario is demanding that his salary increase at the rate of 10% each year.

Serge figures that hiring Mario will increase ticket sales by 35,000 per year. Tickets sell for $20 per game, and total variable costs associated with each customer per game are about $5. In addition, Serge is certain that with Mario, the Flyers will get into the playoffs each year. Getting into the playoffs means sales of at least 50,000 playoff tickets, which sell for $30 each. The variable (unit-driven) cost associated with each playoff ticket is about $5. Because the Flyers have the highest ticket prices in the league and would operate at capacity if Mario were signed, Serge does not expect these numbers to change over the life of Mario's contract.

Serge's only concern is that Mario is demanding a guaranteed contract—that is, he will be paid whether he plays or not. Serge is virtually certain that Mario will play for seven years. However, after that, he is not so certain of the possibilities, but he is certain that whenever Mario stops playing, ticket sales will revert to their current levels.

(a) Prepare a 10-year statement of cash flows associated with this opportunity.
(b) Assume that the Flyer's after-tax cost of capital is 6%. Compute the net present value of this deal if Mario plays for 7 years, 8 years, 9 years, and 10 years. Assume that the Hogtown Flyers face a marginal tax rate of 40% and that any losses on the sports operations can be used to reduce the taxes on other operations.
(c) What would you advise Serge to do?

10-61 *Evaluating a new technology* National Courier Company picks up and delivers packages across the country and, through its relationships with couriers in other countries, provides international package delivery services. Each afternoon couriers pick up packages. In late afternoon, the packages are returned to the courier's terminal, where they are placed in bins and shipped by air to National Courier Company's hub. In the hub, these bins are emptied. The packages are sorted and put into different bins according to their destination terminal. Early the next morning, the bins arrive at the various destination terminals, where they are sorted by route, put onto trucks, and delivered.

An operations study determined that about $2 million of employee time could be saved each year by using a scanning system. Each package's bill of lading would have a bar code that the courier would scan with a hand-held scanner when the package is picked up. The shipment would be scanned again as it reaches the terminal, when it leaves the terminal, when it reaches the hub, when it is placed into a bin at the hub, when it arrives at the destination terminal, when it is sorted onto a courier's truck for delivery, and when it is delivered to the customer. Each scanning would eliminate the manual and less accurate completion of a form, thereby providing courier time savings.

The total cost of the scanning system is estimated to be $10 million. It is thought to have a life of six years when the equipment will be replaced with new technology. The salvage value of the equipment in six years is estimated to be $500,000.

At the end of each shift, the information from all the scanners will be loaded into National Courier Company's main computer, providing the exact location of each shipment. This tracking information provides for increased security, a lower mis-sort rate, and improved service in tracing shipments that have been mis-sorted. The reduced time spent tracing missing shipments accounts for the balance of the estimated employee time savings. The marketing manager believes that the increased security and service will result in an increased contribution margin of about $1 million per year if competitors do not adopt this technology and National Courier Company does. If competitors buy this technology and National Courier Company does not, it will lose $1 million in contribution margin. If everyone buys this technology each competitor will maintain its current sales level.

If National Courier Company's marginal tax rate is 35% and it has an after-tax cost of capital of 6%, should it make this investment? Assume that National Courier Company will use straight-line depreciation to compute depreciation for tax purposes.

11

PLANNING AND CONTROL

[1] You may find the word nexus unfamiliar; however, it suits our purpose precisely in this chapter. A *nexus* is a group of interrelated elements. The important image is one of a system of connected parts designed to achieve a purpose—for example, the parts of an automobile or the players on a sports team.

GOVERNMENT CONTROL

Citizens all over the world criticize their governments for waste, excessive bureaucracy, and inattention to citizen concerns. Over the last 10 years many people have written about re-inventing government, a process of making governments more responsive to citizen concerns and improving the efficiency of activities that governments actually undertake.

Courtesy **Sandra Baker/Liaison International**

A common theme that appears in virtually every commentary on government agencies is that most governments provide no systematic way of measuring the performance of their funded programs—that is, governments do not question systematically whether these programs live up to their proponents' claims. These commentators believe that the lack of specific and measurable performance objectives renders these programs virtually uncontrollable and accounts for many of the complaints people raise about governments' activities.

STAKEHOLDER PERSPECTIVE

An organization's five major stakeholder groups—customers, employees, suppliers, owners, and the community—define its objectives. Stakeholders are the individuals, groups of individuals, and institutions that define an organization's success or affect the organization's ability to achieve its objectives. The challenge for an organization becomes its ability to define and manage its relationships with each of its major stakeholder groups. In fact, the role of strategic planning is to define the relationship that the organization will develop with each of its stakeholder groups.

Strategic Planning

Primary objectives
The organization's objectives as specified by its owners.

The first step in planning is to identify what the owners expect (for example, increased wealth) from their participation in the organization. The owners' expectations become the organization's **primary objectives.** The second planning step is to choose a strategy to achieve the organization's primary objectives. The two elements in choosing strategy that planners must consider simultaneously are these:

1. Identifying the alternatives the organization may use to compete for customers; this is the contract between the organization and customers.

2. Evaluating those competitive alternatives relative to the capabilities and expectations of the organization's stakeholders; this establishes the relationships or contracts between the organization and suppliers, employees, and the community.

Suppose planners choose a competitive strategy based on continuous product innovation; this is part of element 1 above. To do this, the organization must have highly trained and innovative employees, flexible manufacturing and logistical systems, and suppliers who can adapt quickly to changing product requirements. To be acceptable to owners, the plan must provide the expectation of a reasonable return on investment. The plan must also meet the community's expectations with respect to meeting laws and social conventions. These are the components of element 2 above.

Strategic, or long-term, planning consists of developing a nexus of interrelated, explicit and implicit contracts between the organization and its major stakeholder groups. These contracts specify what the organization plans to deliver to each stakeholder group in return for its participation and contributions in helping the organization achieve its primary objectives. Generally this means providing stakeholders with the following: customers with the products having the right mix of cost, quality, and service; owners and suppliers with the profits commensurate with their expectations and the level of their investment in the organization; employees with acceptable working conditions; and the community with an intent to meet its expectations.

The result of planning is the design and implementation of specific processes—including logistical, manufacturing, personnel, customer service, and administrative processes—that the organization uses to carry out its strategies. The organization then monitors the performance on these processes in terms of its primary and secondary objectives.

Secondary Objectives as the Drivers of Primary Objectives

The organization's secondary objectives are very important in securing each stakeholder group's participation. **Secondary objectives** are the things that the organization expects to give to and receive from each stakeholder group other than its owners. For example, the organization may expect to provide employees with satisfaction (through working conditions, wages, and organization culture) and in return receive motivation, skill, and knowledge. These secondary objectives are the means to the end of achieving certain primary objectives; therefore, secondary objectives are not important in their own right. Rather, they are important because planners believe that if the organization achieves these secondary objectives, it will succeed in meeting its primary objectives. In this sense, the secondary objectives are the determinants or drivers of primary objective performance.

> **Secondary objectives**
> Objectives, defined by the organization's relationship with its customers, employees, suppliers, and community, that are thought to improve performance on the organization's primary objectives.

The organization's secondary objectives are important because they reflect these concerns:

1. What the organization expects from each of its stakeholder groups to help it achieve its primary objectives.
2. What the organization must provide to each stakeholder group to secure from that group what the organization needs to achieve its primary objectives.

The role of a performance measurement system is to identify the organization's primary and secondary objectives, measure performance on these objectives, and by doing so help the organization improve its performance on achieving its primary objectives.

The Organization as a Nexus of Contracts

It is useful to think of the modern organization as a nexus of interrelated contracts among its five stakeholder groups. These implicit or explicit contracts define what each stakeholder group expects from and contributes to the organization. This contracting view recognizes two important realities of the modern organization.

> **OBJECTIVE 11.1**
> Understand the organization as a nexus of contracts among its stakeholder groups.

1. Different groups of people often with disparate objectives must *work together within a set of reciprocal relationships* to help the organization achieve its objectives.
2. The *achievement process is give and take*—what each stakeholder group is willing to contribute to the organization reflects what that group expects to receive in return for its cooperation.

Explicit contracts specify exactly what each party contributes.[2] *Implicit* contracts are based on unwritten expectations that develop from trust in a long-term relationship.[3] Whether a contract is explicit or implicit, the organization must de-

---

[2] An explicit contract may specify the nature, quantity, quality, and timeliness of what a supplier is to deliver to the organization and the method, place, and amount of payment that the supplier will receive in exchange net of any penalties for nonperformance.

velop a performance measurement system to assess performance on that contract. Generally, explicit contracts are useful when the product or service is well defined and easy to measure, such as the number of good units of a commodity product made. Implicit contracts are useful when the product or service is intangible and results from the development and application of specialized skill or knowledge. For example, a supplier may agree to use its expertise to design and supply a required component.

The Environment-Defining Stakeholders

The five types of organization stakeholders can be divided into two groups—the environment-defining group and the process-defining group. The **environment-defining group of stakeholders,** which includes owners, customers, and the community, has the role of defining the organization's external environment. We begin by identifying each environment-defining stakeholder group and how it contributes to defining the organization's primary and secondary objectives.

Environment-defining stakeholders
The organization's owners, customers, and community that define the environment in which the organization operates.

Organizations like Ben and Jerry's Homemade and the Body Shop are renowned for having primary organization objectives that reflect a willingness to sacrifice owners' wealth to pursue social objectives such as supporting the local community or achieving environmental objectives. However, most profit-seeking organizations have primary objectives that reflect only owner wealth considerations. *Courtesy* **Steve Hanson/Stock, Boston**

---

[3] An implicit contract may reflect an understanding between the organization and a supplier that the supplier will commit time and resources to develop unique products that meet the organization's requirements in exchange for an opportunity to recover its investment in developing this new product by being allowed to supply the product to the organization over the long run.

OWNERS. The organization's owners provide the organization with its primary source of capital and expect a return on their investment commensurate with their investment risk.[4] Owners are the residual claimants on the organization's assets. For this reason, they have the right to specify the organization's primary objectives.

While the owners' objectives can in principle be anything,[5] we will assume for our discussion that the organization is profit seeking and that the objective specified by the owners is to increase the owners' wealth.[6] Thus owners' requirements constrain an organization's operations by limiting the organization's ventures to those expected to provide returns that exceed the owners' minimum requirements.

The organization's relationships with stakeholders other than owners are defined by and reflect how the organization expects each stakeholder group to contribute to helping the organization achieve its primary objectives.

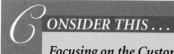

CONSIDER THIS . . .

Focusing on the Customer at Kramer Chemicals

The mission statement at Kramer Chemicals says simply "They want it now."[7] *They* refers to the company's customers and *now* means filling and delivering an order in one day. While this statement has the virtue of being simple and uncompromising, it may suggest to zealous employees that they should do anything to get a shipment to a customer within one day, including incurring excessive shipping charges, shipping incomplete orders or defective products, or going outside the organization's ordinary delivery systems to effect the delivery. A more effective statement would focus on identifying the rights and responsibilities of all the organization's stakeholders as identified in the organization's plan.

CUSTOMERS. The organization's customers play a pivotal role in the organization's affairs. The owners define what the organization wants—its primary objectives—while customers define what the organization must do to meet these primary objectives. Simply stated, customers want products that meet their requirements relating to all dimensions of their experience with the organization and the product.[8]

Therefore, in order to be successful in meeting its primary objectives, the organization must monitor its ability to meet its customers' requirements. Customer requirements relate to the product's cost, quality, and service. These customer requirements become part of the set of the organization's secondary objectives. These deserve mention here because, while customers value lower prices,

---

[4] The other two common sources of capital are debt and trade credit. We will call the providers of debt and trade credit suppliers.

[5] A not-for-profit organization, like a group dedicated to helping the homeless, may have as its objective to reclaim people from the streets, provide any necessary counseling to integrate them back into society, and to train them so that they can find jobs. A profit-seeking organization may pursue social objectives that compete with its other objectives. For example, Ben and Jerry's Homemade, a manufacturer of dairy products, established a policy of sourcing raw materials only from Vermont farmers, while recognizing that raw materials might be less expensive if acquired elsewhere. The Body Shop, a manufacturer of cosmetic products, has developed some sourcing, environmental, and social policies that can create additional costs and may alienate some customers, thereby conflicting with the objective of increasing owner wealth.

[6] Most economics-based treatments of organization objective-setting assume that the shareholders' objective is to maximize their wealth. In practice, limits on managers' cognitive ability to identify and implement wealth-maximization strategies make wealth maximization improbable. In fact, most organizations seem to aim to achieve a return on investment for owners that meets or exceeds the return that owners expect given the risk of their investment—a process that is called *satisficing*. Owners' wealth increases when the return received from their investment exceeds the market-defined return for the level of risk of that investment.

[7] A *mission statement* is an organization's statement of purpose and its commitments to each of its major stakeholder groups. A mission statement sometimes includes a statement of the organization's broad strategies.

[8] In this regard, recall the discussion of service in Chapter 2.

higher quality, and better service, the organization must make important choices about the level of each. Since improving quality, service, and cost performance requires an investment of time and resources, the organization must look at both the costs and benefits of improving each of these performance elements.

COMMUNITY.   The third group of environment-defining stakeholders is the community. The community allows the organization to transact with actual or potential customers, employees, or suppliers. Therefore, rather than creating organization success in themselves, the role of the community is to allow the other elements of success to operate. The community's requirements are more passive and indirect than the requirements of the organization's other stakeholders. The community expects the organization to act ethically in its contracting relationships with customers, employees, suppliers, and owners. In addition, the community imposes two types of requirements on the organization.

1. The first requirement is that the organization's activities do not violate the community's laws. These laws regulate the way that the organization interacts with its stakeholders and include employment laws, laws regulating advertising and selling practices, and laws protecting the environment.

2. The second requirement, which is more of an expectation than a requirement, is that the organization provide social leadership in the community. This expectation is vague and can have many forms. Examples include contributions to community relief programs and to community resources, such as schools and libraries; innovations and leadership in human resource practices and policies; and leadership in environment protection activities. Organizations are seldom penalized for not undertaking these activities, but participat-

---

Most communities expect that organizations will provide leadership in community activities, which includes supporting community resources like universities and colleges. While there is no return promised to organizations that make community contributions, most organizations expect that the goodwill generated by these contributions will enhance the organization's image in the community and, with that, organization sales. *Courtesy* **Lee Snider/The Image Works**

ing in these activities often provides a favorable corporate image in the community that organizations hope will lead to benefits like increased sales, access to better employees, and fewer hassles relating to their operations.

Therefore, community requirements define the legal and moral environment within which the community expects the organization to operate. The penalties for straying outside the limits of what the community finds acceptable consist primarily of legal sanctions, such as fines, or of community ill-will directed toward the organization that inhibits its relationships with its other stakeholders.

The Process-Defining Stakeholders

The **process-defining group of stakeholders,** comprised of employees and suppliers, works within the environment defined and created by the environment-defining group of stakeholders to design, produce, and deliver the organization's goods and services to its customers.

Process stakeholders
The organization's employees and suppliers, who have the primary responsibility of managing the processes of making and delivering goods and services to customers.

EMPLOYEES. The organization's employees constitute the single most important resource that the organization uses to create products for its customers.[9] Employees run the organization on behalf of the organization's owners and are responsible for planning, implementing, and executing the decisions designed to meet the owners' objectives.

Employees provide knowledge, skill, and effort to the organization. In exchange, employees expect competitive wages; a decent working environment, which includes both the physical conditions and the organization's general management style; and, where appropriate, an opportunity to learn and grow in the jobs that they have. Employee expectations define the types of jobs, income, and personnel practices that the organization must provide to attract and maintain the employees it wants.

Many organizations measure employee satisfaction either directly by polling employees or indirectly by measuring employee turnover because they feel that employee satisfaction has a crucial effect on employee effectiveness and efficiency and ultimately on success in achieving the organization's primary objectives.

Employees react in different ways when the organization fails to deliver what they expect in exchange for the contribution of knowledge, skills, and effort they provide. For example, if they feel they are receiving unfair treatment, employees can engage in activities like quitting, striking, working fewer hours, or providing less effort to help the organization achieve its primary objectives. For these reasons, the organization's secondary objectives should reflect employee expectations.

SUPPLIERS. Suppliers are the people or organizations, other than the owners or employees, that provide the organization with the goods and services it needs to design, make, sell, deliver, and maintain the company's products. In addition, there is an important group of suppliers, called creditors, who provide the organization with short term operating funds.

---

[9] As in earlier chapters, when we speak of products we mean both goods and services.

Suppliers have the same primary objectives as the organizations with which they do business. They are looking to increase the wealth of their own owners. Therefore, historically there has been a natural tension between organizations and their suppliers. The tension reflects the common view that the value chain creates a fixed profit to share among its participants and the organization that does the toughest bargaining and receives the biggest share of the profits is the one that has done the best.

A number of organizations, particularly NCR and Xerox, have begun to change the way we think about supplier relations. These and other innovative organizations recognize that increased profitability for all value-chain participants can result when organizations cooperate and develop long-term relationships with their suppliers. In the past organizations simply asked suppliers to bid on supplying a part or component designed by the organization for its products. Organizations like NCR recognized that suppliers have the skill and knowledge to design better components, provided they understand what the organization requires. Therefore, by involving the supplier in the organization's product-design process, the organization usually gets higher-quality, better-functioning, and lower-cost components.

Suppliers are likely to believe that their customers are treating them fairly when they feel that they have a good opportunity to earn reasonable returns for their efforts. When this happens, suppliers often increase their efforts on behalf of the customer organization. However, if suppliers feel that they are being treated unfairly, they withdraw their efforts and provide only the minimum effort expressly provided for in the contract. For these reasons, it is important that the organization's secondary objectives reflect a commitment to good supplier relationships.

Why Do Stakeholder Requirements Matter?

We have argued that what various stakeholders provide to and expect from the organization are important and become part of the organization's secondary objectives because the stakeholders help the organization achieve its primary objectives. Exhibit 11-1 summarizes this give and take.

Stakeholder requirements matter because stakeholders expect to receive something in exchange for what they contribute to the organization. If any stakeholder group feels that what it is receiving from the organization is insufficient for what it contributes to the organization, that stakeholder group will begin to withdraw its contribution from the organization. If owners do not get what they expect from the organization, they will transfer or liquidate their investments. Customers will stop buying the organization's products. The community will either pursue legal sanctions against the organization or campaign against the organization in subtle ways (such as a boycott). Employees will either withdraw their services or reduce their level of commitment and effort. Suppliers will withdraw their services or reduce the level of expertise and effort that they devote to the relationship.

In order to promote effective relationships with its stakeholders, the organization must develop a clear understanding of what it expects from each of its stakeholders to achieve its primary objectives and what each stakeholder group expects from it in return. This is the nature of the contracting process. Contracts between the organization and each stakeholder group create expectations about

EXHIBIT 11-1
Contributions and Requirements of Organization Stakeholders

Group	Contribution	Requirements
Environment-Defining Stakeholders:		
Owners	Capital	Financial rewards commensurate with risk taken
Customers	Purchasing loyalty	Service, quality, and value
Community	Allows the organization to operate or does not actively oppose its operation	Conformance to laws, good corporate citizenship, and occasional social leadership
Process-Defining Stakeholders:		
Employees	Effort, skill, motivation, and commitment	Competitive wages and benefits, job environments that meet expectations, economic security, and proper treatment
Suppliers	Effort, skill, motivation, and commitment	Financial rewards commensurate with time and skill invested, ethical treatment

what is to be given and what is to be received in return. To promote success in pursuing its objectives, the organization must monitor both sides of each contract with its stakeholders.

PERFORMANCE MEASUREMENT AND MONITORING CONTRACTS

One of the most fundamental and important roles of the organization's performance measurement system is to monitor the exchange that takes place between the organization and each stakeholder group. This allows the organization to determine whether contract expectations are being met on both sides and to identify both problem areas and opportunities for improvement. Performance measures represent the organization's secondary objectives. As a result, they are critical because if they are well-chosen they predict, or drive, the organization's performance on its primary objectives. This, in turn, provides the organization with a means to manage its performance on its primary objectives.

To illustrate the difference between managing using primary performance measures and secondary performance measures, consider which of these two reports you would rather have if you were a senior manager:

1. The first report is a primary performance measure. It consists of a comparative income statement that indicates that profits are falling through a combination of revenue and cost changes.

2. The second report includes primary and secondary performance measures. It, too, notes that profits are falling as well as a number of other things.

Customer satisfaction is falling because of poor quality. Employee satisfaction is falling because of the current management style. Suppliers are unhappy because the organization is using a contracting process that provides them with no long-term incentives to engage in new-product design. The community thinks the organization is heartless because it did not contribute to a recent flood-relief program. A number of organization processes, particularly in logistics and manufacturing, are falling far below their expected performance levels in terms of cost and cycle time.

Clearly, the second report provides a basis to evaluate, explain and improve the poor profit performance presented in the first report. This is precisely the role of appropriately chosen secondary measures of performance.

The Role of Organization Planning

Organization planning has two broad aspects:

1. The organization must decide what markets to be in and how to compete in these markets. *This planning process defines the nature of the chosen relationship between the customer and the organization.* Such choices reflect the organization's beliefs about what customers value, which become secondary objectives, and how performance on what customers value translates into improved performance on the organization's primary objectives.

2. The organization must design the specific processes that it will use to meet its customers' requirements. *The specific processes designed and used by the organization define the nature of the relationship between the organization and its employees and suppliers and reflects both community and owner requirements.*[10] These choices reflect the implicit and explicit contracts that the organization undertakes with its stakeholders to design and manage the processes that it uses to develop, make, and deliver products to its customers.

In choosing what products the organization is going to offer and how it is going to compete, the organization must simultaneously consider customer, community, and owner requirements as well as the requirements and capabilities of its suppliers and employees, which include their skills and knowledge in designing and managing processes. Any plan that is unacceptable to any stakeholder group is infeasible and must eventually be revised. For example, if the plan calls for illegal activities or a level of employee skills and motivation that is unavailable, it is necessary to revise the illegal activity and to provide a means of developing the required employee skills and motivation. This reinforces the idea that planning is reciprocal and must simultaneously consider all stakeholder groups.[11] The final plan must be feasible in the sense that it must not require resources or skills that any stakeholder group is unwilling or unable to deliver.

---

[10] This means that the organization cannot design a process that is illegal or socially unacceptable nor should it design and implement products or processes that have no potential to increase owner wealth.

[11] Management texts call this process a *SWOT* analysis, which is a systematic and simultaneous consideration of the organization's strengths, weaknesses, opportunities, and threats.

In this sense, planning sets the nature, scope, and elements of the contracts between the various stakeholder groups. Once the organization has identified a plan that meets all the requirements of the participants, that plan *identifies what contributions are expected from each stakeholder group and what each group expects in exchange.* This becomes the organization's strategy and the focus of the organization's performance measurement system.

The plan defines what needs to be measured. The performance objectives for each stakeholder group are the organization's secondary objectives. If the organization monitors what it is giving and receiving from each stakeholder group, it will predict and manage the performance on its primary objectives.

Relating Secondary and Primary Objectives

Organizations choose plans and processes and develop relationships with stakeholders to achieve their primary objectives.

Managing the performance of the primary objectives requires understanding the causes of that performance and managing those causes effectively—that is, managers must manage the secondary performance measures that are drivers of performance on primary objectives.

Suppose that you use the grades on your course assignments and examinations to identify opportunities to improve your knowledge of the course material. In this process, could you ever imagine that a test or assignment returned to you with only a grade marked on it would be useful? You need more than a simple grade, which is a summary evaluation of your performance. What you need are details about what the grader valued or found lacking in your response. In the same way, managing using results on primary objectives is like trying to improve your course performance using only grades. However, managing using results on secondary objectives is like trying to improve your course performance using the detailed comments that the grader provides to you about your work.[12]

CUSTOMERS.   Consider an organization that manufactures paper products. The organization's two competitive alternatives include:

1. Competing by continuously developing and introducing new niche products
2. Focusing on being a low cost, high-quality, supplier of a single product

In choosing between these two strategies, the organization must balance the capabilities of its production systems, employees, and suppliers with customer requirements.

Suppose that a detailed evaluation of the organization's strengths and weaknesses suggests that its financial, personnel, logistical, and manufacturing resources would not now, or in the foreseeable future, support a competitive strategy based on product innovation. Therefore, the organization chooses to compete based on low cost, high quality, and excellent customer service. The organization has chosen this strategy because, given the skills and potential of its employees and suppliers and the environment defined by its customers, owners, and

> **OBJECTIVE 11.3**
>
> Discuss the importance and interrelationship of primary and secondary organization objectives.

---

[12] Alternatively, imagine that you are the coach of a sports team and that you are trying to improve the performance of your team based solely on reports of the final scores of your team's games.

Meet Kathy Nelson, the manager of one of Whirlpool Corporation's appliance manufacturing plants. Kathy uses non-financial, that is secondary, performance measures to focus employee attention on, and monitor, the facets of plant activity that support the functional-level strategy of improving profitability by lowering production costs. Using the secondary performance measures of flexibility, availability, and quality provides the focus and coordination needed in Kathy's approach to management, which focuses on performance drivers (causes) and not the performance results. *Courtesy* Whirlpool Corporation

the community, this strategy provides the most profitable match between itself and its customers. Therefore, the organization hopes to increase customer satisfaction by using a strategy of low cost, high quality, and excellent customer service. If customer satisfaction increases, then sales should increase. If sales increase, profits should increase. Finally, if profits increase, then the owners' wealth should increase.

One of the most important management roles is to understand the causal relationship between the organization's competitive strategy and its primary objectives. Management must understand and be able to specify how the organization's stakeholder requirements translate into improved performance on the organization's primary objectives. This is the essence of planning and organization learning. Based on experience and information from past performance, the organization must continuously re-evaluate the causal chains reflected in its planning and decision-making choices. This allows the organization to test its beliefs about what is the most effective way of linking customer requirements with the organization's primary objective.[13]

Recall that the secondary objectives of low cost, high quality, and excellent customer service are not important in their own right. These objectives are important only because organization members believe that they advance the cause of meeting the organization's primary objective. Therefore, it is critical that the performance measurement system monitor, evaluate, and manage secondary objectives because if the organization's beliefs are accurate performance on these secondary objectives will predict and lead to enhanced performance on the primary objectives. Moreover, unacceptable performance levels on any secondary objectives should trigger management efforts to identify the cause of the poor

[13] For example, a niche strategy that focuses on meeting specific customer requirements may be more profitable than a strategy that focuses on supplying a low-cost, high-quality, high-service product in a commodity market.

performance and ways to improve future performance. Therefore, we say that the secondary objectives are the drivers, or causes, of primary objectives.

EMPLOYEES. Consider the role of the organization's employees in a setting where the organization has chosen a competitive strategy that includes low cost, high quality, and service. This strategy requires continuous improvement of processes and occasionally a redesign (re-engineering) of the organization's processes. This strategy also requires dedicated and knowledgeable employees who are focused on continuously designing and improving systems to reduce costs, increase quality, and increase customer service. This strategy also requires that employees have the skill and motivation to respond appropriately and quickly to changes in the organization's operating environment.

Highly motivated, highly skilled, and knowledgeable employees do not just walk into the organization off the street. The organization must design and implement human resources practices to attract and keep employees with these traits. Since these types of employees are vital to the organization's competitive strategy and relationship with customers, the organization must monitor directly or indirectly the development of employee motivation, skills, and knowledge.[14]

McDonnell Douglas is an enthusiastic supporter of employees working together to solve problems. Because they deal first-hand with problems, production-level employees often have useful suggestions to improve a process. These employees are part of a group that combined two steps in a product assembly process to make the assembly easier, save assembly time, and improve quality. *Courtesy* McDonnell Douglas

---

[14] Often a variable of interest, such as motivation, skill, or knowledge, must be measured indirectly. For example, an organization may choose to estimate employee skill by using the individual's prior training, knowledge by using the number of years of experience, and motivation by examining demonstrated effort, such as cost reduction or quality improvement.

Employees provide motivation, skill, and knowledge to the organization. These traits are necessary for success in achieving the organization's primary objectives; they actually become part of the organization's secondary objectives because they drive performance on the primary objectives or on other secondary objectives like customer satisfaction. In return for providing these inputs to their employers, employees expect certain things in return. A successful organization identifies employee expectations and measures employee satisfaction and turnover to assess how it is meeting employee expectations. To the extent that employee satisfaction affects the willingness of employees to deliver skills and effort, employee satisfaction becomes an element of the organization's secondary objectives.[15]

The idea here is that improvement on these aspects will lead to improved performance on the organization's processes, which will increase customer satisfaction and in turn lead to higher levels of performance on the organization's primary objective. Employee performance and satisfaction become part of the organization's secondary objectives since they are drivers of the performance on the organization's primary objective.

SUPPLIERS.   Consider the role of the organization's suppliers in supporting a customer strategy that focuses on low cost, high quality, and excellent customer service. Suppliers must cooperate in developing and delivering this strategy. This requires training, experience, and a long-term commitment on the suppliers' part.[16] The organization must monitor its suppliers' ability to support its strategy by delivering low-cost, high-quality goods and services when and where the organization requires them and to be innovative and flexible in responding to new challenges.

As in the case of all stakeholders, the organization cannot afford to focus only on what suppliers provide to the organization. Suppliers are likely to withdraw their contributions from the organization if they cannot meet expectations or objectives within the relationship. Therefore, the organization should monitor whether it is meeting the supplier's expectations that are embodied in the contracts, explicit or implicit, it has with the suppliers.

Therefore, supplier-related measures, including both their realized performance measures on what matters to the organization, such as quality and on-time delivery, and supplier satisfaction, which organizations often assess directly by polling or indirectly by measuring supplier turnover, become part of the organization's secondary objectives.

---

[15] Note that we have assumed that the organization's only primary objective is to increase owner wealth. Given this assumption, the only interest that the organization has in employee satisfaction is how it affects owner wealth. You may object to this and argue that some organizations seem to take a primary interest in employee welfare and do things for employees that are philanthropic. The philanthropic view of organizations simply reflects an organization with a broader primary objective set than what we are assuming here. This does not affect anything that we are saying here other than we must broaden the primary objective set for an organization like this. We do not take a position in this text on the relative merits of stakeholder capitalism and shareholder capitalism. Shareholder capitalism argues that the organization's sole goal is to maximize the return on the owners' investment. Stakeholder capitalism argues that firms should balance the interests of all the organization's stakeholders including shareholders, employees, suppliers, customers, and the community. This chapter's ideas can be adapted to any organization or set of objectives. For a discussion of stakeholder capitalism and shareholder capitalism see "Unhappy Families," *The Economist*, February 10, 1996, pp. 23–25.

[16] For example, many organizations have developed programs to train their suppliers to be low-cost, high-quality, and high-service suppliers. The General Motors *PICOS* system evaluates the performance potential of a supplier's manufacturing process, identifies opportunities for improvement, and helps the supplier to make these improvements.

One form of preventive control is to work with suppliers so that they provide products that meet specification. Motorola is a world leader in developing relationships with suppliers and has invested millions of dollars in training suppliers to deliver what Motorola wants when it is needed. This Motorola employee is helping representatives of one of its suppliers develop methods to improve quality and cut cycle time in their operations. © Michael L. Abramson

COMMUNITY.   Consider the role of the community in supporting a customer-related strategy of low cost, high quality, and excellent customer service. The community's role is primarily to put constraints on the organization's behavior as it designs and negotiates contracts with other stakeholders. For example, in its push to reduce costs, organizations may design systems that put employees at risk. The community may prohibit this type of behavior through its employee welfare laws. Community requirements relating to customer, employee, and supplier relations should be part of the organization's monitoring process to verify that the organization is meeting community requirements. These community requirements become part of the organization's secondary objectives. Community requirements are important not because they increase performance on the primary objectives directly but rather because they reflect societal constraints. When community requirements are not met, the organization will often find that its ability to contract with customers, suppliers, employees, and owners is impaired.

STAKEHOLDERS, INPUTS, AND OUTPUTS.   Organizations should measure and therefore include in their performance measurement system all elements of performance on primary and secondary objectives. Such comprehensive performance measurement allows organizations to test their understanding of these factors:

1. The input/output relationship between what they must give to stakeholders to get what they want from them.

EXHIBIT 11-2
Stakeholder Inputs and Outputs and Organization Performance

Stakeholder Group	Inputs Provided to Stakeholder Group	Results of Providing Inputs to This Stakeholder Group	Effect of Output on the Organization's Primary Objective
Customers	Low cost High quality Good service	Customer satisfaction measured directly by polling or indirectly through increased sales, higher profit margins, warranty claims	Increased sales leading to greater owner wealth
Employees	Wages Incentive compensation Training Good work environment Opportunity for improvement	Employee satisfaction measured by polling or indirectly by employee turnover or by higher employee performance levels	Increased employee motivation and productivity in designing and operating processes to achieve owner objectives
Suppliers	Long-term relationship Fair treatment	Supplier satisfaction measured directly by polling or indirectly by supplier innovations, commitment, profit levels, or turnover	Innovative products at lower cost and higher quality delivered when needed, thereby increasing customer satisfaction and owner wealth
Community	Meeting community laws and expectations with respect to leadership	Community satisfaction measured directly by polling or indirectly by community challenges to organization's operations	Higher sales and owner wealth

2. How contributions by stakeholders and processes contribute to achieving their primary objectives.

This testing is part of the process of organization learning. Therefore, in order to monitor, manage, and improve this causal chain, organizations design and operate performance measurement systems that provide a basis for learning and process improvement. Exhibit 11-2 illustrates this idea.

PROCESSES

The tangible result of specifying an organization's primary and secondary objectives is the organization design. This consists of the set of processes the organization uses to achieve its objectives.

A *process* is any integrated group of activities designed to achieve a specific purpose. All processes use physical elements, such as people and equipment. Some processes have tangible outcomes, like completing or delivering a unit of production; some processes have intangible outcomes, such as customer or employee satisfaction.

Each process must contribute, either directly or indirectly, to some organization objective. Therefore, an organization monitors, evaluates, and improves (that is, manages) processes by focusing on how each process contributes to its objectives. This is known as process control or managing the organization.

Since the relationship between a particular process—for example, processing an employee paycheck—is often only indirectly related to the organization's primary objective of owner wealth, it is more useful and reasonable to relate a process to the organization's secondary objectives—in the case of the paycheck, to employee satisfaction.

Therefore, the performance measurement system focuses on process results and how those results contribute to the organization's secondary objectives. Clearly a given process will not contribute to every one of the organization's secondary objectives. For example, a system designed to monitor and improve customer satisfaction may contribute nothing to employee satisfaction. However, processes can be interrelated. For example, reporting customer satisfaction may contribute to employee satisfaction, which stresses the importance of considering all interrelated performance characteristics. Many organizations routinely circulate or post customer testimonials in a prominent place. The intent of publicizing these testimonials is to provide employees with the opportunity to experience the satisfaction of a job well done. The important point to remember is to assess each organization process in terms of how it contributes to the organization's secondary objectives.

Consider a process that makes the wooden frame for a sofa. This process may be evaluated in terms of a number of things:

1. The cost to make the frame; this relates to the primary objective of owner wealth in addition to the ability to sell the product at a low price—a customer-related issue.

2. The production cycle time and quality; this reflects cost and therefore owner wealth considerations and customer service issues.

3. The ability of employees to make process improvements and product suggestions; this relates to cost, customer service, and employee motivation considerations.

4. The amount of scrap generated by the process; this relates to cost and environmental/community considerations.

5. Employee safety: This relates to employee and community considerations.

This entire process of making a frame might be managed in terms of the five performance dimensions of cost, cycle time, quality, process improvements, and waste.

Some organizations use processes to create intangible results. Consider a customer service system that monitors warranty claims and identifies customers who have experienced trouble with products. The organization would evaluate this system in terms of its ability to do the following:

1. Improve customer satisfaction—a customer-related issue.

2. Identify opportunities to make process improvements—both a cost (owner) and customer-related issue.

3. Identify responsibility for unusual or unacceptable performance—an employee-related issue.

Organizations have invested considerable time and money to develop manufacturing cells, such as the one shown in this picture. These manufacturing cells, which are examples of processes, increase cycle time, improve quality, and generally reduce manufacturing costs. Organizations invest in designing these cells with the expectation that the improved quality and reduced cycle time promised by the cells will increase customer satisfaction, in turn creating higher sales and increased owner wealth. These cells would be evaluated in terms of their ability to meet their objectives of reduced cycle time, increased quality, and reduced costs. *Courtesy* Cincinnati Milicron

In general, the measures that an organization uses to monitor and assess process performance should reflect the choices made during its strategic planning phase. Organizations should evaluate processes based on the contributions of these processes to the organization's primary and secondary objectives. This focuses the attention of the employees who manage an organization's processes on the elements of process performance that matter. It also provides a practical means of coordinating the management of the literally thousands of organization processes on the organization's objectives.

MONITORING AND ORGANIZATION LEARNING

Continuously improving processes so that they result in enhanced performance on secondary objectives and continuously re-evaluating and revising the causal link between secondary objectives and the organization's primary objectives is the essence of organizational learning.[17]

Exhibit 11-3 summarizes this view. Note that there are two groups of stakeholders—the environment-defining group, which defines what the organization has to do to be successful, and the process group, which designs and manages the systems and processes that create success. Note that the environment-defining stakeholders contribute to process design by identifying the outside expectations

---

[17] For example, do increased quality or customer service really increase customer satisfaction leading to increased sales and resulting in increased owner wealth? Do increased levels of employee training and pay result in increased employee motivation leading to process and product improvement that increase owner wealth? Do higher levels of supplier satisfaction result in new purchased products and services that ultimately increase owner wealth?

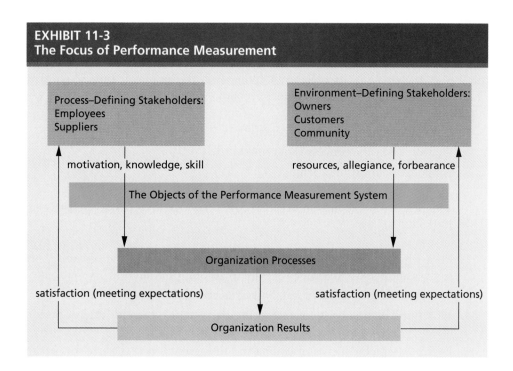

EXHIBIT 11-3
The Focus of Performance Measurement

Process–Defining Stakeholders:
Employees
Suppliers

Environment–Defining Stakeholders:
Owners
Customers
Community

motivation, knowledge, skill

resources, allegiance, forbearance

The Objects of the Performance Measurement System

Organization Processes

satisfaction (meeting expectations)

satisfaction (meeting expectations)

Organization Results

that the organization's processes must meet. The process-defining stakeholders contribute to process design by providing the motivation, knowledge, and skill to design and manage the processes the organization uses to develop, make, deliver, and service its products. Note that the scope of the performance measurement system includes what each group of stakeholders contributes and receives from the organization. The contribution of each stakeholder needs to be calculated in terms of how if affects the organization's primary objectives. What each stakeholder receives from the organization needs to be evaluated in terms of how it affects stakeholder satisfaction and the potential for continued participation in the organization. The evaluation of the give and take for each stakeholder group also supports the process of comparing the net benefit, that is, benefit minus cost, provided by each group other than the owners.

ORGANIZATION CONTROL

The success of the reciprocal relationships among stakeholders determines the organization's performance on its primary objectives. For this reason, stakeholder requirements including what each stakeholder gives and receives become a primary focus of performance measurement—what we have called the organization's secondary objectives.

The process of monitoring, evaluating, and improving performance so that the organization stays on track in achieving its objectives is usually called **organization control.**

Organization control
The tools and systems an organization uses to keep it on track toward achieving its objectives.

In control
A state in which the organization or process is on track toward achieving its objectives.

Out of control
A state in which the organization or process is not on track toward achieving its objectives.

The Nature of Control

Control is the set of methods and tools that the organization members use to keep the organization on track in achieving its objectives. A system is **in control** if it is on a path to achieving its objectives. Otherwise, the system is **out of control.** Three important roles of management accountants are:

1. Help an organization stay in control.
2. Identify when the process is out of control.
3. Support organization learning.[18]

The process of keeping an organization in control involves five steps as Exhibit 11-4 shows:

1. Plan, which consists of developing organization's primary and secondary objectives and identifying the processes to accomplish them.
2. Execute, which consists of implementing the plan.
3. Monitor, which consists of measuring the system's current level of performance.
4. Evaluate, which consists of comparing the system's current level of performance to the objective to identify any variance between the system's objective and actual performance and deciding on corrective action.

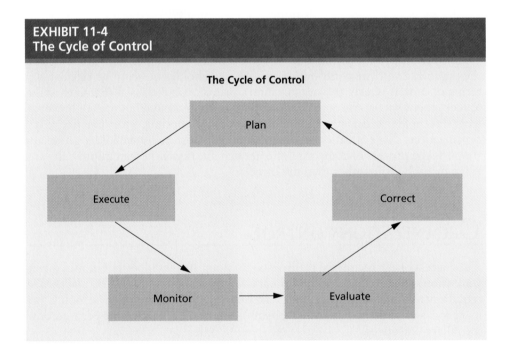

EXHIBIT 11-4
The Cycle of Control

The Cycle of Control

[18] Two other important roles of management accounting are to support planning and decision-making.

5. Correct, which consists of taking any corrective action needed to return the system to being in control.

For the process of control to have meaning, the organization must have the knowledge and ability to correct situations that it identifies as out of control; otherwise control serves no purpose because it cannot correct out of control situations.

Planning sets the environment and focus of control, but control is very complex and means different things in different organizations. Any discussion of control begins by introducing the general issues related to control.

The Timing of Control

The **timing of control** refers to the temporal relationship between the system that is being controlled and the application of the control device. You have been exposed to issues concerning the timing of control in your daily lives. For example, discussions of criminal behavior often reflect the different approaches to control. Some people focus on how to penalize people for criminal behavior in order to provide a disincentive for criminal behavior. Reacting to events in this matter is called **feedback, or reactive, control.** Other people stress monitoring known criminals or situations where there is a potential for crime, for example, advising a community that a person with a criminal record has moved into the community or putting a video camera in a bank. This approach to control is called **concurrent control.** Finally, some people stress prevention approaches to control, such as developing a social environment and job opportunities that make crime less attractive. This approach to control is called **feedforward control.**

Many organizations have found that designing systems to prevent processes from going out of control, a form of feedforward control, is the most effective approach to control. In fact, much of the literature regarding quality is based on the assumption that the cost of designing systems that eliminate the possibility for error is less expensive than the cost of designing and operating systems to identify and correct errors.

Many manufacturing systems use concurrent control processes designed to immediately identify when a process has gone out of control so that it can be shut down and corrected. For example, concurrent control would include a machine that measures the fill rate on a bottling line.

Because they rely on recorded observations, performance measurement systems support either concurrent control or feedback control systems. Although the performance measurement systems described in this chapter are exclusively feedback systems, do not assume that feedback control systems are either the most important or most effective control systems that organizations use. However, feedback systems serve important roles in organizations, particularly in controlling decision-making behavior.

Types of Control Systems

There are two broad types of control systems:

1. Task control (also called command and control)
2. Results control

Timing of control
The temporal relationship between the method and object of control.

Feedback, or reactive, control
An approach to control that reports data on completed activities to decide whether they were completed as planned.

Concurrent control
A control device that operates at the time the work is being done. An example is weighing a box of cereal as it is being filled.

Feedforward control
Often called *preventive control*, this approach to control focuses on preventing an undesired outcome and occurs before the activity is undertaken.

Most organizations require that employees who handle cash provide a cash register receipt to the customer—and some back this up by promising the customer a free meal or a discount if a receipt is not provided. Requiring that the customer receive a cash receipt requires that the sale is entered into the cash register's memory which, in turn, ensures that all incoming cash receipts are recorded—a form of task control that relies on prevention. *Courtesy* David Ulmer/Stock, Boston. Inset: *Courtesy* Taco Bell

Task control
Systems or procedures designed to ensure that employees follow stated procedures or rules.

Preventive control
An approach to control that focuses on preventing an undesired event.

The organization's choice of the general nature of its control systems should reflect its strategy because it has a profound impact on how it should monitor and evaluate employee and process performance.

CONSIDER THIS . . .

An Audit Approach to Task Control

Large fast-food chains, such as McDonald's, have developed elaborate procedures related to customer service and food preparation to ensure quality. They expect every outlet to follow these procedures. Employees from the head office, disguised as customers, visit outlets to ensure that they are following these procedures—a form of audit control. Hotel chains, such as the Four Seasons that have staked their reputation on high levels of customer service hire outsiders, called spotters, to visit their hotels to assess how well hotel staff lives up to service claims often by demanding specialized services at odd or inconvenient hours.

TASK CONTROL.   **Task control** is the process of ensuring that a task is completed in a predetermined manner.[19] One approach to task control is **preventive control,** in which managers design a system that can only be operated in the way intended. For example, an organization manufactured a product that required production employees to drill holes in a sheet of steel. The organization experienced chronic problems with holes that were improperly drilled. The employees who drilled the holes were responsible for investigating and solving the problem. Their solution was to design a small tool that clamped onto the drilling machine. The small tool fixed the steel sheet in its proper position and made it physically impossible for the drill operator to drill holes in the wrong place. This simple solution relied on preventive control to solve a nagging and expensive problem.

[19] Task control is also called action control, input control, and pretransaction control.

The second approach to task control is **audit control,** in which managers train employees to perform a task in a specific way and then use random audits to determine whether the employees are performing as intended. For example, many telephone companies periodically monitor the conversations that their operators have with customers to verify that operators are treating the customers according to specified procedures.[20]

Task control is appropriate in the following situations:

1. Where there are legal requirements to follow specific rules or procedures to protect public safety—for example, in the making of prescription drugs, manufacturing critical aircraft components, and operating nuclear generating facilities.

2. Where employees handle liquid assets to reduce the opportunity for fraud.

3. Where the organization can control some facet of its environment, thereby eliminating environmental uncertainty and the need for the application of judgment. This in turn allows the organization to develop specific rules that employees must follow, for example, preparing food in a chain restaurant. This also requires that the cost of monitoring compliance is not excessive.

RESULTS CONTROL. **Results control** focuses on motivating the organization's employees to pursue the organization's stated objectives.[21] For results control to be effective, the organization must have clearly stated its objectives and communicate them to all organization members so that each person in the organization understands what is important for organization success and how to contribute to that success.

> **Audit control**
> An approach to control that emphasizes checking people's work.

> **Results control**
> A system focused on results or outcomes that is designed to motivate decision-making behavior to achieve the organization's behavior.

ONSIDER THIS . . .

Task and Results Control

Kenneth Arrow divided the problem of organization control into two parts: the choice of *operating rules* that tell organization members what to do and the choice of *enforcement rules* that specify the consequences to employees who do not follow the operating rules.

Arrow observed that when the process is well understood or when it is not too difficult/expensive to monitor employee compliance, control takes the form of **task control,** which tells employees what to do in any situation. In this setting, enforcement rules specify the consequences, such as employee dismissal, of not following the operating rules.

When the process is not well understood or when it is difficult or costly to monitor employee compliance, control takes the form of **results control,** which tells the employees to use their skills and knowledge to do what is best for the organization. In this setting, enforcement rules take the form of rewarding employees for results valued by the organization's owners.

Source: K. J. Arrow, "Control in Large Organizations," *Management Science,* April 1964, pp. 397–408.

---

[20] For audit control to be effective, the audit must either be unexpected or covert. For this reason, many people resent audit control.

[21] Results control is also called decision control, outcome control, and management control.

CONSIDER THIS . . .

Results and Task Control in a University

Your course grade is a good example of results control because it reflects your assessed level of knowledge, which is imperfectly measured by your performance on examinations and assignments that sample your knowledge of some of the course material. Your course grade can be affected by the amount of work that you put into the course; group work that you do; your physical and mental condition when you do your assignments or take your examinations; your ability to communicate your knowledge; whether the material on the examination was the focus of your studies; and, sometimes, your performance relative to others in your course.

Because it is difficult to isolate the individual effort from the other effects on their grades, students often argue that they would prefer a task control system that determines course grades based on the individual's effort—a form of input performance reward system. Beyond the problem of measuring individual effort levels, think about the fundamental issues in deciding whether to use the task or results approach to control.

Unlike task control, which specifies a course of action and assesses penalties for noncompliance, results control rewards people based on their contributions to achieving the organization's objectives. Therefore, effective results control requires that it is possible to monitor and assess contributions to stated organization objectives.

Results control is most effective when these factors apply:

1. The environment is changing. In this setting, the organization cannot develop rules to deal with a situation.
2. Organization members have the knowledge, skill, and authority to respond to changing situations by making independent decisions.
3. Organization members understand the organization's objectives and how they contribute to those objectives.
4. The performance measurement system measures individual contributions so that an individual can be motivated to make decisions that reflect the organization's best interests.

THE ROLE AND IMPORTANCE OF DECENTRALIZATION

Decentralization
Delegating decision-making responsibility to a lower level in the organization.

Most organizations today face dynamic environments that require delegating decision-making responsibility, called **decentralization** or employee empowerment, for two reasons.

1. The people on the front lines are the first to see or sense the need for change. Therefore, they can respond most quickly to a need for change.
2. By virtue of being close to what is going on, the people on the organization's front lines are in the best position to develop the knowledge and skills required to understand needed changes in their own jobs.

Decentralization requires the support of a results control system. The system should provide both a scorecard that employees can use to evaluate the types of changes needed and to assess their own performance. A related use for a results control system is to focus and motivate employee behavior.

The potential of decentralization has been increased by the rise of the so-called knowledge worker. This person has the skills and knowledge necessary to accept decision-making responsibilities. In many companies today, important decisions are being made at levels that even five years ago would have been unimaginable. For example, in many organizations factory floor personnel have the right and responsibility to shut down the production line if they feel there are problems requiring correction. Many first-line sales personnel now have the right and responsibility to make adjustments, such as price reductions or free products, for customers who have had a bad experience with the organization.

Controlling Decentralized Decision Making

An organization's performance measurement system does two things that are vital in supporting the process of controlling decentralized decision-making:

1. The performance measurement system focuses attention on what is important, namely, the organization's primary and secondary objectives. Therefore, the performance measurement system provides the vital link between planning and control.

2. The performance measurement system coordinates decision-making behavior at all levels of the organization. Clearly, each person in the organization

Phyllis Pfeiffer, the President and Publisher of the Marin, California, Independent Journal, feels that 'being a publisher is like being an orchestra leader. You've got to keep all the people playing at the same time. Usually a leader plays one or two instruments, but must understand the scope of how a piece comes together' (*Gannetter*, Gannett Corporation, March/April 1995, page 10). *Photo courtesy* David Austen/Stock, Boston

contributes differently to help the organization achieve its primary and secondary objectives. This works in the same way that each member of an orchestra must play a piece of music that is coordinated with what all the other members of the orchestra are playing. A vital role of the performance measurement system is *to coordinate the activities of different decision makers by providing them with a common set of objectives and indicating how each person contributes to these objectives.*

CONTROL AND ORGANIZATION LEARNING

OBJECTIVE 11.5

Determine the relevance and importance of organization learning.

Effective control implies a control system that can adapt to changes as needed. In conventional control systems, learning is triggered by situations that present unexpected results. In such systems, organization members use performance measurement information to identify the cause of the variance from planned performance and to take corrective action.

Organization learning focuses on three elements of performance:

1. How do organization processes work? What is the internal physical or behavioral mechanism that creates the process results? For example, how does the employee's motivation affect job performance?

2. How do existing organization processes contribute to the organization's secondary objectives? What specific measurable results occur as a result of a particular process. For example, what is the level of motivation created by the existing system of incentive compensation?

3. How do the organization's secondary objectives contribute to the achievement of its primary objectives? What is the effect of changes in a process result on the organization's primary objectives? For example, what is the effect of a change in employee motivation on the organization's primary objectives?

There are two results of organization learning.

1. There are adjustments to existing processes that occur to make them more effective and efficient. This is known as **continuous improvement.**

2. There is the development and implementation of new processes to replace old processes to improve performance in achieving the organization's objectives. This is called **re-engineering.**

Continuous improvement
An approach to process management that emphasizes constantly looking for ways to improve its performance.

Re-engineering
The activity of improving process performance by redesigning the process.

The process of learning is enabled and driven by the organization's performance measurement system for two reasons.

1. The performance measurement system *identifies when the organization is not achieving its objectives.*

2. The performance measurement system by measuring both cause and effect variables identifies *where or why the current system is failing and suggests opportunities for improvement.*

For example, an organization might find that a three-year old program of profit sharing seems to have no effect on increasing the organization's profit per-

---

> ## C ONSIDER THIS . . .
>
> ### Performance Measurement Systems at Amoco Corporation
>
> Amoco Corporation, a multinational petroleum products company, is developing an innovative performance measurement system based on the organization's primary and secondary performance measures, which reflect controllable performance.
>
> The centerpiece of the performance measurement system is a set of performance measures that include both financial and customer service measures. Included in the new performance measurement system is a benchmarking component that compares the organization's performance against companies that are considered world class, both inside and outside our industry.
>
> As part of a trial of the new system, one group developed a performance measurement system that focused on the performance of trucking companies that deliver Amoco's products. "The result is a supplier requirements scorecard that evaluates carriers on such performance as on-time pickup, on-time delivery, safety and insurance issues, and responsiveness to Amoco customer service needs."
>
> *Source: Amoco Torch,* January 9, 1995.

formance. There are three possible explanations for this apparent outcome: (1) profit-sharing plans have no effect on employee performance; (2) in general, profit-sharing plans can have an effect, but this particular plan was poorly designed, poorly implemented, or is being poorly managed; or (3) the profit-sharing plan has increased the employee's desire to increase owner wealth but for some reason has not translated into improved performance.

The organization's performance measurement system should help identify the cause of the failure of profit-sharing. In turn, this should improve performance because it also highlights the elements of management's beliefs about the causal chain between profit-sharing and improved performance on the organization's secondary objectives that are incorrect.

Linking Primary and Secondary Objectives

While all organization learning is important, perhaps the most important knowledge concerns the links in the causal chain between the organization's secondary objectives and its primary objectives. Organization members must continuously monitor and use performance information to understand the drivers of performance on the primary objectives.[22] The links between secondary and primary objectives are important because decision-makers focus on, or manage, the secondary performance measures. For example, managers spend time and money to improve product quality with the expectation that improved product quality will result in increased customer satisfaction. This in turn should eventually lead to

---

[22] You may wonder whether periodically revisiting and testing this understanding would be good enough. The answer is probably no for two reasons. First, organizations can never be sure that they understand an existing relationship fully enough to exploit it to its greatest potential. Second, in a global economy existing relationships change frequently thereby dating existing knowledge.

increased owner wealth. Decision-makers must be given feedback about whether improvements in secondary performance measures, such as quality, customer service, employee training, employee motivation, supplier confidence, supplier turnover, or the community's image of the organization, are leading to improved performance on the organization's primary objectives.

The Tension Between Learning and Accountability

Many organizations are able to motivate desired performance by monitoring and rewarding, or controlling, the results that decision-makers create—what we call results control.

Organizations must confront three major questions when they use results control:

1. *Are they sure about the causal link between secondary results and primary results?* Rewarding behavior for attaining secondary results should create the primary results the organization values.

2. *Can they measure the right thing?* Suppose that there is a reasonable certainty that increased employee motivation will lead to improved performance on primary results. The question then becomes how the organization measures employee motivation. Perhaps there is a psychological test that can measure employee motivation, although such tests may either be inconclusive or barred by the explicit or implicit contract between the organization and its employees.

3. *Is it possible to associate a given result with a given person or decision?* For example, how can organizations attribute improved performance of a manufacturing team to individual members of that team? If it rewards individual performance, there may be an environment of hostility and a preoccupation on individual performance that may adversely affect group performance. If the organization rewards group performance, it may create an environment where some individuals shirk their responsibilities and let others do the work that creates the performance rewards.

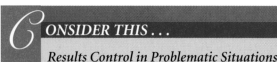

CONSIDER THIS . . .

Results Control in Problematic Situations

The owner of a landscaping services company decided to reward employees based on customer satisfaction, which was assessed by polling customers. Employees complained about the proposed system, pointing out that the appearance of the customer's lawns, trees, and bushes reflected the joint effect of employee care, weather, pollution, and pests. Therefore, a poor appearance may not be caused by poor employee attention to the customer's property. Some employees argued that if their performance was to be based on group performance (the employees worked in teams of three), they wanted the right to pick their team members. No one wanted lazy or inexperienced employees on their team. Some employees pointed out that the pesticide unit (two employees with a truck who did the lawn spraying work and were not part of the landscaping unit) was often careless and the pesticide drifted from the lawn onto bushes, killing some of the more sensitive plants and ruining the landscaping team's work.

It is fair to say that organizations wrestle continuously with these problems and that they have no obvious answers to them. The best course for any organization is to recognize that these problems exist, to identify situations where a problem is creating difficulties for the organization, and to work to mitigate the effect of that problem.

*T*YING PLANNING AND CONTROL TOGETHER

Performance measurement provides the critical link between planning, which identifies the organization's objectives and develops the strategies and processes to achieve those objectives, and control, which makes the organization members keep the organization on track toward achieving its objectives.

> **OBJECTIVE 11.6**
>
> Explain the important role that performance measurement plays in an organization's control function.

Picture this link between planning and control by thinking about the task of riding a bicycle—a task so complex that it would stymie any modern computer, yet a task that most humans find relatively easy. In riding a bicycle, control relies on visual and muscle systems to keep the bicycle on its path and keep the rider from falling over, while also dealing with wind and road hazards, such as cars and potholes. While this may seem both natural and simple to you, it illustrates a very high order of planning and control elements: (1) developing an objective, (2) monitoring and evaluating information to achieve the objective, and (3) comparing actual and planned performance to make adjustments to achieve the objective.

We have argued that a performance measurement system has three primary roles:

1. Focusing organization members on objectives by choosing the primary and secondary objectives in the planning process and then choosing the performance measures for those objectives.

2. Coordinating individual decision-making by ensuring that all organization members understand the primary and secondary organization objectives and how each member contributes to those objectives. To accomplish this role it is necessary to specify the secondary performance measures that each organization member is responsible for managing.

3. Providing a basis for organization learning by providing contemporaneous measures of performance on primary and secondary measures of performance so that organization members can test alternative explanations of the cause-and-effect relationship.

Until very recently, most management accounting systems made little attempt to deal with these three primary performance measurement roles comprehensively or realistically. Common problems included:

1. A preoccupation with primary results, particularly profits, with little interest in or consideration of the causes of primary results. This leads to an inability to assess the effects of various operating objectives, such as improved product quality or increased cycle times on primary results. The effect is to create fads or excesses where people blindly follow advice of so-called management gurus. For example, during the 1980s many organizations pursued quality objectives with either a vague or no understanding of how quality translated into improving performance on primary objectives.

2. A lack of coordination by focusing on individual results that reflect the doctrine of controllability. This doctrine argues that people should be held accountable only for the results that they individually create. This creates the notion that the organization can be viewed as functional silos to be evaluated independently, both in terms of their process contributions and in terms of their contributions to profits rather than viewing the organization as a set of processes integrated in an overall value chain with common objectives. For example, evaluation of a manufacturing unit may be done in terms of the number of units made and its ability to control costs rather than in terms of quality or in terms of its ability to meet production schedules.

3. No basis for learning by failing to link performance on primary and secondary objectives. This limitation reflects the attitude that the management accounting system does not need to measure process results. This attitude reflects the belief that since some objectives are not financial, an employee-motivation system or a customer-satisfaction system are beyond the scope and interest of management accounting.

Today people are beginning to realize that these outdated views of management accounting are both myopic and dysfunctional; organizations are beginning to develop performance measurement systems that reflect the scope and perspectives developed in this chapter. These new performance measurement systems have been given various names, including the balanced scorecard, strategic performance measurement, and comprehensive performance measurement.

THE BALANCED SCORECARD

OBJECTIVE 11.7

Understand the role of the balanced scorecard in organizational control.

The balanced scorecard reflects the first systematic attempt to develop a design for a performance measurement system that focuses on organization objectives, coordination of individual decision-making, and provision of a basis for organization learning.[23] These are the three primary objectives of performance measurement systems previously mentioned. Think of a balanced scorecard as a philosophy rather than a blueprint for a performance measurement system that can be implemented in any organization. The scorecard balances performance measurement by considering both the results and the causes of performance on the organization's primary objectives.

The Bank of Montreal, one of Canada's largest chartered banks, has implemented a full-fledged performance measurement system along the lines of what we have described in this chapter.[24]

---

[23] Robert S. Kaplan and David P. Norton provided the first systematic outline of the balanced scorecard idea in a series of articles. *See* "The Balanced Scorecard—Measures that Drive Performance," *Harvard Business Review*, January-February 1992; "Putting the Balanced Scorecard to Work," *Harvard Business Review*, September-October 1993; and "Using the Balanced Scorecard as a Strategic Management System," *Harvard Business Review*, January-February 1996.

[24] For a brief discussion of several organizations that have implemented performance measurement systems, see Bill Birchard, "Making it Count", *CFO*, October 1995, Vol. 11, No. 10, pp. 43–51.

The Bank of Montreal has developed and implemented a coordinated approach to control which it calls its balanced scorecard. *Courtesy* **Mark Antman/The Image Works**

Objectives and Performance Drivers

The Bank of Montreal identified increasing shareholder wealth as its primary objective and identified shareholders, customers, employees, and communities as its remaining stakeholders.

The Role of Performance Measures

Bank management identified three primary roles of performance measures:

1. Focus decision-makers' attention on what causes/drives performance on the bank's primary objectives.
2. Ensure that both insiders and outsiders understand the bank's strategies to achieve its primary objectives
3. Provide signals and diagnostic measures to the bank's decision-makers to allow them to understand how underlying processes drive performance on the bank's primary objective and to provide a basis for organization learning.

The Nature of Performance Measures

Planners at the Bank of Montreal established measures of how each stakeholder group contributed to owner wealth—secondary performance measures. For each stakeholder group, the bank also identified a second-level set of performance measures that reflected what planners felt were the measurable drivers of the secondary performance measures for that stakeholder group.[25]

---

[25] One may argue that there should be a secondary performance measure relating to satisfaction for each stakeholder group, for example, customer satisfaction, supplier satisfaction, employee satisfaction, community satisfaction, and owner satisfaction. However, a stakeholder group's satisfaction is often either impossible or prohibitively expensive to measure. Therefore, organizations often substitute other secondary performance measures, or auxiliary performance measures, for those they cannot measure directly. For example, an organization may use turnover as a proxy for customer, employee, supplier, or owner satisfaction.

EXHIBIT 11-5
Secondary Performance Measures at the Bank of Montreal

Stakeholder Group	First-Level Secondary Measures	Second-Level Secondary Measures
Owners (shareholders)	Return on common shareholders' investment	Revenue growth Expense growth Equity dilution Capital ratios Liquidity ratios Quality of loans ratios
Customers	Customer satisfaction and quality of service	Customer surveys for different market/product services
Employees	Employee commitment, customer service index, and employee productivity ratio	Employee opinion survey Customer service index Financial ratios of employee costs to total revenues
Community	Public image	External surveys

For example, planners may decide that customer satisfaction is a secondary measure for the customer stakeholder group because it has a direct effect on corporate profitability. Second-level secondary performance measures for customer satisfaction may include service times, error rates, and banking hours.

Exhibit 11-5 summarizes the bank's measures.

Using the Performance Measurement System

Beyond serving as an attention-directing and learning-support device, the performance measurement system at the Bank of Montreal is tied to its reward system. The bank does this by assigning performance standards or targets for each responsibility unit for each primary, secondary, and second-level secondary performance measure. Then decision-makers compare the actual performance level to the target performance level to determine a score. The higher the performance relative to the plan, the higher the score. Then they weight the scores for each performance measure to determine an overall score, which serves as the basis for incentive compensation.

THE MEANING OF BALANCE IN BALANCED SCORECARD

To be balanced, performance measurement systems must meet two requirements:

1. They should reflect the organization's understanding of causes of successful performance on the organization's primary objectives—that is, the perfor-

mance measurement system should monitor both the organization's performance and what management believes are the drivers of performance on the organization's primary objectives. This is the depth requirement of being balanced.

2. The performance measurement system should measure the most critical aspects or differentiators of organization performance. These aspects give the organization its unique abilities to achieve its primary objective. This is the breadth requirement of being balanced.

The focus of the balanced scorecard is a system of performance measurements that the organization uses to track performance on its primary and secondary objectives. In this sense, the organization's planning and strategy, which defines what relationships the organization must develop with its employees, its suppliers, and the community to be successful with its targeted customers, defines the focus and scope of the balanced scorecard. Therefore, the balanced scorecard requires and reflects a comprehensive planning system and an understanding of how organization processes contribute to the organization's primary objectives.

Many organizations find developing a balanced scorecard of performance measures a daunting task. Implementing a balanced scorecard requires many things:

1. *Management must define the organization's primary objectives.* This is usually well done because most profit-seeking organizations have a narrow primary objective, namely, to increase shareholder wealth. In profit-seeking organizations that have primary objectives that include both social and owner wealth objectives, management must stipulate how decision-makers should weight each of these objectives. In not-for-profit organizations like governments, management must state its objectives precisely. Since these objectives are invariably multidimensional—for example, to reduce taxes or operate a balanced budget while maintaining social services—senior management must specify the desired weighting of primary objectives.

2. *The organization must understand how stakeholders and processes contribute to its primary objectives.* Many managers and consultants admit that this is problematic. For example, the organization behavior literature is unclear about whether increased employee motivation necessarily translates into improved employee and profit performance. Many organizations, despite implementing massive quality programs, really do not understand the effect of quality on performance and prefer to speak in platitudes when they say, for example, "quality is not an issue, you have to have quality just to be in the game."

3. *The organization must develop a set of secondary objectives that are the drivers of performance on primary objectives.* This step is perhaps the most challenging and important in implementing the balanced scorecard. Accomplishing this task requires that processes and results come together. The organization must invest resources to back the strategies that it feels will produce results. This task seeks answers to questions like how much should be invested in employee training, a customer satisfaction system, a quality improvement system, or an improved logistical system? Such decisions should be based on an understanding of how increased spending improves process results, such as improved customer satisfaction, which in turn results in improved performance on the organization's primary objectives.

4. *The organization must develop a set of measures to monitor performance on both primary and secondary objectives.* This is the conventional role for management accounting. This step raises issues about how to measure the variable of interest. For example, how does the organization measure employee motivation or commitment to the organization? These performance measures are important because they translate strategy into focus, since the measures that people are told to manage will drive their performance. If the organization chooses the wrong set of measures, it will motivate inappropriate performance. Suppose, for example, that the organization, lacking an ability to measure motivation, equates motivation with lavish incentive compensation and measures motivation by the amount of incentive compensation that it distributes to employees. However, incentive compensation actually may have little incremental effect on motivation.

5. *The organization must develop a set of processes with their attendant implicit and explicit contracts with stakeholders to achieve those primary objectives.* Although this management requirement is well understood, the implied level of complexity required by the balanced scorecard is much deeper than what is done in normal practice. For example, based on 1980s experience, many managers developed the motto of "quality at any cost." Under the balanced scorecard, managers would assess the costs and benefits of schemes to improve quality.

6. *The organization must make specific and therefore public statements about its beliefs concerning how processes create results.* Public statements and specific commitments to courses of action and expected results provide a basis for accountability. Therefore, they represent an element of management risk since management can be questioned more accurately about its failures. Many senior managers may find this level of risk distasteful. However, owners may find such public statements illuminating.

Despite any related problems that a balanced scorecard presents, its development in organizations is critical for two reasons:

1. It provides a method for the organization to systematically consider what it should do to develop an internally consistent and comprehensive system of planning and control.

2. It provides a basis for understanding the difference between successful and unsuccessful organizations.

GOVERNMENT CONTROL REVISITED

One of the primary causes of government ineffectiveness and inefficiency is the inability or unwillingness to develop and monitor specific performance measures for government agencies and projects. To address this problem, the government of New Zealand only approves program-spending proposals if they are accompanied by specific and measurable performance results.

Performance measures for government agencies and programs provide a basis for allocating limited tax revenues among competing spending proposals since they systematically lay out the costs and benefits of different programs. They also provide a basis for accountability and focus in government operations.

Setting performance measures for a program ensures that all the people involved with a particular government program understand both its scope and objectives and how their work contributes to organizational objectives.

Absent performance measurement, there is no basis for organization learning or accountability—two of the critical elements of control. *The United States Senate's Government Performance and Results Act of 1993* shows how planning and performance measurement complement each other and ties together the material discussed in this chapter.

The act specifies the following:

No later than September 30, 1997, the head of each agency shall submit to the Director of the Office of Management and Budget and the Congress a strategic plan for program activities. Such a plan shall contain (1) a comprehensive mission statement covering the major functions and operations of the agency; (2) general goals and objectives, including outcome-related goals and objectives, for the major functions and operations of the agency; (3) a description of how the general goals and objectives in the strategic plan are to be achieved, including a description of internal processes, skills and technology, and the human, capital, information, and other resources required to meet those goals and objectives; a description of how the performance goals included in the plan for the agency . . . shall be related to the general goals and objectives contained in the strategic plan.

Note some of the key attributes of this act:

1. Each agency department identifies its primary stakeholders and both its primary and secondary objectives in a mission statement. This information supports the process of funding programs and also the process of reviewing ongoing programs and provides coordination of and focus for agency employees.
2. By defining outcome-related goals and objectives, agencies identify performance outcomes—the primary and secondary objectives they are seeking. This requires a level of specificity that is absent in most government spending proposals.
3. By requiring a general statement of strategy, a description of the primary processes that the agency will use to achieve its objectives, and the nature of the resources required, the act forces agencies to specifically develop and document their strategic and operating plans and to provide some assurance that the general strategies and detailed operating plans are feasible.
4. By requiring a set of performance goals, the act forces the agencies to indicate how they plan to monitor and assess performance on their primary and secondary objectives; that is, the agencies must specify what measures they will use for their objectives.

The act goes on to provide details about the nature and scope of the performance measures that it expects:

The Director of the Office of Management and Budget shall require each agency to prepare and submit to the Director an annual performance plan covering each program activity set forth in the budget of each agency. Such plan shall (1) establish performance goals to define the level of performance to be achieved by a program activity; (2) express such goals in an objective, quantifiable, and measurable form unless authorized to be in an alternative form . . . ; (3) briefly describe the operational processes, skills, and technology and the human, capital, information, or other resources required to meet the performance goals; (4) establish performance indicators to be used in measuring or assessing the relevant outputs, service levels, and outcomes of each program activity; (5) provide a basis for comparing actual program results with the established performance goals; and (6) describe the means to be used to verify and validate measured values.

By requiring the monitoring and annual reporting of performance results, the act is effectively defining the parameters of a control system. The important elements of this performance measurement system are these:

1. Specific performance targets that provide a basis for setting funding levels for programs and a basis for accountability. In other words, the act implies that funding will be based on what people claim they can accomplish and that they are expected to live up to their claims.

2. By insisting on measurable performance, the act prevents people from specifying performance measures that are either infeasible or impractical that in turn would render the performance measurement system useless.

3. The act requires performance measures for primary goals and for program outputs, which we called secondary goals. Such measures enable the organization to evaluate the relationship between measures of program outputs—for example, in a retraining agency, the number of classes conducted—and measures of overall performance—for example, in a retraining agency, the number of people placed in jobs.

4. By requiring that agencies compare actual results with targets, the act is effectively closing the control loop. Comparing actual results to planned results begins the process of organization learning. This helps to keep the system on track toward achieving its objectives.

The act even included a section designed to establish the basis for organization learning:

Each report on program performance shall (1) review the success of achieving the performance goals of the fiscal year covered by the report; (2) evaluate the performance plan for the current fiscal year relative to the performance achieved toward the performance goals in each fiscal year covered by the report; (3) explain and describe, where a performance goal has not been met (a) why the goal was not met; (b) those plans and schedules for achieving the established performance goal; and (c) if the performance goal is impractical or infeasible, why that is the case and what action is recommended.

These requirements define the basic control steps that include these factors:

1. Measure actual results
2. Compare the results to the plan

3. Identify the variance
4. Study and explain the variance
5. Take corrective action

These steps are necessary because they close the control loop and provide the basis for both accountability and organization learning.

Summary

Today organizations face complex and changing environments that are defined by their customers, owners, and the communities in which they operate. Customers define what the organization must do for them to continue to buy the organization's products. Owners define the organization's primary objectives, which most often reflect wealth considerations but can reflect socially related goals. The community defines the laws and social conventions that the organization must recognize as it interacts with its stakeholders, which includes customers, employees, suppliers, owners, and the community itself.

One of the major roles of management is to define how it will manage the relationships among its stakeholders. The primary focus of planning is to identify a coherent and feasible way for the organization to interact with its customers. For example, what products will the organization make and sell to its customers and, for each product, will the organization compete by offering the lowest prices, by continuously designing new products, or by meeting the specialized requirements of a target group of customers?

The customer-related strategies that the organization chooses must be feasible in the sense that they meet the requirements of all the stakeholders that the organization relies on to help it pursue those strategies. Owners require assurance that the chosen customer strategy will meet the primary objectives set for the organization. Employees require assurance that they will be paid competitive wages and will be provided with the types of jobs and working environments that they feel are consistent with what the organization expects from them. Suppliers, who provide the organization with the goods and services that it uses to create its own products and deliver them to its customers, require assurance that they can meet their own objectives within the relationships that they enter into with the organization. The community requires assurance that the organization will obey its laws and has some expectations that the organization will provide some type of community leadership.

The expectations that the organization and each stakeholder group develop in terms of what they will contribute to the organization and what they will receive in return may be specified in explicit contracts or implied by the implicit contracts that reflect the working relationship between the organization and that stakeholder group. Whatever the form, these expectations are important because they reflect what is required for the relationship to continue to exist between the stakeholder group and the organization. Therefore, these expectations, which we have called the organization's secondary objectives, become important to the organization because they reflect what the organization must deliver to each stakeholder group in order to secure that group's participation in helping the organization achieve its primary objectives.

The planning process identifies the organization's primary objectives and, by choosing the nature and form of the processes that it will use to pursue its primary objectives, also identifies the organization's secondary objectives.

Control is the process that organizations use to keep them on track toward achieving their primary objectives. Control involves the steps of monitoring performance and comparing actual performance to a plan in order to identify situations where the plan is either not being achieved or is unlikely to be achieved. We call this type of situation out of control and it should trigger a learning process that identifies why the process has gone out of control and what steps are required to return the process to being in control.

The central nervous system of control and therefore what ties planning and control together is the organization's performance measurement system. The performance measurement system identifies how the organization will measure performance on both its primary and secondary objectives and provides a means of focusing and coordinating decision-making in the organization. By supporting the process of organization learning, the performance measurement system serves as the primary means of moving the organization toward higher levels of performance on its primary objectives.

Key terms

audit control, p. 523

concurrent control, p. 521

continuous improvement, p. 526

decentralization, p. 524

environment-defining stakeholders, p. 504

feedback, or reactive, control, p. 521

feedforward control, p. 521

in control, p. 520

organization control, p. 519

out of control, p. 520

preventive control, p. 522

primary objectives, p. 502

process stakeholders, p. 507

re-engineering, p. 526

results control, p. 523

secondary objectives, p. 503

task control, p. 522

timing of control, p. 521

■ QUESTIONS

11-1 What is the primary role of organization planning?

11-2 Why do stakeholder requirements matter to the organization?

11-3 What is an organization process?

11-4 Name two things that a customer might give to the organization and two things that a customer might expect from the organization.

11-5 What is organization learning?

11-6 Name two things that an owner might give to the organization and two things that an owner might expect from the organization.

11-7 What are the five steps involved in keeping an organization in control?

11-8 What are stakeholders?

11-9 What is a balanced scorecard?

11-10 What is task control?

11-11 Name two things that an employee might give to the organization and two things that an employee might expect from the organization.

11-12 What is organization control?

11-13 What is concurrent control?

11-14 What does decentralization mean? Does decentralization mean the same thing as employee empowerment?

11-15 What does a nexus of contracts mean?

11-16 How are the organization's primary and secondary objectives related?

11-17 What are secondary objectives?

11-18 Why should organizations manage causes and not results?

11-19 Name two things that a supplier might give to the organization and two things that a supplier might expect from the organization.

11-20 What are primary objectives?

11-21 What is feedback control?

11-22 Give an example of audit control not found in the text.

11-23 What is results control?

11-24 Name two things that the community might give to the organization and two things that a community might expect from the organization.

11-25 Give an example of preventive control not found in the text.

11-26 What is feedforward control?

■ EXERCISES

11-27 *Coordinating the elements of a system* Identify a system that consists of a group of interrelated parts or components. How are the parts in this system coordinated? What is the consequence of not coordinating the parts?

11-28 *Relating primary and secondary objectives* Explain the relationship between secondary and primary objectives by discussing employee motivation.

11-29 *Nonfinancial primary objectives* Can you think of an organization that has a primary objective not related to increasing the owners' wealth? Name the organization and the primary objective and why you think it is a primary objective.

11-30 *Importance of planning* The text indicates that planning is the process where the organization chooses the relationships that it defines with each of its stakeholder groups. Why is planning important?

11-31 *Managing causes* You are trying to explain to a friend why it is important to manage causes and not results. Construct an example that is not in the text that you might use to explain this idea to your friend.

11-32 *Choosing an approach to control* Think of any setting in need of control. Explain why you think that task control or results control would be more appropriate in the setting that you have chosen. Do not use an example from the text.

11-33 *Defining the organization's environment* Identify two ways that each of the owner, customer, and community stakeholder groups define the organization's external environment. Why is each group's requirements important to the organization?

11-34 *The nature of moving inventory* Consider the process of moving work in process around a manufacturing facility. Explain how the organization might evaluate this process.

11-35 *Performance measurement and organization learning* Construct an example to show how a performance measurement system might support a process of organization learning.

11-36 *The timing of control* Construct an example to show why you think preventive control is either more or less effective than either feedback or concurrent control.

11-37 *Designing a balanced scorecard* Consider the manager of store in a fast-food restaurant chain. Construct a balanced scorecard to evaluate that manager's performance.

11-38 *Using results control* A company that sells life insurance to customers has decided to use results control to control the behavior of its sales staff. What form of results control do you think the company should use in this situation? Why?

11-39 *Importance of stakeholder requirement* Using the supplier stakeholder group, explain why stakeholder requirements matter to the organization.

11-40 *Community satisfaction and owner wealth* Identify how an organization might learn about how community satisfaction with the organization might translate into increased owner wealth.

11-41 *Choosing between task and results control* Do you think that results control or task control is better suited for controlling the performance of a professional athlete? Why?

11-42 *Choosing organization objectives* Consider a government agency responsible for finding jobs for its clients. Identify a set of primary objectives and a set of secondary objectives for this agency.

11-43 ***Choosing stakeholder objectives*** Consider the employee stakeholder group. Identify four secondary objectives for that group and state why you think that each is a secondary objective.

■ PROBLEMS

Fundamental Problems

11-44 GenCorp's mission statement includes the following: "Our mission is to continuously improve the company's value to shareholders, customers, employees, and society."

REQUIRED

    (a) Why do organizations need a mission statement?

    (b) Interpret how each of GenCorp's stakeholder groups may interpret the company's value in GenCorp's mission statement and, given each group's interpretation, how it may be measured for each group?

    (c) GenCorp has identified shareholders, customers, employees, and society as its stakeholders. Is any group missing? Why? Should any of these groups be dropped as part of GenCorp's stakeholder group? Why?

11-45 ***Stakeholders and strategy*** Suppose that you are the owner/manager of a business that provides food catering services.

REQUIRED

    (a) Identify your stakeholder groups.

    (b) Identify three different approaches that you may use to compete in the food-catering market.

    (c) Identify how you would choose which one of the three competitive approaches identified in (b) you would actually use.

    (d) Specify what your plan expects to receive from and expects to give to each stakeholder group; from this information, specify your organization's primary and secondary objectives.

    (e) Construct a balanced scorecard to assess the performance of your cooking staff.

11-46 ***Community expectations*** Use business periodicals and general news sources, such as newspapers and magazines, to identify five examples of community expectations concerning organizations. Each example should clearly identify the community's expectation and should indicate your assessment of the consequences to the organization of not meeting that expectation. *Hint:* Editorial pages often contain commentaries on the social responsibility of business.

11-47 ***Approaches to control*** Cite two settings or jobs where each of the following approaches to control would be appropriately applied. Identify what you feel is the definitive characteristic of the setting that indicates the appropriateness of the approach to control that you have identified.

    (a) preventive control

    (b) results control

    (c) audit control

11-48 ***Efficiency considerations in control*** Many people believe that preventive control is more effective (achieves objectives better) and more efficient (costs less) than concurrent control, which in turn is more effective and efficient than feedback control.

Consider the operations of any organization making any product or service. Identify three alternative systems to control the quality of some facet of that product or service: one involving feedforward control; one involving concurrent control; and one involving feedback control.

11-49 *Choosing information for control* Suppose that you are the general manager of a large hotel. Identify the daily, weekly, monthly, quarterly, and annual information that you would want to receive to help you manage the hotel. Assume for the sake of discussion that the hotel is divided into five major areas: customer service, housekeeping, restaurant, maintenance, and administration.

11-50 *Evaluating system performance* Suppose that you are the manager of a production facility in a business that makes plastic items that organizations use for advertising. The customer chooses the color and quantity of the item and specifies what is to be imprinted on the item. Your job is to ensure that the job is completed according to the customer's specifications. This is a cut-throat business that competes based on low price, high quality, and good service to the customer.

Recently you installed a just-in-time manufacturing system. How may you evaluate the performance of this system given the characteristics of your organization?

11-51 *Information to evaluate performance* You have just been made the manager of a group of 45 dry cleaning outlets that are located in a large metropolitan area. Your company has positioned itself as a niche competitor. You offer personalized customer service and prompt cleaning. Because of this your prices are slightly higher than those of most of your competitors. You have just designed and installed a new system that picks up clothing from each of the outlets, delivers the clothing to the dry cleaning plant, and returns cleaned clothing to the outlets. How would you evaluate the performance of this process, given the characteristics of your organization?

11-52 *Information and control* You are the quality manager in the factory of a large consumer products company that has staked its competitive position and its reputation on the quality of its products. For this reason, doing your job well is very important to the company's success.

You are interested in applying some of the principles of control in your job.

REQUIRED

(a) What measures would you use in your job to monitor the quality produced by the manufacturing system?
(b) How would you decide when the manufacturing system is in or out of control with respect to quality?
(c) When you are designing quality-control systems, how would you evaluate the relative merits of preventive, concurrent, or feedback control?
(d) What employee and equipment factors would you consider when deciding on the approach that you will use to quality control?

Challenging Problems

11-53 *Monitoring stakeholder commitments* Harris Company, a manufacturer of electronic systems and equipment, has identified the following stakeholder goals in its annual report:

Customers — For customers, our goal is to achieve ever-increasing levels of satisfaction by providing quality products and services with distinctive benefits on a timely and continuing world-wide basis. Our relationships with customers will be forthright and ethical and will be conducted in a manner to build trust and confidence.

Shareholders	For shareholders, the owners of our company, our goal is to achieve sustained growth in earnings per share. The resulting stock-price appreciation combined with dividends should provide our shareholders with a total return on investment that is competitive with similar investment opportunities.
Employees	The people of Harris are our company's most valuable asset, and our goal is for every employee to be personally involved in and share the success of the business. The company is committed to providing an environment that encourages all employees to make full use of their creativity and unique talents and to equitable compensation, good working conditions, and the opportunity for personal development and growth limited only by individual ability and desire.
Suppliers	Suppliers are a vital part of our resources. Our goal is to develop and maintain mutually beneficial partnerships with suppliers who share our commitment to achieving increasing levels of customer satisfaction through continuing improvements in quality, service, timeliness, and cost. Our relationships with suppliers will be sincere, ethical, and will embrace the highest principles of purchasing practice.
Communities	Our goal is to be a responsible corporate citizen. This includes support of appropriate civic, educational, and business activities, respect for the environment, and the encouragement of Harris employees to practice good citizenship and support community programs. Our greatest contribution to our communities is to be successful so that we can maintain stable employment and create new jobs.

REQUIRED

The role of the management accountant is to help management develop the control and measurement systems it needs to achieve the organization's goals. Identify a set of measures that will help Harris Corporation management identify and track performance that it has specified as relevant for each stakeholder group.

11-54 *University mission statement*   Does your university have a mission statement? If so, find and study it. If not, try to compose one so that it addresses the following questions.

REQUIRED

(a) What stakeholder groups does your university's mission statement specifically identify? Who do you think are the university's stakeholders?

(b) Who is the university's customer? (Be careful, this is a tricky question. Legitimate arguments can be made for each of the following: students, students' parents or sponsors, high-school guidance counselors, and prospective employers.)

(c) Some universities identify either alumni or faculty as the university's customer. Explain why you agree or disagree with specifying alumni or faculty as the university's customer.

(d) Has your university developed specific and measurable performance goals relating to each stakeholder group? If so, what do you think of them? If not, what should they be?

11-55 *Tying stakeholder relationships to competitive strategy*   Pick any organization that you know or for which you can develop the data that you need to complete this question. Identify precisely the strategy that the organization uses to compete for customers. Relate the organization's personnel-related, supplier-related, and community-related practices to the organization's customer-related strategy indicating why you think that each one is either appropriate or inappropriate. What secondary performance measures may this organization effectively use?

11-56 *Designing a balanced scorecard*   The following exhibit appeared in Weirton Steel Corporation's 1990 annual report.

We are bound together in these common beliefs and values. We must . . .

For the Customer

1. Have a total quality commitment to consistently meet the product, delivery and service expectations of all customers.
2. Give customers increased value through processes that eliminate waste, minimize costs, and enhance production efficiency.

For the Employee

1. Reward teamwork, trust, honesty, openness, and candor.
2. Ensure a safe workplace.
3. Recognize that people are the corporation and provide them with training and information that allows for continuous improvement.
4. As employee-owners, obligate ourselves to provide a high level of performance and be accountable for our own actions.
5. Respect the dignity, rights, and contributions of others.

For the Company

1. Continuously invest in new technology and equipment to ensure competitiveness and enhance stockholder value.
2. Manage our financial and human resources for long-term profitability.

For the Community

1. Commit to environmental responsibility.
2. Fulfill our responsibility to enhance the quality of community life.

REQUIRED

Develop a balanced scorecard that Weirton Steel Corporation may use to measure performance on each of these imperatives.

11-57 *The relationship between secondary and primary objectives*   Consider the following causal links. Better working conditions increase employee satisfaction, which in turn increases employee motivation, which in turn causes the employee to work harder, which in turn causes the employee to develop and implement better processes, which in turn cause the organization to be more profitable. The organization is wondering how to evaluate the potential payoff in terms of increased profitability of better working conditions. How would you evaluate this causal chain? Do you think it provides a useful basis to decide whether or not to improve employee working conditions?

11-58 *Mission statements, stakeholders, critical success factors, and key performance measures*   The Liquor Control Board of Ontario is a government agency charged with the acquisition, transportation, storage, and retailing of beverage alcohol in Ontario, Canada's largest province. The following was taken from the LCBO's strategic plan:

Our Commitment

To succeed as a dynamic retailer and progressive organization, the LCBO must continue to foster a climate of trust and co-operation, where corporate values are clearly communicated and responsibilities readily accepted. To our employees, customers, suppliers, government, and communities, we commit the following:

Customers

To exceed our customers' expectations by providing them with service excellence. This will be demonstrated in the selection and quality of our products, the ambiance and convenience of our stores, the professionalism of our employees, and our ongoing commitment to introduce new products and services.

To rigorously test all products sold to our customers to ensure that they exceed established health and quality standards.

To deliver quality customer services throughout our organization by ensuring that every employee's first priority is to serve the customer or to support someone who does.

Employees

To recognize employees' capabilities, empower them to made decisions, impart responsibility for results, and reward their achievements.

To challenge and encourage employees to reach their potential, and coach and support them in their professional development.

To treat employees as individuals, and to value and respect their diversity in experience and perspective.

To create and maintain a workplace environment free from harassment and discrimination.

To respect our employees' right to a healthy and safe working environment, where safe working conditions are promoted and achieved.

To establish a proactive dialogue and positive working relationship with our Union, and to work together with all employees to address the challenges which face the LCBO.

Suppliers

To ensure fairness in our relations with suppliers and trade associations, and to support an equitable system where suppliers can market and sell their products according to customer demand.

Government

To operate our business in a profitable manner on behalf of the people of Ontario, and to support government policies and programs.

Communities

To respond with sensitivity in all our business decisions to the concerns and changing societal values regarding the marketing, distribution, and consumption of beverage alcohol.

To continually consider and address the environmental implications of our business decisions.

To encourage employees to become involved in their communities by supporting charities and cultural programs, and voluntarily contributing their time and talent to community activities.

Recall that, as a government agency, the LCBO's sole shareholder is the government. The LCBO is organized into five operating groups called divisions. These divisions and their charges are the retail division, operating the LCBO's 815 liquor outlets; merchandising division, acquiring the products that will be stocked in the retail outlets; distribution division, transporting products between suppliers and retail outlets; finance and administrative division, providing financial planning and organization control; human resources division, providing services to employees; information technology division, implementing leading-edge technology; and executive offices, reporting directly to the chief executive officer.

REQUIRED

(a) What do you think about the commitment statement?
(b) Name the LCBO's stakeholder groups.
(c) Based on the contents of the commitment statement, identify the LCBO's critical success factors.
(d) For each of the organization's operating divisions, except the executive offices division, identify three critical performance indicators that would reflect that division's contribution to the LCBO's critical success factors.

11-59 *Testing the causal link between secondary and primary performance measures*   The text described two broad areas of organization learning: (1) identifying the causal relationships between secondary and primary objectives and (2) identifying how to evaluate and improve existing processes.

Identify an organization with which you are familiar.

REQUIRED

(a) Specify the organization's primary objectives.
(b) Specify the organization's secondary objectives.
(c) Identify the causal links between its secondary objectives and its primary objectives.
(d) Describe how you would test the accuracy of your beliefs about the causal links between secondary and primary objectives.
(e) Describe what information you would use to identify opportunities for improving or replacing existing processes.

11-60 *Developing a balanced scorecard for a university*   Develop a balanced scorecard that the dean or director of your school may use to evaluate the school's operations. Be specific and indicate the purpose of each balanced scorecard measure.

11-61 *Pursuing noneconomic objectives*   Some people argue that the only relevant stakeholder to consider in a profit-seeking organization is the owner. These people argue that in competitive markets an organization that pursues social or other goals that increase costs is inappropriately diverting economic resources. They also say that firms pursuing social objectives will be disciplined by the market—that they will suffer losses because their prices can be no higher than the competition while their costs will be higher. Despite this we see many organizations that pursue both social and economic goals. How can such a course of action be rationalized with the economic view, or does this phenomenon call the economic view into question? Explain.

■ CASE

11-62 *Implementing the balanced scorecard*   Find either by visiting a site or from a description in a published article a description of the implementation of a balanced scorecard.

REQUIRED

    (a) Document in detail the elements of the balanced scorecard.

    (b) Identify the purpose of each balanced scorecard element.

    (c) Describe, if the facts are available, or infer, if the facts are not available, how the balanced scorecard elements relate to the organization's strategy.

    (d) Evaluate the balanced scorecard by indicating whether you agree that the choice of balanced scorecard measures is complete and consistent with the organization's plan and stakeholder set.

12

FINANCIAL CONTROL

UNITED STATES POSTAL SERVICE

Courtesy **Bob Daemmrich/ Stock, Boston**

In 1990 Marvin T. Runyon was hired as the Postmaster General of the United States Postal Service (USPS). Marvin's mandate was to improve performance in two areas where the USPS was chronically weak: cost control and service performance.

In 1995 these developments occurred:

1. For the first time since 1989, the USPS announced a budget surplus,

2. The independent audit firm Price Waterhouse reported that the USPS achieved an on-time delivery rate of 87%, up from its 83% performance level in 1994.

3. *USA Today* announced that the American Customer Satisfaction Index for the USPS jumped 13% between 1994 and 1995.[1]

Despite these developments, criticisms and complaints about the USPS continued in 1995, no doubt incited by three other factors:

1. A postal rate increase, in January, from 29 cents to 32 cents for a first class letter

2. The USPS debt of $7.3 billion, reflecting the effects of past deficits

3. A General Accounting Office (GAO) report that cited continuing poor labor-management relations in the USPS and an inadequate performance measurement system

In 1995, determined to continue to improve its cost and service performance and to deal with continuing problems, the USPS announced that it was embracing a financial management tool called economic value added. The USPS expected that using this tool would help it control and improve worker productivity leading to reduced costs and improved service.

---

[1] *USA Today* did note parenthetically that interpreting this gain had to be tempered by the realization that USPS was starting almost at the bottom in terms of customer satisfaction.

FINANCIAL CONTROL

Chapters 2 and 11 discussed the organization's goals and control systems and described how many organizations today provide employees with information to help them achieve both local and organizational goals. This chapter addresses the issue of financial control, which involves using financial information for organization control. Decentralization was the phenomenon that prompted the original use of financial control in organizations in the early 1900s.

During the 20th century, most organizations developed and used financial control methods to monitor, assess, and improve operations. Financial control uses financial numbers, such as costs or expenses, as overall indices or measures of the resources used by a process or operating unit. Financial control involves comparing actual financial numbers with targets from a standard or budget to derive variances. An unfavorable variance serves as a warning signal and should trigger a sequence of activities to identify, investigate, and correct the cause of the unfavorable performance.

DECENTRALIZATION

Centralized
Reserving decision-making power for senior management levels.

Decentralized
Delegating decision-making responsibility from senior management to employees at lower levels of the organization.

Chapter 1 indicated that **centralized** organizations reserve most of the decision-making power for senior executives. In contrast, **decentralized** organizations delegate a good deal of decision-making authority to lower-level managers.

Most highly centralized organizations are unable to respond effectively or quickly to their environments; therefore, centralization is best suited to organizations that are well adapted to stable environments. People used to cite utilities and companies such as couriers, fast-food operations, financial institutions, or natural resource industries as examples of organizations facing stable environments. This meant that there were no major information differences between the corporate headquarters and the employees who were responsible for dealing with customers or running the operations that make the organization's goods and services. Therefore, there was no need for a rapid response to a changing environment or for delegation of decision making to local managers.

In such organizations, technology and customer requirements were well understood and the product line consisted mostly of commodity products for which the most important attributes were price and quality. When price is critical, controlling cost and quality becomes critical. To accomplish this, organizations often develop standard operating procedures to ensure that they are using the most efficient technologies and practices to promote both low cost and consistent quality and that there are no deviations from the preferred way of doing things.

For example, McDonald's Corporation has developed the use of standard operating procedures almost to a science. Its restaurant layout, product design, form of raw materials, and prescribed operating procedures are all intended to keep costs low and quality high. McDonald's is not looking for a chef who wants to be creative in either the area of food preparation or the introduction of new items to the menu. Rather, it wants someone who can follow standardized procedures developed to promote consistent quality and low costs.

Today, in response to increasing competitive pressures, many organizations—even utilities, couriers, and financial institutions that were once thought to face stable environments—are changing the way they are organized and the way they do business. This is necessary because they must be able to change quickly in a world where technology, customer tastes, and competitors' strategies are constantly changing.

For example, in the past, financial institutions developed rigid and authoritarian management systems to protect assets and meet regulatory requirements. Although these systems have helped financial institutions protect their assets, in many cases they have not served financial institutions well in dealing with their customers. This requires accommodating customers by remaining open in the evenings, installing automated teller machines to provide 24-hour banking services, offering on-line banking that customers can access via a telephone or a personal computer, offering new products and services, and responding more quickly to customer requests, such as approving a car loan on the spot rather than asking the customer to wait several days for approval or processing a mortgage application in minutes rather than weeks.

Being adaptive generally requires that the organization's senior management delegate or decentralize decision-making responsibility to more people in the organization. Decentralization allows well motivated and well trained organization members to identify changing customer tastes quickly and gives front-line employees the authority and responsibility to develop plans to react to these changes.

There are many degrees of decentralization. Some organizations restrict most decisions to senior and middle management. Other organizations delegate important decisions about how to make products and serve customers to the employees who perform these activities. The amount of decentralization reflects the organization's trust in its employees, the employees' level of training, and the employees' ability to make the right choices. It also reflects the organization's need to have people on the front lines who can make good decisions quickly.

There are three conditions necessary for effective decentralization:

1. Employees must be given, and must accept, the authority and responsibility to make decisions.

In a high-volume business like a courier company, cost control is crucial for success. What is equally important, however, is to provide customers with the service they have been promised. *Courtesy* Federal Express

2. Employees must have the training and skills they need to accept the decision-making responsibility.

3. The organization must have a system in place that guides and coordinates the activities of decentralized decision makers.

OPERATIONS AND FINANCIAL CONTROL

Decentralization requires that someone who has the responsibility to make decisions should know what is important to the organization's success, have the information to help evaluate alternatives, and have the skill to evaluate alternatives and choose the appropriate course of action. Chapter 11 discussed the role of critical success factors used to summarize operating information so that employees can choose the appropriate actions to improve day-to-day and front-line operations.

Operations control The evaluation of control from the perspective of process improvement.

Operations control considers control from the perspective of process improvement, while financial control assesses an organization's financial success by measuring and evaluating its financial outcomes. Operations control focuses on finding the best operating decisions; financial control focuses on an overall assessment of how well operations control is working to improve financial performance. **Financial control** information signals when operations control is not working well and, hence, needs to be evaluated and improved.

Financial control The formal evaluation of some financial facet of an organization or a responsibility center.

The performance measures used for financial control vary. The most widely used measures include revenue, cost, profit, return on investment, and economic value added. Before discussing particular forms of financial control, we must first understand the role of responsibility centers, which are the different types of decentralized units in organizations to which financial controls are applied.

CONSIDER THIS...

Improving Performance at Liz Claiborne

After experiencing extraordinary growth in the 1980s, Liz Claiborne, Inc., a designer of womens' apparel, failed to recognize the change in what women want and are willing to pay for in clothing—a failure that resulted in lost sales and declining profits.

The company hired Paul Charron, an expert in designing and using financial controls, who promised to cut operating costs; eliminate unprofitable lines of clothing; reduce the time to design, make, and deliver clothes to retailers from 40 weeks to 30 weeks; and, in an unusual step in the fashion industry, speak to customers to find out what they want in clothes.

Critics remained skeptical, arguing that Mr. Charron's skills and efforts were misplaced because existing financial controls were already keeping costs reasonably competitive. These critics felt that Mr. Charron should have focused on developing a better system to identify and track changing customer tastes, that is, they felt that the organization should develop a sharper focus on operations control.

Source: James F. Peltz. "Fashioning a New Strategy at Claiborne," *Los Angeles Times*, May 21, 1995, Part D, p. 1.

RESPONSIBILITY CENTERS

A **responsibility center** is an organization unit for which a manager is made responsible. Examples of responsibility centers include a store in a chain of sporting goods stores, a workstation in a production line that makes automobile batteries, the data processing group in a government office that handles claims for payment from suppliers, a claims processing unit in an insurance company, or a shipping department in a mail-order business.

A responsibility center is like a small business and its manager is asked to run that small business to promote the interests of the larger organization. The responsibility center's manager and his supervisor establish goals for the responsibility. Goals provide employees with focus and, therefore, should be specific and measurable. These goals should promote both the long-term interests of the larger organization and the coordination of each responsibility center's activities.

COORDINATING RESPONSIBILITY CENTERS. For an organization to be successful, the activities of its responsibility units must be coordinated. Suppose that we divide the operations in a fast food restaurant into three groups: order taking, order preparation, and order delivery. Imagine the chaos and customer ill will that would be created if the communication links between any two of these organization groups were severed. Unfortunately, in large organizations sales, manufacturing, and customer service activities are often very disjointed, resulting in diminished performance.

Consider the operations of a nationwide courier such as Federal Express. Nationwide couriers establish local stations or collector points (called terminals) from which they dispatch trucks to pick up and deliver shipments. Shipments bound for other terminals are sent to the Federal Express hub in Memphis where they are sorted and redirected. The formula for success in the courier business is

Responsibility center
An organization unit for which a manager is accountable in the form of cost (a cost center), revenue (a revenue center), profits (a profit center), or return on investment (an investment center).

OBJECTIVE 12.1

Discuss the design and use of responsibility centers in an organization.

Kinko's Copy Centers have become successful by designing processes and systems that minimize costs. However, to ensure success, Kinko's Copy Centers have expanded their focus beyond cost control to incorporate quality and service considerations as well. *Courtesy Kinko's, Inc.*®

very simple and involves two key elements: (1) meeting the service commitment to the customer politely, on time, and without damage and (2) controlling costs. The only way to achieve success in the courier business is to ensure that all the pieces of the system work together effectively and efficiently to achieve these two critical elements of performance.

Suppose that management has determined that each terminal is to be treated as a responsibility center. How should the company measure the performance of each terminal, its managers, and its employees?

First, the company can measure the drivers (causes) of terminal efficiency (cost containment). To focus on efficiency, it may measure the number of parcels picked up, sorted, or delivered per route, per employee, per vehicle, per hour, or per shift. To focus on efficiency *and* customer satisfaction, it may count only those shipments that meet customer requirements—for example, on-time pick up and on-time delivery to the right address—in the number of parcels handled for the productivity calculations.

Second, the ability to meet the service commitment to customers in a highly integrated operation like a courier business reflects how well the pieces fit together. The company should measure how each group contributes to the organization's ability to meet its commitments to customers. A courier operation has two important facets of terminal-hub interaction:

1. The proportion of the time that the terminal meets its deadlines, that is, whether the trucks and containers are packed and ready to leave for the hub when they are required to leave[2] (often called a percent correct measure)

2. When terminals are required to sort shipments, how many shipments are sorted to the wrong destination or traveled by the wrong mode[3] (often called a percent defect measure)

Third, the company must also measure service to the customer at a more detailed level. For example, it can measure:

1. The number of complaints (or percent of shipments with complaints) the terminal operations group receive

2. The average time taken by the operations group to respond to complaints

Automobile dealerships provide a ready illustration of the complex of mix of interactions that can take place between departments even in simple organizations. Despite the need for the effective coordination of different activities to ensure overall organization success, to provide a better assessment of profitability and motivation, most organizations divide themselves into subcomponents, or responsibility centers, that are managed as if they were independent businesses. For example, the managers of new car sales, used car sales, leasing, service department, and body shop operations in this dealership may be told by the general manager of this business to manage their respective businesses as if they were independent businesses. *Courtesy* Kagan/Monkmeyer Press Photo

3. The number of complaints of poor, or impolite, service received by the company's customer service line

In general, controlling the activities of responsibility centers requires measuring the nonfinancial elements of performance, such as quality and service, that create financial results. The key message is that properly chosen nonfinancial measures anticipate and explain financial results. Therefore, we must always be careful to use financial results as aggregate measures of performance and rely on nonfinancial results to identify the causes or drivers of the financial results.

ACCOUNTING FOR RESPONSIBILITY CENTERS. Organizations use financial control to provide a summary measure of how well their systems of operations control are working. When organizations use a single index to provide a broad assessment of operations, they usually use a financial number such as revenue, cost, profit, or return on investment.

The accounting report prepared for a responsibility center reflects whether the responsibility center manager controls revenue, cost, profit, or return on investment. When preparing accounting summaries, accountants classify responsibility centers into four types:

1. Cost centers
2. Revenue centers
3. Profit centers
4. Investment centers

> ### CONSIDER THIS . . .
>
> *Choosing Between Operations and Financial Control*
>
> Some people believe that financial control is inappropriate under any conditions and refuse to use financial numbers for control. Instead, these people promote using performance measures like quality, cost, or service, which are defined by the organization's critical success factors, for control purposes. These people believe that, if the organization has chosen critical success factors appropriately, particularly those related to customer satisfaction, financial results will follow.
>
> People who promote the use of financial control believe that it is an overall, shareholder-relevant test of the efficacy of the strategic and operating decisions that the organization has made. Most organizations use a combination of both types of control.

> **OBJECTIVE 12.2**
>
> Understand the issues to consider and basic tools to use in assessing the performance of a responsibility center.

Cost Centers

Cost centers are responsibility centers where employees control costs but do not control revenues or investment level. Virtually every processing group in service operations (such as the cleaning plant in a dry cleaning business or the check-clearing department in a bank) or in manufacturing operations (such as the lumber-sawing department in a sawmill or the steel-making department in a steel mill) is a candidate to be treated as a cost center.

Cost center reporting, especially for repetitive operations such as stamping car body parts, reflects the perspectives and uses of the reporting methods described in Chapters 5 and 6 to provide cost information that managers use to monitor and assess operations. Organizations evaluate the performance of cost

> **Cost centers**
> Responsibility centers whose manager and other employees control costs but not revenues or investment level.

---

[2] The entire courier operating and logistical system is organized around meeting the delivery commitment to the customer. Therefore, the ability to clear a terminal or hub by the time that the truck or plane must leave is critical for organization success.

[3] The ability to sort packages quickly and accurately is a key measure of performance since it reflects both cost and quality of service.

☾ONSIDER THIS...

Using Other Performance Indicators for Cost Centers

A manufacturing facility making computer chips was evaluated using conventional manufacturing cost variances. The facility made computer chips on a large disk called a wafer. The wafer was tested and defective chips were marked, cut out of the wafer, and discarded. Processing costs were not affected by the number of good or bad chips.

In this environment, the facility had little interest in controlling quality. The result was poor quality—the average chip yield was about 60%, meaning that only about 60% of the chips on each wafer were usable.

Then the performance measurement system was changed from assessing the manufacturing group's ability to control costs relative to a standard (a one-dimensional focus on an internal cost standard) to cost per good chip compared to that of a competitor.

The facility quickly became concerned with quality because yields were the critical driver for decreasing the cost per good chip produced. Designs, processes, equipment, and employee training were reevaluated and changed to improve yield. Yield increased, leading to dramatic reductions in the cost per good chip produced.

center employees by comparing the center's actual costs with target or standard cost levels for the amount and type of work done. Therefore, cost standards and variances figure prominently in cost center reports. Moreover, because standards and variances are used to assess performance, the process of setting standards and interpreting variances has profound behavioral effects on employees, particularly relating to misrepresenting performance potential and performance results.

COMPARING BUDGETED AND ACTUAL COSTS. The cost budget shown in Exhibit 12-1 was prepared for the manufacturing unit in Moncton Carpet Products, a manufacturer of carpet cleaning products. This budget represents a cost target for the cost performance of the manufacturing group and shows that total center costs are budgeted at $9,891,820. The actual costs reported by the manufacturing group are $9,978,050. Exhibit 12-2 provides details of these actual costs.

The evaluation of this cost center involves identifying the causes for the differences between the budgeted costs in Exhibit 12-1 and the actual costs in Exhibit 12-2. Exhibit 12-3 provides a summary of these cost differences. The variances reported equal the actual cost minus the budgeted cost.

Because the reported variance equals actual minus budgeted cost, a positive variance means that the actual cost was more than expected. A variance is unfavorable when the actual cost is higher than the planned cost, and a variance is favorable when the actual

EXHIBIT 12-1
Moncton Carpet Products
Master Budget

	Product 1	Product 2	Product 3	Product 4	Totals
Units made	245,000	385,000	636,000	1,250,000	
Units per batch	500	2,500	1,500	5,000	
Number of batches	490	154	424	250	
Cost per unit	$5.40	$3.20	$4.25	$1.45	
Cost per batch	$325.00	$680.00	$400.00	$135.00	
Unit-related costs	$1,323,000	$1,232,000	$2,703,000	$1,812,500	$7,070,500
Batch-related costs	$159,250	$104,720	$169,600	$33,750	467,320
Product-sustaining costs	$125,000	$168,000	$256,000	$355,000	904,000
Facility-sustaining costs					1,450,000
Total costs					$9,891,820

EXHIBIT 12-2
Moncton Carpet Products
Actual Results

	Product 1	Product 2	Product 3	Product 4	Totals
Units made	297,000	345,000	675,000	960,000	
Units per batch	600	2,300	1,800	6,000	
Number of batches	495	150	375	160	
Cost per unit	$5.43	$3.18	$4.33	$1.40	
Cost per batch	$335.00	$670.00	$387.00	$144.00	
Unit-related costs	$1,612,710	$1,097,100	$2,922,750	$1,344,000	$6,976,560
Batch-related costs	$165,825	$100,500	$145,125	$23,040	434,490
Product-sustaining costs	$133,000	$163,000	$259,000	$362,000	917,000
Facility-sustaining costs					1,650,000
Total costs					$9,978,050

EXHIBIT 12-3
Moncton Carpet Products
Simple Cost Analysis

	Master Budget (From Exhibit 12-1)	Variance	Actual Results (From Exhibit 12-2)
Unit-related costs:			
Product 1	$1,323,000	$289,710	$1,612,710
Product 2	1,232,000	(134,900)	1,097,100
Product 3	2,703,000	219,750	2,922,750
Product 4	1,812,500	(468,500)	1,344,000
Total	$7,070,500	($93,940)	$6,976,560
Batch-related costs:			
Product 1	$159,250	$6,575	$165,825
Product 2	104,720	(4,220)	100,500
Product 3	169,600	(24,475)	145,125
Product 4	33,750	(10,710)	23,040
Total	$467,320	($32,830)	$434,490
Product-sustaining costs:			
Product 1	$125,000	$8,000	$133,000
Product 2	168,000	(5,000)	163,000
Product 3	256,000	3,000	259,000
Product 4	355,000	7,000	362,000
Total	$904,000	$13,000	$917,000
Facility-sustaining costs	1,450,000	200,000	1,650,000
Total costs	$9,891,820	$86,230	$9,978,050

cost is less than planned cost. *Therefore, positive cost variances are unfavorable and negative cost variances are favorable.*

Exhibit 12-3 reports a mix of positive and negative variances. For example, for products 1 and 3, the unit-related costs are higher than planned, and for products 2 and 4 they are lower than planned. In total, the unit-related costs and batch-related costs are lower than planned and the product-sustaining and facility-sustaining costs are higher than planned.

Based on this initial analysis, we may conclude that the manufacturing group at Moncton Carpet Products is able to control unit-related and batch-related costs but does not do well controlling its product-sustaining and facility-sustaining costs. A closer examination of Exhibits 12-1 and 12-2, however, casts doubt on the validity of these conclusions. We can see in one of these exhibits that the *number of units produced* differs from the *planned number of units* for each product. Similarly, as we can see from line two of these exhibits, the *actual number of units per batch* differs from the *planned number of units per batch* for each product. Because of these volume differences, it is not meaningful to compare the cost targets in the master budget with the actual cost results. When actual volume differs from budgeted or planned volume, accountants use what is called a flexible budget to evaluate actual costs.

USING THE FLEXIBLE BUDGET.   Producing a product requires production activities that, in turn, create costs. For example, increased production levels require more production activities that, in turn, create higher costs. Now recall the preparation of the master budget occurs before the start of production and is based on the planned level of production and production-related activities. However, organizations seldom realize their production plans exactly. Therefore, there usually are differences between the actual level of production and planned production, causing actual production activity levels to differ from planned production activity levels. Thus, it follows that the cost targets, or budgets, in the master budgets reflect different activity levels than do the actual costs incurred. Therefore, it is inappropriate to compare actual cost results with a budget that reflects cost targets based on a different level of production activities.

Flexible budget
Budget that recasts cost targets in the planned or master budget to reflect the actual level of production.

A **flexible budget** recasts cost targets in the planned or master budget to reflect the actual level of production. *The flexible budget develops the cost target levels based on the actual level of activity.* Thus, flexible budgets allow comparisons of actual results to targets based on the achieved level of production.

Exhibit 12-4 presents the flexible budget for Moncton Carpet Products. The cost standards in this exhibit reflect the same cost per unit or cost per batch standards as the master budget.[4] The only difference here is that there is an adjustment in the volume levels to reflect the achieved level of activity. For example, Moncton Carpet Products actually made 345,000 units of product 2. At the standard batch size of 2500, there should have been 138 (345,000 ÷ 2500) batches of product 2 made. At a standard unit cost of $3.20 and a standard batch cost of $680, the unit-related and batch-related costs for product 2 should have been $1,104,000 ($3.20 × 345,000) and $93,840 ($680 × 138), respectively. We can now adjust the master budget targets for the changes in volume to provide a volume-adjusted cost standard to compare with actual costs. This is done in Exhibit 12-5.

---

[4] Recall that *standard* refers to the cost per unit, whereas *target* or *budget* refers to the product of the standard and some activity measure (number of units).

EXHIBIT 12-4
Moncton Carpet Products
Flexible Budget

	Product 1	Product 2	Product 3	Product 4	Totals
Units made	297,000	345,000	675,000	960,000	
Units per batch	500	2,500	1,500	5,000	
Number of batches	594	138	450	192	
Cost per unit	$5.40	$3.20	$4.25	$1.45	
Cost per batch	$325.00	$680.00	$400.00	$135.00	
Unit-related costs	$1,603,800	$1,104,000	$2,868,750	$1,392,000	$6,968,550
Batch-related costs	$193,050	$93,840	$180,000	$25,920	492,810
Product-sustaining costs	$125,000	$168,000	$256,000	$355,000	904,000
Facility-sustaining costs					1,450,000
Total costs					$9,815,360

EXHIBIT 12-5
Moncton Carpet Products
Flexible Budget Cost Analysis

	1	2	3	4	5
	Master Budget	Planning Variance	Flexible Budget	Flexible Budget Variance	Actual
Unit-related costs:					
Product 1	$1,323,000	$280,800	$1,603,800	$8,910	$1,612,710
Product 2	1,232,000	(128,000)	1,104,000	(6,900)	1,097,100
Product 3	2,703,000	165,750	2,868,750	54,000	2,922,750
Product 4	1,812,500	(420,500)	1,392,000	(48,000)	1,344,000
Total	$7,070,500	$(101,950)	$6,968,550	$8,010	$6,976,560
Batch-related costs:					
Product 1	$159,250	$33,800	$193,050	$(27,225)	$165,825
Product 2	104,720	(10,880)	93,840	6,660	100,500
Product 3	169,600	10,400	180,000	(34,875)	145,125
Product 4	33,750	(7,830)	25,920	(2,880)	23,040
Total	$467,320	$25,490	$492,810	$(58,320)	$434,490
Product-sustaining costs:					
Product 1	$125,000	0	$125,000	$8,000	$133,000
Product 2	168,000	0	168,000	(5,000)	163,000
Product 3	256,000	0	256,000	3,000	259,000
Product 4	355,000	0	355,000	7,000	362,000
Total	$ 904,000	0	$ 904,000	$ 13,000	$ 917,000
Facility-sustaining costs:	1,450,000	0	1,450,000	200,000	1,650,000
Total costs	$9,891,820	($76,460)	$9,815,360	$162,690	$9,978,050

Exhibit 12-5 reconciles the actual cost to the master budget target through the flexible budget. The variances between the master budget (column 1) and the flexible budget (column 3), which accountants call planning variances (column 2), reflect the cost adjustments resulting from the differences in production volume between the master budget (planned volume) and the flexible budget (achieved volume). This *planning variance* is computed by subtracting the master budget amount from the flexible budget amount for each item. A negative variance means a cost reduction due to a lower volume, and a positive variance means a cost increase because of a higher volume.

Planning variances have little meaning in themselves. Their value lies in showing the effect of volume change on revenues, costs, and profits. They facilitate adjustments to the master budget target amounts for differences between planned and actual volumes so that the cost targets become comparable to the actual cost levels.

The flexible budget variances are the focus of cost control in a cost center. We can see that the flexible budget variance for unit-related costs for product 1 was $8910 (column 4), signaling that cost expenditures for unit-related items relating to product 1 were $8910 higher than they should have been given the level of volume achieved. This flexible budget variance is the sum of the price and quantity variances.

For batch-related costs, the flexible budget variance reflects a mix of the difference between the planned and actual cost per batch and the number of batches given the actual level of activity. Note that the variance for batch-related costs for product 1 was −$27,225 (column 4). This favorable variance indicates that batch-related costs were $27,225 less than the target specified in the flexible budget.

This hotel has many facilities that allow it to attract convention business. While, on the surface, the dining rooms or the meeting rooms may not appear profitable, if these services were unavailable, the hotel would be unable to earn the room revenues from the convention business. In many organizations, there is a complex interaction between the different business segments that influence the organization's overall profits. *Courtesy* **Las Vegas Hilton Hotel**

This favorable variance arises from two factors. First, as we can see by comparing the cost targets in Exhibit 12-1 with the actual costs in Exhibit 12-2, the standard cost per batch and actual cost per batch for product 1 were $325 and $335, respectively. Therefore, the batch-related costs for product 1 reflect an increased, or unfavorable, cost, which equals the increased cost per batch of $10 multiplied by the actual number of batches, a total of $4950 ($10 $\times$ 495).

Second, we can see that when comparing the actual results in Exhibit 12-2 with the flexible budget amounts in Exhibit 12-4, given the achieved level of activity, the actual number and standard number of batches were 495 and 594, respectively. The manufacturing group increased the average batch size for product 1 from 500 to 600, thereby reducing the number of batches, to create part of the reported savings in batch-related costs.[5] By reducing the number of batches by 99 (594 − 495) from the planned level, the manufacturing group saved $32,175 ($325 $\times$ 99) in batch-related costs.

The total flexible budget variance for the batch-related costs for product 1 is −$27,225 ($4950 − $32,175) and reflects the combined effect of (1) fewer than the standard number of batches given the production level achieved and (2) a higher than standard cost per batch. We can also investigate the cause of the other flexible budget variances reported for the various costs for each product in a similar manner.

OTHER COST CONTROL APPROACHES. When an organization unit's output mix and output level are constant, it is possible to compare current cost levels with those in previous periods to promote an environment of continuous cost improvement. Interperiod cost comparisons can be very misleading when the production mix or the production level are changing. Under these conditions, there exists non-comparability of cost levels between periods. However, where circumstances warrant, organizations are often able to plot cost levels on a graph and look for downward cost trends, implying improved efficiencies in the processes that are creating costs.

ADDRESSING OTHER ISSUES IN COST CENTER CONTROL. Many organizations make the mistake of evaluating a cost center solely on its ability to control and reduce costs. The Federal Express example illustrates that quality, response time, the ability to meet production schedules, employee motivation, employee safety, and respect for the organization's ethical and environmental commitments are other critical measures of a cost center's performance. If management evaluates cost center performance only on the center's ability to control costs, its members may ignore unmeasured attributes of performance. Therefore, organizations should never evaluate cost centers using *only* the center's cost performance. Rather, performance measures also should reflect the contributions the cost center makes to the organization's success.

Revenue Centers

Revenue center
A responsibility center whose employees control revenues but not manufacturing or product costs or the level of investment.

Revenue centers are responsibility centers where members control revenues but not the manufacturing or acquisition cost of the product or service they sell or the

---

[5] It would be interesting to determine whether these savings were accomplished at the cost of increased warehousing costs.

level of investment in the responsibility center. Examples are a department in a department store, a regional sales office of a national or multinational corporation, and a unit in a large chain of units.

OBJECTIVE 12.3

Recognize the common forms of responsibility centers.

Some revenue centers control price, the mix of stock carried, and promotional activities. In these centers, revenue measures most of their value-added activities and indicates in a broad sense how well they carried out their various activities.

Consider the activities of Napanee Service Center, a gasoline and automobile service station owned by a large oil refiner. The service center manager has no control over the cost of items such as fuel, depreciation on the building, power and heating costs, supplies, and salary rates. This manager has a minor influence on the total labor cost through scheduling and staffing decisions. Levels of gasoline sales and repair activities determine all the other costs. The service manager also has no control over automobile repairs; the head office staff controls them. The central marketing staff controls all promotional activities. The major controllable item in this service station is customer service, which distinguishes the gasoline sales and repair services offered in this outlet from similar outlets and helps to determine this service station's sales levels.

The revenue-center approach evaluates the responsibility center based solely on the revenues that it generates. Most revenue centers incur sales and marketing costs, however, and have varying degrees of control over those costs. Therefore, it is common in such situations to deduct the responsibility center's traceable costs, such as salaries, advertising costs, and selling costs, from its sales revenue to compute the center's net revenue.

Critics of the revenue-center approach argue that basing performance evaluation on revenues can create undesirable consequences. For example, sales staff rewarded solely on sales may (1) promote, or agitate for, a wide product line which, in turn, may create excessive diversity related (both production and logistic) costs or (2) offer excessive customized services. In general, focusing only on revenues causes organization members to increase the use of activities that create costs to promote higher revenue levels.

Profit Centers

Profit center
A responsibility center whose employees control revenues and costs but not the level of investment.

Profit centers are responsibility centers where managers, and other employees control both the revenues and the costs of the product or service they deliver. A profit center is like an independent business except that senior management, not the responsibility center manager, controls the level of investment in the responsibility center. For example, if the manager of one outlet in a chain of discount stores has responsibility for pricing, product selection, purchasing, and promotion, the outlet meets the conditions to be evaluated as a profit center.

Most individual units of chain operations, whether they are stores, motels, or restaurants, are treated as profit centers. It is doubtful, however, that a unit of a corporate-owned fast-food restaurant, such as Burger King, or a corporate-owned hotel such as Holiday Inn, meets the conditions to be treated as a profit center because the head offices make most purchasing, operating, pricing, and promotional decisions. These units are sufficiently large, however, that costs can vary due to differences in controlling labor costs, food waste, and the schedule for the facility's hours. Moreover, revenues can shift significantly based on the unit's service level. Therefore, although these organizations do not seem to be candidates to be treated as profit centers, enough local discretion affects revenues and costs so that they can be treated as profit centers.

Therefore, many organizations evaluate units as profit centers even though the corporate office controls many facets of their operations. The profit reported by these units is a broad index of performance that reflects both corporate and local decisions. If unit performance is poor, it may reflect poor conditions that no one in the organization can control, poor corporate decisions, or poor local decisions. For this reason, organizations should not rely only on profit center results for performance evaluations. Instead, detailed performance evaluations should include quality, material use (yield), labor use (yield), and service measures that the local units can control.

Investment Centers

Investment centers are responsibility centers where the manager and other employees control revenues, costs, and the level of investment in the responsibility center. The investment center is like an independent business.

In 1993 Canada Post, Canada's national postal service, purchased Purolator Canada Limited, a courier service, and announced that Purolator would continue as an independent operation with its own management and policies. Purolator is an example of an investment center within the Canada Post system.

Exhibit 12-6 summarizes the characteristics of the various types of responsibility centers.

Investment center
A responsibility center whose employees control its revenues, costs, and the level of investment.

EXHIBIT 12-6
Summary of Responsibility Centers

Type of Responsibility Center

Factors	Cost Center	Revenue Center	Profit Center	Investment Center
Controlled by center management	Costs	Revenues	Costs, revenues	Cost, revenues, and significant control over investment
Not controlled by center management	Revenues, investment in inventory and fixed assets	Costs, investment in inventory and fixed assets	Investment in inventory and fixed assets	—
Measured by the accounting system	Costs relative to some target (usually a budget)	Revenue relative to some target (usually a budget)	Profit relative to some target (usually a budget)	Return on investment relative to some target
Not measured by the accounting system	Performance on critical success factors other than cost	Performance on critical success factors other than revenue	Performance on critical success factors other than profit	Performance on critical success factors other than return on investment

*E*VALUATING RESPONSIBILITY CENTERS

Using the Controllability Principle to Evaluate Responsibility Centers

Controllability principle
A principle that asserts that people should be held accountable only for results that they can control. The main application of this principle is that a manager should not be held accountable for revenues, costs, investments, or other factors outside her control.

Underlying these accounting classifications of responsibility centers is the concept of controllability. The **controllability principle** states that the manager of a responsibility center should be assigned responsibility only for the revenues, costs, or investment that responsibility center personnel control. Revenues, costs, or investments that people outside the responsibility center control should be excluded from the accounting assessment of that center's performance. Although the controllability principle seems to be appealing and fair, it can be difficult, often misleading, and undesirable to apply in practice.

A significant problem in applying the controllability principle is that in most organizations many revenues and costs are jointly earned or incurred. Consider the operations of an integrated fishing products company that is divided into three responsibility centers: harvesting; processing; and marketing and distribution. The harvesting group operates ships that go out to sea and catch various species of fish. The ships return to one of the company's processing plants to discharge their catches. The plants process the fish into salable products. Finally, the marketing and distribution group sells products to customers.

As in most organizations, the activities that create the final product in this company are sequential and highly interdependent. The product must be of the right species, quality, and cost to be acceptable to the customer. The performance of the harvesting, processing, and marketing and distribution jointly determine the organization's success.

Evaluating the performance of harvesting, processing, and marketing and distribution involves considering many facets of performance. For example, it is possible to evaluate harvesting's operations by measuring its ability to:

1. Catch the entire quota allowed.
2. Minimize the waste and damage done to the fish caught.
3. Minimize equipment failures.
4. Control the costs associated with operating the ships.

Similar measures can be developed for processing, and the evaluation of marketing and distribution may be based on the ability to meet delivery schedules and improve market share.

As part of the performance-evaluation process, the organization may want to prepare accounting summaries of the performance of harvesting, processing, and marketing and distribution to support some system of financial control. The management accountant undertaking this task immediately confronts the dilemma of how to account for highly interrelated organization centers as if they were individual businesses. For example, harvesting's costs are easy to determine, but what are the harvesting revenues? Harvesting does not control sales or prices. Its role is to catch the fish, maintain raw material and product quality, and meet the schedules determined jointly by it, processing, and marketing and distribution. If the company evaluates harvesting as a cost center, what about indirect organization costs such as corporate administration that reflect overhead resources that the cost center uses? What about other important performance facets, such as maintaining quality, catching the full quota of fish, and delivering the required species of fish when required to the processing group? Should harvesting be asked to bear some of the costs of the head office groups, such as personnel, planning, and administration, whose services it uses? If so, how should its share of the costs of those services be determined?

For the same reasons, we could probably conclude that processing should be evaluated as a cost center. However, what about the marketing and distribution group that through its general marketing efforts probably has the most direct impact on sales? But what costs does this group control? It does not control harvesting and processing costs. The only costs that marketing and distribution controls are marketing and distribution costs that, in most integrated fishing products companies, are less than 10% of the total costs. The harvesting group, through its ability to catch fish and maintain their quality, and the processing group, through its ability to produce quality products, are also influential in determining the organization's sales level.

Using Performance Measures to Influence Versus Evaluate Decisions

Some people argue that controllability is not a valid criterion to use in selecting a performance measure. Rather, they suggest that the choice of the performance measure should influence decision-making behavior.

Consider a dairy that faced continuing problems developing performance standards in the face of continuously rising costs. Because the cost of raw materials, which were between 60% and 90% of the final costs of the various products, were market determined and, therefore, thought to be beyond the control of the various product managers, people argued that evaluation of the managers should depend on their ability to control the quantity of raw materials *used* rather than the cost of raw materials.

Senior management of the dairy announced, however, that it planned to evaluate managers on their ability to control total costs. The managers quickly discovered that one way to control raw materials cost was to make judicious use of long-term fixed price contracts for raw materials. These contracts soon led to declining raw materials cost. Moreover, the company could project product costs several quarters into the future, thereby achieving lower costs and stability in planning and product pricing.

This example shows that managers, even when they cannot control costs entirely, can take steps that can influence final product costs. By including more costs or even revenues into performance measures, managers are more motivated to find actions that can influence incurred costs or generated revenues.

Using Segment Margin Reports

Many problems can occur when organizations evaluate responsibility centers as profit centers. These problems concern identifying responsibility for the control of sales and costs. In particular, this means deciding how to assign the responsibility

CONSIDER THIS . . .

Segment Margins and Financial Control

Business Week reports that one of the first activities of Nobuhiki Kawamoto when he took over as the President of the ailing Honda Motor Co. in 1990 was to divide "the company by product lines so that the robust motorcycle and power-equipment groups wouldn't disguise the trouble in cars."

Source: Karen Lowry Miller, Larry Armstrong, and David Woodruff, *Business Week,* September 13, 1993, p. 64.

for jointly earned revenues and jointly incurred costs. Therefore, as we now consider the form of the accounting reports that accountants prepare for responsibility centers, remember the assumptions and limitations that underlie these reports.

Despite the problems of responsibility-center accounting, the profit measure is so comprehensive and motivating that many organizations prefer to treat many of their organization units as profit centers. Because most organizations are integrated operations, one of the first problems that designers of profit center accounting systems must confront is handling the interactions between the various profit center units.

To address this issue, consider the activities at Earl's Motors, a full-service automobile dealership organized into five responsibility centers: new car sales, used car sales, the body shop, the service department, and leasing. Each responsibility center has a manager who is responsible for the profit reported for that unit. The responsibility center managers report to Earl using the quarterly reports such as the one shown in Exhibit 12-7.

Exhibit 12-7 illustrates a common form of the segment margin report for an organization that is divided into responsibility centers. There is one column for each profit center. The revenue attributed to each profit center is the first entry in each column. Variable costs are deducted from its revenue to determine the con-

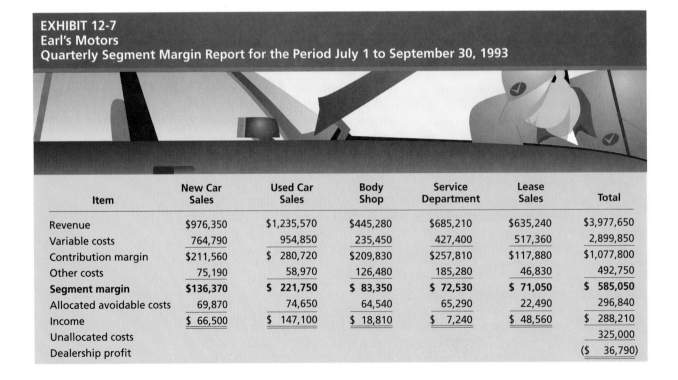

EXHIBIT 12-7
Earl's Motors
Quarterly Segment Margin Report for the Period July 1 to September 30, 1993

Item	New Car Sales	Used Car Sales	Body Shop	Service Department	Lease Sales	Total
Revenue	$976,350	$1,235,570	$445,280	$685,210	$635,240	$3,977,650
Variable costs	764,790	954,850	235,450	427,400	517,360	2,899,850
Contribution margin	$211,560	$ 280,720	$209,830	$257,810	$117,880	$1,077,800
Other costs	75,190	58,970	126,480	185,280	46,830	492,750
Segment margin	**$136,370**	**$ 221,750**	**$ 83,350**	**$ 72,530**	**$ 71,050**	**$ 585,050**
Allocated avoidable costs	69,870	74,650	64,540	65,290	22,490	296,840
Income	$ 66,500	$ 147,100	$ 18,810	$ 7,240	$ 48,560	$ 288,210
Unallocated costs						325,000
Dealership profit						($ 36,790)

Evaluating the department that manufactured this wafer of computer chips would motivate that department's personnel to ignore quality related issues. Performance measures must be broad enough to motivate desired performance—for example cost per *good* chip produced.
Courtesy Tom Tracy/FPG International

tribution margin, which is the contribution made by operations to cover its costs that are not proportional to volume (Other costs in Exhibit 12-7).

Next the costs not proportional to volume are deducted from each center's contribution margin to determine that unit's segment margin, which is the performance measure for each responsibility center. The unit's **segment margin** measures its controllable contribution to the organization's profit and other indirect costs. Allocated avoidable costs are the organization's administrative costs, such as personnel-related costs and committed costs for facilities. These costs can be avoided if the unit is eliminated and the organization has time to adjust its capacity levels by selling excess facilities or by reducing the number of administrative staff. Allocated avoidable costs are deducted from the unit's segment margin to compute its income. Finally, the organization's unallocated costs (sometimes called shutdown costs), which represent the administrative and overhead costs incurred regardless of the scale of operations,[6] are deducted from the total of the five profit center incomes to arrive at the dealership's profit.

Segment margin
The level of controllable profit reported by an organization unit or product line.

EVALUATING THE SEGMENT MARGIN REPORT. What can we learn from the segment margin report for Earl's Motors? First, we know that conventional accrual accounting reports a loss of $36,790 for this quarter. This loss may signal a long-term problem, or it may have been expected. Perhaps this quarter is a traditionally slow quarter and operations in the year's other three quarters make

---

[6] For example, the president's salary and the cost of administrative staff who are not involved with the operation of an individual responsibility center are unallocated costs.

up the deficiency. Perhaps there is a disproportionate amount of committed costs incurred in this quarter and they will be less in subsequent quarters.

WHAT DO THE STATEMENTS TELL THE READER?   As we look at the statements for the individual responsibility centers, we can see that each one showed a positive income. The contribution margin for each responsibility center is the *value added* by the manufacturing or service-creating process before the costs that are not proportional to volume.

A unit's segment margin is an estimate of its short-term effect on the organization's profit. It also represents the immediate negative effect on corporate income if the unit is shut down. The unit's income is an estimate of the long-term effect of the responsibility center's shutdown on the organization's profit after fixed capacity is allowed to adjust. For example, if the lease sales operation is discontinued, the immediate effect is to reduce the profit at Earl's Motors by $71,050. After some period of time, however, perhaps a year or even several years, when capacity has been allowed to adjust for this loss of activity, the estimated net effect of closing the lease operation would be to reduce corporate profits by $48,560. The difference between the unit's segment margin and income reflects the effect of adjusting for facility-sustaining costs, which are committed in the short run.

GOOD OR BAD NUMBERS?   Organizations use different approaches to evaluate whether the segment margin numbers are good or bad. These are the most popular sources of comparative information:

1. Trends of past performance. Is performance this period reasonable given past experience?
2. Comparisons to comparable organizations. How does performance compare to similar organizations?

These evaluations include comparisons of absolute amounts, such as cost levels and revenue levels, and relative amounts, such as each item's percentage of revenue.

For example, in evaluating the performance of Earl's Motors, the manager of the service department may note that variable costs (the costs of flexible resources) are about 62% of revenue. This may compare favorably with past relationships of variable cost to revenue. By joining an industry group that provides comparative information for dealerships in similar size communities, however, Earl's Motors may find that, on average, variable costs in automobile dealerships are only 58% of revenue. This suggests that Earl's Motors should investigate why its variable costs are higher than the industry average. Management at Earl's should make similar evaluations for all the cost items in this report.

OBJECTIVE 12.4

Evaluate the issues and problems created by revenue and cost interactions in evaluating the performance of an organization unit.

INTERPRETING SEGMENT MARGIN REPORTS WITH CAUTION. The segment margin statement may seem to be a straightforward and interesting approach to financial control. Segment margin statements should be interpreted carefully, however, because they reflect many assumptions that disguise underlying issues.

First, as with all approaches to financial control, segment margins present an aggregated summary of each organization unit's performance. It is important to consider other facets relating to critical success factors, such as quality and service. For example, companies may use customer surveys to establish a customer satisfaction index for each department, or they might compute quality statistics that report error or recall rates for each department.

Second, the segment margin report contains numbers that can be quite arbitrary because they rest on subjective revenue and cost allocation assumptions over which there can be legitimate disagreement. (Accountants often call these arbitrary numbers soft numbers.) Each subsequent amount shown down each column becomes less controllable by the responsibility center's manager and is affected more by the assumptions used in allocating costs. Although a unit's segment margin is assumed to be controllable, the manager may have less than complete control over the costs used to compute it. And the manager may have almost no control over the costs allocated to compute the unit's income. In a typical refinery, for example, joint use of facilities creates problems when attempting to allocate the costs of expensive processes, such as the Crude Distillation unit, to the outputs that it produces—naphtha, distillate, gas, oil, and residuals. (See Exhibit 12-8.)

Third, and perhaps most important, the revenue figures reflect important assumptions and allocations that sometimes can be misleading. These assumptions relate to the transfer pricing issue—how the revenues the organization earns can be divided among all the responsibility centers that contribute to earning those revenues.

TRANSFER PRICING

OBJECTIVE 12.5

Discuss transfer pricing alternatives in organizations.

Transfer pricing is the set of rules an organization uses to allocate jointly earned revenue among responsibility centers.[7] These rules can be very arbitrary if there is a high degree of interaction among the individual responsibility centers. Exhibit 12-9 shows the possible interactions among the responsibility centers at Earl's Motors.

Transfer pricing
A set of tools and methods (rules) used by the organization to allocate jointly earned revenues to organization subunits. Common transfer pricing approaches are cost, market, negotiated, and administered.

To understand the issues and problems associated with allocating revenues in a simple organization like Earl's Motors, consider the activities that occur when a customer purchases a new car. The new car department sells the new car and takes in a used car as a trade. Then Earl's must transfer the used car to the used car department, where it may undergo repairs and service to make it ready for sale, or sell it externally, as is in the wholesale market.

The value placed on the used car transferred between the new and used car departments is critical in determining the profitability of both departments. The new car department would like the value assigned to the used car to be as high as possible because that makes its reported revenues higher; the used car department would like the value to be as low as possible because that makes its reported costs lower.

---

[7] In this text we focus on transfer pricing—often called domestic transfer pricing—which is used for internal purposes, primarily to motivate managers. Multinational organizations use transfer pricing to price product transfers between tax jurisdictions—often called international transfer pricing. It is well known that multinational subsidiaries artificially inflate their profits in Ireland because of the low tax rate on corporate profits in that country. International transfer pricing is influenced by countries' tax policies and companies' tax planning and is not discussed in this text.

EXHIBIT 12-8
The Operation of a Typical Mobil Corp. U.S. Refinery

CRUDE INPUT

LPG

CRUDE DISTILLATION
Distillation separates the crude into fractions based on boiling range. The crude is heated until each fraction boils off as vapor and is then condensed and subject to further processing.

NAPHTHA

DISTILLATE

GAS OIL

REFORMER
Reforming is important because it enables refiners to produce the high-octane gasolines required by some of today's cars. Reforming rearranges gasoline molecules into forms with a higher octane rating.

Mobil's U.S. refineries are designed to process low-cost, high-sulfur crude oil to make high-value premium gasoline, distillate, and lube products.

ALKYLATION
In an alkylation unit, light olefins from the FCC are reacted in the presence of an acid catalyst to produce high-octane, premium-quality gasoline blending stock.

GASOLINE

HYDROCRACKING
Hydrocracking is catalytic cracking performed under high pressure in the presence of hydrogen to yield products of higher quality and higher sulfur content.

RESIDUALS

Catalytic cracking is the primary means of upgrading heavy oils into higher–value light products. A catalyst breaks down large hydrocarbon molecules in heavy oil into a mixture of smaller molecules that can be separated by distillation into lighter products such as liquefied petroleum gas (LPG), naphtha (raw gasoline), and heating oil. The gasoline produced by catalytic cracking has a high-octane rating.

FLUID CATALYTIC CRACKER
In a fluid catalytic cracker (FCC), gas or air is forced through a bed of finely powdered catalyst to flow like a liquid. In large units, the catalyst recirculates through the system at up to 80 tons per minute.

GASOLINE

DISTILLATE SULFUR REMOVAL
Distillate sulfur removal typically occurs when sulfur is catalytically removed from distillate streams using fixed bed reactors in the presence of hydrogen. Products include high-quality kerosene, heating fuel, and diesel.

DISTILLATE

DISTILLATE

COKER
The Coker converts residual fuels to lighter components, such as gasoline and diesel oil, using high temperatures; it also produces a solid material called coke, which is typically used as industrial fuel. All Mobil U.S. refineries have cokers.

NAPHTHA

DISTILLATE

SULFUR RECOVERY
Very pure sulfur from the sulfur recovery unit is the result of the various sulfur removal processes in the refinery. Effective sulfur removal/recovery permits the processing of low-cost, high-sulfur crudes.

SULFUR

LUBE/WAX PRODUCTION BLENDING AND PACKAGING
Lube/wax units produce a wide range of lube products at two of Mobil's U.S. refineries. Heavy gas oils go through an extraction and dewaxing process to produce lube blend stocks. These are the basestocks that are blended into a variety of high-quality finished lubes and waxes.

GAS OIL

LUBE/WAX

COKE

This graphic, developed by Mobil Corporation, shows the processing activities used in a typical U.S. refinery to refine a barrel of crude oil into its resulting, or joint, products. The complex and interrelated nature of the products simultaneously produced in a refinery creates profound problems in determining the individual costs of those products. *Courtesy* Mobil Corporation

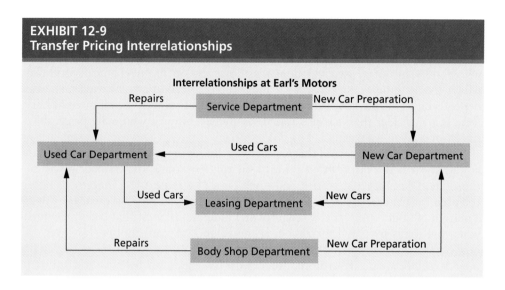

EXHIBIT 12-9
Transfer Pricing Interrelationships

Interrelationships at Earl's Motors

The same considerations apply for any product or service transfer between any two departments in the same organization. The rule that determines the values of the internal transfers will allocate the organization's jointly earned revenues to the individual profit centers and, therefore, will affect each center's reported profit.

Organizations choose among four different approaches to transfer pricing:

1. Market-based transfer prices
2. Cost-based transfer prices
3. Negotiated transfer prices
4. Administered transfer prices

Before we review the basic transfer pricing methods that organizations use, it is worthwhile recalling that the relevance and purpose of transfer prices depends upon whether the transfer price has the intended effect on organization decision makers. Accountants must always remember that the primary purpose of producing management accounting numbers is to motivate desirable behavior regarding managers' planning, decision making, and resource allocation activities, not to create accounting reports.

Market-Based Transfer Prices

If external markets exist for the intermediate (transferred) product or service, then market prices are the most appropriate basis for pricing the transferred good or service between responsibility centers. The market price provides an independent valuation of the transferred product or service and how each profit center has contributed to the total profit earned by the organization on the transaction. For example, the selling division, instead of transferring the good internally, could sell it externally. Similarly, the buying division could purchase externally rather than receiving the internal transfer.

Unfortunately, such competitive markets with well-defined prices seldom exist. Consider Earl's Motors. Dealers trade used cars in well-organized markets that publish prices. A given used car could be valued using this information. The wholesale value of a used car depends, however, on its mechanical condition, which is only imperfectly observable and at a cost. In addition, the used car's value depends on its visible condition, which is a matter of subjective judgment. Therefore, it is not clear that it is possible to easily determine a wholesale price objectively for a given used car.

Some dealerships avoid this problem by asking the used car manager to value any used car being taken in on trade. This value becomes the transfer price. Because people often react to risk and uncertainty by requiring a margin of safety, the used car manager may discount the perceived value of the used car to provide a margin of safety to cover the repair of any hidden problems that become evident when the car is prepared for resale. If the value is excessively low, however, the new car manager complains that this is impeding the ability of the new car department to sell new cars. Therefore, the new car manager may be given the option to shop a potential trade-in to other used car dealers to find a better price. This allows the transfer price to better reflect market forces.

Cost-Based Transfer Prices

When the transferred good or service does not have a well-defined market price, one alternative to consider is a transfer price based on cost. Some common transfer prices are variable cost, variable cost plus some percent markup on variable cost, full cost, and full cost plus some percent markup on full cost.

Proponents of each of these types of transfer prices have arguments to support their respective choices. Economists argue, however, that any cost-based transfer price other than marginal cost (assuming that it can be computed) leads organization members to choose a lower than optimal level of transactions, causing an economic loss to the overall organization.[8] The dilemma here, however, is that if the supplying division charges marginal cost as the transfer price and if marginal costs decline with volume, the marginal cost will be less than average cost and the supplying division will always show a loss.

Cost-based approaches to transfer pricing are inconsistent with the intent that the transfer pricing mechanism support the calculation of unit incomes. Many organization units prefer to be treated as profit centers, not cost centers, because they feel that profit centers are more prestigious.

Transfer prices based on actual costs provide no incentive to the supplying division to control costs since the supplier can always recover its costs. This is a well-known problem in government contracting and utility regulation where prices are often based on actual costs. One solution is to use a standard cost as the transfer price. Under this approach, the difference between the actual costs that a center incurs and the standard costs that are charged out become a measure of the unit's operating efficiency.

---

[8] For example, if the transfer price is higher than the marginal cost, the supplying unit wants to sell more than the optimal quantity and the purchasing unit wants to buy fewer than the optimal quantity. Because supply and demand must be equal, and because no one can be forced to buy or sell more than is wanted, the amount that is ordered and supplied is always the lower amount of what is offered and wanted.

Using a cost-based transfer price assumes that the organization can compute a product's cost in a reasonably accurate way. Chapters 5 and 6 show that developing and operating accurate costing systems is quite a challenge. People are likely to complain and become frustrated if they feel that the organization is using an inaccurate costing system for transfer-pricing purposes.

A final problem with cost-based approaches is that they do not provide the proper economic guidance when operations are capacity constrained. When operating at capacity, production decisions should reflect the most profitable use of the capacity rather than cost considerations only. In this case, the transfer price should be the sum of the marginal cost and the opportunity cost of capacity, where opportunity cost reflects the profit of the best alternative use of the capacity.

One interesting approach to transfer pricing is the so-called dual rate approach in which the receiving division is charged only for the variable costs of producing the unit supplied and the supplying division is credited with the net realizable value of the unit supplied. This procedure has the desirable effect of having short run marginal cost influence the decisions of the buying division while, at the same time, giving the selling division credit for an imputed profit on the transferred good or service.

Another interesting cost-based approach charges the buying division with the target variable cost. That amount includes the number of standard hours

Like all businesses in the natural resource sector of the economy, saw mills take special care to use their raw materials as effectively as possible. This employee at Potlatch Corporation, a diversified forest products company, is using a reducing band saw to cut a squared log, or cant, into lumber. Employees at Potlatch have continuously refined and improved sawing so that the saw operator, using specially designed monitors and computers, can obtain the highest value of products from a given piece of raw material at the lowest possible cost to the company. *Courtesy* Tom Tracy

allowed for the work done multiplied by the standard cost per hour, in addition to an assignment of the supplying division's committed costs. The assignment should reflect the buying division's share of the supplying division's capacity. For example, if the service department acquired capacity expecting that 10% of its capacity would be supplied to the new car department, then the new car department would receive a lump-sum assignment of 10% of the service department's capacity costs, irrespective of the amount of work actually done for the new car department during the period. In this situation, the service department's income is the difference between the actual and target cost of the work it completes.

Cost-based transfer prices raise complex performance measurement, equity, and behavioral issues. Such issues are addressed more thoroughly in advanced texts.

Cost Allocations to Support Financial Control

Despite the difficulties of measuring responsibility center performance, many organizations want to develop responsibility center income statements. In effect, although revenue and cost allocation rules are arbitrary, people seem satisfied as long as the ones chosen and put in place are fair and consistently applied. Because of their arbitrariness, organizations need to design and present responsibility center income statements so that they isolate the discretionary components included in the calculation of each center's reported income. Refer back to Exhibit 12-7, which presents one possible format.

The format shown in Exhibit 12-7 helps to identify what the center controls directly. It shows the revenue and variable costs separately from the other costs in the profit calculation, which are the indirect or joint costs that are allocated. As with the allocation of jointly earned revenues, the allocation of indirect or joint costs can cause considerable distortions and can misdirect decision making.

Consider the operations of Shirley's Grill and Bar, which has three operating units: a restaurant, a billiards room, and a bar. (See Exhibit 12-10.) The segment margin of $110,256 reported for the restaurant includes all revenues from selling food, all food costs, all costs of kitchen and serving staff, and all costs of equipment and supplies relating to the kitchen and the seating area. These revenues and costs are directly attributable to the operation of the restaurant. Indirect costs that

EXHIBIT 12-10
Shirley's Grill and Bar
Responsibility Center Income Statements
Indirect Cost Allocation Based on Benefit

	Restaurant	Billiards	Bar	Total
Attributed revenue	$354,243	$32,167	$187,426	$573,836
Less segment costs	243,987	12,965	127,859	384,811
Segment margin	**$110,256**	**$19,202**	**$59,567**	**$189,025**
Less allocated costs	87,791	15,289	47,430	150,510
Segment income	$ 22,465	$ 3,913	$ 12,137	$ 38,515

are included in the $87,791 allocated to the restaurant operations include depreciation and taxes on the building, advertising, and franchise fees.

In general, the restaurant's accountant can choose among many different activity bases to select a method to allocate indirect costs, for example, a responsibility center's direct costs, floor space, and number of employees. Suppose that Shirley's decides to allocate indirect costs in proportion to the presumed benefit, measured by segment margin, provided by the capacity these allocated costs reflect.[9] Many people believe that allocating indirect costs in proportion to benefit is fair. It is a widely used criterion to evaluate an indirect cost allocation method.

The segment incomes reported in Exhibit 12-10 may seem straightforward and reasonable, but like all results involving indirect cost allocations, the numbers need careful interpretation. Suppose that a cost driver analysis revealed the following:

1. A significant portion of total indirect costs reflects depreciation on the building.
2. Allocating building costs based on floor space is considered to be the most reasonable approach to handling building costs.
3. The amount of floor space occupied by the restaurant, billiards, and bar operations is 40%, 25%, and 35%, respectively.[10]

An allocation of costs based on floor space occupied yields the results summarized in Exhibit 12-11.

Do these alternative results mean anything? On the one hand, we might argue that the indirect cost allocations based on floor space provide more meaningful economic results because the floor space allocation reflects depreciation, the major component of indirect costs, and its driver, floor space. Even if floor space is the cost driver for indirect costs in the short term, the revised results may suggest nothing significant because the allocated depreciation cost is likely to be a committed cost that cannot be avoided in the short term.

EXHIBIT 12-11
Shirley's Grill and Bar
Responsibility Center Income Statements
Indirect Cost Allocation Based on Floor Space Occupied

	Restaurant	Billiards	Bar	Total
Attributed revenue	$354,243	$32,167	$187,426	$573,836
Less segment costs	243,987	12,965	127,859	384,811
Segment margin	$110,256	$19,202	$59,567	$189,025
Less allocated costs	60,204	37,627	52,679	150,510
Segment income	$ 50,052	($18,425)	$ 6,888	$ 38,515

[9] Note that the segment margin for the restaurant is 58.3% ($110,256/$189,025) of the total business segment margin. Therefore, the restaurant is allocated 58.3% of the total costs to be allocated.

[10] Therefore, following this method, the restaurant is allocated 40% of the costs because it occupies 40% of the floor space.

The allocations based on floor space may seem to suggest that the contribution to profit per square foot of floor space is lowest in the billiard operation and that Shirley's should reduce the scope of the billiard operations in favor of adding more floor space to the bar or restaurant. This conclusion, however, does not necessarily follow. Suppose that without the billiard operation to attract customers the bar sales would be cut in half. How could the responsibility center income statements reflect this? They probably cannot. With this supplementary information, it would be possible to determine the economic effect of closing the billiards operation. Conventional segment margin statements cannot capture the interactive effects of such actions.

The message of this discussion is that responsibility center income statements have to be interpreted with considerable caution and healthy skepticism. Responsibility center income statements may include arbitrary and questionable revenue and cost allocations and often disguise interrelationships among the responsibility centers.

Negotiated Transfer Prices

In the absence of market prices, some organizations allow supplying and receiving responsibility centers to negotiate transfer prices between themselves. Negotiated transfer prices reflect the controllability perspective inherent in responsibility centers since each division is ultimately responsible for the transfer price that it negotiates. Negotiated transfer prices, and therefore production decisions, however, may reflect the relative negotiating skills of the two parties rather than economic considerations.

Net realizable value
The difference between a transferred product's selling price and the additional costs needed to put it in the customer's hands.

In an economic sense, the optimal transfer price results when the purchasing unit offers to pay the net realizable value of the last unit supplied for all the units supplied. The **net realizable value** of a unit of transferred material is the selling price of the product less all the costs that remain to prepare the final product for sale. If the supplying unit is acting optimally, it chooses to supply units until its marginal cost equals the transfer price offered by the purchasing unit. This leads to the optimal quantity of the transferred units being supplied. Appendix 12-1 presents an example of these calculations and the determination of the optimal quantity to transfer.

Problems arise when negotiating transfer prices because this type of bilateral bargaining situation causes the supplying division to want a price that is higher than the optimal price and the receiving division to want a price that is lower than the optimal price. When the actual transfer price is different from the optimal transfer price, the organization as a whole suffers because it transfers a smaller than optimal number of units between the two divisions.

Administered Transfer Prices

An arbitrator or a manager who applies some policy sets administered transfer prices, for example, market price less 10% or full cost plus 5%. Organizations often use administered transfer prices when a particular transaction occurs frequently. However, such prices reflect neither pure economic considerations, as market-based or cost-based transfer prices do, nor accountability considerations, as negotiated transfer prices do.

Exhibit 12-12 summarizes the four major approaches to transfer pricing.

EXHIBIT 12-12
Summary of Transfer Pricing Approaches

	Market-Based	Cost-Based	Negotiated	Administered
Measure Used	Market Price	Product Cost	Direct Negotiations	Application of a Rule
Advantage	If a market price exists, it is objective and provides the proper economic incentives.	This is usually easy to put in place because cost measures are often already available in the accounting system.	This reflects the accountability and controllability principles underlying responsibility centers.	This is simple to use and avoids confrontations between the two parties to the transfer-pricing relationship.
Problems	There may be no market or it may be difficult to identify the proper market price because the product is difficult to classify.	There are many cost possibilities and any costs other than the marginal cost will not provide the proper economic signal.	This can lead to decisions that do not provide the greatest economic benefits.	This tends to violate the spirit of the responsibility approach.

Returning to the example of Earl's Motors, Earl may decree that the transfer price for body shop work done for the new and used car departments will be charged out at 80% of the normal market rate. This may seem reasonable and may reflect a practical approach to dealing with the issues associated with market-based and cost-based transfer prices. But this rule is arbitrary and, therefore, provides an arbitrary distribution of revenues and costs between the body shop and the units with which it deals. Administered transfer prices inevitably create subsidies among responsibility centers. Subsidies obscure the normal economic interpretation of responsibility center income and may provide a negative motivational effect if members of some responsibility center believe that the application of such rules is unfair.

TRANSFER PRICES BASED ON EQUITY CONSIDERATIONS. Administrative transfer prices are usually based on cost, that is, the transfer price is cost plus some markup on cost or market. This means that the transfer price is some function, for example, 80%, of the market price. However, sometimes administrative transfer prices are based on equity considerations that invariably are designed around some definition of a reasonable division of a jointly earned revenue or a jointly incurred cost.

For example, consider a situation where three responsibility center managers need warehouse space. Each manager has undertaken a study to determine the cost for an individual warehouse that meets the responsibility center's needs. The costs are as follows: manager A—$3,000,000; manager B—$6,000,000; and manager C—$5,000,000. A developer has proposed that the managers combine their needs into a single large warehouse, which would cost $11,000,000. This represents a $3,000,000 savings from the total cost of $14,000,000 if each manager were to build a separate warehouse. The issue is how the managers should split the cost of this warehouse.

One alternative, sometimes called the relative cost method, is for each manager to bear a share of the warehouse cost that is proportional to that manager's alternative opportunity. This would result in the following cost allocations:

$$\textit{Manager A's Share} = \$11,000,000 \times \frac{\$3,000,000}{\$14,000,000} = \$2,357,143$$

$$\textit{Manager B's Share} = \$11,000,000 \times \frac{\$6,000,000}{\$14,000,000} = \$4,714,286$$

$$\textit{Manager C's Share} = \$11,000,000 \times \frac{\$5,000,000}{\$14,000,000} = \$3,928,571$$

This is fair in the sense of being symmetrical. All parties are treated equally and each allocation reflects what each individual faces. Another approach, which reflects the equity criterion of ability to pay, is to base the allocation of cost on the profits that each manager derives from using the warehouse. Still another approach, which reflects the equity criterion of equal division, is to assign each manager a one-third share of the warehouse cost. Thus, each of the many different approaches to cost allocation reflects a particular view of equity.

ASSIGNING AND VALUING ASSETS IN INVESTMENT CENTERS

When companies use investment centers to evaluate responsibility center performance, there are all the problems associated with profit centers[11] plus some new problems that are unique to investment centers. The additional problems associated with investment centers concern how to identify and value the assets used by each investment center. This presents troubling questions that have no clear answers.

Many organizations follow a pattern of providing their distribution channels with huge quantities of materials that represent a two- or three-month supply. This practice, known as trade-loading, creates huge warehousing and inventory holding costs as well as increases the level of productive capacity the organization needs. *Courtesy* Henry Horenstein/Stock, Boston

---

[11] These problems relate to allocating jointly earned revenues and jointly incurred costs to each profit center.

In determining the level of assets a responsibility center uses, the management accountant must assign the responsibility for (1) jointly used assets, such as cash, buildings, and equipment, and (2) jointly created assets, such as accounts receivable. Once the decision makers have assigned the organization's assets to investment centers, they must determine the value of those assets. What cost should be used—historical cost, net book value, replacement cost, or net realizable value? These are all costing alternatives for which supporting arguments can be made. (See advanced cost accounting texts.)

The culmination of the allocation of revenues, costs, and assets to operating divisions is the calculation of the division's return on investment. To consider this, we return to the Dupont Company, one of the earliest and most prolific users of the return-on-investment criterion.

*E*FFICIENCY AND PRODUCTIVITY ELEMENTS OF RETURN ON INVESTMENT

Referring back to the discussion in Chapter 1 about the Dupont Company, recall that one of Dupont's major challenges was to develop the means to manage the complex structure caused by its diverse activities and operations. In the early 20th century, most organizations were single-product activity operations. These organizations approached the evaluation of the investment level of the organization by considering the ratio of profits to sales and the percent of capacity used. Dupont, however, being a multiproduct firm, pioneered the systematic use of return on investment to evaluate the profitability of its different lines of business. Dupont's approach to financial control is summarized in Exhibit 12-13. At Dupont, the actual exhibit used to summarize operations was extremely detailed and contained 350 large charts that were updated monthly and permanently displayed in a large chart room in the headquarters building.

Recall from Chapter 1 that return on investment (ROI) is the ratio of operating income to investment. The Dupont system of financial control focuses on return on investment and breaks that measure into two components: a return measure that assesses efficiency and a turnover measure that assesses productivity. The following equation illustrates this idea:

$$Return\ on\ Investment = \frac{Operating\ Income}{Investment} = \frac{Operating\ Income}{Sales} \times \frac{Sales}{Investment}$$

Alternatively, we can compute return on investment in two other ways.

$$Return\ on\ Investment = Return\ on\ Sales \times Asset\ Turnover$$
$$Return\ on\ Investment = Efficiency \times Productivity$$

The ratio of operating income to sales (also called return on sales, or sales margin) is a measure of efficiency: the ability to control costs at a given level of sales activity. The ratio of sales to investment (often called asset turnover) is a measure of productivity: the ability to generate sales for a given level of investment.

The Dupont approach to financial control develops increasingly more detailed sub-components for the efficiency and productivity measures by focusing on more detailed calculations of costs and different groups of assets. The upper portion of Exhibit 12-13 shows the efficiency measure factored into its components,

> **OBJECTIVE 12.6**
>
> Understand the use of return on investment and economic value added as financial control tools.

EXHIBIT 12-13
The Dupont Return on Investment Control System

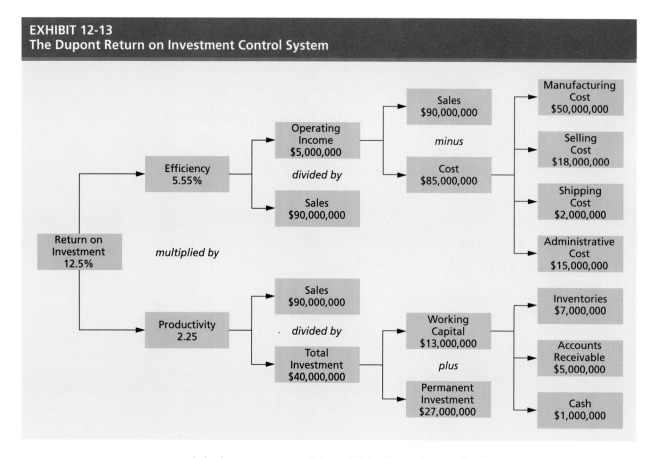

and the lower portion of the exhibit shows the productivity measure factored into its components. For example, by looking at the efficiency ratio of operating income to sales, we can examine the various components of costs (manufacturing, selling, shipping, and administrative), their relationship to sales, and their individual trends to determine whether each is improving. Then it is possible to compare these individual and group efficiency measures to those of similar organization units or to competitors to suggest where to make improvements.

The productivity ratio of sales to investment allows development of separate turnover measures for the key items of investment: inventories, accounts receivable, cash—the elements of working capital—and the elements of permanent investment, such as equipment and buildings. Comparisons of these turnover ratios with those of similar units or those of competitors can suggest where improvements are required.

We now turn to consider the two elements of return on investment. First we will discuss efficiency and then we will discuss productivity, which is one of the most interesting and widely used applications of financial control.

Assessing Organization Efficiency Using Financial Control

Most accounting approaches to assessing efficiency stress comparing costs to some standard. For example, if a standard cost is $10 and the actual cost is $12, the efficiency measure is standard cost divided by actual cost or, in this case, 83.3%. In this particular approach, the benchmark efficiency measure is 100%. An efficiency measure below 100% implies inefficient operations, while a measure above 100% implies efficient operations.

$$\text{Operations Efficiency} = \frac{\text{Standard Cost}}{\text{Actual Cost}}$$

Assessing Productivity Using Financial Control

The most widely accepted definition of productivity is the ratio of output over input. For example, if a worker produces 50 items in a seven-hour shift, the worker's productivity (often called labor productivity) is 7.1 units per hour. Industries that are very labor intensive, that is, where labor costs are a big fraction of total costs, monitor their labor productivity closely.

Organizations develop productivity measures for all factors of production, including people, raw materials, and equipment. For example, in the fishing industry, the ratio of weight of salable final products to the weight of the raw fish is typically about 30%. This ratio of raw material in the finished product to the total quantity of raw material acquired is called raw material productivity or yield. Most organizations in the natural resource industry keep a very close watch on raw material productivity because the cost of acquiring raw materials is such a large proportion of total costs. For example, Weirton Steel, a U.S. steel products manufacturer, estimates that each percentage point increase in its raw material yield is equivalent to a $4.7 million decrease in operating costs. This gives a practical example of how organizations can use a financial control number, like raw material yield, to make inferences about how well the underlying manufacturing operations are working.

Finally, many organizations in continuous-process industries, such as paper manufacturing, monitor their machine productivity ratios (output per hour or per shift of machine time). Investment in the machine represents a huge fixed cost invested in capacity, and profitability depends on how well that capacity is used.[13] Again, a measure like machine productivity provides organizations with an effective method to relate process results and financial results.

ASSESSING RETURN ON INVESTMENT

Using Ratio Trends

Trend analysis and cross-sectional analysis[14] provide useful insights for assessing return on investment. Consider the operations of Dorchester Manufacturing,

---

[13] Note that the numerator in all the productivity measures noted above is in physical unit terms, for example, kilograms or units. Some organizations prefer to use the sales value of the output as the numerator in the productivity ratio. This is particularly important when numerator input (such as labor) can affect the quality of the output, and, therefore, its net realizable value. For example, it does not take any talent to turn a side of beef into hamburger. Similarly, any machine operator can turn out products that are marred and have to be downgraded and sold as seconds or discarded. It takes someone with skill and knowledge to maximize the yield of high-value products.

[14] Trend analysis compares sequential measures for the same organization, for example, comparing this year's productivity measure with last year's. Cross-sectional analysis compares the same measure for different organizations during the same time period, for example, comparing company A's productivity measure with company B's.

which makes custom windows for the residential construction industry. Dorchester Manufacturing's most recent balance sheet and income statement appear in Exhibits 12-14 and 12-15.

The first decision to make when applying the return on investment approach to financial control is to determine how to define investment. This example measures investment as total assets employed net of accumulated depreciation.[15] With this assumption, and using the previous equation for calculating ROI, the return on investment for Dorchester Manufacturing is computed as follows:

$$Return\ on\ Investment\ =\ \frac{Operating\ Income}{Investment}\ =\ \frac{Operating\ Income}{Sales}\ \times\ \frac{Sales}{Investment}$$

$$Return\ on\ Investment\ =\ \frac{\$5,000,000}{\$40,000,000}\ =\ \frac{\$5,000,000}{\$90,000,000}\ \times\ \frac{\$90,000,000}{\$40,000,000}$$

$$Return\ on\ Investment\ =\ 0.0556\ \times\ 2.25\ =\ 12.5\%$$

EXHIBIT 12-14
Dorchester Manufacturing
Balance Sheet

Cash	$ 1,000,000	Accounts payable	$ 2,000,000
Accounts receivable	5,000,000	Other liabilities	1,000,000
Inventory	7,000,000	Long-term debt	7,000,000
Plant and equipment (net)	27,000,000	Shareholders' equity	30,000,000
Total	$40,000,000	Total	$40,000,000

EXHIBIT 12-15
Dorchester Manufacturing
Income Statement

Sales		$90,000,000
Less cost of goods sold:		
Materials and supplies	$25,000,000	
Labor	10,000,000	
Overhead	15,000,000	50,000,000
Gross margin		$40,000,000
Selling expenses	$20,000,000	
Administrative expenses	10,000,000	
Taxes	5,000,000	35,000,000
Net income		$5,000,000

[15] Other commonly used approaches to measure the investment level are total assets at historical cost, total assets at replacement cost, total assets at net realizable value, and shareholders' equity.

Time Series Comparisons

Dorchester Manufacturing earned a return of 12.5% on the net book value of its assets invested. This equals net income of 5.5% of sales multiplied by the 2.25 sales to total assets ratio. It is possible to evaluate trends for these numbers and to compare them with other organizations as shown in Exhibit 12-16. This form of financial benchmarking is common since decomposing an ROI number into its components and evaluating the trend of these components and the performance of competitors provides additional insight about recent performance.[16]

Cross-Sectional Comparisons

The top two lines of Exhibit 12-16 show that Dorchester Manufacturing is earning a lower return on investment than its competitor. The efficiency and productivity portions of the exhibit explain why. The middle portion of Exhibit 12-16 shows that the efficiency of operations (return on sales) at Dorchester Manufacturing is declining while the competitor's efficiency is improving continuously. The bottom portion of the exhibit shows that Dorchester's productivity (asset turnover) is also lower than its competitor's.

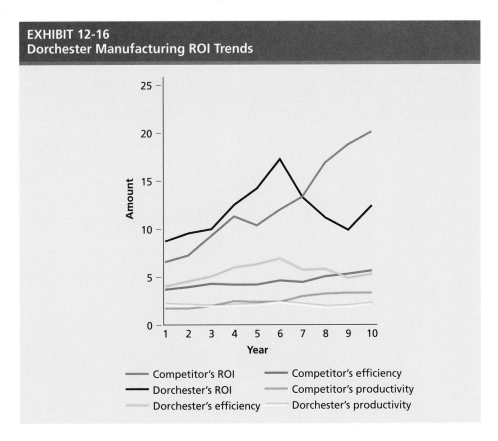

EXHIBIT 12-16
Dorchester Manufacturing ROI Trends

---

[16] Tracking trends and comparing performance to that of a competitor increases the ability of a financial number, or index, to identify an underlying problem.

It is possible to further examine the efficiency and turnover ratios by decomposing them into their individual components. Exhibit 12-17 summarizes the individual components of costs as a cumulative percent of sales for Dorchester Manufacturing and shows a comparison of these numbers to those of its best competitor.

The bar chart for Dorchester Manufacturing shows that materials, labor, overhead, selling, and administrative costs are approximately 28%, 11%, 17%, 22%, and 11% of sales, respectively, and approximately 30%, 9%, 14%, 20%, and 8%, respectively, compared with the best competitor. These figures suggest that labor, overhead, selling, and administrative costs in total are too high at Dorchester Manufacturing relative to the competitor's costs and that it may be advisable for Dorchester to conduct an investigation to determine why these differences exist.

Exhibit 12-18 summarizes the ratios of sales to assets, the productivity contribution to the return on investment, for individual asset accounts and compares these ratios to those of Dorchester's best competitor. It shows that the ratios of sales to cash and sales to inventory are, respectively, about 90 and 15 for Dorchester Manufacturing and about 100 and 55 for the best competitor. This comparison suggests that, given its level of sales, Dorchester Manufacturing holds too much cash and inventory compared with its competitor. Perhaps the competitor is using just-in-time production to reduce costs, reduce the investment in inventory, improve quality, and increase return on investment. This is an important manufacturing strategy that Dorchester Manufacturing can consider.

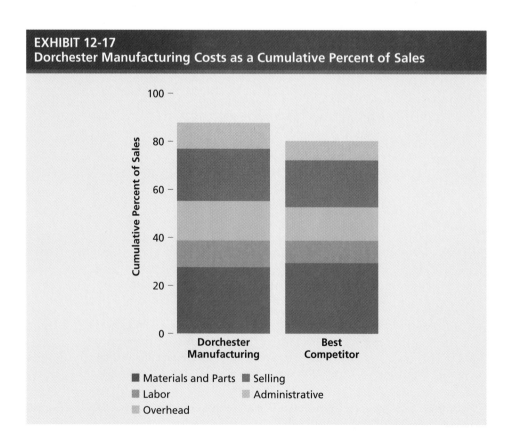

EXHIBIT 12-17
Dorchester Manufacturing Costs as a Cumulative Percent of Sales

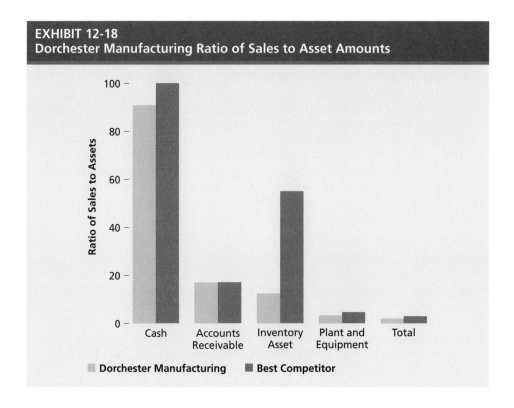

EXHIBIT 12-18
Dorchester Manufacturing Ratio of Sales to Asset Amounts

This discussion illustrates two important attributes of the Dupont method of financial control. First, these measures are most useful when evaluating trends and when comparing the numbers with those of the best competitor.[17] Second, these comparisons do not identify the problem or how to solve it. Rather, they are signals suggesting where to look for a problem.

For most organizations, a major portion of the investment number used to compute return on investment is the commitment made for long-term capacity.[18] Therefore, it is important to recognize that the return on investment criterion is an evaluation of the desirability of a long-term investment rather than a measure of the short-term performance of the manager of a facility.

To see this, consider the plight of a manager who is employed by an organization that owns a chain of fast-food restaurants. The manager has been asked to manage a restaurant located in an area that is turning from residential to commercial and industrial. Because of the lack of a residential base to support sales, the restaurant faces declining sales prospects. As a result, the restaurant's return on investment will be low, indicating that it is a marginal investment and a candidate

---

[17] Recall from Chapter 2 that benchmarking is used to identify best practices in any organization, regardless of whether the organization identified as best at doing something is in the same line of business. Financial information is usually used differently. In comparing financial results, which we might call financial benchmarking, it is necessary to make direct aggregate comparisons between competitors in order to rank them. Unlike conventional benchmarking, there is no intent in financial benchmarking to identify and adapt best practices.

[18] The other significant investment in most organizations is inventory, which reflects the nature of the process the organization uses to make products. In this sense, inventory is a long-term investment because the inventory investment level usually changes only when the production process itself changes.

for liquidation if the property has other uses. A good manager may mitigate or slow the decline of return on investment by organizing innovative promotions to attract business customers at lunch time. In such a case, the manager may do an outstanding job given the circumstances even while the restaurant shows a return on investment below the company's cost of capital.

To evaluate a manager's performance, we must compare actual performance to the performance potential inherent in the circumstances. The desirability of an investment is a different matter, however. An investment may be liquidated because of its declining potential even though a manager has been doing an outstanding job delaying the decline. Therefore, performance evaluation is relative to the potential and circumstances of the setting. The return on investment evaluation is relative to other investment opportunities.

Questioning the Return on Investment Approach

Despite its relative popularity, many people have criticized using return on investment as a means of financial control. Some critics object to the sole use of any financial measures as being too narrow for effective control. They argue that the most effective approach to control is to monitor and assess the organization's critical success factors, such as quality, service, and employee skills and knowledge.

Others who accept the need for financial measures still find weaknesses with the return on investment measure. They observe that profit-seeking organizations should make investments in order of declining profitability until the marginal cost of capital of the last dollar invested equals the marginal return generated by that dollar. Unfortunately, financial control based on return on investment may not yield this result.

For example, consider a manager who is evaluated based on return on investment. Suppose that the current return on investment is 15% and the manager is contemplating an investment that is expected to return 12%. The manager would be motivated to decline this investment opportunity because accepting it would lower the division's total return on investment. This may conflict with what is in the organization's best interests. For example, if the organization's cost of capital were only 10%, the manager should accept the investment because its expected return exceeds the investment's cost of capital.

Using Economic Value Added

Economic value added
Evaluates a product line's financial desirability using its residual income.

People have responded to this criticism of return on investment by creating a different investment criterion. **Economic value added,**[19] previously called residual income, equals income less the economic cost of the investment used to generate that income. For example, if a division's income is $13,500,000 and the division uses $100,000,000 of capital, which has an average cost of 10%, the economic value added can be computed as follows:

[19] The definitive reference for economic value added is G. Bennett Steward III, *The Quest for Value*, Harper-Collins Publishers Inc., 1991.

$$Economic\ Value\ Added\ =\ Income\ -\ Cost\ of\ Capital$$
$$=\ \$13,500,000\ -\ (\$100,000,000\ \times\ 10\%)$$
$$=\ \$3,500,000$$

Like return on investment, economic value added evaluates income relative to the level of investment required to earn that income. Unlike return on investment, however, economic value added does not motivate managers to turn down investments that are expected to earn more than their cost of capital. Under the economic value added criterion, managers are asked to do whatever they think is necessary to make economic value added as large as possible.

For example, return to the example of the manager who is facing an investment opportunity with an expected return of 12% when the cost of capital is 10%. If the project requires an investment of $100,000,000, the economic value added if the investment is made and the expected return is realized is $2,000,000 [$100,000,000 × (12% − 10%)]. Therefore, if the manager is rewarded based on economic value added, the manager will accept this investment opportunity.[20]

ORGANIZATIONS ADOPT ECONOMIC VALUE ADDED FOR DIFFERENT REASONS. SPX Corporation supplies specialty service tools and original equipment components to the automotive industry. In its 1995 Annual Report SPX identified the following reasons for adopting shareholder value analysis:
"SPX adopted EVA because it:

- treats the interests of shareholders and management the same, encouraging SPX people to think and act like owners
- is easily understood and applied
- fits into operational improvement efforts, because success requires continuous improvement of EVA
- correlates closer to market value than any other operating performance measure
- links directly to investor expectations through EVA improvement targets
- focuses on long-term performance by using a bonus bank and predetermined improvement targets
- provides a common language for performance measurement, decision support, compensation and communication."

The notion of a bonus bank, mentioned in the sixth point above, is particularly interesting. In years when performance exceeds the economic value added target, two-thirds of all bonuses are set aside in a bonus bank that is carried forward and is only payable if the manager achieves economic value added targets in subsequent years. When performance falls below target, the bonus is negative and

---

[20] It might occur to you that there is a problem here because the actual return from the investment will only be realized in the future. Therefore, using economic value added as a criterion to provide rewards based on future realizations may promote lying about what the manager's expectations are when the investment is made. This deep problem is called the moral hazard problem and is beyond the scope of this text. However, as a practical matter, many organizations tie rewards to the organization's market value added, which is determined by the value of the organization's shares and which, as we will see below, is directly related to economic value added.

CONSIDER THIS . . .

Economic Value Added at Coca-Cola

In the late 1980s Coca-Cola applied economic value added to its product lines. The analysis suggested that many of Coca-Cola's product lines were unprofitable. As a result, Coca-Cola decided to refocus its attention on its soft-drink business and eliminated investments in many other businesses, including pasta and wine.

is deducted from the bonus bank. The bonus bank turns what is nominally a short run performance measure and reward into a longer run measure.

It is possible to compute the economic value added for every major product or product line to evaluate a product line's contribution to creating shareholder wealth. Recently, economic value added has been extended to adjust GAAP income to correct for the conservative approach that GAAP uses to determine income and value assets.[21]

For example, GAAP requires the immediate expensing of research and development costs; yet, in computing shareholder value analysis income, research and development costs are capitalized and expensed over a certain time period, such as five years. The intent of the adjustments[22] prescribed to compute shareholder-value-added income from GAAP income is to develop an income number that better reflects the organization's long-run earnings potential.

Organizations are beginning to use economic value added to identify products or product lines that are not contributing their share to organization return given the level of investment they require. An organization can use economic value added to make strategic decisions about its product lines. Organizations that are using economic value added have used activity based costing analysis to identify activities and assets with individual products or product lines to assign assets and costs to individual products, services, or customers. This allows the calculation of economic value added by product, product line, or customer.

Organizations can also use economic value added to evaluate operating strategies. Quaker Oats Company, a food manufacturer, used economic value added to support its decision in June 1992 to cease trade loading, which is the food industry's practice of using promotions to obtain orders for two or three months' supply of food from customers. Trade loading produces quarterly peaks in production and sales that, in turn, require huge investments in assets, including the inventory itself, warehouses, and distribution centers. Customers pay for the higher costs caused by the higher inventory levels created by this cyclical pattern of inventory through higher prices. An article[23] in *Fortune* estimated that trade loading is primarily responsible for the $75 to $100 billion in groceries that are in transit between manufacturers and consumers and that supporting this inventory "adds some $20 billion to the $400 billion that Americans annually spend on groceries."

Quaker Oats' economic value added analysis suggests that even though sales levels may be lower by not offering the price reductions associated with trade loading, it is more profitable for Quaker Oats and its trading partners to eliminate these large inventories and the related required warehouse space. Also, to produce

[21] See, for example, G. Bennett Stewart III, "EVA: Fact or Fancy," *Journal of Applied Corporate Finance*, Summer, 1994.

[22] Other recommended adjustments include adding back to income the increase in the bad debt and LIFO reserves, adding back to income the goodwill amortization, and adjusting the tax expense to eliminate the effect of deferred taxes on income.

[23] Patricia Sellers, "The Dumbest Marketing Ploy," *Fortune*, October 5, 1992, pp. 88–94.

food at even levels rather than in peaks reduces the level of production capacity needed. Quaker Oats motivates managers to end trade loading by basing bonuses on efficiency and cycle times rather than on annual sales.

A measure of the increasing importance of economic value added in organizations is the seniority of people who are usually appointed to manage economic valued added implementation projects in organizations. For example, in 1995, Olin Corporation's new president and chief executive officer was heading the company's economic value added steering team at the time of his appointment.

The results of economic value added suggest interesting insights into financial control applied at all levels of the organization. However, they should be treated with caution. As with return on investment calculations, economic value added analysis requires complex allocations of assets, revenues, and costs to divisions, product lines, products, or customers, depending on the focus of the analysis, for it to be an effective motivational and evaluation tool. However, many organizations believe that these problems can be solved and that the insights provided by economic value added analysis are well worth the effort.[24]

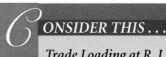

CONSIDER THIS...

Trade Loading at R. J. Reynolds

Although most organizations recognize the cost savings that come with eliminating trade loading, many hesitate to eliminate the practice because sales, and therefore profits, will be depressed while waiting for the glut of inventory to be cleared from the system. For example, R. J. Reynolds saw earnings fall $360 million in the year after its eliminated trade loading because production and sales were curtailed while billions of cigarettes were eliminated from the distribution system. Eliminating the excess inventory is now saving R. J. Reynolds about $50 million a year in inventory-holding costs. Meanwhile, Philip Morris, one of R. J. Reynolds' main competitors, continues to trade load.

THE EFFICACY OF FINANCIAL CONTROL

OBJECTIVE 12.7

Identify the limitations of using financial controls.

Although financial control is widely practiced, many people have questioned its true insights and effectiveness. Critics have argued that financial information is delayed—highly aggregated—information about how well the organization is doing in meeting its commitments to its shareholders and that this information measures neither the drivers of the financial results nor how well the organization is doing in meeting its stakeholders' requirements—a leading indicator of future financial performance.

Financial control may be an ineffective control scorecard for three reasons. First, financial control focuses on financial measures that do not measure the organization's other important attributes, such as product quality, the speed at which the organization develops and makes products, customer service, the ability to provide a work environment that motivates employees, and the degree to which the organization meets its legal and social obligations to society. Because these facets and others are important to the organization's long-term success, they also deserve to be measured and monitored. The argument is that financial control measures only the aggregated results of how the organization achieved its target financial performance. This limitation of financial control led to the development of the balanced scorecard, which we discussed in Chapter 11.

[24] The December 11, 1995 issue of *Fortune* magazine included several articles describing the nature of economic value added analysis and named some of the organizations where it has been applied. Included among the avid users of economic value added analysis are AT&T, Eli Lilly, Georgia-Pacific, and Tenneco.

CONSIDER THIS . . .

Financial Control at Ford Motor Corporation

In the 1940s, Ford Motor Corporation was in big trouble as profits and sales were both falling. In response to this crisis, Ford hired Charles Tex Thornton and a group of 10 people that came to be known as Thornton's whiz kids. The whiz kids revolutionized management at Ford and replaced the autocratic secretive management style at Ford with a disciplined system of financial controls. At the heart of this philosophy was the belief that organizations could and should be controlled by financial numbers and that a detailed knowledge of markets and operations was unnecessary for control.

For many years, these controls worked well and Ford's fortunes improved. Financial control was hailed as a success and Ford's savior. However during the 1970s and 1980s, Ford's fortunes, as well as those of the other big three North American automobile manufacturers, sagged under relentless pressure from Japanese competitors. Many experts attributed the inability of Ford and the North American manufacturers to respond to the competitive pressures presented by the Japanese to their preoccupation with financial control and a lack of a basic understanding of or monitoring of the manufacturing and distribution processes that create financial results.

Second, financial control measures the financial effect of the overall level of performance achieved on the critical success factors[25] and ignores the performance achieved on the individual critical success factors. For this reason, many people believe that financial control does not suggest how to improve either performance on the critical success factors or financial performance. Critics argue that at best financial results only act as a broad signal of how well the organization manages the tasks that create success on the critical success factors that, in turn, create financial returns. The argument is that effective control begins with measuring and managing the elements or processes that create financial returns, rather than measuring the financial returns themselves. This is a problem that the balanced scorecard addresses by focusing on both financial results (such as return on investment) and measures of process performance (such as employee skills, knowledge, and satisfaction; customer satisfaction; cycle times; the rate of process improvement and innovation; and quality that create the financial results).

Third, financial control is usually oriented to short-term profit performance. It seldom focuses on long-term improvement or trend analysis but instead considers how well the organization, or one of its responsibility centers, has performed this quarter or this year. This is the result of the misuse of financial control rather than an inherent fault of financial control itself. The preoccupation with short-term financial results is debilitating, however. It motivates an atmosphere of managing short-term financial results that provides disincentives for the types of management and employee initiatives that promote long-term success, particularly in the area of investing in training, equipment, and process changes. One of the major reasons given for taking public organizations private is to provide senior management with the opportunity to manage for long-term results rather than being inappropriately concerned with short-term performance.

In summary, how should we interpret these facets of financial control? Financial control is an important tool in the process of control. If used properly,

---

[25] The organization's critical success factors are its secondary objectives, which we discussed in Chapter 11.

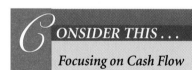

CONSIDER THIS . . .

Financial Versus Operations Control

Consider the following statement by Tom Peters, the management consultant, expressing his views on the efficacy of financial control. This is an articulate presentation of the case some people advance against financial control.

"What do you think of EVA as a barometer of business performance?" asked a participant at a recent seminar in the Netherlands. "Not much," I replied. I'm no expert on the pluses and minuses of Economic Value Added. I admitted as much, and then confessed that neither was I that keen on earnings per share or return on investment.

Sure, I understand the importance of profitability, in my business as well as in others,' and debate over various measures has merit. It is just that they mostly put the cart before the horse.

The horse is what you make. The financial measure—important as that is—is a derivative of the goodness and acceptance of the product.

Source: Tom Peters, "Legacies With Value Added," *The Independent*, February 5, 1995, p. 10.

financial results provide crucial help in assessing the organization's long-term viability and in identifying processes that need improvement. It is a tool to be supported by other tools since it is only a summary of performance.

Financial control does not try to measure other facets of performance that may be critical to the organization's stakeholders and vital to the organization's long-term success. It can, however, provide an overall assessment of whether the organization's strategies and decisions are providing acceptable financial returns. Organizations can also use financial control to compare one unit's results with another. This financial benchmarking signal indicates whether the organization's operations control systems, which seek to monitor, assess, and improve performance on the critical success factors, are operating well enough to deliver the desired financial results.

THE UNITED STATES POSTAL SERVICE REVISITED

Having studied the nature and scope of financial control, we can return to the United States Postal Service and consider why management introduced economic value added as a management tool.

The United States Postal Service wants to improve labor productivity. The economic value added metric helps evaluate spending proposals for new capital and identify the profitability of different operations or products, thereby targeting operations or products for improvements. Used in this way, shareholder value analysis serves as a warning signal that identifies products that require improvement or

CONSIDER THIS . . .

Focusing on Cash Flow

Mike Maskall, director of international tax services at Price Waterhouse, feels that institutional investors do not trust earnings numbers because despite GAAP they can be easily manipulated.

Instead, Mr. Maskall and his colleagues argue that financial control should focus on cash flow (which they feel cannot be as easily manipulated as GAAP income) and have identified what they feel are the seven key drivers of cash flow: sales growth, operating profit margin, cash tax rate, working capital, fixed assets, cost of capital, and the length of the growth period. The idea is to measure performance on these seven elements and benchmark them against competitors or best-in-class performers.

Source: Simon Caulkin, *The Observer*, March 5, 1995, p. 9.

termination. Also, it motivates managers to invest in and manage their assets so that the benefits from using the assets exceed the United States Postal Service's cost of capital. All operating units are to be charged a 12% cost of capital. Given that the United States Postal Service employs almost $15 billion in capital assets, this means that it must earn an income of at least $180 million to cover its capital costs.

SUMMARY

We began this chapter by reviewing the motivation that drives organizations to decentralize decision-making responsibility. Decentralized decision makers create the need for control, and one approach to control is financial control.

The foundation of financial control is the concept of a responsibility center, an organization unit assigned the responsibility to achieve specified financial results. Organizations classify and evaluate their responsibility based on the presumed control that their members exercise over cost, revenues, profits, and return on investment.

A major tool used in financial control is the segment margin report, which computes responsibility center profit. The segment margin provides insights into the financial contribution or loss attributable to a particular responsibility center. Because of the assumptions that underlie this report, particularly relating to cost and revenue allocations, its calculation must be carefully done and should include an understanding of the potential for distortion caused by any arbitrary allocations used to compute the responsibility center's profits.

Transfer pricing is an important tool used to allocate revenues to responsibility centers. Transfer prices can be based on market prices, costs, or negotiation, or they can be set administratively.

Return on investment is a widely used tool in financial control and, when used properly, can provide insights into the profitability of invested assets. Economic value added is an alternative to financial control that overcomes some problems associated with the return on investment criterion.

In summary, the chapter argues that financial control is an important component of control to use with other control tools that monitor and assess the organization's performance on its critical success factors.

KEY TERMS

centralized, p. 550

controllability principle, p. 564

cost centers, p. 555

decentralized, p. 550

economic value added (residual income) p. 586

financial control, p. 552

flexible budget, p. 558

investment center, p. 563

net realizable value, p. 576

operations control, p. 552

profit center, p. 562

responsibility center, p. 553

revenue center, p. 561

segment margin, p. 567

transfer pricing, p. 569

APPENDIX 12-1

Finding the Optimal Quantity to Transfer

Suppose that the cost function for the supplying division in a transfer pricing situation can be approximated as this formula, where x is the number of units made and transferred to the receiving division:

$$\text{Total Cost in Supplying Division} = \$250,000 + 20x - 0.0001x^2$$

The marginal cost of the supplying division is found by taking the derivative of its total cost function with respect to x and equals:

$$\text{Marginal Cost in Supplying Division} = 20 - 0.0002x$$

Note that the marginal cost in the supplying division decreases as x increases. This means that a cost-based transfer price will create negative profits for the supplying division.

Suppose that the receiving division has committed costs of $200,000 and incurs $48 cost per unit to sell the product into a market where the price per unit is:

$$\text{Market Price} = \$100 - 0.0005x$$

Therefore, the net revenue equation for the receiving division is:

$$
\begin{aligned}
\text{Net Revenue of Receiving Division} &= (\text{Price} \times \text{Quantity}) - \text{Costs} \\
&= (\$100 - 0.0005x)x - \$200,000 - \$48x \\
&= (\$52 - 0.0005x)x - \$200,000
\end{aligned}
$$

The net realizable value for a unit that is transferred into the receiving division is found by taking the derivative of the receiving division's net revenue equation with respect to x and equals:

$$\text{Net Realizable Value of Unit } x = 52 - 0.001x$$

The optimal quantity is found when the marginal cost of the supplying division equals the net realizable value in the receiving division:

$$
\begin{aligned}
20 - 0.0002x &= 52 - 0.001x \\
0.0008x &= 32 \\
x &= 40,000 \text{ units}
\end{aligned}
$$

Therefore, the optimal quantity is 40,000 units. We can find the optimal transfer price by substituting 40,000 in either the marginal cost equation of the supplying division or the net realizable value equation of the receiving division.

$$\text{Transfer Price} = \$20 - (0.0002 \times 40000) = \$12$$

$$\text{Transfer Price} = \$52 - (0.001 \times 40000) = \$12$$

Total corporate profit is the net revenue in the receiving division less the total cost in the supplying division.

$$
\begin{aligned}
\textit{Total Corporate Profit} \; &= \; \textit{Net Realizable Revenue of Rec. Div.} \; - \; \textit{Total Cost of Supply. Div.} \\
&= \; [(\$52 \; - \; 0.0005x)x \; - \; \$200{,}000] \; - \; (\$250{,}000 \; + \; \$20x \\
&\quad - \; 0.0001x^2) \\
&= \; -0.0004x^2 \; + \; 32x \; - \; \$450{,}000
\end{aligned}
$$

Substituting 40,000 for x in this equation, we find that the maximum total corporate profit is $190,000.

    The profit reported by the supplying division equals the number of units transferred multiplied by the transfer price minus its costs:

$$
\begin{aligned}
\textit{Profit in Supplying Division} \; &= \; (\textit{Units} \; \times \; \textit{Transfer price}) \; - \; \textit{Costs} \\
&= \; (x \; \times \; \$12) \; - \; (\$250{,}000 \; + \; 20x \; - \; 0.0001x^2) \\
&= \; 0.0001x^2 \; - \; 8x \; - \; 250{,}000
\end{aligned}
$$

Substituting 40,000 for x in this equation, we find that the loss in the supplying division is $410,000.

    The profit reported by the receiving division equals its net revenue minus the number of units transferred multiplied by the transfer price:

$$
\begin{aligned}
\textit{Profit in Receiving Division} \; &= \; \textit{Net Revenue} \; - \; (\textit{Units} \; \times \; \textit{Transfer Price}) \\
&= \; [(52 \; - \; 0.0005x)x \; - \; \$200{,}000] \; - \; (x \; \times \; \$12) \\
&= \; -0.0005x^2 \; + \; 40x \; - \; \$200{,}000
\end{aligned}
$$

Substituting 40,000 for x in this equation, we find that the profit in the receiving division is $600,000.

ASSIGNMENT MATERIAL

■ QUESTIONS

12-1 What is decentralization?

12-2 What does control mean in a decentralized organization?

12-3 What is a responsibility center?

12-4 What does the controllability principle require?

12-5 How do responsibility centers interact?

12-6 What does financial control mean?

12-7 What is a cost center?

12-8 What is a flexible budget?

12-9 What is the assigned responsibility in a revenue center?

12-10 When do organizations use profit centers?

12-11 What is an investment center?

12-12 What is a contribution margin?

12-13 What does segment margin mean?

12-14 What is a transfer price?

12-15 What are the four bases for setting a transfer price?

12-16 What is a soft number in accounting?

12-17 Why must organizations allocate revenues to responsibility centers?

12-18 Why must organizations allocate costs to responsibility centers?

12-19 What is return on investment?

12-20 How does efficiency affect return on investment?

12-21 How does productivity affect return on investment?

12-22 What does economic value added mean?

12-23 What is the role of shareholder value analysis?

■ EXERCISES

12-24 *Issues in decentralization*   What control problems does decentralization create in organizations?

12-25 *University responsibility centers*   Give an example of a responsibility center in a university.

12-26 *Controllability*   Based on your understanding, which of the following—costs, revenues, profits, and investment—does the manager of a cinema control?

12-27 *Controllability and evaluation*   Suppose that you are the manager of a fitness center that is one of many in a chain. Give one example of a cost that you control and one example of cost that you do not control. Why is it important to distinguish between costs that are controllable and costs that are not controllable in this setting?

12-28 *Responsibility centers*   Identify three responsibility centers in a fast-food restaurant and explain how they may interact.

12-29 *The efficacy of financial control*   Is financial control sufficient in itself as an organization control tool? Explain.

12-30 *Cost centers*   Give an example of a responsibility center that is properly treated as a cost center.

12-31 *Master and flexible budgets*   An organization plans to make a product in batches of 25,000 units. Planned production is 1,000,000 units, and actual production is 1,125,000 units. What are the planned (master budget) number of batches and the flexible budget number of batches?

12-32 *Revenue centers*   Give an example of a responsibility center that is properly treated as a revenue center.

12-33 *Investment centers*   Based on your understanding of how they are managed, would you agree or disagree that an outlet of a large department store chain should be treated as an investment center? What about the maintenance department within that outlet? What about a single department within the store?

12-34 *Multinational companies and investment centers*   Many multinational companies create wholly owned subsidiaries to do business in the countries or regions where they operate. Are these wholly owned subsidiaries examples of investment centers? Explain.

12-35 *Computing division income*   A home services company offers renovations, heating, air conditioning, and plumbing services to its customers. Imagine that you are in the process of computing the income for the renovations division. What problems may you encounter in computing this income?

12-36 *Choosing transfer prices*   How might a transfer price be chosen for logs in an organization that cuts down trees and processes the logs in a sawmill to make lumber or in a pulp mill to make paper?

12-37 *Choosing transfer prices*   In a fishing products company, the harvesting division catches and delivers the fish to the processing division that, in turn, delivers the processed fish to the selling division to sell to customers. How can you determine the appropriate transfer price between harvesting and processing and between processing and selling?

12-38 *Soft numbers*   Why did accountants develop the expression soft number?

12-39 *Allocating costs*   A store is divided into four departments: automotive products, home products, paint, and lumber. How would you assign the building costs such as depreciation to each of these departments?

12-40 *Return on investment*   A business reports an income of $1,000,000. How would you compute the return on investment for this business?

12-41 *Single ratio values*   Give an example of why looking at a single value of a financial ratio may give either a misleading or a meaningless result.

12-42 *Characteristic financial ratios*   All organizations face a requirement to earn at least a minimum level return on investment. Some businesses rely on high ratios of income to sales; other businesses rely on high ratios of sales to investment. Give an example of each of these types of businesses and explain what this characteristic implies about the business.

12-43 *Productivity ratio*   Give an example of why using units rather than the value of the products produced in the numerator of a productivity ratio may give a misleading picture of the process that produced that output.

12-44 *Controllability and motivation*   Give an example of a situation where invoking the controllability principle would have a desirable motivational effect and an example of a situation where suspending the controllability principle would have a desirable motivational effect.

12-45 *Domestic and international transfer pricing*   Most organizations use either a transfer pricing system designed to support international transfer pricing or a domestic transfer pricing system designed to achieve motivational objectives. Give a reason why you think that organizations would not use two transfer pricing systems—one for tax purposes and one for motivational purposes.

12-46 *Using market-based transfer prices*   What is the main advantage and the main obstacle in using market-based transfer prices?

12-47 *Computing economic value added*   A business whose investors require a return on investment of 8% after taxes reports an after-tax income of $1,500,000 on an investment of $20,000,000. What is the economic value added for this business?

12-48 *Economic value added in a multi-product company*   Based on an analysis of operations, a company making sporting goods has determined that the income provided by its golf, ski, tennis, and football product lines are $3,500,000, $7,800,000, $2,600,000, and $1,700,000, respectively. The accountant believes that the investment levels in these product lines are $35,000,000, $50,000,000, $45,000,000, and $23,000,000, respectively. Use an economic value added analysis to evaluate the performance of each of these product lines, assuming that the organization requires a 10% return on investment.

■ PROBLEMS

Fundamental Problems

12-49 *Choosing responsibility center type*   For each of the following units, identify whether the most appropriate responsibility center form is a cost center, a profit center, or an investment center and why you have made that choice.

  (a) A laboratory in a hospital
  (b) A restaurant in a department store
  (c) The computer services group in an insurance company
  (d) A maintenance department in a factory
  (e) A customer service department in a mail-order company
  (f) A warehouse used to store goods for distribution in a large city

12-50 *Implementing the controllability principle*   One of the most widely accepted and longest held beliefs is the controllability principle, which says that organization units and people should be held accountable only for things that they can control.

REQUIRED

  (a) For any job you choose, give one example of something you should be expected to control and one example of something that you should not be expected to control.
  (b) Can you think of an example in which making yourself responsible for something that you cannot control would promote a desirable activity?

12-51 *Computing flexible budget variables*   For Moncton Carpet Products, analyze the flexible budget variances for products 2, 3, and 4 using an analysis similar to that used for product 1 in the text on pages 558 to 561.

12-52 *Variances and motivation*   Discuss the possible effect on human behavior of a preoccupation with variances in financial control.

12-53 *Problems in computing economic value added*   A bank is thinking of using economic value added analysis to identify services that require improvement or elimination. What problems may the bank have in computing the economic value added of any of the services that it offers to its customers?

12-54 *Allocating common costs to cost centers* You have decided to divide a factory into cost centers. How would you allocate depreciation expense on the factory building to its individual cost centers?

12-55 *Strategy and control* Many people believe that in a successful organization the focus of control reflects the strategic initiatives in the organization. For each of the following organizations, identify what you think are the three most important items assessed by the organization's financial control system and why each is important. For each organization, what critical information is not assessed by the financial control system?

(a) A company selling cable television services to its subscribers
(b) A symphony orchestra
(c) An organization selling canned soup
(d) A government agency responsible for finding jobs for its clients
(e) An auditing firm
(f) A company selling high-fashion clothing

12-56 *Evaluating the potential of economic value added* The owner of a chain of fast-food restaurants has decided to use economic value added to evaluate the performance of the managers of each of the restaurants. What do you think of this idea?

12-57 *Using economic value added* As a result of an economic value added analysis, the owner of a company that makes and installs swimming pools has decided to shut down the manufacturing operations which show a negative economic value added for the current year. Is this *necessarily* the proper response to this information?

12-58 *Transfer prices and division autonomy* You are a government controller. A division manager being audited objects to the transfer price he is being charged by the audit group for the audit services. The manager observes, "If I have to pay for these services, I should be allowed to buy them from an outside supplier who is prepared to offer them to me at a lower price." You have been asked to mediate this dispute. What would you do?

12-59 *Transfer pricing and outside opportunities* Deseronto Electronics manufactures motherboards for computers. The company is divided into two divisions—manufacturing and programming. The manufacturing division makes the board and the programming division makes the adjustments required to meet the customer's specifications.

The average total cost per unit of the boards in the manufacturing division is about $450 and the average total cost per board incurred in the programming division is about $100. The average selling price of the boards is $700. The company is now operating at capacity and increasing the volume of production is not a feasible alternative.

In the past the managers of the two divisions have negotiated a transfer price. The average transfer price has been about $500, resulting in the manufacturing division recognizing a profit of about $50 per board and the programming division recognizing a profit of about $100 per board. Each of the managers receives a bonus that is proportional to the profit reported by his division.

Karen Barton, the manager of the manufacturing division, has announced that she is no longer willing to supply boards to the programming division. Sam Draper, the senior purchasing executive for Koala Electronics, a computer manufacturer, has indicated that he is willing to purchase, at $650 per unit, all the boards that Karen's division can supply and is willing to sign a long-term contract to that effect. Karen indicated that she offered the boards to the programming division at $625 per board on the grounds that selling and distribution costs would be reduced by selling inside. Neil

Wilson, the manager of the programming division refused the offer on the grounds that the programming division would show a loss at this transfer price.

Neil has appealed Karen's intention to Shannon McDonald, the general manager, arguing that Karen should be prohibited from selling outside. Neil has indicated that a preliminary investigation suggests that he cannot buy these boards for less than about $640 outside. Therefore, allowing Karen to sell outside would effectively doom Neil's division.

REQUIRED

What should Shannon McDonald do in this situation?

12-60 *Return on investment and economic value added*   The Newburg Flyers operate a major sports franchise from a building in downtown Newburg. The building was built in 1940 at a cost of $5,000,000 and is fully depreciated so that it is shown on the company's balance sheet at a nominal value of $1. The land upon which the building was built in 1940 was purchased in 1935 for $10,000 and is valued at this amount for balance sheet purposes. The franchise, which is the company's only other major investment, cost $100,000 in 1940.

The current assessed value of the building is $200,000. The assessed value of the land, which is located in a prime urban area, is $20,000,000 and reflects the net value of the property if the current building is demolished and replaced with an office and shopping complex. The current value of the franchise, assuming that the league owners would approve a franchise sale, is $50,000,000.

REQUIRED

(a) If the team earns approximately $3,000,000 per year, what is the return on investment? (Ignore taxes in this calculation.)

(b) If the team earns approximately $3,000,000 per year, what is the economic value added? Assume that the organization's cost of capital is 15%. (Ignore taxes in this calculation.)

12-61 *Conflicting organization and individual objectives*   Strathcona Paper rewards its managers based on the return on investment of the assets that they manage—the higher the reported return on investment, the higher the reward. The company uses net book value to value the assets employed in the return on investment calculation. The company's cost of capital is assessed as 12% after taxes. The organization's tax rate is 35%.

The manager of the Logistics Division is faced with an opportunity to replace an aging truck fleet. The current net income after taxes of the logistics division is $7,000,000 and the current investment base is valued at $50,000,000. The current net income after taxes and the current investment base, absent any investment in new trucks, are expected to remain at their existing levels.

The investment opportunity would replace the existing fleet of trucks, which have a net book value of about $100,000 with new trucks costing about $50,000,000 net of the trade in allowance for the old trucks. If kept, the old trucks would last another five years and would have no salvage value. The new trucks would last five years, have zero salvage value, and increase cash flow relative to keeping the old trucks (through increased revenues and decreased operating costs) by about $16,000,000 per year. If purchased, the new trucks would be depreciated for both accounting and tax purposes on a straight-line basis.

REQUIRED

(a) From the point of view of the company, should this investment be made? Support your conclusion with relevant calculations.

(b) From the point of view of the manager, should this investment be made?

(c) If the manager was rewarded based on economic value added, would the manager want to make the investment? Show why or why not.

Challenging Problems

12-62 *Coordinating divisional activities*   For many years, automobile companies have been highly decentralized in terms of functions. The most obvious effect of this heavy decentralization of function is apparent when all the groups must work together to accomplish a goal. The highest order of integration occurs in the design of a new automobile.

Reflecting the functional decentralization of automobile manufacturers, the traditional approach to automobile design is for the marketing group to identify a concept. The design group then creates an automobile that reflects the marketing group's idea but incorporates engineering requirements and aesthetics identified by the design group. The purchasing group then identifies the parts required by the design and makes further modifications to it to incorporate parts that can be made or purchased. Finally, the manufacturing group modifies the design to reflect the nature and capabilities of the production process. This process takes up to four years and usually results in a vehicle that is far removed from the initial design.

What went wrong here? How might this process be improved?

12-63 *Organic and mechanistic organizations*   Researchers have defined two extreme forms of organizations. Organic organizations are highly decentralized with few rules. Most people agree that software development companies are very organic. Mechanistic organizations are highly centralized and use many rules to prescribe behavior. Most people agree that government agencies are very mechanistic.

Do you agree with these examples? Give your own examples of each of these types of organizations with your reason for giving the organization the chosen classification.

12-64 *Assigning responsibility for uncontrollable events*   Some people and organizations believe that the discussion of controllable and uncontrollable events is distracting in the sense that it encourages finger pointing and an excessive preoccupation with assigning blame. These observers argue that it is more important to find solutions than to identify responsibility for unacceptable or acceptable events.

REQUIRED

(a) What do you think of this argument?

(b) As an organization moves away from assessing and rewarding controllable performance, what changes would you expect to see in its organization structure?

12-65 *Fairness criteria*   See if you can find three examples of fairness criteria that have been used in the management, accounting, legal, or public regulation literatures. How are the three examples that you have found similar or different?

12-66 *Material yield*   Find an example of a reference to material yield in any type of management or business journal. Identify how the organization uses the material yield measure and why it appears to be an important measure in that organization.

12-67 *Segment margins*   Construct a segment margin statement for a hypothetical organization. Use the segment margin statement to explain why the segment margins reported for an organization unit must be interpreted carefully.

12-68 *Market value added, economic value added, and net income*   If you look through *Fortune*, you will find articles that rank organizations by market value added and economic value added. Find one such article and identify three firms: the one with the highest economic value added, the one with the highest market value added, and the one with the highest reported net income. Compare the three firms. Explain the dif-

CHAPTER 12 / FINANCIAL CONTROL **601**

ference in rankings. (In the event that the top-ranked firms by any two of these criteria are the same, do the above for the second-ranked firms.)

12-69 *Group and individual conflict* Think of an example of an organization where it is important that the various functional areas be closely coordinated to promote the organization's overall success. Show how performance measures that focus solely on the performance of an individual unit could create problems in this organization.

12-70 *Decision-making with return on investment* You are the controller of a chain of dry-cleaning establishments. You are computing the return on investment for each outlet.

Outlet A located in a city core reported a net profit of $130,000. The land on which Outlet A is located was essentially rural when it was purchased for $100,000. Since then, the city has expanded and the land is located in the population center. Comparable undeveloped land in the immediate area of the outlet is worth $2,000,000. The net book value of the outlet building and equipment is $400,000. The replacement cost of the building and equipment is $1,200,000. If the outlet building, equipment, and land were sold as a going concern, the sale price would be $1,500,000. It would cost $250,000 to demolish the building and clear the property for commercial development.

REQUIRED

(a) What is the return on this investment?
(b) How would you decide whether this outlet should continue to be operated, sold as a going concern, or demolished and the land sold?

12-71 *Choices in financial control* Bennington Home Products sells home products. It buys products for resale from suppliers all over the world. The products are organized into groups. A few examples of these groups are floor care products, kitchen products, tool products, and paper products. The company sells its products all over the world from regional offices and warehouses in every country where it operates. Because of differences in culture and taste, the product lines and products within those lines vary widely among countries.

The regional offices have administrative staff that manage the operations, do the ordering, and undertake the usual office administrative functions and a sales staff that does the selling directly to stores within that country. The regional offices are evaluated as investment centers because they have responsibility for revenues, costs, and investment levels. The regional offices make suggestions for new products.

The corporate office manages the regional offices and places the orders received from the regional offices with suppliers. The corporate office does the ordering for three reasons. First, it is believed that one ordering office eliminates duplication in ordering activities. Second, it is believed that one office ordering for all the regional offices gives the organization more power when dealing with suppliers. Third, it is believed that one office can develop the expertise to find and negotiate with suppliers of unique and innovative products.

REQUIRED

(a) Describe an appropriate system of financial control at the regional level.
(b) Describe an appropriate system of financial control at the corporate office level.
(c) Explain why the three systems of financial control should, or need not, mesh.

12-72 *New product opportunities and transfer pricing* Plevna Manufacturing makes and distributes small prefabricated homes in kits. The kits contain all the pieces needed to assemble the home—all that is required is that the builder erect the home on a foundation.

Plevna Manufacturing is organized into two divisions—the manufacturing division and the sales division. Each division is evaluated based on its reported profits. The transfer price between the manufacturing division, where the kits are made, and the selling division, which sells the kits, is variable cost plus 10%, a total of about $33,000. The selling price per kit is about $40,000 and selling and distribution costs are about $5,000 per home kit.

The total costs that do not vary in proportion with volume at Plevna Manufacturing amount to about $2,000,000 per year— $1,500,000 in manufacturing and $500,000 in the selling division. Currently the company is operating at capacity, which is dictated by the machinery in the manufacturing division. Each kit requires about 10 hours of machine time and the total available machine time is 5000 per year. Plevna Manufacturing is making and selling about 500 kits per year. Increasing the plant capacity in the foreseeable future is not a viable option.

Willie Scott is the firm's salesperson. Willie has been approached a number of times recently by people wanting to buy homes to erect on recreational properties. The cottages would be made by modifying the existing home product. The modification process would begin with a completed home kit. The manufacturing division would then incur additional materials and labor costs of $3000 and three hours of machine time to convert a home kit into a cottage kit.

Willie is proposing that the company split the sales division into two divisions—home sales and cottage sales. The new divisional structure would have no effect on existing administrative, personnel, or selling costs.

REQUIRED

Suppose that the new division is created, discuss the issues in choosing a transfer price in this situation. What transfer price for each of the two products, home and cottage kits, would you recommend and why? (If you feel that the appropriate transfer price for each product can be within a range, specify the range.)

12-73 *General Motors and economic value added*   Since the firm of Stern Stewart & Co. began ranking firms based on market value added, General Motors has always been at, or near, the bottom of the list. Undertake an investigation to determine the circumstances that led to this ranking and whether there is any evidence that the situation is improving or getting worse.

■ CASES

12-74 *Computing economic value added*   Consult a reference such as *The Quest for Value* by G. Bennett Stewart III.[26] You will also need a copy of the Coca-Cola's 1994 Annual Report, or at least the financial statement with notes to complete this project. With these references, transform the GAAP income reported by Coca-Cola in 1994 into an income figure that is consistent with economic value analysis. Show all the steps in this calculation.

12-75 *Choosing an organization structure*   You are a senior manager responsible for overall company operations in a large courier company. Your company has 106 regional offices (terminals) scattered around the country and a main office (hub) located in the geographical center of the country. Your operations are strictly domestic. You do not accept international shipments.

The day at each terminal begins with the arrival of packages from the hub. The packages are loaded onto trucks for delivery to customers during the morning hours. In the afternoon, the same trucks pick up packages that are returned to the terminal in late afternoon and then shipped to the hub where shipments arrive from the terminals into the late evening and are sorted for delivery early the next day for the terminals.

[26] G. Bennett Stewart III, *The Quest for Value*, New York: Harper Business, 1991.

Each terminal in your company is treated as an investment center and prepares individual income statements each month. Each terminal receives 30% of the revenue from packages that it picks up and 30% of the revenue from the packages it delivers. The remaining 40% of the revenue from each transaction goes to the hub. Each terminal accumulates its own costs. All costs relating to travel to and from the hub are charged to the hub. The revenue per package is based on size and service type and not the distance that the package travels. (There are two services: overnight and ground delivery, which takes between one and seven days, depending on the distance traveled.)

All customer service is done through a central service group located in the hub. Customers access this service center through a toll-free telephone number. The most common calls to customer service include requests for package pickup, requests to trace an overdue package, and requests for billing information. The company has invested in complex and expensive package tracking equipment that monitors the package's trip through the system by scanning the bar code placed on every package. The bar code is scanned when the package is picked up, enters the originating terminal, leaves the originating terminal, arrives at the hub, leaves the hub, arrives at the destination terminal, leaves the destination terminal, and is delivered to the customer. All scanning is done by hand-held wands that transmit the information to the regional and then central computer.

The major staff functions in each terminal are administrative (accounting, clerical, and executive), marketing (the sales staff), courier (the people who pick up and deliver the shipments and the equipment they use), and operations (the people and equipment who sort packages inside the terminal).

This organization takes customer service very seriously. The revenue for any package that fails to meet the organization's service commitment to the customer is not assigned to the originating and destination terminals.

All company employees receive a wage and a bonus based on the terminal's economic value added. This system has promoted many debates about the sharing rules for revenues, the inherent inequity of the existing system, and the appropriateness of the revenue share for the hub. Service problems have arisen primarily relating to overdue packages. The terminals believe that most of the service problems relate to missorting in the hub, resulting in packages being sent to the wrong terminals.

REQUIRED

    (a) Explain why you believe that an investment center is or is not an appropriate organization design in this company.
    (b) Assuming that this organization is committed to the current design, how would you improve it?
    (c) Assuming that this organization has decided that the investment center approach is unacceptable, what approach to performance evaluation would you recommend?

12-76 *Computing objectives and organization responsibility* Baden is a city with a population of 450,000. It has a distinct organization group, called the Public Utilities Commission of the City of Baden (called the Baden PUC), whose responsibility is to provide the water and electrical services to the businesses and homes in the city. Baden PUC's manager is evaluated and rewarded based on the profit that Baden PUC reports.

Baden PUC buys electricity from a privately owned hydroelectric facility several hundred miles away for resale to its citizens. Baden PUC is responsible for acquiring, selling, billing, and servicing customers. The maintenance and moving of electric wires within the city are, however, the responsibility of the City of Baden maintenance department (called Baden Maintenance). Baden PUC pays Baden Maintenance for work done on its electrical wires.

Over the years, there have been may squabbles between Baden Maintenance and Baden PUC. These squabbles have usually involved two items: complaints by customers about delays in restoring disrupted service and complaints by Baden PUC that the rates charged by Baden Maintenance are too high. The most recent debate concerns a much more serious issue, however.

On July 12, at about 10:30 a.m., a Baden city employee working in the parks and recreation department noticed an electrical wire that seemed to be damaged. The employee reported the problem at about 12:15 p.m. to Baden Maintenance during his lunch break. The report was placed on the maintenance supervisor's desk at 1:15 p.m. where it was found at 2:05 p.m. when the supervisor returned from lunch. The maintenance supervisor then called the Baden PUC dispatch office to report the problem and request permission to investigate the report and make any required repairs. The request for repair was placed on the Baden PUC service manager's desk for approval at 2:25 p.m. The service manager received the message when he returned from a meeting at 4:00 p.m., approved the work, and left a memo for a subordinate to call in the request. The request was then mistakenly called in as a request for routine service by a clerk at 4:50 p.m. and logged by the dispatcher in Baden Maintenance. A truck was dispatched the following day at 3:50 p.m. When the repair crew arrived at the scene, it discovered that the wire was indeed damaged and, if any of the children playing in the park had touched it, it would have caused instant death.

The incident went unreported for several days until a reporter for the *Baden Chronicle* received an anonymous tip about the episode, verified that it had happened, and reported the incident on the front page of the paper as an example of bureaucratic bungling. The public was outraged and demanded an explanation from the mayor, who asked the city manager to respond. The initial response from the Baden City manager that "everyone had followed procedure" only fanned the furor.

REQUIRED

(a) Was what happened inevitable given the City of Baden's organization structure? Explain.
(b) Given the existing organization structure, how might this incident have been avoided?
(c) How would you deal with this situation now that it has happened?
(d) Would a change in the organization structure help prevent a similar situation from occurring in the future? Explain.

12-77 *Variance and cost analysis*   Peterborough Food produces a wide range of breakfast cereal foods. Its granola products are two of its most important product lines.

Because of the complexity of the granola production process, the manufacturing area in the plant that makes these two product lines is separated from the rest of the plant and is treated as a separate cost center. Exhibit 12-19 presents the activity and cost data for this cost center for the most recent quarter. The plan data in Exhibit 12-19 reflect the master budget targets for the quarter.

The factory accountant estimates that, with the increased production in line 1, the labor-related product-sustaining costs and the other product-sustaining costs for line 1 should increase by $20,000 and $100,000, respectively. The factory accountant also indicated that the decreased production in line 2 would require several quarters to be reflected in lower product-sustaining costs.

The factory accountant indicated that the labor-related facility-sustaining costs and the other facility-sustaining costs should increase by $0 and $140,000, respectively, given the net increase in production.

REQUIRED

Prepare an analysis of costs for the granola line cost center.

EXHIBIT 12-19
Peterborough Food: Granola Line Products

	Line 1 Plan	Line 1 Actual	Line 2 Plan	Line 2 Actual	Total Line 1 Plan	Total Line 1 Actual	Total Line 2 Plan	Total Line 2 Actual	Total Plan	Total Actual
Number of boxes	945,000	1,200,000	1,175,000	945,000						
Number of batches	189	200	235	210						
Units per batch	5,000	6,000	5,000	4,500						
Unit-related costs										
Materials										
Grams per box	500	515	350	375						
Cost per gram	$0.0030	$0.0027	$0.0050	$0.0055	$1,417,500	$1,668,600	$2,056,250	$1,949,062	$3,473,750	$3,617,662
Packaging										
Units per box	1.0000	1.0600	1.0000	1.0450						
Cost per unit	$0.0450	$0.0420	$0.0380	$0.0410	$42,525	$53,424	$44,650	$40,489	$87,175	$93,913
Labor										
Hours per box	0.013	0.011	0.009	0.010						
Cost per hour	$18.00	$18.25	$18.00	$18.25	$221,130	$240,900	$190,350	$172,463	$411,480	$413,363
Batch-related costs										
Materials										
Per batch	$1,200	$1,325	$1,525	$1,495	$226,800	$265,000	$358,375	$313,950	$585,175	$578,950
Labor										
Hours per batch	12	11	16	18						
Per hour	$18.00	$18.25	$18.00	$18.25	$40,824	$40,150	$67,680	$68,985	$108,504	$109,135
Product-sustaining costs										
Labor					$256,000	$287,000	$305,000	$323,000	$561,000	$610,000
Other					$2,054,000	$2,123,000	$1,927,000	$2,005,000	$3,981,000	$4,128,000
Facility-sustaining costs										
Labor									$145,000	$152,000
Other									$4,560,000	$4,740,000
Total all costs					$4,258,779	$4,678,074	$4,949,305	$4,872,949	$13,913,084	$14,443,023

13

CONTEMPORARY MANAGEMENT ACCOUNTING: METHODS TO STAY COMPETITIVE

ARCHER COMPANY

Courtesy Hank Morgan/Photo Researchers, Inc.

Bing Low is vice-president of manufacturing at Archer Company, a medium-sized manufacturing concern that produces electronic components in Los Angeles. Bing's firm is engaged in a serious global struggle to bring innovative, high-quality components to market as quickly as possible to respond to customer demand. Over the past year, Archer Company has implemented a just-in-time manufacturing system and invested in state-of-the-art machines, but Bing still does not feel that the organization is competitive. For example, several of Archer's competitors have been underpricing him significantly on two of his product lines.

Unsure of how to fight the competition, Bing asks his management team for advice. His controller, Anne Deakin, mentions that she has heard that one of Archer's competitors is using a total-life-cycle approach to product costing, while another has implemented target costing. Bing thinks these new management accounting methods are worth investigating. Perhaps this is where his competitors are getting their edge.

After reading several articles on these management accounting methods, Bing is certain that he has to find out much more about them but he does not quite know how. Bing calls his colleague, Dick Chaste, to ask him if he knows anything about these methods. Dick mentions that he is about to engage in a benchmarking effort with a small group of companies. Benchmarking, Dick explains, is a method by which organizations can learn about what others within his industry and in other industries are doing.

After more discussions with his colleagues, Bing calls some friends in the industry. He is surprised to learn that some competitors are willing to share information. For example, Homebush Company in Sydney, Australia is very interested in participating in benchmarking with Archer. Now the question becomes what should Bing look for when he benchmarks management accounting methods with other organizations.

ORGANIZING FRAMEWORK

Today's customers are demanding new products and services at an ever increasing rate. The intensity of international competition has forced many organizations to speed product and service innovations to market at the lowest possible cost. Fortunately, at the same time new innovations in management accounting methods also are being developed as tools to measure and evaluate the performance of product design and development activities.

Companies often find it difficult to keep up with the pace of innovation; therefore, they look to others for insight and help. Benchmarking is a method to aid organizations gather and share information of all types.

In this chapter, we focus on some recent innovations in management accounting, especially in relation to reducing the costs of new products and services. In particular, we use an expanded life-cycle model—total-life-cycle product costing—as an organizing framework for managing costs and quality. Within this framework, we focus on three specific methods: (1) target costing to reduce costs, (2) Kaizen costing to reduce costs and (3) quality costing to decrease the cost of nonconformance to quality standards. Finally, we present a model of benchmarking and illustrate how organizations can use it to emulate the best management accounting practices of others. Exhibit 13-1 illustrates the organization of this chapter's topics.

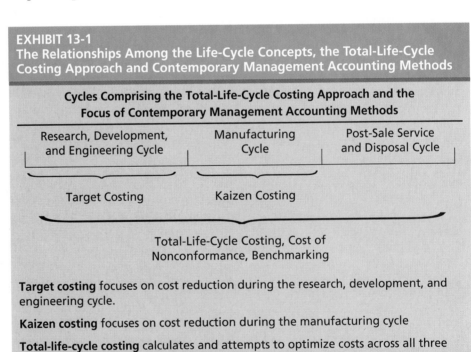

EXHIBIT 13-1
The Relationships Among the Life-Cycle Concepts, the Total-Life-Cycle Costing Approach and Contemporary Management Accounting Methods

Cycles Comprising the Total-Life-Cycle Costing Approach and the Focus of Contemporary Management Accounting Methods

Research, Development, and Engineering Cycle	Manufacturing Cycle	Post-Sale Service and Disposal Cycle

Target Costing   Kaizen Costing

Total-Life-Cycle Costing, Cost of Nonconformance, Benchmarking

Target costing focuses on cost reduction during the research, development, and engineering cycle.

Kaizen costing focuses on cost reduction during the manufacturing cycle

Total-life-cycle costing calculates and attempts to optimize costs across all three cycles.

Cost of nonconformance calculates the cost to the organization of poor quality at all stages of the life cycle.

Benchmarking of other organizations' management accounting methods also applies across all three cycles depending on what is being benchmarked.

TRADITIONAL APPROACHES TO PRODUCT COSTING

Historically, the focus of cost management has been only on manufacturing processes. In the traditional approaches, premanufacturing costs, such as research and development, and post-manufacturing costs, such as service, are period costs. Therefore, companies expense them in the period incurred, which results in not linking these costs to individual products.

Traditional accounting procedures and the way that many organizations have been separated by department or function, for example, design, engineering, manufacturing, marketing, logistics, installation, and post-sale service, often lead managers to focus only on their own department's costs. In particular for the manufacturing function, defining product costs as those solely related to the manufacturing process ignores many costs associated with the entire-life-cycle cost of a product.

TOTAL-LIFE-CYCLE PRODUCT COSTING

Understanding the **total-life-cycle costs** of a product or service, or the product costs incurred before, during, and after the manufacturing cycle, is critical as decision-makers can more realistically analyze and understand what creates product costs. For example, if a company can reduce a product's design and development costs at the premanufacturing stage, it is also possible to reduce all other subsequent product-related (downstream) costs, such as manufacturing and service-related costs. Opportunity costs play a heightened role with a total-life-cycle cost perspective because it is possible to develop only a limited number of products over a particular time period. Thus, organizations have to be very selective about the amount of resources committed to certain products or services they choose to develop, introduce, and support.

Given the rapid development of new products and shorter product life cycles, some organizations have developed a more comprehensive approach to product costing, which we call **total-life-cycle costing** (TLCC).[1] A TLCC system provides information for managers to understand and manage costs through a product's design, development, manufacturing, marketing, distribution, maintenance, service, and disposal stages.[2] It is also known as managing costs from "the cradle" to "the grave."

Numerous life-cycle concepts, such as research, development and engineering, and post-sale service and disposal, have emerged in various functional areas of business. While each concept is useful within its respective area, a TLCC perspective integrates the concepts so that they can be understood in their entirety. Such integration allows managers to see the *big picture* and manage costs in a comprehensive fashion. For example, poor decisions in the design stage may lead to much higher costs in the manufacturing and post-sale service stages. From the manufacturer's perspective, total life-cycle product costing integrates these functional life-cycle concepts: research, development and engineering, manufacturing, and post-sale service and disposal.

Total-life-cycle costs
Costs incurred before, during and after the manufacturing cycle.

OBJECTIVE 13.1

Describe the total-life-cycle costing approach to managing product costs in a comprehensive manner.

Total-life-cycle costing
A costing system that provides information for managers to understand and manage costs through a product's design, development, manufacturing, marketing, distribution, maintenance, service, and disposal stages.

---

[1] Another term sometimes used for total-life-cycle costs is *whole-life* product costing.
[2] While TLCC has its roots in early-life-cycle costing concepts developed by the U.S. Department of Defense in the 1960s, it has been adopted in commercial organizations only recently.

Research, Development, and Engineering Cycle

Research, development, and engineering cycle
The cycle in which customer needs are assessed and the product is designed and developed.

The **research, development, and engineering (RD&E) cycle** has three stages:

1. Using market research to assess emerging customer needs, which leads to generating ideas for new products.
2. Product design, in which scientists and engineers develop the technical aspects of products.
3. Product development, in which the company creates features critical to customer satisfaction and designs prototypes, production processes, and any special tooling required.

Committed costs
Costs which a company knows it will have to incur at a future date.

By some estimates, 80% to 85% of a product's total life costs are committed by decisions made in the RD&E cycle of the product's life.[3] **Committed costs** are those a company knows it will have to incur at a future date. Decisions made in this cycle are critical because an additional dollar spent on activities that occur during this cycle can save at least $8 to $10 on manufacturing and post-manufacturing activities, such as design changes or service costs.[4] Exhibit 13-2 illustrates how costs are committed over the RD&E cycle. Note that many costs are determined in this stage when information on incurred costs is not readily available.

Manufacturing Cycle

Manufacturing cycle
The cycle in which costs are incurred in the production of a product.

After the RD&E cycle, the company begins the **manufacturing cycle** where costs are incurred in the production of the product. Usually at this stage there is not as much room for engineering flexibility to influence product costs and product design because they have been set in the previous cycle. In Exhibit 13-2 the lower curve illustrates how costs are incurred over both the RD&E and the manufacturing cycle. Note the much higher level of costs incurred during the manufacturing cycle relative to the RD&E cycle. Traditionally, this is where product costing plays its biggest role.

Operations management methods, such as facilities layout and just-in-time manufacturing, help to reduce manufacturing life cycle product costs. Over the past decade in an effort to reduce costs, companies have used management accounting methods, such as activity-based cost management to identify and reduce nonvalue-added activities.

Post-Sale Service and Disposal Cycle

Post-sale service and disposal cycle
The cycle which begins once the first unit of a product is in the hands of the customer.

The third cycle is the **post-sale service and disposal cycle.** While the costs for service and disposal are committed in the RD&E stage, the actual service cycle begins once the first unit of a product is in the hands of the customer. Thus, this cycle overlaps the manufacturing cycle.

---

[3] This section is based in part on a paper by M. Shields and S. M. Young, "Managing Product Life Cycle Costs: An Organizational Model," *Journal of Cost Management*, Fall, 1991, pp. 39–52.
[4] M. Shields and S. M. Young, *op cit.* 1991.

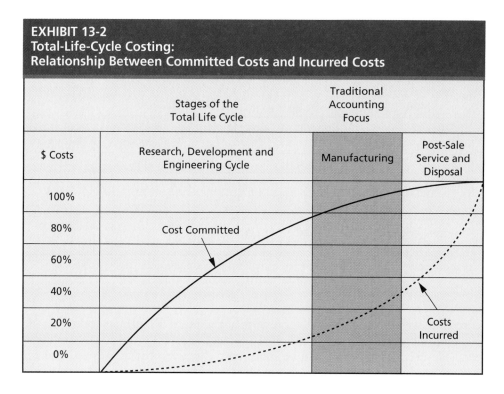

EXHIBIT 13-2
Total-Life-Cycle Costing:
Relationship Between Committed Costs and Incurred Costs

The service cycle typically consists of three stages:

1. Rapid growth from the first time the product is shipped through the growth stage of its sales.

2. Transition from the peak of sales to the peak in the service cycle.

3. Maturity from the peak in the service cycle to the time of the last shipment made to a customer. Disposal occurs at the end of a product's life and lasts until the final unit of a product is retired by the customer.[5]

Disposal costs often include costs associated with eliminating any harmful effects associated with the end of a product's useful life. Products whose disposal could involve harmful effects to the environment, such as nuclear waste or other toxic chemicals, can incur very high costs.

A breakdown of costs for each of the functional life cycles will differ based on the industry and specific product produced. Exhibit 13-3 illustrates four types of products and how the organizations that produce them incur costs over the respective total life cycle of each product.[6]

Exhibit 13-3 shows the variation of costs within the cycles. Traditional accounting focuses on manufacturing costs, thus ignoring a very large portion of total costs. For instance, the manufacturing cost of the commercial aircraft

---

[5] The discussion of the service cycle expands on G. W. Potts', "Exploit Your Product's Service Life Cycle," *Harvard Business Review*, September-October, 1988, pp. 32–36.

[6] The information in this table comes from interviews conducted for Shields and Young (1991) *op. cit.* Specific names of companies and products have to remain anonymous due to confidentiality agreements.

EXHIBIT 13-3
Percent of Life Cycle Costs Incurred Across Four Types of Products

Stage of Life Cycle	Type of Product			
Cycle	Combat Jets	Commercial Aircraft	Nuclear Missiles	Computer Software
RD&E	21%	20%	20%	75%*
Manufacturing	45%	40%	60%	*
Service and Disposal	34%	40%	20%	25%
Average Length of Life Cycle	30 years	25 years	2 to 25 years	5 years

*For computer software, both RD&E and manufacturing are often tied directly together.

company is approximately 40% of total incurred costs. RD&E and post-sale service and disposal incur 20% and 40%, respectively. With an understanding of total-life-cycle costs, there can be more cost-effective product designs and improved product planning, such as how best to ultimately dispose of a particular product.[7] Computer software development requires much time in the RD&E stage in order to create and debug the software. It often costs 100 times more to correct a defect in the operating phase for software than in the design phase.[8]

TARGET COSTING

Target costing
A method of cost planning used during the RD&E cycle that focuses on products that require discrete manufacturing processes and reasonably short life cycles.

OBJECTIVE 13.2

Explain target costing.

Target costing is a method of cost planning that focuses on products with discrete manufacturing processes and reasonably short product life cycles. Exhibit 13-1 shows target costing used during the RD&E stage of a product's total life cycle.

Target costing has been in use in Japanese firms for over a decade. A survey conducted by Kobe University in 1992 showed that of those responding to the survey, 100% of transportation equipment manufacturers, 75% of precision equipment manufacturers, 88% of electrical manufacturers, and 83% of machinery manufacturers stated that they used target costing.[9] The impetus for such widespread use developed as a result of diminishing efficiency gains realized in production from using the just-in-time manufacturing system. The Japanese believed that further gains in both manufacturing and service costs could be made if they shifted the focus on cost reduction to the RD&E cycle.[10]

---

[7] We should note that the distribution of costs between manufacturing and post-sales service can vary considerably depending on how quickly the product is consumed. Toothpaste (compared to weapons systems) is consumed immediately, and the amount of post-sale service for this product is close to zero.

[8] See M. A. Cusumano, *Japan's Software Factories*, New York, New York: Oxford University Press, 1991.

[9] This study is cited in Y. Kato, G. Boer and C. W. Chow, "Target Costing: An Integrated Management Process," *Journal of Cost Management*, Spring 1995, pp. 39–51.

[10] Some information extracted from R. Cooper, *When Lean Enterprises Collide*, Harvard Business School Press, 1995, and Yutaka Kato, *Target Costing: Strategic Cost Management*, Nihon Keizai Shinbunsha, 1993.

CONSIDER THIS . . .

Bristol-Myers Squibb: Pollution Prevention Throughout the Product Life Cycle

In 1992, Bristol-Myers Squibb developed a pollution prevention program called Environment 2000. This program helps the company identify environmental, health, and safety issues at all stages of the product life cycle. Ban Roll-On was one of the first products studied. Repackaging the product in a smaller-size carton resulted in a reduction of 600 tons of recycled paperboard and 55% less shelf space required for display. As a result, pollution was prevented and customer's operating costs reduced.

POLLUTION PREVENTION THROUGHOUT THE PRODUCT LIFE CYCLE

Objective:
To systematically identify opportunities to prevent pollution and gain competitive advantage

Approach:
To highlight how employees from many functional

areas can prevent pollution that is generated throughout a product's life cycle (e.g., product design, manufacture, distribution, sales, consumer use, and ultimate fate) and thereby reduce the environmental impact of our businesses' activities

Benefits:
- Reducing environmental liabilities;
- Increasing cost-effectiveness of complying with environmental regulations;
- Developing safer and more environmentally sound products;
- Minimizing waste of energy and raw materials;
- Differentiating products from the competition; and
- Being recognized as a good environmental citizen

Source: Marc J. Epstein, *Measuring Corporate Environmental Performance*—Best Practices for Costing and Managing an Effective Environmental Strategy, The IMA Foundation for Applied Research, 1996, p. 39.

BMW uses parts made of recycled plastics (blue) and those parts that can be recycled (green). So-called green manufacturing and potential legislation for companies to take back used components illustrates decision making based on the total-life-cycle costing concept. Companies can reuse, refurbish, or dispose of a product's components safely and reduce total-life-cycle product costs. *Courtesy* **BMW Corporation**

In the United States, target costing is gaining momentum as a management method. However, it is not just a method of cost control but a comprehensive approach to cost and profit management. Companies such as Boeing, Eastman Kodak, Texas Instruments, and Chrysler have all adopted target costing in parts of their businesses.

Comparing Traditional Cost Reduction and Target Costing

Traditional cost reduction
Methods of cost reduction in which product designers do not attempt to achieve a particular cost target.

The process involved in **traditional cost reduction** in the United States is significantly different from target costing. As shown in Exhibit 13-4, column 1, the traditional costing method begins with market research into customer requirements followed by product specification. Thus, companies engage in product design and engineering and obtain prices from suppliers. At this stage, product cost is not a significant factor in product design. After the engineers and designers have determined product design, they estimate product cost (C_t) where the t subscript indicates numbers derived under traditional thinking. If the estimated cost is considered to be too high, then it may be necessary to modify the product design. To find the desired profit margin (P_t), it is necessary to subtract the estimated cost from the expected selling price (S_t). The profit margin is the result of the difference between the expected selling price and the estimated production cost.[11] This relationship is expressed in the following equation:

$$P_t = S_t - C_t$$

In another widely used traditional approach, the cost-plus method, an expected profit margin (P_{cp}) is added to the expected product cost (C_{cp}), where the subscript cp indicates numbers derived under cost-plus thinking. Selling price (S_{cp}) simply becomes the result of the sum of these two variables. In equation form this relationship is expressed as this:

$$S_{cp} = C_{cp} + P_{cp}$$

Target selling price (S_{tc})
The selling price in a target costing system of a product based on the company's perceived value of the product to the customer.

Target product volume
The product volume in a target costing system based on the company's perceived value of the product to the customer.

Target profit margin (P_{tc})
The profit margin in a target costing system based on a long-run profit analysis.

Target cost (C_{tc})
The difference between the target selling price and the target profit margin.

In both traditional methods, product designers do not attempt to achieve a particular cost target.

In target costing both the sequence of steps and the way of thinking about determining product costs differ significantly from traditional costing. (See Exhibit 13-4, column 2.) The first two steps, market research to determine customer requirements and product specification, are similar to traditional costing. After these initial steps, the process is quite different. The next step, determining a **target selling price (S_{tc})** and **target product volume,** depends on the company's perceived value of the product to the customer. The **target profit margin (P_{tc})** results from a long-run profit analysis often based on return on sales (net income ÷ sales). Return on sales is the most widely used measure as it can be linked most closely to profitability for each product. The **target cost (C_{tc})** is the difference between the target selling price and the target profit margin.[12] Note that the tc subscript indicates numbers derived under the target costing approach. This relationship for the target costing approach is shown in the following equation:

$$C_{tc} = S_{tc} - P_{tc}$$

---

[11] Robin Cooper developed the structure for comparing costs in this manner in *Nissan Motor Company, Ltd.: Target Costing System,* Harvard Business School Case #9-194-040.

[12] The process of target costing can involve more steps and more iterations. For more details *see* Y. Monden and K. Hamada, "Target Costing and Kaizen Costing in Japanese Automobile Companies," *Journal of Management Accounting Research,* 1991, pp. 16–34, and T. Tanaka, "Target Costing at Toyota," *Journal of Cost Management,* Spring 1993, pp. 4–11.

EXHIBIT 13-4
A Comparison of the Process of Traditional U.S. and Japanese Cost-Reduction Methods

Traditional U.S. Cost Reduction	Japanese Target Costing
Market research to determine customer requirements	Market research to determine consumer needs and price points
⇓	⇓
Product specification	Product specification
⇓	⇓
Design	Target selling price (S_{tc}) (and target product volume)
⇓	−
Engineering	Target profit (P_{tc})
⇓	=
Supplier pricing	TARGET COST (C_{tc})
⇓	⇓
ESTIMATED COST (C_t) (if too high, return to design phase) Desired profit margin (P_t)	Value engineering Supplier pricing pressure
=	(Both value engineering and pressure of suppliers to reduce cost are applied as a result of the target costs for each component)
Expected selling price (S_t) − Estimated cost (C_t)	⇓
⇓	**Manufacturing**
Manufacturing	⇓
⇓	Continuous cost reduction
Periodic cost reduction	

Source: This is a modified version of F. S. Worthy's table in "Japan's Smart Secret Weapon," *Fortune,* August 12, 1991, pp. 72–75.

By the time that these Japanese motor vehicle components reach this stage of production, target costs have already been determined and incorporated into the components. *Courtesy* FUJI Photos/The Image Works

Value engineering
The process of examining each component of a product to determine whether its cost can be reduced while maintaining functionality and performance.

Once the target cost is set, the company must determine target costs for each component. The **value engineering** process includes examination of each component of a product to determine whether it is possible to reduce costs while maintaining functionality and performance. In some cases, product design may change, materials used in production may need replacing, or manufacturing processes may require redesign. For example, a product design change may involve using fewer parts or reducing specialty parts if more common components can be used. Several iterations of value engineering usually are needed before it is possible to determine the final target cost.

Suppliers also play a critical role in making target costing work. As manufacturers with market power, such as Toyota and Nissan, decide that there is a need to reduce the cost of specific components, they will pressure suppliers to find ways to reduce costs. Companies may also offer incentive plans to suppliers who come up with the best cost reduction ideas.[13] Exhibit 13-5 illustrates how to calculate a target cost.

Concerns About Target Costing

While target costing has some obvious advantages, some studies of target costing in Japan indicate that there are potential problems in implementing the system, especially if focusing on meeting the target cost diverts attention away from other elements of overall company goals.[14] These are some examples:

1. Conflicts can arise between various parties involved in the target-costing process. Often companies put excessive pressure on subcontractors/suppliers to conform to schedule and reduce costs. This can lead to alienation and/or failure of the subcontractor. Sometimes design engineers become upset

---

EXHIBIT 13-5
A Target-Costing Example

After conducting a marketing research study, Illumina Company decides to produce a new light fixture to complement its outdoor lighting line. According to estimates, the new fixture can be sold at a target price of $20, and the estimated annual target sales volume is 100,000 light fixtures. Illumina has a 20% expected return on sales target. The target cost is computed as follows:

Target sales (100,000 fixtures × $20)	$2,000,000
Less: Target profit (20% × $20/unit × 100,000 units)	400,000
Target cost for 100,000 fixtures	$1,600,000
Unit target cost per fixture ($1,600,000 ÷ 100,000 fixtures)	$16.00

---

[13] See R. Cooper's *Nissan Motor Company, Ltd.: Target Costing System*, Harvard Business School Case #9-194-040.

[14] See M. Sakurai, "Past and Future of Japanese Management Accounting," *Journal of Cost Management*, Fall, 1995, pp. 21–30 and Y. Kato, G. Boer, and C. W. Chow, "Target Costing: An Integrated Management Process," *Journal of Cost Management*, Spring 1995, pp. 39–51.

when other parts of the organization are not cost conscious; they argue that they exert much effort to squeeze pennies out of the cost of a product, while other parts of the organization (administration, marketing, distribution) are wasting dollars.

2. Employees in many Japanese companies working under target-costing goals experience burnout due to the pressure to meet the target cost. Burnout is particularly evident for design engineers.

3. While the target cost may be met, there may be increased development time because of repeated value engineering cycles to reduce costs, which ultimately can lead to the product being late in coming to market. For some types of products, being six months late may be far more costly than having small cost overruns.

While companies find it possible to manage many of these factors, organizations interested in using the target-costing method should be aware of these concerns before immediately attempting to adopt this cost reduction method. Despite these criticisms, target costing can provide engineers and managers the greatest leverage to reduce product costs in a critical part of the product life cycle.

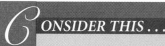

CONSIDER THIS . . .

Target Costing in the Japanese Automobile Industry

The target-costing method used at some of the Japanese automobile companies begins with the corporate planning department. At this level, the goal is to determine the long- and medium-term profits for the entire company as well as the profit targets for each product over specific time periods. The engineering department then receives the new product plan to be developed along with the market-driven requirements for the new model. At this stage, the cost management group estimates the costs of the plan to determine whether it is possible to achieve the target profit.

The next phase involves the development of another plan to determine specific cost factors related to product design. At this time, target price information gathered from domestic and international competition is used to calculate an *allowable cost*. The equation for this is as follows:

Target Sales Price − Target Profit = Allowable Cost

However, *allowable* cost is a very difficult number to achieve; therefore a *target cost* is established. A target cost is one that is considered tight but attainable; it is used so that employees do not become highly discouraged. Once senior management has approved the target cost, then value engineering is used in the design of the product. Value engineering methods focus on (1) material specifications and consumption, (2) yield, (3) number of parts and part numbers, (4) ease of work, and (5) amount of labor. Ultimately, the target cost is decomposed down to the part level by the product designers.

The next step is to draft a trial blueprint for the automobile based on the target cost determined for each part. If there is a discrepancy between the target cost and the estimated cost of the prototype produced, value engineering is applied again until the target cost and blueprint are aligned. The final step involves the production engineering department establishing standards for labor, materials, and overhead. These standards are fixed for a year and become the basic cost. Three months after production begins the target cost is evaluated.

Sources: Y. Monden and K. Hamada, "Target Costing and Kaizen Costing in Japanese Automobile Companies," *Journal of Management Accounting Research*, 1991, pp. 16–34; T. Tanaka, "Target Costing at Toyota," *Journal of Cost Management*, Spring 1993, pp. 4–11.

KAIZEN COSTING

Kaizen costing
A method of cost reduction developed in Japan to reduce costs during the manufacturing cycle.

OBJECTIVE 13.3

Understand the use of Kaizen costing.

Kaizen costing is similar to target costing in its cost-reduction mission except that it focuses on reducing costs during the manufacturing stage of the total-life-cycle of a product. (See Exhibit 13-1.) *Kaizen* is the Japanese term for making improvements to a process through small, incremental amounts rather than through large innovations. The intent of Kaizen is reasonable because the product is already in the manufacturing process. This makes it difficult and costly to make large changes to reduce costs. Kaizen costing contrasts with target costing, which allows many more opportunities to effect change because product design is still taking place while decisions are being made.

Kaizen costing is tied into the profit-planning system.[15] In the Japanese automobile industry, for example, an annual budgeted profit target is allocated to each plant. Each automobile has a predetermined cost base, which is equal to the actual cost of that automobile in the previous year. All cost reductions use this cost base as their starting point.

Target-reduction rate
The ratio of the target reduction amount (in a target costing system) to the cost base.

The **target-reduction rate** is the ratio of the target reduction amount to the cost base. This rate is applied over time to all variable costs and results in specific target-reduction amounts for materials, parts, direct and indirect labor, and other variable costs. Then management makes comparisons of actual reduction amounts across all variable costs to the pre-established targeted reduction amounts. If there are differences, variances for the plant are determined. Kaizen costing's goal is to ensure that actual production costs are less than the cost base. However, if the cost of disruptions to production are greater than the savings due to Kaizen costing, then it will not be applied.[16] Exhibit 13-6 illustrates one example of determining the total amount of Kaizen costs across multiple plants in a Japanese automobile plant.

Comparing Traditional Cost Reduction to Kaizen Costing

The Kaizen costing system is quite distinct from a traditional standard costing system where the typical goal is to meet the cost standard while avoiding unfavorable variances. With Kaizen costing, the goal is to achieve cost reduction targets. Variance analysis under a standard cost system usually compares actual to standard costs. Under Kaizen costing, variance analysis compares target costs with actual cost-reduction amounts. Kaizen costing operates outside of the standard costing system in part because standard costing systems in Japan are oriented towards complying with financial accounting standards.

Another key difference between standard and Kaizen costing has to do with the assumptions about who has the best knowledge to improve processes and reduce costs. Traditional standard costing assumes that *engineers and managers* know

---

[15] This discussion is based on research by Y. Monden and J. Lee, "How a Japanese Auto Maker Reduces Costs," *Management Accounting*, August, 1993, pp. 22–26 and Y. Monden and K. Hamada, "Target Costing and Kaizen Costing in Japanese Automobile Companies," *Journal of Management Accounting Research*, 1991, pp. 16–34.

[16] See R. Cooper, *When Lean Enterprises Collide*, Harvard Business School Press, 1995.

EXHIBIT 13-6
Computing Kaizen Costs for Plants

Cost savings in Japanese automobile plants involve reducing both committed (fixed) and flexible (variable) costs. Since fixed costs are believed necessary for growth, the main emphasis is on reducing variable costs.

In this example, the total amount of Kaizen costs in all plants determined in a Kaizen planning meeting is designated as C in the formulae that follow:

Amount of Actual Cost per Car in the Last Period (A)	=	Amount of Actual Cost in the Last Period	÷	Actual Production in the Last Period
Estimated Amount of Actual Cost for All Plants in This Period (B)	=	Amount of Actual Cost per Car in the Last Period (A)	×	Estimated Production in This Period
Kaizen Cost Target in This Period for All Plants (C)	=	Estimated Amount of Actual Cost for All Plants in This Period (B)	×	Target Ratio of Cost Decrease to the Estimated Cost

The target ratio of cost decrease to the estimated cost is based on attaining the target profit for the year.

The Kaizen cost target for each plant is determined in the following manner:

Assignment Ratio (D)	=	Costs Controlled Directly by Each Plant	÷	Total Amount of Costs Controlled Directly by Plants
Total Kaizen Cost for Each Plant	=	Kaizen Cost Target in This Period for All Plants (C)	×	Assignment Ratio (D)

The amount of Kaizen cost for each plant is subdivided to each division and subdivisions as cost-reduction goals.

Source: Y. Monden and K. Hamada, "Target Costing and Kaizen Costing in Japanese Automobile Companies," *Journal of Management Accounting Research,* 1991, pp. 16–34.

---

best since they have the technical expertise. Thus, they determine procedures that workers are required to perform according to preset standards and procedures. Under Kaizen costing, *workers* are assumed to have superior knowledge about how to improve processes because they actually work with manufacturing processes to produce products. Thus, one of the central goals of Kaizen costing is to give workers the responsibility to improve processes and reduce costs. Exhibit 13-7 summarizes the differences in philosophy between standard-costing and Kaizen-costing methods.

Concerns About Kaizen Costing

Kaizen costing also has been criticized for the same reasons that target costing has—the system places enormous pressure on employees to reduce every conceivable cost. To address the problem, some Japanese automobile companies use a

EXHIBIT 13-7
A Comparison of Standard Costing and Kaizen Costing

Standard Costing	Kaizen Costing Concepts
Cost-control system concept	Cost-reduction system concept
Assumes stability in current manufacturing processes	Assumes continuous improvement in manufacturing
Goal is to meet cost performance standards	Goal is to achieve cost reduction standards
Standard Costing Techniques	**Kaizen Costing Techniques**
Standards are set annually or semi-annually	Cost-reduction targets are set and applied monthly and continuous improvement (Kaizen) methods are applied all year long to meet targets.
Cost-variance analysis involves comparing actual to standard costs	Cost-variance analysis involves target Kaizen costs versus actual cost reduction amounts
Cost variance investigation occurs when standards are not met	Investigation occurs when target cost reduction (Kaizen) amounts are not attained
Who Has the Best Knowledge to Reduce Costs?	**Who Has the Best Knowledge to Reduce Costs?**
Managers and engineers develop standards as they have the technical expertise	Workers are closest to the process and thus know best

Source: Adapted from Y. Monden and J. Lee, "How a Japanese Auto Maker Reduces Costs," *Management Accounting*, August, 1993, pp. 22–26.

grace period in manufacturing just before a new model is introduced. This period, called a *cost-sustainment period*, provides employees with the opportunity to learn any new procedures before the company imposes Kaizen and target costs on them.

Cost of nonconformance (CONC) to quality standards
The cost incurred by an organization if products and services do not conform to quality standards.

COST OF NONCONFORMANCE (QUALITY)

Reducing costs involves much more than simply finding ways to cut product design costs. The premise underlying cost-reduction efforts is to decrease costs while maintaining or improving product quality. In today's environment, quality has become an important commitment in order to be competitive. As discussed in Chapter 2, it is necessary for organizations to assess whether products and services meet quality standards. If products and services do not conform to quality standards, the organization incurs a cost known as the **cost of nonconformance (CONC) to quality standards.** The CONC applies over the total life cycle of the product.

Quality means different things to different people. Quality can be seen as the difference between the promised and realized level of service for the customer. Additionally, quality usually can be viewed as being determined by two major factors:

1. Satisfying customer expectations regarding the attributes and performance of the product, such as its functionality and features.
2. Ensuring that the technical aspects of the product's design and performance, such as whether it performs to the standard expected, conform to standards from the perspective of the manufacturer.

Global competition has led to the development of international quality standards. Company certification under these standards indicates to customers that management has committed their company to follow procedures and processes that ensure the production of high-quality goods and services.

Quality Standards

In Europe in 1987, the International Organization for Standardization (ISO), headquartered in Geneva, Switzerland developed the **ISO 9000 Series of Standards.** The goal of the 96-member nations was to develop globally-recognized quality standards for both products and services. Many types of organizations are interested in becoming ISO-9000 registered in order to accomplish the following:

1. Comply with external regulatory agencies.
2. Meet or exceed customer requirements.
3. Implement a quality-improvement program to remain competitive.

Exhibit 13-8 presents the ISO 9000 Standards and their purposes. The exhibit also provides a sketch of the procedures that organizations need to follow if they wish to be ISO 9000-certified.

The Japanese use **Industrial Standard Z8101-1981** as their standard for quality management. The standard specifies that effective quality control results from cooperation from everyone in an organization. The standard lists all functional areas, such as market research, product planning, purchasing, manufacturing, service, and administration, as being integral to adhering to the standard.

The American Quality Control Society in the United States has developed its own quality standards known as the **Q Series of Quality Standards,** which are similar to those developed in Europe. These are Q90 through Q94. Exhibit 13-9 presents information regarding these standards.

Costs of Quality Control

Our focus in this section on quality is how to interpret quality costs from a management accounting point of view. The best known framework for understanding **quality costs** divides them into four categories:

1. **Prevention costs**
2. **Appraisal costs**
3. **Internal-failure costs**
4. **External-failure costs**

ISO 9000 Series of Standards
International quality standards developed by the International Organization for Standardization (ISO).

Industrial Standard Z8101-1981
The Japanese standard for quality management.

Q series of quality standards
U.S. quality standards developed by the American Quality Control Society.

Quality costs
Costs incurred to prevent quality problems from occurring, determine if problems have arisen, and correct quality problems both internal and external to a company.

Prevention costs
Those costs incurred to ensure that companies produce products according to quality standards.

Appraisal costs
Those cost related to inspecting products to ensure that they meet both internal and external customer requirements.

Internal-failure costs
A cost incurred when a manufacturing process produces a defective component or product and the defect is detected internally.

External-failure costs
A cost incurred when a manufacturing company produces a defective component or product and the defect is detected externally.

EXHIBIT 13-8
The ISO 9000 Standards

ISO guidelines consist of five standards, two of which are general-quality management guidelines (ISO 9000, ISO 9004), and three of which are quality-system models (ISO 9001, ISO 9002, ISO 9003). The quality-system models are listed below.

The first general-quality management guideline, ISO 9000, *Quality Management and Quality Assurance Standards—Guidelines for Selection and Use,* is used to help a potential registrant decide on which of the three quality-system models, ISO 9001, ISO 9002, and ISO 9003 should be selected and followed for a particular application. The second general quality-management guideline, ISO 9004—*Quality Management and Quality System Elements*—explains how to use each of the three quality-system models based on specific elements of the quality-management system.

Once an organization has committed to obtaining ISO 9000 status, it must select a standard from one of the following:

1. ISO 9001 Quality Systems. *Model for Quality Assurance in Design and/or Development, Production, and Installation.* This standard is the most all-encompassing and specifies a supplier's capability to design, supply, and service a product. The standard is designed for the entire life of the product.

2. ISO 9002 Quality Systems. *Model for Quality Assurance in Production and Installation.* ISO 9002 centers on organizations that produce products but whose design and servicing are done by others. The requirements are focused at the production and installation stages of the product's life cycle.

3. ISO 9003 *Model for Quality Assurance in Final Inspection and Testing.* This standard applies to contracts between parties in which the supplier has to be able to detect and control any product nonconformance during final inspection and testing. This is the most-limited aspect of the ISO standard.

Once an organization has decided on which standard it wishes to follow, it can then take the following steps towards ISO 9000 registration.

1. *The company must become organized to achieve the standards.* This involves gaining top-management support, developing quality policies, and establishing a management review committee and implementation teams.

2. *The current quality management system needs to be evaluated.* In many cases, companies determine the current state of their system and identify how big a gap they have to bridge before being able to attain ISO 9000-status.

3. *The quality system must be documented.* The gap analysis will guide the level and kind of documentation needed. ISO 9000 requires careful documentation of objective evidence of performance. Quality manuals, system procedures, work instructions, and quality records need to be developed and/or evaluated.

4. *The quality system must be monitored.* Monitoring involves management reviews of the documented quality system, internal quality audits, and corrective actions.

5. *The organization must be registered as ISO 9000.* After the quality system has been functioning for several months, it can choose to undertake an audit to determine if it can achieve ISO 9000-registration status. An accredited ISO 9000-registrar will undertake a thorough study that will last several days and cost between $5,000 and $20,000 or more depending on the complexity of the organization. A formal audit is conducted and if any nonconformances to the guidelines are found they must be corrected. If the audit team is satisfied with the corrections, the Registrar will award certificates of ISO 9000 registration.

Source: Becoming ISO 9000 Registered, The Society of Management Accountants Canada, 1994.

EXHIBIT 13-9
U.S. Quality Standards

The Q Series of Standards consist of Q90 through Q94. Q90 is the standard that provides an overview of the other standards, definitions used, and the key concepts related to quality. U.S. organizations wanting to be certified under the Q Series of Quality Standards have to consider and choose one of Q91-Q94.

1. Q91 is the general standard that is used for design, development, manufacturing, installation, and servicing of products and services.

2. Q92 is meant to provide finer details than Q91 for organizations that engage in manufacturing, installation, and servicing of products or services.

3. Q93 provides finer details than Q91 for organizations that perform inspections and tests and for distributors and value-added contractors.

4. Q94 presents the guidelines for managing and auditing a quality-control system.

Source: J. Heizer and B. Render, *Production & Operations Management,* Prentice Hall, 1995.

The framework results from experience which shows that it is much less expensive to prevent defects than to detect and repair them after they have occurred. The framework highlights the categories and their respective tradeoffs.

PREVENTION COSTS. Companies in the 1980s discovered that they were spending as much as 20% to 30% of total manufacturing costs on quality-related processes, such as detection and internal and external failure. Prevention costs are incurred to ensure that companies produce products according to quality standards. Quality engineering, training employees in methods designed to maintain quality, and statistical process control are examples of prevention costs. Prevention costs also include training and certifying suppliers so that they can deliver defect-free parts and materials.

APPRAISAL COSTS. Internal customers have the task of performing a function on the output of a previous process stage. An external customer purchases the product from the manufacturing organization. Appraisal costs most often are related to inspecting products to make sure that they meet both internal and external customers' requirements. Inspection costs of purchased parts/materials and costs of quality inspection on an assembly line are considered to be appraisal costs. Examples include inspection of incoming materials, maintenance of test equipment, and process control monitoring.

INTERNAL-FAILURE COSTS. An internal-failure cost occurs when the manufacturing process produces a defective component/product and detects this fact internally. The cost of downtime in production as a result of discovered defects in moving from one stage of the process to another is one example of internal-failure costs. Others include scrap and rework. Engineers have estimated that in some discrete part of manufacturing processes, the cost of defects rise by an order of magnitude for each stage that the defect goes undetected. For example, inserting a defective $1 electronic component leads to $10 of scrap if detected at the first stage, $100 at the next stage, and perhaps $10,000 if not detected for two more stages of assembly.

EXTERNAL-FAILURE COSTS. External-failure costs are detected by the customer upon receipt of a product. All costs associated with correcting the problem—repair of the product, warranty costs, service calls, and product liability recalls—are examples of external failure costs. For many companies, this is the most critical quality cost to avoid. Not only are costs required to fix the problem in the short run, but also customer satisfaction and the reputation of the manufacturing organization may be in jeopardy over the long run. Exhibit 13-10 provides examples of the quality costs in each category.

A **cost-of-quality report** using the categories shown in Exhibit 13-10 appears in Exhibit 13-11. Consider the hypothetical business Renwal Company, with $100,000,000 in sales, that is deciding how to manage its quality costs. In studying this report, note that total prevention costs are 1.04% of sales, appraisal costs are 2.225% of sales, internal failure costs are 2.66% of sales, and external failure costs are 10.895% of sales.

The most obvious problem at Renwal is the extremely high external-failure costs of almost 11%. Since as a norm many companies would like to keep their quality costs below 4% to 5% of sales, Renwal Company's quality costs are out of line. Note in particular that product-liability lawsuits, warranty claims, and product recalls are the biggest external-failure costs. Renwal must find out why its products seem to be failing in the field.

Renwal should first turn to an analysis of its other quality costs. Quality costs are incurred throughout the total life cycle of a product. If Renwal does not control quality costs early in the RD&E stage by ensuring good product design, then design problems will lead to increased quality costs later on.

At Renwal both prevention and appraisal costs are a relatively small percent of total quality costs (1.04% and 2.225% respectively). Renwal should consider putting more effort into quality training and engineering and statistical process

Cost-of-quality report
A report that details the cost of quality by the categories prevention, appraisal, internal failure and external failure.

EXHIBIT 13-10
Examples of Quality-Related Costs

Prevention Costs	**Appraisal Costs**
Quality engineering	Inspection/testing of incoming materials
Quality training	Maintenance of test equipment
Statistical-process control	Process-control monitoring
Supplier certification	Product-quality audits
Research of customer needs	

Internal-Failure Costs	**External-Failure Costs**
Downtime due to defects	Product liability lawsuits
Waste	Repair costs in the field
Net cost of scrap	Returned products
Rework costs	Product liability recalls
	Service calls
	Warranty claims

These Motorola employees are discussing ways to prevent defects from occurring on printed circuit boards. Preventing errors at the earliest possible stage will reduce quality costs significantly over the product's life cycle. *Courtesy* Motorola Corporation

control. The company should also determine whether to spend more money on appraisal. There could be a problem with Renwal's test equipment that would require the company to incur higher maintenance costs.

With regard to internal-failure costs, Renwal also apparently incurs a great deal of rework costs. The product seems to require many additional costs that need not be incurred if the company could produce it correctly the first time. Perhaps the production process is at fault, or maybe Renwal's workers are sloppy or not highly skilled.

Exhibit 13-12 shows a graph of the data by quality-cost category. Note that *actual quality costs* for Renwal Company are very low at the prevention stage. They increase for the appraisal and internal-failure cost categories. Under external-failure costs, the level of costs are extremely high. This pattern of quality costs is what most organizations hope to avoid since they indicate that the highest level of quality costs are occurring in the field when products are in customers' hands.

The more *desirable quality-cost* trend would be to reverse the actual pattern described above to have the greatest proportion of quality costs incurred in the prevention stage. By increasing training and quality engineering costs during this stage, a company can reduce other quality costs. Using the same quality-cost numbers that have been derived for the Renwal Company and reversing the categories in which we place the costs, there is a more desirable trend of increased costs in prevention and very low external-failure costs. Thus, even though Renwal's quality costs are still very high, quality costs are being incurred in such a way that the company's products are failing much less in the field. This will help their

EXHIBIT 13-11
Quality-Cost Report for Renwal Company for 1997

Quality Cost Category	Annual Cost	Percent of Sales*
Prevention Costs:		
Quality training	$ 125,000	0.125%
Quality engineering	500,000	0.500%
Statistical process control	250,000	0.250%
Supplier certification	90,000	0.090%
Research of customer needs	75,000	0.075%
Total	$ 1,040,000	1.040%
Appraisal Costs:		
Inspection of and testing of in-coming materials	$ 400,000	0.400%
Maintenance of test equipment	350,000	0.350%
Process-control monitoring	1,000,000	1.000%
Product-quality audits	475,000	0.475%
Total	$ 2,225,000	2.225%
Internal Failure Costs:		
Waste	$ 700,000	0.700%
Net cost of scrap	635,000	0.635%
Rework costs	1,200,000	1.200%
Downtime due to defects	125,000	0.125%
Total	$ 2,660,000	2.660%
External Failure Costs:		
Product-liability lawsuits	$ 4,500,000	4.500%
Repair costs in the field	850,000	0.850%
Warranty claims	2,345,000	2.345%
Returned products	1,200,000	1.200%
Product recalls	2,000,000	2.000%
Total	$10,895,000	10.895%
Total Quality Costs:	$16,820,000	16.820%

*Total sales for 1997 were $100,000,000.

reputation and overall customer satisfaction. The next step for Renwal will be to find ways to reduce both prevention and appraisal costs.

While this is a hypothetical example, the most important idea to note is that a cost-of-quality report will highlight problem areas over the total life cycle of a product and allow for corrective action. If a company can reduce quality costs and hence quality problems early in the design and manufacturing stages, the benefits will ripple through the entire life cycle and ultimately reduce costs in the other quality cost categories.

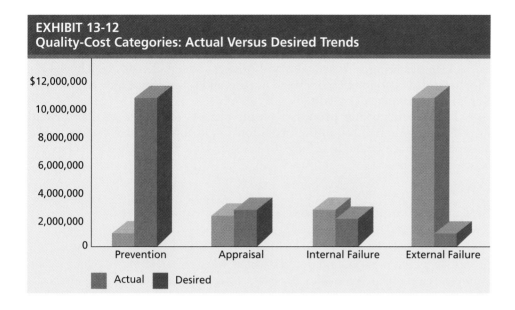

EXHIBIT 13-12
Quality-Cost Categories: Actual Versus Desired Trends

Benchmarking[17]

The opening vignette to the chapter posed several questions concerning how Bing Low, vice-president of Archer Company, would go about learning about management accounting methods from other organizations. Organizations interested in a new management accounting method usually choose one of three ways to learn about and adopt a method.

1. The first is to bring in outside consultants to implement a particular method. Outside consultants can be effective, but costly.

2. A second approach is for organizational members to develop their own systems internally with little or no assistance from outside consultants. While this approach can be satisfying, it can be highly costly and time consuming, especially if the organization fails in its first few attempts at change.

3. The third approach, known as benchmarking, requires that organizational members first understand their current operations and approaches to conducting business and then look externally to the practices of other organizations for guidance on improving.

We addressed benchmarking in Chapter 2 and now expand on the definition presented there (an organization's search for implementation of the best way of doing something as practiced by another organization).

This chapter focuses on the process of benchmarking. Benchmarking allows organizations to gather information regarding the *best practices* of others. It is often highly cost effective since organizations can save time and money avoiding the mistakes that other companies have made or by avoiding reinventing a process/method that other companies have already developed and tested.

[17] This section is based on a paper by D. Elnathan, T. Lin, and S. M. Young, "Benchmarking and Management Accounting: A Framework for Research," *Journal of Management Accounting Research*, 1996.

The Xerox Corporation advanced the benchmarking process to better management in the United States. After Xerox lost its leading position in the copier business to IBM, Kodak, and several Japanese firms in the late 1970s, Xerox studied its manufacturing cost structure and pricing strategy. Xerox's benchmarking effort revealed that competitors were pricing and selling machines at or below Xerox's own manufacturing cost.[18]

Benchmarking process
A five-stage process of gathering information regarding the best practices of others.

The **benchmarking process** typically consists of five stages that include several organizational/diagnostic, operational, and informational factors.[19] We present each stage below by listing their key factors. Exhibit 13-13 depicts the benchmarking process.

Stage 1: Internal Study and Preliminary Competitive Analyses

OBJECTIVE 13.5

Understand a model for benchmarking the best practices of other organizations.

In this stage, the organization decides which *key areas to benchmark for study*, for example, the company's activities, products, or management accounting methods. Then the company determines how it currently performs on these dimensions by initiating both *preliminary internal competitive analysis* using internal company data and *preliminary external competitive analyses* using, for example, industry comparisons on quality via publications such as *Consumer Reports or J. D. Powers and Associates Reports*. Both of these types of analyses will determine the *scope and significance of the study* for each area.

Stage 2: Developing Long-Term Commitment to the Benchmarking Project and Coalescing the Benchmarking Team

In Stage 2, the organization must develop its commitment to the benchmarking project and coalesce a benchmarking team. Because significant organizational change, such as adopting a total-life-cycle costing approach, can take several years, the level of commitment to benchmarking has to be a long-term rather than a short-term commitment. Long-term commitment requires (1) obtaining the support of *senior management* to give the benchmarking team the authority to spearhead the changes, (2) developing *a clear set of objectives* to guide the benchmarking effort, and (3) *empowering employees* to make change.

The benchmarking team should include individuals from all functional areas in the organization. Developing a target costing system, for example, would benefit from a total-life-cycle costing perspective, which requires employees from

---

[18] Benchmarking gained more momentum with its inclusion as a component of the Malcolm Baldrige National Quality Award. A number of major institutions, such as the Consortium for Advanced Manufacturing International (CAM-I), The American Productivity and Quality Center in Houston (which established the International Benchmarking Clearinghouse), and The Institute of Management Accountants (IMA-Continuous Improvement Center,) have started benchmarking-initiatives to pool their resources to act as information clearinghouses.

[19] The five-stage approach in this chapter is used for illustrative purposes. Not all organizations would classify their approach using the same five stages; however, there will probably be a great deal of similarity in the variables that most organizations find important.

EXHIBIT 13-13
Stages of the Benchmarking Process

Stages of the Benchmarking Process	Factors to Consider
Stage 1: Internal Study and Preliminary Competitive Analyses	Preliminary internal and external competitive analyses Determine key areas for study Determine scope and significance of the study
Stage 2: Developing Long-Term Commitment to the Benchmarking Project and Coalescing the Benchmarking Team	*Developing Long-Term Commitment to the Benchmarking Project:* Gain senior management support Develop a clear set of objectives Empower employees to make change *Coalescing the Benchmarking Team:* Use an experienced coordinator Train employees
Stage 3: Identifying Benchmarking Partners	Size of partners Number of partners Relative position within and across industries Degree of trust among partners

Stage 4:
Information Gathering- and Sharing-Methods
	Type of Benchmarking Information:
	Product
	Functional (process)
	Strategic (includes management accounting methods)
	
	Method of Information Collection:
	Unilateral
	Cooperative:
	  Database
	  Indirect/third party
	  Group
	
	Determine performance measures
	
	Determine the benchmarking performance gap in relation to performance measures

Stage 5: Taking Action to Meet or Exceed the Benchmark	Comparisons of performance measures are made

many functional areas. An *experienced coordinator* is usually necessary to organize the members' team and develop *training* in benchmarking methods. Lack of training will often lead to the failure of the implementation.

CONSIDER THIS . . .

Benchmarking Speed to Market of Automobile Manufacturers

Benchmarking can take many forms. As the data below illustrate, there is wide variation in the time it takes Japanese and U.S. automobile manufacturers to move from concept approval to the manufacturing of a vehicle. Decreasing the time for development is a critical goal for automobile manufacturers worldwide, since faster development times reduce costs and help manufacturers respond to customer preferences quickly. The data below can be used as a first step to begin the benchmarking process. For example, armed with this information, a competitor may approach Chrysler Corporation to find out how it is able to bring automobiles from concept approval to production in 29 months. The specific approach used to gather the information varies with the kind of relationship that one firm has developed with another.

Source: V. Reitman and R. L. Simison, "Japanese Car Makers Speed Up Car Making," *Wall Street Journal*, December 29, 1995, pp. B1, B5.

QUICKER CARS

Time it takes to develop new vehicle from concept approval to production

Auto Maker	Current Average (months)	Goal (months)	Record Time (Model)
Mazda	21	15–18	17 months (Capella)
Toyota	27*	18*	15 months (Ipsum, Starlet)
Mitsubishi	24	18	19 months (FTO)
Nissan	30	20	Not available
Honda	36*	24*	24 months* (CR-V)
Chrysler Corp.	29	24	24 months (Sebring)
Ford	37	24	18 months (European Escort restyling)
GM	46	38	26 months (Yukon, Tahoe)

Source: Auto makers   *Includes design time before concept approval

Stage 3: Identifying Benchmarking Partners

The third stage of benchmarking includes identification of partners. Some of the critical factors to consider are these:

1. The size of the partners
2. The number of partners

3. The relative position of the partners within and across industries
4. The degree of trust among partners

SIZE. The size of the benchmarking partner will depend on the specific activity or method being benchmarked. For example, if an organization wants to understand how a very large organization with a number of divisions coordinates its suppliers, then the organization would probably seek another organization of similar size for benchmarking. However, size is not an always an important factor. For instance, Chrysler Corporation studied L.L. Bean's warehousing method of flow-charting wasted motion. As a result, Chrysler implemented a method that led to significant changes in the ways that its workers were involved in organizational problem solving.

NUMBER. Benchmarking partners benefit from initial increases in the number of participants. However, as these numbers increase, there are issues of coordination, timeliness, and concern over proprietary information disclosure. Researchers argue that today's changing business environment is likely to encourage a larger number of participants because increased competition and technological progress in information-processing increases benchmarking benefits relative to costs.

RELATIVE POSITION WITHIN AND ACROSS INDUSTRIES. Another factor is the *relative position* of the organization within an industry. In many cases, *industry newcomers* and those whose performance on leading indicators has declined are probably more likely to seek a wider variety of benchmarking partners than those who are established industry leaders. Those who are *industry leaders* may benchmark because of their commitment to continuous improvement.

DEGREE OF TRUST. From the benchmarking organization's point of view, developing *trust* among partners is critical to obtaining truthful and timely information. Most organizations including industry leaders operate on a *quid-pro-quo* basis, with the understanding that both organizations will obtain information they can use.

These managers are engaged in a benchmarking exercise. They are studying the performance of one of their products to that of their competitors. *Courtesy* **Richard Pasley/ Stock, Boston**

Stage 4: Information-Gathering and -Sharing Methods

Two dimensions relating to information gathering and sharing emerge from the literature.

1. The type of information that benchmarking organizations collect
2. The method of information collection

TYPE OF INFORMATION. There are three broad classes of information on which firms interested in benchmarking can focus. *Product benchmarking* is the long-standing practice of carefully examining other organizations' products. *Functional (Process) benchmarking* is the study of other organizations' practices and costs with respect to functions or processes, such as assembly or distribution. *Strategic benchmarking* is the study of other organizations' strategies and strategic decisions, such as why organizations chose one particular strategy over another. Since management accounting methods have become an integral part of many organizations' strategies, benchmarking of these methods would occur as part of the management accounting function.

METHODS OF INFORMATION GATHERING. Management accountants play a key role in gathering and summarizing information used for benchmarking. There are two major methods of information collection for benchmarking. The most common can be described as **unilateral (covert) benchmarking,** in which companies independently gather information about one or several other companies that excel in the area of interest. Unilateral benchmarking relies on data that companies can obtain from industry trade associations or clearinghouses of information.

A second method is called **cooperative benchmarking.** Cooperative benchmarking involves the voluntary sharing of information through mutual agreements. The major advantage of cooperative benchmarking is that information sharing occurs both within and across industries. Within cooperative benchmarking there are three subcategories which we call *database, indirect/third party,* and *group*.

Companies that use **database benchmarking** typically pay a fee and in return gain access to information from a database operator who collects and edits the information prior to making it available to users.[20] In most cases, there is no direct contact with other firms, and the identity of the source of the data often is not revealed. The database method has the advantage of including a large amount of information in one place. However, insights regarding what the data mean for the firm and how to use the information are often not available.

Indirect/third party benchmarking involves the hiring an outside consultant to act as a liaison among firms engaged in benchmarking. The consultant supplies information from one party to the others and handles all communica-

---

[20] Industry surveys are a form of benchmarking, which often involve the collecting and analyzing of marketing data. Usually, though, only aggregate or average results are available. Industry associations also collect information from member firms, such as market data and wage and employment-level information used for labor negotiations and lobbying purposes. Associations focused on specific organizational functions, such as procurement or facilities management, provide another form of benchmarking. While associations engage mainly in technical training and professional certifications of their membership, many publish an annual review of key statistics of their membership and the industry, which can be used in the early stages of a benchmarking effort.

OBJECTIVE 13.6

Show how to apply the benchmarking model to learning about advances in management accounting methods.

Unilateral (covert) benchmarking
One method of benchmarking in which one company obtains information about another through industry trade associations or information clearing houses.

Cooperative benchmarking
A benchmarking method in which information is shared voluntarily between parties.

Database benchmarking
One approach to cooperative benchmarking in which companies can pay a fee in order to gain access to information from a database operator.

Indirect/third-party benchmarking
One approach to cooperative benchmarking in which an outside consultant acts as a liaison between two companies engaged in benchmarking.

tions. Often the consultant participates in the selection of partners. Since the members may be competitors, these groups pass information through a consultant so that members can learn about best practices. This approach requires that the sources of the information remain confidential.

Participants following **group benchmarking** meet openly to discuss their methods. They coordinate their efforts, define common terminology, visit each other's sites, and generally have a long-run association. Typically, firms that engage in cooperative benchmarking abide by a code of conduct that they agree upon prior to the study. As in most interactions, direct contact offers the opportunity for better understanding of the other parties involved and usually is the most effective benchmarking method. However, this method also is the most costly to implement; therefore, firms must evaluate the cost-benefit tradeoffs. This approach is probably the most useful technique for benchmarking management accounting methods as there is much more ability to gain insight through direct interaction with other companies.

> **Group benchmarking**
> One approach to cooperative benchmarking in which participants meet openly to discuss their methods.

After the information-gathering process is complete, the participants conducting the benchmarking study determine a **benchmarking or performance gap** by comparing their organization's own performance with the "best" performance that emerges from the data. The performance gap is based on specific performance measures on which the firm would like to improve. Performance measures may include *reduced defectives, faster on-time delivery, increased functionality, or reduced life-cycle product costs*. Other more qualitative measures may include *changes in employee decisions* concerning ways to work or how to solve problems, *increased motivation and satisfaction*, and *improved cooperation and coordination* among workgroups and employees. Financial measures, such as reduced product costs, usually occur as a result of addressing the relevant nonfinancial measures involved. Since most financial gains may take a significant amount of time, organizations should monitor the nonfinancial variables in the short term. Simply judging the effects of a benchmarking effort in the short term based on financial indicators may often lead to premature abandonment of what has been learned during the benchmarking project.

> **Benchmarking/performance gap**
> A comparison of one organization's performance to the "best" performance of other organizations.

For benchmarking to be successful, it is crucial to understand the incentives for benchmarking organizations as decision makers will only select courses of action where the expected *benefits* exceed the expected *costs*.

Stage 5: Taking Action to Meet or Exceed the Benchmark

In the final stage, the organization takes action and implements change as a result of the benchmarking initiative. After implementing the change, the organization makes comparisons to the specific performance measures selected. In many cases, the decision may be to perform better than the benchmark to be more competitive.

ARCHER REVISITED

If Bing Low, the vice-president of manufacturing at Archer Company wants to learn more about new management accounting techniques, he can begin by following the first three stages of the benchmarking approach. These stages—

conducting an internal study and performing a preliminary competitive analysis, developing a long-term commitment to the benchmarking project and coalescing the benchmarking team, and identifying benchmarking partners—are often similar regardless of whether an organization is benchmarking a product, function, or firm strategy. Where Bing has to begin to think specifically about benchmarking management accounting methods is in stage 4, which relates to information-gathering and information-sharing methods.

For example, in benchmarking how other organizations develop and use their total-life-cycle product costing system, Bing would want to determine:

1. The way that organizations define their life cycle concepts
2. The way organizations account for costs during each stage of the life cycle
3. What the level of committed costs for each phase of the life cycle is
4. What organizational structure and coordination processes exist to manage the total-life-cycle costing process

Exhibit 13-14 lists several factors that Bing may wish to consider if he is interested in implementing the methods discussed in this chapter.

For target costing, Archer Company would study how target prices, sales volume, targeted profit, and target costs are set. Because the target-costing process is so different from traditional product-costing methods, Bing would have to understand the kinds of philosophical and organizational changes necessary across the functional areas in his company. Two other key aspects for him to consider relate to whether he can develop the necessary supplier relationships that would be critical for target costing to succeed. Bing also would have to determine whether he could apply value engineering given his current organizational design. Since cost reduction under target costing can be very taxing on employees and suppliers, Bing would have to make a cultural assessment of whether his organization would be able to handle the changes.

Similarly, for Kaizen costing Bing would investigate how to derive the cost reduction targets and how often to revise them. Working around the standard costing system is also a consideration when implementing Kaizen costing as many employees will be well entrenched in trying simply to meet cost standards. Like the situation described with target costing, Kaizen costing requires significant changes in organizational culture. Again Bing would have to assess the chances of being able to foment organizational change.

Finally, quality costing involves knowledge of how and why organizations categorize costs into prevention, appraisal, internal failure, and external failure. This is a necessary first step to benchmarking the system. Some organizations, for example, will classify one particular quality cost into one category while another may choose a different category. However, simply understanding the categories is not enough. Bing also will want to understand the ways that different types of quality costs interact and how managing one set of costs, such as prevention costs, will have rippling effects on all the other costs. Deriving a useful quality-costing system requires cooperation among all functional areas in the organization. Archer Company will need to determine whether it is possible to obtain such cooperation in the organization.

For all of these management accounting methods, understanding the organizational structure and culture in place is necessary to manage any significant or-

EXHIBIT 13-14
Benchmarking Management Accounting Methods

Management Accounting Method	Factors to Benchmark
Total-life-cycle costing	The ways that other organizations define their life-cycle concepts
	How other organizations account for costs during each life cycle
	The level of committed costs for each phase of the life cycle
	The organizational structure and culture in place for life-cycle cost management
Target costing	The method by which target prices are set
	The method by which target costs are set
	Supplier relationships
	The role of value engineering in target costing
	The organizational structure and culture to manage target-costing
Kaizen costing	The overall cost-reduction system concept
	How to set cost-reduction targets
	How frequently to revise cost-reduction targets
	The organizational structure and culture used to manage Kaizen costing
Quality costing	How the organization classifies its quality costs into these categories: Prevention costs Appraisal costs Internal-failure costs External-failure cost
	The organizational structure and culture used to manage quality costs

ganizational change. Often decision makers may believe that the adoption of a technique, such as target costing, is simply a numerical accounting method. As illustrated in the chapter, each method requires decision-makers to understand the big picture related to these methods, which requires taking the ever-important first step of understanding the total life cycle of their products and services.

SUMMARY

In this chapter, we have discussed some of the contemporary management accounting methods being implemented in organizations. One critical point stressed is that decision makers should consider adopting a total-life-cycle-product perspective when developing new products or rejuvenating existing products.

A total-life-cycle perspective is essential, since simply focusing on manufacturing costs ignores an enormous percent of the costs to which the organization commits. With the total-life-cycle perspective, managers can make decisions during the RD&E cycle that can directly influence all costs during the rest of the whole life cycle.

In addition, the chapter also describes three management accounting methods—target costing, Kaizen costing, and quality costing—as ways of reducing costs and improving quality over the product life cycle. Finally, we presented a model of benchmarking that organizations can use to obtain information about their competitor's products, processes, and strategy. Benchmarking is becoming much more widely used in management accounting as organizations begin to use management accounting methods as a source for competitive advantage.

KEY TERMS

appraisal costs, p. 621

benchmarking (performance) gap, p. 633

benchmarking process, p. 628

committed costs, p. 610

cooperative benchmarking p. 632

cost of nonconformance (CONC), p. 620

cost-of-quality report, p. 624

database benchmarking, p. 632

external-failure costs, p. 621

group benchmarking, p. 633

indirect/third party benchmarking, p. 632

Industrial Standard Z8101-1981, p. 621

internal-failure costs, p. 621

ISO 9000 standards, p. 621

Kaizen costing, p. 618

manufacturing cycle, p. 610

post-sale service and disposal life cycle, p. 610

prevention costs, p. 621

Q Series of Quality Standards p. 620

quality costs, p. 621

research, development and engineering life cycle, p. 610

target cost (C), p. 614

target costing, p. 612

target product volume, p. 614

target profit margin (P), p. 614

target-reduction rate, p. 618

target selling price (S), p. 614

total-life-cycle costs, p. 609

total-life-cycle costing, p. 609

traditional cost reduction, p. 614

unilateral (covert) benchmarking, p. 632

value engineering, p. 616

ASSIGNMENT MATERIAL

■ QUESTIONS

13-1 What is the total-life-cycle costing approach? Why is it important?

13-2 Identify and explain each of the three major cycles of the total-life-cycle costing approach.

13-3 What is the difference between committed costs and incurred costs?

13-4 What are the three stages of the research, development, and engineering cycle?

13-5 What is the post-sale service and disposal cycle?

13-6 What is target costing?

13-7 What are the two essential elements needed to arrive at a target cost?

13-8 What is value engineering?

13-9 In which stage of the total life cycle of a product is target costing most applicable?

13-10 What is Kaizen costing?

13-11 When is a cost-variance investigation undertaken under Kaizen costing?

13-12 Why is it said that the Kaizen costing system operates "outside of the standard costing system"?

13-13 What is meant by the term "the cost of nonconformance"?

13-14 Waste, rework, and net cost of scrap are examples of what kinds of quality costs?

13-15 Quality engineering, quality training, statistical process control, and supplier certification are what kinds of quality costs?

13-16 List three examples for each of the following quality costing categories:
(a) prevention costs
(b) appraisal costs
(c) internal-failure costs
(d) external-failure costs

13-17 What is ISO 9000? Why is it important?

13-18 What is the Q Series of Quality Standards?

13-19 What is benchmarking and why is it used?

13-20 What are the five stages of the benchmarking process?

13-21 What are the two general methods of information gathering and sharing when undertaking a benchmarking exercise?

13-22 What are the three types of sharing and gathering information under the cooperative form of benchmarking?

13-23 What are the three broad classes of information on which firms interested in benchmarking can focus? Describe each.

13-24 What is a "benchmarking (performance) gap"?

13-25 What stage of the benchmarking process is the most important for benchmarking management accounting methods? Why?

■ EXERCISES

13-26   *Total-life-cycle costing*   How does the total-life-cycle costing approach differ from traditional product costing? Explain.

13-27   *Benefits of total-life-cycle costing*   What are the benefits of using a total-life-cycle costing approach to product costing? Explain.

13-28   *Problems with traditional accounting focus*   What is the traditional accounting focus in managing costs over the total life cycle of a product? What is the problem with this focus?

13-29   *Costs committed versus costs incurred*   Review Exhibit 13-2 showing the relationship between committed costs and incurred costs over the total life cycle of a product. Explain what the diagram means and what the implications are for managing costs.

13-30   *Post-sale and disposal cycle*   When does the disposal phase of the post-sale and disposal cycle of a product begin and end?

13-31   *Target costing*   How does target costing differ from traditional cost-reduction methods? Explain.

13-32   *Target costing equation*   Express the target-costing relationship in equation form. How does this equation differ from the other two types of traditional equations relating to cost reduction? Why is this significant?

13-33   *Value engineering*   What is the relationship between value engineering and target costing?

13-34   *Target costing: profitability measure*   What is the most widely used profitability measure to develop the target profit margin under target costing?

13-35   *Implementing target costing*   What are potential problems in implementing a target-costing system from a behavioral point of view?

13-36   *Kaizen versus standard costing*   What factors differentiate Kaizen costing from standard costing?

13-37   *Target costing versus Kaizen costing*   What is the major difference between target costing and Kaizen costing?

13-38   *Kaizen costing: knowledge*   According to the Kaizen-costing approach, who has the best knowledge to reduce costs? Why is this so?

13-39   *Kaizen meaning*   What do the terms "Kaizen" and "Kaizen costing" mean? In which stage of the total life cycle of a product is Kaizen costing most applicable? Why?

13-40   *Kaizen costing*   Under what condition will the cost savings due to Kaizen costing not be applied to production?

13-41   *ISO 9000*   Describe the ISO 9000 standards. How do ISO 9000 and ISO 9004 differ from ISO 9001, ISO 9002, and ISO 9003?

13-42   *ISO 9000: process*   What is the process that an organization has to go through to become ISO 9000 certified? Explain.

13-43   *Quality-cost categories*   Regarding the quality-costing categories, how do prevention costs differ from appraisal costs? How do internal-failure costs differ from external-failure costs?

13-44   *Quality-cost categories*   Of the four quality-costing categories, which quality cost is the most damaging to the organization? Explain.

13-45   *Cost-of-quality report*   What is the purpose of the cost-of-quality report? What kinds of decisions can be made with it?

13-46 *Benchmarking partners* What are the key factors in identifying benchmarking partners? Explain.

13-47 *Benchmarking and types of information* What are the three types of information on which firms benchmark? In what category do management accounting methods fall? Why?

13-48 *Benchmarking a target costing system* As a manager asked to benchmark another organization's target costing system, on what factors would you gather information? Why?

■ PROBLEMS

Fundamental Problems

13-49 *Total-life-cycle costing* Consider the following situation. Your manager comes to you and says, "I don't understand why everyone is talking about the total-life-cycle costing approach to product costing. As far as I am concerned this new approach is a waste of time and energy. I think we should just stick to what we know and that is the traditional approach to product costing."

REQUIRED

Write a memorandum critiquing your manager's view. In the memo, discuss the benefits of adopting the total-life-cycle costing approach.

13-50 *Total-life-cycle costing versus traditional methods* Gene Brooks is a traditional manufacturing manager who is only concerned with managing costs over the manufacturing cycle of the product. Arguing that since traditional accounting methods are focused on this cycle, he should not bother with the RD&E cycle because it is separate from his area of manufacturing.

REQUIRED

Write an essay discussing Gene's view. What types of structural and functional changes in organizations may be necessary to help Gene overcome his traditional view?

13-51 *Target costing: unit cost* Ajax Company is contemplating introducing a new type of pen to complement its existing line of writing instruments. The following data are available. The target price of the pen is $10; annual sales volume is 250,000 pens. Ajax has a 15% return-on-sales target.

REQUIRED

Compute the unit target cost per pen.

13-52 *Target costing: return on sales* Frank Stein, vice-president of Monsters, Inc., a toy manufacturer in Hollywood, California, has been trying to decide whether one of his branch managers, Billy Mummy, has been achieving the company-wide return-on-sales target of 20%. Frank has just been given data from his new target costing system regarding Bill's operation. Bill's estimated target sales volume is 250,000 toys with a target selling price of $25 at a unit target cost of $19.50.

REQUIRED

Help Frank determine whether Bill's return-on-sales target has been met. Has Bill done a good or a poor job? Explain.

13-53 *Target costing: implementation issues* Gaston Mirro, manager of Satellite Corporation, is thinking about implementing a target-costing system in his organization.

Several managers have taken him aside and have expressed concerns about implementing target costing in their organization.

REQUIRED

As an expert in target costing, you have been called in to discuss these concerns and offer advice as to how to overcome them. Write a memorandum discussing the concerns that managers have with target costing. In the memo, state how you would remedy these concerns.

13-54 *Benchmarking*   As a manager interested in learning more about target costing, you are contemplating three approaches to obtaining the best information about target costing. The first is to bring in an outside consultant; the second is to develop your own system inside your organization with little to no outside assistance; and the third is to engage in a benchmarking project with several other firms.

REQUIRED

Critique each of the these approaches, discussing their pros and cons. On what basis will you select your approach to learning about target costing? Explain.

13-55 *Traditional cost reduction versus target costing*   Traditional cost reduction in the U.S. differs significantly from the Japanese method of target costing.

REQUIRED

Discuss the similarities and differences in the process by which cost reduction under both systems occurs. Be specific in your answer.

13-56 *Kaizen costing: behavior issues*   Kaizen costing is a method that many Japanese companies have found effective in reducing costs.

REQUIRED

From a behavioral point of view, answer these questions:
(a) What are the biggest problems in using Kaizen costing?
(b) How can managers overcome these problems?

13-57 *ISO 9000: field exercise in a company*   Attaining ISO 9000 certification has become a goal of many organizations. The process of attaining certification is both difficult and time consuming.

REQUIRED

Identify a company close to your university that has attained ISO 9000 certification. If there are no companies close by, try to locate a company with the help of your professor, a relative, or a friend. Visit or call the company, and ask them if they will discuss the process of ISO 9000 certification with you. Then write a report discussing what you have found out. What did you learn from this exercise?

> ### Challenging Problems

13-58 *Target-costing versus transitional cost-reduction methods*   According to the chapter, the target-costing and traditional cost-reduction methods approach the relationships among cost, selling price, and profit margin quite differently.

REQUIRED

Write an essay that illustrates how the target-costing and traditional cost-reduction methods differ, using the appropriate symbols and equations. In addition to the equations, describe how the process differs in deriving costs.

13-59 *Standard costing versus Kaizen costing*   Many companies are interested in adopting a Kaizen-costing approach to reducing costs. However, they are not sure how their current standard-costing system will fit with the Kaizen-costing approach.

REQUIRED

How do the standard-costing system and the Kaizen-costing system differ? Can the two systems coexist? Explain.

13-60 *Quality costing: balancing category costs* Managers concerned with improving quality sometimes have a difficult balancing act given the four types of quality costs that they have to manage. As a new manager, you are trying to figure out a strategy for managing $2 million of quality costs; your total quality costs cannot exceed 4% of sales.

REQUIRED

You need to decide on how much should go into each of the four quality-cost categories. How would you go about allocating these costs? What tradeoffs would you have to make as you allocate the costs?

13-61 *Benchmarking: field exercise with other students* Assume that you are an average student who has a desire to be one of the best students in your class. Your professor suggests that you benchmark the working habits of the best student in the class. You are somewhat skeptical but decide to take on the challenge.

REQUIRED

How would you go about this benchmarking exercise? In answering this question, describe the process that you would undertake in benchmarking the best student, the factors that you would be trying to study, and how you would implement changes to your working habits.

13-62 *Benchmarking: field exercise in a company* Benchmarking a product, process, or management accounting method takes a great deal of time and effort. Companies have many choices when it comes to conducting a benchmarking study. For example, in following the five stages of the benchmarking process, companies have to decide on how to proceed, who to select as benchmarking partners, and what information they are willing to share and to gather.

REQUIRED

Locate a company in your local community that has engaged in a benchmarking study. Try to arrange a visit to the company (perhaps through your professor, relative, or friend) in order to talk to employees who have been involved in the benchmarking effort. Using the five-stage process, critique the approach that this company followed. What are the similarities and differences between what this company did and the process described in this chapter? Be specific about the procedures that were used and the variables that were assessed. Finally, what were the results of the benchmarking exercise at this company? Was it a success or a failure? Why?

13-63 *Target costing and service organization* Imagine that you are the manager of a large bank. Having heard about a management accounting method called target costing, you are wondering whether it can be applied to the banking industry. In particular, you are trying to determine how to benchmark other organizations to gain more information.

REQUIRED

(a) Can target costing be applied to the banking industry? To what products or services can target costing be applied?
(b) Devise a benchmarking plan for the bank. Your plan should include which banks to benchmark with and the kinds of information sought.

13-64 *Kaizen costing versus standard costing* Your organization, located in Worthington, Ohio, is contemplating introducing Kaizen costing to help with cost reduction. As someone who has an understanding of management accounting, you have been asked for your opinion. Specifically, some of your colleagues are wondering about the differences between standard costing and Kaizen costing.

REQUIRED

Write a report discussing the following:
(a) The similarities and differences between standard costing and Kaizen costing.
(b) Under what conditions Kaizen costing can be adapted to U.S. organizations.

13-65 ***Managing with a cost-of-quality report*** As a quality manager with the Multiple Products Company, you are approached by Lucy S. Diamonds, the manufacturing manager, who asks you to help her set up a quality costing system that will generate a cost-of-quality report. Lucy also wants to know how to use the report.

REQUIRED

(a) Describe the categories of quality costs and what types of costs go into each category.
(b) Given the quality-cost categories, what should Lucy try to do to manage each?
(c) How will managing one category affect the others?

■ CASES

13-66 ***Preparing a cost-of-quality report*** The information below has been gathered from the PECO Company.

Item	Amount
Quality engineering	$1,000,000
Warranty claims	120,000
Product-liability lawsuits	200,000
Research of customer needs	800,000
Maintenance of test equipment	350,000
Returned products	200,000
Rework costs	600,000
Quality training	305,000
Process control monitoring	1,000,000
Inspection of and testing of in-coming materials	900,000
Repair costs in the field	250,000
Statistical process control	650,000
Product recalls	300,000
Waste	300,000
Net cost of scrap	435,000
Supplier certification	400,000

Total sales for 1997 were $175,000,000.

REQUIRED

Prepare a cost-of-quality report by quality-cost category and a memorandum discussing your findings and recommendations to PECO management.

13-67 ***Preparing a cost-of-quality report*** The following data have just been gathered on quality costs at the Ideal Company.

Cost Category	Amount
Product recalls	$ 325,000
Downtime due to defects	600,000
Warranty claims	420,000
Inspection of and testing of in-coming materials	300,000
Product liability lawsuits	500,000
Process quality audits	350,000
Rework costs	2,000,000
Quality training	150,000
Process control monitoring	350,000
Repair costs in the field	375,000
Statistical process control	300,000
Waste	900,000
Net cost of scrap	1,500,000
Supplier certification	350,000
Quality engineering	200,000
Returned products	380,000

Total sales for 1997 were $75,000,000.

REQUIRED

As manager of quality at the Ideal Company your task is to make sense of the data. Prepare a cost-of-quality report that organizes the data. How do you interpret the data? What actions would you take as the quality manager at Ideal?

14

COMPENSATION ISSUES

FRIEDMAN-JACOBS COMPANY

Courtesy **Dick Luria/FPG International**

Consider the following real story about a small appliance dealer whose owner, Arthur Friedman, decided to let his employees set their own pay.[1]

Friedman first unleashed his proposal at one of the regular staff meetings. "Decide what you are worth," he said, "and tell the bookkeeper to put it in your envelope next week. No questions asked. Work any time, any day, any hours you want. Having a bad day? Go home. Hate working Saturdays? No problem. Aunt Ethel from Chicago has dropped in unexpectedly? Well, take a few days off, show her the town. Want to go to Reno for a week, need a rest? Go, go, no need to ask.

If you need some money for the slot machines, take it out of petty cash. Just come back when you feel ready to work again."

This is what happened.

"It was about a month before anyone asked for a raise," recalls Stan Robinson, 55, the payroll clerk. "And when they did, they asked Art first. But he refused to listen and told them to just tell me what they wanted.

I kept going back to him to make sure it was all right, but he wouldn't even talk about it. I finally figured out he was serious."

"It was something that I wanted to do," explains Friedman. "I always said that if you give people what they want, you get what you want. You have to be willing to lose, to stick your neck out. I finally decided that the time had come to practice what I preached."

Soon the path to Stan Robinson's desk was heavily traveled. Friedman's wife, Merle, was one of the first; she figured that her contribution was worth $1 an hour more. Some asked for $50 more a week, some $60. Delivery truck driver, Charles Ryan, was more ambitious; he demanded a $100 raise.

In most companies, Ryan would have been laughed out of the office. His work had not been particularly distinguished. His truck usually left in the morning and returned at five o'clock in the afternoon religiously, just in time for him to punch out. He dragged around the shop, complained constantly, and was almost always late for work. Things changed.

[1] Martin Koughan, "Arthur Friedman's Outrage: Employees Decide Their Pay."

"He had been resentful about his pay," explains Friedman. "The raise made him a fabulous employee. He started showing up early in the morning and would be back by three o'clock, asking what else had to be done."

Instead of the all-out raid on the company coffers that some might expect, the fifteen employees of the Friedman-Jacobs Company displayed astonishing restraint and maturity. The wages they demanded were just slightly higher than the scale of the Retail Clerks union to which they all belonged (at Friedman's insistence). Some did not even take a raise. One serviceman who was receiving considerably less than his co-workers was asked why he did not insist on equal pay. "I did not want to work that hard," was the answer.

THE ROLE OF COMPENSATION IN ORGANIZATION CONTROL

An element of control is motivating employees to pursue the organization's interests as they undertake their daily jobs. Thus, the major role of motivation is to align the individual's interests with those of the organization. An important element of motivation is compensation, which is the topic of this chapter.

THE ROLE OF MANAGEMENT ACCOUNTING IN COMPENSATION

Motivation
A person's interest or drive to act in a certain way.

An organization seeks to motivate its employees to act in the organization's best interests. Many factors can affect an employee's **motivation,** which we define as a person's interest or drive to act in a certain way. These factors include the employee's personal traits, the organization's culture, and the general management style of the organization's key people. We discuss compensation here because management accountants play a critical role in compensation practice.

In general, the objective of compensation policy is to tie the individual's and the organization's interests together by rewarding employees for actions that benefit the organization. Conventional compensation practice focuses on tying employee rewards to outcomes that the organization values, such as profits, number of good units of production a machine operator produces, positive labor efficiency variances, or high customer service ratings. The higher the valued outcome, the higher the employee's reward. Since the foundation of most compensation contracts is measured performance, one of the major roles of management accounting practice is to measure and report the outcome measures that define compensation contracts.

While this may seem quite simple, designing effective compensation contracts actually is quite difficult. First, outcomes often reflect the joint effect of decision and environmental uncertainty. A bad outcome may reflect an unfortunate and uncontrollable uncertainty rather than poor effort, skill, knowledge, or execution on the part of the decision maker. For example, suppose that you are preparing an assignment that has a fixed due date. You have carefully researched the subject, developed numerous references, and written up your response using a word processor. Then disaster strikes. When you try to access the file on your diskette to print your response, you find that the file has been accidentally erased. You have no proof of the hours, effort, and thought that you have put into this project.

Because of the potential for such an uncontrollable uncertainty to affect measured outcomes, compensation is sometimes based on inputs rather than outputs. For example, rewards may be based on the number of hours employees work or the skill or training that they bring to their jobs. Although people feel that rewards based on inputs rather than outputs are motivationally inferior, organizations often have to use them as a reward basis.

A second major problem in compensation practice is that outcomes are often the result of the activities of many different people, which makes it difficult to isolate and reward individual contributions. In this case, organizations often resort to rewards based on group performance. However, rewarding group behavior creates the opportunity for people to share in the hard work and efforts of others. This, in turn, creates an incentive for people to let others do the work (shirking).

A third major problem in compensation practice is that there is considerable disagreement among experts about the precise effect of compensation on motivation. At one extreme some individuals believe that performance-based rewards are necessary to provide motivation. At the other extreme, some people believe that performance-based rewards are both demeaning and ineffective. These arguments suggest that different things motivate different people and that no one person can say definitively what compensation practice works best in a given situation.

Finally, organizations often choose inappropriate performance measures that motivate dysfunctional and suboptimal performance. For example, a courier company that rewarded managers of local terminals based on their ability to clear mail out of the terminal before a deadline encouraged managers to send out mail that they knew had been sorted incorrectly. This, in turn, created serious service problems that were corrected only when the terminal managers where charged back for the related cost and service problems. Consider the example of an organization that manufactured motherboards for computers. The company had three major divisions—manufacturing, assembly, and sales. The manager of each division was rewarded based on meeting production or sales quotas, which fostered an environment where each division felt that it operated independently of the other divisions. Therefore, each division blamed other divisions for its inability to achieve its own objectives. For example, manufacturing often transferred problem boards to assembly because it received rewards based on the number of units transferred. The sales division often made promises to customers for custom production without consulting manufacturing and inflicted heavy special order and expediting costs on the manufacturing unit.

In general, it is virtually impossible to provide a rational set of individual rewards in a highly integrated and balanced value chain. However, as organizations move toward providing group rewards, they face the problem of people who coast along, taking advantage of the work of others.

OBJECTIVE 14.1

Understand the role of motivation in organizations.

OBJECTIVE 14.2

Discuss the significant elements of two influential theories of motivation.

*T*HEORIES OF MOTIVATION

In most organizations, pay is more than simply what is required to keep an employee from leaving the organization. Pay is part of the complex bundle of factors that motivate people to work in the organization's best interests. Therefore, organizations must consider pay issues within the larger context of motivation.

People who study human behavior have developed many alternative theories to explain what motivates behavior. We will discuss two of these theories here—Herzberg's two-factor theory and Vroom's expectancy theory. These two theories are not necessarily the most widely accepted. Rather, they provide a good framework for our discussion of compensation systems and, in particular, help identify the role of management accounting in supporting those systems.

Herzberg's Two-Factor Theory of Motivation

Herzberg's two-factor theory of motivation
A theory that maintains that two groups of factors with different roles—hygiene and satisfier—motivate individual behavior.

Hygiene factors
A group of factors in the Herzberg theory that relate to job context. They are thought to be necessary to provide the environment for motivation rather than being motivators themselves.

Based on interviews with hundreds of people, Frederick Herzberg came to believe that two groups of factors—hygiene factors and satisfier factors—affect behavior. This idea became known as **Herzberg's two-factor theory of motivation.**[2] Exhibit 14-1 summarizes these factors.

Hygiene factors relate to the job context and define the individual's work environment. Herzberg believed that, when hygiene factors are poor, the employee becomes dissatisfied and job performance suffers. Herzberg believed that improving hygiene factors makes employees less dissatisfied. However, Herzberg argued that hygiene factors by themselves do not motivate or satisfy employees. Rather, they establish the potential for motivation, which is provided by what Herzberg called *satisfier factors.*

Think of hygiene factors as constraints. If an organization fails to meet minimum conditions relating to hygiene factors, employees are not motivated to do their jobs well no matter what else the organization does. Hygiene factors are to motivation as the foundation of a house is to the house. The foundation provides the potential for the living space to provide comfort and shelter to the occupants of the home but, by itself, provides no comfort or shelter.

EXHIBIT 14-1
Herzberg's Two-Factory Theory of Motivation

Hygiene Factors	Satisfier Factors
Working conditions	Achievement
Base pay	Recognition
Organization policies	Responsibility
Interpersonal relationships	Opportunity for growth
Supervisory quality	

[2] Frederick Herzberg, "One More Time: How Do You Motivate Employees?," *Harvard Business Review,* January-February 1968, pp. 53–62.

Routine tasks undertaken in busy office environments may offer employees little in the way of hygiene factors, thereby reducing the potential for satisfier factors to motivate those employees. *Courtesy* **Tom Campbell/ FPG International**

Satisfier factors relate to the job content and define how workers feel about their jobs. Herzberg believed that when satisfier factors are poor, employees derive no satisfaction from their jobs and have no motivation. He believed that improving satisfier factors makes employees more satisfied with their jobs and therefore more highly motivated. Satisfier factors can motivate performance if hygiene factors are in place. In essence, satisfier factors provide the motivation for people to do their jobs well.

Pay has two roles in Herzberg's theory. Base pay is a hygiene factor. If employees believe that their base pay is too low, they will be dissatisfied with their jobs and satisfier factors will be unable to motivate performance. Any discretionary part of pay that the employees perceive as an achievement or a recognition of performance is a satisfier factor.[3] However, if the discretionary part of pay is perceived as an extension of base pay, it serves as a hygiene factor not a motivating factor. Management accountants are particularly interested in discretionary pay because it is often based on information or numbers provided by the organization's management accounting system.

Satisfier factors
A group of factors in the Herzberg theory that relate to job content. They are thought to provide motivation when the environment for motivation has been properly prepared.

Vroom's Expectancy Theory

Victor Vroom[4] developed a model of motivation he called **expectancy theory.** Exhibit 14-2 shows the relationship of various elements in Vroom's expectancy theory, which includes the following:

1. *Effort.* What the person contributes to the job, including knowledge, skill, time, and effort.
2. *Expectancy.* The individual's expectations about whether the application of knowledge, skill, time, and effort will affect measured performance.
3. *Performance.* The way that the performance measurement system assesses what the individual has put into the organization. This can include factors

Vroom's expectancy theory
A theory that maintains that motivation is a product of expectancy, instrumentality, and valence.

---

[3] A sense of achievement and recognition can come in many other forms that do not involve pay, such as personal satisfaction and commendations from superiors. This is important to remember. Many people assume that monetary rewards are the only device that organizations can use to motivate employees.
[4] Victor H. Vroom, *Work and Motivation*, New York: Wiley, 1964.

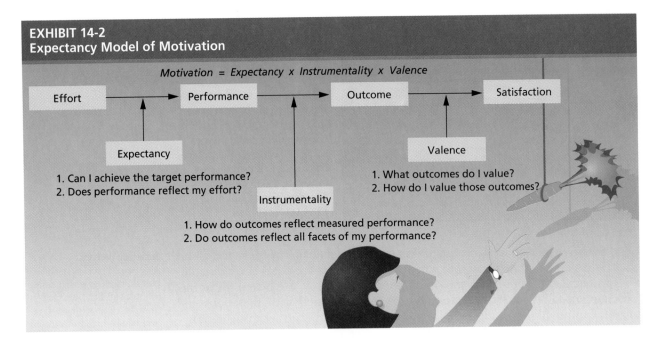

EXHIBIT 14-2
Expectancy Model of Motivation

Motivation = Expectancy x Instrumentality x Valence

Effort → Performance → Outcome → Satisfaction

Expectancy
1. Can I achieve the target performance?
2. Does performance reflect my effort?

Instrumentality
1. How do outcomes reflect measured performance?
2. Do outcomes reflect all facets of my performance?

Valence
1. What outcomes do I value?
2. How do I value those outcomes?

that the individual controls and those that the individual does not control, depending on the accuracy of the performance measurement system. Performance measurement is the domain of the organization's management accounting system.

4. *Instrumentality.* The relationship between the individual's measured performance and the outcomes provided by the organization, such as pay for performance or recognition. This reflects the details of the compensation contract between the individual and the organization.

5. *Outcome.* The set of rewards that the person experiences or receives based on measured performance.

6. *Valence.* The value assigned by the individual to the outcomes.

7. *Satisfaction.* The value of the outcome to the individual.

This expectancy model is one approach to explain how employee skill and knowledge, the organization's performance measurement and reward system, and the individual's personal values combine to determine individual motivation. A **motivation system** is a performance measurement and reward system that provides benefits or recognition to employees.

Motivation system
A system of performance measurement and rewards that provides employee benefits or recognition based on measured performance.

FACTORS AFFECTING INDIVIDUAL MOTIVATION

OBJECTIVE 14.3

Understand how organizations tie individual objectives to organization objectives.

The Herzberg and Vroom theories offer different but reinforcing perspectives on the role for rewards and management accounting systems in organizations. Herzberg's theory recognizes that hygiene factors are not motivators, but that they are necessary for organizations to provide in order for satisfier factors, or motivators, to have their effects. Many current debates about motivation focus on:

The Ford Motor Company employee was a member of a team that streamlined the ordering process for dealers, thereby improving service while reducing costs. This employee may have been motivated by being given the responsibility to make changes and from succeeding in improving a customer-related process. *Courtesy* Ford Motor Company

1. Whether a particular reward is a hygiene factor or a satisfier factor
2. The strength of satisfier factors in motivating performance

For example, most articles advocating employee empowerment focus on the value and role of opportunity for personal growth that can be motivated by proper job design. Herzberg's theory indicates that, for rewards to act as a satisfier factor, individuals must have a clear understanding of how their activities affect measured performance and how measured performance affects the rewards provided by the organization to the individuals. Therefore, the performance measurement system plays a crucial role in providing the effect of performance-based pay as a satisfier factor.

Vroom's theory provides a specific structure in which to consider the role and effect of the key management accounting function of performance measurement. Exhibit 14-2 shows that the performance measurement system lies at the heart of the motivation system. If the reward system ties the performance measurement directly to outcomes that the employee values, the employee substitutes performance measures for outcomes. Then the performance measures become the employee's goals because valued outcomes follow directly. Therefore, according to this theory, the key is to ensure that while pursuing performance measures the employee takes actions that meet the organization's objectives. Therefore, the performance measurement system must monitor and reward those elements of performance that contribute to the organization's goals. Exhibit 14-3 summarizes this perspective of linking personal and organization goals.

The vertical axis reflects the organization's perspectives and shows the link between its objectives, the results that employees create in the organization, and the outcomes that the organization values. The horizontal axis reflects the employee's perspective and shows the link between what the employee puts into the organization, the results that effort produces, and the rewards that the employee values.

Results are the link between the employee and the organization. Results must lead to rewards that the employee values and to outcomes that the organization values. The first step is for the organization to identify what results it wants.

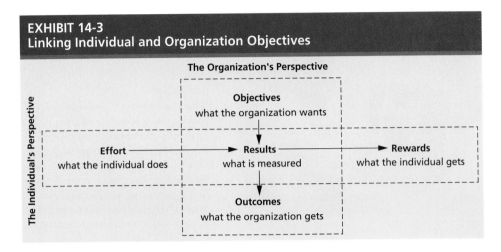

EXHIBIT 14-3
Linking Individual and Organization Objectives

The next step is to establish the link between the employee and the organization by designing a reward system that rewards employees for results that the organization values because they produce desired outcomes.

Intrinsic Rewards

Organizations use two broad types of rewards, intrinsic and extrinsic, to motivate employees. **Intrinsic rewards** relate to the nature of the organization and the design of the job. They come from inside the individual and reflect the satisfaction that a person experiences from doing the job and from the opportunity for growth that the job provides. One of management's most important tasks is to design jobs and develop an organizational environment and culture that lead to employees valuing intrinsic rewards. Because of the nature of intrinsic rewards management accounting has little effect on them.[5]

Intrinsic rewards
Rewards relating to the nature of the organization and the design of the job that people experience without the intervention of anyone else.

Extrinsic Rewards

Based on assessed performance[6] an **extrinsic reward** is any reward that one person provides to another person to recognize a job well done. Examples of commonly used extrinsic rewards are meals, trips, cash bonuses, stock bonuses, and recognition in the organization's newsletter and on plaques.

Extrinsic rewards
Rewards, based on performance, that are provided to the individual by the organization.

*C*ONSIDER THIS . . .

Using Nonfinancial Extrinsic Rewards

A number of organizations have found that recognition rewards may be more effective in motivating performance than bonus awards. In a study of incentives, four of the top five incentives mentioned by employees required little or no money: congratulations by manager, a personal citation, public recognition, and a morale boosting meeting.

Source: Bob Nelson, "Motivating Employees with Informal Rewards," *Management Accounting,* November 1995, Volume 77, Number 5, pp. 30–34.

[5] An exception is that employees sometimes find the internal control systems that management accountants design and operate intrusive and demeaning. When this happens, performance measurement systems can create a dysfunctional environment that can prevent people from experiencing intrinsic rewards.

[6] While the assessment can be formal or informal, that is there is a specific rule that ties rewards to performance, and be based on formal performance measurement or informal information, the vast majority of extrinsic reward systems are formal systems based on formal performance measurements provided by management accounting systems.

Extrinsic rewards are impersonal rewards that reinforce the notion that the employee is distinct from the organization. Many people believe that extrinsic rewards reinforce the common perception that the wage compensates the employee for a minimally acceptable effort and that the organization must use additional rewards or compensation to motivate the employee to provide additional effort.

OBJECTIVE 14.4

Explain several approaches to rewarding performance and the nature of intrinsic and extrinsic rewards.

Choosing between Intrinsic and Extrinsic Rewards

Many compensation experts believe that organizations have not used intrinsic rewards enough. They claim that, given proper leadership, intrinsic rewards may have as strong or even stronger motivational effects than extrinsic rewards. In the context of the Herzberg model, these experts argue that organizations have undervalued:

1. The importance of the job's structure (a hygiene factor)
2. The motivational effect of designing a job that promotes employee satisfaction and personal growth in the job

In the context of the expectancy model, organizations have undervalued the valence that people have for intrinsic rewards relating to pride of accomplishment.

The issue of the effectiveness of intrinsic and extrinsic rewards is a topic of heated debate in the management literature. This requires judgment in evaluating opposing arguments to form an opinion of what seems appropriate. Here very briefly are the opposing arguments prompted by a single article on this topic.

In a provocative article,[7] Alfie Kohn argued that conventional incentive plans that tie rewards to measured performance are fundamentally and irreparably flawed. Kohn observed, "At least two dozen studies over the last three decades have conclusively shown that people who expect to receive a reward for completing a task or for doing that task successfully do not perform as well as those who expect no reward at all." Kohn argues that, although this result holds over a wide range of tasks, people, and rewards, the result is strongest when the job requires creative skills. Kohn's explanation for these results is that "pay is not a motivator," which echoes the Herzberg argument that pay is a hygiene factor, rather than a satisfier (motivator) factor. Kohn cites studies that suggest that pay is well down on the list, often the fifth or sixth item, of important job characteristics.

Kohn's argument is built around the idea that the preoccupation with extrinsic rewards undermines the effectiveness of reward systems and that the design of organizations and jobs should allow employees to experience intrinsic rewards. Kohn urges organizations to spend more time developing an

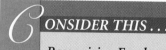

CONSIDER THIS . . .

Recognizing Employee Contributions

Wheeling-Pittsburgh Steel Corporation recognizes employee contributions in its employee publication *Windows*, which features the pictures and contributions of employees. Not only does this recognition acknowledge the contribution of the named employees, but it also provides a description of their ideas. This, in turn, suggests to others the contributions that they may make. In a similar way, McDonnell-Douglas developed the Golden Eagle President's Award to commend its employees for outstanding performance. An important feature of the McDonnell-Douglas award is that fellow employees nominate the recipients.

[7] Alfie Kohn, "Why Incentive Plans Cannot Work," *Harvard Business Review*, September-October 1993, pp. 54–63.

*C*ONSIDER THIS . . .

Providing Results-Based Extrinsic Rewards

Lincoln Electric, a manufacturer of electrical components, has carried rewarding performance to the limit. Its production workers are paid on a piece-rate system. These workers receive no holiday pay, sick leave, or family leave, nor do they receive medical or other benefits. Piece-rate workers at Lincoln Electric are literally paid only for the work that they do. Workers who are highly trained, skilled, motivated, and who can work fast find the Lincoln Electric system very attractive. The company claims that its production employees are the highest paid in the world.

Despite the high rate of pay, the turnover rate is 20% because many new workers find adapting to the rapid pace of work difficult. Some social commentators have observed that in general piece-rate systems are socially undesirable because, if workers slow down due to health or age, they suffer financially through no fault of their own.

In late 1995, the company announced its plans to review this program arguing that the time may have come to use a mix of wage and incentive compensation.

environment in which employees are empowered and can collaborate and in which the job content offers the potential for personal growth. These conditions allow employees to experience intrinsic rewards.[8]

Like all commentaries in this area, Kohn's observations generated many responses, some strongly supporting his views and some fiercely rejecting them.[9] While some responses failed to deal with the substance of his argument, others argued that he was naive, and that[10] their personal experience suggested that extrinsic, particularly monetary, rewards are the most effective motivators of performance.

The issue remains unresolved; however, one thing is clear. Most organizations have ignored and continue to ignore the role of intrinsic rewards in motivation and blindly accept the view that only financial extrinsic rewards motivate employees. Many people believe that financial extrinsic rewards are both necessary and sufficient to motivate superior performance. Both systematic and anecdotal evidence suggest, however, that financial extrinsic rewards are not necessary to create effective organizations and that performance rewards do not necessarily create them. Whether nonfinancial extrinsic and intrinsic rewards are more or less effective than financial extrinsic rewards in motivating behavior is unresolved. Nonfinancial extrinsic and intrinsic rewards do have a role to play in most organizations, however.

Beyond the debate about the relative effectiveness of intrinsic and extrinsic rewards, some people argue that incentive compensation programs in any form are unacceptable. They suggest that organizations must strive to be excellent to survive in a difficult and competitive world. Therefore, these people argue that superior and committed performance is necessary for organizations to survive and is part of the contract of employment, not something that merits additional pay.

Because of the lack of systematic evidence about the role and effectiveness of nonfinancial extrinsic and intrinsic rewards, this chapter focuses on financial extrinsic rewards that are usually based on measures provided by management accounting systems. This does not mean, however, that nonfinancial extrinsic and intrinsic rewards are unimportant. Rather, it reinforces the idea that financial extrinsic rewards tend to be based on more formal systems that require more explanation.

---

[8] Alfie Kohn, "For Best Results, Forget the Bonus," *The New York Times*, October 17, 1993, p. F11.

[9] "Rethinking Rewards," *Harvard Business Review*, November-December 1993, pp. 37–49.

[10] One respondent called Kohn a communist; another suggested that Kohn was a self-promoter seeking consulting opportunities. Unfortunately, these types of responses are typical of the poor quality of debate surrounding this issue.

EXTRINSIC REWARDS BASED ON PERFORMANCE

Incentive compensation, or pay-for-performance systems, are reward systems that provide monetary (extrinsic) rewards based on measured results. **Pay-for-performance** systems base rewards on achieving or exceeding some measured performance. The reward can be based on absolute performance, performance relative to some plan, or performance relative to some comparable group. Examples of measures of *absolute performance* include these:

1. The number of good units made (such as a piece-rate system)
2. The organization's results (such as profit levels or measures from an organization's balanced scorecard—measures of customer or employee satisfaction, quality, and rate of successful new product introductions)
3. The performance of the organization's share price (such as a stock option plan)

Examples of rewards based on *relative performance* are those tied to the following:

1. The ability to exceed some performance target level (such as paying a salesperson a bonus for sales above a quota or paying a production group a bonus for beating a benchmark performance level)
2. The amount of a bonus pool (such as sharing in a pool defined as the organization's reported profits less a stipulated return to shareholders)
3. Exceeding the average performance level of a comparable group

Incentive compensation
A system that provides pay for performance.

Pay-for-performance
A system that provides rewards for performance to motivate achieving or exceeding measured performance targets.

This Harris Corporation employee was part of a team that produced integrated circuits (ICs) used in Ford Motor Company automobiles. The Ford assembly operations began to reject many ICs supplied by Harris Corporation, which led to downtime, missed production schedules, and income losses for the Ford employees. This employee of Harris Corporation said that she "felt terrible about how they [the Ford employees] thought about us" and joined a team that worked with the Ford production workers to solve the problem. This cooperative venture went so well that the Ford workers asked that Harris Corporation become the exclusive supplier of the part. This employee was motivated by pride in her work, an intrinsic reward, and by how the employees at Ford felt about her work, an extrinsic reward. *Courtesy* Theo Anderson/Harris Corporation

To reward performance, organizations need performance measurement systems that gather relevant and reliable performance information.

Occasionally, compensation policy can be affected by government regulations. For example, since 1994 in the United States most organizations cannot claim as an expense for the purpose of computing taxable income the portion of any employee's salary that exceeds $1 million. This will certainly (1) *reduce* the use of salary and perquisites (such as company cars and club memberships) and (2) *increase* the use of monetary rewards based on performance.

EFFECTIVE PERFORMANCE MEASUREMENT AND REWARD SYSTEMS

OBJECTIVE 14.5

Identify what makes effective reward systems.

When an organization has decided to reward performance, it turns to the management accountant to design the performance measurement systems needed to support the reward system. A systematic approach to rewarding performance has six broad attributes designed to ensure that the performance measurement system can motivate desired performance.

First, the employees must *understand their jobs and the reward system and believe that it measures what they control and contribute to the organization.* This attribute ensures that the employee perceives the reward system as fair and predictable. In expectancy model terms, this establishes the expectancy between effort and performance and the instrumentality between performance and outcome.

If employees do not understand their jobs or how to improve their measured performance, a reward system based on performance measures is ineffective. In this case, employees perceive no relationship between effort and performance and ultimately outcomes. Similarly, if the reward system is complex, employees are unable to relate perceived performance improvements to changes in outcomes, and the motivational effect of the reward system will be lost. [11] Finally, if the reward system does not measure employees' controllable performance, they conclude that measured performance is independent of their efforts and again the incentive effect of the reward system is lost. Specifying and developing a clear relationship among effort, performance, and result and ensuring that all employees understand this relationship is a critical management role.

Therefore, *the centerpiece of incentive compensation systems is the performance measurement system,* which becomes the focus of the employees' attention. The decisions that employees make in pursuing the performance measures that ultimately provide valued personal outcomes move the organization toward achieving its goals if the performance measures are aligned with the organization's goals.

CONSIDER THIS . . .

Abandoning Individual Rewards in Favor of Group Rewards

In 1992 Hoechst Celanese, a manufacturer of chemical and pharmaceutical products, announced that "in order to focus more attention on employee performance and development, the (individual) performance rating categories (Exceptional, Quality, or Requires Improvement) are being eliminated. . . . The elimination of these categories is consistent with the company's Quality Values, which place a high degree of importance on continual improvement, teamwork, and participative goal setting."

---

[11] In terms of the expectancy model, the expectancy and instrumentality of the reward and performance measurement systems will be low.

Second, and related to the first attribute, the performance measurement system must make a careful choice about whether it measures employees' inputs or outputs. In general, the greatest alignment between employees' and the organization's interests is provided when the performance measurement system monitors and rewards employee outputs that contribute to the organization's success. However, outputs often reflect circumstances and conditions that are beyond the employee's control, and when they do, the expectancy between individuals' efforts and measured results is reduced, thereby decreasing the motivation provided by the reward system. Under circumstances where outcome measurement is problematic, organizations often choose to monitor and reward inputs (such as employee learning, demonstrated skill, and time worked). The choice of the mix of performance measures and whether those measures are input based, output based, or a combination of measures is one of the most difficult issues in the design of performance measurement and compensation systems.

Third, the elements of performance that the performance measurement system monitors and rewards should reflect the *organization's critical success factors.* This attribute ensures that the performance system is relevant and motivates intended performance—performance that matters to the organization's success. Moreover, the performance measurement system must consider all facets of performance so that employees do not sacrifice performance on an unmeasured element for performance on an element that the reward system measures. This is the role and purpose of measuring and rewarding employees across a set of balanced and comprehensive measures as proposed in the balanced scorecard. For example, if a supervisor tells a telephone operator that productivity (such as the number of help requests handled per shift) is important, the operator may sacrifice the quality and courtesy offered to customers in order to handle as many questions as possible.

Fourth, the reward systems must set *clear standards* for performance that employees accept. In the context of the expectancy model of motivation, this helps employees assess whether their skills and efforts create results that the performance measurement system captures and reports as outcomes. This attribute determines employees' beliefs about whether the performance system is fair. If performance standards are either unspecified or unclear to employees, the relationship between performance and outcome is ambiguous and therefore reduces the motivational effect of the performance reward system.

Fifth, the performance measurement system must be able to *measure the objects of measurement systematically and accurately.* This attribute ensures that the performance measurement system establishes a clear relationship between performance and outcome. (In expectancy theory terms, this linkage is referred to as improved instrumentality).

Sixth, when it is critical that employees coordinate decision making and other activities with other employees, the reward system should *reward group, rather than individual, performance.* Many organizations

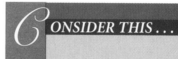

CONSIDER THIS . . .

Motivating Team Performance

Based on survey results received from 37 manufacturing organizations, two researchers concluded that rewards play an important role in motivating teams but are rarely the primary driver of performance. An analysis of what factors drove team performance suggested that the factors in order of importance were worker pride, company culture, competitive pressures, performance rewards, and job security. A majority of responding organizations indicated that they use both financial and nonfinancial (recognition) rewards. Moreover, many organizations design work environments in which employees experience intrinsic rewards.

Source: Christian M. Ellis and Lea A. P. Tonkin, "Survey Report: Rewards for Mature Teams," *Target,* Volume 10, Number 5, p. 22.

now believe that, to be effective, employees must work effectively in teams. These organizations are replacing evaluations and rewards based on individual performance with rewards and evaluation based on group performance.

Conditions Favoring Incentive Compensation

Some organization tasks are better suited to incentive compensation than others.[12] The incentive compensation system designer must consider many items when evaluating an incentive compensation system's potential to motivate performance. Moreover, the organization's culture must support the application of any incentive compensation system.

Not all organizations are suited to incentive compensation systems. Centralized organizations require most of the important operating decisions to be made in the head office. Such organizations are unsuited to incentive compensation systems for their front line employees because employees in these organizations are expected to follow rules and have no authority to make decisions. In fact, it is more appropriate to call compensation systems in these organizations enforcement systems, since employment continues if people follow the rules and standard operating procedures. In these centralized (often called command and control) organizations, the primary role of performance measurement is enforcement—to ensure that people are following rules. Here the task of the management accountant is to design internal control systems and conduct internal audits to verify that people are following rules and procedures.

Incentive compensation systems work best in organizations in which employees have the skill and authority to react to conditions and make decisions. We previously discussed organizations that face environments that are changing continuously—ones in which it is either impractical or impossible to develop standard operating procedures to deal with these changing conditions. Such organizations can develop incentive compensation systems to motivate employees to identify changes in the environment, to apply their skills and knowledge accordingly, and to make decisions that best reflect the organization's goals.

When the organization has empowered its employees to make decisions, it can use incentive compensation systems to motivate appropriate decision-making behavior. In these organizations, the focus of control changes from telling people what to do to asking employees to use their skills and delegated authority to do their best to help the organization achieve its objectives.

Incentive Compensation and Employee Responsibility

The incentive compensation system must focus on organization results that the employee influences or affects. Consider an incentive compensation plan that rewards the performance of a production worker based on achieving a target sales level. Because the sales department rather than production controls sales, such a plan would be ineffectual. In expectancy theory terms, this incentive compensa-

---

[12] One of the first and most definitive discussions of when incentive plans do and do not work well can be found in Arch Patton, "Why Incentive Plans Fail," *Harvard Business Review*, May-June 1972.

This team of Unocal employees earned a team bonus for designing a system to reduce the time taken to perform the annual maintenance on a natural gas liquids plant from 8 days to 3.5 days. The faster turnaround saved Unocal maintenance costs and reduced the amount of lost production time. Asked to describe his reaction to the reward, the employee shown on the far right seemed to derive more satisfaction from having his views "listened to and acted on" than from the monetary reward. The satisfaction expressed by this employee is a form of intrinsic reward related to satisfaction from a job that provides an opportunity for thinking and contribution. *Courtesy* Alan Whitman/ Unocal

tion plan is low on expectancy. The production worker controls quality, the amount of resources used, and the delivery date of the production. Therefore, these items, to the extent that they are important in determining the organization's performance, should be the focus of the production employee's performance incentive system.

Employees' incentive compensation should reflect the nature of their responsibilities in the organization. Employees whose roles are to plan, coordinate, and control day-to-day activities should receive rewards based on their ability to manage these daily operations effectively and to make the best short-term use of available resources. Their rewards should be tied to short-term performance measures, such as efficiency and the ability to meet customer quality and service requirements.

Employees whose roles are to plan intermediate-term projects, such as putting equipment and systems in place, should be rewarded based on their ability to identify, plan for, and install equipment and systems that improve the organization's performance. Their rewards should be tied to measures of the system's adequacy in meeting cost and response time targets, results of post-implementation

Executive Compensation at Campbell Soup Company

In 1993, as a means to tie executive compensation more closely to performance and promote what it called corporate governance principles, Campbell Soup Company announced a new compensation plan that required that between 60% and 75% of senior executive compensation be based on the company's financial performance. Moreover, as many as 60% of the organization's senior executives would be required to hold up to three times their salaries in the company's stock.

audits of the project's effectiveness, and comparisons with the operating results of other organizations.

Employees whose roles are to undertake the organization's long-term planning should be rewarded based on the long-term growth or improvement in the organization's operations that results from their strategic choices. These rewards should be based on the organization's performance compared with similar organizations.

Rewarding Outcomes

A second consideration in the design of effective incentive compensation systems concerns how they measure performance.

We know that organizations should reward employees based on the *outcomes* they create for the organization's stakeholders rather than on the employees' inputs or outputs. This principle argues that success in using the time, knowledge, and skills that the employee brings to the organization—rather the amount of time, knowledge, and skill used—is the proper focus of an incentive compensation system. Moreover,

John Deere & Co. has signed a union contract in which some hourly employees are given pay raises after they complete technical courses and put their new learning into practice. With diversified skills, these employees undertake roles usually not associated with production line workers. The employee shown in this picture is a production line worker who has been temporarily assigned to demonstrate the company's new products to its dealers and customers. *Courtesy* **Michael L. Abramson**

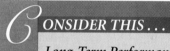

ONSIDER THIS . . .

Tailoring Rewards at Amoco Corporation to Unit Contributions

Amoco Corporation developed its variable incentive plan to motivate, and provide rewards for, performance that exceeds the performance of the highest performing competitors. In 1993 the payouts from this plan varied from 4.6% to 5.4% of the employee's earnings. The plan's payout is the sum of two components—tier one and tier two.

The tier one component is based on the parent Amoco Corporation's return on average capital employed. In 1993, Amoco Corporation's return on average capital employed was 10.6% versus an average of 9.7% for its three highest performing competitors. Amoco's performance resulted in a payout of 2.8% of employee earnings.

The tier two component reflects the financial and strategic performance of the operating company where the employee works. Each operating company uses a unique set of performance measures that correspond to its characteristics and contributions to the parent corporation.

For example, Amoco Chemical Company used return on assets as its financial measure, and Amoco Chemical exceeded the average of its highest four competitors. For strategic measures, Amoco Chemical Company used strategic thrust, progress, environment, health and safety, and people management and development. The total tier two payout for Amoco Chemical Company was 2.5%, giving the employees in this operating unit a total payout of 5.3% (2.8% + 2.5%).

incentive compensation based on outcomes requires that organization members understand and contribute to the organization's objectives. When it is impossible to measure outcomes consistently, when outcomes are affected by factors beyond the employee's control, or when outcomes are expensive to measure, rewards are based on inputs.

Input-based compensation measures the time, knowledge, and the skill level that the employee brings to the job with the expectation that the unmeasured outcome is correlated with these inputs.

Many organizations use some form of *knowledge-based remuneration*. This type of remuneration bases the rate of pay on an employee's training and job qualifications, which can be upgraded by on-the-job training. The employee's compensation is the product of the number of hours worked (time input) and the hourly rate (a reflection of the deemed level of skill input). Organizations use knowledge-based pay to motivate employees to continuously upgrade their job skills, thereby allowing them to receive a higher base pay.

Economic Value Added and Incentive Compensation Plans

Because of the strong link between economic value added and shareholder wealth, economic value added is being strongly touted by consultants as a basis for

ONSIDER THIS . . .

Long-Term Performance Incentives

A Conference Board survey report indicated that most industry sectors use long-term performance plans designed to link the employee's interests with the organization's. The primary method of securing commitment to long-term goals is to link employee rewards to the achievement of financial performance goals over a time period of three to five years.

The survey report also indicated that participation in these plans is usually limited to a small group of senior executives in the organizations surveyed and that less than one half of one percent of employees regularly receive long-term incentive rewards.

The report suggested that the size of the performance rewards are correlated with the individual's position in the organization and range from 48% for CEOs to 21% for the lowest level individuals—the average being 32%.

Source: BNA Pension & Benefits Reporter, June 26, 1995, Volume 22, Number 26, p. 1486.

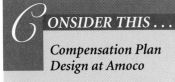

Compensation Plan Design at Amoco

In September 1995, Amoco Corporation, a manufacturer and distributor of petroleum products, announced that it would use the following principles as the basis for its compensation systems: (1) benchmark performance and compensation against competitors; (2) market-based targets for base and incentive pay; (3) compensation that reflects employee performance level; (4) commitment to all employees that they will have an opportunity to earn significant performance-based pay; (5) commitment to all employees that they will have the opportunity to buy and hold Amoco stock to link employee interests to the long-term performance of the company; and (6) open and detailed communication about compensation at all levels of the company.

performance measurement and incentive compensation. Under this approach, executives would receive bonuses based upon how much their performance increased the economic value added over some period of time.

Managing Incentive Compensation Plans

Considerable evidence indicates that organizations have systematically mismanaged incentive compensation plans, particularly those relating to senior executives. Many articles have appeared in influential business periodicals arguing that executives, particularly executives of U.S. corporations, have been paid excessively for mediocre performance.

Some experts stand on both sides of the question of whether conventional incentive compensation systems are effective. They debate whether compensation systems motivate goal-seeking behavior and whether they are efficient, that is, whether they pay what is needed and no more. Some studies show a positive correlation between executive compensation and shareholder wealth.[13] Other studies report finding no, or even a negative, correlation between organization performance and executive compensation.[14] Consider the following observation:

> From 1966 to 1970 corporate performance and shareholder value began to decline. And, since 1970, shareholder value has drifted steadily downward, while executive compensation has climbed ever higher. In light of the prospects that the trend in rising CEO pay will continue, it is particularly inappropriate for companies to continue operating compensation systems in which executive rewards bear no relation to corporate performance.[15]

Rosabeth Moss Kanter summarized the effect of these issues:

> Every year, routine company surveys show fewer employees willing to say that traditional pay practices are fair. In particular, top management compensation has been assailed as unjustifiably high, especially when executives get large bonuses while their companies suffer financial losses or are just recovering from them.
>
> Despite economic data showing an association between executive compensation and company performance, many professionals still argue that the amounts are excessive and reflect high status rather than good performance.[16]

[13] See, for example, Kevin J. Murphy, "Corporate Performance and Managerial Remuneration: An Empirical Analysis," *Journal of Accounting and Economics*, April 1985, pp. 11–42.

[14] See, for example, a summary in Alfie Kohn, "Why Incentive Plans Cannot Work," *Harvard Business Review*, September-October 1993. The different conclusions reflect different assumptions and different measures of performance that have been used in various studies.

[15] Louis J. Brindisi, Jr., "Creating Shareholder Value: A New Mission for Executive Compensation," *Corporate Restructuring and Executive Compensation*, ed. Joel M. Stern, G. Bennett Stewart III, and Donald H. Chew, Ballinger Publishing Company, 1989.

[16] Rosabeth Moss Kanter, "The Attack on Pay," *Harvard Business Review*, March-April 1987, pp. 60–67.

These beliefs reflect broadly based feelings of unfairness and a degree of cynicism about incentive compensation that organizations must address to restore the motivational effect that incentive compensation is intended to create.

Types of Incentive Compensation Plans

The most common incentive compensation plans are cash bonuses, profit sharing, gainsharing, stock options, performance shares stock, stock appreciation rights, participation units, and employee stock ownership plans (usually called ESOPs). These different plans pose varying challenges for the management accounting system.

We can group compensation plans into two broad groups: (1) those that rely on internal measures, invariably provided by the organization's management accounting system and (2) those that rely on performance of the organization's share price in the stock market.

The primary interest of management accountants revolves around rewards that are based on performance that the organization's management accounting system monitors and reports. Most employees who participate in incentive plans that provide financial rewards take them very seriously. They are both interested in, and concerned about, the performance measurement system that monitors and reports performance measures that provide the basis for computing and distributing financial rewards. Many practicing management accountants have found that the most contentious debates about management accounting practice arise from issues relating to performance measurement designed to provide the basis for financial rewards. Therefore, management accountants take the matter of developing performance measures for financial reward systems very seriously.

<table>
<tr><td>

OBJECTIVE 14.6

Explain the broad types of monetary rewards that organizations use.

</td></tr>
</table>

CASH BONUS. A cash bonus, also called a *lump-sum reward, pay for performance*, and *merit pay*, is a payment of cash based on some measured performance. Such a bonus is a one-time award that does not become part of the employee's base pay in subsequent years.

Cash bonuses can be fixed in amount and triggered when measured performance exceeds the target or they can be proportional to the level of performance relative to the target. Cash bonuses can be based on individual or group performance and can be paid to individuals or groups.

For example, in the late 1980s, General Motors eliminated automatic salary increases based on increases in the cost of living and replaced them with a pay-for-performance system that rewarded managers based on their results. Managers were required to group their employees into three groups: high performers (the top 10%), good performers (the next 25%), average performers (the next 55%), and the

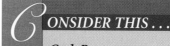

CONSIDER THIS . . .

Cash Bonuses at Chrysler Corporation

In February 1994, Chrysler Corporation announced that it would give many of its executives cash bonuses for performance during 1993. For the 200 most senior executives, the cash bonuses were about 100% of salary. For the next 100 executives, the bonuses amounted to about 80% of salary. Lower-level executives received much less.

The Chrysler bonus plan rewards performance on quality (measured by warranty claims), customer satisfaction (measured by surveys), and profitability. The size of the bonus pool available for distribution reflects whether performance targets are met in all 3 areas. If performance targets are not met in some areas, the bonus pool is reduced proportionately. If goals are exceeded in all 3 areas, the bonus pool expands to 125% of its original size. The bonus pool for 1993 achieved the maximum amount.

low performers (the last 10%). Supervisors used these groupings to award merit pay and enforce salary differences based on assessed performance.

Profit sharing
A cash bonus system in which the total amount available for distribution as cash bonuses is a function of the organization's, or an organization unit's, reported profit.

PROFIT SHARING. **Profit sharing** is a cash bonus that reflects the organization's, or an organization unit's, reported profit. Therefore, profit sharing is a group incentive compensation plan focused on short-term performance.

All profit-sharing plans define what portion of the organization's reported profits is available for sharing, the sharing formula, the employees who are eligible to participate in the plan, and the formula for each employee's share.

Many profit-sharing plans stipulate that the reported profit will be reduced by some percent (say 15%) of the shareholders' investment in the organization.[17] This allotment provides the shareholders with the required return on their investment. The resulting pool is shared between employees and shareholders on some fractional basis, such as 40%/60%. The plan also may specify a limit on the total amount of profits that can be distributed to employees.

Finally, the profit-sharing plan specifies how it will distribute the money in the pool to each employee. Some plans provide equal distribution; others distribute the bonus pool based on the employee's performance relative to individual performance targets.

In the performance compensation approach, employees receive a performance score that reflects how well they achieved specific performance goals for that year. The employee's score divided by the total of the scores of all the employees in the profit-sharing agreement is the individual's share of the pool total. Some profit-sharing plans distribute rewards to each employee in an amount proportional to the base wage or salary because their designers believe this reflects the employee's contribution to the overall result.

Profit sharing plans require a number of contributions from the organization's accounting systems, in general, and from the management accounting system, in particular. First, the organization must prepare a means to calculate profits. This process usually is monitored and attested to by an external auditor. Second, when a deduction is to be made from the pool that is based on the owners' investment, the management accounting system must provide a measure of invested capital. Third, when the profit sharing is based on some measured level of performance, for example, a composite score that reflects the employee's ability to meet a set of performance targets, the management accounting system must provide the underlying measures of performance and the overall performance score.

Gain sharing
A cash bonus system in which the total amount available for distribution as cash bonuses is a function of performance relative to some target (usually the difference between the actual and the target level of labor cost).

GAIN SHARING. **Gain sharing** is a system for distributing cash bonuses from a pool when the total amount available is a function of performance relative to some target. For example, employees in a designated unit receive bonuses when

---

[17] The idea is to provide shareholders with the required return on their investment before making distributions to employees. Many plans base the reduction on the book value of the investment, that is, the reduction is 15% of invested capital as measured by net book value. However, some people argue that this historical cost-based measure of investment is inappropriate and that the actual level of investment is the market price, or liquidation value, of the investment.

their performance exceeds a performance target. Gain sharing is a group incentive, unlike the pay-for-performance cash bonus, which is an individual reward.[18]

In its usual form, gain sharing provides for the sharing of financial gains in organizational performance. The gain sharing plan usually applies to a group of employees within an organization unit, such as a department or a store. Gain sharing uses a formula to specify the amount and distribution of the rewards and a base period of performance as the benchmark for comparing subsequent performance. This benchmark is not changed unless there is a major change in process or technology. When performance exceeds the base period performance, the gain sharing plan pays a bonus pool.

CONSIDER THIS...

Gain Sharing at A&P

When A&P, a large grocery chain, faced a need to reduce costs, it developed and put in place a gain sharing plan. This plan provided employees in individual stores a bonus of one percent of store sales when employee costs were kept below 10 percent of sales. This plan lowered employee costs and increased profits dramatically.

Gain sharing promotes teamwork and participation in decision making. It requires that employees have the skills to participate and that the organization encourages participation. Consider these companies that have used gain sharing effectively:

- The Herman Miller Company, a furniture manufacturer that is frequently rated as one of the 10 best-managed U.S. corporations, has used a gain sharing plan for many years. The company also uses a strategy of employee involvement that supports and enhances the motivational effect of the gain-sharing plan.

- Grumman Corporation developed a performance bonus plan for the crew in its Long Life Vehicle project that it used in conjunction with its Grumman Quality program. Employees focused on processes that involved rework, scrap, and excessive maintenance costs. Half the savings from improved performance were divided equally among the crew members working on the project.

The three most widely used gain sharing programs are Improshare, the Scanlon plan, and the Rucker plan:

1. **Improshare** (Improved Productivity Sharing) is a widely used gain sharing program that determines its bonus pool by computing the difference between the target level of labor cost given the level of production and the actual labor cost (the direct labor efficiency variance). The plan specifies how the difference will be shared between the shareholders and the employees and how to calculate the amount distributed to each employee.

2. The **Scanlon plan** is based on the following formula computed using the data in some base period.[19]

Improshare
An incentive program that pays cash bonuses to employees based on labor savings relative to a target or plan.

Scanlon plan
An incentive program that pays cash bonuses to employees based on the relationship between the ratio of payroll costs and the value of product produced and a target on standard.

[18] For a detailed discussion of gain sharing approaches to motivation, see Robert L. Masternak, "Gainsharing: Overcoming Common Myths and Problems to Achieve Dramatic Results," *Employment Relations Today*, December 22, 1993.

[19] This plan, developed by Joseph Scanlon during the 1930s, promotes and recognizes employee contributions through suggestion systems and participation with management in analyzing and improving operations.

$$Base\ Ratio\ =\ \frac{Payroll\ Costs}{Value\ of\ Goods\ or\ Services\ Produced}$$

For example, if in the base period payroll costs are $25,000,000 and the deemed value of production or service is $86,000,000, the base ratio would be 0.29 ($25,000,000 ÷ $86,000,000).

In any period in which the ratio of labor costs to the value of production or service is less than the base ratio, the deemed labor savings are added to a bonus pool. Therefore, continuing the above example, if in a subsequent period actual payroll costs were $28,000,000 in a period when the deemed value of production was $105,000,000, the amount added to the bonus pool would be this:

$$
\begin{aligned}
Amount\ Added\ to\ Bonus\ Pool\ &=\ (Value\ of\ Production\ This\ Period\ \times\ Base\ Ratio)\\
&\quad -\ Actual\ Payroll\ Costs\\
&=\ (\$105,000,000\ \times\ 0.29)\ -\ \$28,000,000\\
&=\ \$2,450,000
\end{aligned}
$$

When labor costs are more than the base ratio, some organizations deduct the difference from the bonus pool. Periodically, usually once a year, the pool is apportioned between the company and the employees in the pool using the plan ratio, which is often 50%/50%.

Rucker plan
An incentive program that pays cash bonuses to employees based on the relationship between the ratio of payroll costs to production value and a target on standard.

3. The **Rucker plan** is based on the following formula, which reflects the data from a representative period:

$$Rucker\ Standard\ =\ \frac{Payroll\ Costs}{Production\ Value}$$

where production value is measured as *Net Sales − Inventory Change − Materials and Supplies Used*. As in the Scanlon plan, the idea in the Rucker plan is to define a baseline relationship between payroll costs and the value of production and reward workers who improve efficiency. Efficiency is measured as lowering the ratio of payroll costs to the value of production. When actual labor costs are less than the Rucker standard, the employees receive a bonus.

Gain sharing plans must reflect performance levels that are reasonable in order to work. As you might expect, management and the employees who are subject to these plans often have very different ideas about what is fair. Management usually seeks tighter standards or targets, and employees want the opposite. This requires that management, the management accountant, and employees participate in seeking the performance level that will serve as the standard or benchmark for the plan. Many management accountants relish this role as the honest brokers between management and the employees who are subject to these plans.

The people who designed gain sharing plans believed, from the beginning, that monthly or even weekly performance awards are best. This provides rapid feedback and therefore provides additional motivation since it reinforces the desired type of behavior. While rapid feedback may improve the motivational effect of rewards (expectancy), short-cycle feedback can put strains on the organization's management accounting system as the need for recording and accruing labor costs increases both the cost and potential for error in the management accounting system.

Recall that since gain sharing plans are team-based rewards, they have associated with them the problem of some team members not doing their fair share and earning rewards based on the work of others. For example, students often complain about group projects, particularly when they cannot choose their own groups, because there is often someone in the group who refuses to do or is incapable of doing the work. Students, like employees, are often uncomfortable about disciplining, or reporting, their peers. The early proponents of gain sharing recognized this phenomenon and observed that, for gain sharing to work, the organization culture must promote cohesive relationships within the group and between the group and management.

Finally, corporate culture has a significant effect on the potential of gain sharing plans. Gain sharing programs rely on employee commitment and involvement. Therefore, a corporate culture that respects employees, encourages their involvement, and actively supports employee learning and innovation reinforces the motivational potential of a gain sharing program. Finally, like all incentive programs, gain sharing programs work best when they are simple to understand and monitor. A test of this attribute is whether employees can compute their own bonuses. In addition, such programs should be perceived as fair, as being directly affected by employee performance, and as being conducive to promoting teamwork.

Stock option
A right to purchase stated number of the organization's shares for a specified price (the option price).

Gain sharing plans usually rely on performance measures reported by an organization's management accounting system, which plays a primary supporting role in the gain sharing process. Most gain sharing plans focus on management accounting measures relating to labor costs and the relationship of actual labor cost to some standard, or budgeted, level of labor cost. Therefore, the key issues in performance measurement relate to measuring labor costs accurately and consistently and to having the ability to establish a cost standard that is perceived as fair.

STOCK OPTIONS AND OTHER STOCK-RELATED COMPENSATION PLANS. Judging by the published remarks of compensation experts, stock options are the most widely known, misused, and maligned approach to incentive compensation. A **stock option** is the right to purchase a unit of the organization's stock at a specified price, called the option price.

A common approach to option pricing is to set the option price at about 105% of the stock's market price at the time the organization issues the stock option.[20] This is intended to motivate the employee who has been granted the stock options to act in the long-term interests of the organization, thereby increasing the value of the firm so that the market price of the

ONSIDER THIS . . .

Profit-Sharing Stock Option Plans at Wal-Mart

Bob Ortega observed that "Wal-Mart Stores Inc. has relied on stock incentives to motivate otherwise low-paid employees, giving them a feeling of ownership and hopes for wealth." This strategy worked well while the stock price was increasing. However, since February 1993, the stock price has been on a downward trend, which has created a number of problems at Wal-Mart.

Incentive plans should be used for motivation purposes, not to replace part of the employee's market wage. The consequence of violating this suggestion is apparent at Wal-Mart. With rising stock prices no longer providing the capital gains that employees relied upon to bolster their low wages, discontent is setting in. The article implies that this discontent is beginning to adversely affect the company's vaunted corporate culture.

Source: Bob Ortega, "Life Without Sam . . . ," *The Wall Street Journal,* January 4, 1995.

---

[20] This choice reflects both motivational issues (to encourage the employee to work to improve the market's valuation of the organization) and taxation issues (to avoid having tax authorities deem that the organization has given the employee something whose value does not depend on the employee's subsequent actions).

This employee is part of a gain sharing plan at Georgia-Pacific, a paper products manufacturer. The plan pays employees cash bonuses based on productivity improvements. A motivationally desirable feature of the Georgia-Pacific gain sharing plan is that it pays these productivity bonuses even when the company's net income is negative.
Courtesy **John Chiasson/Gamma Liaison Network**

stock will exceed the option price. For this reason, compensation system designers usually restrict stock options to senior executives because they believe that senior executives have the greatest effect on increasing the market value of the organization. Some people have argued, however, that operations staff, as they carry out short-term operating plans, can make significant and sustainable process improvements. This would provide the organization with a competitive advantage, thereby increasing the organization's market value.

The critics of stock option plans have argued that organizations have been too generous in rewarding senior executives with stock options. For example, the organization may issue a senior executive many thousands of stock options with an option price that is very near, or even below, the market price at the time the stock option is issued. This is an implementation issue, not a fundamental defect of stock options. Some critics have argued, however, that stock price increases often reflect general market trends that have nothing to do with the performance of the individual organization. For this reason, many incentive compensation experts have argued that the stock option price should be keyed to the performance of the organization's shares relative to *the performance of the prices of comparable shares.* Therefore, the stock option would be valuable only if the organization's share price increases more rapidly than the share prices of comparable organizations. Since management accountants are often involved in studies or systems that rely on external benchmarks, organizations often delegate the role of developing the appropriate performance standards for relative stock option plans to a team that includes a management accountant.

Organizations use many other forms of stock-related incentive compensation plans, including performance shares stock, stock appreciation rights, participation units, and employee stock ownership plans that are beyond the scope of issues in management accounting. These plans provide incentive compensation to the participants when the stock price increases. The idea behind such plans is to motivate employees to act in the long-term interests of the organization by engaging in activities that increase the organization's market value. Therefore, all these plans assume that stock markets will recognize exceptional behavior in the form of increased stock prices.

In general, the use of employee stock ownership plans assumes that employees will work harder when they have an ownership stake.[21] Avis, the automobile rental company, used an employee stock ownership plan to improve employee motivation, which, in turn, resulted in both higher sales and a higher margin on sales.

Salomon Brothers, a Wall Street investment house, provided huge bonuses for high-performing employees during the 1980s and early 1990s. For example, one bond trader was paid a $23 million bonus in 1990. Reacting to this, Salomon Brothers' largest shareholder, Warren Buffett, whom *Forbes* identified as the wealthiest person in the United States in 1993, became interim chairman and indicated that he wanted Salomon Brothers' employees to earn rewards through owning shares not by free riding on the owners' investment. To align the interests of the firm's employees and its shareholders and provide for more reasonable performance rewards, Mr. Buffet, through the Salomon Brothers' Compensation

---

CONSIDER THIS . . .

Research About Incentive Rewards

In a widely read and quoted study, Jensen and Murphy made three recommendations: (1) that CEOs should be required to have considerable shareholdings in the companies that they manage; (2) that compensation should be more closely tied to performance; and (3) that executives should be terminated for inadequate performance.

Source: M. Jensen and K. J. Murphy, "CEO Incentives: It's Not How Much You Pay But How," *Harvard Business Review*, May-June, 1990, pp. 138–153.

Based on a careful review of the incentive compensation literature, Scott and Tiessen concluded that, while firms do seem to maintain a relationship between compensation and performance, there is no clear evidence to suggest that tying compensation to shareholder wealth is desirable. They also concluded that tying financial rewards more closely to performance seems to have only a modest effect on long-term financial performance. Finally, the authors concluded that, while extrinsic rewards are undoubtedly important, intrinsic rewards likely have a significant effect on performance.

Source: E. L., Pavlik, Thomas W. Scott, and Peter Tiessen, "Executive Compensation Issues and Research," *Journal of Accounting Literature*, Volume 12, 1993, pp. 131–189.

---

[21] Of course, as owners, the employees should have some say in how the company is run. Therefore, a real system of employee involvement should accompany the use of employee stock ownership plans.

Like their counterparts in most large corporations, these senior executives at ASARCO International, a producer of nonferrous metals, are members of a stock incentive plan designed to reward them for actions they take to increase the firm's market value. *Courtesy* Chris Jones/ASARCO, Inc.

Committee, developed an incentive plan that paid employees up to half their pay in company stock, issued at below market prices, that could not be sold for at least five years after issue. However, Mr. Buffet failed to weigh a consideration that is vital in designing any compensation plan, namely, how other investment banking firms were compensating their employees. While many people applauded the rationality of Mr. Buffet's plan, many employees left the firm to join other investment banking firms, which were using compensation practices that were similar to the practices abandoned at Salomon Brothers. These departures precipitated a crisis which, eventually, led to the scrapping of the new plan.

OTHER INCENTIVE PLANS. In the current era when employees can develop important information that is valuable to the organization, some people have proposed rewarding employees based on the value of the information they develop and communicate to organization planners. The two best known of these plans are the Soviet incentive system and the so-called Groves Mechanism.

The Soviet incentive system was developed and used in the former Soviet Union to support the operation of a centralized economy in which a central planner coordinated the production decisions of manufacturing facilities, which were called enterprises. The primary purpose of the Soviet incentive model was to obtain accurate forecasts of production levels so that the central planner had good information upon which to base her production and logistical planning.

The Soviet incentive system was based on the formulas below where:

y_A is the actual production level achieved

y_T is the target level of production chosen by the manager

α is a positive constant

β is a positive constant

γ is a positive constant

If $y_A \geq y_T$:

$$\textit{Manager's Compensation} = \textit{Fixed Wage} + \beta y_T + \alpha(y_A - y_T)$$

If $y_A < y_T$:

$$\textit{Manager's Compensation} = \textit{Fixed Wage} + \beta y_T - \gamma(y_T - y_A)$$

This formula shows that the enterprise manager's reward increases as the target level of production increases and for a given target as production increases. The target level of production was important information in the centralized Soviet economy because central planners used it to make logistical decisions to coordinate value chain activities that made products and delivered them to customers.

This part of the reward structure provides an incentive for the manager to set a higher target level. However, on its own, it would encourage the manager to misrepresent the true target level of production. This incentive to misrepresent is balanced by the second term, which pays a bonus to the manager if the actual level of production exceeds the target level of production and exacts a penalty if the actual level of production is less than the target level of production. For this incentive system to work properly, the following relationship must exist between the incentive model parameters

$$0 < \alpha < \beta < \gamma$$

Moreover, if the enterprise manager acts as an expected value maximizer, that is, if the manager does not expect to be compensated for taking risk, when facing uncertainty, the manager will communicate the mean value of the assessed probability distribution of production if:

$$\gamma = 2\beta - \alpha$$

This model reflects a specific approach to providing an incentive to both provide an honest estimate and work as hard as possible to achieve the target production level.

A second approach to rewarding knowledge is the Groves Mechanism, named after the author who first proposed this approach. This incentive mechanism can be written as follows:

$$\textit{Manager's Compensation} = \textit{Fixed Wage} + \beta(\textit{Organization's Target Profits})$$
$$+ \beta(\textit{Actual Profit of the Manager's Division} - \textit{Division's Target Profits})$$

Like all incentive systems that reward information, this system assumes that a central planner needs information to coordinate the activities of individual divisions. In this model, the central planner controls a factor of production, such as operating capital, that must be allocated to division managers who have productive use for that resource. The division manager submits a target level of profit that, in effect, says "If you give me a certain amount of this resource, this is the profit level that I think that I can produce." If the division managers are rewarded based on division profits, each division manager would want to acquire this scarce resource until the marginal value of the last unit acquired is zero. Therefore, it is likely that the total demand by all the division managers for the scarce resource will far exceed the amount available.

Therefore, this incentive function makes the division managers consider the value of the resource to the firm. Under this incentive function, the manager's reward increases with the expected value of the firm's production decisions; therefore, the manager is motivated to provide honest information to help ensure allocations of the scare resource in the best possible way. The last element in the incentive function is used to make sure that all the managers have an incentive to deliver on expectations. This is done to prevent the managers as a group from misrepresenting profit potential to achieve high bonuses.

Incentive schemes that reward information are rarely found in practice since most planners are more comfortable with rewarding results rather than beliefs. However, as organizations continue to try to motivate the development of expert knowledge and to exploit that knowledge, they may begin to consider incentive schemes that reward information. When this happens, it is quite likely that management accountants will be asked to help in the design and implementation of these reward systems.

FRIEDMAN-JACOBS COMPANY REVISITED

Recall our introductory discussion of Arthur Friedman's appliance store. Charles Ryan was clearly an unhappy and unmotivated employee, as every facet of his behavior suggested. In fact, most organizations would not have tolerated his behavior. The Herzberg theory of motivation suggests that poor hygiene factors and his own attitudes explain Charles's behavior. In the matter of having employees determine their own pay, one employee, George Tegner, 59, an employee for 14 years, observed: "You have to use common sense; no one wins if you end up closing the business down. If you want more money, you have to produce more. It can't work any other way. Anyway, wages aren't everything. Doing what you want to is more important."

Arthur's style and approach to dealing with the pay issue reflected and determined the working conditions, organization policies, interpersonal relationships, and supervisory quality in this organization. The clear signal from Arthur to the employees was, "I trust you to do the right thing. I want to give you what you think is fair."

Arthur Friedman believed that the poor hygiene factor for Charles was his feeling that his base pay was too low. Once the base pay problem was corrected, Charles became a model employee. Because there is no evidence that any other conditions were changed, the other hygiene factors in this organization seemed to have been acceptable to Charles.

Given that the removal of the poor hygiene factor relating to base pay caused such an improvement in motivation, we assume that the satisfier factors must have already been in place. Certainly, employees exhibited a high element of responsibility after they were allowed to determine their own pay. In any event, this anecdote shows, for one employee at least, how one poor hygiene factor can prevent all the positive satisfier factors from motivating an employee. When the poor hygiene factor was removed, the satisfier factors provided for a satisfied and highly motivated employee.

This was a unique experiment that we should be careful in generalizing to other organizations. It seems that most employees at Friedman-Jacobs were happy with their base pay; the company had objective evidence in the form of union pay scales that the employees were relatively well paid. It had a positive organization culture that included mutual respect and trust between Arthur and the employees. This was a small company and everyone knew each other. Arthur's offer was an extension of trust that employees seemed to feel self-conscious about breaching. This implies that the employees had a positive attitude toward their work and that there was a group norm that they should be paid only for the value of their work. Note that the company had no measurement system to enforce pay for performance, as evidenced by Charles, the serviceperson who turned down a raise because he felt that he did not deserve it.

The article about Arthur Friedman also provided a summary of the results as a follow-up in a later time period:

> In the past five years, there has been no turnover of employees. Friedman estimates that last year his 15 workers took no more than a total of three sick days. It is rare that anyone is late for work and, even then, there is usually a good reason. Work is done on time and employee pilferage is nonexistent.
>
> As part of the new freedom, more people are given keys to the store and the cash box. If they need groceries, or even some beer money, all they have to do is walk into the office, take what they want out of the cash box, and leave a voucher. Every effort is made to ensure that no one looks over their shoulders.
>
> There has only been one discrepancy. "Once our petty cash was $10 over," recalls Friedman. "We could never figure out where it came from."
>
> Skeptics by now are chuckling to themselves, convinced that if Friedman is not losing money, he is just breaking even. The fact is that net profit has not dropped a cent in the last five years; it has increased. Although volume is considerably less (the store discontinued selling televisions and stereo equipment to concentrate on refrigerators, washers, and dryers) and overhead has increased at what some would consider an unhealthy rate, greater productivity and efficiency have more than made up for it.[22]

---

[22] Martin Koughan, *op. cit.*

SUMMARY

One of senior management's most important leadership roles is to design and manage reward systems that appropriately measure and reward superior performance and to create an organization environment where employees experience intrinsic rewards.

The chapter presents two significant theories of motivation. The Herzberg theory maintains that two types of factors affect motivation. The hygiene factors provide the framework for motivation and the satisfier factors provide the motivation itself. The major insight of the Herzberg theory is that only satisfier factors provide motivation, although hygiene factors must be present to allow the satisfier factors to have their effect.

Another important motivation theory, Vroom's expectancy theory, maintains that motivation is a function of these factors:

1. The relationship that employees believe exists between what they do and measured performance results (expectancy)

2. The relationship employees believe exists between the measured performance results and the reward that they receive (instrumentality)

3. The value employees place on rewards (valence)

The organization's performance measurement system has a critical effect on expectancy and instrumentality, thereby having a critical effect on motivation.

Effective reward systems are clear and unequivocal and focus organization employees on the relevant and measured performance that they control. Organizations that face rapidly changing external environments and give the employees the authority to use their knowledge and skills are the best candidates for incentive compensation systems.

Effective incentive compensation systems reflect employee responsibilities. Therefore, incentive compensation systems for employees who focus on the effective and efficient management of daily activities will be different from incentive compensation systems for employees who identify and implement tactical-level or strategic-level strategies, which are longer term.

Incentive compensation systems should, if possible, reward outcomes achieved (such as customer satisfaction for a customer relations specialist) rather than inputs (such as number of hours worked or previous training). They also should clearly distinguish between base salary, which reflects market conditions, and incentive rewards, which reflect measured performance. Depending on the employee's contribution and the organization's needs, rewards can reflect either individual or group performance and can focus on short- or long-term results. An incentive compensation system's effectiveness can be judged by sampling employee attitudes about its relevance, fairness, and comprehensiveness.

The most common forms of incentive compensation are cash rewards based on short-term performance and stock-related rewards for long-term performance. An ideal combination for many organizations is to use a combination of profit-sharing or stock-related plans to encourage coordination and company-wide thinking and gain sharing plans to encourage and reward local initiatives.

KEY TERMS

extrinsic reward, p. 652

gain sharing, p. 664

Herzberg's two-factor theory of
    motivation, p. 648

hygiene factors, p. 648

improshare, p. 665

incentive compensation, p. 655

intrinsic rewards, p. 652

motivation, p. 646

motivation system, p. 650

pay-for-performance system, p. 655

profit sharing, p. 664

Rucker plan, p. 666

satisfier factors, p. 649

Scanlon plan, p. 665

stock option, p. 667

Vroom's expectancy theory, p. 649

ASSIGNMENT MATERIAL

■ QUESTIONS

14-1 What is the Herzberg theory of motivation?

14-2 What is a hygiene factor?

14-3 What is a satisfier factor?

14-4 What is the expectancy theory?

14-5 What does expectancy mean?

14-6 What is instrumentality?

14-7 What is valence?

14-8 What is an intrinsic reward?

14-9 What is an extrinsic reward?

14-10 What is incentive compensation?

14-11 What are the five attributes of effective performance measurement systems?

14-12 What type of organization is best suited to incentive compensation? Why?

14-13 What are the four guidelines for designing effective incentive compensation systems?

14-14 What is a cash bonus?

14-15 What is profit sharing?

14-16 What is gain sharing?

14-17 What is a stock option plan?

■ EXERCISES

14-18 *Herzberg's theory*   Explain, in everyday words, Herzberg's two-factor theory of motivation.

14-19 *The element of motivation*   Explain how hygiene factors and satisfier factors combine to provide motivation.

14-20 *Role of satisfiers*   How do satisfier factors motivate?

14-21 *Expectancy and performance measurement*   Explain how Vroom's expectancy theory specifies the attributes of an effective performance measurement system.

14-22 *The nature of intrinsic rewards*   Do you believe that people value intrinsic rewards? Give an example of an intrinsic reward that you would value and explain why. If you value only extrinsic rewards, explain why.

14-23 *The environment of intrinsic rewards*   How do leaders provide an environment within which employees experience and value intrinsic rewards? Give an example of such a leader.

14-24 *Fairness in distrubuting rewards*   The text claims that providing extrinsic rewards or employment benefits such as parking and dining facilities to one group of employees, tends to alienate employees who are not in that group. Do you agree or disagree? Why?

14-25 *Role of extrinsic rewards*   Why are extrinsic rewards important to people?

14-26 *Understanding performance measurement*   Why is it so important that people understand what performance is measured, how performance is measured, and how outcomes (employee rewards) relate to measured performance?

14-27 *Controllable performance*   Why should performance measurement systems and rewards focus on performance that employees can control?

14-28 *Scope of performance measurement*   Why is it important that the performance measurement system include all the elements of employee performance? Can you give an example of the consequence of not including some element of performance in the performance measurement system?

14-29 *Environment for incentive compensation*   Why are incentive compensation plans unsuited to organizations in which employees for the most part are simply expected to follow rules? Can you give an example of such an organization?

14-30 *Tailoring performance measurement to the job*   In a company that takes telephone orders from customers for general merchandise, explain how you would evaluate the performance of the company president, a middle manager who designs the system to coordinate order taking and order shipping, and an employee who fills orders. How are the performance systems similar? How are the performance systems different?

14-31 *Choosing what to reward*   Why is it important to reward outcomes rather than outputs or inputs?

14-32 *Rewarding knowledge*   Can you give an example of knowledge-based pay?

14-33 *Nature of incentive compensation*   Do you believe that organizations should pay extra for superior performance?

14-34 *Choosing the reward level*   You work for a consulting firm and have been given the assignment of deciding whether a particular company president is overpaid both in absolute terms and relative to presidents of comparable companies. How would you undertake this task?

14-35 *Pay equity*   Some people believe that pay equity is a critical hygiene factor and that one element of pay equity is vertical structure of the pay scale. What do you think of the principle of keeping the ratio of the highest pay to the lowest pay in the organization below some target value like 20?

14-36 *The rule of confidence in incentive compensation*   Is it important for employees to believe that the incentive compensation system pays for measured, relevant, and controllable performance? Explain.

14-37 *Using cash bonuses*   When should an organization use a cash bonus?

14-38 *Using profit sharing*   When should an organization use profit sharing?

14-39 *Using gain sharing*   When should an organization use gain sharing?

14-40 *Using stock options*   When should an organization use stock options?

14-41 *Rewarding group performance*   How would you reward a group of people that includes product designers, engineers, production personnel, purchasing agents, marketing staff, and accountants, whose job is to identify and develop a new car? How would you reward a person whose job is to discover a better way of designing crash protection devices in cars? How are these two situations similar? How are they different?

■ PROBLEMS

Fundamental Problems

14-42 *Performance rewards at Hoechst Celanese*   Hoechst Celanese, a pharmaceutical manufacturer, uses a profit-sharing plan, which it calls the Hoechst Celanese Performance Sharing Plan, to motivate employees. The Hoechst Celanese Executive Committee sets a target earnings from operations (EFO). This target is based on the company's business plans and the economy's expected performance. The Performance Sharing Plan also uses two other critical values: the earnings from operations threshold amount and the earnings from operations stretch target. The targets for 1994 are shown in the accompanying figure.

If earnings from operations fall below the threshold value, there is no profit sharing. If earnings from operations lie between the threshold amount and the target, the profit sharing percent is prorated between the threshold award of 1% and the target payment of 4%. For example, if earnings from operations were $285 million, the profit sharing percent would be 2.5%:

$$Profit\ Sharing\ Percent\ =\ 1\%\ +\ 3\%\ \times\ \left[\frac{285\ -\ 250}{320\ -\ 250}\right]\ =\ 2.5\%$$

$$Profit\ Sharing\ Pool\ =\ 2.5\%\ \times\ \$285{,}000{,}000\ =\ \$7{,}125{,}000$$

If earnings from operations are between the target and the stretch target, the profit sharing percent is prorated between the target payment of 4% and the stretch-sharing payment of 7%. For example, if earnings from operations were $350 million, the profit sharing percent would be 5.29% and the profit sharing pool would be $18,500,000:

$$Profit\ Sharing\ Percent\ =\ 4\%\ +\ 3\%\ \times\ \left[\frac{350\ -\ 320}{390\ -\ 320}\right]\ =\ 5.29\%$$

$$Profit\ Sharing\ Pool\ =\ 5.29\%\ \times\ \$350{,}000{,}000\ =\ \$18{,}500{,}000$$

If earnings from operations equal, or exceed, the stretch target level, the profit sharing pool would be $27,300,000:

$$Profit\ Sharing\ Pool\ =\ 7\%\ \times\ \$390{,}000{,}000\ =\ \$27{,}300{,}000$$

REQUIRED

(a) List, with explanations, what you think are the desirable features of the Hoechst Celanese Performance Sharing Plan.

(b) List, with explanations, what you think are the undesirable features of the Hoechst Celanese Performance Sharing Plan.

(c) The EFO for 1994 was $332,000,000. Compute the size of the profit sharing pool.

(d) In 1995 the Performance Sharing Plan parameters were threshold EFO—$420,000,000; target EFO—$490,000,000; and stretch EFO—$560,000,000. What do you think of the practice of raising the parameters from one year to the next?

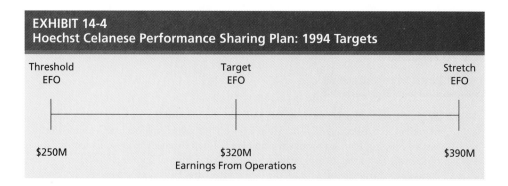

EXHIBIT 14-4
Hoechst Celanese Performance Sharing Plan: 1994 Targets

Threshold EFO — $250M
Target EFO — $320M
Stretch EFO — $390M
Earnings From Operations

14-43 *Designing a compensation plan* Suppose that you are the owner/manager of a house-cleaning business. You have 30 employees who work in teams of three. Teams are dispatched to the homes of customers where they are directed by the customer to undertake specific cleaning tasks that vary widely from customer to customer.

Your employees are unskilled workers who are paid an hourly wage of $8. This wage is typical for unskilled work. Turnover in your organization is quite high. Generally, your best employees leave as soon as they find better jobs. The employees that stay are usually ones who cannot find work elsewhere and have a poor attitude.

The hourly rate charged customers per team hour is $40. That is, if a team spends 1.5 hours in a customer's home, the charge is $60.

You want to develop an incentive system to use in your organization. You would like to use this incentive system to motivate good employees to stay and motivate poor workers either to improve or to leave. What type of system would you develop? If the system relies on any measurements, indicate how you would obtain these measurements.

14-44 *Motivating desired performance* Darlington Engineering is a research and development company that designs equipment for nuclear generating stations. The company consists of an administrative unit, a research laboratory, and a facility used to develop prototypes of new designs. The major costs in this company are the salaries of the research staff, which are substantial.

In the past, the research scientists working at Darlington Engineering have been rewarded based on their proven scientific expertise. Salaries of these research scientists are based on the level of education achieved and the number of research papers published in scientific journals. At a recent board of directors meeting, an outside director criticized the research and development activities with the following comments:

> "There is no question that we have the most highly trained scientists in our industry. Evidence of their training and creativity is provided by the number of research publications that they generate. However, the knowledge and creativity are not translating into patentable inventions and increased sales for this company. Our organization has the lowest rate of new product introduction in our industry, and we have one of the largest research and development teams. These people are too far into basic research, where the rewards lie in getting articles published. We need these people to have more interest in generating ideas that have commercial potential. This is a profit-seeking organization, not a university research laboratory."

REQUIRED

(a) Assuming that the director's facts are correct, do you agree that this is a problem?

(b) The board of directors has ordered the president of Darlington Engineering to increase the rate of new products and the time for new product development. How should the president go about this task?

14-45 *Profit sharing* Peterborough Medical Devices makes devices and equipment that it sells to hospitals. The organization has a profit sharing plan that is worded as follows:

The company will make available a profit sharing pool that will be the lower of the following two items:

1. 40% of net income before taxes in excess of the target profit level, which is 18% of net assets or

2. $7,000,000

The individual employee is paid a share of the profit sharing pool equal to the ratio of that employee's salary to the total salary paid to all employees.

REQUIRED

(a) If the company earned $45,000,000 of profits and had net assets of $100,000,000, what would be the amount available for distribution from the profit sharing pool?

(b) Suppose that Marg Watson's salary was $68,000 and that total salaries paid in the company were $25,000,000. What would Marg's profit share be?

(c) What do you like about this profit sharing plan?

(d) What do you dislike about this profit sharing plan?

14-46 *Gain-sharing* Lindsay Cereal Company manufactures a line of breakfast cereals. The production workers are part of a gain-sharing program that works as follows. A target level of labor costs is set based on the achieved level of production. If the actual level of labor costs is less than the target level of labor costs, the difference is added to a cumulative pool that is carried from year to year. If the actual level of labor costs exceeds the target level, the amount of the excess is deducted from the cumulative pool.

If the balance of the pool is positive at the end of any year, the employees receive half the balance of the pool as part of a gain sharing plan and the balance of the pool is reset to zero. If the balance of the pool is negative at the end of any year, the employees receive nothing and the negative balance is carried to the following year.

In any year when the target level of costs exceeds the actual level of costs, the target level for the following year is based on the actual level of cost performance in the previous year.

REQUIRED

(a) Suppose that the target level of performance is set using the following labor use standards: (1) 0.15 labor hours per case of cereal A, (2) 0.10 labor hours per case of cereal B, (3) 0.20 labor hours per case of cereal C, and (4) 0.25 labor hours per case of cereal D.

During the last year, production of cereal A, B, C, and D were 200,000 cases, 220,000 cases, 130,000 cases, and 240,000 cases, respectively. The company used 120,000 labor hours during the year, and the average cost of labor was $16 per hour. What is the amount available for distribution to employees under this gain-sharing program?

(b) What do you like about this program?

(c) What do you dislike about it?

14-47 *Why intrinsic rewards matter* Intrinsic rewards are rewards that people value because of their commitment to their job or pride in their work. Examples of intrinsic rewards include pride in a job well done and value placed in personal growth in a job.

REQUIRED

(a) Why do intrinsic rewards work?

(b) Do intrinsic rewards work for everyone? Why or why not?

14-48 *Organization structure and incentive compensation* Identify an organization that is hierarchical and leaves little discretion for employees to exercise. Explain why an incentive compensation system is or is not well suited to the organization that you have identified.

14-49 *Designing reward structures* Answer these two questions about the organization units listed below:

■ What is an appropriate incentive system?

■ What behavior should be rewarded?

(a) A symphony orchestra

(b) A government welfare office

(c) An airline complaint desk

(d) A control room in a nuclear generating facility

(e) A basketball team

14-50 *Rewarding individual and group behavior*   Experts in incentive compensation argue that rewards should be based on group performance when people must work together to achieve some objective, and rewards should be based on individual performance when work can be decomposed into autonomous work units.

REQUIRED

  (a) Identify a situation that you think is well suited to using a group reward, that is, a reward based on the performance of the overall group. Indicate why you think a group reward is appropriate in this situation and precisely how you would divide the rewards among the individual members of the group.

  (b) Identify a situation that you think is well suited to using individual rewards, that is, individuals are rewarded based in their individual performance. Indicate why you think individual rewards are appropriate in this situation and precisely how you would reward each individual.

14-51 *Risk incentive compensation*   Read the article: "Life Without Sam" by Bob Ortega, *The Wall Street Journal*, January 4, 1995. This article describes the employee profit-sharing plan at Wal-Mart, which the article says is the only pension plan at Wal-Mart for nonexecutives. "Wal-Mart, which put about $166 million in the plan in both fiscal 1994 and 1993, says the plan invests heavily in Wal-Mart stock because that is what ESOPs do. . . . The board sets the total company contribution each year, and the contribution to the employee's account is based on his or her earnings." The article claims that this plan, through its lack of diversification, puts employee retirement funds at risk, a matter of increasing employee concern.

REQUIRED

  (a) What do you think of the practice of putting employee retirement funds at risk using a plan like this?

  (b) What are the positive elements of this plan?

  (c) What are the negative elements of this plan?

14-52 *Scanlon plan*   Bathurst Company manufactures household paper products. During a recent quarter, the value of the products made was $50,000,000 and the labor costs were $3,000,000. The company has decided to use a Scanlon plan with this quarter being used to establish the base ratio for the plan.

The formula is to be applied quarterly with differences, positive or negative, added to the bonus pool. The pool is to be distributed on a 35%/65% basis between the employees and the company at the end of the fourth quarter.

The following production and cost levels were recorded during the first year of the plan's operation.

Quarter	Production Value	Payroll Costs
1	$45,000,000	$2,475,000
2	60,000,000	3,480,000
3	55,000,000	3,575,000
4	48,000,000	2,832,000

REQUIRED

  (a) How much would be distributed to the employees at the end of the year?

  (b) What assumptions does the Scanlon plan make about the behavior of payroll costs?

(c) What formula should be used to determine each employee's share?

(d) Management proposes to adjust the base ratio using the lowest ratio experienced in any year. Do you think this is a good idea?

Challenging Problems

14-53 *Evaluating a compensation plan*   Tambrands, Inc., a manufacturer and distributor of personal hygiene products, made the following disclosures about its compensation program:

> Our compensation philosophy is based on two simple principles: (1) we pay for performance; and (2) management cannot benefit unless our shareholders benefit first.
>
> Executive compensation at Tambrands consists of three elements: base salary, bonus, and stock awards. Frankly, we see base salaries and the underlying value of restricted stock as what you have to pay to get people in the door—fixed costs, if you will. Incentives, in the form of annual cash bonuses and gains tied to increases in the price of our stock, are the performance drivers of our pay equation—the variable costs.
>
> The first element is base salary. Our philosophy is to peg salary levels at median competitive levels. In other words, we pay salaries that are sufficient to attract and retain the level of talent we require.
>
> The second element of our executive compensation is our bonus plan. This plan is based on management by objectives. Each year, the compensation committee approves objectives and performance measures for the corporation, our divisions, and our key individual managers. At year end, bonuses are paid on the basis of measurable performance against these objectives.
>
> The third element of our executive compensation program is stock incentives, namely, restricted stock and stock options.
>
> Our restricted stock program is very straightforward. Stock option grants are made each year at market value. Our options vest over time periods of two to six years to encourage long-term equity holding by management.
>
> In 1991, we instituted an innovative stock incentive plan called the Stock Option Exchange Program. Under this program, management can purchase stock options by exchanging other forms of compensation, such as the annual bonus or restricted stock, for the options. The price charged for the options is determined by an independent investment banker using standard pricing mechanics.
>
> Our compensation committee is made up entirely of independent outside directors. There are no interlocking directorates, in which I serve on the compensation committee of one of my director's companies and he or she serves on mine. The compensation committee uses outside advisers chosen independently to ensure that recommendations are fair to all shareholders.

What do you think of this incentive compensation plan?

14-54 *The mix of salary and commission*   Belleville Fashions sells high-quality women's, men's, and children's clothing. The store employs a sales staff of 11 full-time people and 12 part-time people. Until recently, all sales staff were paid a flat salary and participated in a profit-sharing plan that provided benefits equal to about 5% of wages. Recently, the manager and owner of Belleville Fashions announced that in the future all compensation would be commission based. The initial commission rate was set equal to the rate that would have caused the actual wage bill based on the old system to be equal to what the wage bill would have been under the commission system. Profit sharing was discontinued.

REQUIRED

(a) What do you think of this change?

(b) Describe some of the reactions that the owner might hear from the sales staff when announcing this change.

(c) Do you think that the method of determining the commission rate was appropriate?

(d) Describe what you think will happen under the new system.

14-55 *Motivating employees*   Sam Walton, the founder of the Wal-Mart chain, was an inspirational leader. Although some industry surveys suggest that Wal-Mart employees were paid salaries that were lower than the average salaries paid in the department store industry, the employees were enthusiastic and productive supporters of the organization and its objectives.

REQUIRED

(a) What is management's role in motivation?

(b) How do inspirational leaders lead? Why are employees sometimes willing to work for less than what they could earn elsewhere?

(c) Could an inspirational leader like Sam Walton be successful in any organization? For example, if Sam Walton had been made the president of IBM, could he have created the same success there as he did at Wal-Mart? Explain.

14-56 *Measuring units of work done*   In an effort to cut costs, a company in the Bell Telephone system developed productivity standards for its employees. Each employee was expected to deliver services to customers within the allowed time. As part of this process, installers were allowed a certain amount of time to install residential telephones.

A new customer in a home that was already wired requested a service connection. Because the home was already wired and the customer indicated that the telephone jacks were already in the house, the installer was allowed 30 minutes to visit the customer, give the customer the telephone, and ensure that the line had been activated properly.

When the installer arrived at the customer's home, the customer asked about having a second line installed. The installer inspected the lines in the home and told the customer that the second line into the home had a short circuit and that a second line could not be installed. The installer left the customer's home.

About a year later, the customer was experiencing problems with the line and an installer was dispatched to fix the problem. In the course of identifying the problem, the installer discovered an old telephone transformer that had been used by a previous owner of the home plugged into an electrical outlet in an unused corner of the basement. This transformer was causing the short circuit associated with the second telephone line into the home. Shortly after, the second line was installed in the home. The customer had been without a second line, for which the monthly rental was about $15 for a year. When asked why the first installer had not taken the time to find the cause of the short-circuit, the second installer replied:

> He was probably a new fellow who was rushing to meet the productivity standard for the call. Finding the short circuit would have solved the problem but created problems for him since the system would not have given him credit for doing that work. I don't care. I have been around too long to worry about productivity measurement systems. They are not going to fire me; I have too much seniority.

REQUIRED

(a) What do you think of this Bell Telephone Company's performance measurement system? What went wrong?

(b) Recognizing the need to have a system that provides the proper motivation for customer service and truthful reporting, what type of performance measurement system would you recommend?

14-57 *Salary and job responsibilities*   Marie Johnston, the manager of a government unemployment insurance office, is paid a salary that reflects the number of people she supervises and the number of hours that her subordinates work.

REQUIRED

(a) What do you think of this compensation scheme? What incentives does this compensation scheme provide to Marie?

(b) What would you recommend as an appropriate performance measurement and reward system?

14-58 *Vertical pay equity*   Many compensation experts have proposed a 20:1 compensation rule for the sake of equity. The idea is that the total compensation paid to the highest-paid person in the organization must not exceed 20 times the total compensation paid to the lowest-paid person in the organization. *The Wall Street Journal*, April 13, 1994, estimated the average ratio of the salary of a chief executive to the average worker's pay to be about 117.

Ben and Jerry's Homemade, Inc., is a manufacturer and distributor of dairy products located in Vermont. The compensation ratio at Ben and Jerry's Homemade, Inc., was originally set at 7:1, then moved to 10:1, and has since risen to about 12.5:1.

REQUIRED

(a) Do you think that compensation rates reported by *The Wall Street Journal* article could create motivational problems?

(b) Do you think that there could be some practical problems using a compensation rule like the one that Ben and Jerry's uses?

14-59 *Choosing what to reward*   During the late 1970s, Harley-Davidson, the motorcycle manufacturer, was losing money and was very close to bankruptcy. Management believed that one of the problems was low productivity and, as a result, asked middle managers to speed up production. The employees who made the motorcycles were told that the priority was to get the motorcycles made and shipped on schedule, which was usually very tight. Middle managers were judged by their ability to meet shipment schedules.

REQUIRED

(a) What is the rationale that would lead to a desire to speed production in the face of increasing costs and declining productivity?

(b) What type of behavior do you think that this performance measurement system would create in the sense of the priorities that middle management would establish for the production process?

(c) What type of problems would this performance measurement system create?

(d) How, if at all, would you modify this system?

14-60 *The Soviet incentive system*   The text claims that the appropriate relationship between the Soviet incentive system parameters is $0 < \alpha < \beta < \gamma$. Explain why this is so.

14-61 *Choosing parameters in the Soviet incentive system*   (Advanced: requires differentiation skills.) The text claims that the following relationship will cause the enterprise manager in the Soviet incentive system to report the mean of the distribution of expected production:

$$\gamma = 2B - \alpha$$

Show that this is true.

14-62 *The Groves Mechanism*   Suppose that a company manufactures three products using a single manufacturing facility. The capacity of the facility is 6000 hours per year. The number of units of each product that can be made per hour on the machine are as follows: product 1 — 125, product 2 — 150, product 3 — 100. The contribution margins of the three products are as follows: product 1 — $80, product 2 — $50, product 3 — $90.

The three product managers have estimated the demands for the three products as follows. These individual beliefs are known only to the individual managers.

product 1   The product manager believes that the demand for this product will be somewhere between 280,000 units and 360,000 units with every amount on this interval equally likely.

product 2   The product manager believes that the demand for this product will be somewhere between 180,000 units and 220,000 units with every amount on this interval equally likely.

product 3   The product manager believes that the demand for this product will be somewhere between 220,000 units and 280,000 units with every amount on this interval equally likely.

The three product managers are expected value decision makers who only value wealth. There is a central planner who is responsible for allocating time on this machine to the three product managers.

REQUIRED

    (a) From the point of view of the firm, what is the best allocation of the 6000 hours of machine time?

    (b) If the division managers are rewarded on the basis of division profits, what will be their motivation in communicating their beliefs to the central planner?

    (c) Suppose that the three product managers are each paid an annual salary of $60,000 and are rewarded using the Groves Mechanism with $\beta = 0.01$. What will be the result in terms of the beliefs that they communicate to the central planner?

14-63 ***Distributing a bonus pool***   These are the four broad approaches to distributing the proceeds of a bonus pool in a profit-sharing plan:

    (1) Each person's share is based on salary.

    (2) Each person receives an equal share.

    (3) Each person's share is based on position in the organization (larger payments to people at higher levels).

    (4) Each person's share is based on individual performance relative to some target.

REQUIRED

    (a) For each of these alternatives, give two reasons to support the alternative.

    (b) For each of these alternatives, give two reasons to oppose the alternative.

    (c) Pick the alternative that you think is best and support your choice with an argument of no more than 100 words.

■ CASES

14-64 ***The effect of rewards on performance***   Dorothy Webster was the supervisor of a special claims processing group in the Eastern Insurance Company. This group processed medical claims that involved complex injuries and claims that involved elective surgery. One of the group's major roles was to respond to requests seeking authorization for cosmetic surgical procedures.

The claims processing clerks in Dorothy's department were all highly experienced. Most had worked in the company's regular claims processing group for at least five years. The clerks needed a comprehensive knowledge of the company's different insurance plans and the options in each plan. They needed good general medical knowledge since they often had to read and discuss medical reports with physicians who submitted proposals for elective surgery.

The clerks had to make three determinations when processing a claim. For claims involving required surgery, the clerks had to verify that the claimant's insurance covered the claim, that all procedures were necessary given the nature of the accident or illness, and that the charges reflected the plan's reimbursement schedule. The same considerations applied to claims for elective surgery with two additional considerations. First, any elective procedure costing more than $3000 had to be approved in advance by a special claims processing unit. Second, each procedure in an elective surgery and its rate had to be approved separately.

The insurance company dealt only with companies that established medical plans for their employees. The role of the insurance company was really that of an administrator rather than an insurer. The annual premiums charged each company reflected that company's claim experience and the insurance company's administrative costs in dealing with claims from that company. On average, the margin provided by each company's business was about 3% of premiums collected from that company, that is, 3% of the insurance premiums from each customer went toward covering the insurance company's general overhead.

The insurance business was very competitive. There were three critical success factors: (1) response time and accuracy in dealing with a claim, (2) keeping administrative costs low so that premiums would provide an adequate margin, and (3) rejecting invalid, unauthorized, or excessive claims to keep the group's claims experience as low as possible, thereby minimizing premium increases.

The clerks in Dorothy's department were the highest-paid nonsupervisory staff in the company. Their average pay was about $65,000 per year. The pay consisted of an annual salary of about $40,000 and incentive pay that averaged $25,000 per year. Incentive pay was proportional to the number of points that the clerk earned. Dorothy rated each claim on a scale of 5 to 10 points, depending on the claim's complexity. The processing clerk earned that number of points when the claim was completed. Points for claims that proved later to have been processed incorrectly were deducted from the clerk's accumulated total. In addition, a penalty was deducted for incorrectly processed claims. A manual described each type of error and the penalty that would result from it. The clerks understood the incentive and penalty scheme and were satisfied with it. Turnover in the group was less than 5%. Most clerks who left the company went to supervisory positions in similar groups in other insurance companies. The clerks in the special claims processing group were widely regarded in the medical insurance industry as the best trained and most highly motivated.

During the past year, several changes had taken place in the special claims processing group. First, the company had grown rapidly through several acquisitions, and the number of clerks in the group had increased from 73 to 104 in less than one year. Dorothy had assigned each new clerk to an experienced clerk for one month's training and supervision. This role had cut down on the experienced clerk's ability to earn bonuses, and the average incentive pay had fallen 20% to $20,000. This had created considerable discontent. Second, a study of the group's operations had proposed a major change. The study suggested that the group's response time was below the industry average and needed to be improved.

One of the problems was the excessive amount of time required to process the most complex claims involving elective surgery. These claims often involved conferences with the insurance company's medical staff that often took days to schedule and usually required travel to another office for the meeting. It seemed that these claims became orphans in the system, and eventually Dorothy herself processed many of them. The study proposed that clerks work in groups with representatives from other company groups, including medical, legal, and sales, to improve response time for these claims. When asked, the clerks admitted that they avoided these claims because, relative to the huge amount of time they consumed, the clerks received relatively little credit for processing them. Moreover, the most experienced clerks who did the majority of these claims objected to Dorothy's practice of giving them the claims because they were the most experienced. For the first time ever, the special claims processing group was experiencing requests for transfers to other groups within the company, and this year seven experienced claims clerks left the company.

Using the expectancy theory model, discuss the incentive plan used in the special claims processing group.

14-65 *Rewarding long-term performance* In 1983 Johnson Controls Inc. developed a seven-year performance plan for two of their most senior-level executives. In each of the seven years, the base amount of the plan (consisting of $300,000 and $100,000 for the two executives, respectively) is multiplied by a percentage that varies between 0% and 150%. The determination of each percentage is based upon the ratio of the average annual total shareholder return for Johnson Controls (over the 10-year period ending with the current year) to the average total shareholder return for a peer group of Fortune 500 companies over the same period. Then each of the yearly awards is invested in a hypothetical portfolio consisting of the stock of Johnson Controls. The payment of the total value of this hypothetical portfolio is deferred until the end of the seven-year performance period.

There are several interesting aspects of this performance plan. First, the term of the contract extends approximately three years beyond the retirement of the two executives. This feature appears to be an attempt to lengthen the decision-making horizons of the two executives, especially in the case of those near retirement age. This contract explicitly motivates the executives to consider the impact of their decisions on the company after they leave the corporation.

Second, the scorecard for the annual changes in the value of the performance plan is formally tied to changes in shareholder wealth over the prior 10 years. This is unusual because performance plans are typically based on earnings per share or return on equity growth rates. One explanation for the choice of changes in shareholder wealth is that the board of directors is attempting to lengthen the executive's decision-making horizon by selecting a scorecard that has a longer performance evaluation horizon than yearly accounting numbers.

Finally, the performance plan is based on relative changes in shareholder wealth. This appears to be an attempt to isolate that portion of changes in shareholder wealth that is under management's control from economy- and industry-wide effects. The choice of a 10-year period for assessing the performance of the company may be an attempt to wash out other random effects that affect performance in a single year.

Comment on this incentive compensation plan. Identify what you like and what you do not like about it.[23]

[23] Richard A. Lambert and David F. Larcker, "Executive Compensation, Corporate Decision-Making and Shareholder Wealth: A Review of the Evidence," *Corporate Restructuring and Executive Compensation*, ed. Joel M. Stern, G. Bennett Stewart III, and Donald H. Chew, Ballinger Publishing Company, 1989.

15

MANAGEMENT ACCOUNTING AND CONTROL SYSTEM DESIGN: BEHAVIORAL FACTORS AND CHANGE MANAGEMENT

CHAPTER OBJECTIVES

After reading this chapter, you will be able to

1. discuss managerial approaches to motivation and, in particular, the human resources model

2. identify the characteristics of well-designed management accounting and control systems (MACS) and the links among the concepts of motivation, ethics, control, and performance

3. evaluate the behavioral consequences of poorly designed MACS

4. understand the behavioral implications of implementing a new MACS or changing a current MACS

AUTOMOBILE MANUFACTURING

Courtesy **Toyota Motor Corp.**

Susan Wu has just been appointed as a senior manager of a major automobile manufacturing company in Los Angeles. Susan is on the fast track, having graduated with concentrations in operations management and management accounting from a southern California business school only six years earlier. Her most recent job as a manager has been very straightforward, and with her strong accounting background she has developed a strong reputation as being able to move in and out of the management accounting and control system with ease. Even the current controller goes to Susan for help when stuck. In short, Susan is considered a whiz with numbers.

The corporation has just decided to change its entire cost system as the current system has been identified as inadequate for cost control and product costing. Apart from the outmoded system, reports from other divisions of the organization are noncomparable and often unreadable in their current format. Further, because of the amount of information required on reports and the lack of staff, the reports are always notoriously late. Also, the system only gathers quantitative financial information, which Susan finds inadequate given the organization's new focus on quality and speed to market. Finally, there are many stories about how managers felt they had to "game" the system to make their numbers look good for senior management. Given her background, Susan is sent to a week-long seminar on new costing methods.

Susan gains much insight from the seminar. She realizes that she now has a rare opportunity to redesign a system that can produce many benefits for the company. Susan thinks that system redesign can be easy because she can combine her business school knowledge and her work experience to design a new system and implement the necessary changes. Susan's first step is to meet with area managers in marketing, operations, engineering and material management, and finance to discuss the needed changes. Susan explains how the new system can overcome the problems that they all had experienced in the past. She begins to outline the changes, when several area managers protest loudly. While managers agree that the existing system is flawed, they feel that at least they understand it and are used to the way it works. Managers comment that they are under severe competitive pressure, requiring all their energies to be devoted to getting the product out the door. They don't have the time or energy to cope with installing and understanding a new cost system. A new system can potentially change cost assignments, performance measurements, resource allocation, and their bonuses. Until they can evaluate all of the implications of the cost system, they want it put on hold.

Susan is dismayed at this initial response. Her previous belief about how easy change can be could not have been more wrong. How can she make everyone realize the benefits from updating the system? Can she help them overcome their fears and concerns? Is it possible to lead the change in the face of such resistance? Finally, what principles must she follow that would help guide the change?

MANAGEMENT ACCOUNTING AND CONTROL SYSTEMS AND BEHAVIORAL SCIENCE

In previous chapters, our discussion presented many aspects of management accounting information from a conceptual and technical point of view. By way of review, the goals of a management accounting and control system (MACS) are as follows:

1. To aid the organization in *planning* for the future.
2. To *monitor* events in the external environment and their effects on the design and functioning of the MACS.
3. To *measure* and *record* the results of activities occurring inside the organization to ensure that decision makers are well informed.
4. To *motivate* individuals and groups who are affected by and who affect the MACS.
5. To *evaluate the performance* of individuals and groups in the organization.

Because people are involved with each of these goals, the study of management accounting methods and systems must be connected to the study of human behavior. Fortunately, accounting scholars have studied ideas developed in fields of human behavior, such as sociology, organizational behavior, and social psychology, and learned how to apply these ideas to management accounting contexts in organizations. These ideas help us understand how individuals and groups are motivated, how to evaluate their performance, and how to coordinate their actions.

This chapter focuses on the behavioral and organizational issues that arise in the design and use of management accounting information and the overall MACS. The opening vignette to this chapter highlights issues that are becoming more commonplace, especially during turbulent economic times. Our discussion focuses on ways to resolve these issues when introducing a new MACS.

We begin by presenting some fundamental ideas about human motivation and then link these ideas to the characteristics of a well-designed MACS and the behaviors that a well-designed system promotes. Next, we discuss the consequences of poor MACS design, especially the lack of goal congruence and failure to follow ethical guidelines. Finally, in the last section of the chapter, we consider behavioral factors that companies should address when they alter their existing MACS.

Managerial approaches to motivation

In Chapter 14, we discussed two psychological theories of individual motivation—Herzberg's two-factor theory and Vroom's expectancy model. In contrast, there are numerous theories of management thought regarding the best way to motivate people to improve their performance at work. This chapter emphasizes how management thinking has evolved since the early 1900s regarding people and work and how the changes in thinking affect MACS design.

> **OBJECTIVE 15.1**
>
> Discuss managerial approaches to motivation and, in particular, the human resources model.

The earlier attempts to explain motivation differ from more recent models based on the assumptions made about people's preferences and tastes for work. These assumptions have shifted from a viewpoint of valuing employees primarily for their physical contribution to seeing them as an important intellectual and creative force.

1. The earliest model of motivation, developed at the turn of the century in accordance with the **scientific management school of motivation,** assumed that most people found work objectionable, that money was the only driving force behind good performance, and that individuals cared little for exercising creativity on the job. Then the task for management was to tightly monitor and control employee behavior and to break down tasks in such a way that employees could follow tightly prescribed procedures without having to make decisions. Management believed that with very little discretion, employees would focus their attention exclusively on improving production.

   Scientific management school of motivation
   A school of motivation in which people are viewed as finding work objectionable, motivated only by money, and as having little knowledge to contribute to the organization.

2. The second significant development in motivational theory arose with the **human relations movement** beginning in the late 1930s. This movement recognized that people had needs that go well beyond a simple repetitive task at work and that financial compensation was only one aspect of what workers desired. Employees wanted respect, discretion over their jobs, and a feeling that they contributed something valuable to their organization. Thus, a focus began on developing interpersonal relations, improving morale, and increasing job satisfaction.

   Human relations movement
   A model of human motivation that considers that people have many needs and aspirations at work and that they are motivated by things other than money.

3. The most recent model of motivation, based on the **human resources model,** advances our understanding even further. Although this model retains some aspects of the earlier models, under the strong influence of Japanese management practices it introduces a high level of employee participation in decision making. The central assumptions of the human resources model are that people do not find work objectionable and that they want to participate in developing objectives and attaining goals in a work environment that has grown increasingly complex. Another assumption is that individuals have a great deal to contribute to the organization in terms of the information and knowledge they possess about their jobs, that they are highly creative and responsible, and that they desire opportunities to effect change in their organizations. The task for management is to understand

   Human resources model of motivation
   An approach to human motivation that emphasizes that individuals do not find work objectionable, that they have knowledge to contribute, and that they are creative.

that a mix of psychological factors (such as the supervisory approach—authoritarian versus participative, the nature of working conditions, and the needs of the individual) and economic factors (such as the type of incentives) influence motivation. In this chapter, we use the human resources model as the basis for understanding the design of the MACS.

With the human resources model in mind, managers usually focus on three key aspects of employee motivation:

1. *Direction*, or where an employee focuses attention at work
2. *Intensity*, or the level of effort the employee expends
3. *Persistence*, or the duration of time that an employee will stay with a task or job.

As mentioned in earlier chapters, the ideal situation for management occurs when employees voluntarily have aligned their individual goals with those of the organization so that they can attain their goals as they perform their jobs well. We refer to this situation as achieving **goal congruence.**

Goal congruence
The alignment of individual and organizational goals.

Creating goal congruence for employees involves many factors. Among these is the need to provide strong organizational leadership, satisfying work, appropriate rewards, opportunities for advancement, and a supportive work environment for an organization's workers. If goal congruence is possible to attain, then managing direction, intensity, and persistence is easier. But if goal congruence cannot be attained, which is often the case, then management's task becomes much more challenging.

A well-designed and functioning MACS can help the organization achieve goal congruence among its employees. We present the characteristics of a well-designed MACS next.

OBJECTIVE 15.2

Identify the characteristics of well-designed management accounting and control systems (MACS) and the links among the concepts of motivation, ethics, control, and performance.

CHARACTERISTICS OF WELL-DESIGNED MANAGEMENT ACCOUNTING AND CONTROL SYSTEMS

A well-designed MACS should include the following:

1. A consistent, global, technical structure that also allows for flexibility at the many local levels (specific groups or operating units) in the organization and a structure that fosters continuous improvement. We label this the **multiple perspectives approach to management accounting systems design.**

Multiple perspectives approach to management accounting system design
The development of a consistent organization-wide management accounting system that also allows for local input and tailoring.

2. The incorporation of the organization's code of ethical conduct into system design to motivate appropriate behavior.

3. The development and use of both quantitative and qualitative information in a timely fashion for control, motivation, and performance evaluation.

4. The participation and empowerment of employees in system design and improvements and also in continuous education to understand how the system functions, how to interpret its information meaningfully, and what decisions will be made and actions taken with this information.

5. Development of mechanisms such as reward systems tied to performance to promote motivation and goal congruence between the organization and employees.

The Multiple Perspective Approach to MACS Design

Traditionally, in many organizations, the controller's office has had responsibility for MACS design with the main responsibilities of developing and maintaining information system design including the management accounting and control function. The controller and other members of the MACS design team have two tasks as they implement the multiple perspectives approach to system design.

1. **Consistency.** They must structure the MACS to provide a consistent framework for information that can be applied globally across the units or divisions of an entity. Consistency means that the language used and the technical methods of producing management accounting information do not conflict within various parts of an organization. For example, having two divisions with different costing systems makes it more difficult to understand and compare results across divisions. If one division of an organization uses activity-based costing principles and another division, especially one that is very similar in goals and function to the first, uses volume-based overhead allocation methods, the organization is not operating under the same MACS philosophy. Or consider the difficulties that would arise if divisions classified the same expense differently, e.g., fringe benefits of workers classified as direct labor expenses versus indirect labor expenses.

2. **Flexibility.** MACS designers, however, must allow employees to use the system's available information in a flexible manner so they can customize its application for local decisions. If flexibility is not possible, an employee's motivation to make the best decision may be lessened for the decision at hand, especially if units engage in different types of activities. For instance, if one division of a company located in Pasadena is involved in new product development and another division in Taipei performs final assembly, each division probably will have different data needs and may use different cost drivers in making its decisions. The critical success factors for managing new product development in Pasadena will be quite different from the factors that the Taipei assembly division must use to manage effectively. A well-designed MACS should be able to accommodate the local needs of each division. If not, inaccurate ad hoc local systems may develop, which can lead to poor decisions and confusion between the company's division and upper management.

Designers of management accounting systems should attempt to meet the needs of as many relevant parties involved as possible. Thus, the first step in system development is to agree on the underlying principles of the MACS. The second step is to tailor local systems to address specific information needs of system users in a manner that is consistent with the underlying philosophy of the MACS. Fortunately, as mentioned in Chapter 1, managers in every organization can become party to the multiple perspectives approach because they can devise their

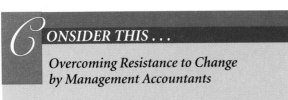

Overcoming Resistance to Change by Management Accountants

An article on activity-based costing stated, "Most bean-counters don't like activity-based costing when they first see it, perhaps because it demands a minute understanding of how a company works. 'It forces accountants into the factory,' says Marlene D. Smith, controller for the plant of Toledo-based Dana Corp. that makes axles for off-highway vehicles. Yet many become converts, says Tom E. Pryor, former head of the cost-management program at Computer-Aided Manufacturing International, a consortium of manufacturers that has championed ABC's development: 'Their resistance vanishes once they realize ABC makes the finance function more vital to the company's success.'"

Source: "A Bean Counter's Best Friend," *Business Week*, Special Issue on Quality, 1991, pp. 42–43.

own systems for internal decision making. Such flexibility does not apply to systems designed primarily to produce information to comply with external financial reporting information requirements.

Earlier we stated that individuals in the controller's office traditionally have been responsible for MACS design. Since the early 1980s, however, employees working in various functional areas of companies who were frustrated with existing systems began to develop their own formal and informal management accounting systems. For example, in many companies, industrial and design engineers or manufacturing managers have taken the lead in developing their own costing systems due to the inadequacy of existing systems. In such cases when employees outside the controller's office develop local ad hoc systems, conflict arises between them and the individuals in the controller's office who are formally charged with MACS design. Developers of the new costing systems, such as activity-based costing, have historically believed that many management accountants were inflexible regarding change and that financial reporting requirements would keep management accountants from being able to make key cost management changes. In other organizations, management accountants have embraced the changes made to the existing systems, which were obsolete. These individuals realized that without adopting new systems they would be hindering progress. In many organizations today, both local users and employees responsible for system design have realized that they are all better off by joining forces and agreeing on how changes should be made.

Ethical Considerations in MACS Design

A well-designed MACS should incorporate the principles of an organization's code of ethical conduct into its system design. Ethics is a discipline involving the study of standards of conduct and moral judgment. By incorporating ethical considerations in a MACS, ethical principles can play an important role in affecting the behavior of all organizational participants.

For system designers such as management accountants, in addition to their organization's code of ethical conduct, their professional association, the Institute of Management Accountants (IMA), has established ethical standards. Certified Management Accountants (CMAs) are required to be competent and to always maintain confidentiality, integrity, and objectivity.[1] Having a clear set of ethical standards guides motivation, especially regarding the direction of effort, and should help reduce nongoal-congruent behavior by users. In order to incorporate

---

[1] See "Standards of Ethical Conduct for Management Accountants," *Management Accounting*, February 1992, p. 11.

ethical principles into the design of a MACS, management accountants might attempt to ensure the following:

1. The organization has formulated, implemented, and communicated to all employees a comprehensive code of ethics.
2. All employees understand the organization's code of ethics.
3. A system exists to detect and report violations of the organization's code of ethics.

Although management accountants may find some variations in codes of ethics in various countries, such codes are remarkably similar in purpose.

System design will influence the behavior of all users. The key user group, managers, interacts a great deal with the MACS. Often managers are subject to intense pressures from their jobs and from other influential organizational members to suspend their ethical judgment in certain situations. These pressures include the following:

1. Requests to tailor information to favor particular individuals or groups
2. Pleas to falsify reports or test results or approve false reports or claims
3. Requests for confidential information
4. Pressures to ignore a questionable or unethical practice

AVOIDING ETHICAL DILEMMAS.   Most organizations attempt to address ethical considerations and avoid ethical dilemmas by developing a code of ethics. Although there is no universal hierarchy of ethical principles, these five categories capture the broad array of ethical considerations:

1. Legal rules
2. Societal norms
3. Professional memberships (CPAs, CMAs, etc.)
4. Organizational or group norms
5. Personal norms

This hierarchy is listed in descending order of authority. For example, an action that is prohibited by law should be unacceptable by society, by one's profession, by the organization and, finally, by each person. An action that is legally and socially acceptable, such as strategically underestimating product costs, may, however, be professionally unacceptable and, in turn, unacceptable to the organization and its employees. Unfortunately, any hierarchy of this sort has a number of gray areas, and yet, it provides general guidelines for understanding and dealing with ethical problems which arise.

The ethical hierarchy presented above provides a set of constraints on a decision. In this scheme, ethical conflicts arise when one system of values diverges from a more fundamental system of values. For example, suppose that the organization's code of ethics commits it to meeting only the letter of the law regarding disclosure of a product fault of one of its manufactured goods that could prove to be hazardous to consumers. However, a broader societal expectation is that organizations be aggressive in identifying and disclosing potential product problems.

Thus, an individual decision maker may face an ethical conflict when the organizational code of ethics implies doing nothing about a product fault, since there is no definitive evidence of a product problem. In such cases, broader societal expectations would imply that disclosure is necessary because there is persistent evidence of a problem.

DEALING WITH ETHICAL CONFLICTS.   Organizations that formulate and support specific and unambiguous ethical codes can create an environment that will reduce ethical conflicts. One step in avoiding ambiguity or misunderstanding is to maintain a hierarchical ordering of authority. This means that the organization's stated code of ethics should not allow any behavior that is either legally or socially unacceptable. Because most professional codes of ethics reflect broad moral imperatives, such as loyalty, discretion, and competence, an organization would create public relations problems for itself if its stated code of ethics conflicted with a professional code of ethics.

Another critical variable that can reduce ethical conflicts is the way that the chief executive and other senior managers behave and conduct business. If these individuals demonstrate exemplary behavior at work, others will follow. Organizations whose leaders evidence unethical behavior cannot expect their employees to act differently.

In some cases, when organizations develop a formal code of ethics, they can create the potential for explicit ethical conflicts to arise with the code itself. The conflicts that appear most in practice are those that occur between the law and the organization's code of ethics, conflicts between the organization's practiced code of ethics and common societal expectations, and conflicts between the individual's set of personal and professional ethics and the organization's practiced code of ethics. Any conflicts that remain relate primarily to personal values and norms of behavior that were acceptable prior to the adoption of the organization's new code of ethics but that are now in question.

CONFLICTS BETWEEN INDIVIDUAL AND ORGANIZATIONAL VALUES.   People bring personal codes of ethics with them into the organization. If the organization's code of ethics is more stringent than an individual's, conflicts could arise. But, if adherence to the organization's ethical code is required and enforced, it is possible to diminish ethical conflicts if, as part of the employment contract, the individual is asked and expected to pursue a more stringent code of ethics. Another possible, and probably more desirable, outcome is that individuals may raise their own ethical standards without conflict.

Difficult issues may arise when the individual's personal code of ethics prohibits certain types of behavior that are legal, socially acceptable, professionally acceptable, and acceptable to the organization. Potential for conflicts in such situations will arise when the action that is unacceptable to the individual is desirable to the organization. As an example, an employee may have deep religious objections to doing business in any form on a holy day. Working for an organization may require that the person, under these circumstances, do things that he or she finds unacceptable. In this case, the individual is confronted with a personal choice. Unfortunately, the employee may have little institutional support in this situation but can lobby within or outside the organization to prohibit working on a holy day. This may be effective, or the affected employee may choose not to work for that organization depending on what he or she decides is important.

CONFLICTS BETWEEN THE ORGANIZATION'S STATED AND PRACTICED VALUES.

In some cases, employees will observe management or even senior management engaged in unethical behavior such as management fraud. This type of conflict is the most difficult because the organization is misrepresenting its ethical system, which forces the employee to make a choice between going public or not. In this setting, the employee is in the position of drawing attention to the problem by being a whistle-blower, which many have found to be a unique and lonely position. In many instances, though, whistle-blowers have chosen personal integrity over their loyalty to the organization.

Experts who have studied this problem advise that the individual should first make sure that the facts are correct and that a conflict does exist between the organization's stated ethical policy and the actions of its employees in practice. Second, the individual, by speaking with superiors, should determine whether this conflict is institutional or whether it reflects the decisions and actions of only a few people.

Faced with a true conflict, the individual has several choices, among them:

1. Point out the discrepancy to a superior and refuse to act unethically. This may lead to dismissal, the need to resign from the organization, or the experience of suffering hidden organization sanctions.

2. Point out the discrepancy to a superior and act unethically. The rationale for this choice, which is incorrect, is that the employee believes this affords protection from legal sanctions.

3. Delay taking action and take the discrepancy to an ombudsperson in the organization, if one exists.

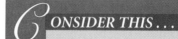

CONSIDER THIS . . .

Cheats on the Links Are Cheats at the Job

A survey by Hyatt Hotels and Resorts, *Golf and the Business Executive,* found that almost half of the 401 executives surveyed agreed that "the way a person plays golf is very similar to how he or she conducts business affairs." The statistics were very telling: 55% of the surveyed executives admitted cheating at golf at least once, including moving the ball to get a better lie (41%), not counting a missed tap-in (19%), intentionally miscounting strokes (8%), and secretly pocketing a fresh ball while pretending to look for a lost ball in the woods (6%). A third of the executives who admitted cheating also admitted to pulling fast ones on the job.

Source: M. Quinn, "It's All in the Lie," *Time,* July 26, 1993, p. 54.

CONSIDER THIS . . .

Whistleblowing and the IMA Standards

Whistleblowing inside or outside an organization can lead to opposition to employer conduct. The Standards of Ethical Conduct of the Institute of Management Accountants (IMA) provide guidance for management accountants faced with whistleblowing. Management accountants are advised to resolve their conflicts within the organization. If a satisfactory resolution cannot be obtained in this manner, the alternative sanctioned by the Standards (SMA Number 1C, 1983) is "to resign from the organization and to submit an informative memorandum to an appropriate representative of the organization." This action is a form of internal whistleblowing. According to the standards, communication of such problems to "authorities or individuals not employed or engaged by the organization (external whistleblowing) is not considered appropriate," unless required by law.

Source: G. Rechtschaffen and J. A. Yardley, "Whistleblowing and the Law," *Management Accounting,* March, 1995, p. 40.

4. Delay taking action and work with respected leaders in the organization to change the discrepancy between practiced and stated ethics.

5. Delay taking action and go outside the organization to publicly resolve the issue.

6. Delay taking action and go outside the organization anonymously to resolve the issue.

7. Resign and go public to resolve the issue.

8. Resign and remain silent.

9. Delay taking action, do nothing, and hope that the problem will go away.

Although most experts recommend following the course stated in item 4 on this list, it is not our place to discuss the efficacy of any of these alternatives other than to mention that there are circumstances that can make any of them appropriate. If the organization is serious about its stated code of ethics, it should have an effective ethics control system to ensure and provide evidence that the organization's stated and practiced ethics are the same. Part of this control system should include a means for employees to point out inconsistencies between stated practices and ethics without fear of retribution. Any organization that does not provide a system to protect employees in these situations is either not taking its code of ethics seriously or has an inadequate ethics control system.

Ethical control system
A system that reinforces the ethical responsibilities of all firm employees.

THE ELEMENTS OF AN EFFECTIVE ETHICAL CONTROL SYSTEM.
To promote ethical decision making, management should implement an **ethical control system.** The elements of this ethical control system should include the following:

1. A statement of the organization's values and code of ethics stated in practical terms, along with examples so that the organization's employees can relate it to their individual jobs.

2. A clear statement of the employee's ethical responsibilities for every job description and a specific review of the employee's ethical performance as part of every performance review.

3. Adequate training to help employees identify ethical dilemmas in practice and learn how to deal with those they can reasonably expect to face.

4. Evidence that senior management expects organization members to adhere to its code of ethics. This means that management must:
   ■ Provide a statement of the consequences of violating the organization's code of ethics.
   ■ Establish a means of dealing with violations of the organization's code of ethics promptly, ruthlessly, and consistently with the statement of consequences.
   ■ Provide visible support of ethical decision making at every opportunity.
   ■ Provide a private line of communication (without retribution) from employees directly to the Chief Executive Officer, Chief Operating Officer, Head of Human Resource Management, or someone else on the Board of Directors.

5. Evidence that employees can make ethical decisions or report violations of the organizations stated ethics (the whistleblower) without fear of reprisals from superiors, subordinates, or peers in the organization. This proof usually takes the form of an organization ombudsperson who has the authority to investigate complaints, wherever they lead, and to preserve the confidentiality of people who report violations.

6. Providing for an ongoing internal audit of the efficacy of the organization's ethical control system.

STEPS IN MAKING AN ETHICAL DECISION. Formal training is part of the process of promoting ethical decision making. After gathering the facts relating to a particular decision and evaluating the alternative courses of action, the decision maker can eliminate possible courses of action that are ethically unacceptable. The decision model in Exhibit 15-1 is one approach to eliminating unacceptable alternatives.[2]

In summary, the MACS represents one of the organization's central information systems, and the organization's code of ethics must underlie its design. Both designers and users of the system should remember this and rectify any deviations from the code of ethics that the system explicitly or implicitly promotes.

Developing and Using Both Quantitative and Qualitative Information

A well-designed MACS should ensure that it captures and uses both quantitative and qualitative information for decision making.

THE NEED FOR MULTIPLE MEASURES OF PERFORMANCE. There is a saying in business that "what gets measured gets done." In other words, the ways in which organizations and individuals use management accounting and other types of information and the particular kinds of measures that the organization establishes send signals to all employees and stakeholders about what the organization considers to be important. For many years, it has been recognized that without well-defined measures of performance, employees will engage in noncongruent behavior. For instance, if a firm uses management accounting information to set up a performance evaluation system that rewards a vendor only for the on-time delivery of product, this will be the variable on which the vendor's employees will focus. Since this evaluation would not consider the quality of the goods sent, vendors who supply the merchandise may sacrifice quality for the sake of meeting promised delivery dates—the measured variable—or they may quote excessively long lead times. Either act could work to the long-term detriment of the organization and the vendor.

Department store managers have found that when salespeople are compensated solely by sales commissions, their attention will be focused on selling as much expensive merchandise as possible. Employees faced with such a situation initially may find that their sales volume is increasing. But, as the competition for customers develops, the work environment may become hostile as disputes arise

[2] This decision model was developed initially to teach cases in accounting with an ethics perspective.

EXHIBIT 15.1
Decision Model for Resolving Ethical Issues

1. **Determine the Facts—What, Who, Where, When, How.**
   What do we know or need to know, if possible, that will help us define the problem?

2. **Define the Ethical Issue.**
   - List the significant stakeholders
   - Define the ethical issues
   Make sure precisely what the ethical issue is, for example, conflict involving rights, questions over limits of disclosure obligation, and so on.

3. **Identify Major Principles, Rules, Values.**
   Determine key principles such as integrity, quality, respect for persons, societal benefits, and costs.

4. **Specify the Alternatives.**
   List the major alternative courses of action, including those that represent some form of compromise or point between simply doing or not doing something.

5. **Compare Values and Alternatives.**
   Determine if there is one principle or value, or a combination, which is so compelling that the proper alternative is clear, for example, correcting a defect that is almost certain to cause loss of life.

6. **Assess the Consequences.**
   Identify short- and long-term positive and negative consequences for the major alternatives. The common short-run focus on gains or losses needs to be measured against long-run considerations.

7. **Make Your Decision.**
   Balance the consequences against your primary principles or values and select the alternative that best fits.

Source: William W. May (Ed.), *Ethics in the Accounting Curriculum; Cases and Readings,* American Accounting Association, Sarasota, Florida, 1990, p. 1.

over whose customer it was or who really made the sale. Another consequence of relying solely on commissions as a motivating tool is that other aspects of the sales function, such as straightening up merchandise after customers have been browsing or restocking shelves, may become lower priorities for salespeople. Also, customers may return merchandise that has been oversold to them. Ultimately, the department store can be heading for trouble in such circumstances.

Given the problems of using a single performance measure, organizations should attempt to evaluate employees by using more than one performance measure. Not only will this expand employee vision, but it may also motivate employees consistently with organizational goals. It is important to use multiple performance measures that reflect the complexities of the work environment and the variety of contributions that employees make. In many manufacturing and service environments today, many employees, or associates or operators as they are often called, are being cross-trained to perform a variety of tasks. Further, as in the case at General Motors' Saturn plant, many employees are organized into self-managed work teams or they follow a product's manufacture from beginning to end. Thus, organizations have an opportunity to design multiple measures to assess the work that is actually being done. Using multiple performance measures also will cause employees to recognize the various dimensions of their work and to be less intent on trying to maximize their performance on a single target at the expense of other aspects of their jobs.

QUANTITATIVE AND QUALITATIVE MEASURES. Individuals who design MACS must think very carefully about the organization's mission and objectives and the ways to operationalize them. Additionally, the challenge for managers has been to expand their views of the kinds of information to supply for effective control, motivation, and performance evaluation. For instance, only within the past few years have management accountants become aware of the need for measures of quality, speed to market, cycle time, flexibility, complexity, innovation, and productivity. Historically, some of these measures, such as quality, were in the hands of industrial engineers, while others, such as speed to market or flexibility, were not measured directly.

There are other new organizational realities that managers should also keep in mind. Faced with increasing competitive pressures, many organizations have begun to move away from traditional hierarchical organizations with many layers of management, sometimes referred to as tall organizations, to those with fewer and fewer layers, or flat organizations. General Electric, for example, has reduced its hierarchical structure significantly. As the barriers to various functional areas, such as engineering design, manufacturing, accounting, finance and marketing, are being eliminated, employees are working increasingly in cross-functional teams. Another significant corresponding change involves business process re-engineering, which involves designers who begin with a vision of what organizational participants would like their process or product to look like or how they would like it to function and then radically redesign it. Such an approach is significantly different than starting with an existing product or process and then making slight incremental changes. Further, re-engineering design changes have led to the need for new informational requirements and measures related to the costs and benefits of innovation. Thus, development of new measures of performance must take into account group-level performance measures and cross-functional business process measures, not just efficiency and spending measures for functional departments.

The traditional focus of performance measures in management accounting has been to use quantitative financial measures such as cost and profit, rather than quantitative nonfinancial and qualitative measures. Examples of quantitative, nonfinancial measures include yield, cycle time, schedule adherence, number of defectives, market share, and customer retention. Variables such as the image of a product or service, the level of caring of the staff in a hospital, or the reputation of a company are examples of qualitative variables. While qualitative variables may be more subjective than quantitative variables, many qualitative variables can now be assessed using psychometric methods developed in the behavioral sciences. Customer satisfaction, for instance, is a qualitative measure which can now be quantified by using psychological scales. Clearly, measures such as customer satisfaction and employee morale are crucial for both the short- and long-term success of any organization.

Are management accountants responsible for reporting all of the relevant quantitative and qualitative variables? The answer to this question varies a great deal depending on the specific organization. In many ways, the answer depends on the view of the role of the MACS in the organization. In some situations, there is an attempt to develop and integrate both quantitative and qualitative measures into the MACS; others may keep certain types of measures distinct from the MACS. If management believes, however, that the organization is not being supplied with the key information that it needs to be competitive, it should help supply the most pertinent information to the MACS, regardless of the type of information that is relevant.

Since producing and supplying information is costly, whoever designs the information system has to worry about two interrelated issues: (1) reducing redundancy in information generation and (2) increasing coordination among the different parties.

First, organizations should avoid duplication in generating a measure of the same variable. Two automobile assembly divisions operating in different locations but within the same organization should be assessing the defect rate in the same way. It makes little sense for each division to devise vastly different measures to assess defects, for example, because comparisons between divisions become extremely difficult and confusing as to which measure to use.

Second, because information at each level of the organization is aggregated for use at the next level, there must be timely and accurate coordination among those levels producing the various kinds of information and the measures themselves. While reducing redundancy and increasing coordination of information is a topic with a long history in management accounting, today's competitive environment has brought this issue to the forefront for many information system designers.

Participation, Empowerment, and Education of Employees in MACS Design

A well-designed MACS must provide employees the opportunity to participate in decision making and empowering them in the workplace.

PARTICIPATION AND EMPOWERMENT.   Organizations often do not realize that their greatest asset is the people they employ. Except in highly automated industries, people still perform the major portion of work and have the best understanding of how jobs get done and, consequently, how to improve products and processes. Therefore, asking them to participate in decision making and empowering them to suggest and make changes is central to fostering all aspects of motivation as well as good MACS design.

For example, employees in the Sydney branch of ANZAC Company will know more about the way their branch functions than will central headquarters located in Melbourne. Therefore, MACS designers should strongly consider enlisting the participation of the Sydney employees. The same concept applies within a division. Assembly line operators usually know more about the process on which they work than their managers do. Apart from being consistent with the multiple perspective approach, research has shown that participation and communication between local and central offices and between superiors and subordinates results in the transmission of critical information to which central management would otherwise not have access. Further, research indicates that the equally important benefit of employee participation in decision making can lead to greater motivation, increased job satisfaction, improved morale, and greater commitment to decisions.

CONTINUOUS EDUCATION AND UNDERSTANDING INFORMATION.

Organizations need to address another key issue—whether their employees understand the information that they use and on which they are evaluated. Many executives believe that only managers need to understand the information generated by the MACS. Lately, however, managers have realized that employees at all levels must understand the organization's performance measures and how they are computed in order to be able to take actions that lead to superior performance. For example, if employees do not understand how their actions affect a variable like cycle time (the time it takes for a product or service to be produced or performed from start to finish), then they will not know how to alter their actions to improve cycle

CONSIDER THIS...

The Importance of Qualitative Measures of Performance: The Case of Corporate Reputations

For the second year in a row, Rubbermaid was voted "America's Most Admired Company." Microsoft was rated second, followed by Coca-Cola. While many believe that quarterly financial results are the most important variables for a company's reputation, respondents to *Fortune's* survey stated that *quality of management* and the *quality of products and services* were a company's most important attributes. Other variables that were assessed on the survey included innovativeness; community or environmental responsibility; financial soundness; value as a long-term investment; use of corporate assets; and ability to attract, develop, and keep talented people.

Source: R. Jacob, "Corporate Reputations," *Fortune,* March 6, 1995, pp. 54–64.

Employees at Grand Rapids Spring & Stamping, Inc. are shown participating in a meeting and making suggestions for process improvements. *Courtesy* Grand Rapids Spring & Stamping, Inc.

This multifunctional team of employees is involved in a brainstorming session at Xerox's high performance workroom in Rochester, New York. *Courtesy* **Xerox Corporation**

employees in a manufacturing plant are performing unnecessary actions on an assembly line or are idle, for example, the cycle time performance of their group will be affected. Similarly, at the point of service, or the point where organizational employees interact with customers, delays in the processing of claims will increase cycle time as well.

Consider an airline whose intent is to improve its public image. From time to time, some airlines ask customers to fill out a customer satisfaction survey. If flight attendants have not been educated regarding how each of their actions (such as being rude or slow to produce service) directly affects customer satisfaction, then the airline has failed to do its part to ensure satisfactory performance of one of its key indicators for flight attendants. This is also true in many other types of service organizations. In restaurants or department stores, customers often become frustrated with the level of service. For example, assigning waiters and waitresses in a restaurant to too many tables can cause them to forget customer requests, or if they have annoying personal habits or are extremely clumsy, customers remember the negative experience and may not return. Consider a department store in which sales personnel may be too pushy, too difficult to find for service, or too arrogant. A customer may become very irritated with this experience and vow never to shop at that store again.

Unless restaurant owners and department store managers educate their employees about how their actions affect customer perceptions of service quality and repeat business, the energy devoted to improving customer satisfaction is wasted. Studies have shown that, on average, five times as many customers who are dissatisfied with a product or service tell other people about their experience than customers who are satisfied with a product or service. Thus, the reputation of organizations that offer a poorly produced product or a poorly delivered service can be ruined very quickly. In general, poor or nonresponsive service by employees who have direct contact with customers is usually evidence of poor management, poor training, and poor education rather than an indicator that the employee is not a good worker.

In order for MACS to function well, employees have to be constantly re-educated as the system and its performance measures change. Without continuous updating of everyone's education, companies cannot be leaders or even players in international markets. In the United States, the lack of training problem is quite severe. Some studies have shown that U.S. employees receive only about one-tenth of the training that Japanese employees do, for example. Thus, U.S. management cannot expect its employees to be globally competitive if management does not supply them with the necessary training. Ultimately, the concept of continuous education should become so ingrained in employees that continually mastering new skills becomes a job requirement. Organizations that foster such an environment have been labeled "learning organizations."

Reward Systems for Goal Congruence

Chapter 14 discussed reward systems. A few additional points are worth considering here regarding overall MACS design. The backbone of most MACS consists of the many types of performance measures they generate and what these measures communicate to employees. Throughout this text, we have discussed a variety of

---

Rick Hunter, a junior scientist with Rohm & Haas, worked his way up from a janitorial job to studying agricultural biology. His focus on continuous education continues to improve his job skills and employment prospects. Here he inspects a lima bean plant. © Bob Sacha

such measures, including budgets, standards, measures of quality, and productivity. However, the art involved in developing an effective MACS design includes attempting to understand what standards to use and where the level of these standards should be set for motivational purposes.

System designers have many types of mechanisms that they use to resolve such issues. One mechanism that we have already talked about is to use participative decision making. By allowing subordinates to participate in standard setting and budgeting decisions, management can obtain a better understanding of what kinds of standards to use and how such standards motivate subordinates to achieve certain levels of performance. The other mechanism is to design incentive systems that are tied to standard or budget attainment. Academics in and practitioners of management accounting have spent a great deal of time devising such systems. Typically, incentive system designers are concerned with the level of uncertainty of overall goal achievement associated with particular degrees of difficulty regarding standard attainment. At the same time, system designers try to consider the risk attitudes and work ethic of individuals when devising these systems.

A well-designed MACS must develop appropriate reward systems to foster goal congruence between employees and the organization. Goal congruence implies that the actions that employees take and their personal goals are consistent with those of the organization. In today's uncertain work environment, it is unrealistic to simply hope that employees inherently feel that they have congruent goals with those of the organization. Thus, choosing the reward system that is most motivating for the individual or group and also consistent with organizational goals is very difficult.

Many companies are trying to use incentives to motivate employees. At some auto repair companies, such as MasterCare, managers pay mechanics for customer retention. This approach also helps them retain mechanics. © Jeff Greenberg/Photo Researchers Inc.

Fostering goal congruence is complicated further once employees are organized into teams because teams can still have goal congruence problems, both within the team and with the organization, especially if the MACS design has not been accomplished well.

BEHAVIORAL CONSEQUENCES OF POORLY DESIGNED MEASUREMENT SYSTEMS

Up to this point, we have discussed five key characteristics in the design of an effective MACS. What happens, though, when the MACS is poorly designed or does not promote the kinds of motivation and behaviors that the organization desires? In this section, we address the issue of poor MACS design. Our working definition of *poor design* is a system that is lacking at least one or a combination of the five key characteristics.

> **OBJECTIVE 15.3**
>
> Evaluate the behavioral consequences of poorly designed MACS.

Employees can become dissatisfied with a MACS for many reasons. Clearly, a system that produces inconsistent information, gathers only quantitative information when a mix of quantitative and qualitative information is necessary, does not operate under the organization's code of ethics, omits participation and input on the parts of employees in decision making, and does not reward good performance will reduce motivation and increase nongoal-congruent behavior. In this section of the chapter, we present three behaviors that employees use to manipulate their way around the MACS for their own ends. Keep in mind the following three questions as we discuss these behaviors.

1. Are these behaviors unethical?
2. What are the consequences of these behaviors?
3. Is it possible to design MACS so that employees will not be tempted to engage in these behaviors?

Nongoal-Congruent Behavior

For any number of reasons, subordinates engage in a variety of behaviors to improve their own situations in an organization. For example, if employees feel that they are not getting the rewards that they deserve for their performance or that they are not being heard by their superior, they may resort to increasing their bonuses or position in the organization by trying to outwit the MACS. The MACS may be manipulated in such a way that the reports or data that are generated affect a superior's behavior. Numerous methods allow the manipulation of information including *smoothing*, *gaming*, and *data falsification*.

Smoothing occurs when individuals either accelerate or delay the preplanned *flow* of data without altering the organization's activities. For example, a manager who is close to meeting his or her performance target, such as a net income or ROI number, may decide to defer expenses incurred in the current period to a future period. Similarly, he or she may attempt to book future revenues into the current period to increase net income. Over the long run, such behavior will lead to the same bottom-line financial outcomes, but the cost to the organization is that it does not obtain a clear picture of performance for a defined time

Smoothing
The act of affecting the preplanned flow of information without altering actual behavior.

period in order to plan effectively and make sound decisions. Excessive amounts of smoothing are probably the result of inappropriate standards or a poorly conceived reward system.

Gaming
An alteration of an employee's planned actions as a result of a particular kind of performance indicator.

The technique of **gaming** is said to exist whenever a subordinate alters his or her actions specifically in an attempt to manipulate a performance indicator through job-related acts. While gaming was illustrated in Chapter 9 within the budgeting context, there are many other types of gaming that can arise. For example, in order to meet sales quotas, a salesperson may ask a colleague to give him or her the credit for some of the colleague's sales bookings for a particular performance period. In return, the salesperson requesting the favor will return it if the colleague needs help in a subsequent period. Gaming is different from smoothing in that the flow of information is not altered, but the actions taken to affect key indicators are.

Data falsification
The act of knowingly falsifying information.

Data falsification or illegal acts occur when someone falsifies a piece of information. For example, in the late 1980s, senior management at MiniScribe, feeling enormous pressure to meet sales targets imposed on them by their autocratic CEO, engaged in a series of illegal acts. Senior managers packed bricks in crates and shipped them as disk drives or shipped faulty disk drives. The shipments were then recorded as sales. When the shipments were returned, MiniScribe added the shipment to its inventory of disk drives, further inflating inventory. The company also accumulated scrap components that had been written off and added these to inventory. This massive fraud led MiniScribe to file for bankruptcy, and both the firm and its auditors had to pay bondholders millions of dollars in settlement.

Smoothing, gaming, and data falsification result from pressures that come with having to meet performance targets, many of which are designed by the management accounting system. These behaviors also can result from having inadequate internal control systems or systems that tolerate unethical behavior. Certainly it is not possible to completely eliminate these behaviors, but the MACS should be designed well enough so that individuals are not inclined to manipulate performance indicators.

Are all of these behaviors unethical? Certainly the last action, data falsification, is both highly unethical and illegal. If ethical principles are not both internalized by employees and evident in MACS design, then the type of behavior which occurred at MiniScribe will be repeated over and over again. Smoothing and gaming, on the other hand, may violate an individual's code of ethics and the organization's values, but they are not really illegal. One could argue that as long as employees are meeting the targets specified by the organization, both of these actions are not unethical. Smoothing, however, does involve altering the preplanned flow of information. For example, if an employee does not appropriately defer revenues into the next period, the organization would book these revenues and increase sales, inflating the current period's performance results. Gaming, in the form of building in slack resources, also can be viewed as a way for subordinates to deal with the risk involved of meeting performance targets. Building slack or additional resources into the activities plan allows some leeway for the employee in case something unforeseen occurs in the work environment. Once again, if performance indicators are met, it is difficult to say whether gaming is unethical. The organization may experience increased costs or inefficiencies in the form of wasted resources, but employees also may be able to function better at work knowing that there is some built-in cushion available in case the work environment changes significantly.

*B*EHAVIORAL CONSIDERATIONS WHEN IMPLEMENTING NEW MANAGEMENT ACCOUNTING SYSTEMS

Many firms still use management accounting systems that are not keeping pace with all of the changes that are occurring in their industries and around the globe. Since the late 1970s and early 1980s, however, many other firms have changed their accounting systems. Regardless of why changes are taking place, one thing is certain. Changing to a new MACS can be accomplished more easily if the original system was constructed using the five key characteristics discussed at the beginning of the chapter. This is so in part because the five characteristics often serve as goals of new systems. However, very few systems, especially those that were developed before the early 1980s, have these five principles.[3]

> **OBJECTIVE 15.4**
>
> Understand the behavioral implications of implementing a new MACS or changing a current MACS.

In this section, we will focus on the behavioral factors to consider when making changes from an existing MACS to a new system, such as an activity-based cost management system. An understanding of such behavior has become even more relevant with mixed results about the relative success of many new management innovations such as total quality management and re-engineering efforts.[4]

There are two different phases of implementation: phase 1 *involves designing and building the new MACS* while phase 2 involves *using the new MACS*.

Designing and Building the New MACS

Before implementing any new costing system, responsible employees in the organization should spend a great deal of time benchmarking other systems; forming a multifunctional team and a senior management steering committee; defining purposes, goals, and users; and developing the technical details of the system.

BENCHMARKING. As discussed in Chapter 13, benchmarking is a process by which firms strive to use the best practices of others, both within their own and other industries, to improve their own organizations. One way to begin the process of a MACS change is for the firm to engage in benchmarking activities with other organizations. Benchmarking another organization's MACS can involve obtaining benchmarks for the general technical structure of the company's management accounting system or collecting information about the number of cost pools; activity centers and drivers; and value-added versus non-value added costs or burden rates.[5] Benchmarking also can be used to identify system goals and users as well as how the company accomplished the change to a new system.

SENIOR MANAGEMENT SUPPORT. Senior management support is critical for success in making changes in an organization's MACS. As an example, when

---

[3] See M. D. Shields and S. M. Young, "A Behavioral Model for Implementing Cost Management Systems," *Journal of Cost Management*, Winter 1989, pp. 17–27.

[4] See Fred R. Bleakley, "The Best Laid Plans—Many Companies Try Management Fads, Only to See Them Flop," *Wall Street Journal*, July 6, 1993, p. 91.

[5] See D. Elnathan, T. W. Lin and S. Mark Young, "Benchmarking and Management Accounting: A Framework for Research," *Journal of Management Accounting Research*, 1996, for more details.

Chrysler Corporation decided to implement ABCM, Robert Lutz, the president of Chrysler, publicly supported ABCM implementation and also produced a video that was shown to management describing the ABCM's benefits. In some cases, senior management convenes a multifunctional team to provide direction and support for the change, including a change champion, senior managers from other functional areas, and other employees.

CHANGE CHAMPION AND MULTIFUNCTIONAL TEAM.   A **change champion** is the key person or persons who lead any change in an organization. Typically, a MACS champion is an individual who sees the need for significant change. As portrayed in the opening vignette to this chapter, Susan Wu is a change champion. The champion is often a risktaker who is very intrapreneurial and entrepreneurial. Usually, the champion is someone at a reasonably high level within an organization who has the authority and influence to foment any major modifications. In some instances, there are champions at the middle-manager level, but often such managers are responsible for changes only in their divisions. Regardless of who the champion is, this person must garner the support of top management in order to have credibility with many organizational members.

> **Change champion**
> An individual who takes the initiative and the risk to make significant changes in an organization.

The champion has to understand the sources of resistance to change and have the requisite verbal and interpersonal skills to overcome resistance and defensive behavior. This person also must be able to obtain the required level of financial resources. Without the money needed for personnel, the development of software, and so on, the change will not occur.

The champion has to coordinate a multifunctional team of individuals from various areas for assistance in providing various types of information and support. The team usually consists of technical people who are well-versed in operations management and cost accounting and also often includes manufacturing managers, purchasing managers, human resource managers, marketing managers, and information system managers among others. In some organizations employees other than management are included as part of the team. For example, hourly workers have been included in multifunctional teams because of their experience on the shop floor.

If the champion is not a management accountant, and in many instances this is the case, management accountants must become part of the change team because they can provide useful information about the existing cost system.

Using the New MACS

Phase 2 of implementation involves getting organizational members to use the new MACS. The design phase (phase 1) is never completely independent of phase 2 in that the multifunctional team has to try to gauge whether the new system will be used while it is designing the system. Thus, there will always be some assessment on the part of the multifunctional team about what to expect as the new system is introduced to the organization.

CHANGE PROCESS.   System planners should realize that there are always some differences between what people say they will accommodate and their actual behavior as changes occur. In this section, we will discuss four topics related to the change process that the multifunctional team should consider as it begins to implement change:

1. Knowledge of the organizational culture
2. Knowledge of current manufacturing or service practices
3. Types of resistance to change
4. Aspects of employee compensation

KNOWLEDGE OF ORGANIZATIONAL CULTURE.   Organizational culture[6] can be described as the "mindset of employees, including their shared beliefs, values, and goals." Before implementing the new MACS, those involved need to develop a clear understanding of the kind of culture that currently exists within the organization. Although cultures can vary a great deal, three general types emerge: (1) strong functional, (2) strong dysfunctional, and (3) ill-defined. Some believe that the *ideal* culture is a strong functional one whose culture has clearly articulated beliefs, values, and goals or a clear organizational mission statement. Often these goals are expressed in slogans such as General Electric's "We Bring Good Things to Life," or Toshiba's "In Touch With Tomorrow," which serve as rallying points for employees and clearly define the firm's mission and focus to external stakeholders. A great deal of employee involvement, goal congruence of subordinates and managers, strong feelings of teamwork, work stability, and continuous improvement characterize a strong functional culture.

> **Organizational culture**
> The mindset of organizational participants including goals, values, and attitudes.

At the other extreme is a strong dysfunctional culture, which is characterized by internal conflict between superiors and subordinates typically arising from stringent top-down control of employees by management. With little employee involvement, poor worker attitudes and behaviors and low morale can result. Often employees are scared to voice their opinions and do not feel a strong commitment to the workplace. Interestingly enough, performance can be high under this type of culture because sometimes people work hard out of fear.

The third type of culture is ill-defined. Such cultures have employees who do not have a sense of mission and whose beliefs, values, and goals are not congruent. Leadership is often lacking in these organizations and employees tend to plod along without clear direction.

If the culture of an organization is not assessed or if it is misread, successful changes are unlikely to occur. Furthermore, experience has shown that strong, functional cultures can be changed more easily than either strong dysfunctional or ill-defined cultures.

KNOWLEDGE OF CURRENT MANUFACTURING AND SERVICE PRACTICES.   One of the initial problems facing employees who desired to change MACS was how the changes would fit with existing technology. One prominent example occurred as organizations switched from traditional manufacturing methods to the just-in-time (JIT) manufacturing philosophy discussed in Chapter 8.

---

[6] This discussion follows M. D. Shields and S. M. Young, "A Behavioral Model for Implementing Cost Management Systems," *Journal of Cost Management*, Winter 1989.

Researchers found that early attempts to implement JIT were quite successful from a technical point of view. In other words, it was possible to change the actual methods of production relatively easily. What organizations did not realize was that many other aspects of their entities, including the existing MACS, were not automatically changing with the adoption of JIT. Instead, the organizations used existing MACS to measure, control, and evaluate performance, which made it hard to clearly evaluate whether the implementation of the JIT system was successful. As one example, an underlying principle of the JIT system in its purest form is to have virtually no raw materials on hand and no work in process or finished goods inventories at the end of a production period. A central feature of the traditional cost accounting model is the tracing of the flow of inventories through the system. With no inventories in the new JIT system, the old MACS system either was imprecise about what to record or attempted to record tens of thousands of inventory transactions as material flowed continuously through the plant on a JIT basis. In either case, the information system was producing irrelevant and useless information, and employees became frustrated as it was not possible to evaluate their work clearly.

Another set of issues relates to the motivational and control aspect of the JIT system. Japanese firms relied on a different kind of cultural control in the development of the JIT system than did traditional U.S. manufacturing firms. In the United States, many workers adhere to the notion of **primary control,** or rather it is hard-wired into them. Under a system of primary control, individuals try to modify the existing social and behavioral factors surrounding them (their environment), including attempting to influence other coworkers or their bosses. They may also try to alter specific events in their favor. By shaping their environment, individuals in the U.S. feel that they will increase their personal rewards.

In contrast, in Japan, under what is called secondary control, individuals increase their rewards and are motivated in a completely different manner. **Secondary control** calls for employees to accommodate themselves to the current environment by adjusting their expectations, their goals, and their own attitudes. In other words, individuals subordinate their needs to those of their workgroup and their organization. The principles that underlie the JIT system rely on the notion of secondary control. For instance, the idea of cross-training workers in workgroups relies on a sense of group cooperation and not on notions of every individual for him- or herself.

It is quite easy to see that trying to introduce the JIT system to U.S. employees who have not been brought up or trained with secondary control ideas might be met with resistance, which certainly was the case.[7] This example illustrates that not only do system designers have to consider the culture of the organizations in which they work, but they also may have to take into account aspects of others' national culture when applying management concepts.

Thus, the mixed success of the JIT system in the early 1980s was due in part to inappropriate MACS design and to system designers who were not aware that the types of cultural control used in Japan were different from those used in the United States. In the 1990s, however, with the benefit of experience many JIT systems in the United States are now comparable to those operating in Japan.

Primary control
A method of control in which employees further their own ends by trying to influence their environment.

Secondary control
A method of control in which employees adapt themselves to their environment rather than trying to change the environment.

---

[7] This issue is discussed at length in S. M. Young, "A Framework for Research on Successful Adoption and Performance of Japanese Manufacturing Practices in the United States," *Academy of Management Review*, 1992, pp. 677–700. This paper is included in *Readings in Management Accounting*.

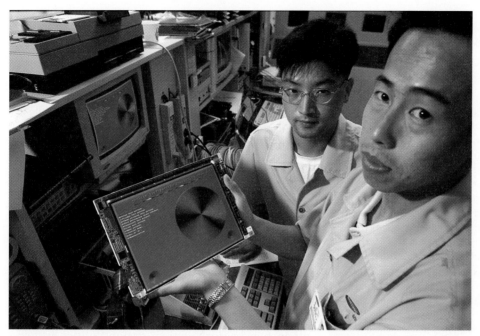

Manufacturing methods developed in other countries often are tied to cultural work norms. If companies in another culture attempt to adopt these methods without understanding the work culture from which the methods arise, then implementation problems can occur. Pictured are Samsung employees showing a new product innovation in LCD screens. © 1995 Greg Girard/Contact Press Images

As the use of benchmarking increases, organizations attempt to implement new manufacturing and service practices and procedures, not only from companies within their own industries, but also from firms in other industries and other countries. This means that system designers have to become fully aware of the ramifications of such changes before they proceed with implementation.

RESISTANCE TO CHANGE.   Resistance to change is the biggest stumbling block that change agents face, as noted in Susan Wu's company. The difficulties are as follows:

1. The defensive response when people and organizations set in their ways are forced to change[8]
2. The cost of change, which can be very high, both in terms of employees' compensation and other rewards and in the amount of time it takes to make change
3. The shift in an organization's balance of power

As an example, consider a product line manager who historically has been incorrectly allocated a small amount of factory overhead. This manager has been operating a business unit for 10 years, and because of the favorable allocation of

---

[8] See Argyris and Kaplan's article, "Implementing New Knowledge: The Case of Activity-Based Costing," *Accounting Horizons,* September 1994, pp. 83–105 for an excellent discussion on managing change.

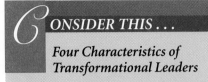

Four Characteristics of Transformational Leaders

Strong leadership during organizational change is absolutely critical to success. In a recent article according to Robert J. House at the Wharton School of Management, transformational leaders who emerge during major organizational changes exhibit four characteristics. First, they have a vision for a better future for the organization—one that the organization deserves and of which it can be proud. Second, leaders have shown their commitment to the organization through self-sacrifice. Third, they respect their followers but also have high standards for them. Fourth, they do not pursue money or power but are driven by satisfaction of building the organization, seeing people develop, and accomplishing things through others. The most effective leaders do not push their vision on others but help others buy it.

Source: Thomas A. Stewart, "How to Lead a Revolution," *Fortune,* November 28, 1994, pp. 48–61.

overhead has been able to show very good bottom-line results. If an ABC system more accurately reflects cost drivers and changes the way the allocation of overhead is made to this person's product line, the business unit's product line will look unprofitable, which indeed it is. This manager will probably resist any of the changes that the new ABC system calls for because such changes will affect the unit's profit and potentially the level of expected bonus. In the worst case, the entire business unit could be dropped due to poor profitability.

Another reason for resistance to ABCM is that many employees do not necessarily want their superiors to know what they do. Many managers value their privacy relative to their superiors. Thus, when employees reflect on their original job descriptions, it is highly unlikely that what they actually are doing on the job currently is the same as their initial job description. Some may have chosen to engage in more tasks in order to advance in the organization while others may be shirking their responsibilities by doing fewer jobs and parceling them out to others. The threat to managers is that one of the first things that activity analysis does is to assess how people are spending their time. This analysis is intended to uncover many actions and behaviors that employees at all levels of the firm would prefer to hide. Those who are engaging in additional activities may become concerned that there will be reallocation of these activities or that the activities will become part of their formal job description. Those who know that their activities are being subsidized by others may fear they will have more work to do.

For example, it is not uncommon in manufacturing firms for managers to engage in some customer service because part of their jobs is to understand what customers desire. Some customer service is necessary to maintain customer relations, but the sales and customer service departments usually perform this function. However, some manufacturing managers may spend as much as 30% of their time performing such service duties. If short-staffed, the customer service manager relies on help from the manufacturing manager. However, activity analysis, whose purpose is to reflect what people are and are not doing relative to their assigned duties, may identify this situation and preclude the manufacturing manager from performing this service in the future.

One of the most notable reasons for resistance to change relates to ABCM employees' fears about cost cutting. Beginning in the late 1970s and continuing through to the present, many organizations have engaged in significant, if not continuous, cost-cutting activities. In the United States, this has occurred most typically by reducing headcount. Even at IBM, a company that had an implicit system of permanent employment, employees have been laid off in large numbers. What are the results of these kinds of layoffs and cost-cutting decisions?

First, organizational decision makers may be making a tremendous mistake by eliminating people and jobs arbitrarily. Employees have a great deal of information about how work gets done, and they develop substantial knowledge about their work domain. Employees also develop working networks within and across divisions and with other organizations of which upper-level management may be unaware. If management bases decisions using only the out-of-pocket cost of the employee and ignores the knowledge and capabilities each person contributes to the organization, then the organization will lose vital resources. Cost cutting by arbitrarily laying off employees may yield short-run benefits, such as reducing payroll costs, but the organization may have sacrificed knowledge and capabilities required for its long-term success.

Another disadvantage of arbitrary personnel layoffs occurs when other employees who remain in the organization have to assume the duties of the laid-off workers. In the short term, at least, employees may be willing to absorb the extra work. Eventually, however, motivation drops as burnout from the higher workload occurs. Further, cutting people does not help to build trust among organizational members, and the level of efficiency at work may decrease due to concerns regarding who is next to be laid off. The human resources model of motivation focuses on building and fostering workgroups and teams. Arbitrary firing decisions can adversely affect the gains previously made by investing in people's knowledge and capabilities.

The scope of change is another critical variable. Organizations and managers often make the mistake of trying to make too many changes simultaneously in too many areas of their organizations. If attempts to complete conversion to a new system across all functions and divisions should fail simultaneously, the organization may never have the opportunity again to make the change. To avoid this problem, some organizations implement change beginning in a single workgroup or business unit. In some instances, the old MACS is run alongside the new system, thus making it possible to work out many bugs before changing the entire organization. Once final conversion and debugging is accomplished, the old MACS can be turned off so that users work with only a single system.

Overcoming resistance to change is critical to the success of any new system. Susan Wu and thousands of managers like her face the problem of overcoming resistance constantly as organizational innovations are always being suggested. One of the best approaches to overcome resistance to change is to understand and anticipate the fear and embarrassment that managers sometimes feel when confronted with modifications to an existing technical system. The organization should invest in educational programs to introduce the overall philosophy of the new method or innovation to all employees well before the changes are to occur. Everyone should understand why the changes are necessary, including the benefits that all employees will realize as a result of them. The benefits include a more secure work environment; a better run and more profitable organization; a fairer performance evaluation system; and a stronger tie between each employee's contribution and organizational rewards. Then, each operating unit should develop several short-term attainable goals that are consistent with the changes. After the company attains these goals, managers and employees begin to build confidence that more significant changes are possible.

COMMITMENT AND CONTINUOUS EDUCATION. Once both top management and other employees have committed to the change, the immediate quest for change is significantly complete. The most difficult aspect of commitment is sustaining it. Changing to new management accounting systems is costly both in monetary and personal terms. The level of energy required to change can be staggering on the parts of everyone in the organization. As commitment to change can easily erode, managers must stay focused on the change process.

Employees need **continuous education**—available educational programs for employees on an ongoing basis—to keep abreast of system developments and the required related skills. Employees' skills can erode or become outdated very quickly given the many changes occurring in manufacturing, service, and information technology. Therefore, providing employees with the information about needed skills keeps them up to date. In addition, it can foster more employee commitment because they believe that the organization is investing in them.

Continuous education
A commitment on the part of the organization to provide educational programs for employees on an ongoing basis.

COMPENSATION.   Often before an organization implements an ABCM system, it performs an activity analysis. A common outcome of this analysis is that work becomes reorganized according to business processes that involve teams of individuals. Performance then is the result of team effort. Thus, compensation systems must be designed to reward the outcomes of team-managed business processes.

As an example of the old functional organization of work, the design, manufacture, costing, pricing, and sales of a product used to be done in a linear, step-by-step fashion. Design engineers would design a product. Upon completing the design, they would pass it over the wall to manufacturing engineers who laid out the shop floor and selected processes to produce the product in an efficient manner. Then the cost accountants would work from the product design and the process characteristics to develop the product's cost. Then marketing personnel would determine the price, and sales people would attempt to sell the finished product.

In contrast, in today's manufacturing environment, this linear process has changed substantially. The new work environment involves teams of design, manufacturing, and industrial engineers; accountants; operations personnel; and marketing people meeting together to share their information and expertise about all aspects of launching a new product. The product is likely to have a better chance of appealing to the market due to the consideration of marketing research on the features customers want and because of costing information during the design phase. Also, the process often increases the speed at which the product reaches the market.

Many other types of teams exist in the new work environment. We have already described how employees on shop floors in service organizations are organized in "cells" to perform specific tasks. Members of these teams are cross-trained so that they can perform the jobs of several others in their team.

Numerous types of compensation systems currently exist to reward team performance. In Chapter 14, we discussed profit-sharing and gain sharing plans. In the examples just given, the product design and development team might be compensated based on how quickly the new product can be brought to market, on the number of parts deleted from an existing product to make manufacturing less complex, or on the product's price or functionality. Each new situation, especially ones involving major changes, deserves special consideration regarding development of the most motivating kind of compensation system.

SUMMARY

Our focus in this text has been to present a new view of management accounting. This view incorporates the disciplines of strategy, operations management, ethics, and the organizational sciences with a perspective on management accounting that is organized around the activities that occur in the organization.

This chapter presents a human resources model of human motivation and a discussion of how the design of a management accounting and control system should be consistent with this model. Additionally, since many traditional management accounting systems have and will be changing to an activity-based approach, we have discussed issues and variables related to the change process in an activity-based-cost-management environment. Because the implementation of ABCM can meet with resistance, cost management champions and their teams should pay a great deal of attention to behavioral and organizational issues to increase their chances of being successful.

KEY TERMS

change champion, p. 710

continuous education, p. 716

data falsification, p. 708

ethical control system, p. 698

gaming, p. 708

goal congruence, p. 692

human relations movement, p. 691

human resources model of
   motivation, p. 691

multiple perspectives approach to
   management accounting system
   design, p. 692

organizational culture, p. 711

primary control, p. 712

scientific management of motivation,
   p. 691

secondary control, p. 712

smoothing, p. 707

$\mathcal{A}$SSIGNMENT MATERIAL

■ QUESTIONS

15-1 What are the goals of a management accounting and control systems (MACS)?

15-2 What is the scientific management view of motivation?

15-3 What is the human relations school view of motivation?

15-4 What is the human resources view of motivation?

15-5 The human resources view of motivation focuses on three key aspects of motivation. What are they?

15-6 What is goal congruence?

15-7 List and describe the five characteristics of a well-designed MACS.

15-8 What is the multiple-perspectives approach to MACS design?

15-9 What are the four requirements of ethical conduct by which certified management accountants (CMAs) have to abide?

15-10 What are the choices that individuals can make when ethical conflicts arise?

15-11 What is an ethical control system?

15-12 List three quantitative financial measures of performance in a *manufacturing* organization of your choice.

15-13 List three quantitative financial measures of performance in a *service* organization of your choice.

15-14 List three quantitative nonfinancial measures of performance in a *manufacturing* organization of your choice.

15-15 List three quantitative nonfinancial measures of performance in a *service* organization of your choice.

15-16 List three *qualitative* measures of performance.

15-17 What is employee empowerment?

15-18 What is the working definition of poorly designed MACS?

15-19 What is smoothing?

15-20 What is gaming?

15-21 What is data falsification?

15-22 What is benchmarking?

15-23 What is a strong, functional culture?

15-24 What is a strong, dysfunctional culture?

15-25 What is primary control?

15-26 What is secondary control?

15-27 What is a change champion?

15-28 What is resistance to change?

■ EXERCISES

15-29 *Managerial approaches to motivation*   How do the scientific management, human relations, and human resource schools differ in their views on human motivation?

15-30 *Characteristics of a MACS: multiple perspectives*   Why is having a multiple perspectives approach to MACS design important?

15-31 *Characteristics of a MACS: ethical issues*   List and describe the hierarchy of ethical considerations.

15-32 *Characteristics of a MACS: ethical issues*   What should a person do who faces a conflict between his or her values and those of the organization?

15-33 *Characteristics of a MACS: ethical issues*   What should a person do when the organization's stated values conflict with practiced values? What are the individual's choices?

15-34 *Characteristics of a MACS: multiple performance measures*   What is the advantage of having multiple measures of performance?

15-35 *Characteristics of a MACS: participation*   What are the advantages for the *individual* in being able to participate in decision making in the organization?

15-36 *Characteristics of a MACS: participation*   What are the advantages for the *organization* in allowing the individual to participate?

15-37 *Behavior consequence*   What are the behavioral consequences of a poorly designed MACS?

15-38 *Characteristics of a MACS: rewards*   Can goal congruence be increased, if rewards are tied to performance? Explain.

15-39 *Nongoal-congruent behavior*   Are gaming and smoothing illegal activities? Explain.

15-40 *Nongoal-congruent behavior*   What distinguishes data falsification and gaming activities?

15-41 *Nongoal-congruent behavior*   List some methods of gaming performance indicators.

15-42 *Nongoal-congruent behavior*   Can gaming and smoothing ever be completely eliminated in organizations?

15-43 *Nongoal-congruent behavior*   Can you think of instances when gaming behavior is appropriate in an organization?

15-44 *Implementation: cultural issues*   How do strong functional cultures differ from strong dysfunctional and ill-defined cultures?

15-45 *Implementation: cultural issues*   How does primary control differ from secondary control? What are the significant implications of these differences?

15-46 *Implementation: change champion*   What factors will help a change champion to be successful?

15-47 *Implementation: resistance*   What is resistance to change, and how can it be overcome?

■ PROBLEMS

Fundamental Problems

15-48 *MACS design: motivation*   Why is an understanding of human motivation essential to MACS system design?

REQUIRED

Write an essay discussing this issue.

15-49 ***Characteristics of MACS design*** List the characteristics that will lead to good MACS system design. What are the benefits of each?

REQUIRED

Write an essay to answer this question.

15-50 ***Nongoal-congruent behavior*** Describe the acts of smoothing, gaming, and data falsification. Are they unethical and how can they be overcome?

REQUIRED

Write an essay to justify your answers.

15-51 ***Characteristics of MACS: types of information*** Under what circumstances should both quantitative and qualitative performance measures be used to evaluate employee, workgroup, and divisional performance?

REQUIRED

Write an essay and provide examples to justify your answer.

15-52 ***Characteristics of MACS design: types of information*** Is it possible to design a single performance measure to capture all aspects of an employee's performance?

REQUIRED

If your answer is yes, provide a context and an example.

15-53 ***Characteristics of MACS design: rewards*** What are the pros and cons of tying an individual's pay to performance?

REQUIRED

Write an essay citing concrete examples of both pros and cons.

15-54 ***Implementation issues*** Discuss the key variables that system designers have to consider when trying to implement an ABCM system.

REQUIRED

Write an essay discussing this issue.

15-55 ***Implementation: organizational culture*** Why is a knowledge of organizational culture critical to bring about lasting change?

REQUIRED

Write an essay discussing this question.

15-56 ***Characteristics of MACS design: participation*** Discuss whether participation in decision making and employee empowerment is important in MACS design.

REQUIRED

Write an essay discussing this issue.

15-57 ***Implementation phases*** Discuss how the two phases of implementation differ. Are both phases necessary for successful implementation of change?

REQUIRED

Write an essay discussing these questions.

Challenging Problems

15-58 ***Implementation: managing change*** Tobor Company is a large manufacturer of industrial robots and has been using the same management accounting system for the past 25 years. Faced with increasing international pressure, Sarah Tobor, president of Tobor Company, has decided that one of the major changes that she must make is to implement a new management accounting and control system.

REQUIRED

What key variables does Sarah have to manage very carefully during this transition? Why?

15-59 ***Characteristics of MACS design: participation vs. imposition*** Denver Jack's is a large toy manufacturer. The company has 100 highly trained and skilled employees who are involved with six major product lines, including the production of toy soldiers, dolls, etc. Each product line is manufactured in a different city and state. Denver Jack has decided to make all of the production decisions for the toy lines himself, including which products to eliminate. The managers of each toy line believe he is making a mistake.

REQUIRED

What are the pros and cons of Denver Jack's approach?

15-60 ***Implementation: cost reduction*** Archer Company, a high-tech manufacturing firm, has faced severe losses over the past three years. Archer's stakeholders have demanded that the company make some significant changes and improvements to its operations over the next two years. Faced with a very hostile group of shareholders at a board meeting, the president of Archer, Roger Slothand, quickly lays out a plan to lay off 20% of its workforce. The thinking is that this reduction in people will make Archer's financial statements look better. The irate shareholders seem to believe this plan may work.

REQUIRED

What are some likely results of Slothand's actions? Will the shareholders be happy two years from now? Please explain.

15-61 ***Characteristics of MACS design: types of information*** Is customer satisfaction a qualitative variable, a quantitative variable, or both?

REQUIRED

Write an essay that states your position and use examples to support it.

15-62 ***Characteristics of MACS design: ethical issues*** During data collection for the transition from an old management accounting system to a new ABCM system, you see a manager's reported time allotments—those of Sherrie Louis. You know that the data supplied by the manager is completely false. You confront the manager and she states that she is worried that if she reports how she actually spends her time and resources that her job will be altered, and it will also be found out that she is really not performing very well. She implores you not to tell anyone.

REQUIRED

What actions should you take? Please explain.

15-63 ***Characteristics of MACS design: ethical issues*** As a management accountant working in the controller's office, Rick Koch, a very powerful executive, approaches you in the parking lot and asks you to do him a favor. The favor involves falsifying some of his division's records on the main computer. The executive states that if you do not do as he asks, he will have you fired.

REQUIRED

What do you do? Please explain.

15-64 ***Implementation: resistance*** You are the change champion for the new MACS (an ABCM system) that your organization is going to implement. You have been working on the change for 18 months and firmly believe that it is the best system for your organization. Along the way you have met with a great deal of resistance to change, primarily from managers who fear that their product line profitability will change as a result of the ABC system.

REQUIRED

(a) Discuss how you would deal with the managers. What key arguments would you put forth to convince them that they should lower their resistance to the new system?

(b) What steps would you take to smooth the transition to the new system?

15-65 *Implementation: cultural issues*   What are the consequences of implementing a new technology that relies on secondary control into a work environment that has historically operated on primary control?

REQUIRED

Write an essay discussing this question.

■ CASES

15-66 *Characteristics of MACS design: types of information*   Chow Company is an insurance company in Hong Kong. Chow hires 55 people to process insurance claims. The volume of claims is extremely high and all claims examiners are kept extremely busy. The number of claims that have mistakes runs about 10%. If a claim has an error, it must be corrected by the claims examiners. After looking at the data, Judy Choy, senior manager of the division, was not satisfied with the volume of claims processed. She instructed Anne Wu, the manager, to motivate the claims examiners to work faster. Judy believes that the claims examiners are working as fast as they possibly can. She is also concerned that, by working faster, the examiners will make more errors.

REQUIRED

(a) How should Anne Wu handle this situation?

(b) On what performance measures is the organization relying?

(c) What performance measures should the organization use?

15-67 *Implementation: resistance*   Ian Hopwood, vice-president of manufacturing of the Marx Plastics Company in Manchester, England, has been asked to implement an activity-based costing and management system in his organization. Ian has had some training in ABCM, but none of his managers knows anything about the method. Mary Sentra is the manager of the best performing division of Marx Plastics. Two of her ten product lines, SuperX and SuperY, make the most money of any products in the entire company. For years, Mary has boasted endlessly about the success of these products, and she gets a great deal of satisfaction knowing that these are the company's most successful products.

Recently, Ian has begun to wonder about SuperX and SuperY. As he has learned more about ABC/ABM, he realizes that he has been using direct labor as an allocation base for overhead in all of Mary's divisions and for all of his products. He now realizes that there are two other drivers that seem to be the most appropriate for Mary's division. These drivers are direct materials and machine hours.

Ian's preliminary figures show that if he uses these drivers, the cost to produce both products SuperX and SuperY is much higher than anyone ever thought. In fact, the costs are so high that, at the current price, both SuperX and SuperY lose money. However, at the same time, some of his other products begin to look a lot more attractive. Ian has a hunch that Mary will strongly resist the ABC system, given her strong ego-involvement with SuperX and Super Y.

REQUIRED

(a) How should Ian approach this problem?

(b) What should he tell Mary?

(c) What actions are recommended if Mary is adamantly opposed to changing to different allocation bases? Why?

15-68 *Characteristics of MACS design: ethical issues*   You are employed as a senior manager in an insurance organization. One of your responsibilities is to randomly review claims for reimbursement that have been submitted by people who have traveled on the organization's behalf.

By accident, you have pulled a claim that was submitted by Susan, one of your closest friends. You decide to confront your friend with your findings. Susan, knowing you are a friend, replies: "Sure the claim contains false items. Everybody does it and it is almost expected!"

Stunned by her confession, you tell her that she has to resubmit an accurate reimbursement claim. Susan responds: "Look Mark, I don't feel that I get paid enough in this lousy organization and this is my way of getting a few extra dollars each month. You know how they have been working all of us to death after the layoffs. I'm entitled to this, and I refuse to resubmit the claim."

REQUIRED

(a) What do you think of Susan's argument?
(b) Should you have approached her differently?
(c) What should you do now and why? Please explain.

GLOSSARY

Activity   A unit of work, or task, with a specific goal. Examples of activities are grading a student's examination, issuing a Medicare check, and painting an automobile.

Activity analysis   An approach to operations control that involves applying the steps of continuous improvement to an activity (also known as value analysis).

Activity cost driver   Unit of measurement for the level (or quantity) of the activity performed.

Activity cost driver rate   Ratio of the cost of resources to provide an activity to the level of the capacity made available by those resources.

Activity-based costing   A procedure that measures the costs of objects, such as products, services, and customers. Activity-based costing (ABC) first assigns resource costs to the activities performed by the organization. Then activity costs are assigned to the products, customers, and services that benefit from or are creating the demand for the activities.

Activity-based costing systems   Product costing systems that assign support costs to products in the proportion of the demand each product places on various activities.

Activity-based management   The management processes that use the information provided by an activity-based cost analysis to improve organizational profitability. Activity-based management (ABM) includes performing activities more efficiently, eliminating the need to perform certain activities that do not add value for customers, improving the design of products, and developing better relationships with customers and suppliers. The goal of ABM is to enable customer needs to be satisfied while making fewer demands on organizational resources.

Administrative and discretionary spending plan   An operating plan that summarizes administrative and discretionary expenditures.

Aggregate planning   An approximate determination of whether the organization has the capacity to undertake a proposed production plan.

Annuity (*a*)   An investment that promises a constant amount each period for a stated number of periods—also known as an *n*-period annuity; the equal amount received or paid at the end of each period for *n* periods.

Appraisal costs   Those cost related to inspecting products to ensure that they meet both internal and external customer requirements.

Appropriation   An authorized spending limit in a government department.

Audit control   An approach to control that emphasizes checking people's work.

Authoritative budgeting   A top-down approach to budgeting in which a superior tells a subordinate what the budget will be.

Avoidable costs   Costs that are eliminated when a part, a product, a product line, or a business segment is discontinued.

Balanced Scorecard   A measurement and management system that views a business unit's performance from four perspectives: financial, customer, internal business process, and learning and growth.

Batch-related activities   Activities whose levels are related to the number of batches produced.

Benchmarking   The process of studying and comparing how other organizations perform similar activities and processes. The other organizations can be either internal or external to the firm and are selected because they are known to have excellent performance for the benchmarked process.

Benchmarking/performance gap   A comparison of one organization's performance to the "best" performance of other organizations.

Breakeven point   Production level at which sales volume results in zero profit.

Budget   A quantitative expression of the money inflows and outflows to determine whether a financial plan will meet organizational goals.

Budget games   Attempts by managers to manipulate information and targets to achieve their budgets and to attain high bonuses.

Budget slack   The result of subordinates either (1) building excess resources above and beyond what they need to achieve their budget objectives or (2) distorting information about their ability to achieve a budget.

Budgeting   The process of preparing budgets.

Capacity constraints   Limitations on the quantity that can be produced because the capacity committed for some activity resources (such as plant space or number of machines) cannot be changed in the short run.

Capital budget   The management document that authorizes spending for resources, such as plant and equipment, that will have multiyear useful lifetimes.

Capital budgeting   A systematic approach to evaluating the economic desirability of a long-term investment.

Capital spending plan   An operating plan that specifies when long-term capital expenditures such as acquisitions for buildings and special-purpose equipment must be made to meet objectives.

Cellular manufacturing   Organization of the plant into a number of cells so that within each cell, all machines required to manufacture a group of similar products are arranged sequentially in close proximity to each other.

Centralized   Reserving decision-making power for senior management levels.

Centralized control   The management process by which senior executives receive periodic information about decentralized divisional operations to ensure that division managers are making decisions and taking actions that contribute to overall corporate goals.

Certified supplier   A specially selected supplier who is assured a high level of business for conforming to high standards for quality and delivery schedules.

Change champion   An individual who takes the initiative and the risk to make significant changes in an organization.

Committed costs   Costs which a company knows it will have to incur at a future date.

Committed resources   Resources made available before their demand is known precisely; cannot be reduced if demand is lower than planned.

Concurrent control   A control device that operates at the time the work is being done. An example is weighing a box of cereal as it is being filled.

Consultative budgeting   A budgeting process in which a subordinate is asked to discuss ideas about the budget, but no joint decision making occurs.

Continual budgeting   A budgeting process that plans for a specified period of time, usually one year, and is organized into budget subintervals, usually a month or a quarter.

Continuous education   A commitment on the part of the organization to provide educational programs for employees on an ongoing basis.

Continuous improvement   An approach to process management that emphasizes constantly looking for ways to improve its performance.

Contribution margin per unit   Difference between the price and variable cost per unit.

Contribution margin ratio   Contribution margin expressed as a percent of sales.

Control   The set of methods and tools that organization members use to keep the organization on track toward achieving its objectives.

Controllability principle   A principle that asserts that people should be held accountable only for results that they can control. The main application of this principle is that a manager should not be held accountable for revenues, costs, investments, or other factors outside her control.

Controller   An organization's senior finance and accounting executive; prepares and interprets financial information for managers, investors, and creditors.

Conversion costs   Costs of production labor and support activities to convert the materials or product at each process stage.

Cooperative benchmarking   A benchmarking method in which information is shared voluntarily between parties.

Cost behavior   The way costs change with changes in activity cost driver or with production volume.

Cost centers   Responsibility centers whose manager and other employees control costs but not revenues or investment level.

Cost curve   Graph of costs plotted against activity cost driver or production volume.

Cost driver rate   Ratio of normal cost for a support activity to normal level of cost driver for the activity.

Cost of capital   The return that the organization must earn on its investments in order to meet its investors' return requirements. This is the interest rate that organizations use in their time value of money, discounting, or compounding, calculations.

Cost management systems   Information systems that report on the costs of an organization's activities, processes, products, services, and customers; used for a variety of decision-making and improvement activities.

Cost of nonconformance (CONC) to quality standards   The cost incurred by an organization if products and services do not conform to quality standards.

Cost pool   Each subset of total support costs that can be associated with a distinct cost driver.

Cost variances   Differences between actual and standard costs.

Cost-of-quality report   A report that details the cost of quality by the categories prevention, appraisal, internal failure and external failure.

Costs   Resources used to provide a product or service.

Critical performance indicators   Performance measures used to assess an organization's performance on its critical success factors.

Critical success factors   Elements of performance required for an organization's success, for example, for *customers*, service, quality, and cost; for *employees*, job satisfaction and safety; for *partners and owners*, an adequate return on investment; and for *the community*, conformance to laws.

Critical success factors   The elements, such as quality, time, cost reduction, innovativeness, customer service, or product performance, that create long-term profitability for the organization.

Customer costing   The process of assigning marketing, selling, distribution, and administrative costs to individual customers so that the cost of serving each customer can be calculated.

Customer lead time   The time from when a customer first requests a good or service until the customer receives the requested good or service. For example, the lead time for receiving a hamburger from a fast food outlet could be 6 minutes, for receiving a mortgage approval could be 21 days, and for receiving a complex medical instrument could be 8 months.

Cycle times   The time required to perform a process. For example, the cycle time to install a muffler could be 36 minutes, to transport a case of goods from a warehouse to a retail outlet could be 22 hours, and to produce a semiconductor chip from raw materials could be 18 days.

Data falsification   The act of knowingly falsifying information.

Database benchmarking   One approach to cooperative benchmarking in which companies can pay a fee in order to gain access to information from a database operator.

Decentralization   Delegating decision-making responsibility to a lower level in the organization.

Decentralized   Delegating decision-making responsibility from senior management to employees at lower levels of the organization.

Decentralized responsibility   Senior corporate managers give local division managers the rights to make decisions on pricing, product mix, customer relationships, resource acquisition, materials sourcing, and operating processes without having to seek approval from higher-level managers. Decentralized responsibility allows local managers to make decisions rapidly based on their superior access to information about local opportunities and threats.

Demand forecast   An estimate of the market demand, or sales potential, for a product under specified conditions.

Direct allocation method   A simple method to allocate service department costs to production departments that ignores interdependencies between service departments.

Direct manufacturing costs   Costs that can be traced easily to the product manufactured or service rendered.

Discounting   The process of computing present value.

Discretionary costs   Costs resulting from strategic and tactical decisions of managers; examples include advertising, publicity, and research and development.

Discretionary expenditure   An expenditure whose cost has no direct relationship between the level of spending on an activity and active production levels.

Diseconomies of scale   Increasing average costs with increases in production volume.

Economic value added   Evaluates a product line's financial desirability using its residual income.

Economies of scale   Decreasing average costs with increases in production volume.

Effective   A process characteristic that refers to the ability of a process to achieve its objectives.

Efficient   A process characteristic that refers to its ability to use the fewest possible resources to produce something.

Employee empowerment   Managers give employees who are closest to operating processes, customers, and suppliers the rights to make decisions. Employees are encouraged to solve problems and devise creative new approaches for performing work and satisfying customers.

Engineered expenditure   An expenditure whose short-term cost is directly determined by the proposed level of activity.

Environment-defining stakeholders   The organization's owners, customers, and community that define the environment in which the organization operates.

Ethical control system   A system that reinforces the ethical responsibilities of all firm employees.

External-failure costs   A cost incurred when a manufacturing company produces a defective component or product and the defect is detected externally.

Extrinsic rewards   Rewards, based on performance, that are provided to the individual by the organization.

Facility-sustaining activities   Activities performed to provide the managerial infrastructure and to support the upkeep of the plant.

Feedback, or reactive, control   An approach to control that reports data on completed activities to decide whether they were completed as planned.

Feedforward control   Often called *preventive control*, this approach to control focuses on preventing an undesired outcome and occurs before the activity is undertaken.

Financial accounting   The process of producing financial statements for external constituencies—people outside the organization, such as shareholders, creditors, and governmental authorities. This process is heavily constrained by standard-setting, regulatory, and tax authorities and the auditing requirements of independent accountants (contrast with management accounting).

Financial budgets   Budgets that summarizes the expected financial results from the chosen operating plans.

Financial control   The formal evaluation of some financial facet of an organization or a responsibility center.

First-level variance   Difference between actual and estimated costs for a cost item.

Fixed costs   Costs that are independent of the level of production (or sales).

Flexible budget   A forecast of what expenses should have been given the actual volume and mix of production and sales.

Flexible resources   Resources that are acquired as needed; their costs vary with production activity; examples include indirect materials and electric power to operate machines.

Full costs   Sum of all costs (direct materials, direct labor, and support) assigned to a product.

Future value (*FV*)   The amount to which an amount invested today will increase over a stated number of periods at a stated periodic rate of return; the ending value of an investment *n* periods from now at a stated rate of interest.

Gain sharing   A cash bonus system in which the total amount available for distribution as cash bonuses is a function of performance relative to some target (usually the difference between the actual and the target level of labor cost).

Gaming   An alteration of an employee's planned actions as a result of a particular kind of performance indicator.

Goal congruence   The alignment of individual and organizational goals.

Group benchmarking   One approach to cooperative benchmarking in which participants meet openly to discuss their methods.

Herzberg's two-factor theory of motivation   A theory that maintains that two groups of factors with different roles—hygiene and satisfier—motivate individual behavior.

Human relations movement   A model of human motivation that considers that people have many needs and aspirations at work and that they are motivated by things other than money.

Human resources model of motivation   An approach to human motivation that emphasizes that individuals do not find work objectionable, that they have knowledge to contribute, and that they are creative.

Hygiene factors   A group of factors in the Herzberg theory that relate to job context. They are thought to be

necessary to provide the environment for motivation rather than being motivators themselves.

Improshare   An incentive program that pays cash bonuses to employees based on labor savings relative to a target plan.

In control   A state in which the organization or process is on track toward achieving its objectives.

Incentive compensation   A system that provides pay for performance.

Incremental budgeting   An approach to developing appropriations for discretionary expenditures that assumes that the starting point for each discretionary expenditure item is the amount spent on it in the previous year.

Incremental cost per unit   The amount by which the total costs of production and sales increase when one additional unit of that product is produced and sold.

Incremental costs/revenues   The amount by which costs/revenues change if one particular decision is made instead of another.

Indirect manufacturing costs   All manufacturing costs other than direct manufacturing costs.

Indirect/third-party benchmarking   One approach to cooperative benchmarking in which an outside consultant acts as a liaison between two companies engaged in benchmarking.

Industrial Standard Z8101-1981   The Japanese standard for quality management.

Internal rate of return (*r*)   The rate of interest earned on an investment.

Internal-failure costs   A cost incurred when a manufacturing process produces a defective component or product and the defect is detected internally.

Intrinsic rewards   Rewards relating to the nature of the organization and the design of the job that people experience without the intervention of anyone else.

Investment   The monetary value of the assets that the organization gives up to acquire a long-term asset.

Investment center   A responsibility center whose employees control its revenues, costs, and the level of investment.

ISO 9000 Series of Standards   International quality standards developed by the International Organization for Standardization (ISO).

Job bid sheet   Format for estimating job costs.

Job cost sheet   Format for recording actual job costs.

Job costs   Total of direct material, direct labor, and support costs estimated for or identified with a job.

Job order costing system   System for estimating costs of manufacturing products for a job.

Just-in-time manufacturing Making a good or providing a service only when the customer who may be internal or external requires it.

Kaizen costing A method of cost reduction developed in Japan to reduce costs during the manufacturing cycle.

Labor hiring and training plan An operating plan that schedules the hiring, releasing, and training of people that the organization must have to achieve its activity objectives.

Line of credit A short-term financing arrangement, with a prespecified limit, between an organization and a financial institution.

Make-or-buy decision Decision either to make a part or component in-house or to purchase it from an outside supplier.

Management accounting The process of producing financial and operating information for organizational employees and managers. The process should be driven by the informational needs of individuals *internal* to the organization and should guide their operating and investment decisions.

Management accounting information Financial and operating data about an organization's activities, processes, operating units, products, services, and customers; e.g., the calculated cost of a product, an activity, or a department in a recent time period.

Management control The process of providing information about the performance of managers and operating units.

Managing by the numbers An approach to cost-cutting that focuses on reducing the budget, or cost allowance, allowed for a particular activity.

Manufacturing costs All costs of transforming raw materials into finished products; classified as direct and indirect costs.

Manufacturing cycle The cycle in which costs are incurred in the production of a product.

Manufacturing cycle efficiency (MCE) Method of assessing process efficiency based on the relationship between actual processing time and total cycle time.

Manufacturing support costs Indirect cost of transforming raw materials into finished product; indirect manufacturing costs.

Marginal revenue (cost) The increase in revenue (cost) for a unit increase in the quantity produced and sold.

Markup or margin Amount of profit added to estimated job costs to arrive at bid price.

Markup rate Ratio of the markup amount to the estimated costs for a job.

Master budget The budget that encompasses all operating and financial budgets.

Materials purchasing plan An operating plan that schedules purchasing activities.

Materials requisition note A note instructing the stores department to issue materials to the shop floor in order to commence production.

Mixed costs Costs comprising both fixed and variable cost components.

Motivation A person's interest or drive to act in a certain way.

Motivation system A system of performance measurement and rewards that provides employee benefits or recognition based on measured performance.

Multiple perspectives approach to management accounting system design The development of a consistent organization-wide management accounting system that also allows for local input and tailoring.

Multi-stage process costing system System for determining product costs in multi-stage processing industries.

Net present value The sum of the present values of all the cash inflows and cash outflows associated with a project; also known as residual income and economic income.

Net realizable value The difference between a transferred product's selling price and the additional costs needed to put it in the customer's hands.

Nonmanufacturing costs All costs other than manufacturing costs.

Nonvalue-added activity An activity that presents the opportunity for cost reduction without reducing the product's service potential to the customer.

Normal unit cost The average cost of the activity when the demand for the activity exactly equals the capacity made available by the resources committed to the activity.

Number of periods (n) In capital-budgeting analysis, the number of periods, usually measured in months, quarters, or years, whose cash flows a proposed long-term investment will affect.

Objectives The broad purposes of an organization that reflect the objectives of the stakeholders whose interests the organization deems primary.

Operating budget The document that forecasts revenues and expenses during the next operating period, typically a year. The operating budget also authorizes spending on discretionary activities, such as research and development, advertising, maintenance, and employee training.

Operating costs Indirect costs of producing services in a service organization.

Operational control   The process of providing feedback to employees and their managers about the efficiency of activities being performed.

Operations control   The evaluation of control from the perspective of process improvement.

Opportunity costs   The amount of lost profit when the opportunity afforded by one alternative is sacrificed to pursue another alternative.

Organization control   The activity of assessing the value chain's performance from the perspective of the organization's objectives.

Organizational culture   The mindset of organizational participants including goals, values, and attitudes.

Out of control   A state in which the organization or process is not on track toward achieving its objectives.

Outcome   The value attributed to the result of an activity by the customer, for example, the number of good units of production and the amount of client satisfaction generated by a service.

Output   A physical measure of production or activity, such as the number of units produced or the amount of time spent doing something.

Outsource   The process of selecting an outside organization (a supplier) to provide a good or service previously produced internally. Outsourcing is typically done because the outside supplier can supply the good or service at lower cost or higher quality.

Outsourcing   Purchasing a product, part, or component from an outside supplier instead of manufacturing it in-house.

Participative budgeting   A method of budgeting in which superiors and subordinates jointly set the budget.

Pay-for-performance system   A system that provides rewards for performance to motivate achieving or exceeding measured performance targets.

Payback period   The number of periods required to recover a project's initial investment.

Penetration pricing strategy   Charging a lower price initially to win over market share from an established product of a competing firm.

Performance measurement   The measuring of the performance of an activity or a value chain.

Period costs   Costs treated as expenses in the period in which they are incurred because they cannot be associated with the manufacture of products.

Periodic budget   A budget that is prepared for a specified period of time, usually 1 year.

Post-implementation audit   Re-assessing the decision to purchase a long-lived asset.

Post-sale service and disposal cycle   The cycle which begins once the first unit of a product is in the hands of the customer.

Present value (*PV*)   A future cash flow's value at time zero; the value at the current moment in time of an amount to be received *n* periods from now and given a rate of interest.

Prevention costs   Those costs incurred to ensure that companies produce products according to quality standards.

Preventive control   An approach to control that focuses on preventing an undesired event.

Price setter   A firm that sets or bids the prices of its products because it enjoys a significant market share in its industry segment.

Price taker   A firm that has little or no influence on the industry supply and demand forces and consequently on the prices of its products.

Primary control   A method of control in which employees further their own ends by trying to influence their environment.

Primary objectives   The organization's objectives as specified by its owners.

Pro forma statement   A forecasted or estimated statement.

Process control   The activity of assessing the operating performance of a single process or the entire value chain in meeting customer requirements.

Process layout   Organization system in which all similar equipment or functions are grouped together.

Process stakeholders   The organization's employees and suppliers, who have the primary responsibility of managing the processes of making and delivering foods and services to customers.

Processing time   Time expended in making a product.

Product costing   The process of measuring and assigning the costs of the activities performed to design and produce individual products (and services, for nonmanufacturing companies).

Product costs   Costs associated with the manufacture of products.

Product layout   Organization of equipment or functions to accommodate the production of a specific product.

Product-sustaining activities   Activities performed to support the production of individual products.

Production departments   Departments directly responsible for some of the work of converting raw materials into finished products.

Production plan   An operating plan that identifies all required production.

Production volume   Overall measure, such as number of units, of various products manufactured in a given time period.

Profit center   A responsibility center whose employees control revenues and costs but not the level of investment.

Profit sharing   A cash bonus system in which the total amount available for distribution as cash bonuses is a function of the organization's, or an organization unit's, reported profit.

Project funding   An approach to developing appropriations for discretionary expenditures that organizes appropriations into a package with a focus on achieving some defined output.

Pseudo-participation   An approach to budgeting in which a subordinate believes he or she will have an influence on the budget process but actually does not have any effect.

Q series of quality standards   U.S. quality standards developed by the American Quality Control Society.

Quality   The difference between the promised and the realized level of service; conformance to specifications.

Quality costs   Costs incurred to prevent quality problems from occurring, determine if problems have arisen, and correct quality problems both internal and external to a company.

Rate of return   Ratio of net income to investment (also called *return on investment*).

Re-engineering   The activity of improving process performance by redesigning the process.

Reciprocal allocation method   A method to determine service department cost allocations simultaneously that recognizes the reciprocity between pairs of service departments.

Relevant costs/revenues   The costs/revenues that differ across alternatives and therefore must be considered in deciding which alternative is the best.

Relevant range   The range of production levels over which the classification of a cost as fixed or variable is appropriate.

Research, development, and engineering cycle   The cycle in which customer needs are assessed and the product is designed and developed.

Responsibility center   An organization unit for which a manager is accountable in the form of cost (a cost center), revenue (a revenue center), profits (a profit center), or return on investment (an investment center).

Results control   A system focused on results or outcomes that is designed to motivate decision-making behavior to achieve the organization's behavior.

Return   The increased cash flows in the future attributable to the long-term asset.

Return on investment   The calculation that relates the profitability of an organizational unit to the investment required to generate that profitability. Often written as the return on sales multiplied by the ratio of sales to assets (or investment) employed.

Revenue center   A responsibility center whose employees control revenues but not manufacturing or product costs or the level of investment.

Rucker plan   An incentive program that pays cash bonuses to employees based on the relationship between the ratio of payroll costs to production value and a target on standard.

Sales plan   A document that summarizes planned sales for each product.

Satisfier factors   A group of factors in the Herzberg theory that relate to job content. They are thought to provide motivation when the environment for motivation has been properly prepared.

Scanlon plan   An incentive program that pays cash bonuses to employees based on the relationship between the ratio of payroll costs and the value of product produced and a target on standard.

Scientific management of motivation   A school of motivation in which people are viewed as finding work objectionable, motivated only by money, and as having little knowledge to contribute to the organization.

Second-level variance analysis   Analysis of a first-level variance into efficiency and price variances.

Secondary control   A method of control in which employees adapt themselves to their environment rather than trying to change the environment.

Secondary objectives   Objectives, defined by the organization's relationship with its customers, employees, suppliers, and community, that are thought to improve performance on the organization's primary objectives.

Segment margin   The level of controllable profit reported by an organization unit or product line.

Sensitivity analysis   An analytical tool that involves selectively varying key estimates of a plan or budget. Sensitivity analysis includes an investigation of the effect of a change in a parameter on a decision.

Sequential allocation method   A method that recognizes interdependencies between service departments and allocates service department costs one service department at a time in a sequential order.

Service   The product's tangible and intangible features promised to the customer; service is also known as value in use.

Service departments Departments that perform activities that support production but are not responsible for any of the conversion stages.

Signal Information provided to a decision maker. There are two types of signals: (1) a warning that there is a problem and (2) a diagnostic that identifies the problem.

Skimming price strategy Charging a higher price initially from customers willing to pay more for the privilege of possessing a new product.

Smoothing The act of affecting the preplanned flow of information without altering actual behavior.

Stage 1 allocations Identification of costs with individual production and service departments (step 1), followed by allocation of service department costs to production departments (step 2).

Stage 2 allocations Assignment of costs accumulated in production departments to individual products.

Stakeholders Groups of people who, or institutions that, have a legitimate claim on having an organization's objectives reflect their requirements. Stakeholders include customers, employees, partners, owners, and the community.

Standard costs Efficient and attainable benchmarks established in advance for the costs of activity resources that should be consumed by each product.

Step fixed costs Costs that increase in relatively wide discrete steps.

Step variable costs Costs that increase in relatively narrow discrete steps.

Stock option A right to purchase a stated number of the organization's shares for a specified price (the option price).

Storyboarding Using a chart to depict all activities involved in a process.

Strategic control The process of providing information about the competitive performance of the overall business unit, both financially and in meeting customers' expectations.

Strategic information Information that guides the long-term decision making of the organization. Strategic information can include the profitability of products, services, and customers; competitor behavior and performance; customer preferences and trends; market opportunities and threats; and technological innovations.

Stretch budgeting An approach to budgeting in which an organization attempts to achieve much higher goals than normal with the current budget.

Stretch targets Those targets that represent significant increases in the targeted amount, or goal, above the existing targets or goals.

Sunk costs Costs of resources that have already been committed and, regardless of what decision managers make, cannot be changed by any current action or decision.

Target cost (C_{tc}) The difference between the target selling price and the target profit margin.

Target costing A method of cost planning used during the RD&E cycle that focuses on products that require discrete manufacturing processes and reasonably short life cycles.

Target product volume The product volume in a target costing system based on the company's perceived value of the product to the customer.

Target profit margin (P) The profit margin in a target costing system based on a long-run profit analysis.

Target selling price (S) The selling price in a target costing system of a product based on the company's perceived value of the product to the customer.

Target-reduction rate The ratio of the target reduction amount (in a target costing system) to the cost base.

Task control Systems or procedures designed to ensure that employees follow stated procedures or rules.

Time card Record of hours spent by each worker each day or week on different jobs.

Time value of money The primary concept in capital budgeting, which states because money can earn a return, its value depends on when it is received.

Timing of control The temporal relationship between the method and object of control.

Total quality management A management philosophy that attempts to eliminate all defects, waste, and activities that do not add value to customers; also refers to an organizational commitment to customer satisfaction.

Total-life-cycle costing A costing system that provides information for managers to understand and manage costs through a product's design, development, manufacturing, marketing, distribution, maintenance, service, and disposal stages.

Total-life-cycle costs Costs incurred before, during and after the manufacturing cycle.

Traditional cost reduction Methods of cost reduction in which product designers do not attempt to achieve a particular cost target.

Transfer pricing A set of tools and methods (rules) used by the organization to allocate jointly earned revenues to organization subunits. Common transfer pricing approaches are cost, market, negotiated, and administered.

Unilateral (covert) benchmarking One method of benchmarking in which one company obtains information about another through industry trade associations or information clearing houses.

Unit-related activities Activities whose levels are related to the number of units produced.

Value chain A sequence of activities whose objective is to provide a product to a customer or to provide an intermediate good or service in a larger value chain.

Value engineering The process of examining each component of a product to determine whether its cost can be reduced while maintaining functionality and performance.

Value-added activity An activity that, if eliminated in the long run, would reduce the product's service to the customer.

Variable costs Costs that change proportionally with production (or sales) volume. They represent resources whose consumption can be adjusted to match the demand placed for them.

Variance The difference between actual results and the budget plan.

Variance analysis Decomposition of differences between actual and estimated costs into amounts related to specific factors causing the variance between actual and estimated costs.

Vroom's expectancy theory A theory that maintains that motivation is a product of expectancy, instrumentality, and valence.

What-if analysis A strategy that uses a model to predict the results of varying a model's key parameters or estimates.

Zero-based budgeting An approach to developing appropriations for discretionary expenditures that assumes that the starting point for each discretionary expenditure is zero.

SUBJECT INDEX

COMPANY NAME INDEX